INTERPRETING
TWENTIETH-CENTURY
AMERICA
a reader

INTERPRETING TWENTIETH-CENTURY AMERICA
a reader

Edited by
RICHARD LOWITT
University of Kentucky
and
JOSEPH F. WALL
Grinnell College

THOMAS Y. CROWELL COMPANY
New York Established 1834

Library of Congress Cataloging in Publication Data

LOWITT, RICHARD comp.
Interpreting twentieth-century America.

Includes bibliographical references.
1. United States—History—20th century—Addresses, essays, lectures. I. Wall, Joseph Frazier, joint comp. II. Title.
E742.L68 973.9 72-13854
ISBN 0-690-44612-8

 Published simultaneously in Canada by Fitzhenry & Whiteside, Ltd., Toronto.

Manufactured in the United States of America

1 2 3 4 5 6 7 8 9 10

PREFACE

This volume of supplementary readings is designed to serve a dual purpose: first, it introduces some important themes in twentieth-century American history that, owing to space and time limitations, are seldom mentioned in textbooks or in the classroom; and, second, by presenting case studies, it gives insight or perspective to major issues in twentieth-century American history. In no sense are these readings designed to replace basic textual material. Nor do they follow a problem approach by introducing similar articles with different points of view, which, in effect, ask the reader to decide which are the more valid, thus giving the impression that all that need be said about the topic has been presented and that the student can now proceed to the next problem. Rather they are supplementary readings that reveal the roots of problems and issues that confront Americans today. Very few of these selections have appeared in previously published books of readings. Obviously, other selections might have been made, but it is hoped that the range and diversity of these readings will assist the student and the instructor in interpreting recent American history.

CONTENTS

The Perils of PAULINE
THE BIG RED SCARE
Ford
ELLIS ISLAND
VOTES FOR WOMEN
THE OCTOPUS by FRANK NORRIS
"Speak Softly a
Carry a Big Stic
Teddy Roosevel

PART ONE

1900-1920

As a young historian at the University of Wisconsin in 1893, Frederick Jackson Turner was to give historical significance to the brief statement by the Superintendent of the Census in reporting the census figures for 1890 that "at present the unsettled area has been broken into . . . that there can hardly [be] said to be a frontier line. . . . It cannot, therefore, any longer have a place in census reports." An era beginning in 1607 had ended. Thirty years later, it might well have been noted by alert social scientists that another historical period had come to a conclusion, for the census of 1920 recorded the fact that for the first time a majority of Americans now lived in an urban environment. America in 1920 had become urbanized and industrialized.

The readings in Part I are concerned with the first two decades of the twentieth century, which mark this period of transition from ruralism to urbanism. After the depression of the early 1890's, America had entered joyfully into the great imperial contest of Western powers for the control of Asia and Africa, and the United States emerged in 1898 with its own noncontiguous empire, scattered over the broad Pacific. Following that "splendid little" venture, Americans again turned their attention to the domestic scene. The phrase "politics of joy," which seemed singularly incongruous when used by a presidential candidate in 1968, is an appropriate slogan for this period. Inspired by the vigorous leadership of Theodore Roosevelt, Americans faced the problems of social and economic transition with naïve optimism. "An air of contentment and enthusiastic cheerfulness characterized the thought and temper of the American people," wrote William Graham Sumner at the outset of the twentieth century. While much of significance was accomplished in this period of Progressivism, the full magnitude of the task of reform, or as John Dewey would say, of "the reconstruction of American life" to meet the social realities of the period, was not realized. As these essays indicate, certain specific problems were identified and attacked, but few were resolved, and future generations would have to grapple with those persisting issues that were but dimly perceived in this period. And never again would Americans enjoy the "contentment and enthusiastic cheerfulness" that characterized the thought and action of the period from 1900 to 1920.

The essays in this section suggest some of the currents in American life that frequently receive inadequate attention in American history courses. The Progressive approach is examined and the confusion and frequent conflicting attitudes of the reformers are revealed. Of the nine articles here, six focus on the years prior to World War I and examine aspects of both rural and urban American life.

Although the Progressive period was primarily interested and achieved its most notable success in dealing with the problems of the city, there was also a continuing and real concern for the land, its natural resources, and the people who farmed, mined, or simply exploited it for immediate material gain. In the first essay Clayton Ellsworth shows how the Roosevelt administration attempted to deal with the persistent farm question, which was as much a social as it was an economic problem. Roderick Nash in his essay presents a version of the classic conflict between pragmatic progress and nostalgic preservation that disturbed the conservation movement to which Theodore Roosevelt was vociferously committed. This particular conflict of interest among well-meaning conservationists is no longer central to the movement, but is still perhaps implicit in the present conservation crisis as ecology becomes a paramount issue in American life today.

Joseph Frazier Wall's article highlights the sense of stewardship, paternalism, and noblesse oblige that some of the great entrepreneurs expressed in the doctrine of the Gospel of Wealth as they turned from getting to giving, from acquisitive despotism to benevolent despotism with the naïve belief that the dispensation of great fortunes could solve our basic social problems. In contrast, Robert Buroker shows how a dedicated group of practical reformers dealt with a specific problem, the newly arrived immigrants to Chicago, in a pragmatic way.

Not all of the middle-class, Anglo-Saxon citizens of Illinois felt as kindly toward the new immigrants as did the Immigrants' Protective League. Humbert Nelli's essay analyzes the more typical response toward the Italian immigrant and the Italian community's own concern with the problem of urban crime. Charles Crowe turns his attention to the urban centers of the South, shedding light on a major race riot by revealing the ugly face of racism, of the use by southern whites of Progressivism as a more effective disguise for racial suppression than were the sheets of the Ku Klux Klan.

The remaining three essays in this section pertain to the period of World War I. Richard Lowitt examines the initial twentieth-century confrontation between president and Congress over who can declare war by reviewing the famed congressional crisis that developed over the arming of the merchant ships in 1917. Unlike most accounts of this incident, here the focus is upon the legislative rather than the executive department.

Melvin Urofsky and Robert Cuff deal with an important topic that has not received the attention it deserves—the relationship between government and business during World War I. Their article suggests that government supervision of the wartime economy did not necessarily entail undue hardship for important sections of the business community. Quite the contrary, the war provided the precedent for Herbert Hoover's trade associations, Franklin Roosevelt's National Recovery Administration, and the military-industrial complex of the Cold War.

Finally, Alan Cywar examines the ideas of an American intellectual and political radical, John Dewey, who surveyed the first two decades of the twentieth century with disappointment, but, like the earlier Progressive reformers, faced the third decade with optimism as he called for a genuine reconstruction of American society.

1

THEODORE ROOSEVELT'S COUNTRY LIFE COMMISSION

Clayton S. Ellsworth

At the turn of the century the phrase "country life movement" designated a varied group of activities having as its main concern the social and cultural welfare of rural Americans. This concern was not new. It had been a motivation for the Granger movement in the immediate post-Civil War period, and had been implicit in the goals of the later farm alliances that led to the Populist revolt. But as Mr. Ellsworth states in the following essay, the significance of Theodore Roosevelt's Country Life Commission lay in the fact that "it was the first comprehensive attempt to learn the status of farming" and "the first recognition by a federal agency that the production of more excellent citizens on the farm was at least as important as the production of more . . . hogs and cotton." Today, six decades later, because of better roads, rural electrification, television and radio, the farmer is no longer isolated from the mainstream of American social life. The values of the rural life, however, are still threatened, and the recent controversy over the appointment of Purdue Dean Earl Butz as secretary of agriculture highlighted some of the same concerns that are expressed in this article.

Clayton S. Ellsworth is a professor at the College of Wooster in Ohio. He is a scholar in American social history. An abbreviated version of this article, published in 1960, was first presented as a paper before a joint meeting of the Agricultural History Society and the Mississippi Valley Historical Association.

Unfavorable assays of farm life in the United States became persistent after the Civil War. Embattled farmers who had banded together to form the first farm organization, the Patrons of Husbandry or the Grange, protested in the "Farmers'

Source: *Agricultural History*, Vol. 34, No. 4 (1960), pp. 155–172. Reprinted by permission of the author and the Agricultural History Society.

Declaration of Independence" on July 4, 1873, against oppression by the railroad monopoly which had established an absolute tyranny over the farmers "unequalled in any monarchy of the Old World." Two decades later the platform of the Populist party added the idea that an inadequate currency system stemming from governmental injustice was impoverishing the farmers and producing two great classes—"tramps and millionaires."

During the last two decades of the nineteenth century, such leading clergymen as Josiah Strong and Roland Hyde Hartt looked at the country churches from their New England pulpits, and saw them as dying institutions, consisting of prophetless ministers who mouthed an obsolete theology as they indulged in bitter sectarian rivalries, and a laity which was degenerate and declining in numbers. "The Report of the Committee of Twelve on Rural Schools," prepared for the National Education Association in 1897 by leading school administrators headed by the farm-born Henry Sabin, was merciless in its evaluation of the cherished one-room country schools. Literary men like Hamlin Garland in *Main-Travelled Roads* (1891) created a farm picture showing weary men and women struggling in vain against cultural barrenness, mounting mortgages, and steaming manure piles. One writer in the *Atlantic Monthly* walked off the deep end by recommending that the first step that should be taken in the direction of intellectual development and rational social enjoyment was the abandonment in the open country of prairie farm homes and the establishment of farm villages.[1]

I. THE SLOW BIRTH OF THE COMMISSION

These strictures were dwarfed in 1909 by the *Report* of the Country Life Commission appointed by President Theodore Roosevelt, the first president in the industrial age to acquire a sympathetic understanding of modern farm problems. Since the Commission was appointed by the popular "Teddy" and the members were such distinguished and respectable men as Chairman Dean Liberty Hyde Bailey of the College of Agriculture, Cornell University, Kenyon Butterfield, President of Massachusetts College of Agriculture, Walter H. Page, Editor of *World's Work*, Gifford Pinchot, Chief United States Forester, and "Uncle Henry" Wallace, beloved Presbyterian preacher and editor of *Wallaces' Farmer*, it probably carried more weight with conservative Americans than did the protest of more fervent crusaders.

The *Report*, which proclaimed that the underlying problem was "to develop and maintain on our farms a civilization in full harmony with the best American ideals," was far more than just one of the many documents written in the Muckraking period when Americans were noted more for their critical self-analysis than they were for their complacency.[2] It was the first comprehensive attempt to learn the status of farming, the traditional occupation of the United States of America, under the impact of industrialism. The *Report* was the first recognition by a

[1] E. V. Smalley, "Isolation of Life on Prairie Farms," *Atlantic Monthly* 72: 378, 382 (September, 1893).

[2] *Report of The Commission On Country Life With an Introduction by Theodore Roosevelt*, (Chapel Hill, N. C., 1944), 24. Hereafter, this document will be cited as the *Report*. It was originally published as Senate Document No. 705, 60th Congress, 2d Session for use by Congress in 1909.

federal agency that the production of more excellent citizens on the farm was at least as important as the production of more, bigger and better hogs and cotton, and that the current emphasis upon more scientific production would not solve a host of farm problems. In the fifty years that have followed, the *Report* has been the central charter of farm people in their democratic quest for their just share of the material and spiritual things of life.

The Commission was not created by an unpremeditated act of a president famed for swift, vigorous deeds. The action that preceded the formation of the Commission gained momentum as slowly as many a nineteenth-century novel. Once organized, however, the action of the Commission occurred at the speed of a twentieth-century television play timed to twenty-eight minutes.

An intelligent awareness of farm problems by the city-born Roosevelt, whose early knowledge of farmers had been limited to those farmers who could be observed from the windows of passenger trains, cowboys, and policemen recruited from the farms, was acquired as a mature man. Before he died he had come to the conclusion that the status of the farmer was the most fundamental issue in the United States, "the one issue which is even more basic than the relations of the capitalist and working man."[3] The farmer was Roosevelt's last hero as he was Jefferson's first. As he saw it, upon the farmer rested the heavy responsibility of the preservation of the fertility of the soil, and of feeding a world which "is never more than a year from starvation." The farmer, moreover, represented the best hope that America had of perpetuating a mighty breed of men. Farmers were, as a class, law-abiding, intelligent, energetic, and deeply devoted to the family and private property. Unlike the urban birth rate, which was dropping, the farm birth rate was holding its own. Should the drift of farm people to the city continue, leaving only a small and inferior farm population, the future of all America would be endangered by impoverished soil, less food, and a biologically inferior citizenry.

One of Roosevelt's first farm tutors was Tom Watson, the Populist leader. After Roosevelt had publicly recanted in the fall of 1896, of some ignorant and heedless remarks that he had made about Watson and other Populist leaders earlier in the heated presidential "cross-of-gold" campaign, a friendship developed between the two men. From Watson, Roosevelt acquired a knowledge of the hardships of farm women. In Watson, Roosevelt found a loyal political supporter who saw in Roosevelt's "trust-busting" a policy similar in intent to what the early Populists had attempted. In 1908, Watson, who was still nominally the Populist candidate for the presidency, offered to withdraw if Roosevelt would run again. Roosevelt refused. And in 1912 when Roosevelt did run again, Watson announced that he would "vote the Bull thing ticket."[4]

A second tutor was the incredible Sir Horace Plunkett, a wealthy Irish heir, an Oxford graduate, a member of Parliament, a hatcher of innumerable plots and schemes, whose home was finally dynamited as a result of his participation in the Irish Home Rule controversy. A few of these schemes were highly valuable and workable. He had been the founder in the 1890s of the Irish Agricultural

[3] Albert B. Hart and Herbert R. Ferleger, eds., *Theodore Roosevelt Cyclopedia* (New York, 1941), 6.

[4] C. Vann Woodward, *Tom Watson: Agrarian Rebel* (New York, 1938), 305–307, 364, 397, 430; *Theodore Roosevelt, An Autobiography* (New York, 1914), 427.

Organization Society which successfully fostered dairy cooperatives, and the Irish Department of Agriculture and Technical Instruction.[5] Since 1879, he had also been a part owner of a ranch in Wyoming which he visited annually. Without this ranching experience which included annual financial deficits, round-ups, and sleeping three in a bed with snoring cowboys, Plunkett would never have appealed much to Roosevelt. The Oxford graduate and absentee Wyoming cattleman did not meet the Harvard graduate and Dakota rancher until the two lunched together in the White House in 1901. During the next four years when Roosevelt was preoccupied with his attack upon the "trusts," the two met only once. In 1905, Plunkett, in search for a fresh idea for the Irish Department of Agriculture, of which he was Secretary, asked for an interview. It was granted. During this meeting, Plunkett intensified Roosevelt's interest in rural affairs and gave him, upon request, a famous formula for a sound agriculture, "better farming" (the application of science), "better business" (the organization of farm co-operatives), and "better living" (mostly better schools and modern conveniences). Plunkett's main point was that as industry had become stronger and better organized in the United States, agriculture had become weaker and woefully disorganized. The Grange which had started cooperatives had deserted them for political activities. The only salvation of farming was the revival of cooperatives by the voluntary action of the farmers aided by the protection and encouragement of the federal government.[6]

Plunkett's request for an interview had come at the right moment, for Roosevelt realized that his first term had not been marked by much significant farm legislation. A Reclamation Act providing federal funds for irrigation pleased western ranchers; a determined policy of withdrawing federal timber and forest lands from sale displeased westerners. His most popular deed among farmers everywhere was his emphatic pronouncement in his annual message to Congress in 1902, "Rural free delivery service is no longer in the experimental state: it has become a fixed policy."[7] This endorsement closed the debate. It also showed that Roosevelt was aware of the economic benefits that rural free delivery had brought to farmers and business men, and that one of the highest justifications for rural free delivery was that "it makes farm life pleasanter and less isolated, and will do much to check the undesirable current from country to city." Almost simultaneously, he approved the building of good roads which would also end the isolation of farmers, and make farm life more attractive to those contemplating leaving the farm. Roosevelt continued annually to rejoice in the steady expansion of rural routes, and in 1907, he had the honor of being the first president to recommend the carrying of parcels by rural postmen.[8]

Bailey and Pinchot proved to be Roosevelt's most influential advisers in agricultural matters. They were a remarkable combination. Pinchot, a member of a prominent eastern family, a member of Roosevelt's Tennis Cabinet, one of the President's closest friends, and a prophet of conservation, supplied administrative push and political talent in addition to ideas. These ideas were obtained from his work in forestry which had brought him in contact with farm life in many parts

[5] Margaret Digby, *Horace Plunkett* (Oxford, 1949), 39–64, 84–116.
[6] Digby, *Horace Plunkett,* 122, 123.
[7] James Richardson, *Messages and Papers of the President* (20 vols., New York, 1917), 15:6724.
[8] *Ibid.*, 6798.

of the United States where he said, "I had seen so little of its hardships, and especially of hardships of farm women."[9] Although Pinchot had not been a farmer, Bailey had been. Born on a Michigan farm where he did not see a railroad until he was eighteen, educated at Michigan State College of Agriculture, Bailey had, by the time the story opened, an international reputation as a horticulturist. As a member of the Cornell University faculty and later as Dean of the College of Agriculture, he had transformed a department of agriculture into the world-famed New York State College of Agriculture. This feat was accomplished by securing funds and authority from the New York legislature. In winning the battle, Bailey had to contend with economy-minded legislators who listened with much sympathy to the pleas of some of the farmers who thought that a college education at Cornell University was an unnecessary preparation for learning how to milk a cow. More formidable were some of the learned professors in the traditional departments of the University who unctuously objected to a College of Agriculture, a "Cow College," on the grounds that liberal education and higher agricultural educations were a contradiction of terms. Perhaps what some of them really wanted to do was to spend in their own departments the federal funds already allotted to the University for agricultural purposes according to the Morrill Land Grant Act. To complicate matters, a Chancellor of a nearby university made pious protests while fixing hungry eyes on these funds for the establishment of a College of Agriculture in his own university. Bailey, who was a lip-service Democrat, a scientist rather than a politician, none-the-less displayed much skill in winning farmers to his side by giving talks that they understood, and in influencing legislators through personal conversations.[10]

Bailey communicated to Roosevelt his views on the improvement of country life that were as deceptively disarming as they were heretical. During the tragic depression years from 1893–1897, Bailey turned his thoughts from time to time from his studies of the evolution of unlike species of plants to a study of the causes of rural depressions. Bailey was badly shaken when he discovered that his previous preliminary study of the conditions of fruit growing in western New York, which was concerned solely with the scientific aspects of orcharding, gave not even a single clue to the hard times among the fruit growers.[11] What was needed for this purpose, he concluded, was a new type of study, then virtually non-existent in the United States, a comprehensive fact-finding survey of all the factors, political, economic, and social, involved in fruit-growing in New York. This method of research was also essential to an understanding of farming in other regions of the United States and to the success of off-campus extension education and scientific research. "We conceive," Bailey wrote in 1896 in his *Second Report upon Extension Work in Horticulture,* "that it is impossible really to extend the Experiment Station and the University impulse to the people in such a manner that it shall come to them as a living and quickening force,

[9] Gifford Pinchot, *Breaking New Ground* (New York, 1947), 340.

[10] Andrew Denny Rodgers, III, *Liberty Hyde Bailey; A Story of American Plant Sciences* (Princeton, 1949), *passim;* George H. M. Lawrence, *Liberty Hyde Bailey, 1858–1954. An Appreciation,* reprinted from *Bailey* (March, 1955), 3:26–40; Philip Dort, *Liberty Hyde Bailey. An Informal Biography* (Ithaca, N.Y., 1956), *passim.*

[11] L. H. Bailey, *Report upon Conditions of Fruit-growing in Western New York,* Cornell University Experiment Station, Bulletin 19 (1890).

without first studying the fundamental difficulties of the farmer's social and political environment."[12] Here in this confession was implicit an idea that Bailey repeated again and again in the years that followed, namely that the agricultural scientist with his indispensable emphasis upon improvements in production cannot solve most of the important problems of farm life without the assistance of the social scientist, the moralist, and even the poet.

The new vision of agricultural research was followed by several studies of orchard and poultry industries[13] done under Bailey's direction. In 1906, Professor George F. Warren and several of his colleagues began a more comprehensive survey of "all the conditions that surround the business of farming and the people on the farm" in Tompkins County, New York.[14] This study, which marked the beginning of the survey method on a large scale in the United States, soon led one observer to comment, "We are living in an age of surveys." It included an investigation of soils, capital, expenses, size of farms, abandoned farms, systems of farming, types of tenure, farm buildings, distance from markets, family labor, women as farmers, size of families, age and education of farmers, rural free delivery and telephone.

A comprehensive study of the status of agriculture was to Bailey the first step in the direction of better farm life. The next step was to be sought in better education.[15] Just as the survey should encompass the whole of rural America, better agricultural education should direct itself to the whole farmer. It should include at all levels the conventional time-honored subjects which are essential for an understanding of the spiritual and moral nature of man. It should also include new unconventional subjects, the laboratory sciences, nature study, courses in agriculture which would serve the farmer in his capacity as scientific and business farmer, homemaker, and citizen. Science and nature study were especially valuable in opening the eyes of country people to an appreciation of the beauty and mysteries of nature that unfold daily. In recognition of his prominence in the growing army of educators that shared his views of education, Bailey was asked by the National Education Association and the U. S. Bureau of Education to summarize in 1907, current thought and practice about the teaching of vocational agriculture and industrial courses in the public schools.

Although Bailey and Roosevelt had become aware of each other when Roosevelt was governor of New York 1898–1900, their paths did not intertwine until May, 1907. The occasion was the Semi-Centennial Celebration of the Founding of Agricultural Colleges held at Michigan State College (now Michigan State University) at Lansing, where the two men spoke from the same platform. As President of the Association of Land Grant Colleges, which held its annual con-

[12] Cornell University Agricultural Experiment Station, Bulletin 122 (December, 1896), 534; L. H. Bailey, *The Survey Idea in Country Life Work* (1911), 4; H. C. M. Case and D. B. Williams, *Fifty Years of Farm Management* (Urbana, 1957), 27, 32, 58; Olaf F. Larson, "Liberty Hyde Bailey's Impact on Rural Life," in *Bailey*, 6:12–18 (Ithaca, N. Y., March, 1958).

[13] Cornell University Experiment Station Bulletins 204 (1902), 212 (1903), 226 (1905), 229 (1905), 271 (1909).

[14] Cornell University Agricultural Experiment Station, Department of Farm Management, *An Agricultural Survey. Tompkins County, New York*, Bulletin 295 (March, 1911), 377.

[15] L. H. Bailey, *Agricultural Education and Its Place in the University Curriculum* (Ithaca, N. Y., 1893); Rogers, *Liberty Hyde Bailey*, 350–353.

vention in connection with the Celebration, Bailey delivered the annual presidential address. The brilliant idea of securing the President of the United States to speak came from the inventive mind of Jonathan L. Snyder, President of Michigan State who had "but one over-weening ambition": to build the reputation of his school.[16] Writing on February 6, 1906, to Congressman Charles Jay Monroe and President of the Board of Trustees, Snyder explained with his customary persuasiveness, "On my way to chapel yesterday morning a thought struck me; it was this: Why not make an effort to have President Roosevelt with us at our Semi-Centennial? This meeting, if carried out as we now anticipate, will be one of the greatest educational meetings ever held in this country. It commemorates the fiftieth anniversary of the new type of education."[17] Congressman Monroe approached Roosevelt immediately. After being beseeched for five months by letters, inspired by Snyder, from educators, politicians, and leaders of farm organizations, Roosevelt, who had announced that he would travel no more during his term as president, finally accepted the invitation.[18]

Pinchot and Plunkett created the memorable, working partnership of the colorful Roosevelt and the talented Bailey. This partnership would accomplish two things according to Pinchot's reasoning: Bailey's assistance in the preparation of the Lansing speech; and Bailey's consent to be the head of a new federal department of "Rural Social Economy" which Pinchot and Plunkett hoped that they could persuade Roosevelt and Congress to establish. Pinchot arranged for a three-man meeting with Bailey and Plunkett in the Century Club in New York early in January, 1907.[19] During the conference on the proposal to create a new federal department, some mention was made, probably by Pinchot, that suggestions which would aid the President in his Lansing speech should be sent to Roosevelt. Bailey thought no more of the matter until a few weeks later when he was surprised to receive a follow-up letter from Pinchot begging for help in securing facts and ideas for the speech. He would have been more surprised if he had known that Plunkett in Ireland was also trying to get ideas to send Roosevelt from Bailey by way of Pinchot.[20] Bailey stalled for time and escape, as he pleaded that he, too, had a speech to deliver at Lansing, and that since he was scheduled to speak before Roosevelt did, it would be embarrassing if he anticipated the

[16] Letter from Madison Kuhn, Professor of History, Michigan State University, to the author June 18, 1958. The author is indebted to Professor Kuhn for the kindness of photocopying the thirty pages of correspondence in the archives of the University which are relevant to negotiations involved in securing Roosevelt's agreement to come to Lansing.

[17] Snyder to the Honorable C. J. Monroe, Washington, D. C., February 6, 1906, MS, courtesy of Professor Madison Kuhn.

[18] Wm. Loeb, Jr., Secretary to the President, to the Honorable S. W. Smith, M. C., Pontiac, Michigan, August 1, 1906. MS, courtesy Professor Madison Kuhn.

[19] Gifford Pinchot Diary, January 13, 1907, Gifford Pinchot MSS, Correspondence Box 3320 Manuscript Division of the Library of Congress (hereinafter cited as DLC); Gifford Pinchot to Professor Irving Fisher, New Haven, Connecticut, January 11, 1907, Gifford Pinchot MSS, Correspondence Box 100, DLC; Digby, *Horace Plunkett*, 123–125; Plunkett to Pinchot February 19, 1907, and Pinchot to Plunkett March 14, 1907, Gifford Pinchot MSS, Correspondence Box 102, DLC.

[20] Plunkett to Pinchot, February 19, 1907, Pinchot to Plunkett, March 14, 1907, MSS in Pinchot Correspondence Box 102, DLC; Bailey to Pinchot, March 18, 1907; Pinchot to Bailey, March 20, 1907, MSS in Pinchot Correspondence Box 100, DLC.

President's speech. Finally after Pinchot had written in desperation that Roosevelt had given him just ten more days to round up material for the Lansing speech, and had also assured Bailey that Roosevelt would use the facts in such an original manner that there would be no duplication of ideas, Bailey consented to send his ideas to Pinchot.[21] Pinchot had bagged an adviser on country life problems for the President.

The heart of the long letter which Bailey sent Pinchot just exactly in time to meet the deadline set by "T. R." stressed Bailey's mature elaboration of the idea that he had expressed so many times since 1896. The central effort of the agricultural college and the United States Department of Agriculture had been to increase the producing power of the farmer. But the time had come "when not only the colleges but all public agencies must now unite in an effort to improve the social welfare of the persons who live on the land. In other words, all experimental and educational effort in agriculture must work out to social ends. . . ."[22]

In the meantime, Bailey retaliated by appointing Pinchot to a Commission to study the elimination of duplication of research by federal and state agricultural institutions.[23] Pinchot signed the Report but presented a dissenting opinion that the Commission had not stressed enough the responsibilities of these institutions to the public, and the lack of cooperation between the agencies.[24]

Pinchot drew upon Bailey's letter for a statement, "Betterment of the Social Condition of the Farming Population," which he submitted to Roosevelt, who, in turn, used the facts contained in the statement in preparation of the Lansing address.[25]

In his address at Lansing, "The State and the Farmer," Bailey avoided an excessive duplication of the ideas that he had given Roosevelt by stressing, as a student of country life, how rural governments, banks, schools, churches, and fairs could be made more effective. Although Bailey continued to emphasize self-help, he asked for more state-help through funds for agricultural education at all levels, credit, and legislation to protect the farmer from exploitation from industrial tariffs, inequitable taxation, and monopolies. Governmental funds, when used to help the farmer whom Bailey called "the forgotten man," were not gifts to a special class. They were investments that would help the entire United States, and were due the farmer for the handicaps that industry had placed upon him by legislation.[26] This address Bailey expanded into a book with the same title the next year.

[21] Bailey to Pinchot, March 28, 1907; Pinchot to Bailey, March 28, 1907; Pinchot to Bailey, April 8, 1907, MSS in Pinchot Correspondence Box 100, DLC.

[22] Bailey to Pinchot, April 17, 1907, Gifford Pinchot MSS, Correspondence Box 1741, DLC.

[23] Commission on Agricultural Research of the Association of the American Agricultural Colleges and Experiment Stations, *Report* (November, 1908).

[24] Pinchot to Bailey, April 23, 1907, Pinchot MSS, Box 1741, DLC.

[25] Pinchot to Bailey, April 23, 1907, Gifford Pinchot MSS, Box 1741, DLC. On the communication from Pinchot to Roosevelt are written these words, "Prepared by Mr. Gifford Pinchot for the President's use in a speech at Lansing, Michigan, May 31, 1907," Pinchot MSS, Box 1737, DLC.

[26] Liberty Hyde Bailey, "The State and the Farmer" (*Ithaca Journal*, reprint, no date).

The theme of the President's characteristic long address, "The Man Who Works with His Hands," was that the new task of the farmer, the United States Department of Agriculture, legislative bodies, the colleges and public schools, was to elevate farming to a dignity and quality equal to that of any other profession. The President approved the major reforms prescribed by the crusaders for farm betterment: higher agricultural education which would include business management courses, "a more practical curriculum in the schools," good roads, telephones, and rural free delivery.[27] The content of the speech was trite except for the Bailey-inspired dictum that the United States Department of Agriculture which had been heretofore dealing with growing crops, "must hereafter deal also with living men." None-the-less, the Lansing address was important. For the first time, a president of the United States had recognized the need for agricultural reform, and had spelled out a plan of action. There was much truth to the flattering request that James Wilson, Secretary of Agriculture, made when he wrote to Roosevelt for a copy of the speech: "It is something no president has ever done, and it is so readable and so applicable to present conditions, that I would like to print it."[28]

When the aged Wilson, who had been Secretary of Agriculture since 1897, so long that he had been dubbed "the Irremovable," learned that Roosevelt's plans included the establishment of a new-fangled bureau of rural life in the Department of Agriculture, his warm enthusiasm turned to a guarded but cold hostility. By the end of that year, Wilson's objections had apparently become so intense, despite the efforts of Pinchot, Roosevelt, and Bailey to overcome them, that plans for the new government agency had to be dropped.[29]

Pinchot was not the kind of man who could be thwarted easily. He then turned to his favorite approach to a governmental problem, the commission which consists of a number of disinterested and distinguished experts who are appointed to study a particular problem. Although the resort to commissions was not original with Pinchot, his emphasis upon them was. At his suggestion, President Roosevelt, who was impressed by the way that a commission could summon the services of experts outside governmental circles without the permission of a reluctant or even hostile Congress, appointed six major commissions including the Country Life Commission and the Commission on the Conservation of Natural Resources which were created simultaneously in 1908. Bailey, likewise, liked the Commission approach. But since his energies were fully absorbed by administrative embroilments and by research and writing, he was reluctant to serve on a commission. After some correspondence and one conference, Pinchot finally persuaded the busy Bailey to come to the White House for a conference about the Commission with Roosevelt and him at 9:30 P.M. on April 10. Bailey, who was the kind of man who seldom ever took a vacation,

[27] *The Works of Theodore Roosevelt* (Executive edition, VI), New York, 1283, 1284.

[28] James Wilson to Wm. Loeb, Jr., Secretary to Theodore Roosevelt, June 5, 1907, Record Group 16, United States Department of Agriculture, National Archives.

[29] Digby, *Horace Plunkett*, 125; Pinchot to Plunkett, December 3, 1907; Pinchot to Frissell, December 6, 1907, Pinchot MSS, Correspondence Letter Box 100, DLC; Bailey to Pinchot, March 14, 1908, Pinchot MSS, Box 1741, DLC.

never ceased to marvel at the energy of Roosevelt who scheduled still another appointment that evening after the one with him. At last, Bailey had met a man who could outwork him.[30]

At the White House Conference, Bailey apparently agreed to serve as chairman of the proposed commission.[31] Bailey confided at the time that his dislike of the publicity and responsibility involved as chairman was outweighed by his willingness to put himself at the service of President Roosevelt, "whom I greatly admire not only for his abilities, but also for his frankness, directness, and intensely human qualities."[32] Shortly afterwards, in a long crucial letter requested by the President, Bailey suggested afresh the philosophy that would guide the Commission. In addition to the old Bailey idea that "the great rural interests are human rather than technically agricultural," it contained new details.[33] Although American farmers were more efficient and better off economically than they ever had been before, economic progress was spotty. Since the older social institutions of the open country, the one-room school, the lyceum, the one-room church, and local trade centers were dying out, able public men, whose attention hitherto had been directed exclusively to solution of industrial problems, should find constructive solutions to new rural problems.

Thanks to months of planning by Pinchot and Bailey, President Roosevelt was able to send formal letters of appointment to the Commission by August 10. Besides Bailey and Pinchot, Butterfield, Wallace, and Page were named. From the very beginning, Butterfield had been slated for a position on the Commission.[34] A close friend of Bailey, and Bailey's first choice, Butterfield had been born on a dairy farm at Lapeer, Michigan. And Butterfield, like Bailey, had graduated from Michigan State. Later he was editor of the *Michigan Grange Visitor* and President of the Rhode Island College of Agriculture, where in 1904 he taught the first course in rural sociology ever taught in an agricultural college.[35] Two years later he was called to the presidency of the Massachusetts Agricultural College. He was one of the outstanding advocates of federal aid for vocational agricultural courses and popular extension work.[36]

Wallace was chosen because he was an intimate friend of Secretary James Wilson and because he was regarded as perhaps the most prominent agricultural

[30] Theodore Roosevelt MSS, Diaries, Appointment Book 1907–1908, A. C., 2064, 165, DLC, Friday, April 10, 1908; Bailey to Pinchot, March 2, 1908; Pinchot to Bailey, March 9, 1908; Bailey to Pinchot, March 14, 1908; Pinchot to Bailey, March 23, 1908; Bailey to Pinchot, April 6, 1908, Pinchot MSS, Correspondence Box 104 and Box 1741, DLC; L. H. Bailey, *Some Reminiscences of the Development of the American Country Life Movement* (mimeographed, no date), 2. In these recollections made when Bailey was 85, he recalled two appointments after his. The President's *Appointment Book* indicates only one, the Director of Reclamation.

[31] Pinchot to Bailey, April 13, 1908; Bailey to Pinchot, April 17, 1908; Pinchot to Bailey, April 24, 1908, Pinchot MSS, Box 1741, DLC.

[32] Bailey to Pinchot, April 13, 1908, Pinchot MSS, Box 1741, DLC.

[33] Bailey to Theodore Roosevelt, April 28, 1908, Pinchot MSS, Box 1741, DLC.

[34] Pinchot to Roosevelt, June 29, 1908, Pinchot MSS, Box 1741, DLC.

[35] The first course in rural social life taught in this country was offered by Professor C. R. Henderson at the University of Chicago in 1894–1895 (John Phelan, ed., *Readings in Rural Sociology* (New York, 1922), 619.

[36] Allen Johnson, ed., *Dictionary of American Biography* (22 vols., New York, 1946), 21–22: 144.

editor of the Middle West.[37] As a result of an intimate knowledge of education, sanitary conditions, and farming in the South, the name of Editor Page of the *World's Work* was suggested early to Pinchot by Doctor H. B. Frissell, Principal of Hampton Institute.[38]

Later, following the protest of the Atlanta, Georgia *Southern Ruralist*, a second southerner, C. S. Barrett, President of the Farmers Union of Union City, Georgia, was added as a member of the Commission.[39] At the same time, to give greater importance to the Far West, W. A. Beard, editor of the *Great West Magazine*, Sacramento, California was added to the Commission.

Dr. Charles W. Stiles, zoologist, professor of medicine, and consulting government health official who had discovered an American species of the hookworm, accompanied the Commission as a medical attaché. Stiles was anxious to prove to the South that the hookworm was more prevalent than commonly admitted, that it could be cured by a simple remedy of capsules of thymol and salt taken over a period of eighteen hours, and that reinfection could be averted by wearing shoes and by sanitary latrines. . . .

II. THE COMMISSION AT WORK

The next snag that the new-born Commission hit was financial. "Uncle Henry" Wallace found it difficult to accept Roosevelt's view that if the Commissioners received no compensation, they would perform a better job. A Scotsman, "Uncle Henry" wanted at least his traveling expenses.[40] Finally, Page secured a confidential grant of $5000 from the Russell Sage Foundation which covered a portion of the traveling expenses.[41] Payment of most of the remainder of the expenses came out of the pockets of Bailey, Page, and Pinchot.

After . . . the problems of the purse were resolved, the Commission encountered only minor procedural difficulties. It had been charged by Roosevelt to report on the condition of country life, and upon the means for supplying the deficiencies discovered. The Commission decided to secure the facts not already known from circulars which consisted of twelve questions formulated with the help of the Census Bureau. Over one-half million of these were mailed to farmers living on rural free delivery routes and to other farmers who requested them. Circulars were also sent to rural leaders whose names had been suggested by public school officials and farm editors. Everyone was invited to supplement the circulars with

[37] Roosevelt to James Wilson, August 5, 1908, in Theodore Roosevelt's President's Letter Box 159, DLC; Telegram Pinchot to Roosevelt, August 3, 1908, Pinchot MSS, Box 1743, DLC.

[38] H. B. Frissell to Pinchot, April 11, 1908, Box 1742, DLC; Pinchot to Bailey, April 13, 1908, Pinchot MSS, Box 1741, DLC; Walter H. Page to Pinchot, April 5, 1908, Pinchot MSS, Box 1743, DLC; indicates that Page had early learned of the proposed Commission and was interested enough in it to suggest that its report should be in the form of a short book, and written in a popular style.

[39] H. E. Stockbridge, Atlanta, Georgia, September 15, 1908, to President Theodore Roosevelt in Bailey MSS in the Bailey Hortorium, Cornell University.

[40] Henry Wallace, *Uncle Henry's Own Story of His Life. Personal Reminiscences* (3 vols., Des Moines, 1917–1919), 2: 103; Bailey, September 3, 1908, to Gifford Pinchot in Bailey Hortorium; Pinchot to Bailey, September 22, 1908, MSS in Bailey Hortorium.

[41] John M. Glenn, Secretary Director, Russell Sage Foundation, New York, N. Y., October 28, 1908, to Bailey, MS in Bailey Hortorium.

letters to the Commission. A gratifying number of letters, and about one hundred and fifteen thousand circulars, about one out of five, were returned. At Bailey's suggestion Roosevelt asked the farmers to meet in district schools to discuss the questions on the circulars. Returns from about 200 of these meetings in all but 12 states were returned. Hearings were held by the Commission in 30 places scattered over the United States. And the Commissioners as individuals conducted special investigations. Incredible as it may seem, the Commissioners handed the *Report* to the President on January 23, 1909, less than a month after the deadline and only five months from the day Bailey accepted the chairmanship. It is hard to recall a commission which did so much in such a short period of time as did this pioneering one.

Originally, a question about the rural church had been scheduled to appear on the circulars. But Wallace, who privately admitted the weaknesses of the country church, objected to an investigation by the government. In deference to his wish, no question was asked about the churches. Bailey did ask Butterfield to make a special report on the church.[42] An evaluation which described the indebtedness of American agriculture to the immigrant, and the superiority of the immigrant farm hand to the native farm hand, was trimmed from several pages to a paragraph upon the violent protest of Commissioner C. S. Barrett who wrote from Georgia, "I am surer of nothing on this earth, than that the overwhelming majority of the farmers in the south and west are unalterably opposed to foreign immigration."[43]

The Commission side-stepped a third flammable issue. W. E. Burghardt Du Bois, President of Atlanta University, requested that the Commission study a widespread system of peonage in the South varying all the way "from a share system with a systematic cheating and company stores, to practical slavery."[44] With the explanation that the Commission did not have time to make a thorough study of race relations, this request was denied.[45] To avoid raising race relations to a fever pitch, the Commission, upon the advice of Page, cancelled a stop at Tuskegee Institute.[46] A committee of Negroes was received, however, at the hearings at Spartansburg, South Carolina; and the Commission attempted, under the direction of Page, Pinchot, and especially Wallace, to make an impartial study of renters and farm laborers, of which Negroes were a part.

The purpose, methods, and personnel of the Commission appealed strongly to the American people. Pinchot wrote to Plunkett, that seemingly the President had reached more people by this action than he had done before.[47] Letters of praise were numerous. The depth of appreciation is shown in a letter written to Roosevelt by a farm woman who said, "It must have been divine inspiration that

[42] Bailey to President K. L. Butterfield, September 29, 30, October 28, 1908, MSS in Bailey Hortorium.

[43] C. S. Barrett, Union City, Georgia, January 16, 1909, to Bailey, MS in Bailey Hortorium. The section on the immigrant was deleted from the sixth draft of the *Report* now in the Bailey Hortorium.

[44] W. E. Burghardt du Bois, Atlanta, Georgia, to Bailey, November 23, 1908, MS in Bailey Hortorium.

[45] Bailey to C. J. Blanchard, October 26, 1908, MS in Bailey Hortorium; Bailey to du Bois, December 3, 1908, MS in Bailey Hortorium.

[46] Bailey to C. J. Blanchard, October 26, 1908, MS in Bailey Hortorium.

[47] Pinchot to Plunkett, October 17, 1908, Gifford Pinchot MSS, Box 108, DLC.

caused you to try to understand the loneliness of a farmer's life."[48] Newspaper clippings preserved in the Bailey papers indicate that the tour of the Commissioners received about the same amount of favorable space as a big-league baseball team on a barnstorming tour would have received in that era. The lovable bearded "Uncle Henry," well-known through his writings in *Wallaces' Farmer* for his religious idealism and for his ability to speak the language of the honest "straight-up-and down" farmer, was greeted like a hero. When Bailey could not account for the absence of Wallace at a hearing, he knew the editor-preacher had slipped away to preach a sermon. The agricultural press, with a few exceptions, blessed the venture.

There was some criticism in the urban press which described the Commission either as just an election trick or as an unconstitutional paternalistic act. Typically, one editor wrote:

> *This is a sociological Administration, and President Roosevelt will go out of office in less than four months. After that he is going to Africa to hunt lions. Any farmer whose barn roof leaks, or whose daughter finds compound fractions too hard, or whose hired man goes off to town Saturday night, and does not come home until Monday morning, ought to write to Washington at once. The time is short.*[49]

During the early days of the Commission, cartoonists pictured the Commissioners as men wearing plug hats and Prince Albert coats going out in the country to milk the farmer's cows.[50]

The interest of Dr. Stiles in studying the prevalence of the hookworm in the South offended some sensitive Southerners. One minister took issue with the mosquito theory, which was held by Stiles and other doctors regarding some diseases, and insisted, instead, that the eating of pearl grits and the use of kerosene lamps without chimneys produced illness.[51]

III. THE REPORT

The *Report* was divided into two parts: one was an introductory summary which was written by Page and Pinchot for the use by the newspapers; the other, a longer statement of about 115 pages which had been written in eight drafts by Bailey before it had received the approval of all of the Commissioners.[52] Inasmuch as the Commissioners had planned to publish and edit the facts at greater length later, the *Report* contained only general statements and conclusions. This was an unfortunate decision, since most of the circulars fell into hostile hands in the United States Department of Agriculture and were destroyed before they could

48 Mrs. H. B. Rose, Middlefield, Ohio, September 5, 1908, to Roosevelt, MS in Bailey Hortorium.

49 Unidentified clipping in Bailey Hortorium. The *Literary Digest* 37:235 (August 22, 1908), cites hostile opinion in the New York *Evening Post, Times,* and *Journal of Commerce*. For a summary of the attitude of farm papers see *Literary Digest* 37:965 (December 26, 1908). The author is indebted to Alice Cluetts, a graduate student in history at Ohio State University for calling his attention to these citations in the *Literary Digest*.

50 Henry Wallace, *Uncle Henry's Own Story,* 103.

51 Aiken (S.C.) *Journal,* November 17, 1908.

52 The eight editions are in manuscript in the Bailey Hortorium.

be published. Fortunately, a few of the circulars which were not forwarded to Washington have survived in the Bailey Hortorium at Cornell University. The Census Bureau made a statistical summary of the returns from the circulars for Bailey's use in writing the *Report*. This has also survived in part at Cornell. Minutes of the *Hearings* have been preserved in the Gifford Pinchot papers, now in the Library of Congress. These fortuitous remnants gave us some detailed idea of what farmers were thinking at that time, and the kind of newly acquired information that influenced the Commission.

Although the *Report* conceded that the American farmers were more prosperous than they had ever been, and that farm life was becoming more attractive, there was "more or less serious agricultural unrest in every part of the United States, even in the most prosperous regions."[53] The widespread movement of farmers of all ages to town and city was merely one symptom of agrarian discontent. American farm life was not to be measured in terms of what it had been, but in terms of its possibilities, and in terms of the advantages enjoyed by non-farmers.

A. Findings

Country life possessed two basic handicaps. One was "the lack of a highly organized rural society," in other words, the excessive individualism of the farmer.[54] In pioneer days, self-reliance had been a priceless asset. It still was, if modified. But modified it had to be. Now a farmer stood practically alone, a small capitalist in a world of vast industrial organizations. With the exception of those who belonged to the Grange and the Farmers Union, the farmers possessed no power similar to what the unions secured for the industrial worker or what the corporation and trade association secured for the industrialist. As a detached man, the farmer suffered.

A realization by the farmers themselves of their weakness in economic bargaining was disclosed in their replies to two questions on the circular pertaining to marketing. The response to the question, "Are the farmers and their wives in your neighborhoods satisfactorily organized to promote their mutual buying and selling interests?" was clear-cut.[55] Farmers and their wives and nine other rural occupational groups such as clergymen, teachers, judges and lawyers, merchants and manufacturers responded with 4.4 times as many nays as yeas. Merchants and others who made a living selling and buying from the farmer, saw the least need for business organization among the farmers. The replies from all census regions as well as from all occupational groups were negative. The ratio of nays to yeas—7.2 in the South Atlantic region, and 5.0 in the South Central region—was higher than elsewhere in the United States.

The responses of farmers and their wives to the question, "Do the farmers in your neighborhood get the returns they reasonably should from the sale of their products?," showed more regional variations.[56] In the South Central, South

[53] The *Report*, 38.
[54] The *Report*, 19, 111.
[55] "Farmers' Organization for Buying and Selling," a four-page typed summary sent by L. G. Powers, Chief Statistician Census Bureau to Bailey, December 26, 1908, MS in Bailey Hortorium, 2, 4.
[56] "Farmers' Returns From the Sale of Their Products." submitted by Powers to Bailey, December 26, 1908, MS in Bailey Hortorium, 1–7.

Atlantic, and Western states, the nays exceeded the yeas. In the southern states many farmers believed that they were being defrauded of a part of their earnings by the system of future selling of cotton and other products. Western farmers were influenced by the high costs of transporting their crops long distances to markets. In the North Atlantic and North Central states, there was a slight excess of favorable replies from farmers except from Missouri, Wisconsin, and North Dakota, the future breeding site of the radical Non-Partisan League.

A second fundamental source of woes according to the *Report* was the lack of a proper kind of education. Then, as in the Sputnik era, the school became the scapegoat. In 1908, they were held responsible for "ineffective farming, lack of ideals, and the drift to town." No other subject loomed as large as education in the hearings, correspondence, and in the schoolhouse meetings. No other question in the circulars evoked more responses than the one, "Are the schools of your neighborhood training boys and girls satisfactorily for life on the farm?" There was a heavy excess of nays over yeas in the replies from all occupational groups.[57] The proportion of replies of farmers unfavorable to the schools was 2 to 1. The ratio of unfavorable replies was higher from teachers, clergymen, and lawyers who had a poorer opinion of the schools than other occupational groups including the farmers. The proportion of replies favorable was highest from manufacturers and merchants.

Incompetent teachers, poor physical equipment, poor support from stingy taxpayers, and lack of federal support for schools, especially those for Negroes, were among the shortcomings attributed to the schools. The most frequent charge hurled at the schools was that the courses were not practical or vocational, and that they did not teach the advantages and possible enjoyment of country life.[58] Expressions for and against consolidated schools were about equally divided. No one summarized better the magic which the schools were expected to perform than did an illiterate farmer who asked, "Why not have schools in the country that can edgericate our children and raise them to as high in financial circle as did Abraham linken and Gerge Washington in thare days of growing up."[59]

After mentioning the two primary deficiencies, lack of organization and the proper kind of education, the Commission suggested a series of secondary shortcomings. The first specific deficiency mentioned, as opposed to the two basic handicaps, was the violation of the inherent rights of the men who till the soil by the mining, manufacturing, merchandise, and transportation corporations.[60] This was evidenced by unjust tax systems; the ownership by certain investors in the West and South of large areas of land for speculation which had resulted in so much tenancy and absentee farming that the Commissioners had been asked to demand laws limiting the size of holdings; the monopolistic control of streams

[57] "The Condition of Rural Schools With Reference to Agricultural Education, As Reflected In the Answers to Inquiries by the Commission on Country Life," a summary submitted to Bailey by L. G. Powers, Chief Statistician, Bureau of the Census, December 26, 1908, MS in Bailey Hortorium, 1, 2.

[58] "Memorandum of Contents of Reports of Farmers' Meetings," submitted by A. C. True, Director of Office of Experiment Stations, January 6, 1908, MS prepared by that office and the Census Bureau in Bailey Hortorium, 103, and appendix.

[59] Reply in a circular from Denison, Texas, MS in Bailey Hortorium, no date.

[60] The specific deficiencies are described in the *Report*, 59–106.

which worked a hardship upon irrigation farmers, and which prevented the development of water-power for the transmission of electricity. Forests which prevented soil erosion had been wasted. And finally, the inherent right of a farmer to a fair market had been jeopardized by restraints in trade in the form of tariffs and exorbitant charges by middlemen.

Another defect in farming was the depletion of the soil, which, in accordance with the old proverb, "Poor land, poor people," was held responsible for the evil of tenancy. Exploitation of virgin soil had been characteristic of the general pioneer farmers of the North who had escaped the consequences of robbing the holy earth by moving westward to unoccupied lands. Now that escape to virgin land was no longer possible, northern farmers had either to become skilled farm operators, as many were doing, or to sink into tenancy and degradation as many others in the North were doing. A one-crop system, except perhaps when applied to vegetables and fruits, produced sad results. The ill effects upon the soil and upon the income of farmers of exclusive hay selling in the Northeast, of exclusive corn-growing in the Middle West unless the corn was fed to livestock, and of exclusive wheat-growing on the Great Plains were easily discernible. The most pathetic effect of the one-crop system was to be seen in the cotton South where the depleted soil did not yield an average income of over $150 a year to a tenant farmer growing cotton. There, the tenant was virtually in economic bondage to landlords, who in many counties were little better off than the tenants, since they were trapped on poor soil and were victimized by money-lending merchants and financial manipulators of the prices of cotton.

The answers from the South Atlantic and South Central regions to the question in the circular, "Are the renters of farms in your neighborhood making a satisfactory living?" revealed a deep awareness of the shortcomings of tenancy in Dixie. Not only the answering farmers and their wives, who were primarily landowners rather than renters or croppers, but all occupational groups replied that they thought tenants did not receive proper remuneration for their efforts.[61]

A third specific deficiency was highways. The advantages of good roads were mentioned without end. Improved roads would make it feasible for the federal government to establish more rural free delivery routes and to satisfy the mounting demand for parcel post in the open country. Good roads would make it possible for the farmer to drive his team to town on a weekly shopping trip with comparative ease, comfort, and speed, and to haul his produce whenever the price was best. They would make it possible for a farmer and his family to drive to town to attend church or a concert or a lecture in the schoolhouse whenever they chose in the muddy seasons. A farm woman who lived near Cleveland, Ohio, registered a characteristic complaint. She and her husband yearned for "the music and sermons which we heard a few years ago in the city of Cleveland."[62] But now they could not take full advantage of the limited cultural advantages offered by the nearest villages of Burton and Middlefield, since the main road from their

[61] "Living of Renters," summary sent by L. G. Powers, Chief Statistician, Bureau of Census, December 26, 1908, MS to Bailey in Bailey Hortorium. Farmers and farmers' wives supplied 4,444 yeas and 7,697 nays; school teachers 240 yeas, 442 nays; all others 3,333 yeas, 3,650 nays. *Ibid.*, 2.

[62] Mrs. H. B. Rose, Middlefield, Ohio, October 22, 1908, MS to Norval D. Kemp, Bailey's Secretary, in Bailey Hortorium.

farm to these places was made well-nigh impassable by the roadmaster who plowed it annually just before the fall rains.

The demands for better roads was doubtlessly influenced by the opinion expressed in the circulars by the majority of the farmers in 16 states that the service of the railroads was inadequate.[63]

A fourth specific black spot was farm labor. Employers and farm hands were dissatisfied but for different reasons. From the point of view of farm employers, the situation was hopeless, although the best farmers complained the least. High wages paid by the factories had diminished the supply of competent workers and had forced farm wages to an exorbitantly high level. A majority of the farmers in all of the census regions recorded their opinion that the living conditions and wages of hired men were satisfactory. The farmers of the North Central region with a vote of 3.1 to 1 were most certain that the hired men were faring well; the farmers of two census regions, the South Atlantic and South Central, were least certain with votes of 1.7 to 1.[64] Hired men, for their part, were equally unhappy as a result of seasonal unemployment, low pay, an absence of satisfactory companionship, and long hours. In a few words one of their spokesmen expressed the most frequently mentioned grievance: "Some people hire men and expect them to work night and day which is not right and should be stopped. The days of slavery are past."[65]

Some health conditions were found to be in urgent need of improvement. Farmers and their wives in all but three states gave an excess number of nays over yeas in reply to the question, "Are the farm homes in your neighborhood as good as they should be under existing circumstances?" The states were Virginia, Kentucky, and Texas.[66] The Commission observed that numberless farmhouses and schoolhouses did not have rudimentary sanitary arrangements. It discovered the nationwide prevalence of milk and water pollution and unsanitary slaughterhouses in the open country. Epidemics of typhoid fever were common in some localities. One reply amused Roosevelt so much that he put it in his *Autobiography*. It was from a farmer who reported, "In one well on a neighbor's farm I counted seven snakes in the wall of the well, and they used the water daily: his wife [is] dead now and he is looking for another."[67] The Commission also noted the universality of patent medicines and quack advertising, that physicians were farther apart, and that boards of health were less common than in the cities. In some areas the cost of medical care was found to be high. In the South there was an extensive spread of the hookworm disease and malaria.

Woman's work on the farm was cited as another seamy aspect of the country.

[63] "Services of Railroads, Highroads, Trolley Lines, ETC.," 2; and "Postal and Rural Telephone Service," transmitted by Powers to Bailey, December 26, 1908, MSS in Bailey Hortorium, 1, 2.

[64] "Conditions Surrounding Farm Labor," 1, 2, and "Supply of Farm Labor," 1–3, typewritten summaries from Census Bureau, December 26, 1908, in Bailey Hortorium.

[65] Reply fastened to Circular from Ura Embry, Sherman, Texas, MS in Bailey Hortorium, no date.

[66] "The Condition of Farm Homes as Reflected by the Answers to Inquiries by the Commission," transmitted to Bailey by the Census Bureau, December 26, 1908, MS in Bailey Hortorium, 1–3.

[67] *Roosevelt, An Autobiography*, 430.

Poverty, and a lack of ideals often resulted in the purchase of labor-saving devices for the husband's use rather than in the purchase of conveniences for the home. Consequently, on many farms, burdens fell harder upon the lonely women than upon the men.

The Commission in its limited religious survey found the country churches in the North deficient in size, in scope of operations, in adequately trained resident ministers, and in salaries. Denominational rivalries often impaired the effectiveness of the churches.[68]

B. Recommendations

Unfortunately for the historian of today, a tabulation by the Census Bureau of the replies of farmers to the last and perhaps the most crucial question on the circular, "What, in your judgment, is the most important single thing to be done for the betterment of country life?" which was sent to Bailey, has been lost. The Commission itself, however, had access to this tabulation when it made its concise description of what should be done to overcome the handicaps of farm life.

Following the principle that knowledge was essential to improvement, much emphasis was placed upon a "re-directed" education. Congress was urged to establish a nationwide system of extension education, emanating from the agricultural colleges and involving lectures, correspondence courses, and demonstration work on the farm and in the home. The program was designed to teach sanitation and homemaking in addition to instruction in the science and business of agriculture. Congress was requested to enlarge the United States Bureau of Education to enable it to stimulate and coordinate the educational activities of the nation. And since the work of the Commission had merely been preliminary, Congress was urged to set in motion a series of thorough-going surveys of all of the agricultural regions of the United States; and to establish some kind of central agency to guide the development of rural civilization. Shades of the old Social and Economic Bureau! Further, with and without federal support, the public schools were asked to incorporate courses in vocational agriculture and nature study into their curricula. The Commission also recommended that the powers of the federal government in the field of public health be expanded to include more publicity and greater jurisdiction in the supervision and control of communicable diseases. The expansion of a federal highway engineering service to assist the states in building better roads was requested.

On the principle that organization or collective strength was essential to the betterment of country life, the Commission made several additional recommendations. The Commission requested Congress to re-examine the effects of existing tariffs, control of corporations, and water legislation upon the welfare of the farmer. It urged the establishment of parcel post and postal savings banks. It urged that special attention be paid to the improvement of the credit facilities of country banks. Some substitute should be found for the crop-lien system of credit which cursed the South. The Commission leaned heavily upon the formation of cooperatives to shore up the economic low spots of country life. Cooperatives of all kinds were recommended, ranging from the simplest voluntary

[68] The *Report,* 137–141.

club organized for recreational purposes to credit, telephone, and electricity. Cooperatives might well attempt "to establish prices and to control production."[69] Although the success of the cooperatives would depend ultimately upon the ability of private individuals, the Commission hinted that cooperatives would probably have to be stimulated and protected by federal and state laws.

Acting upon the principle that powerful spiritual forces were at least as essential as knowledge and organization, the Commission urged the country churches to supply ideals. Specifically, there was an urgent need for the churches to persuade prosperous, land-hungry men to invest their money in better schools and community projects, and in conveniences for the home, rather than in more land. To increase their effectiveness, the churches were tactfully advised to become social centers of their communities, and to educate their pastors to understand scientific agriculture and the operation of the industrial forces that could do so much to either help or break the farmer.

Since the Commissioners realized that they were prescribing goals that would take a long time to realize, they recommended that three movements be started at the earliest possible moment: an exhaustive inventory or survey of all the conditions that influenced farming and the people who live on the farm; a nationalized extension work; and a crusade for rural progress involving the holding of local, state, and even national conferences designed to unite all diverse organizations into one forward movement for the rebuilding of country life.

With the exception of a statement of these three movements that the Commission wished to set in motion immediately, and perhaps the recommendations for health, rural electrification, and water power, there was very little else in the *Report* that was original.[70] What was said about schools, roads, and the economic and political impotency of the individual farmer had been said over and over again in cracker-barrel discussions and in farm newspapers. "Uncle Henry," who confessed that he was exceedingly anxious to make the *Report* "a masterpiece, something of which our children may be proud," was also correct in complaining that the wording of the *Report* was not vivid enough.[71] The *Report* did not have the emotional appeal of the *Communist Manifesto* or the platform of the Populist Party. But the *Report* was a masterpiece in the only way that ultimately matters. A half century later, prominent farmers, educators, ministers, educators, and legislators implored Congress at hearings to create another Country Life Commission which they hoped would be as effective as the first one.[72]

C. Official Repudiation

When the President read the summary of the *Report* which Bailey delivered in person, he exclaimed, in the Rooseveltian way which won so many warm admirers, "By George this is a crackerjack, and it makes me as happy as Punch."[73]

[69] The *Report*, 132.
[70] Bailey to Pinchot, January 29, 1909, MS in Bailey Hortorium.
[71] Wallace to Bailey, January 4, 1909, MS in Bailey Hortorium.
[72] U. S. House of Representatives, 86th Cong., 1st Sess., Committee on Agriculture, *Hearings*, County Life Commission, H.R.5010, H.R.5022, and H.R.5517, May 6, 7, 1959 (Washington, 1959). The powerful *Farm Journal* gave its sanction to a second Country Life Commission in 1957. *Farm Journal*, 82 (July, 1957), 134.
[73] Bailey to Page, January 16, 1909, MS in Bailey Hortorium.

The political enemies of Roosevelt felt differently. When the chief executive transmitted to Congress the *Report*, which he said contained information so accurate and vital "as to disturb the serenity of the advocates of things as they are," he asked that $25,000 be included in an annual Sundry Civil Expenses Appropriation bill. This money was to be used to circulate the *Report* widely, and to assist the Commissioners in studying and publishing the circulars and other valuable material amassed by the Commission.

Apparently, hostile steps had been taken already by Secretary Wilson, who naturally, and with some justification, had become embittered. The work had been done outside his Department of Agriculture. And more insulting, Plunkett and others had made strenuous efforts to persuade Roosevelt's successor, Taft, to appoint a Secretary of Agriculture more sympathetic with rural social and economic reform than Wilson was.[74] The Secretary of Agriculture demanded that Bailey and the Census Bureau deliver the circulars to him.[75] Bailey partially complied by ordering some of the circulars sent to Wilson. Subsequently, unsuccessful efforts were made by the Commissioners, the Association of Agricultural Colleges and Experiment Stations, and others to secure an extensive publication of these papers.[76] As a result, the circulars remained stored in the Department of Agriculture where, as one official explained, no one dared touch them since there was a "specie of outlawry attached to them."[77] When the Taft administration was replaced by the Wilsonian administration, the circulars were ordered burned, upon the advice of two subordinates, by D. F. Houston, new Secretary of Agriculture, as waste paper no longer of any value.[78]

Secretary Wilson was joined by Roosevelt's enemies in Congress led by James A. Tawney, Chairman of the House Appropriations Committee and a man who, in Roosevelt's opinion, was "one of the most efficient representatives of the cause of special privilege as against public interest to be found in the House. . . ."[79] Tawney killed Roosevelt's request for an appropriation to complete the work of the Commission by an amendment which forbade expenditures for any commission not authorized by Congress, and which forbade the appointment in the future of commissions without authorization by Congress. The amendment was

[74] Digby, *Horace Plunkett*, 126, 127; *Proceedings*, Twenty-Second Annual Convention of Association of Agricultural Colleges and Experiment Stations, November 18–20, 1908, USDA, Office of Experiment Stations, Bulletin 212 (1909), 48; Early Vernon Wilcox, *Tama Jim* (Boston, 1930), 160.

[75] James Wilson to Bailey, January 19, 1909, January 22, 1909, January 28, 1909, MSS in Record Group 16, National Archives; and letters from Bailey to Wilson, January 16 and January 25, 1909, MSS in Bailey Hortorium.

[76] *Proceedings*, Twenty-Third Annual Convention of Association of Agricultural Colleges and Experiment Stations held at Portland, Oregon, August 18–20, 1909, USDA, Office of Experiment Stations, Bulletin 228 (1910), 44, 99; E. E. Slosson, July 13, 1909, to L. H. Bailey in Box 1741, Pinchot MSS, DLC; W. M. Hays to Bailey, August 18, 1910, and Edwin A. Smith to William Jennings Bryan, March 13, 1913, in Country Life File, National Archives.

[77] Edwin A. Smith to William Jennings Bryan, March 13, 1913, MSS in Country Life File, in Record Group 16, National Archives; W. M. Hays to Bailey, August 18, 1910; Henry Wallace to Bailey, June 29, 1910, MS in Bailey Hortorium.

[78] Charles J. Brand, September 9, 1915, to R. M. Reese, and E. W. Allen to R. M. Reese; and Special Order of D. F. Houston to R. M. Reese, September 23, 1915, MSS, Record Group 16, USDA, National Archives.

[79] *Roosevelt, An Autobiography*, 430; *Congressional Record*, 60th Congress, 2d Session, 2080, 3119, 3120.

passed, and the Commission came to a full stop. The last official act of Roosevelt was to denounce the Tawney Amendment as unconstitutional (which it was not, with the exception of the provision which forbade future presidents to appoint a commission without the consent of Congress), and to assert that if he were to remain in office, he would not obey it.

The *Report* did fare somewhat better than the circulars. As a result of the intercession of Senator Jonathan P. Dolliver from "Uncle Henry's" state, a limited number of copies, about 2000, were circulated as a Senate document.

Taft remained indifferent and inactive during the controversy. He acknowledged the importance of the work done by the Commission, and during the early months of his administration apparently assumed that the Commission was merely dormant awaiting Congressional appropriations, which, according to Pinchot, the President promised to request.[80] Taft did push a serious and able study of the European systems of farm credit. Otherwise, Taft's efforts were so languid that the Commission was permitted to die. And his administration did not enact into law any of the major recommendations of the Commission for farm legislation except in the twilight of the administration when parcel post was inaugurated.

Disappointment over Taft's ineptitude soon became apparent. By June, 1909, "Uncle Henry" had warned Taft in the editorial pages of *Wallaces' Farmer* that if the smiling, golf-playing Taft did not continue the Roosevelt policies, the people of the West would look "for a successor who will do the business, and that is very likely to be the man now in Africa."[81] By the time of the Congressional elections of 1910, the editorial dictum of *Wallaces' Farmer* was that Roosevelt "is today the most valuable asset of the American people." And upon denying press reports that he had criticized Taft for not continuing the work of the Country Life Commission, Bailey withdrew completely and permanently from political affairs.[82]

Naturally, ex-president Roosevelt was indignant. In a comprehensive evaluation of his presidency which he had given to an English journalist in December, 1908, Roosevelt claimed as a major accomplishment, "I also started the movement for the betterment of country life."[83] In the same month, Roosevelt had written to his successor expressing the opinion that of all the legacies of trouble he was leaving to Taft, none was dearer to his heart than the great problems of American country life.[84] Taft's subsequent abandonment of the Country Life Commission was, according to Roosevelt, "the last straw," and "the capstone, the climax" in a series of things that produced the break between him and Taft.[85]

80 Pinchot to L. H. Bailey, June 8, 1909, in Box 1741, Pinchot MSS, DLC; Bailey to Page, April 14, April 17, 1909, MSS in Bailey Hortorium; W. H. Taft to Bailey, August 6, 1910, MS in Bailey Hortorium.

81 "What About Taft?" in *Wallaces' Farmer*, 34:834 (June 18, 1909), "The Greatness of T. R." in *Ibid.*, 35:1243 (September 23, 1910).

82 Taft to Bailey, August 10, 1910, MS in Bailey Hortorium.

83 Roosevelt to Sydney Brooks, December 28, 1908, MS in the President's Personal Letter Box 161, DLC.

84 Elting Morison, ed., *The Letters of Theodore Roosevelt* (Cambridge, 1950–52), 6: 1433.

85 From the diary of John J. Leary, Jr., *Talks with T. R.* on April 8, 1916, (Houghton Mifflin, 1920), 25–27, cited in the *Theodore Roosevelt Cyclopedia* (1941), 596.

As a candidate of the Progressive party for the presidency in 1912, Roosevelt announced emphatically that if he were elected he would re-establish the Country Life Commission and foster a comprehensive program of farm legislation.[86] As a result of the split in the Republican Party, both Taft and Roosevelt were defeated by Woodrow Wilson.

IV. ULTIMATE VICTORY

The Country Life Commission had lost the first battle, but in the end, it won a long war. Within two years after Congress had refused to appropriate money for the popular publication of the *Report*, it had been published by the Spokane Chamber of Commerce for distribution in the Northwest, and by a private commercial firm in New York City. In 1944, long after the bitter fires of controversy had died out, it was published again. This time it was honored by the scholarly University of North Carolina Press. The history of a better rural America has been, to a significant extent, the history of the adoption of the recommendations of the Commission. The Presbyterian Church of the United States of America (the northern branch) under the leadership of William Warren Wilson immediately established a department of country life, which conducted, in the years that immediately followed, comprehensive surveys of churches and schools in several states. Today, almost all of the major denominations and the National Council of Churches have departments of country life.

In 1909, Stiles, the medical attaché, sat up nearly one whole night in a hotel room describing the devastations of the hookworm to Wallace Buttrick, then Secretary of the General Education Board financed by John D. Rockefeller. Buttrick then rushed to Frederick T. Gates, principal adviser to Rockefeller in philanthropy as well as business. Gates was deeply stirred and persuaded Rockefeller to pledge one million for a Sanitary Commission to prevent and cure the hookworm in the South. One problem of the Sanitary Commission was to overcome the objection voiced by one Georgia paper which asked, "Where was this hookworm or lazy disease, when it took five Yankee soldiers to whip one Southerner?"[87] The Sanitary Commission was, nevertheless, so successful that it was expanded into the justly famed International Health Division of the Rockefeller Foundation. Another effect of the attack upon the hookworm disease was to demonstrate the importance of local health agencies as mentioned by the Country Life Commission. By 1911, county health boards had been started in three widely separated states. During the next ten years, they spread to 186 counties in 23 states. By 1953, more than 70 per cent of the counties of the United States were organized for full-time local health services. Many of them were, however, operating with a minimum of services. Although the rapid spread

[86] Henry Beach Needham, "Is the Farmer Getting a Square Deal," an interview with Theodore Roosevelt in *Country Gentleman*, 77:2–3 (June 1, 1912), and "What the Candidates Promise Farmers," 77:9 (August 31, 1912). For the disgust with which some of Roosevelt's supporters regarded Taft's inaction see letter of B. F. Harris of Champaign, Illinois, and President of the Illinois Bankers' Association to Frank Harper, Roosevelt's secretary, March 18, 1912, MS, and letter from Harris to J. Clyde Marquiss, editor of the *Country Gentleman*, March 18, 1912, MS in Box 20, Letters Received, Roosevelt MSS, DLC.

[87] Raymond Fosdick, *The Story Of The Rockefeller Foundation* (New York, 1952), 10.

of the public health movement dates from 1909, the many individuals and organizations other than the Commission had been responsible for its beginning and spread. As a result of the *Report*, farm newspapers and the mail-order houses soon broke out with a rash of advertisements of septic tanks, central heating systems, deep well pumps, electric lighting plants for the home, and power washing machines.

The Wilson administration acted vigorously upon other measures outlined by the Commission. Farm organizations were exempted from the anti-trust laws by the Clayton Anti-Trust Act of 1914; a national system of extension education based upon county agricultural agents came into existence through the Smith-Lever Act of 1914. Three years later vocational education in the high schools was made a reality by the Smith-Hughes Act. The possibility of dispelling the nightmare of bad roads became apparent when Congress passed the Federal Aid to Roads Act of 1916. More adequate rural credit facilities were provided by the Federal Reserve Banking Act of 1913, the Federal Warehouse Act (1916), and the very important Federal Land Bank Act, which marked in 1916, the beginning of the first of the gigantic federal credit arrangements. Industrial tariffs were lowered somewhat by the Underwood-Simmons Tariff. The probing of the monopolistic practices of the packers and grain traders provided facts for federal regulatory legislation in the next decade. Major credit for the passage of these legislative landmarks belongs to farm organizations and the many unnamed men and women who had crusaded for decades in behalf of these legislative reforms. Yet, much credit for giving authoritative benediction for the necessity of these reforms belongs to the Commission.

The recommendation for a central agency to guide improvements in rural life did not become a reality until 1919, when the present Division of Farm Population and Rural Life was started. This governmental agency, which is primarily a research body, has not yet become the powerful policy-forming department envisaged by Pinchot and Plunkett. In the same year, the present-day National Country Life Association was formed largely through the leadership of Butterfield who became its first president. Composed mainly of rural sociologists and ministers who meet in annual conventions, the Association has sustained an enlightened interest in country problems in a civilization preoccupied with urban and international affairs. Rural sociology became a separate and thriving academic discipline as a result of the prestige given to it by the Country Life Commission. It received another lift from the federal government in 1924 when the Purnell Act authorized federal funds for instruction and research. As a result, innumerable sociological surveys of country life have been made annually. A full-fledged Bureau of Agricultural Economics was not instituted until 1922 under the leadership of Secretary of Agriculture Henry C. Wallace, son of "Uncle Henry," who did not live to see the fulfillment of this dream. This splendid bureau became a powerful and proficient institution until it was dismantled by its foes in the middle of the 1950s.

Rural electrification did not become universal until mid-century. Voluntary cooperation, especially economic cooperation, has not, perhaps, replaced excessive individualism as rapidly as the Commission had hoped. The genius, however, of the Country Life Commission was that it made only one major incorrect diagnosis. It believed that the exodus of the farmers to the city and decline of farm population were undesirable. One-half century later, farm economists, with full knowledge of how socially attractive life in the open country had become and how remunerative farming had become for large-scale farmers, were rejoicing in the precipitous decline in farm population. The reasons for this reversal in thinking are primarily economic. Some farmers have left farms where small acreage, poor soil, and adverse climate have usually made profitable farming impossible. Vastly more significant, fewer and fewer farmers who live on good soil and who adopt up-to-date scientific and technological practices can produce, and do produce, fabulous surpluses of foods and fibers which cannot be sold at a profit.

These developments had not been prognosticated by the members of the Country Life Commission. In justice to these men and to President Theodore Roosevelt, it should be recalled that they realized that merely to increase the physical productivity of agriculture by the wonderful wand of science would not automatically solve the great problems of farm life. This awareness was a principal reason, if not the principal reason, for the very existence of the first Country Life Commission.

2

JOHN MUIR, WILLIAM KENT, AND THE CONSERVATION SCHISM

Roderick Nash

The protection of the resources of man's physical environment is now a major problem of civilization since man himself is faced with extinction unless a sensible ecological balance is achieved. The conservation movement in the United States came to public attention late in the nineteenth century with the realization that the resources of the continent were not inexhaustible. Dramatized by Theodore Roosevelt and his associates, who were motivated by the need to prevent waste and by the desire to punish perpetrators of fraud and evasion under the prevailing land laws, the controversy discussed in this article occurred among the conservationists themselves and revealed a critical fissure in their camp.

Roderick Nash specializes in conservation history. Following the appearance of his book Wilderness and the American Mind *(New Haven, 1967), he has compiled two sets of readings dealing with conservation and published* The Nervous Generation: American Thought, 1917–1930 *(Chicago, 1970). This article is the basis of a crucial chapter in his* Wilderness and the American Mind. *He is presently on the faculty at the University of California, Santa Barbara.*

In March, 1868, a self-styled "poetico-trampo-geologist-bot. and ornith-natural, etc!-!-!-!"[1] named John Muir arrived in San Francisco and, allegedly, immediately asked to be shown "any place that is wild."[2] His search took him into the Sierra, and in the following decades Muir became the leading interpreter of these

[1] John Muir to Robert Underwood Johnson, Sept. 13, 1889, as quoted in "The Creation of Yosemite National Park," *Sierra Club Bulletin*, XXXIX (1944), 50.

[2] Muir, *The Yosemite* (New York, 1912), 4.

Source: *Pacific Historical Review*, Vol. 36, No. 4 (1967), pp. 423–433.

mountains as well as America's foremost publicizer of wilderness values in general.[3] Three years after Muir came West, another young man, fleeing the great Chicago fire, arrived in California. William Kent also sought the wilderness—to such an extent that he could state without much exaggeration: "My life has been largely spent outdoors."[4] Independently wealthy and of a reforming temperament, Kent pursued a political career in which conservation played a major part.[5] Inevitably his trail crossed Muir's. Indeed in 1908 Kent insisted that the tract of virgin redwood forest he gave to the public be called the Muir Woods National Monument. But in the next five years San Francisco's attempt to secure the Hetch Hetchy Valley in Yosemite National Park as a reservoir site created an issue that caused a major schism among conservationists. The friendship of John Muir and William Kent was one of the casualties of the Hetch Hetchy fight. Faced with the need to choose between different definitions of "conservation," they ended in opposing camps, learning that in regard to conservation the most intense conflicts are often family affairs.

Rising north of the Golden Gate in Marin County, Mt. Tamalpais dominates San Francisco Bay, and its western slope affords a favorable environment for the towering coast redwood and a lush understory of alder, laurel, and fern. William Kent's home was near Tamalpais, and in 1903 it came to his attention that one of its last unlogged canyons was for sale. Kent knew the area and confessed that "the beauty of the place attracted me, and got on my mind, and I could not forget the situation."[6] But the $45,000 asking price was formidable even for Kent. Still, when his wife protested, he simply asked: "If we lost all the money we have and saved those trees it would be worthwhile, wouldn't it?"[7] The purchase of almost three hundred acres in Redwood Canyon followed. Kent had hopes of "a wilderness park for San Francisco and the Bay Cities."[8] Commenting in September, 1903, on the plan, he explained that "whatever occupation man may follow, there is planted within him a need of nature, calling . . . to him at times to come and . . . seek recuperation and strength." Crowded cities, he added, produced "physical, moral, and civic degradation" and, at the same time, the need to escape to wilder environments.[9]

With this attitude John Muir was in full sympathy. "Civilized man chokes

[3] Roderick Nash, *Wilderness and the American Mind* (to be published in 1967 by the Yale University Press), Chap. 8. Linnie Marsh Wolfe, *Son of the Wilderness: The Life of John Muir* (New York, 1945) is the standard biography.

[4] Autobiographical fragment, Kent Family Papers (hereafter *KFP*), Historical Manuscripts Room, Yale University Library, Box 95.

[5] For Kent's career, see Elizabeth T. Kent, *William Kent, Independent: A Biography* (privately published, 1951) (hereafter cited as *Kent*), and Gilson Gardner, Life of William Kent (unpublished typescript, ca. 1933), *KFP*, Box 152; these must now be supplemented with Robert Woodbury's "William Kent: Progressive Gadfly, 1864–1928" (doctoral dissertation, Yale University, 1967). I also profited from Woodbury's manuscript article on Kent as a conservationist.

[6] William Kent, "The Story of Muir Woods" (undated typescript), *KFP*, Box 111.

[7] *Kent*, 179, fn. 10.

[8] Undated manuscript fragment, *KFP*, Box 99.

[9] "Tamalpais as a National Park" (text of an address of Sept. 12, 1903, at Ross Valley, California), *KFP*, Box 111. Kent has commented on his many wilderness experiences in "Out Doors," *KFP*, Box 100, and in his only book, *Reminiscences of Outdoor Life* (San Francisco, 1929).

his soul," he noted in 1871, "as the heathen Chinese their feet."[10] He believed that centuries of primitive existence had implanted in human nature a yearning for adventure, freedom, and contact with nature which city life could not satisfy. Deny this urge, and the thwarted longings produced tension and despair; indulge it periodically in the wilderness, and there was both mental and physical reinvigoration. Steeped as he was in Transcendentalism, Muir never doubted that nature was a "window opening into heaven, a mirror reflecting the Creator."[11] And *wild* nature, he believed, provided the best "conductor of divinity" because it was least associated with man's artificial constructs.[12] Summing up his philosophy, Muir declared: "In God's wildness lies the hope of the world—the great fresh, unblighted, unredeemed wilderness."[13]

Like Kent, Muir recognized the necessity of the formal preservation of wild country if future generations were to have any left. In 1890 he was a prime mover in the establishment of Yosemite National Park. Two years later he became president of the Sierra Club, an organization dedicated to wilderness enjoyment and preservation.[14] After the turn of the century Muir emerged as a major figure in both the nature-writing genre and the conservation movement.

In 1907 William Kent returned to Marin County from a Hawaiian vacation to find that the North Coast Water Company was beginning condemnation proceedings against his land in Redwood Canyon for the purpose of creating a reservoir. Convinced that wilderness preservation took precedence over private development of water resources, Kent searched for a way of obtaining permanent protection for the area. When the Antiquities Act of 1906 came to his attention, he recognized its possibilities at once. The statute enabled the president to issue executive orders designating tracts of land in the public domain with exceptional historical or natural interest as national monuments. The federal government might also accept gifts of private land for this purpose. Taking the act at its word, in December, 1907, Kent informed Chief Forester Gifford Pinchot and Secretary of the Interior James R. Garfield that he wished to give Redwood Canyon to the government. Photographs and descriptions of the trees, some of the latter by John Muir, accompanied the application. Kent himself described the area as "the most attractive bit of wilderness I have ever seen."[15]

A final draft of the deed went to Secretary Garfield on December 26, and on January 9, 1908, President Theodore Roosevelt proclaimed the land a national monument. Naming the monument proved more complicated. Although

[10] *John of the Mountains: The Unpublished Journals of John Muir*, ed. Linnie Marsh Wolfe (Boston, 1938), 82.

[11] Muir, *My First Summer in the Sierra* (Boston, 1911), 211.

[12] Muir, *Journals*, 118.

[13] *Ibid.*, 317. Extended investigations of Muir's mind are available in Norman Foerster, *Nature in American Literature* (New York, 1923), 238–263, and Edith Jane Hadley, "John Muir's Views of Nature and their Consequences" (doctoral dissertation, University of Wisconsin, 1956). Daniel Barr Weber's "John Muir: The Function of Wilderness in an Industrial Society" (doctoral dissertation, University of Minnesota, 1964) is less satisfactory. A bibliography, largely complete except for some posthumous collections, may be found in the *Sierra Club Bulletin*, X (1916), 41–59.

[14] Holway R. Jones, *John Muir and the Sierra Club: The Battle for Yosemite* (San Francisco, 1965) is definitive for the club's origins and early history.

[15] Kent to James R. Garfield, Dec. 23, 1907, *KFP*, Box 6. Kent described his involvement with Redwood Canyon in "The Story of Muir Woods," *KFP*, Box 111.

he did not know Muir personally, Kent had long admired him as an interpreter of wilderness values and determined to name the reserve in his honor. But late in January he received a letter from the president asking permission to use "Kent" in its title. Kent responded on January 30, thanking Roosevelt for the proclamation and encouragement in saving "more of the precious and vanishing glories of nature for a people too slow of perception." But Kent refused to accept the change in name. If his sons could not keep the family name alive, he was willing it should be forgotten. When Roosevelt conceded "By George! You are right," the designation Muir Woods National Monument was confirmed.[16]

The wide publicity Kent received for his philanthropy pleased him on several counts. In the first place the land involved was still subject to condemnation; Kent wanted an aroused public opinion on his side. Second, his political ambitions, which carried him to the House of Representatives in 1910, were beginning to stir, and "conservation" was a potent, if vaguely defined, word in the Progressive vocabulary. The attention accorded Kent the donor of Muir Woods could not fail to help Kent the candidate. And praise poured in from all sides. *Sunset*, *Collier's*, and the *Sierra Club Bulletin* ran illustrated articles on the new national monument while newspapers throughout the country picked up the story. The Sierra Club made Kent an honorary member, and in June, 1908, Yale awarded him an honorary Master of Arts. Meanwhile, Kent received numerous congratulatory letters applauding him for upholding esthetic and spiritual qualities in a materialistic age.[17]

Kent's gift and personal tribute deeply touched John Muir. On the day Roosevelt created the monument, Muir wrote that in view of the "multitude of dull money hunters" usually associated with undeveloped land, it was "refreshing" to find someone like Kent.[18] Five days later he wrote Kent personally, calling Muir Woods "the finest forest and park thing done in California in many a day." "How it shines," Muir enthused, "amid the mean commercialism and apathy so destructively prevalent these days." Early in February he again thanked Kent for "the best tree-lover's monument that could be found in all the forests of the world." Protecting the redwoods, in Muir's view, was "a much needed lesson to saint and sinner alike, and a credit and encouragement to God." It astonished Muir that "so fine divine a thing should have come out of money-mad Chicago" and he ended by wishing Kent "immortal Sequoia life."[19]

The three years following the establishment of Muir Woods National Monument marked the zenith in the relationship of Kent and Muir. They even discussed the possibility of collaborating in "the general cause of nature preservation."[20] But friction was already mounting within the conservation movement. Those who would preserve undeveloped land for its esthetic, spiritual, and recreational values as wilderness found themselves opposed to resource managers with plans for efficiently harvesting nature's bounties. In the fall of 1897 Muir abandoned his efforts to support professional forestry and, as a consequence, feuded

[16] Roosevelt to Kent, Jan. 22; Kent to Roosevelt, Jan. 30; Roosevelt to Kent, Feb. 5, 1909, *KFP*, Box 6.

[17] Kent carefully preserved clippings and correspondence in regard to Muir Woods: *KFP*, Boxes 6 and 162.

[18] Muir to Catherine Hittell, Jan. 9, 1908, *KFP*, Box 6.

[19] Muir to Kent, Jan. 14 and Feb. 6, 1908, *KFP*, Box 6.

[20] Kent to Muir, Feb. 10, 1908, *KFP*, Box 6.

with Gifford Pinchot, the leading exponent of the "wise use" school.[21] Thereafter Muir poured all his energies into the cause of preservation, particularly the national park movement. Yet Pinchot, W. J. McGee, Frederick H. Newell, Francis G. Newlands, and James R. Garfield among others were directing federal resource policy toward utilitarianism and even succeeded in appropriating the term "conservation" for their viewpoint. The Pinchot-dominated governors' conference on the conservation of natural resources held at the White House in 1908 revealed the depth of the schism. Spokesmen for the protection and preservation of nature, including John Muir, were kept off the guest lists in favor of practical men who interpreted conservation to mean the maintenance of an abundance of important raw materials.[22] The frustrated advocates of wilderness preservation had no choice but to call Pinchot a "deconservationist."[23]

Meanwhile William Kent was construing conservation in his own way. For him the central issue was the future of republicanism. If private interests took precedence over the people's voice in regard to natural resources, democracy was endangered as well as the land.[24] Kent became concerned about this possibility in 1909 and campaigned vigorously against what he conceived to be the attempt of the Truckee River Power Company to obtain rights to Lake Tahoe detrimental to the public interest.[25] The following year the controversy over a private company's rights to Alaskan coal lands brought Kent to Pinchot's side in opposition to Secretary of the Interior Richard A. Ballinger. In Kent's mind it was the archetype Progressive cause with "predatory interests" standing against "the birthright of Americans."[26] Indeed, he conceived of conservation as the people's best weapon against concentrated wealth. If the conservationists and the democratic impulse they expressed did not prevail, Kent believed "there is nothing ahead of us but a trend toward peonage."[27] Understandably, Kent could encourage Pinchot in January, 1910, that his battle with Ballinger was "a crisis in the history of the country which, if settled one way, will lead to progress along

[21] Nash, *Wilderness*, Chap. 8, discusses Muir's break with Pinchot and the forestry in 1896–1897. Samuel P. Hays' *Conservation and the Gospel of Efficiency: The Progressive Conservation Movement, 1890–1920* (Cambridge, Mass., 1959), especially 141–146 and 189–198, examines the broad pattern of ideological conflict within American conservation.

[22] With the exception of the speeches of J. Horace McFarland, George F. Kunz, and Charles Evans Hughes, the participants in the conference reiterated the utilitarian line: *Proceedings of a Conference of Governors in the White House . . . May 13–15, 1908*, ed. Newton C. Blanchard *et al.*, *House Doc. 1425*, 60 Cong., 2 sess. Robert Underwood Johnson's *Remembered Yesterdays* (Boston, 1923), 300–307, and an open letter, Johnson to "Dear Sir," June 3, 1911, Robert Underwood Johnson Papers, Bancroft Library, Berkeley, Box 1, suggest the bitterness the conference engendered.

[23] Robert Underwood Johnson to Senator [Hoke] Smith, Dec. 1, 1913, Johnson Papers, Box 1.

[24] Leonard J. Bates, "Fulfilling American Democracy: The Conservation Movement, 1907–1921," *Mississippi Valley Historical Review*, XLIV (1957), 29–57, and Grant McConnell, "The Conservation Movement—Past and Present," *Western Political Quarterly*, VII (1954), 463–478, discuss the democratic impulse to conservation.

[25] *KFP*, Boxes 102 and 117. The sections in *Kent*, 310–337, concerning public control of water resources are largely the work of Judson King.

[26] *KFP*, Box 95.

[27] *Kent*, 191.

democratic lines, and if settled the other way will be a harbinger of revolution."[28] In this frame of mind Kent welcomed the idea of *public* control of natural resources as a panacea for land policy as well as for American government. And most importantly for his relationship to Muir, Kent's conception of conservation accorded greater value to democratic development of natural resources than to wilderness preservation.

Shortly after the Ballinger-Pinchot dispute, the Hetch Hetchy controversy moved into the conservation spotlight, deepening the rift in conservation ranks and bringing the friendship of John Muir and William Kent to an abrupt end. Situated on a dry, sandy peninsula, the city of San Francisco faced a chronic fresh-water shortage. In the Sierra, about one hundred and fifty miles distant, the erosive action of glaciers and the Tuolumne River had scooped the spectacular, high-walled Hetch Hetchy Valley. Engineers had long recognized its suitability as a reservoir and source of hydro-electric power, but in 1890 the act creating Yosemite National Park designated the valley and its environs a wilderness preserve. Undaunted, San Francisco applied for Hetch Hetchy shortly after the turn of the century, and, riding a wave of public sympathy generated by the disastrous earthquake of 1906, obtained preliminary federal approval of its plans.[29]

John Muir, however, determined to arouse a nation-wide protest over what he conceived to be a needless sacrifice of wilderness values and a betrayal of the whole idea of national parks. In the five years after 1908, while the Hetch Hetchy question was before Congress, Muir labored to convince his countrymen that wild parks were essential, "for everybody needs beauty as well as bread, places to play in and pray in where Nature may heal and cheer and give strength to body and soul alike."[30] As such a statement implied, nature, for Muir, was steeped in spiritual truth. Its desecration for material reasons was sacrilege. He had no doubt that he was doing the Lord's battle in resisting the reservoir. San Francisco became "the Prince of the powers of Darkness" and "Satan and Co."[31] This conviction that he was engaged in a battle between right and wrong prompted Muir and his school of conservationists to issue vituperative outbursts against the opposition. In a popular book of 1912 Muir labeled them "temple destroyers" who scorned the "God of the Mountains" in pursuit of the "Almighty Dollar."[32] Using such arguments, and playing upon the growing American

[28] As cited in *Kent*, 193. Although there is no reason to suspect Kent's sincerity in this sentiment, it is true that he derived considerable political advantage from siding with the influential Pinchot who campaigned actively on Kent's behalf in 1910 and 1912; *Kent*, 213, 252; George Mowry, *The Era of Theodore Roosevelt and the Birth of Modern America, 1900–1912* (New York, 1958), 250–257.

[29] Histories of the Hetch Hetchy issue, largely political in nature, are Jones, *John Muir and the Sierra Club*, 82–169; Elmo R. Richardson, "The Struggle for the Valley: California's Hetch Hetchy Controversy, 1905–1913," *California Historical Society Quarterly*, XXXVIII (1959), 249–258; John Ise, *Our National Park Policy: A Critical History* (Baltimore, 1961), 85–96; and Suzette Dornberger, "The Struggle for Hetch Hetchy, 1900–1913" (Master's thesis, University of California, Berkeley, 1935). Nash, *Wilderness*, Chap. 10, examines the controversy's significance for American attitudes toward nature.

[30] Muir, "The Tuolumne Yosemite in Danger," *Outlook*, LXXXVII (1907), 488.

[31] Muir to Robert Underwood Johnson, March 23, 1913, John Muir Papers, American Academy of Arts and Letters, New York; Muir to "Kelloggs Three," Dec. 27, 1913, John Muir Papers, Bancroft Library, Berkeley, Box 1.

[32] *The Yosemite* (New York, 1912), 261–262. Compare Muir's "The Hetch-Hetchy Valley," *Sierra Club Bulletin*, VI (1908), 220.

enthusiasm for wildness in both man and nature,[33] Muir succeeded in stimulating a remarkable amount of public concern for Hetch Hetchy.

As a California congressman and well-known conservationist, William Kent could not ignore the Hetch Hetchy question. On March 31, 1911, a few weeks after he arrived in Washington to begin his first term, Kent received a personal letter from John Muir. Assuming that Kent, the donor of Muir Woods, would champion the cause of wilderness preservation, Muir simply encouraged him to watch developments concerning Hetch Hetchy closely and "do lots of good work."[34] But for Kent the matter was not so simple. He realized Hetch Hetchy was an extraordinary wilderness area and part of a national park. But he also knew that the powerful Pacific Gas and Electric Company wanted Hetch Hetchy as a step toward tightening its hold on California hydro-electric resources. Municipal control of Hetch Hetchy's water would block this plan and at the same time be a significant victory for the ideal of public ownership. The sacrifice of wilderness qualities, Kent concluded, was regrettable but in this case necessary for a greater good. Making this point in a letter to Muir's colleague, Robert Underwood Johnson, Kent stated his conviction that conservation could best be served by granting the valley to San Francisco.[35]

In 1913 the Hetch Hetchy struggle entered its climactic phase, and as a second-term congressman and key member of the house committee on the public lands, Kent was in a position to exert considerable influence. He began by helping draft a bill granting the valley to San Francisco and insuring that the resulting electricity would be publicly controlled; then he opened his home to the city's supporters as a campaign headquarters. The fact that Kent was known as the donor of Muir Woods lent extra weight to his opinions. Certainly *he* would not dismiss the claims of wilderness preservation lightly. Kent exploited this advantage fully. When the Hetch Hetchy bill was under consideration in the house, he rose to answer the preservationists' arguments: "I can lay claim to being a nature lover myself. I think that is a matter of record." He then proceeded to defend the reservoir plans as "the highest and best type of conservation."[36] The same technique appeared in a letter to President Woodrow Wilson where Kent asserted that in the cause of protecting nature he had "spent more time and effort . . . than any of the men who are opposing this bill."[37] And there was, in fact, much truth in this claim.

The final stages of the Hetch Hetchy controversy revealed just how far apart Muir and Kent had drawn. "Dam Hetch Hetchy!" cried Muir, "as well dam for water-tanks the people's cathedrals and churches, for no holier temple has ever been consecrated by the heart of man."[38] Mustering the Sierra Club and wilderness advocates throughout the country, the elderly Californian threw his remaining energy into what he regarded as the most crucial conservation struggle of his lifetime. Kent's emphasis, on the other hand, was all on the beneficence of public ownership. Speaking in the house, he declared that "the ideal conservation is

33 See Nash, "The American Cult of the Primitive," *American Quarterly*, XVIII (Fall, 1966), 517–537.
34 Muir to Kent, March 31, 1911, *KFP*, Box 26.
35 Kent to Johnson, April 6, 1911 (carbon), *KFP*, Box 17.
36 *Cong. Record*, 63 Cong., 1 sess., L, Pt. 4 (Aug. 30, 1913), 3963.
37 Kent to Wilson, Oct. 1, 1913, Woodrow Wilson Papers, Library of Congress, File VI, Box 199, Folder 169.
38 *Yosemite*, 262.

public social use of resources of our country without waste." Non-use, Kent explained, which the preservation of wilderness entailed, was waste. Searching for a dramatic illustration, he declared it his sentiment that if Niagara Falls could be totally used up in providing for humanity's need for water, he would be "glad to sacrifice that scenic wonder."[39] According to Kent, "all things are relative," and the benefits of having a wild Hetch Hetchy must yield to the greater advantages involved in producing hydropower and creating a water supply "upon which not a cent of private profit shall ever be made."[40] He had made up his mind that "real conservation meant proper use and not locking up of natural resources" and the furtherance of democracy through their public development.[41]

It remained for Kent, as an acknowledged admirer of Muir, to provide public explanation for their divergence over Hetch Hetchy. He did so in the summer of 1913 in a series of letters to his congressional colleagues. To Representative Sydney Anderson of Minnesota he wrote:

> *I hope you will not take my friend, Muir, seriously, for he is a man entirely without social sense. With him, it is me and God and the rock where God put it, and that is the end of the story. I know him well and as far as this proposition is concerned, he is mistaken.*

Similarly he wired Pinchot that the Hetch Hetchy protest was the work of private power interests using "misinformed nature lovers" as their spokesmen.[42] In October Kent told a public gathering in California that because Muir had spent so much time in the wilderness he had not acquired the social instincts of the average man.[43]

The nearest Kent came to accounting directly to Muir was an undated memorandum to the Society for the Preservation of National Parks, of which Muir was a director. After commending the group for its statement on Hetch Hetchy, Kent reiterated his conviction that the "highest form of conservation" called for a reservoir that would provide Californians with an abundant supply of cheap water. "I make these comments," Kent concluded, "with the utmost regard for your sincerity of purpose, and with a full understanding of your point of view."[44]

Muir never responded directly to these remarks, but in the year of his life that remained after the reservoir plan received federal approval in December, 1913, he must have felt betrayed. The man who had done him his greatest honor in creating Muir Woods became an influential opponent in the Hetch Hetchy

[39] *Cong. Record,* 63 Cong., 1 sess., L, Pt. 4 (Aug. 30, 1913), 3963.

[40] Senate Committee on Public Lands, *Hearings, Hetch Hetchy Reservoir Site,* 63 Cong., 1 sess. (Sept. 24, 1913), 70.

[41] As quoted in Gardiner, "Life of William Kent," 347–348. See also Kent's dispatch on the passage of the Hetch Hetchy bill in the San Francisco *Bulletin,* Dec. 20, 1913. A fellow Progressive, Senator George W. Norris of Nebraska, agreed with Kent that the crucial issue in the Hetch Hetchy affair was public ownership of water resources not wilderness preservation: Norris, *Fighting Liberal* (New York, 1945), 163 ff.; Richard Lowitt, "A Neglected Aspect of the Progressive Movement: George W. Norris and Public Control of Hydro-electric Power, 1913–1917," *Historian,* XXVII (1965), 350–365.

[42] Kent to Anderson, July 2, 1913, *KFP,* Box 26. Kent to Pinchot, Oct. 8, 1913, Gifford Pinchot Papers, Library of Congress, Box 1823.

[43] San Rafael *Independent,* Oct. 21, 1913, seen in *KFP,* Box 171. Compare Kent's statement as quoted in Gardiner, "Life of William Kent," 349–350.

[44] *KFP,* Box 116.

fight. But it was not that Kent changed his mind about wilderness after 1908. At the very time he was helping draft the bill authorizing a reservoir in Hetch Hetchy, he asked Gifford Pinchot for a statement in support of a state park on Mount Tamalpais. Specifically, Kent wanted Pinchot to show "the advantage of such a wilderness, particularly near San Francisco."[45] And after Hetch Hetchy, Kent went on to author the bill establishing the National Park Service (1916), participate in the founding of the Save-the-Redwoods League (1918), and add more land to Muir Woods National Monument (1920). At his memorial service in 1928 one of the chief speakers was William E. Colby, president of the Sierra Club. Kent's problem was that the necessity to decide about Hetch Hetchy left no room for an expression of his ambivalence. The valley could not simultaneously be a wilderness and a publicly owned, power-producing reservoir.

In spite of their common interest in wilderness, Kent and Muir ultimately gave it a different priority. The result was a bitter conflict. Yet both men were sincere and energetic proponents of conservation. Indeed, few Americans after their generation openly opposed it. But that hardly ended the controversy over the value and uses of nature in America. One man's conservation was frequently another's exploitation,[46] which is another way of saying that conservationists neither were nor are a homogeneous interest group or political bloc. As the relationship of Kent and Muir revealed, the dynamics of the history of the American landscape in the twentieth century comes not so much from "conservationists" embattled against greedy, wasteful exploiters, but from the conflict of diverse interpretations of the meaning of conserving natural resources.

[45] Kent to Pinchot, March 5, 1913, Pinchot Papers, Box 164.

[46] Donald Swain's *Federal Conservation Policy, 1921–1933* (Berkeley, 1963), especially 123–143, shows how the United States Forest Service and National Park Service perpetuated the conservation schism into the 1930's. Two decades later the Echo Park battle, remarkably similar in circumstances to Hetch Hetchy, pitted the bureau of reclamation and its conception of conservation for use against the Sierra Club and others believing in wilderness preservation: Nash, *Wilderness*, Chap. 12.

3

THE RICH MAN'S BURDEN AND HOW ANDREW CARNEGIE UNLOADED IT

Joseph Frazier Wall

In 1889, Andrew Carnegie published in the North American Review *a two-part essay entitled "Wealth," which quickly became popularized as the Gospel of Wealth. Its thesis was simple—the man of great wealth was only the steward for that wealth, and he had the obligation and, perhaps even more importantly, the talent to dispense that wealth for the betterment of society during his lifetime. Here was the millionaire's answer to the Populists, the Anti-Monopolists, and the Socialists of the time who would by one political device or another correct the maldistribution of wealth. Here also was the raison d'être for the millionaire himself. Carnegie's gospel, both in theory and practice, as shown in this essay, reveals some basic assumptions held by most Americans of that time—and later: popular education could solve all problems; the welfare state was debilitating to the beneficiaries of that welfare; and continuing poverty was indicative of individual defects of character, not of social malfunctioning. The modern philanthropic foundations of Carnegie, Ford, Rockefeller, and many others, which have played so influential a role in present-day society, owe their genesis to this Gospel of Wealth.*

Joseph Frazier Wall is Parker Professor of History, Grinnell College. This essay is taken from his biography Andrew Carnegie, *published by Oxford University Press in 1970 and awarded a Bancroft Prize in History in 1971.*

On one of the last nights of the year 1868, Andrew Carnegie, who had recently moved to New York from Pittsburgh and was living with his mother in the elegant St. Nicholas Hotel, sat down at his desk to total up his various investments

Source: *American Heritage,* Vol. 21, No. 6 (October 1970), pp. 58–67, 90–93.

and his annual returns from those investments. It was an impressive statement of accomplishment for a man who, as a child of thirteen, had accompanied his parents in steerage class from Scotland to America and had found his first employment as a bobbin boy in a textile mill at $1.20 a week. Now, twenty years later, he had assets of four hundred thousand dollars and an annual income of $56,110. How gratifying it all should have been! Yet, in a curious way, it was not entirely satisfying. Carnegie had for some time realized that most of the successful men he had encountered were men with one ambition—money, and with but one talent—the ability to get it. He could not help comparing these business associates with the heroes of his childhood, Uncle Tom Morrison, Uncle George Lauder, and his father, radical Chartists who would discourse at length upon literature, history, politics, and economics.

The end of the year for a Scottish Calvinist is a time for sober reflection, for pondering upon man's sinful frailty and God's awesome majesty. Carnegie had, to be sure, never accepted the Calvinist view of either man or God, but the ethos of Scotland was bred into him. With all the introspection of a Jonathan Edwards or a John Knox, he took a hard, unpitying look at himself. Then he wrote down another kind of balance sheet to accompany his statement of business holdings:

> *Man must have an idol—The amassing of wealth is one of the worst species of idolitary* [*sic*]. *No idol more debasing than the worship of money. Whatever I engage in I must push inordinately therefor should I be careful to choose that life which will be the most elevating in its character. To continue much longer overwhelmed by business cares and with most of my thoughts wholly upon the way to make more money in the shortest time, must degrade me beyond hope of permanent recovery. I will resign business at thirty five . . .*

Carnegie, however, did not resign business at thirty-five. For the next thirty-two years he continued to "push inordinately," and by 1900 he had built a steel empire so vast and so independently powerful that it endangered even the complex, interlocking financial world of J. P. Morgan. In February, 1901, Morgan, representing all of those interests in steel products and railroads that were threatened by Carnegie's ever-expanding empire, offered to buy Carnegie Steel and quickly accepted Carnegie's price of $480,000,000. Paying a visit to Carnegie's home, Morgan shook the Scotsman's hand and said, "Mr. Carnegie, I want to congratulate you on being the richest man in the world!"

And, during all of these years, Carnegie's note, written in 1868 and addressed to himself, had lain in his desk, undisturbed, yet ever disturbing to his self-esteem. Now with this vast fortune in first mortgage, 5 per cent gold bonds of the newly created United States Steel Corporation in his possession, Carnegie turned his full attention away from getting to giving—to debasing the idol at whose altar he had so long and so successfully worshipped. Carnegie was under no illusions about the problems that would confront him. His friend John Morley, an English statesman, had written him a month after the sale to Morgan had been consummated, "I say to you what Johnson said to Burke, when B. showed him his fine house, 'I don't envy, I do admire.' You'll have some difficulty, tho' in adapting the principles of accumulation to the business of distribution." To which Carnegie wrote in answer, ". . . I don't see it needs the same principles as acquisition—but it needs some of these. Tenacity and steady sailing to the haven we clear for—supreme confidence in one's own ideas, or conclusions rather, after thought—and above all, placing use above popularity." These were qualities of character with which Carnegie had proved himself to be well endowed, but he also showed a quality of capriciousness that often made his philanthropic gestures—or lack of them—an enigma to those soliciting him for aid.

Yet Carnegie would always believe that his philanthropic practices, like his business practices, were based upon rational, systematic principles. These principles in some respects made his task of giving more difficult but, he felt, far more socially significant and beneficial than the simple random distribution of largess. He had explained his system in a remarkable two-part essay entitled "Wealth," which appeared in the June and December, 1889, issues of the *North American Review*.

Carnegie's essay created a considerable stir when it first appeared, and deservedly so. The editor of the *North American Review*, Allen Thorndike Rice, called it the "finest article I have ever published in the Review." It was quickly picked up in Britain, where it appeared in *Pall Mall Gazette* under the title "Gospel of Wealth." It caught the attention of the reading public of two nations because of its candor, its specific proposals for the distribution of wealth, and, of course, because of its author—a well-known American millionaire who was openly critical of his own class.

The thesis of the "Gospel" was simply and boldly stated: "The problem of our age is the proper administration of wealth." To Carnegie there appeared only three alternatives by which a man of great wealth could dispose of his fortune: he could leave it to his family, he could bequeath it in his will for public purposes, or he could administer it during his lifetime for public benefit. Of the three, the least desirable both for society and for the individual was the first, and on this point Carnegie gave his oft-repeated homily on the evils of inherited wealth. The wife and daughters should be provided with moderate sources of income, he believed, but as for the sons, he felt that "The thoughtful man must shortly say, 'I would as soon leave to my son a curse as the almighty dollar,' and admit to himself that it is not the welfare of the children, but family pride, which inspires the legacies."

The second alternative, while socially more responsible, is frequently thwarted by disappointed heirs contesting the will, he wrote. Even when a philanthropic bequest is successfully carried out, "it may be said that this is only a means for the disposal of wealth, provided a man is content to wait until he is dead before he becomes of much good in the world." Carnegie approved of heavy inheritance taxes, or "death duties," to ensure society's reaping some benefits from the accumulation of wealth if either of the first two alternatives was chosen.

"There remains, then," he wrote, "only one mode of using great fortunes; but in this we have the true antidote for the temporary unequal distribution of wealth, the reconciliation of the rich and the poor—a reign of harmony. . . . It is founded upon the present most intense Individualism and . . . under its sway we shall have an ideal State, in which the surplus wealth of the few will become, in the best sense, the property of the many, because administered for the common good, and this wealth, passing through the hands of the few, can be made a much more potent force for the elevation of our race than if distributed in small sums to the people themselves." In short, the rich man should spend his fortune during his lifetime in ways that will most effectively benefit and advance society. "This, then, is held to be the duty of the man of wealth: To set an example of modest, unostentatious living, shunning display or extravagance; to provide moderately for the legitimate wants of those dependent upon him; and, after doing so, to consider all surplus revenues which come to him simply as trust funds which he is called upon to administer . . . the man of wealth thus becoming the mere trustee and agent for his poorer brethren, bringing to their service his superior wisdom, experience, and ability to administer, doing for them better than they would or could do for themselves."

In the second part of his essay, Carnegie, at the request of the editor, presented "some of the best methods of performing this duty of administering surplus wealth for the good of the people." First, the millionaire who adheres to the gospel must "take care that the purposes for which he spends it shall not have a degrading pampering tendency upon its recipients, but that his trust shall be so administered as to stimulate the best and most aspiring poor of the community to further efforts for their own improvement. It is not the irreclaimably destitute, shiftless, and worthless which it is truly beneficial or truly benevolent for the individual to attempt to reach and improve. For these there exists the refuge provided by the city or the State, where they can be sheltered, fed, clothed . . . and, most important of all—where they can be isolated from the well-doing and industrious poor. . . ."

The specific fields of philanthropy in which the wise trustee of surplus wealth would invest, according to Carnegie, were seven, listed in descending order of importance: (1) universities—the founding of universities, of course, being possible only "by men enormously rich"; (2) free libraries—for Carnegie himself, he said, this "occupies first place"; (3) the founding or extension of hospitals "and other institutions connected with the alleviation of human suffering"; (4) parks; (5) halls suitable for meetings, concerts, etc; (6) "swimming baths"; and (7) churches—but only the building, not the maintenance of the church activities, which should be done by the entire congregation. "It is not expected," Carnegie added, "that there should be general concurrence as to the best possible use of surplus wealth. . . . There is room and need for all kinds of wise benefactions for the common weal."

It is fortunate that Carnegie did not expect "general concurrence" on his list of proper fields for philanthropy, for he certainly did not get it. Ministers and mission boards, in particular, were outraged to find churches seventh on the list—just after swimming baths. Artists, writers, and musicians also wanted their share of patronage, as did private schools, orphanages, and other charitable institutions.

But Carnegie's fundamental assumptions were not allowed to go unchallenged either. A sharp critique of Carnegie's gospel was offered by William Jewett Tucker, the liberal American theologian, professor of religion at Andover Theological Seminary, and later to be the distinguished president of Dartmouth College. Writing a review of "The Gospel of Wealth" in 1891 for the *Andover Review*, Tucker, as no other critic of the time did, examined the essence of Carnegie's gospel—and found it fallacious. First, Tucker pointed out, it was based upon a false assumption of inevitability. He quoted Carnegie as saying, "We start with a condition of affairs [referring to the prevailing competitive system] under which the best interests of the race are promoted, but which inevitably gives wealth to the few." This Tucker found unacceptable. "[T]he assumption . . . that wealth is the inevitable possession of the few, and is best administered by them for the many, begs the whole question of economic justice now before society, and relegates it to the field of charity, leaving the question of the original distribution of wealth unsettled, or settled only to the satisfaction of the few. . . ."

Tucker also found fault in Carnegie's plan for the redistribution of wealth, generous and praiseworthy as it seemed to be. "Just as formerly it was contended that political power should be in the hands of the few, because it would be better administered, so now it is contended—I quote Mr. Carnegie's words, slightly transferring them, but not changing their meaning—that 'the millionaire is intrusted for the time being with a great part of the increased wealth of the community, because he can administer it for the community far better than it could or would have done for itself.' This, of course, if accepted and carried out in any complete way, becomes patronage . . . and, in the long run, society cannot afford to be patronized."

This was striking at the real inner defense line that protected Carnegie's self-esteem and provided a justification for his life. In an essay, "The Advantages of Poverty," Carnegie made one brief statement that was far more revealing of his own motivation for philanthropy than he probably ever intended or realized. In discussing the question of why the very rich should avoid extravagant living, he wrote, "they can, perhaps, also find refuge from self-questioning in the thought of the much greater portion of their means which is being spent upon others." It is the phrase "perhaps, also find refuge from self-questioning" that is the tip-off. This is the kind of refuge Carnegie must have been seeking for twenty years, ever since as a young man in 1868 he had warned himself against the degradation of money worship. But the old doubts persisted. What was really happening to an America in which one man could accumulate a fortune that ran into nine figures? Carnegie had to justify his life to himself. Unlike some of his contemporaries—Fisk, Gould, Drew—he could not accept for himself the innocent animal amorality of the freebooter, nor on the other hand could he, having rejected the tenets of orthodox religion, now retreat with John D. Rockefeller into pious Baptism and say, "The Good Lord gave me my wealth."

Carnegie must have felt that he had at last found justification for plutocracy by his gospel of wealth: a man may accumulate great wealth in a democracy, but he has a responsibility to return that wealth in a way that will not destroy society's own responsibility to preserve individual initiative. To give through the usual charitable outlets is wrong, for such charity is primarily concerned with the hopeless "submerged tenth." It keeps the weak weak and upsets the equality of opportunity. To give library buildings with the provision that the community must then furnish the books is right, for this makes available opportunities for all—it encourages the salvageable "swimming tenth" and at the same time respects the responsibility of the community. And who is better prepared for the responsible task of being steward for a nation's accumulated wealth than the man who, starting with nothing, has through his own initiative gathered in this wealth? Carnegie must have felt with the writing of his "Gospel of Wealth" that he had at last made peace with his conscience, had at last found that "refuge from self-questioning."

He, of course, had begun to practice long before he had had a gospel to preach. That is why he was convinced that he was a "scientific philanthropist." His principles of philanthropy, he felt, were pragmatically based upon experience. His earliest philanthropic bequests, however, were based on no discernible system. Sentiment and his own idiosyncratic interests dictated his choice more than any rational philosophy. By the time his essay "Wealth" appeared in 1889, he had given a swimming bath and library to Dunfermline, the Scottish town in which he was born, a library to Braddock, Pennsylvania, and a pipe organ to the small Swedenborgian church in Allegheny, Pennsylvania, that his father and aunts had attended in the 1850's. His only gift to higher education was a grant of six thousand dollars extended over a five-year period to the Western University of Pennsylvania (later to be the University of Pittsburgh). This is not a tremendously impressive list, and sentiment was clearly a major factor. But the list is interesting in its diversity. It is evident that these early gifts determined his ideas about "the best fields of philanthropy."

After the appearance of his famous essay Carnegie began in earnest to follow his own dictates. As he had indicated in "Wealth," libraries were to be his specialty in this early phase of his philanthropic career. After his first two library gifts to Dunfermline and Braddock, in which he furnished not only the library building but provided an endowment for the acquisition of books and the maintenance of the library, Carnegie would give only the building and insist upon the town's taxing itself for the books and maintenance. He was to make only three exceptions to this rule after having established it: at Duquesne and Homestead, Pennsylvania, and the borough of Carnegie, a suburb of Pittsburgh. Fifty years later, a report on the Carnegie library system by Ralph Munn, which appeared in the *Library Journal*, showed the wisdom of that rule. The only four libraries in the United States to receive an endowment from Carnegie, Munn reported, "still have exactly the same endowment which he gave them in the 1890's and the cities have firmly refused to give them any local financial support."

It was much easier at first for Carnegie to give libraries in Scotland than in the United States, for there were no taxation restrictions on British municipalities. They could tax themselves for the support of libraries, while many cities of the United States could not. Pittsburgh, for example, could not accept Carnegie's offer to provide a library building in 1881 because the city council ruled that the laws of Pennsylvania did not provide for municipal property-tax assessments to be used to maintain a free library. Shortly thereafter, however, the Pennsylvania legislature specifically provided for tax assessments for libraries, and Pittsburgh quickly requested a renewal of the offer. The renewal came multiplied several times over, for Carnegie now had in mind a great civic center, the Carnegie Institute, which would include not only an imposing library but a great museum, a music hall, and an art institute, located at the edge of Schenley Park.

This was Carnegie's first great philanthropic endeavor, and in these early days he could still allow himself the luxury of considering almost every detail, from the architectural design of the buildings to the question of nudity in the copies of classical statuary. "I strongly recommend nude to be draped since question has been raised," he wired W. M. Frew, the president of the Carnegie Library

Commission. "Remember my words in speech. We should begin gently to lead people upward. I do hope nothing in gallery or hall will ever give offense to the simplest man or woman. Draping is used everywhere in Britain except in London. If we are to work genuine good we must bend and keep in touch with masses. Am very clear indeed on this question." For weeks he fussed with Frew about the names that would be carved in stone on the entablature. When he saw the proposed list in the Pittsburgh *Dispatch,* he exploded to Frew: "I cannot approve the list of names. . . . Some of the names have no business to be on the list. Imagine Dickens in and Burns out. Among painters Perugini out and Rubens in, the latter only a painter of fat, vulgar women, while a study of the pictures of Raphael will show anyone that he was really only a copyist of Perugini, whose pupil he was. Imagine Science and Franklin not there. This list for Music seems satisfactory. Palestrina rightly comes first. Have been entranced by his works, which we have heard in Rome. As I am to be in Pittsburgh very soon, I hope you will postpone action in regard to the names."

Library giving, except for so large an undertaking as the Carnegie Institute of Pittsburgh, quickly became a business, as efficient and standardized as the filling of orders for steel billets at Homestead or Duquesne. A town council would apply for a Carnegie Library, and Carnegie's secretary, James Bertram, would acknowledge the request and inform the municipal government of the specifications to be met before the grant could be made. The town would first have to provide a site, if possible centrally located in the town. Then the governing board of the community would have to pledge an annual appropriation for books and maintenance that would amount to 10 per cent of the Carnegie gift. The size of Carnegie's gift was based upon the population of the town, usually two dollars per capita, which worked very well indeed for cities from twenty-five thousand to one hundred thousand in population. In the latter instance, for example, Carnegie would give two hundred thousand dollars for the building, and the city would pledge twenty thousand dollars a year for maintenance. But in many of the very small villages that also received gifts of libraries, the annual amount pledged in order to receive the gift might be as low as two hundred dollars a year. In fact, the only major criticism made by the Munn report of 1951 was that it would have been much better if small neighboring towns had "pooled their resources for a single library," much as communities would later do in consolidating public-school systems. From the professional librarian's point of view this is certainly a justifiable criticism, but who can say how many youths or lonely old people living in towns like Idaho Springs, Colorado, or Flora, Indiana, or Sanborn, Iowa, in those pre-radio-television days, found their only intellectual excitement or companionship in the Carnegie Free Public Library? In any event, Carnegie liked to think this was true. As he wrote to one applicant for a library building, "I believe that it outranks any other one thing that a community can do to benefit its people. It is the never failing spring in the desert."

At first Carnegie made no attempt to provide building plans along with his grant of money for the building, leaving the architectural design to be determined by each locality. But there were so many bad buildings erected in these early years of library giving, and so many complaints from librarians who had to contend with functional problems, that Carnegie, and later the Carnegie Corporation of New York, sent out standard plans along with the monetary grant. What may have been gained in functional efficiency, however, was lost in architectural variety. Soon, in small towns all over America, there came to be an architectural style, popularly known as Carnegie Classical, that was as easily identifiable as that other standardized small-town architectural style known as Wesley Romanesque. A stranger in the community seldom had difficulty in spotting the Carnegie Library and the Methodist church, which in many towns confronted each other across the square.

The public generally believed that Carnegie insisted that his name be engraved above the front entrance of the libraries he gave. This was not true. But certainly he never objected to its being done, and, upon request, he would provide the library with a photograph of himself, which would hang in the place of honor just inside the main door. As he made clear to applicants, the one thing he did desire was "that there should be placed over the entrance to the Libraries I build a representation of the rays of a rising sun, and above 'LET THERE BE LIGHT,' and I hope you can have this on the building." Not all communities complied with this request, however. Perhaps the Methodists across the way found it a bit presumptuous for a secular institution thus to arrogate to itself Jehovah's own first command.

Carnegie frequently attended the dedication ceremonies of a major new library, particularly if it was in Britain, for there it usually meant that he would be granted the Freedom of the City, a medieval rite that he thoroughly enjoyed. He began collecting "Freedoms" in the early 1890's. The parchment scroll signifying this honor was encased in a small casket, and each town in Britain seemed to be trying to outdo its neighbor in the elaborateness of the casket design. Carnegie, who had never before been infected with the collector's mania —neither stamps nor paintings nor rare old books ever having had an appeal for him—entered into this hobby with all the zest of the most fanatic philatelist. It was a proud day when he broke the previous record, held by Gladstone, of fourteen Freedoms. He really hit top form when he received six Freedoms in six days. They came so fast, in fact, that even the London *Times*, usually so reliable, became confused and on one occasion reported that Carnegie was to receive the Freedom of Bromley-by-Bow the following week. The citizens of that small London suburb were alarmed when they read their papers on that day, for it was the first they had known about it—no casket, no parchment, nothing was prepared. The *Times* hastily carried the next day one of its few retractions. It appeared that it was Bromley, Kent, that was prepared to honor Carnegie that week.

"How dog-sick you must be of all these meetings, addresses, and Hallelujah business," Morley wrote Carnegie, who was then on one of his whirlwind collecting tours. "I shouldn't wonder at your longing for Skibo [Carnegie's castle in Scotland] and what Mr. Smith calls 'the quiet stream of self-forgetfulness'—blessed waters for all of us." But this was the kind of "quiet stream" that Carnegie never cared to fish in, and Morley's sympathy was quite wasted on him. Carnegie, for all his loudly proclaimed radical republicanism, dearly loved the pomp and circumstance of the medieval ritual—riding in an open carriage through the old twisting streets lined with crowds and flags, being met at the town hall by the Lord Mayor, resplendent in his robes and silver medallion of office, who made the formal presentation of the Freedom of the City to Carnegie. Finally came the opportunity to address the assembled crowd and to spread his gospel of wealth.

How sweet it all was! "Never so busy, never so happy," Carnegie would frequently write to his Cousin Dod or friend Morley, neither of whom could understand why he was either.

Carnegie would always insist that these shows were all for the purpose of dramatizing and publicizing the gospel of wealth, in the hope that other millionaires might be converted. As he wrote to one friend in explanation of his "Hallelujah business": "Well do I remember my apprehensions when you advocated keeping all you did quiet. *No show.* No advocacy. Only go on & do the work in a quiet way, when I knew that advertizing was essential for success, i.e. to spreading abroad what could be done. . . . Of course its disagreeable work & puts me forward as a vain trumpeter but one who isn't willing to play this part *for the good* to be done, isn't much of a man."

Carnegie enjoyed his trumpeting too obviously to convince anyone that he found it disagreeable work. The ceremonies and speeches continued, and ultimately he was to collect the Freedom of fifty-seven cities, the all-time record for Great Britain. For a time after World War II it appeared that Winston Churchill might surpass it, but he never quite equalled this total.

The flamboyant public displays of course enhanced Carnegie's already notorious reputation for being a publicity seeker. It was generally believed both in Britain and in America that he never gave a cent that was not returned to him tenfold in public adulation. Poultney Bigelow, who worked with Carnegie for the establishment of the New York Public Library system, wrote one of the harshest indictments of the philanthropist:

> *Never before in the history of plutocratic America had any one man purchased by mere money so much social advertising and flattery. No wonder that he felt himself infallible, when Lords temporal and spiritual courted him and hung upon his words. They wanted his money, and flattery alone could wring it from him. Ask him for aid in a small deserving case or to assist a struggling scientific explorer—that would be wasted time. He had no ears for any charity unless labelled with his name. . . . He would have given millions to Greece had she labelled the Parthenon Carnegopolis.*

Such criticism, while understandable, was quite unfair, and although Carnegie generally ignored such comments, on occasion he felt it necessary to speak out. When he offered to match the six-hundred-thousand-dollar endowment of the Franklin Institute in Boston, he was greatly disturbed to receive an inquiry from Charles Eliot, president of Harvard, one of the trustees of the institute, asking if this meant that Carnegie expected the name to be changed to the Franklin-Carnegie Institute. Carnegie felt obliged to deny this at some length:

> *The idea of tampering with Franklin's name never entered my mind any more than when I duplicated Peter Cooper's gift of six hundred thousand. . . .*
>
> *I find it difficult to avoid having gifts for new things called after the donors. Carnegie Hall New York was called by me* The Music Hall a la *Boston. Foreign artists refused to appear in "A Music Hall"—London idea.*

> *The Board changed it in my absence in Europe without consulting me. . . . "The way of the Philanthropist is hard" but I don't do anything for popularity and just please my sel'—do what I think is useful. I never reply to attacks. Altho I confess I was surprised that you should have for a moment imagined there was a man living who could dream of coupling his name with Franklin* or with any founder.

There were many instances of Carnegie's philanthropy that, at his express order, received no publicity whatsoever. He had many people on his private pension lists, from obscure boyhood friends in Dunfermline to such celebrities as Rudyard Kipling and Booker T. Washington. The publicity he did seek and get for his gospel of wealth after 1890, however, resulted in an almost unbelievable torrent of letters from individuals requesting aid for themselves or for some project in which they were interested. His faithful secretary, James Bertram, who handled all of this correspondence, estimated that Carnegie received on the average of four to five hundred letters a day, and after the announcement of some large benefaction, this number might increase to seven hundred a day. The great majority of these letters Carnegie, of course, never saw. They came from all over the world, from writers who could not get their books published, from inventors with patents to revolutionize industry, from persons who claimed kinship with Carnegie, or simply from desperate people having no other recourse but the blind hope that a simple scrawled message to that magical name would be the open-sesame to help.

No one, however, was too important or too proud, it would appear, to write a begging letter to Carnegie. Those letters from friends and distinguished persons he would have to see and to answer. On one day alone, he had letters from John Morley, Herbert Spencer, and William Gladstone. Morley, who never begged, had simply written a personal letter, but Spencer was begging for help for some sociological study a friend was engaged in, and Gladstone wanted Carnegie to give money to the Bodleian Library. Carnegie was impressed. "Just think," he wrote in reply to Gladstone, "one mail brought me three letters.

One from you—Gladstone
One from Herbert Spencer
One from John Morley

I am quite set up as no other one can say this. A.C." But not set up enough to become softheaded. Carnegie politely but firmly turned down both Spencer and Gladstone.

Mark Twain, who was a frequent correspondent and who always addressed Carnegie as Saint Andrew, wrote the most delightful begging letters of all those that Carnegie received. Sometimes it would be a joke:

> *You seem to be in prosperity. Could you lend an admirer a dollar & a half to buy a hymn book with? God will bless you. I feel it. I know it. N.B. If there should be another application this one not to count. P.S. Don't send the hymn-book, send the money. I want to make the selection myself.*

Sometimes it would be a serious request for Carnegie to enter some business venture with him or to rescue him from one in which he was already caught. Either way, he took Carnegie's refusals with good grace.

On an early spring morning in 1901, when Carnegie sailed for Europe, having sold out to Morgan and leaving behind him safely locked in a vault in Hoboken the world's largest negotiable fortune, he had some understanding of the size of the task that lay before him. Just prior to his departure he had sent to the managers of the Carnegie Company, now a subdivision of United States Steel, five million dollars of those bonds to be held in trust for the following purposes:

> *Income for $1 million to be spent in maintaining Libraries at Braddock, Homestead & Duquesne works.*
>
> *Income from other $4 million to be applied:*
>
> *1st, to provide for employees of Carnegie Company injured in service and for dependents of those killed.*
>
> *2nd, to provide small pensions to employees after long service, help in old age. Not to be regarded as a substitute for what the Company is already doing. . . . I make this first use of surplus wealth upon retiring from business, as an acknowledgement of the deep debt I owe to the workmen who have contributed so greatly to my success.*

He also left letters granting $5,200,000 to New York City for sixty-five branch libraries throughout the five boroughs, under the same conditions as applied to all of his library gifts; and to St. Louis, one million dollars for branch libraries. Thus, by three letters written in a single day, Carnegie had given away $11,200,000. All of his previous gifts up to that date had totalled $16,363,252. But the interest on his bonds and other investments alone amounted to over fifteen million dollars a year. Carnegie knew he would have to do much better than this if he were to make any substantial cut into his vast amount of capital.

But for the next ten years Carnegie gamely ran on in a race that he had set for himself, with handicaps that were self-imposed. Library giving, which he regarded as his specialty, took care of $60,364,808 of his fortune by providing 2,509 free public libraries throughout the United States, the British Isles, Canada, New Zealand, Australia, and South Africa. But spectacularly popular as this field of philanthropy proved to be, it amounted to only one seventh of his total fortune.

The question remained: What other fields could he enter in view of the restrictions he had laid upon himself? He would not enter the medical field, for he felt that this had been pre-empted by John D. Rockefeller. Giving to churches, and particularly to missionary enterprises, was antithetical to his most fundamental beliefs. The substantial exception he made to this rule was in providing church organs—a form of philanthropy into which he rather inadvertently stumbled when he presented the organ in 1873 to the small Swedenborgian church in Allegheny. Once this gift became publicized, other requests began to come in, and soon Carnegie found himself involved in a major operation. Knowing the prejudice of Scottish Calvinists against instrumental music in church, particularly the pipe organ—"a kist fu' o' whistles"—Carnegie took a certain delight in seeing a Scottish Presbyterian church swallow its pride and ask for an organ, in the hopes that this would induce Carnegie to make other and more holy contributions to the congregation. After a time this game, however, became no longer a sport but a big business. By 1919 Carnegie had given 7,629 church organs throughout the world at a cost of $6,248,312—a chest full of whistles large enough to have impressed John Knox himself.

Still the interest on his bonds continued to accumulate, and the years of grace left to him in which to dispose of his fortune were fast slipping by. Ruling out medicine, religion, and charitable social work, he had left to him only one major field in which to dispense his largess—education. Here the need was great, the opportunities many, the demands unlimited. But Carnegie was exceedingly cautious. University presidents throughout the United States and Great Britain were more than eager to help relieve Carnegie of his money, but he remained as deaf as Ulysses' sailors to the siren calls from Harvard, Yale, Oxford, and Cambridge.

When he finally entered the field of higher education, it was by the back door, and only then by violating his own cardinal principle of not making charitable gifts to a whole class of impoverished individuals. It was Henry S. Pritchett, the president of the Massachusetts Institute of Technology, who was to open this door to Carnegie by raising the question of teachers' pensions. Like most men of very limited formal education, and particularly men of European background, Carnegie held college professors in awe. To discover that college professors might teach for several decades and not achieve a salary above four hundred dollars a year, with no provisions for retirement, was for Carnegie a shocking revelation. Office clerks at Carnegie Steel earned as much or more.

The low salaries that prevailed throughout the academic profession were of particular concern to Pritchett, who, as head of a scientific technological school, had a great deal more difficulty in recruiting able men than did the administrative officers of the traditional liberal-arts colleges. Now that many of the basic industries were following Carnegie's early example of employing chemists, physicists, and professionally trained mechanical engineers, educational institutions, even those as distinguished as M.I.T., did not find it easy to compete for personnel with companies that paid salaries three to five times higher. Another college personnel problem resulted from the fact that there were no pension plans for professors. Out of purely humanitarian concern, a college was often obliged to keep on its active teaching staff an elderly faculty member who should have been retired, thus denying a place to a young and valuable instructor. This situation further discouraged young men from going into the teaching profession.

Carnegie listened intently to Pritchett's arguments, and by the spring of the year 1905 he was ready to announce his latest philanthropic foundation, the Carnegie Teachers Pension Fund, with an endowment of ten million dollars. Under the terms of this grant as proposed by Carnegie, a board of trustees, composed of twenty-two of the leading college and university presidents in the United States and Canada, was to establish pensions for faculty in private but nonsectarian colleges and universities "under such conditions as you [the trustees] may adopt from time to time."

Had Carnegie simply set up a pension fund for all college teachers in private institutions, the trustees would have had little to do but see that there was a proper administration of the funds. It was Carnegie's strong bias against sectarianism, plus the phrase "under such conditions as you may adopt," that encouraged this able group of college administrators to set standards for higher education. The fund, at first incorporated under the laws of New York State, within a year received a national charter by act of Congress under a more appropriate name: The Carnegie Foundation for the Advancement of Teaching.

The first act of the trustees was to send out a questionnaire to 627 institutions of higher education throughout the United States and Canada, asking each college the size of its endowment, what educational standards it had established for admission and for graduation, what its relation to the state or province was, and what, if any, sectarian ties or obligations it had. Replies were received from 421 institutions, and the trustees then proceeded to establish standards for admission to the pension fund. They first decided that no school with an endowment of less than two hundred thousand dollars would be considered. No school that received a substantial portion of its operating funds from the state was eligible. No school that required a majority of its trustees to belong to a particular denomination or that had a sectarian requirement for its president, faculty, or student body, or that had a required course in a particular religious creed or sect would be eligible. Finally, no school that did not require of its students what the Carnegie board of trustees regarded as a minimum of preparation prior to admission to the college could qualify. Of the 421 original applicants, the trustees accepted only fifty-two for admission into the pension plan.

There were some surprising rejections. Northwestern and Brown universities were kept out on sectarian grounds. The University of Virginia, a private university founded by Thomas Jefferson, was eliminated because its admissions standards were too low. Of the fifty-two institutions selected, twenty-two were located in New England and New York State. Only one southern school, Tulane University, was admitted. Vanderbilt and Randolph-Macon, both of whose educational standards were acceptable, were rejected on sectarian grounds.

In those schools that had not been selected, the anguished cries and threats of faculty members shook college administrations with a violence that Carnegie and Pritchett could hardly have imagined. There were emergency sessions of boards of trustees throughout the country, and charters that had once been considered inviolate were in many places quickly changed to remove sectarian requirements. Bates College went to the state legislature of Maine and successfully pushed through a new act of incorporation that changed its former relations with the Free Baptist Church. The University of Virginia raised its standards of admission, which had an immediate impact upon secondary schools throughout Virginia and in other parts of the South. Inadvertently, Carnegie, with his pension plan, had done more in a year to advance the standards of higher education within the United States than probably any carefully conceived program to accomplish that goal could ever have done.

By 1909 it was quite apparent to anyone interested in higher education that the Carnegie Foundation had become the national unofficial accrediting agency for colleges and universities. Good teachers were accepting positions on the basis of whether or not the school was a participant in the pension fund, prospective donors used participation as a major criterion in determining the direction and size of their gifts, and the program even had an indirect effect upon admissions.

It is not surprising that schools like Northwestern and Brown should be concerned over exclusion. No president was more importunate in his demands that his faculty be included within the pension plan than was President Abram Harris of Northwestern. He even persuaded the President of the United States to come to his aid. "Northwestern is no more sectarian than Princeton," Theodore Roosevelt, with some heat, wrote Carnegie. But Northwestern would not change the provision in its charter that required a majority of its trustees to be Methodists, and not even T.R.'s big stick could force Carnegie and Pritchett to yield to sectarianism.

They did give in to the demands of the state institutions, however. In 1908 Carnegie agreed to permit state institutions, at the request of the state legislatures and governors, to participate in the pension program, and he added an additional five million dollars to the fund to accommodate these requests. This extension proved to be the undoing of the whole program. By 1915 it was apparent to the trustees that the free pension system could not be continued indefinitely. Two years later an independent legal reserve life-insurance company was created, chartered under the laws of New York State, and called the Teachers Insurance and Annuity Association of America. From 1918 on T.I.A.A. entered into contractual relationships with individual institutions of higher education and established life insurance and annuity programs for faculty and college administrators on a contributory basis. The free pension plan had proved to be infeasible within twelve years after its inauguration, but it was a noble and elevating experiment. Had a regular insurance system such as T.I.A.A. been adopted from the beginning in 1905, we should not have had the sorely needed evaluation of higher education that the Carnegie Fund trustees forced on the colleges and universities. The *Times* of London was quite correct in calling the foundation one of Carnegie's most significant accomplishments "in the supremely difficult art of spending large sums of money in undertakings to be of permanent advantage to the public."

By 1910 Carnegie was more than willing to agree with the *Times* as to how "supremely difficult" the art of spending was. He had given away $180,000,000 of his fortune, but he had almost the same amount still left in his possession. The capitalistic system at 5 per cent worked faster than he could. He told his good friend Elihu Root that it appeared that he would have to die in disgrace as a man of great wealth after all. Root had a simple solution. Why didn't he set up a trust, transfer the bulk of his fortune to others for them to worry about, and then die happy in a state of grace?

And so it was done. Carnegie created the Carnegie Corporation of New York in November, 1911, and transferred to it the bulk of his remaining fortune, $125,000,000, "to promote the advancement and diffusion of knowledge among the people of the United States." As United States Steel had been the supercorporation in industry, so the Carnegie Corporation of New York became the first supertrust in philanthropy.

"Now it is all settled," Carnegie wrote his Scottish solicitor, John Ross, in February, 1913. For years the newspapers of New York had run a box score on the philanthropic gifts of Carnegie vs. Rockefeller. Now the New York *Herald* printed the final score: "Carnegie, $332 million; Rockefeller, $175 million." It was no longer a contest. The public had lost interest, and so had Andrew Carnegie.

4

FROM VOLUNTARY ASSOCIATION TO WELFARE STATE: THE ILLINOIS IMMIGRANTS' PROTECTIVE LEAGUE 1908–1926

Robert L. Buroker

In contrast to the underlying philosophy of the Gospel of Wealth, which, as William Jewett Tucker pointed out, implied reform through patronage by the wealthy, the following essay deals with an important aspect of the Progressive movement, reform through voluntary association, a persistent American phenomenon that greatly impressed Tocqueville in the 1830's. This article finds the greatest strength of the Progressive movement in its concern for isolating and dealing with a specific problem in a particular locality. Progressivism was most effective at the local level—municipal reform, conservation, and social amelioration. Only very recently, after many years of attempting reform on a national scale with the New Freedom, the New Deal, the Fair Deal, and the Great Society, is there once again a renewed interest in dealing with specific issues in the immediate locality.

Robert L. Buroker is presently a graduate student at the University of Chicago. This essay received the Pelzer Award for 1971 from the Organization of American Historians.

With the decline in recent years of the welfare state as a major political issue, it is perhaps now time to trace its administrative history. American historians, fascinated by the partisan and ideological struggles of American liberalism, have produced a substantial literature on the intellectual and political movements which culminated in the New and Fair Deal. They know much less, however,

Source: *Journal of American History*, Vol. 58, No. 3 (1971), pp. 643–660. Reprinted by permission of the Organization of American Historians.

about the social and technological changes which made a national welfare state possible, and they have little knowledge of earlier state and local contributions. This was a crucial phase in the modernization of American government, and social scientists and public officials as well as historians might profit from examining how bureaucracies began and what experiences prior to 1933 made such innovations possible.

What happened in early twentieth-century America to spur the development of public welfare bureaucracies? Modernization, after all, implies that certain types of changes have made other types of changes much more probable. Before a welfare state is feasible a society must have at least the following: (1) a permanent group of people who are continually occupied with social problems and who develop the expertise to deal with them; (2) provisions for the expansion and transmission of such expertise; (3) organization and techniques to integrate that expertise into public recognition and state action.[1] While not exhaustive, these three criteria are necessary conditions for the development of a modern welfare state. How were they fulfilled during the Progressive era?

The years between 1900 and 1920 saw an enormous proliferation of voluntary associations to assist a variety of disadvantaged groups, including the impoverished immigrant with his unique set of problems. The history of the Illinois Immigrants' Protective League (IPL) during the Progressive era suggests how progressive movements contributed to the welfare state in America. What kinds of people were involved and why? How successful were their efforts to fulfill the three necessary conditions for a welfare state? What was the relationship between voluntary associations and subsequent government agencies?

Illinois, and Chicago in particular, experienced a massive influx of immigrants between 1890 and 1910 (see Tables I and II). In 1910 there were 974,013 foreign born in Illinois. Between 1910 and 1919 there were 362,756 new arrivals from abroad. The League was organized in 1908 in response to the problems encountered by immigrants in the Chicago area. The idea for such a league came from a committee of a women's trade union group, which was formed to visit immigrant girls and women. One of the first efforts of IPL was to take over that work.[2]

Each year about 20 percent of the women and girls leaving Ellis Island destined for Chicago were unaccounted for at their destinations.[3] Most were never found. Women and girls who did arrive often had incorrect addresses; some

[1] These criteria were formulated after consulting a number of works, the most helpful of which were: Maurice Bruce, *The Coming of the Welfare State* (London, 1961); Philip Klein, *From Philanthropy to Social Welfare: An American Cultural Perspective* (San Francisco, 1968); Roy Lubove, *The Professional Altruist: The Emergence of Social Work as a Career 1880–1930* (Cambridge, Mass., 1965); Ralph E. Pumphrey and Muriel W. Pumphrey, eds., *The Heritage of American Social Work: Readings in Its Philosophical and Institutional Development* (New York, 1961); and Harold L. Wilensky and Charles N. Lebeaux, *Industrial Society and Social Welfare: The Impact of Industrialization on the Supply and Organization of Social Welfare Services in the United States* (New York, 1958).

[2] Illinois Immigrants' Protective League, "Eleven Years of Community Service" (Jan. 1920), 2, Box 60, Supplement II, Records of the Illinois Immigrants' Protective League (IPL) (Preston Bradley Library, University of Illinois, Chicago Circle).

[3] League for the Protection of Immigrants, *Annual Report (1909–1910)* (Chicago, 1911), 6.

TABLE I

FOREIGN BORN IN ILLINOIS BETWEEN 1910 AND 1919*

Nationality	*Foreign Born in Illinois, 1910*	*Admitted Aliens Giving Illinois As Their Destination, 1910–1919*
German	311,680	45,875
Scandinavian	166,812	34,561
English, Irish, Scotch, and Welsh	214,161	44,207
Greek	10,487	24,088
Italian	73,085	77,489
Lithuanian and Lett	32,662	22,920
Polish	148,809	86,910
Russian	2,595	15,199
Slovak	13,722	11,507

* Grace Abbott, "Memorandum as to Work to be Immediately Undertaken by the Immigrants Commission (March 19th, 1920)," 1, Supplement II, Box 58, Records of the Illinois Immigrants' Protective League.

were taken to saloonkeepers or houses of prostitution by cabbies and expressmen. Many were picked up by policemen and "placed" in the homes of Chicago residents who had contacted the police department for just that purpose. Quite a few officers were involved in the racket, and many girls never reached their families.[4] In 1910 Jane Addams wrote of the heartbreak these abuses caused:

> *Every year we have heard of girls who did not arrive when their families expected them, and although their parents frantically met one train after another, the ultimate fate of the girls could never be discovered; we have constantly seen the exploitation of the newly arrived immigrant by his shrewd countrymen in league with the unscrupulous American; from time to time we have known children detained in New York and even deported whose parents had no clear understanding of the difficulty.*[5]

A related problem was the protection of all immigrants upon arrival at Chicago's railroad stations. Unscrupulous cabbies and expressmen used official-looking costumes and badges and a stock of foreign phrases to lure immigrant families into their vehicles, usually to charge them exorbitant fares, but often to transport them to labor camps in the Chicago area. The League planned to assist immigrants at the railroad stations and to support proposals for a federal protective bureau for immigrants in Chicago.[6]

There were also flagrant malpractices by employment agencies which specialized in immigrant workers. Charging exorbitant rates, they often delivered

[4] Illinois Immigrants' Protective League, "Eleven Years of Community Service," 4–5.

[5] League for the Protection of Immigrants, *Annual Report (1909–1910)*, 4.

[6] Illinois Immigrants' Protective League, "Eleven Years of Community Service," 5.

TABLE II

IMMIGRANT ALIENS ADMITTED TO, EMIGRANT ALIENS DEPARTED FROM, ILLINOIS, AND NET INCREASE OR DECREASE IN POPULATION, FROM 1892 TO 1928*

Year	*Immigrant Aliens Admitted*	*Emigrant Aliens Departing*	*Net Increase or Decrease*
1892	46,012		
1893	45,686		
1894	22,783		
1895	16,798		
1896	22,093		
1897	12,067		
1898	12,129		
1899	18,795		
1900	27,118		
1901	30,509		
1902	45,845		
1903	63,378		
1904	57,457		
1905	72,770		
1906	86,539		
1907	104,156		
1908‡	58,733	28,725	+30,008
1909	63,379	14,485	+48,894
1910	93,340	13,165	+80,175
1911	76,565	21,157	+55,408
1912	67,118	28,355	+38,763
1913	107,060	24,178	+82,882
1914	105,811	23,637	+82,174
1915	19,062	11,682	+7,380
1916	418	6,612	−6,194
1917	10,690	2,182	+8,508
1918	2,748	3,488	−740
1919	3,951	4,638	−687
1920	16,964	17,951	−987
1921	48,358	17,652	+30,706
1922	22,410	14,039	+8,371
1923	35,612	4,582	+31,030
1924	46,254	3,977	+42,277
1925	20,382	4,557	+15,825
1926	20,176	4,377	+15,799
1927	20,723	3,911	+16,812
1928	19,165	3,802	+15,363

* "Immigrant Aliens Admitted to, Emigrant Aliens Departed from Illinois," Main Collection, Box 47. Records of the Illinois Immigrants' Protective League.
‡ No departure figures are available before 1908.

men and women to employers in seasonal labor camps, many as far away as Wisconsin and Iowa. The immigrant was later discharged without any way of returning to Chicago. The League decided to investigate the situation and to recommend appropriate city and state legislation.[7]

In general IPL tried to help the immigrant adjust to American life. As an article in the by-laws of the League stated:

> *The objects of this organization shall be to apply the civic, social and philanthropic resources of the city to the needs of foreigners in Chicago, to protect them from exploitation, to cooperate with the Federal, State and local authorities and with similar organizations in other localities, and to protect the right of asylum in all proper cases.*[8]

Time and time again the League lamented its own and the public's colossal ignorance of immigrant life. One purpose from the beginning was to collect as much information as possible on the problems of various immigrant groups in Chicago. In this respect IPL was starting to develop the expertise necessary to manage a social problem. Acting on its information, according to the first *Annual Report*, the League would welcome newcomers and see that they reached their destination; guard them against wrongs at railroad stations, labor camps, and employment agencies; assist them in finding work; advise and encourage them to take advantage of the many co-operating educational facilities furnished by night schools, settlements, churches, YMCA, and others; supplement these when necessary; protect women and girls from prostitution and the white slave trade; personally visit to assist newcomers and to follow up assistance; confer with local, state, and national authorities, and especially with police.[9]

Among IPL's founders were Margaret Dreier Robbins, social economist, suffragette, educator, and wife of the prominent progressive politician Raymond Robbins; Ernst Freund, University of Chicago law professor and later president of the American Political Science Association; Julius Rosenwald, chairman of the board of Sears, Roebuck and Company; Julian Mack, a judge on federal circuit court of appeals; and Samuel N. Harper, professor of Russian language and literature at the University of Chicago and son of William Rainey Harper, president of the University of Chicago. The most active members were the social workers. Addams was instrumental in getting IPL started, although after that her other duties kept her from being more directly involved. Sophonisba P. Breckinridge, a social worker and professor of social economy at Chicago, was active as an advisor to the League. Grace Abbott, later to become director of the Federal Children's Bureau, was the moving force behind the League. As executive secretary throughout most of its first twenty years, her professional approach to social work, her valuable experience, and her influential contacts in Illinois and throughout the country were indispensable to the League's operation.

These eight people were the most famous League leaders, but they represent only a small portion of the total leadership. Between 1908 and 1917 there were sixty trustees, officers, and executive committee members. Enough biographical

[7] League for the Protection of Immigrants, *Annual Report (1909–1910)*, 27–29.

[8] "The Immigrants' Protective League in 1930," 2, Box 60, Supplement II, Records of IPL.

[9] League for the Protection of Immigrants, *Annual Report (1909–1910)*, 5–6.

information is available for forty of them to reveal definite patterns of occupation, age, religion, politics, education, and geographic backgrounds.[10] A majority were members of a profession or the wives of members of a profession (see Table III). The businessmen all worked for large-scale enterprises. Most were high-level managers in corporations, and not one worked in or owned a small business. The lawyers either had successful private practices in commercial law or worked in corporate legal departments.

Of those whose politics are known, nine were Republicans and four were Democrats. They ranged in age from twenty-six to sixty-seven, the mean age being forty-five. In leadership this was not a young organization, although several young women worked on the staff throughout this period. Of the twenty-one leaders whose religious preferences are known, fourteen were Protestants, five were Jews, and two were Catholics. Among those whose place of birth is known, there were thirty native Americans and only five foreign born. Those who had been born in the United States came from a variety of geographic backgrounds. Seven had been born in Chicago, eleven in other large cities, four in rural or small-town Illinois, and seven in rural areas or small towns outside Illinois. It was a highly educated group (see Table IV). Almost two-thirds of them had a college degree, and over one-third of them had doctorates.[11]

A leader of the League was thus likely to be a Protestant, well-educated, middle-class, native-stock American. This is a familiar portrait of progressive reform, but while it discloses something about the people who participated in organizations like IPL, it does not explain why they chose to do so. Indeed, the most troublesome question for progressive historiography is simply raised again. Why, beginning around 1900, did so many of the American middle class decide that their country needed urgent reform? By most standards those were prosperous times, and materially the middle class was doing well. Discontent among workers, farmers, and immigrants seems logical, but not within the ranks of the relatively well-to-do.

The traditional and most enduring explanation is that progressivism was their response to industrialism. Through the state they wanted to remove the evils of the city and factory, aid the underprivileged, to regulate a capitalist economy, and democratize the American political system. It is a testament to the power of this thesis that over the years historians of widely divergent perspectives have reasserted it. Still, a crucial question remains unanswered. Why did some members of the middle class participate in progressive movements while others con-

10 Biographical information was obtained primarily from John W. Leonard, ed., *The Book of the Chicagoans* (Chicago, 1905), and Albert Nelson Marquis, ed., *Who's Who in Chicago* (Chicago, 1926).

11 It is interesting to see how the social make-up of IPL differed from that of its most vociferous opponent on immigrant questions, the Chicago area Ku Klux Klan. No direct comparison is possible because the Klan figures do not distinguish between leaders and members. Nevertheless, Kenneth T. Jackson gives a useful occupational breakdown of those Chicago residents whom the Catholic magazine *Tolerance* reported to be members of the Klan in 1922 and 1923. Jackson found that 20 percent were businessmen, 29 percent were white collar clerical workers, and 39 percent were blue collar workers, while only 4.6 percent were lawyers and 5.4 percent were other professionals. The League reformer appears to have been a different social type from those who tried to exclude the newcomers from American society. Kenneth T. Jackson, *The Ku Klux Klan in the City, 1915–1930* (New York, 1967), 108.

TABLE III
OCCUPATIONS OF FORTY LEAGUE LEADERS, 1908–1917

Occupation	*Number*	*Percentage*
Lawyer	7‡(1)*	20.0‡
Businessman	8 (1)	22.5
Professor	8 (1)	22.5
Social Worker	5	12.5
Physician	1 (2)	7.5
Journalist	3 (1)	10.0
Public School Administrator	1	2.5
Politician	(1)	2.5
Total	40	100.0

* Parentheses include the number of wives whose husbands practiced each profession.
‡ Total number and percentages include occupations of the husbands whose wives served as League leaders.

TABLE IV
HIGHEST EDUCATIONAL LEVEL ACHIEVED BY THIRTY-THREE LEAGUE LEADERS

Level	*Number*	*Percentage*
High School Only	10	30.3
Some College	2	6.1
Bachelor's Degree	7	21.2
Master's Degree	3	9.1
Doctorate	11	33.3
Total	33	100.0

tinued to support McKinley-Taft conservatism? An adequate explanation should be able to tell historians the relevant differences between these two groups. Moreover, the precise connections between aspects of industrialism and the responses to them are often left undefined. Several historians, including Samuel Hays, Robert Wiebe, Gabriel Kolko, and James Weinstein,[12] have explored those linkages for businessmen in the new corporate economy, but other dimensions of progressivism (and especially social welfare movements) have yet to receive such explicit treatment.

In 1955 Richard Hofstadter offered a persuasive interpretation. According to Hofstadter, anxiety over declining status often motivated progressives to reform efforts.

[12] Samuel P. Hays, *The Response to Industrialism: 1885–1914* (Chicago, 1957); Gabriel Kolko, *The Triumph of Conservatism: A Reinterpretation of American History, 1900–1916* (Glencoe, 1963); James Weinstein, *The Corporate Ideal in the Liberal State: 1900–1918* (Boston, 1968); Robert Wiebe, *Businessmen and Reform* (Cambridge, Mass., 1962).

> *[T]he United States was a nation with a rather broad diffusion of wealth, status, and power, in which the man of moderate means, especially in the many small communities, could command much deference and exert much influence. The small merchant or manufacturer, the distinguished lawyer, editor, or preacher, was a person of local eminence in an age in which local eminence mattered a great deal. In the absence of very many nation-wide sources of power and prestige, the pillars of the local communities were men of great importance in their own right.*[13]

After the Civil War this began to change, and the result was a severe sense of dislocation on the part of the social groups which had traditionally provided community leadership.

> *The newly rich, the grandiosely or corruptly rich, the masters of great corporations, were bypassing the men of the Mugwump type—the old gentry, the merchants of long standing, the small manufacturers, the established professional men, the civic leaders of an earlier era . . . . [T]he America [of the traditional groups] they knew did not lack opportunities, but it did seem to lack opportunities of the highest sort for men of the highest standards. In a strictly economic sense these men were not growing poorer as a class, but their wealth and power were being dwarfed by comparison with the new eminences of wealth and power. They were less important, and they knew it.*[14]

The status revolution thesis explains the behavior of many progressives. It is not so applicable to people like those who founded and directed the League. For one thing the status anxious progressives often resented the immigrant because he was a source of political power for the corrupt city machine. Moreover, it is unlikely that the people participating in IPL were experiencing status anxiety. The majority were well-educated professionals, and many were the first of their families to receive a college education. Several, instead of being replaced by the new plutocracy, were active participants in it. All but one of the lawyers worked for large corporations. Among the businessmen there was not a single small merchant or manufacturer. To a man they were part of the élite of the new economic order, and, in addition, several of them were self-made men, stock boys who became corporation presidents. The university professors and the social workers were members of professions which were rapidly growing as distinctive occupational groups. Thus, far from resenting the changes which industrialization and urbanization had brought to American society since the Civil War, the leaders of the League had every reason to feel self-confident since they were riding the crest of those changes. They represented the new occupations of corporate management and professional skill which were to become the élite strata of twentieth-century America.

Recent investigations of professionalism and bureaucratization during the Progressive era suggest another social basis for reform movements. The growing post-Civil War professional middle class is the subject of an important chapter in Wiebe's *The Search for Order: 1877–1920*. During this period most modern

[13] Richard Hofstadter, *The Age of Reform: From Bryan to F. D. R.* (New York, 1955), 135–36.

[14] *Ibid.*, 137.

professional associations were organized, and those which practiced specialized skills became an integral part of urban-industrial America. Their self-awareness further accentuated rural-urban differences, and living primarily in the larger cities they understandably tried to focus increasing political attention on the problems of the city environment.[15] Roy Lubove's *The Professional Altruist* describes the growth of social work as a profession. After using recent refinements of the sociological literature on bureaucracy and professions to explain the history of both social work and the public welfare agency, he concluded:

> *Specialization and the idealization of expertise, the growth of an occupational subculture, and bureaucratization were instrumental in shaping the character of twentieth-century social work. These typical features of an urban-industrial society have affected not only the professions but most spheres of life, and their controlling influence will undoubtedly remain potent.*[16]

Hays discovered an important political result of these developments when he analyzed the social bases of municipal reform movements. Professionals as well as businessmen dominated these groups, and Hays found that what distinguished these reformers from their less active colleagues in business and the professions was their relatively recent arrival on the social and political scene. The businessmen came from large-scale industries which were but a half century old, and the professionals were "in the vanguard of professional life, seeking to apply expertise more widely to public affairs."[17]

These insights suggest a more adequate explanation for why so many ostensibly comfortable people became at least social welfare progressives. By 1900 a social class based on specialized expertise had become numerous and influential enough to come into its own as a political force. Educated to provide rational answers to specific problems and oriented by training if not by inclination toward public service, they sensed their own stake in the stability of the new society, which increasingly depended upon their skills, and quite predictably turned their attention to the misery of the urban lower classes. In this sense they were responding to the evils of industrialism and urbanism. They were themselves, however, as much a part of the modernization process as the sweat shop and the tenement.

The history of the League is consistent with this interpretation. Clearly IPL was concerned primarily with integrating the immigrant into American society. The leaders were not fundamentally dissatisfied with the American system, and they urged no radical changes. They were trying to solve problems of limited scope. Social theorists have often commented on the stabilizing influence which professionals seem to exercise. Indeed, as Talcott Parsons notes, "The development and increasing strategic importance of the professions probably constitute the most important change that has occurred in the occupational system of

[15] Robert H. Wiebe, *The Search for Order: 1877–1920* (New York, 1967), 111–32.

[16] Lubove, *The Professional Altruist*, 220.

[17] Samuel P. Hays, "The Politics of Reform in Municipal Government in the Progressive Era," *Pacific Northwest Quarterly*, 55 (Oct. 1964), 160.

modern societies."[18] A professional class can prevent serious conflict in a modernizing social system with glaring inequalities in wealth, status, and power. Professionals become experts at alleviating problems and adjudicating conflicts which might otherwise develop into significant disruptions.[19]

Prior to the Progressive era the professions had been growing at an unprecedented rate. Between 1870 and 1900 the number of professionals per 100,000 population almost doubled. The professional labor force increased 245 percent in contrast to a 125 percent rate of growth for the total labor force. The expansion was greatest in architecture, teaching, and journalism.[20] Most League leaders were members of the professional classes, and the plight of immigrants became a focus for their expertise. Whatever their differences, the social science professor, the journalist, the corporation lawyer, and even the corporate executive shared a belief that American society needed their special skills.

Another dimension to IPL leadership deserves special consideration. Thirteen among the forty IPL leaders were women, and most of the staff workers were young women in their twenties. Abbott was the moving force behind the League in its first two decades. A social worker, Marion Schibsby, directed the staff work throughout much of this period and stayed with her work during the financial crisis years of the early 1920s. The participation of women in reform movements is nothing new to progressive historiography.

Indeed, the suffragette and the female social worker had already become classic American types. One historian, however, has put these women in a most interesting perspective. Arthur Mann notes something fundamentally different between Addams' generation and generations of earlier female reformers. By 1900 the legal emancipation of women was almost completed, and a new social type was emerging. The career woman was replacing the feminist. Speaking of Vida D. Scudder, Addams, and their contemporaries, Mann states, "All these women the modern American will recognize as completely modern, whereas the feminists, whether Lucy Stone or Alice Stone Blackwell, Julia Ward Howe or Elizabeth Stuart Phelps, savor of an age unlike our own."[21]

Addams recalled in *Twenty Years at Hull House* how, when she graduated from Rockford College, her first concern was to find a useful purpose for her training. She went to Europe, discovered the settlement house concept, returned to Chicago, and found her role at Hull House.[22] With minor variations, her story is the story of many of these women. They were the first American generation of their sex to leave the household in large numbers and contribute significantly to the society outside the home. Women like Breckinridge and Abbott became highly competent social scientists and administrators. Like the corpora-

[18] Talcott Parsons, "Professions," David L. Sills, ed., *The International Encyclopedia of the Social Sciences* (17 vols., New York, 1968), XII, 536.

[19] Joseph Ben-David, "Professions in the Class System of Present-Day Societies," *Current Sociology La Sociologie Contemporaine*, XII (1963–1964), 249.

[20] Alba M. Edwards, *Comparative Occupational Statistics for the United States, 1870 to 1940* [Department of Commerce, Bureau of the Census, *Sixteenth Census of the United States: 1940 Population*] (Washington, 1943), 111.

[21] Arthur Mann, *Yankee Reformers in the Urban Age: Social Reform in Boston, 1880–1900* (New York, 1954), 227.

[22] Jane Addams, *Twenty Years at Hull House: With Autobiographical Notes* (New York, 1911), 65–88.

tion lawyer, the industrial executive, and the university professor, they were, as Mann suggests, part of the first generation of modern America. Far from being anxious to preserve their traditional roles, they were assertive career women, a new and permanent type in American society. In Boston, Scudder spoke for all such women when she wrote:

> *Into this world . . . life with bewildering and contradictory theories, yet bent, as no other age has ever been, in the analysis of social evil and the right of social wrong—into this world we are born—we, the first generation of college women. In a sense, we represent a new factor in the social order. . . . Surely, I may at least say, that we make ourselves significant if we will.*[23]

In Chicago, the organizers of IPL were part of the larger search by an emerging professional class for the expertise to direct the advance of the new order.

How successfully did the League translate its objectives into results? The evidence indicates that between 1908 and 1926 it managed an impressive quantity of private and public social work. Operating with a staff which rarely exceeded ten or twelve people, it collected information on Illinois immigrant groups, established a case work service, aided new arrivals, improved the employment agency situation, and pressed for state and federal legislation. Its work went a long way toward fulfilling many of the functions of a modern welfare state agency.

The League began in 1908 to locate lost immigrant girls. It obtained their names through private agencies in New York and later through the United States Immigration Service. Representatives of IPL who were familiar with the language and European backgrounds of newcomers made regular visits. It helped to locate missing family members. Girls who needed assistance were put in touch with night schools and various available social agencies. From 1909 to 1915 the League contacted and helped 19,512 immigrant girls.[24]

To protect all immigrants upon arrival in Chicago the League worked closely with newspapers to publicize the problem. In July 1910, the Chicago and Western Indiana Railroad donated a small building across the street from the Dearborn station. There the League established offices, reception rooms, bedrooms, and baths.[25] For the next eighteen months it was a well-matched battle between the female IPL workers and the cabbies and expressmen. There were numerous altercations, but the women won out, and the number of people aided by the League at the Dearborn station increased steadily through 1913.[26] Between July and December 1910, the League helped 1,903 people. In 1911 the number increased to 5,204. The next year it tripled to 15,537, and in 1913 it increased to 41,322.[27]

[23] Quoted in Mann, *Yankee Reformers in the Urban Age*, 201.

[24] Illinois Immigrants' Protective League, "Eleven Years of Community Service," 3–4.

[25] *Fifth Annual Report of the Immigrants' Protective League (1913)* (Chicago, 1914), 8–9.

[26] Illinois Immigrants' Protective League, "Eleven Years of Community Service," 5.

[27] *Ibid.*, 6.

Throughout this period IPL negotiated with federal officials in an effort to obtain a federal bureau to protect immigrants in the Chicago railroad stations. In this effort they received the support of a number of influential Chicago civic associations, including the prestigious Commercial Club.[28] In 1913 Congressman Adolph J. Sabath of Illinois introduced a bill to establish federal bureaus at stations like Dearborn. It became law in July 1913. The government rented a building near the station which was equipped with reception rooms, baths, laundry, and beds. These facilities, however, were rarely used. The government's most frequent excuses were the decline in immigration beginning in August 1914 and the fact that there were no provisions for getting people from the station to the federal building. The League offered to transport the immigrants, but in the end it had to carry on most of the station work itself. Congress failed in later years to appropriate sufficient funds, and IPL continued as the sole protector of new arrivals from abroad.[29]

One of the first League projects was a thorough study of Chicago employment agencies. Abbott's research team discovered that of 289 licensed agencies in Chicago in 1908, there were 110 which specialized in immigrant workers.[30] On the basis of the published reports of malpractices by many of these agencies, the legislature in 1909 passed amendments to the employment agency licensing laws which provided for stricter standards and better enforcement.[31]

Besides these major activities, the League carried on a number of other projects designed to help immigrants adjust to American life. For several years, for example, until it persuaded the Bureau of Immigration to take over the task, IPL compiled a list of all children, aged six through sixteen, who came to Illinois by way of Ellis Island. These lists were furnished to truant officers and school superintendents in Illinois communities.[32] During American participation in World War I the League handled 2,840 draft cases involving immigrant men. League members explained to alien registrants their rights and obligations under the laws and acted as interpreters in communications with draft boards.[33] Beginning in the autumn of 1918 the League began to assist aliens in connection with the new income tax laws. There were a number of ambiguities in the laws relating to non-citizens, and IPL was able to get some of the regulations clarified. Case workers also assisted immigrants in filing their forms.[34]

In 1918, at a time when the League was experiencing severe financial difficulty resulting from the war, the Illinois state legislature established the Immigrants Commission within the State Department of Registration and Education. The League had been publicizing the need for such a commission for some time. On July 1, 1919, the new agency began its work. Abbott was named director, and, for all practical purposes, the staff of the League became the staff of the

28 League for the Protection of Immigrants, *Annual Report (1909–1910)*, 6.

29 *Sixth Annual Report of the Immigrants' Protective League (1914)* (Chicago, 1915), 6–7.

30 Grace Abbott, "The Chicago Employment Agency and the Immigrant Worker," *American Journal of Sociology*, XIV (Nov. 1908), 289.

31 League for the Protection of Immigrants, *Annual Report (1909–1910)*, 6.

32 Illinois Immigrants' Protective League, "Eleven Years of Community Service," 8.

33 *Ibid.*, 8–9.

34 *Ibid.*, 9.

new Immigrants Commission.[35] According to the authorizing statute, the new Commission was to:

> *Make a survey of the Immigrant, alien born, and foreign-speaking people of the State, and of their distribution, conditions of employment, and standards of housing and living. Examine into their economic, financial and legal customs, their provisions for insurance, and other prudential arrangements, their organization, and their education needs; keeping in friendly and sympathetic touch with alien groups and co-operating with State and Local officials, and with immigrant or related authorities of other States and of the United States.*[36]

The Commission operated on a budget of $15,000 for the biennium. This sum did not compare favorably with the budgets for similar commissions in three other large states. For equal periods the California commission had $140,000; the New York commission had $51,200; and the Massachusetts commission had $56,000.[37] In the following two years, however, the Commission was surprisingly active. Under Abbott's direction two massive studies were completed and well-publicized by the press in 1921. One involved the educational needs of immigrants in Illinois, and the other reported the results of investigations on the immigrant and the coal mining communities in Illinois. Both studies prompted a variety of state actions. One, the attack on adult illiteracy, was especially productive.

Abbott's study of the immigrants' education first brought to light the problem of illiteracy in Illinois. The report noted that Illinois ranked twenty-third among the states in the amount of money spent on schools for each $100 of taxable wealth. As a result, Abbott commented, "It was not surprising that the commission found that 96.9 percent of the women and 88.6 of the men interviewed in the course of its investigation . . . were not able to read and write English, and that 53.5 percent of the women and 24.2 percent of the men could not speak English."[38]

Following the Commission's report, both the Commission and the League, now just a paper organization, made a concerted effort to collect as much data as possible on the problem of illiteracy in the state. They compiled a memorandum, "Startling Statistics on Illiteracy in Illinois," which did, indeed, include some startling findings. Illinois, it was discovered, ranked twenty-second among the states in the percentage of illiteracy and twenty-fifth in the percentage of native white illiterates. In 1910 there had been 168,294 illiterates in the state, and by 1920 the number had increased to about 174,000.[39]

The most serious obstacle was a state law which forbade local communities

[35] Reprint of "Immigrants' Protective League," *Social Service*, 3:8 (Chicago: Chicago Council of Social Agencies, May, 1926), 3, in Box 62, Main Collection, Records of IPL.

[36] "The Illinois Immigrants' Commission," memorandum (April 8, 1929), 8, Box 47, *ibid.*

[37] "Memorandum as to Appropriations of other Commissions, Boards or Bureaus charged with duties similar to those of the Illinois Commission," *ibid.*

[38] Reprint from Chicago *Daily News*, March 23, 1921, *ibid.*

[39] "Startling Statistics on Illiteracy in Illinois," 1–5, memorandum, *ibid.*

from providing educational facilities for people over the age of twenty-one. The Commission, the League, and a number of other voluntary organizations including the Illinois League of Women Voters began a publicity campaign to amend the statute. Six years later they were successful. The legislature passed a bill that gave the communities of the state the power "to establish classes for the instruction of persons over twenty-one years of age, and to pay the necessary expenses of the same out of the school funds of the district."[40] At the end of the decade there was significant improvement. By 1930 the number of persons ten years of age and over unable to read and write English had decreased to 153,507. The percentage of illiteracy in Illinois had been 3.4 percent in 1920. In 1930 it was 2.4 percent.[41]

The illiteracy studies were only one example of the skill with which the League and the Commission collected statistics on social problems in Illinois. Abbott and her co-workers in IPL had long been known for their ability to conduct massive survey research. In 1914 Abbott and some other Chicago social workers were invited by the state of Massachusetts to conduct a statewide survey of immigrant problems. Their efforts were instrumental in the success of the Massachusetts Immigration Commission.[42] It would have been impossible for a national welfare system to develop without the now commonplace tools of social statistics. Their refinement was primarily a nineteenth-century development, and IPL leaders were no exceptions among social workers in Europe and America in recognizing the usefulness of the innovations in applied mathematics. The Chicago School of Civics and Philanthropy, founded in 1903 by Addams, Abbott, Breckinridge, and others, offered regular courses to those wishing to join the new profession of social service administration. From the very first year one of the required courses was "Methods of Social Investigation," a class taught by Abbott and Breckinridge. It dealt with a variety of social research techniques including "the application of statistical methods to social problems, the collection and tabulation of data, the use and misuse of averages, index numbers and weighting."[43] Since many IPL staff members were trained at this school, it is not surprising that the League and the Commission were able to ascertain both the quality and the magnitude of immigrants' problems in Illinois.

The Illinois Commission maintained a large and growing load of case work, primarily in the Chicago area. The Commission case load for a three month period increased from 332 in January-March 1920, to 874 during the same three months of the next year.[44] The Commission also carried on IPL's work in supervising the assistance of immigrants at railroad stations. In the last three months

[40] Mrs. Kenneth F. Rich, "Opportunity Under the New Adult Education Law," *Bulletin of the Illinois League of Women Voters* (Nov. 1927), 1, reprint, in *ibid.*

[41] National Advisory Committee on Illiteracy, *Illiteracy Statistics for the State of Illinois* (Washington, 1930), 1–3, in *ibid.*

[42] Illinois State Department of Public Welfare, *Grace Abbott: November 17, 1878 to June 19, 1939* (Springfield, Illinois: Nov., 1940), 11, in Box 3, Supplement II, *ibid.*

[43] Chicago School of Civics and Philanthropy, *Bulletin,* 1 (July 1909), 23.

[44] "Protective Case Work in Chicago and its Immediate Vicinity," memorandum in Box 58, Supplement II, Records of IPL; Illinois Immigrants Commission, "First Quarterly Report of the Executive Secretary for January, February, and March, 1921," typewritten draft in *ibid.*

of 1920, 942 people received assistance, and 1,218 received Commission aid at Chicago railroad stations in the first quarter of 1921.[45]

Despite the Commission's successes, its functions were terminated by Governor Lennington Small's veto of its next biennial appropriation on June 30, 1921. In his farewell address the previous governor, Frank Lowden, had urged that the legislature continue to support the work of the Commission. The lawmakers had responded by voting a $58,000 budget for the years 1921 to 1923. Small's veto was part of a last minute economy move which included vetoes of appropriations for a number of state agencies.[46]

The Commission and League members were stunned on the evening of June 30, when they received word through the press that as of the next day, the beginning of a new fiscal year, the Illinois Immigrants Commission would cease to exist. At that time the Commission was working on about 500 cases, but it had to vacate its offices in Springfield and Chicago within a few hours.[47] On July 2, the trustees of the League met to decide what to do in the face of the veto crisis. There was enough money to pay two people to finish the existing case load. The Girls' Protective Bureau at Hull House donated office space, and through July 118 cases and 117 new ones were either handled or referred.[48] After August 1, Abbott and Schibsby handled case work themselves, and together during the next month they helped 145 new clients.[49]

The trustees decided to try to raise about $5,000 each year for casework and to wait for the state to reactivate the Commission which still retained its legal existence.[50] They had trouble raising the money, but by 1924 they were able to add four new case workers to the staff, making a total of six. During the next two years the League handled about 4,000 new cases. Finally, after five years of waiting and lobbying, the League decided to reconstitute itself as a private organization, a status which it has maintained to this day.[51]

What can be concluded about the work of the League and the Commission through 1926? The evidence suggests that IPL, in both its private and public capacities, fulfilled the necessary conditions for a modern welfare state agency. It constituted a group of people who were continually concerned with social problems and who became experts on such matters. Through the Chicago School of Civics and Philanthropy, several League members laid the groundwork for the growth of an expertly trained profession of welfare administration. They collected and analyzed mass data. They publicized problems and thereby facilitated public recognition and state action. Finally, they actually performed welfare service work on a surprisingly large scale. They set an example of the type of organization which was necessary to administer a modern welfare system.

The League was only one of hundreds of voluntary associations founded between 1900 and 1920. There is no reason to believe that its experience was

[45] Illinois Immigrants Commission, "Fourth Quarterly Report of the Executive Secretary, 1920," typewritten draft in *ibid.*

[46] "The Present Program of the Immigrants' Protective League and a Sketch of its Reorganization," memorandum (1926), 1, Box 57, Main Collection, *ibid.*

[47] *Ibid.*, 2.

[48] *Ibid.*

[49] Ernst Freund to IPL members, Dec. 12, 1921, Box 47, *ibid.*

[50] Abel Davis, memorandum, July 31, 1925, *ibid.*

[51] "Present Program of the Immigrants' Protective League and a Sketch of its Reorganization," 2, Box 57, *ibid.*

unique within its own reform era or throughout the history of American reform. Alexis de Tocqueville wrote of Jacksonian America that, "Wherever, at the head of some new undertaking, you see the government in France, or a man of rank in England, in the United States you will be sure to find an association."[52] This perceptive observer captured something essential to the growth of American government. In a country where decision-making was highly decentralized and where the natural impulse was always toward local autonomy and a suspicion of government, the voluntary association assumed a crucial role in developing the expertise and the organization necessary to manage social problems. When the state finally acted, the minimum requirements of knowledge, personnel, and procedure were already available in the experience of private groups.

Mann has noted the absence of thorough histories of a number of important voluntary associations.[53] Closer study of these groups might substantiate the thesis that in the United States voluntary organizations formed the basis not only for the welfare state but for the whole development of modern public bureaucracies. One can think of numerous examples of people involved in private organizations who assumed newly created government positions in areas where they possessed special skills. Perhaps this is only part of a larger pattern involving a characteristic if not unique American system of public administration, a system in which the voluntary association has usually laid the necessary foundation.

If this is so, the Progressive era deserves reinterpretation as a key transition period in American history. Historians have overemphasized the extent to which progressive reform was a reaction against industrialization and urbanization. Granted it was a response to the more severe evils of the city and the factory, but many progressive leaders were themselves a part of the emerging system. The corporation lawyer, the business executive, the social science professor, the career woman—all were the results of forces transforming a nineteenth-century nation.

If the experience of the League holds true generally, there were many influential progressives who were quite at home in urban-industrial America. They formed associations, and within those associations they developed and professionalized new skills. Max Weber saw professionalization and technical efficiency as two characteristics of the ideal type bureaucracy. Perhaps the Progressive era was among other things the era of proto-bureaucratic association, a necessary link between agrarian, town meeting America and the America of the managed metropolis.

52 Alexis de Tocqueville, *Democracy in America,* Richard D. Heffner, ed. (New York, 1956), 198.

53 Arthur Mann, "The Progressive Tradition," John Higham, ed., *The Reconstruction of American History* (New York, 1962), 176.

5

ITALIANS AND CRIME IN CHICAGO: THE FORMATIVE YEARS, 1890–1920

Humbert S. Nelli

Crime can be regarded as a universal phenomenon, a function of group life evident in all societies and on all levels. The varied forms antisocial conduct takes, however, and the reaction it engenders are variables dependent on the cultural status and social organization of the group. With the rapid growth of American cities in the first decades of the twentieth century, crime became a national issue, and it has remained a concern ever since. In 1968 a poll revealed that crime in the cities was second only to the Vietnam War as the major concern of the American people. Criminal statistics have been used to suggest an ethnic or racial base to the criminal class. Though such an approach has little basis in reality, it does indicate a desire to find a rational explanation of crime as well as to suggest both the fears and prejudices of large numbers of people. The high rate of crimes of violence in southern Italy has often been explained in terms of racial inheritance as has the high homicidal rate of Italian immigrants in the United States. It is to the problem of Italians and crime that Professor Nelli addresses himself.

Humbert Nelli is an ethnic-urban historian whose book The Italians in Chicago, 1880–1930: A Study in Ethnic Mobility *(New York, 1970) appeared in the urban history series edited by Richard Wade. Professor Nelli teaches at the University of Kentucky and is at work on a major study of ethnic groups and crime in the United States.*

I

Americans reacted to crime among Italian newcomers with a frenzy of emotion aroused by no other immigrant activity. Official reports, books, pamphlets, magazine articles, and newspaper stories criticized and analyzed, lamented and decried

Source: *The American Journal of Sociology*, Vol. 74, No. 4 (January 1969), pp. 373–391.

Italian criminality which, in the period to 1921, invariably meant the Black Hand, or Mafia. Some writers argued that Italians naturally possessed criminal inclinations, others blamed slum conditions in American cities, and still others denied the existence of lawbreaking organizations in the United States patterned after the Sicilian Mafia or the Neapolitan Camorra.[1]

Contemporaries emphasized problems such as possible operating procedures of the Black Hand among Italians in America, whether Italian crime represented a reaction to new-world conditions or a carry-over of old-world traditions, and whether Italian criminals worked from centralized headquarters or as independent groups and individuals. Preoccupation with these and similar aspects obscured factors of deeper and more long-lasting significance. First, the groundwork of Italian dominance of Chicago's crime after 1920 was laid in the years prior to national prohibition legislation. In addition, Italian lawbreaking in the era before 1920 involved a wide variety of operations, many of them with no Black Hand connections. In those years also—a time of mass immigration from the Italian kingdom—crime served a useful (although not necessarily desirable) function as one facet of group adjustment to a new environment. Finally, two separate and relatively distinct levels of criminal activity involving Italians developed during the formative period of Italian crime in Chicago. One was entirely within the immigrant community and affected only its residents; the other took place as Italians began to move into "big time" crime which operated within the American community. Before January 16, 1920, most Italian crime took place only within the colony. Prohibition encouraged many to move into organized crime, which they eventually came to dominate in Chicago.

II

A series of events that began in New Orleans in 1890 had a profound effect on the Chicago Italian community. On October 15, 1890, New Orleans Superintendent of Police David C. Hennessy was murdered. City residents assumed Sicilians to be responsible, for Hennessy had been engaged in a crackdown on

[1] For a variety of opinions on the questions of Italian criminality and whether the Black Hand existed see: John Chetwood, Jr., *Immigration Fallacies* (Boston: Arena Publishing Co., 1896), pp. 141–42; Arthur Train, *Courts, Criminals and the Camorra* (New York: Charles Scribner's Sons, 1912), p. 214; U.S. Senate, *Reports of the Immigration Commission* (1911), IV, 209; Isaac A. Hourwich, *Immigration and Labor: The Economic Aspects of European Immigration to the United States* (New York: B. W. Huebsch, Inc., 1912), pp. 358–61; Eliot Lord, John J. D. Trenor, and Samuel J. Barrows, *The Italian in America* (New York: B. F. Buck & Co., 1905), pp. 209–10, 216; William S. Bennet, "Immigrants and Crime," *Annals of the American Academy of Political and Social Science*, XXXIV, No. 1 (July, 1909), 120–21; Arthur H. Warner, "Amputating the Black Hand," *The Survey*, XXII (May 1, 1909), 167; Editor's Note to anonymous article, "The Black Hand Scourge," *Cosmopolitan*, No. 47 (June, 1909), p. 31; Gaetano D'Amato, "The 'Black Hand' Myth," *North American Review*, CLXXXII (April, 1908), 544; Tomasso Sassone, "Italy's Criminals in the United States," *Current History*, XV (October, 1921), 23; *Chicago Record-Herald*, March 26, 1910; John Landesco, *Organized Crime in Chicago. Part III of the Illinois Crime Survey* (Chicago: Association for Criminal Justice, 1929), pp. 938, 941–42; *L'Italia* (Chicago), January 24, 1891, October 8, 1892, December 7, 1919; *Vita Nuova* (Chicago), April, 1925; *La Parola dei Socialisti* (Chicago), March 28, 1914.

crime in the Italian community. In a city-wide atmosphere of near hysteria, the police arrested hundreds of Italians for the crime and brought nine to trial. To the consternation of the American community, the jury found six defendants "not guilty" and could reach no verdict on the other three. Rumors of bribery and intimidation of witnesses filled New Orleans; public officials and city newspapers demanded that "the failure of justice" be remedied. With widespread local support, a mob raged to the parish prison, dragged from it eleven Italian prisoners, and lynched them.

The incident quickly grew into a national crisis and an international affair. Italy demanded punishment of the lynch mob and financial compensation for the victim's families. For a short time in 1891, war between Italy and the United States appeared to be a distinct possibility. President Harrison eased the situation somewhat when he spoke of the New Orleans affair in his annual message to Congress (on December 9, 1891) as "a most deplorable and discreditable incident, an offense against law and humanity." Relations between the two countries improved in the following months, and the breach healed rapidly after Harrison offered an indemnity payment.[2]

Chicago's Italian leaders sympathized with the New Orleans Italian community and subscribed money to pay for the defense of the nine accused men. They emphasized the need for group solidarity and co-operation and tended to view the New Orleans affair as part of a general pattern of anti-Italian attitudes on the part of Irish policemen and English-language newspapers in New Orleans, Chicago, and other American cities. Applauding the Italian government's involvement on behalf of the families of the eleven murdered men, they strongly supported the mother country in her diplomatic exchanges with the United States. They were shocked by Italy's acceptance of the American government's offer to pay what *L'Italia* described on March 19, 1892, as "a small indemnity" without recognizing or suitably condemning American responsibility in the affair.

Prior to 1890, crime in Chicago's Italian community had consisted of illegal activities in employment, child labor, crimes of passion growing out of alcoholic indulgence or presumed insults to female family members, and vendettas from the old country. Outlaws within the community had not organized, and the term "Mafia" received little attention in the city's newspapers in connection with the city's Italians. The New Orleans affair marked a complete turning point.

To their horror, Italians in Chicago found themselves objects of open fear and contempt during the course of the affair. The word "Mafia" now appeared frequently in Chicago's newspapers, and many tabloids proclaimed the criminal inclinations of all Italians, doubtless as an outgrowth of the popular assumption that the Mafia had effected Hennessy's murder. Americans concluded that the Mafia flourished wherever "Southerners" (Sicilians and mainland Italians from the area south of Rome) lived. This belief strongly affected Chicagoans, for by 1891–92 the city contained a sizable and rapidly growing Italian community composed largely of "Southerners." Italian leaders reacted for personal reasons (in order to gain American acceptance), as well as through ethnic pride, by

[2] John E. Coxe, "The New Orleans Mafia Incident," *Louisiana Historical Quarterly*, XX, No. 4 (October, 1937), 1067–1110; John S. Kendall, "Who Killa de Chief?" *Louisiana Historical Quarterly*, XXII, No. 2 (April, 1939), 492–530; A. Pierantoni, *I Fatti di Nuova Orleans e il Diritto Internazionale* (Rome, 1891).

denying the existence of the Mafia in Chicago. Some, like Oscar Durante, editor and publisher of Chicago's *L'Italia,* insisted that it did not exist even in Italy.[3]

In order to make clear to Americans that old-world criminal patterns and groups did not carry over in immigrant-colony crime, Italian-language papers began, shortly after the turn of the century, to use the term "Black Hand" to identify crimes within the immigrant community. This term became favored by both American and foreign-language journals in the first two decades of the twentieth century. From 1904, for example, "Black Hand" supplanted "Mafia" as the preferred term for crimes committed by Italians against each other, at least so far as *L'Italia* was concerned, and the replacement remained in use until the 1920's.[4]

Whichever name they used to publicize crimes, Italian-colony newspapers at first denied the existence of organized gangs. In an article entitled, "The 'Black Hand' in Chicago, Threatening Letter Causes Panic," printed in 1904, Durante repeated a belief he had often stated in the past in *L'Italia*: "The 'Black Hand' does not exist, the crimes must be treated singly as individual events which do not have any relation with organized groups." Over the passage of time, the press attributed an increasing number of crimes to the Black Hand. Even *L'Italia* credited a quantity of blackmailings, bombings, and murders to the secret society: "Black Hand in Chicago. Blackmail Letter for $300" (July 14, 1906); "Italians on Trial. 32 Italians Accused as Members of the Black Hand" (April 27, 1907); "Once Again the Black Hand" (June 5, 1909).[5]

In 1910 *L'Italia* reported the arrest of Black Hand leaders and hopefully echoed city authorities: "Chicago police are elated over the arrest of four Italians accused of being leaders of the so-called Black Hand organization of Chicago." As in earlier cases, however, crimes continued after the reported capture of Black Hand leaders and the smashing of criminal societies.[6]

[3] *L'Italia,* October 25, November 1, 8, 22, and 29, December 13 and 27, 1890; March 7, 14, 21, and 28, April 4, 18, and 25, May 9 and 23, July 18, August 8, September 12, November 28, December 12, 1891; February 6, March 19, April 16, 1892.

[4] Several theories have been offered to explain the appearance of the term "Black Hand" to describe certain types of Italian colony crime. Alessandro Mastro-Valerio, publisher and editor of *La Tribuna Italiana Transatlantica* (Chicago), February 1, 1908, claimed that Carlo Barsotti, editor of New York's *Il Progresso Italo-Americano,* had coined the term in order to avoid using the word "Mafia," and in hopes that the offenses thus identified would be viewed as responses to American conditions. Perhaps the most acceptable was one advanced by Gaetano D'Amato, a New York City Italian community leader and friend of police Lieutenant Joseph Petrosino of New York's Italian detective squad, in a 1908 article, "The 'Black Hand' Myth," p. 548. D'Amato stated that "the term 'Black Hand' was first used in this country about ten years ago, probably by some Italian desperado who had heard of the exploits of the Spanish society, and considered the combination of words to be high-sounding and terror-inspiring. One or two crimes committed under the symbol gave it a vogue among the rapacious brotherhood; and, as it looked well and attracted attention in their headlines, the newspapers finally applied it to all crimes committed by the Italian banditti in the United States."

[5] *L'Italia,* August 27, September 10, 1904; July 14, 1906; April 27 and August 10, 1907; March 7, 1920. See also *La Tribuna Italiana Transatlantica,* November 9, 1907; February 8, 1908.

[6] *L'Italia,* April 16, 1910; August 10, 1901; *La Tribuna Italiana Transatlantica,* February 8, 1908.

Oscar Durante admitted in February, 1911, that "if we continue at the present rate, the Italian colony of Chicago will soon take the lead over that of New York, in the matter of bombings, murder, and blackmail." In fact, the number of criminal activities in the Italian colony increased as the community grew in inhabitants, although few contemporaries recognized the relationship between crime and population growth. The editor blamed Italian-Americans for the fear-ridden situation, for "when they are questioned by the police, they become as dumb as fish and answer with the usual shrug of the shoulders so that . . . the criminal element flourished until its effect is felt from one end of the city to the other." Betraying his middle-class orientation, he complained that these conditions worked "to the detriment of the better class Italians."[7]

Although in April, 1910, *L'Italia* congratulated the police on their activities against the Black Hand—"This arrest is proof that the forces of law and order in our city are always on the alert"—one year later Durante held local officials responsible for the Black Hand's existence. "There have been 34 murders in the past two years, and not one of these murders has been solved by the police. This lack of capacity shown by the police gives criminals the courage to strike again. The police must cooperate with us to clear up this situation." Mastro-Valerio and other community spokesmen agreed that corrupt, incompetent police encouraged or permitted widespread criminal activity in the Italian colony. Many Americans reached the same conclusion. The Black Hand, they argued, could not possibly function without police complicity or inability. The Massachusetts Commission of Immigration, for example, identified police corruption, "which takes the form of protection of criminals," as the factor primarily responsible for Black Hand successes in cities outside Massachusetts, including Chicago.[8]

Fear and concern pervaded the Italian community because of the Black Hand's notoriety. Editor Mastro-Valerio warned in *La Tribuna Italiana Transatlantica* of the all-encompassing menace of the secret crime society: "Yesterday this one, today that one, tomorrow it may strike even you." Durante felt compelled to publicize the seriousness of the Black Hand problem, which he had for so long denied: "Day after day, week after week, more and more crimes are being committed, the perpetrators of which are invariably Italians." Admitting that almost every crime involved the name of the Black Hand, he described a typical method of acquiring money. Blackhanders simply demanded cash "from innocent people who work for a living." If the gangsters received nothing, they murdered their victim; should they spare his life, they bombed his home. "Naturally, these frequent crimes give a bad impression of the Italian colony to other nationalities. . . . Italians! We must do something to prevent these crimes."[9]

As the numbers of Chicago's "Southerners" increased, they became an increasingly tempting source of money, more readily intimidated by threats because of the reputation of the Mafia in Sicily. After the publicity surrounding the New Orleans affair, the American press quickly labeled all crimes in the immigrant community Mafia acts. The successes or failures of Chicago's Italian-

[7] *L'Italia,* February 4, 1911.

[8] *L'Italia,* April 1, 1911; *La Tribuna Italiana Transatlantica,* November 9, 1907; Grace Abbott, *Immigration Problems in Massachusetts. Report of the Commission on Immigration* (Boston: Wright & Potter Printing Co., 1914), pp. 105–6.

[9] *La Tribuna Italiana Transatlantica,* November 9, 1907; *L'Italia,* April 1, 1911.

community gangs, however, depended less on old world techniques and personnel than on local conditions and opportunities.[10]

III

In 1907 and 1908 leaders of the Italian community co-operated with leaders of the press in a concerted effort to combat and eliminate Black Hand crimes. On November 11, 1907, they organized the White Hand Society, largely through the efforts of Italian consul Guido Sabetta. The Unione Siciliana played a leading role in the formation and operation of the White Hand, a significant fact in the light of that society's involvement with criminals in the 1920's and the last years of the preceding decade. The Unione's unfortunate entanglement with criminals in later years should not detract from its sincere concern in 1907 and 1908 over the unfavorable image which Black Hand activities presented of "Southerners" and especially Sicilians, and its efforts to eradicate crime within the immigrant community.

Community newspapers, particularly *L'Italia* and *La Tribuna Italiana Transatlantica*, gave full support to the new organization, as did the Italian ambassador in Washington and the Italian Minister of Foreign Affairs in Rome. The organizers felt that a glorious era had begun with their "war without truce, war without quarter." Bubbling enthusiasm filled early meetings, held to plan action against the enemy.[11]

By the end of November the idea of the White Hand had spread to other cities, and the founders conceived the notion of organizing a White Hand "in all the cities which contain large Italian colonies, which suspect the existence of mafiosi or cammoristi in their midst." The eventual goal, "the day in which the Italian colonies, free of the festering evil of the Black Hand, will become models among the foreigners," unintentionally publicized the problem of crime among Italians in the United States. Ironically, many of the leaders who formulated this goal had minimized the seriousness of Italian crime or publicly denied the existence of the Black Hand. Some continued to deny its existence while supporting White Hand activities against it.[12]

The White Hand was legally incorporated in December, 1907. Joyously the members announced that at last Chicago's *cafoni,* or ignorant "Southern" peasants, too often the victim of Black Hand hoodlums, had "a protector in the White Hand." As stated in the society's constitution, the White Hand intended "to paralyze and eradicate individual and organized crime which exists in the midst of the Italian colony, forcing it to submit to threats and violence," to eliminate a pervasive atmosphere of "mystery and terror," and to "present to the American public the truth concerning Italy and the Italians, frequently misrepresented by incorrect reports."[13]

[10] The Italian "White Hand" Society in Chicago, Illinois, *Studies, Action and Results* (Chicago, 1908), pp. 25–26.

[11] *La Tribuna Italiana Transatlantica,* November 16 and 23, 1907; *L'Italia,* November 16, 1907.

[12] *L'Italia,* November 30, 1907. For the appearance of the White Hand in New Orleans see *La Tribuna Italiana Transatlantica,* December 7, 1907.

[13] *La Tribuna Italiana Transatlantica,* December 14 and 28, 1907. See Italian

In January, 1908, the White Hand . . . announced its first tangible success, claiming that it had driven ten of Chicago's most dangerous criminals out of the city. By February the society listed additional successes in Chicago and similar achievements in other American cities. *L'Italia* jubilantly announced, "Black Hand in Hot Water. The Arrest of One of the Heads Places the Black Hand in the Hands of the Police." The White Hand's attorney, Stephen Malato, played a major role in this capture.[14]

Never again did the White Hand achieve such glory, although it remained in existence for a number of years. It soon became a dead letter, failing in large part because of inadequate financial support. White Hand leaders lamented as early as 1908 that "so wealthy a colony as that of Chicago should have given such niggardly support to a movement intended to . . . purge it" of the Black Hand menace. Indifference, a more basic factor, lay behind this financial distress. Reluctantly the society's leaders admitted that they could not gain, much less hold, the support of immigrant-community residents, the American public, or the police. The society maintained that immigrants believed that it planned to use the money collected from impoverished workers "to defend the lives and wealth of the prominent men of the colony." Among upwardly mobile members of the community the conviction had grown that, by admitting the gravity of the problem of crime among Italians, the White Hand, had "thrown suspicion and discredit upon the Italian name."[15]

More fundamental to rank-and-file immigrants, however, was their sense of self-preservation which, rather than apathy or desire to protect their Italian good name, determined their behavior. "Southerners" knew that crime pervaded their communities; they knew also that authorities could or would do little to terminate it. They believed the White Hand to be powerless in the face of official corruption or tolerance of corruption, and they had no desire to involve themselves with it.[16]

While this situation existed in Chicago, it did not necessarily operate elsewhere. Local factors at work in individual cities strongly influenced and determined the course taken by Black Hand gangs. The Illinois Crime Commission noted that "in some American cities where the law is effectual, the 'black handers' have ceased to operate." According to John Landesco of the Illinois Crime Survey, who observed conditions in Chicago and Milwaukee for a number of years, the Black Hand in Milwaukee had a much shorter life, and "Southerners" adjusted to their new surroundings with a minimal amount of crime and dealings in corrupt politics. John S. Kendall stated that in New Orleans the Sicilian immigrants "under the leadership of the better elements of their own

---

"White Hand" Society, *Studies, Action and Results,* pp. 21–22, for aims of the organization. (The text is in both Italian and English.)

[14] *La Tribuna Italiana Transatlantica,* January 11, February 1, 15, and 22, March 7, 1908; *L'Italia,* February 15, March 14, May 23, 1908.

[15] Italian "White Hand" Society, *Studies, Actions and Results,* p. 24. Also *Chicago Record-Herald,* March 20, 1911; *La Parola dei Socialisti,* March 28, 1914. American lack of support rested on the belief that the entire situation was the problem of immigrants alone, so long as the criminals victimized only other "Southerners." The 1920's brought a change, both in victims and in attitudes.

[16] Local Community Research Committee, *Chicago Communities,* Vol. VI, "East Side," Document 8. See also Vol. VI, "West Englewood," Document 1a; *La Tribuna Italiana Transatlantica,* November 9, 1907.

nationality, . . . set their faces against the activities of such organizations," with the result that the Black Hand disappeared in that city in the years after 1907.[17]

The adjustment of Italians in Boston and elsewhere in Massachusetts contrasted even more sharply with the Chicago experience. In a study published in 1902, social worker Robert A. Woods maintained that few murders committed by Italians in the North End of Boston could be attributed to premeditation, for in the majority of cases impulse and passion formed the motivating forces. Furthermore, no murder had been traced "directly or indirectly" to the Mafia. Twelve years later the Massachusetts Commission on Immigration reported that "so-called 'Black Hand' crimes are practically unknown in Massachusetts," although Italians committed criminal violations. As a "very large proportion" of the immigrants came from the "South," the Commission considered the absence of Black Hand crime to be proof that "local American conditions are responsible for those criminal organizations elsewhere."[18]

Even more striking in indicating the impact of local conditions on crime were differences between Italian colonies in the United States and those in Latin America, specifically Brazil and Argentina, the countries of major Italian immigration. Radicalism, rather than crime in the Chicago style, constituted the most serious social problem involving Italian immigrants in South America. Argentines, for example, viewed socialism and anarchism among Italians as grave difficulties, in contrast to the more limited appeal which these doctrines exerted upon "Southerners" in the United States. Efforts to prevent the immigration of undesirables or to extradite those already in the country by passing laws like the "Residence of Strangers Law" (1902), "Social Defense Law" (1910), and "Italo-Argentine Sanitary Convention" (1913) had little effect.[19]

While southern Italians committed violent crimes in Latin America, neither Brazil nor Argentina exhibited any indication of the Black Hand or any equivalent of Anthony D'Andrea or Al Capone. The principal reason for this difference (as the White Hand society accurately observed in 1908) was that in the United States, and Chicago in particular, "social and political conditions are so favorable to the rise and spread of crime."[20]

Chicago displayed, and continued into the twentieth century to possess, many characteristics of a frontier town, some commendable and others execrable. It was vigorous, brash, lusty, optimistic, energetic. It also contained labor violence, corruption in civic and business affairs, apathy toward poverty, inadequate hous-

[17] Landesco, *Organized Crime*, pp. 947–48, 953–54; Kendall, "Who Killa de Chief?" p. 504.

[18] Robert A. Woods, ed., *Americans in Process* (Boston: Houghton Mifflin Co., 1902), pp. 207–9; Abbott, *Immigration Problems in Massachusetts*, pp. 105–6.

[19] Robert J. Alexander, *Labor Relations in Argentina, Brazil and Chile* (New York: McGraw-Hill Book Co., 1962), pp. 147–49, 162–65, and *Communism in Latin America* (New Brunswick, N.J.: Rutgers University Press, 1957), p. 155; Robert D. Ochs, "A History of Argentine Immigration, 1853–1924," unpublished Ph.D. dissertation, University of Illinois, 1939, pp. 149–57; James Bryce, *South America, Observations and Impressions* (new ed.; New York: Macmillan Co., 1914), p. 320.

[20] Charles Wagley, *An Introduction to Brazil* (New York: Columbia University Press, 1963), pp. 181–83; Thomas F. McGann, *Argentina, the United States and the Inter-American System* (Cambridge, Mass.: Harvard University Press, 1957), p. 193; Robert E. Foerster, *The Italian Emigration of Our Times* (Cambridge, Mass.: Harvard University Press, 1919), pp. 439–40.

ing, unsanitary living conditions, vice, and organized crime. . . . Lincoln Steffens characterized Chicago: "First in violence, deepest in dirt, loud, lawless, unlovely, ill-smelling, irreverent, new; an overgrown gawk of a village, the 'tough' among cities, a spectacle for the nation." Into this environment, with its unparalleled economic opportunities, optimism, mobility, corruption, filth, and violence, arrived increasing numbers of southern Italian and Sicilian immigrants in the years after 1880.[21]

Many Chicago policemen worked illegally and in close harmony with criminals and politicians. Models of success in the city's immigrant communities often turned out to be (as Chicago's few but vociferous socialists claimed and as the White Hand society found to its distress) corrupt politicians and lawbreakers who operated under the protection of the guardians of the law. They displayed all the outward signs of economic achievement: expensive clothes and cars, quantities of ready money, food and drink of excellent quality. They also commanded attention, often respect, from the American community and the Italian-language newspapers. Socialists blamed the Italian-language press, "with few exceptions," for permitting itself to be "the main lever for the elevation of these rascals" and "an accessory to all the disgraceful things befalling our colonies."[22]

Socialists might well have had Anthony D'Andrea in mind, for he exhibited characteristics decried by the socialist press as typical of Italian-community leaders. He (and, during the 1920's, other presidents of the Unione Siciliana) commonly associated with criminal friends and businessmen, involved himself in gangland activities and rivalries, and held a criminal record. Before his death, D'Andrea had been not only president of the Unione, but also president of a labor union and candidate for political office. He and those like him gained leadership of the Unione and other societies through their own personal power and connections. They aspired to such offices because of the prestige and influence that accompanied these positions, including some measure of political power through control of members' votes on election days. On the other hand, members of societies willingly or knowingly elevated men of questionable reputation to positions of authority, possibly through hope of financial reward or fear of personal injury.[23]

For many Chicagoans, however, poverty was the most degrading and deplorable crime. Dishonesty, bribery, and misuse of power simply provided ready methods of overcoming lack of money. Native-born as well as immigrant residents of the city held this view, as concerned Chicagoan Samuel Paynter Wilson observed in 1910.[24] . . .

Black Hand activities in Chicago virtually disappeared in the 1920's. At least three factors caused this decline. First, the supply of simple, pliable victims dwindled soon after the termination of immigration in the years following 1914.

[21] Lincoln Steffens, *The Shame of the Cities* (New York: McClure, Phillips & Co., 1904), p. 163.

[22] John Landesco, "Crime and the Failure of Institutions in Chicago's Immigrant Areas," *Journal of the American Institute of Criminal Law and Criminology*, XXIII (July–August, 1932), 224; *La Parola dei Socialisti*, March 28, 1914.

[23] *L'Italia*, October 12, 1913; November 2, 1919.

[24] Samuel Paynter Wilson, *Chicago and Its Cesspools of Infamy* (11th ed.; Chicago: N.P. [1910?]), p. 29.

Action by federal authorities made up a second factor. Enforcement of laws prohibiting use of the mails to defraud forced personal delivery of threatening Black Hand notes, potentially a dangerous activity because of possibilities of being recognized.[25]

While the preceding two factors limited opportunities for criminals in the ethnic colony, a vast new field of endeavor had presented itself in the American community because of new federal laws prohibiting the manufacture and sale of alcoholic beverages. American drinking tastes and capacities did not adjust to the new regulations, and enterprising young men found themselves in a position to reap immense profits. Many American robbers, murderers, blackmailers, burglars, and thieves left their former fields of labor for the more lucrative work offered through Prohibition and for which their former professions had provided good training. It is likely that many well-qualified blackhanders also forsook the less profitable extortion rackets of the Italian quarter in order to join the liquor-traffic scramble. Thus immigration restriction, along with Prohibition, marked the end of the Black Hand era and introduced many who had been involved in crime within the Italian community into the mainstream of American gangsterdom.[26]

IV

Black Hand activities—mainly extortion and terrorism—received most publicity inside and outside the immigrant community, but many other types of crimes existed within the colony. Over the years Chicago's Italian-language newspapers described a wide range of wrongdoings not limited to the Black Hand. These included padrone (or labor agent) abuses and the illegalities of immigrant bankers, among others.

Labor agents prospered in Chicago because of the city's prominence as a transportation center. While they fulfilled a vital function for newly arrived immigrants as well as for American businessmen, padroni generally did so by cheating and shortchanging their less knowledgeable, more gullible compatriots until effective safeguards frustrated or hampered their efforts.[27]

Immigrant bankers flourished in every part of the country where newcomers from southern and eastern Europe had gathered in any considerable numbers. The principal financial transaction of these bankers consisted of receiving deposits and sending money abroad. Most also served as steamship ticket agents, and often conducted some other business as well. Hence some "banks" could be found in grocery stores, saloons, or other natural gathering places. Investigators of the Immigrants' Protective League visited fifty-five Chicago bankers of Italian birth or extraction in the spring of 1912. Of these, thirty-five were also steamship

[25] Landesco, *Organized Crime*, pp. 946–47. Harvey Warren Zorbaugh, *The Gold Coast and the Slum: A Sociological Study of Chicago's Near North Side* (Chicago: University of Chicago Press, 1929, pp. 170–74), described Black Hand activities in the "Little Sicily" colony on the Near North Side. Zorbaugh does not indicate dates, but the sources he cited described the period before 1920.

[26] John Landesco, "Prohibition and Crime," *Annals of the American Academy of Political and Social Sciences*, CLXIII (September, 1932), 125.

[27] For a detailed examination of padrone methods as well as the factors responsible for the system's decline, see Humbert S. Nelli, "The Italian Padrone System in the United States," *Labor History*, V, No. 2 (Spring, 1964), 153–67.

ticket agents, fifteen were labor agents, eleven operated grocery stores, four ran drugstores, two owned saloons, one owned a barber shop, and one owned a real estate office.[28]

The typical banker had little experience in business methods, operated with a minimal accumulation of capital, and for the most part worked freely outside legal controls. Immigrants' bankers were not, for example, restricted as to the kinds of investments they could make with money deposited (restrictions which applied to state and national banks). As a result, speculative ventures of private bankers often ended in disaster, particularly for immigrant depositors; since they had no adequate legal safeguards, they lost their savings. Immigrants who transmitted money to Italy provided bankers with lush opportunities to defraud, either by using the money for investment purposes with the intention of sending some of it overseas when investments paid off, or else by simply accepting the money and keeping it. Because of the conditions under which they operated, many immigrant bankers went out of business, some through inefficient business methods, others because they had absconded with customers' savings.[29]

The last two decades of the nineteenth century provided Italian bankers with almost unlimited opportunities for exploiting their customers. Conditions for depositors improved somewhat after the turn of the century. By the Italian Emigration Law of 1901, the Bank of Naples became designated as the financial institution entrusted with transmission of savings from all parts of the world, including the United States. The Bank of Naples, therefore, exerted a strong influence in forcing immigrant bankers to improve services for their clients, modify rates of exchange, and lower charges for transmission of money.[30]

In addition, after 1900 various states which contained large immigrant populations enacted legislation intended to regulate immigrant banking operations. Massachusetts, New York, New Jersey, Pennsylvania, and Ohio passed such laws, which were far less stringent than regulations governing state and national banks. In Illinois, rural private American bankers effectively opposed regulations which might have limited their own free and easy activities. As a result, adequate state legislation controlling immigrant banks and American private banking operations was not enacted or enforced until the 1930's, following the failure of numerous banks, both American and immigrant. Consequently, Italians (and other immigrant bankers) continued to operate in Illinois with few restrictions throughout the period of large-scale immigration.[31] Legislation on the books did not mean, of course, that police enforced the laws, that illegal activities ceased, or that the native community supported the new statutes. During Prohibition, for example, Americans ignored existing legislation and patronized illegal bars

[28] Immigrants' Protective League, *Annual Report for the Year Ending January 1, 1913*, p. 18.

[29] U.S. Senate, *Immigration Commission*, XXXVII, 203–25; Immigrants' Protective League, *Annual Report, 1910–1911*, pp. 20–21, and *Annual Report for the Year Ending January 1, 1913*, pp. 18–20.

[30] Gino C. Speranza, "What Italians Send Back," *New York Evening Post*, reprinted in *Immigration*, II, No. 10 (March, 1911), 269.

[31] U.S. Senate, *Immigration Commission*, XXXVII, 280; Immigrants' Protective League, *Annual Report, 1913*, pp. 19–20; Grace Abbott, *The Immigrant and the Community* (New York: Century Co., 1917), chap. iv; *L'Italia*, April 13, 1912; May 5, 1915.

("speakeasies") operated by Italians and others, and city police did little to halt the liquor business.

Other businessmen in the immigrant colony supplied needed services and products and lined their own pockets by overcharging or otherwise cheating their compatriots. Among these were quack doctors, shyster lawyers, and merchants who adulterated their wares—storekeepers, for example, who mixed linseed oil with olive oil and sold the mixture as pure Sicilian or Luccan oil. Italian-language journals reported these and many other crimes, including robbery, embezzlement and misappropriation of funds, arson, counterfeiting, election fraud, and a number of rackets and sharp practices. . . . In addition, corruption and violence often marked the organization and operation of Italian labor union locals.[32]

The neighborhood gang filled an important social void for ethnic-colony youth. It also served to introduce many boys and young men to lives of crime. Although Italians lived in areas which had high delinquency rates, not every child turned to, or was forced into, a criminal career. Even for youngsters inhabiting slum areas, there existed a number of alternatives to crime.[33] Nevertheless, young Italian-Americans, as Alberto Pecorini noted in 1916, "furnished an alarmingly high percentage of young criminals." He maintained that all immigrant groups, from Irish and German to Italian and Jewish, had passed through the same experience. This juvenile lawbreaking stemmed in large part from the fact that criminal activity offered opportunities for quick and substantial monetary gain and therefore success.[34] . . .

Despite the wide range of immigrant community illegalities, most "Southerners" led law-abiding lives. The bulk of arrests and convictions involving Italians in Chicago resulted from minor offenses (misdemeanors), particularly violations of city ordinances, rather than Black Hand crimes. In 1908, the last year in which the Department of Police *Annual Report* listed city ordinance violations separately from state misdemeanors, Italians committed a total of

[32] *La Tribuna Italiana Transatlantica,* May 23, 1903; August 16, 1914; *La Parola dei Socialisti,* April 18, 1908; January 4, May 31, 1913; *La Parola Proletaria* (Chicago), August 26, 1916; *L'Avanti!* (Chicago), November 15, 1918; *Il Messaggiere Italo-Americano* (Chicago), July 5, 1888; *L'Italia,* January 28, 1899; February 11, November 5, 1905; December 4, 1909; March 23, April 13, 1912; March 21, 1913; April 26, 1914; May 5, 1915; June 3, 1917; August 4, 1918; November 7 and 23, 1919.

[33] Clifford R. Shaw *et al., Delinquency Areas: A Study of the Geographic Distribution of School Truants, Juvenile Delinquents and Adult Offenders in Chicago* (Chicago: University of Chicago Press, 1929); Clifford R. Shaw and Henry McKay, *Juvenile Delinquency and Urban Areas* (Chicago: University of Chicago Press, 1942); David Matza, *Delinquency and Drift* (New York: John Wiley & Sons, 1964), p. 65; Albert J. Reiss, Jr., and Albert Lewis Rhodes, "The Distribution of Juvenile Delinquency in the Social Class Structure," *American Sociological Review,* XXVI, No. 5 (October, 1961), 729. Also Thorsten Sellin, *Culture Conflict and Crime,* Bulletin 41 (New York: Social Science Research Council, 1938); Robert K. Merton, "Social Structure and Anomie," *American Sociological Review,* III (October, 1938), 672–82; Robert E. Park and Herbert A. Miller, *Old World Traits Transplanted* (New York: Harper & Brothers, 1921), esp. pp. 238–58.

[34] Alberto Pecorini, "The Child of the Immigrant," *La Fiaccola* (New York), August 31, 1916, reprinted from *Il Cittadino;* William Foote Whyte, "Social Organization in the Slums," *American Sociological Review,* VIII (February, 1943), 38; *L'Italia,* April 1, 1911.

1,935 criminal offenses. Felonies accounted for 294, while the other 1,631 offenses were misdemeanors, of which 1,276 involved city ordinances.[35]

The Chicago City Council Committee on Crime, under the chairmanship of Alderman (and University of Chicago political science professor) Charles E. Merriam, presented in March, 1915, a comparison of arrest and conviction statistics for native-born (white and black) and foreign-born groups. The Committee found a considerably greater percentage of arrests and convictions among native groups than their ratio of the population. Foreign-born elements, on the other hand, showed "almost uniformly" smaller percentages than their proportion of the population. Italians exhibited an excess of one-tenth of one per cent in convictions (misdemeanors and felonies combined); the Committee remarked, "This is surely so small as to be negligible!"[36]

The professional criminal knew, or had ready access to lawyers who knew, the nuances of the law and how to avoid retribution for antisocial actions. He had money and connections with politicians, as well as with corrupt policemen, who would delay or circumvent efforts to bring him to justice. He also could arrange intimidation of witnesses and victims so that they kept silent.[37] The average immigrant Italian, on the other hand, often faced arrest and severe punishment for violating laws and ordinances about which he, and most newcomers, knew nothing. If the immigrant spoke no English, he labored under an additional disadvantage because most court interpreters lacked knowledge of court proceedings, were unacquainted with the various dialects used by Italian residents of the city, and often had a limited familiarity with the English language. In some courts police officers served as interpreters, in others court officials (usually clerks) translated, while in still others the officials simply "got along the best they could" by picking a bystander who claimed to speak the language. Court decisions based on the work of such interpreters often showed little justice or impartiality.[38]

V

Within the immigrant colony, bankers and padroni, blackhanders and other lawbreakers realized small but important profits by swindling or terrorizing compatriots. Another level of illegal activity involved Italians. Organized crime, business operations reaping vast profits in and from the American community, offered almost limitless opportunities for promotion within its hierarchy.

Chicago's organized crime had its origins in the 1870's with the activities of

[35] City of Chicago, Department of Police, *Report of the General Superintendent of Police of the City of Chicago, to the City Council, for the Fiscal Year Ending December 31, 1908* (Chicago, 1909), p. 34.

[36] Chicago City Council, *Report of the Committee on Crime* (Chicago, 1915), pp. 52–56.

[37] Edith Abbott, "Recent Statistics Relating to Crime in Chicago," *Journal of the American Institute of Criminal Law and Criminology*, XII, No. 3 (November, 1922), 330.

[38] Gino Speranza, "The Relation of the Alien to the Administration of the Civil and Criminal Law," *Journal of the American Institute of Criminal Law and Criminology*, I, No. 4 (November, 1910), 563–72; Kate Holladay Claghorn, *The Immigrant's Day in Court* (New York: Harper, 1923), pp. 205–6, 209–10, 222–23; Grace Abbott, *The Immigrant and the Community*, chap. v.

TABLE I
NATIVITY OF MALE PERSONS ARRESTED AND CONVICTED FOR FELONIES, 1913

	Arrests		*Convictions*		
Nativity	*No.*	*%*	*No.*	*%*	*Percentage Distribution**
American					
White	5,756	56.3	2,241	56.9	43.1
Colored	882	8.6	354	9.0	2.6
Foreign:					
Austrian	401	3.9	158	4.0	11.2
English	166	1.6	79	2.0	5.2
French	22	0.2	10	0.3	. . .
German	815	8.0	366	9.3	12.6
Greek	139	1.4	29	0.7	0.6
Hollanders	19	0.2	8	0.2	0.7
Irish	186	1.8	98	2.5	4.4
Italian	392	3.8	108	2.7	3.2
Russian	1,027	10.0	331	8.4	8.5
Scandinavian	214	2.1	93	2.4	6.7
Other	218	2.1	64	1.6	1.2
Total foreign	3,599	35.1	1,344	34.1	54.3
Total	10,237	100.0	3,939	100.0	100.0

* Of male population of Chicago 21 years of age and older.
Source.—Chicago City Council, *Report of the Committee on Crime* (Chicago, 1915), p. 56.

Michael Cassius McDonald. Except for a brief eclipse during the mayoralty of John A. Roche (1887–89), McDonald controlled virtually all city politics from 1879 until the mid-1890's. Recalling the McDonald era on August 18, 1907 (a few days after his death), the *Chicago Record-Herald* stated that "he never held office, but he ruled the city with an iron hand. He named the men who were to be candidates for election, he elected them, and after they were in office they were merely his slaves." . . . With his political power established following Carter Henry Harrison's mayoral success in 1879, "Mike" McDonald turned to organizing the city's first "syndicate," which centered on gambling. During his reign McDonald, as political party boss and head of the "syndicate," forged the powerful and highly effective coalition of criminals, politicians, and compliant policemen which the Torrio-Capone organization utilized so successfully during the 1920's.[39]

Following the assassination of Mayor Harrison in October, 1893, McDonald's

[39] Herbert Asbury, *Gem of the Prairie: An Informal History of the Chicago Underworld* (New York: Alfred A. Knopf, 1940), pp. 142 ff.; Alson J. Smith, *Syndicate City: The Chicago Crime Cartel and What To Do About It* (Chicago: Henry Regnery Co., 1954), pp. 25–30.

TABLE II
NATIVITY OF MALE PERSONS ARRESTED AND CONVICTED FOR MISDEMEANORS, 1913

	Arrests		*Convictions*		
Nativity	*No.*	*%*	*No.*	*%*	*Percentage Distribution**
American					
White	50,999	58.5	23,656	59.6	43.1
Colored	4,741	5.4	2,179	5.5	2.6
Foreign:					
Austrian	3,282	3.8	1,492	3.8	11.2
English	1,240	1.4	537	1.3	5.2
French	181	0.2	90	0.2	. . .
German	6,942	8.0	2,977	7.5	12.6
Greek	1,592	1.8	947	2.4	0.6
Hollanders	209	0.3	115	0.3	0.7
Irish	2,354	2.7	901	2.3	4.4
Italian	2,972	3.4	1,333	3.4	3.2
Russian	7,519	8.6	3,314	8.3	8.5
Scandinavian	2,857	3.3	1,330	3.3	6.7
Other	2,268	2.6	819	2.1	1.2
Total foreign	31,416	36.1	13,855	34.9	54.3
Total	87,156	100.0	39,690	100.0	100.0

* Of male population of Chicago 21 years of age and older.
Source.—Chicago City Council, *Report of the Committee on Crime* (Chicago, 1915), p. 56.

star began to fade, and a number of new independent organizations or "syndicates" formed. By 1907, when "Mike" died, various spheres of interest controlled gambling in Chicago. Mont Tennes gave orders on the North Side, James O'Leary on the South Side, and Alderman Johnnie Rogers on the West Side. First ward political bosses "Hinky Dink" Kenna and "Bathhouse John" Coughlin, early patrons of "Diamond Jim" Colosimo, presided over gambling in the Loop.[40]

After years of gang warfare most of McDonald's former gambling empire centered in the hands of Mont Tennes, who ruled in turn until the 1920's, when the Torrio-Capone group pushed him aside and seized control of gambling as well as other illegal activities in the Chicago area. Although the real entry of Italians into big-time crime, and most of their successes therein, came after 1920—that is, during Prohibition—they did make a strong beginning under Colosimo in the first two decades of the twentieth century.

While still a boy, Colosimo left Calabria for the United States in the 1880's.

[40] Landesco, *Organized Crime*, chap. xix, "Tennes as Vice Chief"; Virgil W. Peterson, *Barbarians in Our Midst, A History of Chicago Crime and Politics* (Boston: Little, Brown & Co., 1952), pp. 84–91.

His first employment in this country, and the work that took him to Chicago, was that of waterboy for a railroad section gang, at the age of sixteen. Before the turn of the century Colosimo became a street sweeper and established his residence in the first ward. Colosimo organized his fellow street sweepers (or "white wings") who resided in the first ward into a political bloc which he led as a unit to the polling station at election time in order to vote for candidates supported by the Democratic machine. This action quickly brought him to the attention of Aldermen Kenna and Coughlin, who had dominated first ward politics since 1893. They made "Big Jim" a precinct captain, and he delivered the vote so successfully for his patrons that before his death he rivaled Kenna and Coughlin as a political power in the ward.[41]

In the meantime, Colosimo and his wife, Victoria Moresco, acquired a string of brothels and saloons as well as a legitimate business, a nationally known restaurant called "Colosimo's Cafe." (Socially prominent Chicagoans patronized it along with theater and opera personalities, including George M. Cohan and Enrico Caruso.) By 1914 "Big Jim" and associates had built a "syndicate," the first one organized by Chicago Italians, based on vice operations, especially prostitution and gambling. In that year State's Attorney Maclay Hoyne launched a grand jury investigation of vice in Chicago's first ward and found the existence of three vice rings or "syndicates." The first and largest consisted of the Colosimo-Torrio outfit, headed by "Big Jim" and his chief lieutenant, Johnny Torrio.[42]

Black Hand extortion threats had prompted Colosimo to bring Torrio from New York in 1909 for personal protection. Within five years, effective and ruthless methods had advanced Torrio to second-in-command and a power in his own right through his organization of gambling in the city and some nearby suburbs. (At this time Torrio resided in the same building as "Big Jim," 101 West 21st Street.) In 1919 Henry Barrett Chamberlain, Operating Director of the Chicago Crime Commission, described increasingly efficient "syndicate" crime: "Modern crime, like modern business, is tending toward centralization, organization, and commercialization. Ours is a business nation. Our criminals apply business methods. . . . The men and women of evil have formed trusts."[43]

When the National Prohibition Enforcement Act (the Volstead Act) went into effect on January 16, 1920, the Colosimo-Torrio organization expanded from prostitution and gambling into an even more lucrative business, the manufacture and distribution of liquor. Colosimo did not live long enough to reap the full financial harvest of his bootlegging ventures, for he was murdered on May 11, 1920.[44]

After Colosimo's death, Johnny Torrio succeeded to the first ward based Italian "syndicate" throne, which he occupied until his retirement in 1925. An able and effective leader, Torrio excelled as a master strategist and organizer and quickly built an empire which far exceeded that of his predecessor in wealth,

[41] Fred D. Pasley, *Al Capone: The Biography of a Self-Made Man* (Garden City, New York: Garden City Publishing Co., 1939), pp. 9–14; Emmett Dedmon, *Fabulous Chicago* (New York: Random House, Inc., 1953), pp. 289–90.

[42] Landesco, *Organized Crime*, pp. 850–57.

[43] Henry Barrett Chamberlain, "Crime as a Business in Chicago," *Bulletin of the Chicago Crime Commission*, No. 6 (October 1, 1919), p. 1.

[44] *Chicago Daily News*, May 12, 1920.

power, and influence. He received invaluable aid from his chief lieutenant, Alphonse Capone, who in turn ruled the empire. Italian domination of Chicago's organized crime had made a strong beginning.[45]

VI

Several factors facilitated Italian successes in the highly competitive (and deadly) business of organized crime. Some related to old world backgrounds and characteristics, others to conditions and opportunities in the host society. Mafia expert Michele Pantaleone has presented a brilliant exposé of the Sicilian Mafia in a recent book. His comments on Sicilians in American crime, however, raise more questions than they answer. According to Pantaleone, men schooled in the Sicilian Mafia "founded and organized gangsterdom in America fifty years ago"—that is, in the decade following 1910. These criminals operated in "St. Louis, Chicago, Kansas City, Detroit, New Orleans, New Jersey and other cities." Boston and Milwaukee are significantly absent from this list. Also pointedly missing are, first, any indication that "organized gangsterdoms" existed in Chicago, New York, and other cities long before 1910, and, second, the fact that when an Italian "syndicate" developed after 1910 in competition with organizations composed of members of other ethnic groups, it was not staffed solely by Sicilians or even entirely by Italians, any more than Irish, Jewish, or Polish criminal organizations were made up only of members of these groups. Thus many alleged *capo mafiosi* (leaders) of Chicago's Italian "syndicate" had no Sicilian ancestry, while others born in Sicily emigrated as children and grew to maturity in urban America. James Colosimo, for example, was born in mainland Italy (Calabria) and arrived in Chicago as a boy; Naples-born John Torrio grew up in Brooklyn; Al Capone was born in Brooklyn of Neapolitan parents; while Jake Gusick (or Jack Cusick), the "so-called brains of the Capone organization," was only one of many non-Italian members of the "American Mafia hierarchy."[46]

More significant than the Sicilian origin of some criminals were the ethnic cohesion and group loyalty exhibited by the Italian criminal element in its struggle to dominate Chicago's organized crime. The Sicilian or southern Italian origin of the bulk of the city's Italians included a background of clan traditions held to be sacred from "outside" interference. Doubtless these traditions and connections provided a ready-made nucleus for criminal gangs in the new world and insured a fierce loyalty to the group's laws and rituals rather than to "outside" rules and regulations, as some writers on Italian-American criminality have pointed out.[47]

[45] Lloyd Wendt and Herman Kogan, *Lords of the Levee: The Story of Bathhouse John and Hinky Dink* (Indianapolis: Bobbs-Merrill, 1943), pp. 430–42; Virgil W. Peterson, "Chicago: Shades of Capone," *Annals of the American Academy of Political and Social Sciences*, CCCXVII (May, 1963), 31–32.

[46] Michele Pantaleone, *The Mafia and Politics* (London: Chatto & Windus, 1966), pp. 38–39 (also see the Preface to the English edition written by Denis Mack Smith, pp. 17–18); Peterson, *Barbarians in Our Midst*, p. 135; Frederic Sondern, Jr., *Brotherhood of Evil* (New York: Farrar, Strauss, & Cudahy, 1959), p. 69.

[47] Among others, Sondern, *Brotherhood of Evil*, p. 66; Ed Reid, *Mafia* (rev. ed., New York: New American Library, 1964), chap. ii; Rudolph J. Vecoli, "Contadini

To a southern Italian or Sicilian living in the Kingdom of Italy during the period from 1890 to 1920, however, the concept of *paesi* ("homeland") meant village of birth, outside of which existed nothing but strangers. Residents of other towns and provinces, regarded as foreigners, became objects of suspicion or contempt. Political scientist Edward C. Banfield, in a recent study widely accepted by immigration scholars and students of Italian history, described a Sicilian–southern Italian society dominated by amoral familism. In the homeland Banfield found peasants and gentry alike unable to act "for any end transcending the immediate, material interests of the nuclear family." If this study is accurate, one can reasonably conclude that community and group consciousness among "Southerners" in the United States did not cross the Atlantic, but developed in the new world.[48]

In America this expanded sense of loyalty and patriotism manifested itself in celebrations supporting the Italian Kingdom, membership in mutual aid and fraternal societies based on regional or national groupings, and support of an "Italian" press and Italian Catholic parishes. In the new homeland, therefore, village loyalties grew to become national loyalties, and members of the ethnic group came to look upon non-Italians, rather than people from outside a particular village in Italy, as "outsiders." "American" Italians (those born or raised in the United States) who established and operated the Chicago Italian "syndicate" excluded members of other ethnic groups until they had proven themselves worthy of acceptance. Conditions in Chicago offered fertile ground for the activities of outlaws (a similar situation existed also in New York City). Long before "Southerners" arrived, gangs composed predominantly of other ethnic groups—Irish, German, Scandinavian—operated openly and often under the protection of the law and elected officials. This "favorable" situation could not be found in all urban areas to which Italians migrated, with the significant result that members of the second generation were prominently involved in organized crime in some cities and not in others. Hence local conditions permitting or even encouraging lawlessness clearly occupied a place of basic importance in Italian successes within Chicago's organized crime.[49]

Chicago attracted professional Italian crooks, generally from Sicily, because of opportunities available to extort money from fellow Sicilians, unimpeded by police, under the magic name "Black Hand."[50] In the Illinois Crime Survey,

---

in Chicago: A Critique of The Uprooted," *Journal of American History*, LI (December, 1961), 409.

[48] Edward C. Banfield, *The Moral Basis of a Backward Society* (Glencoe, Ill.; Free Press, 1958), p. 10. Among others who accept the Banfield position are Herbert J. Gans, *The Urban Villagers: Group and Class in the Life of Italian-Americans* (New York: Free Press, 1962), p. 203; and Norman Kogan, *The Politics of Italian Foreign Policy* (New York: Frederick A. Praeger, 1963), pp. 4–5.

[49] Harold Ross, "Crime and the Native Born Sons of European Immigrants," *Journal of the American Institute of Criminal Law and Criminology*, XXVIII (March–April, 1938), 202–9. Significantly, Italian residents of Latin American countries apparently indicated no propensity to indulge in crime for profit.

[50] The Italian Kingdom encouraged criminals to leave the country. Many eventually settled in American cities. This was not a process unique to Italians; it had existed with other, and earlier, groups. In an article published in 1909, entitled "Immigrants and Crime," p. 118, William S. Bennet, Congressman from New York and a member of the U.S. Immigration Commission, pointed out that "thirty years ago societies were actually organized for the purpose of sending to this coun-

John Landesco reported the results of a study of more than 300 crimes attributed to the Black Hand. He found that these crimes were "limited almost entirely to the Sicilian neighborhoods" of Chicago. Writing in 1909, Arthur Woods, Deputy Police Commissioner of New York City, reported a similar situation. New York police found that "in almost every case" Black Hand crimes were committed by men who had been involved in criminal activities in Italy and who had immigrated to New York in order to continue "fattening off the main body of their fellow-countrymen." In this period, such criminals were not, however, members of a tightly organized, highly centralized structure. "The Black Hand is not a cohesive, comprehensive society, working with mysterious signs and passwords," maintained Woods. "Given a number of Italians with money, and two or three ex-convicts, you have all the elements necessary for a first-rate Black Hand campaign." Landesco reached a similar conclusion concerning the Black Hand in Chicago but went a step further to conclude, "It is the purest banality to excuse the nefarious, bloody practices and wide-spread tribute paid by the victims, that the historical explanation that blackmail and the conspiracy of silence are old-world traits transplanted." Rather, the Black Hand's success in Chicago grew out of local conditions which "have favored the rise, spread and persistence of extortion by violence" even among groups "which did not import the pattern" from the old world. Undoubtedly many Sicilian black-handers moved into the "syndicate," but "American" Italians provided the leadership.[51]

Chicago's Italian-community youngsters . . . could and did turn to work in legitimate lines and found success in commercial, trade, and professional occupations. Nevertheless, illegal activities appeared to offer the quickest means available for monetary gain. Many immigrant-community youngsters early realized that in the highly competitive, mobile, and rootless society in which they lived, achievement, measured in financial terms, had high value, while the methods used to realize success received little attention or condemnation.[52] . . .

Children of "Southern" immigrants arrived at maturity at a time when educational requirements were becoming ever more important in order to qualify for jobs in public as well as in private employment. The fluid political, social, and financial patterns which had aided (and in fact had speeded) the assimilation of Germans, Irish, Bohemians, Poles, Swedes, and Norwegians in the three decades following 1870, were in the process of growing more rigid and unyielding as Chicago slowly grew out of its frontier-town stage and as earlier immigrant elements became entrenched. These earlier arrivals sought to establish barriers to prevent later arrivals from other ethnic backgrounds from challenging their positions.[53]

"Southerners" realized some success in gaining patronage jobs, but they were,

---

try criminals, paupers, old people, and the class that we call unfortunate women. . . . That was all before the South European immigration had started, and from countries from which the very best of our immigrants, according to the universal acceptation, have come."

[51] Landesco, *Organized Crime*, pp. 937, 947–48; Arthur Woods, "The Problem of the Black Hand," *McClure's Magazine*, XXXIII (May, 1909), 40.

[52] Landesco, "Prohibition and Crime," p. 124, and "Crime and the Failure of Institutions," p. 240.

[53] Richard G. Ford, "Population Succession in Chicago," *American Journal of Sociology*, LVI (September, 1950), 160.

TABLE III
FOREIGN-BORN POPULATION OF CHICAGO, BY COUNTRY OF ORIGIN

Nativity	*1884**	*1898†*	*1914‡*
Germany	209,631	207,310	191,168
Ireland	114,005	104,354	68,305
Norway	18,292	22,248	27,562
Sweden	23,755	56,862	66,287
Bohemia	28,281	40,516	49,074
Poland	23,509	44,325	124,543
Italy	4,091	12,585	58,782

* City of Chicago, Board of Education, *School Census of the City of Chicago. Taken May, 1884. Total Population of the City. Over 21 Years and under 21 Years of Age. By Wards and By Divisions of the City* (Chicago, 1884), p. 31.
† "School Census of 1898," printed in City of Chicago, Board of Education, *Proceedings, July 13, 1898 to June 28, 1899* (Chicago, 1899), pp. 254–58.
‡ City of Chicago, Board of Education, *School Census of 1914 and Annual Report of the Superintendent of Compulsory Education* (Chicago, 1914), p. 6.

as one early Italian politician bitterly complained, "the dollar-and-a-half-a-day 'jobs' of sweeping the streets" while Irish aldermen gave "the-four-dollar-a-day 'jobs' of sitting in an office to Irishmen." If at all possible, ethnic-group members tried to "look after their own," whether in politics, crime, organized labor, or the professions. (Early-arriving northern Italians did not consider "Southerners" to be "of their own.") Thus Anton J. Cermak, whether in his capacity as alderman, president of the Cook County Board of Commissioners, or mayor, made sure that his fellow Bohemians (Czechs) received patronage jobs and also support when they tried for elective office. Lacking established "patrons," southern Italians did not move up the political ladder of success in Chicago—to appointive and elective offices, patronage jobs, and exemptions from the law—until the 1920's. Then, under the leadership and guidance of Johnny Torrio and Al Capone, "Southerners" found politics and its urban handmaiden, crime, to offer an increasingly important source of money, as well as a means of social mobility.[54]

At the time when "American" Italians were arriving at maturity only to find economic advancement made difficult (but not impossible) by inadequate education, social and ethnic background, and lack of political connections, a new field of endeavor appeared, requiring as qualifications only ambition, ruthlessness, and loyalty. Prohibition provided a powerful and attractive force with fast, lush financial opportunities which appealed to many qualified young men—and which they regarded as nothing more than a new form of business enterprise. "Prohibition is a business," Al Capone stoutly maintained. "All I do is to supply a public demand. I do it in the best and least harmful way I can." He and others like him undoubtedly convinced themselves that they were simply labor and

[54] Jane Addams, *Democracy and Social Ethics* (New York: Macmillan Co., 1902), p. 259; Alex Gottfried, *Boss Cermak of Chicago: A Study of Political Leadership* (Seattle: University of Washington Press, 1962), pp. 68–70, 86, 268–69.

distribution organizers in a strongly competitive field. . . . Prohibition "opened up a new criminal occupation, with less risk of punishment, with more certainty of gain, and with less social stigma than the usual forms of crime like robbery, burglary, and larceny."[55]

During the 1920's, the Torrio-Capone "syndicate" fought other organizations for control of the liquor business in the Chicago area. The composition of gangland organizations was based largely, but not entirely, on ethnic origin. Thus, not only did the Capone group contain Slavic, Jewish, Irish, and other non-Italian elements; but Italians, foremost among them "Schemer" Drucci and the nine Aiello brothers, worked for Capone's major rival, the North Side gang led by Barney Bertsche, Dion O'Banion, Hymie Weiss, and George "Bugs" Moran. More than 500 gangland murders took place during the decade as competing organizations attempted to eliminate rivals, not always by superior management techniques. By 1930, according to a careful study of 108 kingpins of organized crime in Chicago prepared by William F. Ogburn and Clark Tibbitts, "American" Italians constituted 31 per cent of the leadership group, while 29 per cent came of Irish background and 20 per cent were Jewish.[56]

Each group reaped financial returns, and found itself pushed aside by a new, ambitious ethnic element, eager in its turn to gain economic benefits to be realized from crime and corrupt politics. In his collection of readings about organized crime in America, Gus Tyler maintained that Italians at first operated "almost exclusively" within the Italian colony. "Then they entered into warfare against the other ethnic gangs. Then they merged. And then they became the dominant element in the merger." The last of the large masses of "white" ethnic groups, Italians, however, remained in power at the top of the crime syndicate because no new ethnic mass came along to force them out of their positions of leadership. Perhaps the logical successors, Negroes, have been prevented from exerting pressure in large part because of segregation and color. Not only do Negroes lack a tradition of co-operative group action, but residential segregation and color render attempts to move illegal activities out of the ghetto community and into the larger white society extremely hazardous. Perhaps group awareness growing out of civil rights movements or the Black Power movement, along with society's increasing emphasis on equality regardless of color, will encourage Negroes to demand more remunerative and responsible positions in the hierarchy of organized crime than the lowly places they now occupy.[57]

[55] Edward Dean Sullivan, *Chicago Surrenders* (New York: Vanguard Press, 1930), p. 205; Landesco, "Prohibition and Crime," p. 125; Andrew Sinclair, *Era of Excess: A Social History of the Prohibition Movement* (New York: Atlantic Monthly Press, 1964), p. 220.

[56] Edward Dean Sullivan, *Rattling the Cup on Chicago Crime* (New York: Vanguard Press, 1929), especially chaps. iv, v, ix, and xviii; Denis Tilden Lynch, *Criminals and Politicians* (New York: Macmillan Co., 1932), chaps. vi and x; William F. Ogburn and Clark Tibbitts, "A Memorandum on the Nativity of Certain Criminal Classes Engaged in Organized Crime, and of Certain Related Criminal and Non-Criminal Groups in Chicago," p. 9, unpublished manuscript dated July 30, 1930, in the Charles E. Merriam Papers, University of Chicago Library.

[57] Gus Tyler, ed., *Organized Crime in America: A Book of Readings* (Ann Arbor: University of Michigan Press, 1962), p. 336.

VII

Chicago's Italians enjoyed great success in criminal activities, whether within the immigrant community through Black Hand and other extortion methods or by "syndicate" techniques in the larger American environment. The Black Hand existed, but as a method of criminal action, a modus operandi, and not a formal organization. As the White House society pointed out in 1908, many other Italian community residents who did not see themselves as Black Hand types, among them bankers, interpreters, labor agents, and small businessmen, worked diligently to extort fellow immigrants at every opportunity. They employed more subtle and refined methods than did Black Hand thugs, "but they too are means of exacting tribute from the sweat of the Italian working man, who pays because of his ignorance, and because of the absolute lack of any assistance and protection in a foreign land."[58]

Profits gained through Black Hand methods in the immigrant community seemed small when compared with the lucrative returns won by "syndicate" gangsters from Prohibition law violations, gambling, prostitution, and dope peddling. Italians born or raised in Chicago quickly learned to adapt American business techniques to crime by organizing compatriots (and acceptable "outsiders"), centralizing the chain of command, and controlling and directing the flow of money. In this process of "Americanizing" Italian criminal activities, "American" Italians established the Italian "syndicate."

Crime even facilitated immigrant adjustment. The "syndicate" required the repression of lingering old-world prejudices against fellow members from other provinces or countries because of the overriding importance of co-operation in the common quest for money, the symbol and substance of success. In the new urban home—cynical, cruel, vulgar, avaricious Chicago—Sicilians and Italians, northern as well as southern, joined together for mutual benefit and profit. Because of its function as a means of economic betterment and social mobility, crime occupied a place in the acculturation of Italian immigrants to the United States, along with community institutions, education, the padrone system, and politics.

[58] Italian "White Hand" Society, *Studies, Action and Results,* p. 27; Landesco, *Organized Crime,* p. 937.

6

RACIAL VIOLENCE AND SOCIAL REFORM–ORIGINS OF THE ATLANTA RIOT OF 1906

Charles Crowe

Racial violence with its attendant shock, fear, and bewilderment has become a commonplace facet of American life. A recent national advisory commission concluded that "our nation is moving toward two societies, one black, one white—separate and unequal." Throughout American history rigid barriers—social, legal, economic, and political—have prevented racial minority groups, and particularly black Americans, from participating in the mainstream of American life. The problem became intensified and nationalized in the twentieth century as black Americans moved from the relative isolation of the rural South into the ghettos of our cities, both North and South. While seeking equality in American society, blacks have had to accommodate as best they could to the prevailing patterns of prejudice. This essay explores the sordid background of a notorious twentieth-century race riot and the perversion of the ideals of Progressive reform into a means to further debase a whole minority group.

Charles Crowe teaches at the University of Georgia. He has published a biography of George Ripley *(Athens, Ga., 1967) and edited an authoritative book of readings,* The Age of Civil War and Reconstruction, 1830–1890 *(Homewood, Ill., 1966), among other works. Currently he is engaged in a major project examining "Racial Violence and Repression in the Progressive Era." This article is part of that study.*

In the bloody wake of the Atlanta race riot of 1906 the prophets of prohibition and Negro political repression swept on to victory. Both causes appeared under the sponsorship of Georgia Progressives who frequently cloaked anti-Negro mea-

Source: *Journal of Negro History*, Vol. 53, No. 3 (July 1968), pp. 234–256.

sures in the garb of reform and linked them with other popular goals such as a "clean" franchise or the destruction of the "liquor traffic." "Conflict eliminating" Jim Crow laws presumably served "the public interest" as much as bills for the regulation of railroad rates. By the same token, "progress" demanded that the drive to improve the education of men "with the actual burden of governing" be accompanied by efforts to limit "the black servant class" to appropriate "domestic" and "industrial" training.[1]

Civic leaders drafted reform credentials even for chicanery and violence. In a classic instance Georgians borrowed from a Mississippi politician the argument that the plunder of Negro educational funds was actually a service to black people. During the gubernatorial campaign of 1902, James K. Vardaman, proclaiming the educated white man to be "the Negro's best friend," insisted that the money "squandered" on Negroes "without citizenship" since the State Constitutional convention of 1890 would be more wisely spent in white schools creating "more best friends of Negroes."[2] Atlantans who accepted this absurd "reasoning" had no difficulty finding traces of God's Providence in racial conflict or even hearing His voice in the whirlwind of violence. Clerical and civic leaders in 1907 freely granted that the recent triumph of prohibition would have been impossible without the devastating race riot and the "epidemic of rape" which allegedly preceded it. As if to confirm the intimate relationship of reform, racial repression and violence, the jubilant leaders commemorated "the moral victory of the century" at the Henry Grady monument, where riot terrorists a few months earlier had brought in symbolic tribute the mutilated corpses of three black victims.[3]

The prohibitionist movement developed during the eighteen eighties, and the slogan "Keep whiskey from the Negro" originated in Reconstruction times, but not until the two issues were persistently linked in an explosive political atmosphere did "dry" victory become a strong possibility. In the summer of 1906, after gubernatorial candidates Hoke Smith and Clark Howell had competed with each other for more than a year in a bitter Negrophobe campaign, anti-saloon forces added their contribution to the furor. By September virtually the whole city pulpit had preached enthusiastically on the topic, and the Reverend Sam P. Jones promised to conduct in mid-month a major revival for a full week with "the liquor traffic" as the central theme. Jones, second only to Billy Sunday among American evangelists of the Progressive era, gave once his famous "For Men Only" talk on the triple temptations of prostitution, self-abuse, and Negro women, before proceeding to a series of addresses on the "world dooming" consequences of whiskey. In sermon after sermon Jones stressed the special and intolerable evils which sprang from the consumption of alcohol by Negroes. The same subject was thoroughly discussed by Dr. John E. White, Pastor of the Second Baptist Church and commonly acknowledged dean of the city pulpit.

[1] See A. J. McKelway, "State Prohibition in Georgia and the South," *Outlook*, v. 86 (1907), 947–959. The published material on disfranchisement is vast. See Archibald Grimke and others, *The Negro and the Elective Franchise* (Occasional Papers of the American Negro Academy, 1905), and A. J. McKelway, "Suffrage in Georgia," *Outlook*, v. 87, 63–66, v. 90, 507 (1908).

[2] See Vardaman's newspaper, *Commonwealth*, Oct. 10, Nov. 7, 14, 28, 1902.

[3] McKelway, "State Prohibition," and L. P. Winter, "Prohibition in Georgia," *Independent*, v. 63 (1907), 422–444. Much information on the subject can be found in the Hoke Smith and Rebecca Felton papers at the University of Georgia.

The sermons and public statements of White and Jones inspired other ministers to imitate their example and encouraged a round of energetic discussions and activities by the newly formed Atlanta Anti-Saloon League, the Women's Christian Temperance Union and the Businessmen's Gospel Union.[4] . . .

After the "rape epidemic" and the riot, both of which were blamed on the saloon, civic leaders tried to find a "legal" way of depriving Negroes alone of alcohol. John E. White argued that while such a measure could be described as discriminatory, it was really "a discrimination which a stronger race owed to a weaker race." James R. Gray, successor to Hoke Smith as editor of the *Atlanta Journal,* made the candid suggestion that the sale of whiskey to Negroes be made a felony, but the proposal clearly went beyond the standard forms of chicanery allowed by the U.S. Supreme Court. A more popular plan promised to close most Negro saloons by requiring keepers to pay a license fee of $2,000 and to thwart the few who could afford so large a sum through a fraudulent administration of the law. This plan closely resembled Hoke Smith's proposal to administer an "understanding" suffrage clause by giving easy sentences to the white registrant and impossibly difficult ones to the black registrant. In the last analysis, however, the Smith approach was an untested novelty and "partial" prohibition promised to be very cumbersome. Many civic leaders then chose to make a virtue of necessity by describing universal prohibition as a form of noblesse oblige. According to the child-labor reformer, A. J. McKelway, the prohibition bill sprang from a determination of the "stronger" race to "forego personal liberty" in order to protect the "inferior" race from its own "weakness and folly." McKelway and other Atlanta leaders believed that they had made possible "a popular uprising against a known cause of bestial crime."

As recently as 1899 it had been difficult to link the causes of prohibition and disfranchisement because many "dry" leaders feared that the most likely restrictive device, an educational qualification for voters, would provide a great stimulus to Negro education. In 1906 the prohibitionists took a different point of view and now insisted on disfranchisement as the necessary prelude to "closing the saloons." As spokesman the Reverend Sam Jones often called for the expulsion from the polls of the element that "invariably sells out to the highest bidder." The vote was worthless to the Negro for "it is not counted when cast," and "the Yankees" who originated the whole idea of Negro suffrage had long since admitted their mistake. The ballot, Jones concluded, served only to debauch the Negro, pervert the democratic process, and preserve the saloon.[5]

[4] Ms. copies of the "For Men Only Sermon" and several prohibition sermons of 1906 are in the Jones papers at Emory University. See also "Sam Jones, The Scourging Evangelist," *Literary Digest,* v. 33 (1906), 721–722; John E. White, "Prohibition: The New Task and Opportunity of the South," *South Atlantic Quarterly,* v. 7 (1908), 130–142; and Booker T. Washington to Wallace Buttrick, Sept. 30, 1906, B.T.W. Papers, Library of Congress. Schemes on licensing can be followed in the ms. Notes of the Atlanta City Council still kept at City Hall.

[5] *Atlanta Journal,* Mar. 24, 1906; Jones sermons cited in note 4; John Temple Graves, "Georgia Pioneers the Prohibition Crusade," *Cosmopolitan,* v. 45 (1908), 83–90; Thomas J. Morgan, *The Negro in America* (American Baptist Publication Society Pamphlet, 1900); and ms. Minutes of the Georgia Baptist Association, espec. 1903, 1906, Mercer University, microfilm copy at the University of Georgia.

Preachers and politicians alike during the long gubernatorial campaign of 1905–1906 demanded "the purification of the suffrage." The institutional battle for "pure" polls had begun at the turn of the century with the party primary which was championed more as a "reform" measure to exclude the "corrupt" Negro vote than as a means of bringing nominations "to the people." In 1906 at a time when the Democratic white primary had become the only significant election and the Georgia Negro was nearly without power, Hoke Smith and his allies waged a primary campaign largely on the alleged need to "reform" the suffrage through devices which would totally exclude Negroes from all elections "without disfranchising a single white man." The other leading candidate, Clark Howell, wasted no good will on the Negro, but did propose a substantially different political strategy. Howell as editor of Henry Grady's old newspaper the *Atlanta Constitution* stressed the idea that Smith irresponsibly agitated a problem solved by "the great Robert Tombs" in the Constitutional Convention of 1877. A Negro rush to the polls, Howell reasoned, would be discouraged by many devices including a cumulative poll tax so rigid that it would compel a new voter over 50 years of age to pay taxes for twenty-nine years. The unimpressed Smith retorted that nothing prevented "Yankee millionaires from corrupting the suffrage by paying the back taxes for thousands of Negroes." In response to the fact that only ten percent of male adult Negroes voted in the unimportant general election, Smith insisted that the great goal of complete political purity demanded the total elimination of "the corrupt and purchasable" vote "even as a potentiality." It seemed that the apparently effective white primary by its very existence raised the spectre of counter "black primary" which could carry dozens of Georgia counties. The embattled Howell could only try ineffectually to answer Smith's emotional charges by accusing him of "raising the old cry of nigger" in a state which was already "a blessed white man's country."[6]

The very origins of the Smith campaign can be traced to the desire for the complete exclusion of the Negro from politics. James R. Gray, editor of the *Atlanta Journal* and a leading exponent of more racial repression, began in 1904 to negotiate for an ultra-racist ticket that could win the primary of 1906. In his eagerness Gray approached a political enemy, Tom Watson, with a plea to put aside "mere finance for the one great cause . . . that [is] near to your heart . . . the question of white supremacy." Watson, then singing the swan song of Southern Populism as Presidential candidate, was not quite persuaded, but he did grant that the great reform movement of the age was the drive to end forever in Georgia "the threat of Negro domination." In 1905 Congressman (later Senator) Tom Hardwick, who had spent much of his time as a state legislator working on repressive measures, brought together Hoke Smith, Gray of the *Journal*, and Tom Watson's loyal band of "Old Populists." In an urgent and confidential letter Hardwick asked Watson to support Smith for "the controlling and paramount reason" of a "purified" franchise, a cause for which all "patriotic" Georgians "ought to sink all personal feeling, run all political risks, and help rid the state of this curse. . . ." Without the total elimination of the Negro as "a political potentiality," the South "will never again" have "freedom

6 Nearly all of Smith's speeches and many political editorials are in the Smith Scrapbooks, vols. 60–64, University of Georgia. See also editorials, *Atlanta Constitution*, May 18, 1906.

of thought or independence of action." Thus, Hardwick, Watson, Smith and Gray united in common agreement that new political repression of the Negro was the foundation stone on which all other reforms must rest.[7]

In the campaign Smith said much about railroad reform but so did Howell, and it is difficult to know how serious either man was about the issue. Smith proposed to outlaw stock ownership in Georgia railroads by "foreigners" (i.e., non-Georgians), so if he was a bona fide railroad reformer his mind contained a curious mixture of xenophobia and reform sentiment. Smith's biographer, plagued by the apparent paradox of reform and ultra-racism juxtaposed in the same person, argued that Smith was a sincere and ardent reformer whose Negrophobe campaign sprang largely from "opportunism."[8] Unfortunately for this line of reasoning, Smith was a great admirer of Cleveland and Parker, an opponent of Bryan's platform in 1896, and a consistent gold Democrat at a time when the currency question commonly provided the touchstone of reform. Smith, who had used the "infamous" president of the "infamous" Southern Railroad to secure a $50,000 note, opposed the gubernatorial reform candidate in 1904 and supported Governor Terrell, whom he was to denounce during the campaign of 1906 as "a puppet of the railroad ring." His early efforts in "railroad reform" seem to have consisted largely of efforts to secure lower rates and better terms for his clients, the merchants of the Atlanta Freight Association. Nor do his two terms as U.S. Senator suggest that he was one of the unsung heroes of the New Freedom. If we had to choose the reformer or the racist, Smith's life-long commitment to white supremacy and black repression suggests that his reform interests were heavily tinged with opportunism and his demand for disfranchisement was sincere and central to his thought.

Smith's ally, Tom Watson, poses similar problems of interpretation. To explain Watson, his biographer conjures up an admirable Populist Dr. Jekyll and a ranting Negrophobe, anti-Semitic, anti-Catholic, demon-ridden Mr. Hyde of the Progressive era.[9] A badly needed reassessment of Southern Populism cannot be undertaken here, but it now seems clear that the extent of Negro participation in the movement has been much exaggerated. Many white Georgia Populists worried as much about the Lodge "Force Bill" as they did about the need for railroad regulation, and in North Carolina Fusion the thrust for Negro participation came more from the Republicans than the Populists. Although much importance has been attached to Watson's "disillusionment" after the Democrats "stole" elections with "purchased Negro votes," vote selling was a pastime of both races and the Populists made their contribution to competitive ballot stuffing. Finally, it is doubtful if Georgia had an entirely honest election in the post-Reconstruction era. . . .

The change in the attitudes and conduct of Southern politicians can be

[7] C. Q. DeFrance to A. J. Ledford, Aug. 11, 1906; Gray to Watson, July 21, 1904; Thomas Hardwick to Watson, June 21, Sept. 30, 1905; all in Watson Papers, U.N.C. at Chapel Hill. See the Gray-Watson exchange of Nov., 1903 and a clipping from the *Augusta Chronicle*, July 28 [1905] in the same collection as well as "Deluded Fanaticism," *Atlanta Journal* clipping, Rebecca Felton Scrapbook #32, University of Georgia. See also Dewey W. Grantham, ed., "Some Letters from Thomas W. Hardwick to Tom Watson Concerning the Georgia Gubernatorial Campaign of 1906," *Georgia Historical Quarterly* v. 34 (1950), 328–340.

[8] Dewey W. Grantham, *Hoke Smith and the Politics of the New South* (1958).

[9] C. Vann Woodward, *Tom Watson, Agrarian Rebel* (1938).

traced to the fact that Negroes lost the last remnants of real power between the Populist and the Progressive eras. With the Negro more effectively excluded from politics the white politicians, consistent in devotion to racist ideology in both eras, could easily accelerate the process of repression in ways which would have been difficult if not impossible ten or twenty years earlier. Even the greater degradation of the Negro made it easier to think of new oppression as necessary social reform, and the internal tendency toward repressive politics gathered strength from the rising tide of white supremacy in the South, the nation and the world. Thus the Smiths and the Watsons were neither colorful freaks missing all the wider meanings nor "Dixie demagogues" exploiting "poor whites" but rather representative leaders "reforming" their states and serving values treasured by all classes of their racist constituents.

In Smith's mind the cause of a "reformed suffrage" justified the harshest measures. No statement was too extreme and no action too radical in this increasingly bitter campaign for total Negro political exclusion as "the solution to the race problem." Since the Negro's nature "fitted him only for bondage," the "blessing of slavery" deserved the highest praise for taking the "animalistic" black from the jungle where his brothers "still ate raw meat and sometimes each other." Although American bondage brought the Negro some rudiments of civilization, he degenerated morally and physically after 1865 until his wretched descendant of 1906 stood as a living reproach to "mistaken philanthropy and deluded fanaticism." The Republicans compounded the error of emancipation and committed the "crime of the century" by treating blacks as fellow citizens and voters. According to hundreds of Smith's speeches the Negro voter was ignorant, illiterate, savage, vicious, inhuman, unendurable, venal, arrogant, brutish, venomous, lust-ridden, and so on.[10]

Smith repeatedly asserted that "the white men who made this country" did not mean to have the Negro "interfere" or take any part except that of passive submission to the will of white people. Even submission itself provided more evidence of Negro inferiority, because white men in a similar situation "would rather die than submit." By any standards, he asked, why should "grossly inferior" blacks have rights denied women and young men of the "superior" race? Without the strongest barriers would not the tide of 117,000 Negro adult males "sweep away white civilization" in Georgia? If even a few thousand Negroes became the "balance of power" would not that situation constitute "Negro domination" and "the humiliation of white intelligence?" Was not "the terrible burden" of a Negro legislator in McIntosh County alone enough to justify a "war of liberation?" . . .

A. J. McKelway, another reformer and the leading Southern advocate of child labor laws during the Progressive era, . . . believed that the evasion of the fifteenth amendment had been necessary "to save civilization" and that only the complete expulsion of the Negro from politics could rid the state of fraud, civic corruption and the saloon influence. To these arguments Smith supporters added the allegedly happy experience of other states. Dr. J. B. Hawthorne, a prominent Baptist clergyman, reported that Virginia disfranchisement had "saved

[10] Smith speech in Smith Scrapbook #64, University of Georgia. On the Wilmington riot, see the *Atlanta Journal*, May 19, 1906 and Helen G. Edmonds, *The Negro and Fusion Politics in North Carolina* (1951), 158–178.

the honor of the state," and even made whites "kinder" and Negroes "better." James R. Gray of the *Atlanta Journal* reported even more success in Alabama where "racial harmony" as well as "a perfect white supremacy" reigned, and the voteless Negroes flocking from the city back to the farm "had returned to work." Naturally, Gray added, under such conditions "the Negro loses all hope and becomes permanently docile and quiet."[11]

Even when Atlantans could look forward to a "clean" franchise and a "dry" future, much remained to be done. For example city controlled utilities and transportation, parks and playgrounds were defended both for their own intrinsic value and because they provided fresh opportunity to improve the "separation of the races" in the name of "public peace and order." Segregation as civic reform was a commonplace idea among Southern Progressives, and most segregation laws were prefaced with a declaration of the intent to "improve race relations" or "to prevent race conflict." Ray Stannard Baker, among many other Northern Progressives, thought that Jim Crow car laws were "beneficial" to Southern Negroes, and certainly the Atlanta press never tired of stressing their "benevolence."[12] . . .

Another "social evil" offensive to the reformers was Negro "vagrancy." Emancipation had not prevented Southern whites from continuing to believe that they had a legitimate right to command Negro labor. Atlanta Progressive leaders in 1906 expressed a particularly sharp anger, even rage, over the "vagrant" Negro who by simply not working evoked charges of "criminal evasion" and "fraud" against white people. With righteous indignation, civic leaders demanded "better" vagrancy laws and more rigorous enforcement policies. Laws regulating vagrancy, labor contracts and labor recruiting, along with the practice of annual contracts and jail sentences for violators, helped to keep most rural Negroes in a state of quasi-peonage and debt servitude. White supremacy courts explained their sentences by arguing that they punished Negroes not for debt but for fraud, breach of contract, taking money under fraudulent conditions, and the like. In the cities, where most of the task of repression fell on police hostility and vagrancy laws, the Calvin law of 1903 (amended in 1905) represented a high plane of legal control and the result of years of agitation. Jury trials became even more difficult to get, bond posting passed beyond the means of nearly all Negroes, the right to immediate dismissal on finding gainful employment was lost, and the daily maladministration of the law in local courts seemed to get worse. In 1906 the state supreme court upheld the law and ruled that even a man with "a fixed abode" could be a vagrant, particularly when "his offence is loafing and loitering around pool halls, bar rooms, dives, lewd houses and

[11] A. J. McKelway, "Suffrage in Georgia," *Outlook*, v. 87, 63–66, v. 90, 507 (1908); Gray editorial on the Smith-Howell debate, *Atlanta Journal*, Jan. 10, 1906; and Gray editorial in the *Journal*, Mar. 29, 1906.

[12] Ray Stannard Baker, *Following the Color Line* (1908). Baker did not of course advocate these practices for the North but, as his notes in the Library of Congress on the 1906 Southern trip show, he was told that Jim Crow laws created conflict. Nevertheless in print he held to the theory of conflict minimization. See also "Jim Crow Measure," *Atlanta News*, Sept. 1, 1906; editorial in the same issue; editorial of Sept. 4; and Charles E. Wynes, "The Evolution of Jim Crow Laws in Twentieth-Century Virginia," *Phylon*, v. 28 (1967), 416–425.

653969

D. C. Heath and Company

QUAN.	CATALOG NO.	DESCRIPTION
1	081158	WEBER WEST TRAD 3 ENL-PRESENT
		NO CHARGE

APR 24 3 25 PM '73

SENT TO YOU WITH THE COMPLIMENTS OF D.C. HEATH AND COMPANY.

IF YOU DESIRE FURTHER INFORMATION,
PLEASE CALL US TOLL FREE AT:
1-800-225-1388
(IN NYC 800-225-1388
IN MA. 1-800-842-1211)

OR CONTACT YOUR DISTRICT MANAGER:
L.F. (RED) JURECKA
1800 BLDG.N.E. LOOP 410
SUITE 102
SAN ANTONIO, TEXAS 78217

FORM 16-0152 REV. 11/71

similar places." Needless to say, any Negro establishment might at any time be described by a local court as a "dive."[13]

Urban "vagrancy" drives took a sharp upward turn during the summer of 1906 as police in Macon, Savannah, Augusta, Atlanta and elsewhere used the law with special severity. In Savannah, police systematically raided without warrants, arrested employed Negroes during off-duty hours, roughed up Negro leaders, and arrested property owners in their own houses as vagrants. Similar events took place in Atlanta where a militantly angry press and public opinion provoked an escalation of raids which ended only with the outburst of rioting on September 22. White Georgians automatically classed black people not at work as vagrants, and the concept of a property-holding or leisure class among Negroes hardly penetrated the Southern imagination. When the white man spoke about the very humble "good Negro" he did not have W. E. B. DuBois in mind, or even Booker T. Washington. The only real category of common perception other than field hand, town laborer or servant was the criminally inclined "dude" Negro who clearly "belonged on the chain gang." The subject of "vagrants" (unemployed Negroes), routinely described as "petty thieves and black beasts," moved editors in the crisis of 1906 to headlines such as "DRIVE THEM TO THE CHAIN GANG" and even "KILL THE VAGRANTS."[14]

The war on vagrancy and civic corruption seemed to lead logically to an anti-vice campaign. Charles Daniel, crusading young editor of the *Atlanta News*, applauded the seizure by Anthony Comstock and the New York police of art school catalogues which according to the Atlanta editor contained some "very hot nude figures . . . fit only for the seclusion of a dressing room or a locked bath room." In the "plain, homespun talk" of an editorial entitled "The Nude and the Lewd are Twins," Daniel "demonstrated" that "art means immorality and indecency" because "familiarity with the nude form of either sex perverts all morality . . . destroys the sense of spiritual shame" and produces only "passion and lust." Even Clark Howell of the *Constitution*, the most restrained of the Atlanta editors, sharply attacked "nudes" in art reproductions and on theater billboards. ("Nude" meant any representation of a woman not fully clothed.) According to Howell, one particularly offensive "health" billboard with a "nude figure" and the caption "Tonight!" represented exactly the kind of thing which aroused the Negro criminal.

The anti-vice and prohibition causes found a common enemy in the "dives" where Negroes commonly drank cheap gin from bottles with images of "nude" white women on them. Thus the "primitive" black with his "strong, sudden impulses" absorbed both "the toxic heat" and the "suggestion of aphrodisiacs" in the bottle. With every drink the Negro stared at the "obscene" label "drinking in the invitation" to the act of "assault." Because of this "ever-present danger"

13 *Statutes of Georgia*, Code of 1895, sections 453, 1039; *Public Laws of Georgia* (1905), 109; *Statutes of Georgia*, Code of 1905, No. 57, 141, 150; *Georgia Reports*, the Carter, Glover, Darby and other cases, v. 126 (1906), 567–570, v. 127 (1907), 46. On anti-vagrancy drives in Savannah, see the *Savannah Tribune*, Aug. 18, Sept. 15, and later issues, 1906. All the Atlanta papers carried stories and editorials on Negro vagrancy at the end of August and the beginning of September.

14 Article on Atlanta dives, *Atlanta Constitution*, Aug. 6, 1906; editorial, *Constitution*, Sept. 22, 1906; story on "Decatur Dives," *Atlanta Georgian*, Sept. 18, 1906; and editorial "Reign of Terror," *Georgian*, Aug. 21, 1906.

John Temple Graves insisted on a "clean and decent family newspaper" and refused to take advertisements relating to whiskey, medicine for veneral diseases, or "improper representations" of the white woman. Graves frequently demanded inspection of the dives to prevent replicas of white women from being displayed. On the day before the Atlanta riot the press featured news about the seizure of "nude pictures" in the dives.

If the habit of associating closely vice and Negroes had early origins, the reformers gave more substance to the notion by concentrating most prostitution and vice in Negro districts. Around Decatur Street in Atlanta where many saloons served both races, the white man (and the black man more circumspectly) could find all basic types of sexual activity. The very phrase "Decatur Street Dive" symbolized luridly drunken debauchery and the violation of Southern taboos. According to the highly respected Baptist leader, John E. White, the dives were a "breeding place of lust and animal insanity" where Negroes drank and schemed until "insanely reckless and devilish." Presumably, no other city in the world, had "as much of the prurient devil congested in so small a place" as Decatur Street with its "low-browed, whiskey loving Guinea Negro from which comes the rapist."[15]

If the black man as sexual criminal illustrated ultimate evil, "the most precious flower of Southern womanhood" before "defilement" represented the highest good. Leaders reminded Georgians that society existed first of all to protect "the imperious beauty, the immaculate virtue of Caucasian women," the "most beautiful and purest women . . . in all of history." While her "Christ-like" chastity and loveliness lay beyond description, the unceasing effort to find the proper terms was taken to be a mark of racial identity. "Caucasian virtue" constantly faced the peril of "the most murderous and beastly of crimes" and during August and September of 1906 Atlantans began to believe that a new and dangerously "torrid wave of black lust and fiendishness" placed them "in a state of siege." Tom Watson and John Temple Graves, among others, took up the theme of "the black terror" and "the red death," the "ordeal worse than death," the "nightmare" which "our wives, mothers and daughters live every day." Men like Watson and Graves could hear "the agony and the pitiful cries of the defenseless white woman . . . crying out in pain from the awful . . . attacks," the "shrieks of the poor victim of beastly lusts . . . the heart broken sobs . . . the blood stains in the earth."[16]

This frenzied rhetoric—which obviously contained identity problems, status anxieties, sexual guilt and repression, the massive projection of sexual fantasies—at times even cloaked political and economic repression with sexual symbols. What might be called "the sexual interpretation of Southern history" obsessed many Southerners and gained a large audience in the North. George Harvey presented in *Harper's Weekly* a representative version of the fable. Allegedly

[15] Will Irwin, "More About Nigger Gin," *Collier's* v. 45 (Aug. 15, 1908), 19; *Atlanta Constitution*, Aug. 6, 1906; Daniel's editorial on "The Nude and the Lewd," *Atlanta News*, Aug. 10, 1906; *Atlanta Constitution*, Sept. 28, 1906; *Atlanta News*, Aug. 23, 1906; and editorial in the *Nation* v. 83 (Sept. 27, 1906), 253.

[16] *Atlanta Georgian*, Aug. 21, 25, Sept. 18, 1906; *Atlanta Journal*, Aug. 6, 1906; *Watson's Magazine*, v. 4 (1906); 7–8, 501–502; and *Watson's Jeffersonian Magazine*, v. 1 (1907), 166–169.

"the peculiar institution," as a system of "social control" with complete protection of white women, gave way during Reconstruction to the "War Amendments" which assumed "the absolute equality of the races" along with "the inevitable corollary . . . of racial amalgamation."[17] . . .

By 1906 when this "New Negro Crime" had reached "epidemic proportions," reformers clamored not so much for new legislation as for drastic changes in criminal procedure or new ways to evade the law in the "punishment" of "sex criminals." The statute of 1896 defined assault as "the *attempt* to commit violent injury" and the law on rape explained the crime as "the *attempt* to know a female forcibly against her will." Moreover, the higher courts allowed assault and even rape convictions to stand when no physical contact had taken place, and Atlanta editors followed established custom by describing all incidents which involved black men and white women as "assaults." John Temple Graves made the point clear in September, 1906: "The mere suggestion of the slightest familiarity of a black and filthy Negro with a refined and gentle Caucasian girl stirs the blood to fever heat, but the monstrous and unspeakable horror of a more serious and brutal assault wakes the blood to complete frenzy." In a representative remark Charles Daniel was even more specific: "All Negroes must understand that any contact under any circumstances by accident or design with a Southern woman" would result in lynching. In effect the statutes, the courts, the editors, public opinion in all classes handed to the white woman who wished to use it the death warrant for any black man. A misinterpreted step, an unexpected presence, an unexplained word, a stare, a hysterical girl, a vengeful female, a woman with something to hide—all could lead to death.[18]

For about five weeks prior to September 22 the "usual" tensions became a continuing sexual hysteria, and later many leaders attributed the riot itself to the "epidemic of Negro assaults." The "epidemic," first discovered in early August by editors Graves and Daniel, obsessed populace and press by mid-month. Banner headlines recorded each "assault" until the count reached twelve on September 21 with four more added on the afternoon of the riot. Even a precursory investigation exposes most of these "assaults"—one woman drawing her shades saw a strange Negro on the sidewalk, another woman attempted to conceal a bungled suicide—until one probable rape and several instances of bodily harm remain as events which actually took place. Still, as the history of witchcraft suggests, collective belief in the non-existent can lead to very tangible and violent results.

For men who believed that a solution existed for every "social evil," black "sexual crime" seemed to be a maddeningly intractable problem. The dives could be closed and the "corrupt" Negro disfranchised, but Atlanta opinion leaders searched vainly for the appropriate "reform" to end "the nameless crime." Mere amelioration could not satisfy a mortal totalitarianism which regarded even one black "assault" as absolutely intolerable. Due process seemed too slow and uncertain for the "most damnable of all crimes," and Judge George Hillyer, gen-

17 Harvey, "The New Negro Crime," *Harper's Weekly*, v. 47 (1903), 1577; editorials, *Atlanta Georgian*, Aug. 21, 25, Sept. 1, 22, 1906; and editorial, *Atlanta News*, Aug. 16, 1906.

18 See *Georgia Reports*, v. 128 (1907), 41–47, 102–115; Superior Court Dockets, Fulton County, Georgia, 1906; and editorials, *Atlanta News*, July 27, Sept. 1, 1906.

erally on the side of political moderation, now demanded "reformation" of criminal procedures in "assault" cases so that no more than three days lapsed between arrest and execution. In cases of this kind any action at all by U.S. Courts was bitterly denounced as "Federal interference." Thus, when a Chattanooga mob in 1906 lynched a prisoner under U.S. Supreme Court protection, they were heartily congratulated for "having promptly and properly meted out swift justice."

According to the most strident—and probably the most numerous school—lynching seemed to be the only remedy for "sexual assault." Often a qualifying clause was added, "when the law broke down," or "when the law failed to act," and according to the most common accounts mobs did not actually murder Negroes. Instead, the "brute" or "fiend" was "properly dispatched to his doom," or "met his just fate," or encountered "summary punishment" and "swift justice" at the hands of "patriotic citizens," "juries in the woods," "the people sitting as the high court of justice," the "people's court and jury," a "group of determined avengers," a "posse of firm purpose and cool determination," or "citizens of patriotic purposes." Charles Daniel, who announced that an Atlanta lynching of July 31, 1906, "gave great satisfaction to the community," offered a $1,000 reward for lynching, and insisted that it was

> *a cowardly evasion of public duty . . . to say that these devils are entitled to long drawn out trials . . . the usual technical details, appeals, application for pardon, interference of the Federal Courts, and possible final escape.*

Even more explicit was Mrs. Rebecca Felton, plantation mythmaker and lynch advocate as well as prohibitionist, suffragette, civil reformer and the first woman to sit in the U.S. Senate. Mrs. Felton dismissed "maudlin sentiment" and observed that:

> *It is not possible to inflict upon the black rapist, any punishment comparable to the suffering already endured by innocence and virtue. If he was torn to pieces limb by limb and burnt with slow fire, or hung by the thumbs until the buzzards swarmed around him, he would still be saved some of the revolting torture already inflicted upon a harmless victim. In dealing with such ravenous beasts there can be no dealings with human souls and the best thing to do is to promptly rid the earth of such vile and dangerous cattle.*[19]

Editor Daniel agreed that for assault "lynching is too good . . . and hanging is a mercy," and Graves added that laws related only "to human beings." In September, 1906, Graves began to wonder if lynching was enough. After all, some Negro preachers allegedly promised heaven to the lynched "assailant," the offenders became "heroes" and "martyrs" in the "more demoralized" black communities and some publicity crazed Negroes seemed to assault in order to gain the dramatic and spectacular death by rope, and even by faggot. One approach, Graves suggested, would be to set up a scientific study to discover "the germ of the rapist." Or possibly Atlantans might find "a new and mysterious mode

[19] Felton letter to the *Atlanta Journal* [1905], clipping, Box 5, "Race Problems Folder," Felton Papers, University of Georgia; Felton ms. "Racial Antipathy," Ibid.; Daniel editorials, *Atlanta News,* Aug. 15, 16.

of killing" in which the assailant before a large gathering of Negroes would pass over "a slender bridge into a dark chamber where in utter darkness he perished by a terrible means never known to Negroes." Another proposal by Graves would prescribe for all Negroes involved in incidents with white women castration and branding on both cheeks with the letter "R." The public response to Graves's suggestions ranged from offers to do the branding and castrating to assertions that the safety of white women required the castration of all black men. (One proposal suggested that Negro women must be "unsexed" to prevent another generation of Negro rapists from arising.) Other citizens called for some form of the old slave patrol, the assignment of white "overseers" to every Negro, arming all white women and providing them with shooting schools, or a system of rewards which would pay $10,000 to every white female of any age who killed a black "assailant."[20]

The word "genocide" did not exist in 1906, but the conditions which made general slaughter a real possibility were present before, during, and after the Atlanta riot. In the midst of the riot the relatively moderate *Atlanta Constitution* proclaimed RIOT'S END ALL DEPENDS ON NEGROES/IN THEIR POWER TO STOP TROUBLE OR BRING ON A WAR OF EXTERMINATION. *Constitution* Editor Clark Howell warned T. Thomas Fortune of the *New York Age* that his call for retaliatory violence if acted on by even a few "irresponsible and vicious Negroes" would lead immediately to "either extermination or wholesale banishment." John Temple Graves, who frequently discussed total physical "separation," colonization and deportation as final solutions, warned Negroes that any "rational" plan was beside the point if the current "wave" of Negro crime continued and "provoked" mass slaughter.[21] Indeed, the most impatient ones denounced public discussion as irrelevant to the "race crime" of assault, for which Negroes were collectively responsible. For more than one citizen of this persuasion, "the code of chivalry" called for genocide. "The once proud Anglo-Saxon lords of Creation" had failed to inflict upon Negroes the general destruction which black sexual assaults deserved, and "Chivalry" demanded that Anglo-Saxons overcome their low economic desire to exploit black labor. "Yes," concluded the Southern "knight," "let the war of extermination begin now."[22]

If a full-scale "race war" failed to develop, massacre and rioting did come to Atlanta and many of the rioters regarded themselves as moral agents of the community—even "reformers." Moreover, the riot was not an isolated event but one of more than forty major riots in the decade from 1898 to 1908 and part of a pattern of violence which also included several hundred lynchings a year and countless acts of individual terrorism. Bishop Henry Turner's estimate of one thousand to fifteen hundred racial killings a year may have been correct. The period from 1880 to 1892 which saw the most rapid advances of Negroes

[20] *Atlanta Georgian*, Aug. 21, 25, Sept. 1, 10, 15, 18, 1906; *Atlanta News*, Aug. 7, 15; and many other issues as well as issues of the *Atlanta Journal* and the *Atlanta Constitution*. See also Clark Howell to Thomas Nelson Page, Nov. 5, 1906, Page Papers, Duke University.

[21] *Atlanta Constitution*, Sept. 25, 1906; *Atlanta Georgian*, Sept. 24, 26, 1906. For an account of Graves' lecture before a national audience on the virtues of lynching and the possible "annihilation of the Negro race," see "Chatauqua Conference on the Mob Spirit," *Outlook*, v. 74 (1903), 959–960. The conference was a typically American effort to discuss fairly and freely the good and the bad sides of a subject, i.e. racial murder.

[22] Letter to the editor, *Atlanta Georgian*, Aug. 26, 1906.

in the acquisition of liberty and property, was followed by an era of disfranchisement, Jim Crow laws, attacks on Negro property and education, and pervasive violence. Even the Progressive movement itself served mainly to provide new occasions for racial aggression in the Southern search for a system of social control to replace slavery.[23]

Almost any form of non-subservient behavior raised "the spectre of Negro domination" and challenged the feeling of racial superiority which constituted the deepest sense of identity among Southern whites. Because Smith, Vardaman and other reformers sought a massive and secure power which could be insured only by the social stability of the region and by national action, they frequently clamored for the repeal of "the War Amendments." Southern leaders were not satisfied by the fact that the nation largely ignored the fourteenth and fifteenth amendments; they demanded repeal as the minimum price of social peace and would have asked for national caste legislation if there had been any prospects of success. Meanwhile, frustrated white leaders raged over the incompleteness of their "freedom" to rule and the inadequacy of local institutions to repress more effectively a rising Negro population. Private violence was far from incidental or merely "criminal." It was instead a loosely institutionalized force which filled the void between large claims of mastery and limited institutions for racial control. Because the South feared Federal "intervention" in "local affairs," and regarded the nation as a standing threat to racial mastery, the violence tended to be specific, limited and sporadic rather than general and unlimited. If public and private comments on Georgia Negroes seem stridently hysterical in relation to the realities of power, the stridency sprang at least partly from the fact that socially functional violence took place in the realm of individual initiative and free enterprise. "Isolated" and routine acts of racial aggression served to create caste behavior, to drive Negroes into subservient personal relationships with individual whites, and to make life difficult for those who remained outside the pale of protection.[24]

Many Southern whites publicly deplored violence, but few or none rejected caste gains or tried to alter the society served by riots, lynching, and terrorism. Atlanta leaders agitated public feeling in such a way as to make violence inevitable and afterward presumed to criticize the rioters for their misdeeds. Even the arch-instigators, Hoke Smith and John Temple Graves, assumed a public mask of racial fairness. Smith boasted that he had sheltered Negroes in his house and Graves proudly reported that when a delegation of East Point Negroes came humbly to his back door he agreed to help keep rioting out of the neighbor-

[23] Louis Harlan has demonstrated clearly Negro educational losses at a time of improving white education in *Separate and Unequal* (1958), but the precise account of economic losses has not been published. The best unpublished accounts are LaWanda F. Cox, "Agricultural Labor in the U.S., 1865–1900, With Special Reference to the South," Doctoral Dissertation, California at Berkeley, 1942, and E. A. Gaston, "A History of the Negro Wage Earner in Georgia, 1890–1940," Doctoral Dissertation, Emory University, 1957. For general political background on Georgia Negroes during this period, see Clarence A. Bacote, "Some Aspects of Negro Life in Georgia, 1880–1908," *Journal of Negro History*, v. 43 (1958), 186–214. On Turner's remarks, see *Savannah Tribune*, Nov. 17, 1905.

[24] See John Edward Bruce, Ms. Notes on Lynching, Schomberg Collection, N.Y. Public Library; Robert E. Park to Emmett Scott, [Sept., 1906], Booker T. Washington Papers, Library of Congress.

hood. Undoubtedly some households both sheltered Negroes and sent out rioters, and the choice of embracing or rejecting violence was itself a luxury provided by the system of white supremacy.[25]

[25] W. E. DuBois, "The Atlanta Race Riot," *World Today*, V. 11 (1906), 1173–1179. For an apologia, see Clark Howell to Thomas Nelson Page, Nov. 5, 1906, Page Papers, Duke University.

7

THE ARMED-SHIP BILL CONTROVERSY: A LEGISLATIVE VIEW

Richard Lowitt

The following article deals with a filibuster that never occurred, though almost every textbook and monograph says it did and President Wilson denounced its perpetrators as willful men. To filibuster is to delay or defeat legislation through the use of dilatory parliamentary tactics such as excessive and organized oratory, continuous quorum calls, and moves to correct the record. Whether successful or not, those resorting to the filibuster at least make a good show of their opposition. Richard Lowitt examines a critical incident in the crisis leading to American entrance into World War I. Behind it was a conflict between the president and some senators as to the constitutional role of the executive and Congress in declaring war. This theme has taken on a particular relevance in the years since the Tonkin Bay resolution of 1964.

Richard Lowitt specializes in recent American history. He is a professor at the University of Kentucky, where he is preparing a biography of George W. Norris, of which two volumes (Syracuse, 1963 and Urbana, 1971) already have been published. This article develops a point touched upon in George W. Norris, The Persistence of a Progressive, 1913–1933 *(Urbana, 1971).*

Almost every college textbook in American history makes note of the "little group of willful men," as Woodrow Wilson called the United States Senators, "who representing no opinion but their own have rendered the great government of the United States helpless and contemptible."[1] They allegedly talked the armed-ship bill to death in the last days of the Sixty-Fourth Congress.

[1] Wilson was particularly sensitive on the subject of filibusters. The first and only major defeat he thus far suffered at the hands of Congress occurred as a result of

Source: *Mid-America*, Vol. 46, No. 1 (1964), pp. 38–47. Reprinted by permission of the publisher.

Having severed diplomatic relations with Germany on February 3, 1917, because of her intention to violate the "Sussex Pledge" of May, 1916, not to engage in ruthless submarine warfare against passenger and freight-carrying vessels, Wilson after some hesitation asked Congress on February 26 to grant the government the power to place navy gun crews aboard merchant ships. After the measure gained rapid approval in the House by an overwhelming 403 to 14 vote on March 1, a few senators, led by Robert M. La Follette, were excoriated, ridiculed and denounced as traitors because they dared to oppose the protective arming of American merchant ships. In an atmosphere charged with excitement and tension, in part caused by the release on March 1, 1917, of the Zimmerman telegram suggesting that Mexico "reconquer the lost territory in Texas, New Mexico and Arizona" with German aid in event of war, these men exhibited foolhardiness of courage by filibustering in opposition to the Administration's wishes which were backed by apparently overwhelming public sentiment. It is the purpose of this paper to re-examine this important incident on the road to American participation in the First World War. It will give attention to legislative details and note who and what were involved in the controversy.

First of all, who participated in this filibuster? On February 7, 1917, five senators: Asle J. Gronna, William F. Kirby, Robert M. La Follette, James K. Vardaman and John D. Works voted against a resolution approving Wilson's action of February 3, in severing diplomatic relations with Germany. Of the five only Kirby and Vardaman were Democrats, and Works was a "lame duck" whose term would end with the session. All five were opposed to the passage of the armed-ship bill.[2]

On the other hand Moses E. Clapp, Albert B. Cummins, Wesley L. Jones, William S. Kenyon, George W. Norris and William J. Stone were among the 78 senators who voted in favor of Wilson's action, though later in the month all but Kenyon were openly opposed to the arming of merchant vessels. Of this group Clapp was a "lame duck" and only Stone was a Democrat. Indeed it was Stone, the Chairman of the Foreign Relations Committee, who had introduced the resolution "approving the President's course in severing diplomatic relations." Among those not voting owing to absence from the Senate were Thomas P. Gore, Harry Lane and James A. O'Gorman. All were Democrats; all were later opposed to the armed-ship bill. O'Gorman was a "lame duck" and Gore was not present for the remainder of the session owing to illness. Though Gore was opposed to the measure and would have favored the filibuster, he was unable to aid in the cause.

The Zimmerman telegram had been released to the press on March 1, 1917, and that same day, as already noted, the House approved an armed-ship bill, a

filibustering in the Senate against the ship-purchase bill during the short session of the Sixty-Third Congress in February, 1915. Wilson yielded in his support of the measure so that the Senate could consider necessary appropriation measures, thereby avoiding the necessity of calling the new Congress into immediate extra session.

[2] On February 12, 1917, Senator La Follette introduced a joint resolution (S. J. Resolution 211) making it unlawful for armed merchant vessels of the United States in time of peace to depart from American ports or any of its territories for foreign countries. The resolution was tabled; *Congressional Record*, 64th Congress, 2nd Session, p. 3064.

measure that did not give the President the full authority he desired.[3] The next day, March 2, a more complete bill (S.8322) was presented to the Senate. A motion to consider the measure was made by Senator Stone and it carried 64 to 15 with 17 members not voting. Among the fifteen senators who did not want to consider the measure, eight (Clapp, Cummins, Gronna, Jones, Kirby, La Follette, Norris and Works—Kirby the only Democrat in the group) would actively oppose it. On the other hand Lane, O'Gorman, and Stone—all Democrats—voted with the majority. Vardaman did not vote.

Thus with the Sixty-fourth Congress scheduled to end on March 4, 1917, on March 2 the Senate, with numerous appropriation measures still to be enacted, amid the usual end of the session rush and confusion, agreed in an atmosphere compounded by mounting tensions and clamors to consider without previous hearings a highly controversial measure. By this action a special session of the Sixty-fifth Congress was virtually insured so that necessary appropriation measures could be enacted. Regular Republicans, as distinguished from the progressive faction of the party, were pleased. Though most of them agreed to the arming of merchant vessels, they nevertheless wanted Congress to be in session as relations with Germany deteriorated so that the President could not act with an entirely free hand.[4]

A bill drafted by the Senate Foreign Relations Committee to carry out the policy of armed neutrality urged by President Wilson was introduced in the Senate on the evening of February 27th by Senator Stone, chairman of the committee, and was read for the first time. Once debate got underway on March 2, Gilbert M. Hitchcock, who directed the fight for the bill after Stone had announced his opposition, requested unanimous consent to lay aside the Senate bill (S.8322) for the one which had already passed the House (H.R.21052). This maneuver was designed to save precious time by eliminating the parliamentary necessity of ironing out differences between the two bills in conference and then having the compromised version enacted by Congress. Hitchcock was successful in this tactic, but at very high cost. He had to approve a recess until 10 o'clock Saturday morning, March 3.[5] By this recess the opponents of the

[3] See *New Republic*, vol. X (March 24, 1917), 218–219 for an interesting analysis revealing that Congressmen from the Mid-West and Far West were far more sympathetic to barring arms and gunners to merchant vessels than the 403 to 14 vote indicated. The *Christian Science Monitor* on March 1, 1917, reported that "The Flood bill [the armed-ship bill] . . . is not wholly acceptable to the White House."

[4] *The Washington Post* on February 24, 1917, reported: "In a conference lasting an hour and a half yesterday, Republican members of the Senate decided that Congress shall be in session while the international situation remains in its present grave position. . . . Senator Lodge wants Congress to remain in session to hold up the hands of the President: to prevent him from 'running away' as one Senator said. Senator La Follette wants Congress to restrain the executive from going too far." And on February 26 the *New York Times*, a morning paper, reported that the Republicans might filibuster not primarily to kill bills but to require a special session. It also reported that there was a general feeling among Republicans that the President should not be left until December to handle the foreign crisis without Congress. That same afternoon (February 26) Wilson asked Congress for the power to arm merchant ships.

[5] *Congressional Record*, 64th Congress, 2nd Session, p. 4781.

armed-ship bill were assured of the success of their endeavors. Thereafter in efforts to obtain unanimous consent to limit debate and fix a time for voting, Hitchcock met rebuff after rebuff.

It was Hitchcock too who designated the number of opposition Senators when on March 4 as the session drew to an end he claimed that "nine tenths of the Senate are ready to vote and are anxious to vote for this bill, but that they are being prevented by 12 Senators . . . who refuse us [sic] an opportunity to vote."[6] An examination of the *Record* reveals, however, that most of the talking was done by supporters rather than opponents of the measure.

On March 4, 1917, early in the morning with the debate reaching a bitter climax, Senator Ellison D. Smith of South Carolina requested action on a conference report on the agricultural appropriation bill. This measure displaced the armed-ship bill and gave Senator Gronna, who had been demanding unsuccessfully a right to be heard at length on the arming of merchant vessels, opportunity to discuss rural matters. He spoke for more than one hour, mostly reading statistics about different grades of wheat.[7] Then as it became evident that the armed-ship bill could not be enacted, its supporters devoted themselves chiefly to keeping La Follette from talking. Throughout his remarkable career in the Senate, hardly a bill in which he was vitally interested had come to a vote without his managing to make the closing speech. Thus the leader of the opposition to the armed-ship bill was frustrated. He was forced to hear Hitchcock discuss the measure until the clock ran out and the Sixty-Fourth Congress expired.[8]

If one examines the speeches on the bill once the Senate proceeded to its consideration during the last three days of the session the following pattern emerges:[9]

[6] *Ibid.*, p. 4988. Seventy-five senators signed a "round-robin" statement dated March 3, 1917. As published in the *Record* that statement said the senators favored the passage of S.8322. But by unanimous consent on March 2, S.8322 had been replaced by H.R.21052. Only two progressive Republicans, Miles Poindexter and William E. Borah, signed the round-robin. Of the seventy-five signing senators 45 were Democrats and 30 were Republicans. Of the twelve in opposition (thirteen, if Kenyon, a Republican who played no role, is included) five were Democrats and seven were Republicans. All the Republican opponents of the bill except Wesley L. Jones were of the progressive faction. The remaining senators were either absent from the Senate or were not asked to sign. Finally, it might be of further interest to note that Hitchcock had opposed the bill in committee. But with the publication of the Zimmerman telegram he accepted responsibility for the measure forced upon him by Stone's opposition.

[7] While Gronna sadly read statistics on the floor, Democrats and Republicans were shouting with laughter in the Democratic cloakroom over imitations of senators by Joseph O'Toole, chief of pages; *New York Times*, March 4, 1917.

[8] For an exciting account of La Follette's predicament at the closing of the session see Belle C. and Fola La Follette, *Robert M. La Follette*, 2 Vols., New York, 1953, I, 615–625. The account of the filibuster in this volume (Chapter XLIII) is the best available. The most satisfactory brief account is to be found in Arthur S. Link, *Woodrow Wilson and the Progressive Era*, New York, 1954, 271–274.

[9] The individuals mentioned held the floor. Those whose names appear in capital letters opposed the bill. They answered questions, debated or orated. Rarely did they speak continuously. The unaccounted-for pages were concerned with Senate business other than consideration of the armed-ship bill.

Friday, March 2.	Hitchcock	*Record* pp.	4747–48
	Lodge		4748–54
	Walsh		4754–59
	Poindexter		4759, 4764–68
	Thomas (Colo.)		4768–71
	KIRBY		4771–72
	McCumber		4772–74
Hitchcock seeks unanimous consent to substitute H. R. 21052 for Senate measure.			
	La Follette objects		4774–77
	VARDAMAN		4777–78
	Brandagee obtains floor		4780–81

Senate recessed at 12:40 A.M. to 10 A.M. Saturday, March 3, 1917.

Saturday, March 3.	Brandagee	*Record* pp.	4858–69
	Fall		4869–76
	STONE		4877–93
Hitchcock asks unanimous consent to limit speeches 15 minutes.			
	Cummins and Norris object		4894–95
	Sutherland		4895–97
	JONES		4898–4905
	Townsend		4905–4906
	Hardwick		4906–4907
	CUMMINS		4907–4912
Valedictories for retiring senators			4912–14
Hitchcock requests unanimous consent to limit debate and to fix a time for voting.			
	Clapp and Works object		4914–15
	Reed		4915–17
Sunday, March 4.	Round-Robin presented		4988
Hitchcock requests unanimous consent for an end of debate and for a vote at 6 A.M.			
	Weeks and Gronna object		4989–90
	Williams		4990–91
	WORKS		4992–99
	CLAPP		4999–5002
	LANE		5002–5004
	NORRIS		5004–5009
	Owen		5010–12
	Hitchcock		5013–20

Senate adjourned *sine die* at 12 noon with Hitchcock still holding the floor.

The dramatic features of the situation were heightened by crowded galleries and the attendance of cabinet members and representatives on the floor as spectators. Other notables, including the British ambassador, Sir Cecil Spring-Rice, also appeared during the course of the debate. The gallery reserved for diplomats was filled day and night. Some of its occupants tittered in amusement at this strange spectacle of American legislative procedure. The other galleries were filled to overflowing and long lines of would-be spectators stood patiently outside every door. All of this occurred in an atmosphere of mounting resentment and bitterness toward the little group who opposed the armed-ship bill.[10]

Thus among the group of senators opposed to the measure Kenyon and O'Gorman did not speak. La Follette only raised points of order and objected, while Gronna spoke only on the agricultural appropriation bill. Senator Cummins several days later estimated that the bill was under actual consideration on the floor a little less than thirty-five hours. During this period the "little group of willful men" consumed less than eleven hours in debate while those who were not so castigated consumed more than twenty-four hours. Senator Reed Smoot believed "there would have been a vote upon the armed neutrality bill if the friends of the measure had not taken the time they did in discussing it." He further claimed, and no one objected, that the friends of the measure occupied more time in discussing it than those who were opposed to it.[11]

Those who were against the bill consumed less time in debate than those who favored the bill, a phenomenon not usually associated with filibustering. Moreover, opponents of the measure did not demand frequent roll calls on the absence of a quorum, another technique usually associated with filibustering. Speakers on both sides did not discuss irrelevant matters; almost always they confined themselves to arguments for or against the bill. Considering the important implications of the armed-ship bill the speeches delivered against it were not too long. And, again, the leader of the opposition could not obtain the floor to speak.

George W. Norris, many years later, in an interview granted the biographer and daughter of Robert M. La Follette, recalled revealing incidents during the debates. At least two Democratic senators at different times privately admitted that though they agreed with Norris' position, they were afraid to speak against the armed-ship bill. He asked why they could not help prevent its passage by consuming time speaking for it. The senators agreed and without naming names Norris claimed they did speak. Moreover, before the March 3, 1917, convening of the Senate, after the recess granted by Hitchcock to gain consideration of the House measure, Norris confided to La Follette that he felt certain that the opponents of the bill could prevent its passage.[12] In a letter written at the time Norris summed up the reasons why he and the group that supported his position opposed the armed-ship bill. He wrote, "had the bill become a law as it was before the Senate—and there was no possibility of securing an amendment, it would without doubt, have placed in the hands of the President unlimited authority to make war." He believed the Constitution vested this power in Congress, and, along with the group of willful men, Norris was not willing to "delegate that enormous power to any one man."[13]

What did it all mean? Did the failure to pass the armed-ship bill delay or

[10] *New York Times,* March 4, 1917, and March 5, 1917.

[11] *Congressional Record,* 65th Congress, Special Session, March 8, 1917, 34, 37–38.

[12] Interview: Fola La Follette with George W. Norris, February 15, 1939; George W. Norris Papers, Manuscripts Division, Library of Congress. In his autobiography, *Fighting Liberal,* New York, 1945, Norris reiterated many of the points made in this interview. See Chapter 19, "Death Kiss by Filibuster."

[13] G. W. Norris to A. F. Buechler, March 10, 1917, Norris Papers.

thwart the course of events leading to the United States involvement in the First World War? What effect did it have on the careers of the "little group of willful men?" What was the significance of this controversy? The following comments might suggest some of the answers to these questions.

To begin, as every textbook points out, the failure to enact the bill did not prevent Wilson from quickly finding another mandate to arm merchant vessels. Whether arming merchant vessels was worth the bitterness this controversy engendered is a question that cannot be accurately or easily answered. Military authorities at the time realized that the arming of merchant vessels afforded little or no protection against a surprise submarine attack and that the chance of hitting a submarine by shots fired from a ship were not great.[14]

That the controversy in one way or other impeded or accelerated our entrance into the war is to be doubted. No serious scholar has put forth such a claim. That the debate revealed anti-war sentiment among vast segments of the American people is a point that perhaps needs stressing. David Lawrence, writing at the time, claimed that "not even the extreme proponents of the Armament bill dared to indicate more for the future of American policy than armed neutrality."[15] Of course, Robert M. La Follette argued that "the Armed Ship Bill Means War"[16] and Theodore Roosevelt, more bitter against Wilson than against the "treason committed by the eleven senators," argued, as expected, that "the bill itself is almost worthless. Armed neutrality is nothing but timid war."[17] Yet according to an analysis made at the time of the House vote on the measure, "Practically half of the members of the House from West of the Appalachians" were opposed to an amendment "guaranteeing safe transport of munitions to the Allies."[18] And with the exception of the "lame duck" Senator O'Gorman of New York, who uttered not a word during the debates, all of the willful men came from west of the Appalachians.

Moreover, it can be shown that the supporters of the bill had no one idea of its significance. Rather, they interpreted it largely out of their own background. In the Senate Albert Fall was convinced "that the President would have the right to place guns and men to man them upon ships carrying munitions." Yet Henry Cabot Lodge, who likewise supported the bill, declared:

> *I am assuming that the vessels to which we give arms are not carrying contraband. If we deliberately as a government, put arms on a vessel carrying contraband, of course it is an act of war. I take it that any vessel which is armed by the government will be subjected to careful examination by the officers of the United States to make sure that she is not carrying contraband and that her cargo and voyage are lawful.*

Similar confusion as to what the measure proposed could be shown from statements by its supporters in the House of Representatives. The only statement

[14] For a contemporary comment making this point see the remarks of an officer of the New York Naval Militia in the *New York Evening Post,* March 1, 1917.

[15] *New York Evening Post,* March 3, 1917.

[16] The phrase is the title of a signed front page editorial that appeared in the March, 1917, issue of *La Follette's Magazine,* IX.

[17] Theodore Roosevelt to J. C. O'Laughlin, March 8, 1917; Theodore Roosevelt Papers, Manuscripts Division, Library of Congress.

[18] *New Republic,* X (March 24, 1917), 219.

that can be made with certainty is that those members in the Senate and House who opposed the measure were "resolutely determined not to arm munitions ships with guns and gunners."[19]

One very quick result of the Senate debate was a successful demand for cloture. On March 8, 1917, with only three votes against it,[20] the Senate enacted for the first time in its history a rule limiting debate. And it should be reiterated that the regular Republicans were successful in their policy of obtaining a special session of Congress to consider necessary appropriation bills. Thus Congress was in session as the rupture of relations with Germany eventuated in Wilson's request for a declaration of war. This possibly can help to explain why several regular Republicans were willing to help talk the bill to death as friends of the measure. Indeed, Franklin K. Lane, Wilson's Secretary of the Interior, claimed "it is unjust to charge the whole thing on the La Follette group; they served to do the trick which the whole Republican machine wished done. For the Penrose, Lodge people would not let any bills through and were glad to get La Follette's help."[21]

Somewhat less clear is the result participation in the filibuster had on the political careers of the men opposed to armed neutrality. Examining a list of the senators who spoke against the armed-ship bill or who were opposed to it, one finds thirteen names: Clapp, Cummins, Gronna, Jones, Kenyon, Kirby, La Follette, Lane, Norris, O'Gorman, Stone, Vardaman and Works. Most lists do not include the name of Wesley L. Jones, a regular Republican who by his speech on March 3 associated himself with the opponents of the measure. If one excludes the three "lame duck" senators (Clapp, O'Gorman and Works) whose careers came to an end with the 64th Session of Congress, ten names remain. Of these ten men, six voted in April, 1917, against participation in the First World War: Gronna, La Follette, Lane, Norris, Stone and Vardaman. Of these six senators, Gronna in 1920 and Vardaman in 1918 were unsuccessful candidates for re-election. Lane and Stone died before their terms expired: Lane in May, 1917, and Stone in April, 1918. La Follette and Norris continued their distinguished careers in the United States Senate. Neither man ever regretted his actions during this period.

As for the others, Cummins was re-elected in 1920, but failed to gain renomination in 1926 and died shortly thereafter. Jones was twice re-elected. It was not until 1932 that he failed in his bid to return to the Senate. Kenyon was re-elected in 1918 and resigned in 1922 to become a judge of the United States Circuit Court of Appeals, Eighth Circuit. Finally, Kirby was defeated in his efforts in 1920 to gain renomination.

Thus of the ten senators whose careers continued after March 4, 1917, only three failed to gain renomination when their terms ended. Presumably their opposition to the armed-ship bill was a factor of some significance in their defeat. Whether Lane and Stone would have been able to return to the Senate, had they lived, is a matter of speculation. But for five of the ten senators their role

[19] *Ibid.*, 218–219.

[20] Robert M. La Follette, Asle J. Gronna and Lawrence Y. Sherman voted against cloture. La Follette and Gronna opposed the armed-ship bill.

[21] Franklin K. Lane to George W. Lane, March 6, 1917, in *The Letters of Franklin K. Lane* edited by Anne Wintermute Lane and Louise Herrick Wall, Boston, 1922, 241.

in this controversy and the denunciations that were heaped upon them did not noticeably damage their political lives. They survived and went on to further their careers.

A final and perhaps most important comment upon the significance of this filibuster was made by George W. Norris. He recalled that feeling in the Senate was more intense during the debate on the armed-ship bill than it was later when the war resolution was requested. In the first instance the outcome was uncertain; on the war resolution it was a foregone conclusion.[22] During the armed-ship bill controversy, several senators felt compelled to take a decisive stand based upon conscience and conviction that cut across party lines. But as the round-robin referred to by Senator Hitchcock on March 4, 1917, indicated, Wilson's wishes as to armed neutrality and eventually war would have had the support of a majority of the members of the United States Senate. In short, the debate revealed that though the Constitution gave Congress power to declare war, Congress would follow the President as the crisis situation reached its climax. The "little group of willful men" refused to abdicate their constitutional responsibility in this matter.

[22] Interview: Fola La Follette with George W. Norris, February 15, 1939; Norris Papers.

8

THE STEEL INDUSTRY AND PRICE-FIXING DURING WORLD WAR I

Robert D. Cuff and Melvin I. Urofsky

Business history in the United States until recently usually followed one of two approaches owing to lack of available records. If the author were critical, his chief sources were usually court or legislative records based on evidence unearthed when the corporation was being either prosecuted or investigated. If the author were overtly sympathetic, chances were that he was being paid to present a laudatory history. In recent years, however, as more corporations proceed to make their records available to scholars, and as other archival material is being used, historians are able to present more analytical accounts, seeking comprehension rather than praise or blame. This essay examines a major American industry at a critical juncture and it casts important new light on the relations of government and industry during World War I.

The authors, Robert Cuff at York University and Melvin Urofsky at the State University of New York at Albany, are young scholars working in the field of business history. Professor Cuff has published articles examining the government service of businessmen during World War I, while Professor Urofsky has, in addition to several articles, published Big Steel and the Wilson Administration *(Columbus, 1969),* A Mind of One Piece: Brandeis and American Reform *(New York, 1971), and, with David W. Levy,* Letters of Louis D. Brandeis, *Vol. I (Albany, 1971).*

Our purpose in this article is to analyze the process of adjustment between the steel industry and the Wilson Administration which transpired during World War I in the debate over price controls. From the spring of 1917, when the Administration inaugurated discussions for price reduction on government sup-

Source: *Business History Review,* Vol. 44, No. 3 (1970) pp. 291–306.

plies, to September 24, 1917, when the first price-fixing agreement was reached, tough bargaining and open hostility between industry and government officials resulted in a general impasse that adversely affected the entire munitions program. Yet as soon as the industry and government reached the September settlement, relations improved remarkably and persistent conflict rapidly changed to routinized cooperation. The questions that concern us here are: why were relations so strained in the early months; what factors lay behind the post-September accommodation; and what sustained the spirit of good fellowship until the end of the war. Hopefully the answers to these questions will illuminate a number of significant aspects of business-government relations during the war years.

THE LEGACY OF CONFLICT

On the eve of World War I, relations between the steel industry and the Wilson Administration reflected four years of tempered hostility and conflict. The steelmakers had never trusted the President, who had specifically criticized the Steel Trust in the 1912 campaign, and declining profits in the recessions of 1914 did not alleviate their pessimistic mood.[1] More importantly, from the time he took office, Secretary of the Navy Josephus Daniels had energetically fought the industry on pricing policy, and had even gained Congressional approval in 1916 for construction of a federally-owned armor plate factory.[2] It is with these circumstances in mind that we must understand the industry's unwillingness to cooperate with the Administration as the country inched its way toward war in early 1917. On March 30, 1917, Bernard Baruch privately appealed for voluntary price reductions to Elbert H. Gary, chairman of the United States Steel Company and the president of the American Iron and Steel Institute. He had no success. As the member of the Advisory Commission of the Council of National Defense in charge of raw materials and metals, Baruch had already made such an arrangement with the copper interests in hopes of showing the Administration that big business was not unmindful of the public interest. Gary's forthright refusal soured Baruch on the steel industry, however, and only confirmed Daniels' contention that big business required continuous scrutiny. Daniels took up the cudgels on the Administration's behalf and ultimately had his way with U. S. Steel on prices for the Navy. This clash, however, sharpened tempers further and caused *Iron* Age, the industry's chief trade journal, to grumble about the implicit threat of commandeering it saw in the Administration's "request."[3]

[1] Melvin I. Urofsky, *Big Steel and the Wilson Administration* (Columbus, 1969), 32–36, 41, 63–64, 86–87.

[2] Melvin I. Urofsky, "Josephus Daniels and the Armor Trust," *North Carolina Historical Review*, XLV (Summer, 1968), 237–63.

[3] Daniels to Elbert H. Gary, March 31, 1917, Exhibit 1726, and Memorandum by Bernard Baruch, March 30, 1917, Exhibit 1727, both in the United States Senate, Special Committee Investigating the Munitions Industry, *Munitions Industry Hearings . . .*, 74 Cong., 1 Sess. (Washington, 1935), XXII, 6534 (hereafter cited as *Nye Hearings*). See also Bernard M. Baruch, *Baruch, The Public Years* (New York, 1960), 64–65; Entries for April 3, 4, 5, and 6, 1917, E. David Cronon (ed.), *The Cabinet Diaries of Josephus Daniels* (Lincoln, Neb., 1963), hereafter cited as *Daniels Diary;* and *Iron Age*, April 12, 1917.

Hostility carried over from peace-time squabbles was supplemented by the general uncertainty of the initial mobilization effort. No one in business or government circles knew in April what the exact nature of America's contribution to the war would be, or how long the war might last. Fights over prices, purchases, and the rest abounded in an organizational landscape that grew more chaotic every day. Emergency agencies sprang up in great profusion and aggressively competed for policy-making authority. Steel, like business in general, could not turn to any single source for the direction it required. Baruch strove for the honor of being the government's official link with industry, but the General Munitions Board, the United States Shipping Board, and other agencies claimed authority too, and military department heads intervened at will.

In this welter of contending agencies and personalities, it is hardly surprising that no consensus existed as to how prices should be fixed, or whether they could be fixed at all. The Administration's business advisors argued that at the very least industry deserved some kind of policy statement, so it could stop worrying and get on with production. A decision on price policy, Baruch wrote Wilson in May, would "set loose the great machinery of the Government, and clarify the situation tremendously."[4] Dollar-a-year men prodded the Administration to meet industry halfway in a cooperative effort that would avoid drastic federal controls on the one hand, and laissez-faire economics on the other. A special price committee under the chairmanship of Frank A. Scott, a Cleveland businessman and head of the General Munitions Board, reported in May that "sufficient price regulation" could be obtained "through immediately seeking the cooperation of the great owning and operating interests" of the country.[5] Baruch and Scott placed the onus for unsettled market conditions largely on the Administration's failure to design a policy regarding prices on government supplies and the relationship among prices to the government, to the general public, and to the Allies.

President Wilson was indeed reluctant to move on prices, and his hesitation contributed to the developing impasse between the industry and government during the spring and summer of 1917. Wilson seemed to share Daniels' special hostility to the steel industry as a whole, commenting more than once on the possibility of nationalization. At the same time, he shared the hope of his Secretary of War, Newton D. Baker, that America could wage war without making a dramatic change in the balance of power between the public and private sectors of the economy. Moreover, he seemed uncertain as to the powers available to him on such things as prices, sensitive all the while to those vocal elements on Capitol Hill who challenged every extension of executive authority.[6]

[4] Baruch to Wilson, May 15, 1917, Records of the War Industries Board, Record Group 61, Federal Records Center, File 21A–A4, Box 1147 (hereafter cited as W.I.B. Records). See also Baruch to Daniel Willard and Willard S. Gifford, March 31, 1917, and April 19, 1917, in the Records of the Council of National Defense, Record Group 62, Federal Records Center, Suitland, Maryland, File 2–A8, Box 86 (hereafter cited as C.N.D. Records).

[5] Frank A. Scott to Franklin K. Lane, May 3, 1917, C.N.D. Records, File 2–AB, Box 86.

[6] In May 1917, the President discussed with Daniels a plan by which the government would suggest "good" prices, yielding profits of from 10 to 20 percent, and if the producers refused to cooperate, they would have to declare so in writing. The President could then appeal to the country and demand that they sell at fair levels.

For its part the steel industry adopted a wait and see attitude through the spring, holding firm in its conviction that Washington had no right to interfere in its private domain without invitation. *Iron Age* denied the government had any authority to force large concessions, or to receive more than the usual discount accorded any large purchaser.[7] The industry refused to perceive the federal establishment as anything more than one of a number of groups competing for its resources—just the kind of unyielding stance which so angered Baruch, Daniels, and the President. The industry had far more business than it could handle with high-priced Allied orders, and it felt no obligation to leave this lucrative market for a buyer who demanded lower rates. From big steel's perspective, the Administration seemed to expect industry to compensate for the absence of a rational price policy through a series of voluntary, patriotic sacrifices. Businessmen in government believed such a step necessary in the short-run but they agreed with their colleagues in industry that it was no way to conduct business in the long-run, even in wartime.

The steel industry was no stranger to the idea of business-government cooperation, even though in this instance it wanted to stay clear of Daniels and the Wilson Cabinet. Elbert Gary had frequently tried to enlist Washington in his campaign for trade stability during the progressive era, and had supplemented these efforts at an entente with private dinners among steel executives and an active role in the industry's trade association. He had not had uniform success in these endeavors, but he and the industry had acquired considerable experience in dealing with bureaucracies which they could now usefully enlist against the chaos of wartime economics.[8] As steel prices went sky high in the summer months, pressure grew within the industry for stabilizing measures, and U.S. Steel, the major producer, extended an olive branch to Washington in search of some kind of entente.[9] By this time the industry's leadership wanted to move

Daniels Diary, May 22, 1917. Also see Daniel A. Beaver, "Newton D. Baker and the Genesis of the War Industries Board, 1917–1918," *Journal of American History*, LII (June, 1965), 43–58. Baker argued that neither Congress nor the American people would sanction outright federal control of the steel industry. Baker to Wilson, May 28, 1917, Papers of Woodrow Wilson (Manuscript Division, Library of Congress), hereafter cited as Wilson MSS.

7 *Iron Age*, May 10, 1917.

8 The steel industry at this time was dominated by United States Steel, the Bethlehem Corporation, and the newly formed Midvale Iron & Steel Corporation, which together produced close to two-thirds of the industry's output. Gary had won over the executives of these companies to his programs, but many of the smaller independents still clung to the older beliefs of a free-swinging, competitively-structured market. For all practical purposes, however, Elbert Gary spoke for the entire steel industry during the war, despite occasional flare-ups among the independents. See Gabriel Kolko, *The Triumph of Conservatism* (Chicago, 1967), 30–39 for a brief description of U.S. Steel's unsuccessful but persistent search to end competition before the war.

9 Taking the average price of all steel products from July 1, 1913, through June 30, 1914, as a base of 100, the April, 1917, index stood at 340, and by July had shot up to 435. Pig iron went from $42.20 to $57.45 per gross ton, and billets from $73.75 to $100.00 per g.t. Bars increased from $3.75 to $4.50 per cwt; for the same quantity, beams rose from $3.88 to $4.50, and plates to $9.00 from $5.88. Division of Planning and Statistics, W.I.B., "Steel Price Chart," n.d., copy in Papers of Bernard M. Baruch (Princeton University). The editors of *Iron Age* argued in July that some action was needed to head off a possible market collapse. See *Iron Age*, July 12, 1917.

the whole issue into the area of private negotiations free from the rising clamor of critical opinion.

THE SEARCH FOR COMPROMISE

The industry's desire for a solution was reflected in U.S. Steel's response to a developing controversy with the U.S. Shipping Board in June over steel plate prices. Under chairman William Denman's threats to impose arbitrary prices, James Farrell, U.S. Steel president, proposed that the AISI submit a tentative price schedule to a joint commission of Army, Navy, and Shipping Board representatives, which could then set up a proper scale in consultation with industry representatives. Farrell realized that this step would centralize responsibility for prices on the government side, open the possibility of consistently stable prices, and most assuredly give the industry a large voice in the decision-making process. And finally, such an agreement would take the question out of politics and give it to administrative agencies where bargaining could proceed without charges of immorality and lack of patriotism. Farrell wanted to avoid a uniform price schedule for all customers based on the lower rates he now recognized that the government would demand. To head off the possibility, he recommended that prices be fixed high enough to ensure maximum production of even the high-cost mills, with an excess profit tax instituted to take back exorbitant profits, "if any," from the low-cost producers. This last recommendation was of course a *sine qua non* with the Administration and Congress for the kind of high pricing policy favored by the industry.[10]

The Wilson Administration was not prepared to respond to steel's initiative at this point, much to the disappointment of both Farrell and the government's business advisors. The President had simply not yet made up his mind to act. He preferred to start with a Federal Trade Commission investigation into steel prices and to reach a decision only after he received the commission report. In the meantime, government officials suggested another conference for early July and directed the Army and Navy to have the industry supply their needs at pre-war rates with additional payments to be adjusted at a later date.[11]

It was an unsatisfactory compromise. It was hardly realistic to expect the industry to cooperate happily in this course after the preceding struggle, yet conversely, the Administration lacked the will, or the way, to force the industry to sell at pre-war rates. Steel did not want to make contracts until the uncertainty cleared, while government buyers hesitated to purchase materials for fear of missing future price reductions. The stopgap measure also made business advisors nervous about the chance that Congress would respond to the consequent delay in the war program with drastic, arbitrary controls. "Unless the question of price and the necessary economic readjustment can be settled without involving the military programme as seriously as at present," Baruch and Scott warned Baker, "we may well anticipate not only the gravest military results, but also serious reaction of public and political opinion."[12]

[10] "Memorandum adopted by the Joint Conference of Army and Navy Officers with James A. Farrell, Representing the Iron and Steel Institute, June 21, 1917," Exhibit 1730, *Nye Hearings*, XXXI, 6535.

[11] Baker to Scott, Exhibit 1731, *ibid;* and *New York Times*, June 28, 1917.

[12] Baruch and Scott to Baker, July 5, 1917, W.I.B. Records, File 21B–A3, Box

Wilson remained firmly committed to a preparatory FTC investigation, but in the meantime he skillfully employed the rising tide of outraged public opinion to try to get what he wanted from steel without legislation or long-range policy commitments. By July, secondary manufacturers were demanding action, Congress had launched an investigation into the general price rise, and Senator Atlee Pomerene, an Ohio Democrat, introduced a bill giving the President broad discretionary power over a whole range of products, including steel. This last measure threatened to undermine any hope for a voluntary agreement.[13]

On July 11, 1917, the same day that Administration officials held the first of two meetings with steel executives, Wilson issued an emotional statement proclaiming that henceforth the public and the government must receive identical "just" prices on all goods. While calling on all businessmen not to lose their patriotism in a headlong rush for profits, he hoped to calm the public mind, to satisfy private buyers, and to soften up the steel industry.[14] He achieved more success in the first two endeavors than the third, although the steel makers did agree in principle to the one-price-for-all idea in the day-long conference on the twelfth. But this was about the extent of progress at the end of two days of talks. Solution of the major issues waited on completion of the FTC inquiry; a "just" price lacked definition; and the distribution problems sure to follow government price-fixing remained untouched. In fact, the July conferences did not even settle the one-price-for-all issue because both sides took away different impressions of what had been said regarding the Allies. Secretary Daniels believed the operators had included this group in the agreement and was enraged to learn in August that mills were charging different rates.[15] Judge Gary was willing to concede this point, as it turned out, but only if he could sell through the American government and not directly to the Allies themselves.[16] The president of Midvale Steel, however, balked altogether. "We beg to assure you," he wrote Newton Baker, "that we did not conceive that we were agreeing to supply the needs of the Allies at a price to be later ascertained by the method proposed for our own Government."[17] In his reply, Baker followed the President's lead and expressed hope for an ultimate solution after the FTC investigation.[18]

---

166. Throughout June and July, government purchasing bureaus found it difficult to obtain steel. Robert E. Wood (General Purchasing Officer) to General George Goethals, June 28, 1917, W.I.B. Records, File 21B–A3, Box 166; Daniel Willard to William C. Redfield, July 6, 1917, Records of the Department of Commerce, Record Group 40, National Archives, File #75024/164; also see *Iron Age*, July 19, 1917.

[13] *Iron Age*, June 28, 1917. For evidence relating to the demand by secondary manufacturers for fixing steel prices, see: *American Machinist*, July 26 and August 23, 1917; C. M. Woolley (president of the American Radiator Company) to Burwell S. Cutler (Acting Chief, Bureau of Foreign and Domestic Commerce), July 30, 1917, Department of Commerce Records, File #75024/185.

[14] *New York Times*, July 12, 1917.

[15] *Daniels Diary*, August 1, 1917. See also Col. Edward M. House to Wilson, August 4, 1917, Wilson MSS, Series II, Box 155.

[16] Gary to Baruch, July 18, 1917, Box 149, Papers of Josephus Daniels (Library of Congress), hereafter cited as Daniels MSS.

[17] Alva Dinkey to Baker, July 31, 1917, and similar message in John A. Topping to Baker, August 1, 1917. *Ibid.*, Box 36. Dinkey claimed that only the U.S. Steel Corporation, with its low costs, could afford to make the same price to both the American and Allied Governments; his company, he declared, could not possibly do it.

[18] Baker to Dinkey, August 2, 1917, Baruch MSS. Series VIII, vol. 1.

After further negotiations, a temporary compromise was reached which called for the same price to everyone but with two qualifications designed to appease the steel producers. First, the agreement would be reciprocal: the Allies had to apply the same principle to their own producers who sold to the United States. Second, the arrangement would be limited to war materials, "in order to protect our own industry." Raw materials sold to the Allies could not be diverted to trade or to industry which might subsequently compete with American manufacturers.[19] The steel industry, like American business in general, could never forget for a moment that while European countries might be military allies, in the post-war world they would be America's economic competitors.

During the summer of 1917, the Trade Commission worked as rapidly as an undermanned staff allowed, digesting inadequate information provided for the most part by the steel companies themselves.[20] At the same time, Congressional pressure mounted for regulatory legislation, an outcome which *Iron Age* viewed as an unmitigated evil; it would be far better, the journal declared, if industry and government could meet halfway in devising inflation controls.[21] The War Industries Board, created in late July to replace the General Munitions Board, was not wholly happy with the industry's past conduct. But it too favored a flexible compromise devised outside the bounds of Congressional legislation, and it conferred with "some of the best informed men in the business" throughout early September.[22] In maneuvering for position prior to the final bargaining session, and in securing its public image as public protector, the WIB adopted a carrot-and-stick policy, alternating hints of a liberal price policy with threats of a federal takeover.[23] Such threats, when supplemented by the Pomerene Bill, would prove a significant factor in securing an agreement that month and sweetening the periodic negotiations that would follow. That factor raised the stakes for steel in a way which made the industry's leadership more susceptible to agreement and more eager to maintain the basic compromise. Furthermore, and even more importantly, such threats provided a useful smokescreen behind which businessmen in government and in industry would forge a compromise out of public view, and thus head off the kind of controls which not even the Administration really wanted.

ACCOMMODATION ACHIEVED

The FTC report which arrived on the President's desk on September 19 confirmed the prevalent suspicion that steel profits were indeed astronomical and offered a number of stratagems to curb such excesses. One possibility was making a uniform price on all products sufficiently high to maintain the production of

[19] U.S. Senate, Special Committee Investigating the Munitions Industry, *Minutes of the War Industries Board from August 1, 1917, to December 19, 1918*, Committee Print 4, 74 Cong., 1 Sess. (Washington, 1935), Meeting of Aug. 7, 1917.

[20] For a description of the Federal Trade Commission's general role in price-fixing, see the testimony of William B. Colver in House of Representatives, Select Committee on Expenditures in the War Department, *Expenditures in the War Department, Hearings* . . . , 66 Cong., 1–3 Sess. (Washington, 1919–1921), II, 2673–696.

[21] *Iron Age*, July 19, 1917; and see E. A. S. Clarke (president of Lackawanna Steel) to Baruch, August 10, 1917, W.I.B. Records, File 21A–A4, Box 1147.

[22] *Iron Age*, September 13, 1917.

[23] *Ibid.*, August 23, 1917, and W.I.B. Minutes, September 18, 1917.

even the least sufficient companies, with profits regulated through a discretionary tax system. This plan guaranteed simple administration and full production, but of course it meant outrageous profits for the efficient producers who accounted for roughly 80 percent of the gross tonnage. Any price high enough to sustain the small companies (who produced roughly 20 percent of the output) would, according to FTC estimates, yield Class I and II firms (fully or near-fully integrated) between 25 and 50 percent profit. The commission as a body seemed to favor as an alternative a pooling plan, whereby buyers bought at a uniform price but with profits adjusted to compensate for cost differentials. This course could certainly help restrain prices but it would involve enormous administrative problems and a far more extensive intrusion into the steel business. The FTC report also carried the radical suggestion that only if all existing contracts were renegotiated once new prices were established would the benefit of lower prices reach private buyers, many of whom were already under contract for months in advance. Enacting such a suggestion would literally have torn up the steel market and steel blanched at the prospect.[24]

The WIB was committed to setting a uniform price on all the ingredients involved in finished steel when it met with the sixty-four steel representatives on September 21, and it had resolved to take over the steel plants if necessary. There was a predictably stormy confrontation at this unprecedented attempt to regulate the steel market. Big steel resented the method and manner of federal intervention, and government officials boiled at this persistent challenge to their authority and wisdom. Despite the general emotional hostility, however, each side followed its natural instincts in a bargaining situation and set about to make some kind of deal.[25]

In the end, both government and industry claimed substantial success and appeared satisfied enough with the outcome. Prices did not fall as far as government reports claimed, but some reductions did occur. Conversely, while most operators considered the prices on the low side, Judge Gary described them as "fair and reasonable."[26] *Iron Age* was candid enough to admit that "While the

[24] "Report of the Federal Trade Commission Made Upon the Direction of the President of the United States, on the Costs of Iron Ore, Coke, Pig Iron, Steel, and Certain Steel Products, September 8, 1917," enclosed in William J. Harris to Woodrow Wilson, September 18, 1917, Wilson MSS, Series IV, Case File 4178. Commissioner John Franklin Fort disagreed with the pooling plan in an addendum to the F T C report. Although the FTC favored contract negotiation throughout the war, the WIB never pursued the matter. Undoubtedly, Constitutional proscriptions regarding the sanctity of contracts would have made such a policy, even in wartime, highly questionable. See FTC "Report;" *Iron Age*, October 4, 1917; and the *Annual Report of the Federal Trade Commission for 1917*.

[25] For an account of this meeting see Bernard Baruch, *The Public Years*, 66–68.

[26] Quoted in the *New York Times*, September 25, 1917. *Engineering and Mining Journal* suggested the prices settled upon were close to those quoted for several months whereas the WIB compared the savings with unrepresentative buyers. According to one observer, "The new schedule, while representing a radical reduction in current quotations was not low, even while making allowances for the higher costs of production under war conditions." Abraham Berglund, "Price Fixing in the Iron and Steel Industry," *Quarterly Journal of Economics*, XXXII (August 1918), 597–620, 612. *Iron Age* noted that the WIB statement put the former price of pig iron at $58 per ton when the recent level was $50 or less. It became $33 per ton under the WIB agreement. See *Iron Age*, September 27, 1917. See also *Hardware Age*, October 4, 1917, for a similar observation. The WIB reported the following reductions: coke, then selling at $16.00 per net ton, reduced to $6.00; pig iron from

new prices on plates, shapes and bars are lower than some of the steel conferees were prepared to accept . . . it is to be considered that they are not far from the average prices on contract shipments in the past six months, on which the profits of integrated companies as well as some that are but partly integrated have been quite satisfactory."[27] In subsequent months, *Iron Age* came to see how the September agreement could achieve industrial stability without federal control. As the willingness of the WIB to let the industry regulate itself became more apparent, the journal adopted the agreement as its own, defending it against criticism from both without and within the industry. The editorial page trumpeted the arrangement as "the beginning of a new era"[28] in business-government relations.

The industry appreciated the fact that the WIB had steered clear of every radical proposal. It had ignored the pooling and varied price concept; it had dismissed the idea of contract renegotiations; and it had not encouraged passage of the Pomerene Bill.[29] Indeed, one of the central goals of the September agreement was to prove these measures were really unnecessary.

The rhetoric which hinted darkly at government takeovers was worlds apart from the working relationship ultimately devised. Even after all the delays and hardships caused by the steel conflict, the government not only accepted an ethos of bargaining and compromise, but even went so far as to ask the industry to work out the bulk of the price structure on semi-finished goods and finished goods, subject of course to the WIB's final approval. After all the hostility and the gossip about nationalization, the actual denouement was not far from the kind of suggestion James Farrell had made the previous June. *Iron Age* became positively euphoric as the implications became clearer in subsequent months. The WIB was "taking a minor position in price fixing,"[30] it noted happily in November. The commodity committees of the AISI were in complete command. "The whole movement indicates that a broad spirit of confidence is reposed in the representatives of the steel makers."[31]

During October and November, the steel industry's pessimism about the Wilson Cabinet gave way to optimism about the future of business-government relations. Gary, in particular, after initial suspicion, began to see in the WIB a forum where businessmen might talk to each other without the company of meddlesome, obtuse politicians. At a meeting on December 10 to discuss the expiration of the September agreement, which was to terminate on January 1, 1918, Gary asked the board to use its influence to have all potential buyers consult the industry before they plunged into the market in hopes of eliminating competition among the government bureaus. He also emphasized the advantages of stable prices at this time and asked the board to extend the existing price structure for another period.[32] The FTC seconded this suggestion and the WIB forthwith sanctioned the agreement for three months until April 1, 1918.

$58.00 to $33.00 per gross ton; bars from $5.50 per hundred weight to $2.90; shapes from $6.00 to $3.00; and plates $11.00 to $3.25. Robert S. Lovett to Gary, September 25, 1917, in *W.I.B. Minutes*, September 28, 1917.

[27] *Iron Age*, September 27, 1917.

[28] *Ibid.*

[29] The specter of the Pomerene Bill remained to haunt the industry for some months, but it never did reach the statute books.

[30] *Iron Age*, November 1, 1917.

[31] *Ibid.*

[32] *W.I.B. Minutes*, December 10, 1917; "Conference of Steel Manufacturers and

Later in the war, *Iron Age* noted that the steel industry had been eager for a partnership with government for a long time but, "apparently the Government lacked the desire, while business felt it had good reason to doubt the ability of the Government to be a good partner. These difficulties have been removed."[33] The changing nature of Washington government and Washington officialdom fed Gary's growing enthusiasm for cooperation. Dollar-a-year men dominated the scene far more than had been the case in the early months so that industry was now free of Daniels, Baker, and other men it mistrusted. Moreover, the intense organizational fragmentation of the previous spring, while never wholly eliminated, was at least reduced as the WIB established itself more firmly in Washington. As the mobilization process gained strength and form, administrative lines stabilized and business-government relations moved from politics to administration, from public conflict to private negotiations. Businessmen both inside and outside government were obviously more comfortable in this environment and as a result a mood of good fellowship spread.

This trend reached its apogee with the formation of the Price Fixing Committee of the WIB set up in March, 1918 under the chairmanship of Robert S. Brookings, a retired lumber magnate. Brookings had long shared Judge Gary's belief in associationalism in industry, and as a member of the National Civic Federation in the progressive era he had espoused the ideology then fashionable among corporate hierarchies which stressed business-government cooperation and social stability.[34] Both men subscribed to the values of advanced corporate capitalism and easily reached agreement on all major points. To the end of the war, Brookings and Gary stood united in their commitment to long-term price stability and cooperative understandings as against short-run profits and competitive bargaining.

The way in which the two men handled the pressure for price hikes from small, independent steel producers is illustrative of their quest for stability. As early as December, high-cost firms had complained that they could not make a profit under the September price schedule and their discontent increased thereafter. Just two weeks before a meeting held to discuss the December extension, *Iron Age* observed a sharp difference between the small companies which favored

---

Members of War Industries Board . . . December 10, 1917," W.I.B. Records, File 21A–A1, Box 2; and Daniel Willard to Wilson, December 22, 1917, Wilson MSS.

[33] *Iron Age*, May 2, 1918.

[34] Hermann Hagedorn, *Brookings: A Biography* (New York, 1937), *passim*; James Weinstein, *The Corporate Ideal and the Liberal State* (Boston, 1968), ch. 8. The other members of the committee were: F. W. Taussig, Chairman of the Tariff Commission, a noted authority on the tariff and highly respected in the business community; William B. Colver of the FTC; Harry A. Garfield, president of Williams College and wartime Fuel Administrator; Hugh Frayne, labor representative on the WIB; Henry C. Stuart, former governor of Virginia, representing agricultural interests; and W. W. Phelps, a New York financier who served as secretary. In addition, at Secretary Daniels' request, Wilson had agreed that the Army and Navy should each have a representative on the committee. Commander John Hancock represented the Navy; Lieutenant Colonel Robert H. Montgomery sat in for the Army. Both service representatives took very little part in P.F.C. discussions; their main function was to insure that their own service's special contracts and arrangements were not jeopardized by PFC rulings. In addition, Bernard Baruch held *ex officio* status.

a general increase and the large producers who sought an extension of existing prices.[35] Brookings and Gary wanted to avoid bringing steel prices into the public arena once again, so they arranged to have the matter settled privately within the industry itself.

Gary volunteered to see to it that the less fortunate firms received their raw materials at reduced prices through some kind of pooling arrangement. Brookings made his contribution to the stratagem by ignoring this violation of the antitrust law. Brookings was pleased to have a short cut to stability, and he agreed with Gary that the whole arrangement ought to be kept from the public lest it be misconstrued. "You have saved us the necessity of consuming our gray matter," he told Gary, "of securing additional legislation for the handling of a problem by volunteering practically what is a pooling proposition."[36] September brought more complaints, this time from the pig and ore groups, and once again Brookings turned the issue over to the AISI. However, in this case the protesters were not so easily appeased and the Price Fixing Committee had to sanction a price increase in both pig iron and iron ore.[37]

Brookings and Gary devised a mutually protective arrangement that went far beyond the formal connection of regulator and regulated anticipated when Wilson originally established the committee. Brookings relied on Gary and the AISI to administer and enforce the agreements they worked out together.[38] Gary was obliged to define the WIB's committee to industry just as Brookings was compelled to justify steel prices to the rest of the Washington bureaucracy. Brookings moved from price-fixer to price apologist. He stood firmly with Gary and steel when the Railroad Administration tried to lower rail prices in the summer and fall of 1918; and he objected to the growing demand within government circles for the kind of pooling system and varied price arrangement which the FTC had outlined in September, 1917.[39] By the end of the war, Brookings had become a virtual peacemaker between steel and its critics. When government purchasing agents complained about extravagant steel profits, he called attention to increasing production costs, especially the advances in transportation and labor; he argued that under proposed excess profit taxes the industry would

[35] *Iron Age*, March 14, 1918.

[36] Senate, Special Committee Investigating the Munitions Industry, *Minutes of the Price Fixing Committee of the War Industries Board*. Committee Print No. 5, 74 Cong., 2 Sess. (Washington, 1936), Minutes of March 20, and 21, 1918 (hereafter cited as *P.F.C. Minutes*).

[37] *Iron Age*, September 11 and 26, 1918; *P.F.C. Minutes* September 19, 1918.

[38] John Kenneth Galbraith has suggested that governmental pricing is more successful in industries where some sort of pricing cooperation existed than in ones where competitive markets prevail. The case of steel during World War I would seem to support this hypothesis. Despite some breakdowns, the steel industry had for the most part followed U. S. Steel's pricing policy since 1903, and the basing-point system of "Pittsburgh-plus" had further assisted in informally stabilizing prices. The WIB and PFC had no difficulty establishing pricing mechanisms after the September, 1917, agreement, since the industry had already informally established such mechanisms. See Galbraith, *A Theory of Pricing Control* (Cambridge, 1952), and for "Pittsburgh-plus," Louis Marengo, "Basing Point Pricing in the Steel Industry" (Ph.D. dissertation, Harvard University, 1950).

[39] Brookings to John Skelton Williams (Director, Purchasing and Finance Division, United States Railroad Administration), August 23, 29, 30, 1918, W.I.B. Records, File 21A–A3, Box 34; and Brookings to the Price Fixing Committee, September 16, 1918, *ibid*, Box 38.

emerge with only a small proportion of its profits.[40] It should be noted in fairness to Brookings, however, that by the fall of 1918 even he had become skeptical about some of the claims made by the less integrated companies and began to demand that a balance sheet accompany cost complaints. Moreover, as the end of the war drew near, he also began to feel that in the future the integrated companies would use the exaggerated claims of small companies as an excuse for a general price advance.[41]

November 11 arrived before Brookings could test his intuition on this point or become involved in any controversy that might ultimately have disrupted the entente. With the Armistice, Brookings and Gary directed themselves to developing a strategy which would ease the steel industry into the post-war world. They pursued their quest for stability with even more zeal and urged the government departments to maintain their steel purchases at a high level.[42] By this time, however, the WIB was in the process of winding up its affairs and by the middle of December when steel and the Price Fixing Committee met for the last time, Brookings was no longer in a position to legitimize Gary's price schedule. Gary tried throughout December and well into the spring to revitalize the wartime entente with its federally-endorsed price scale, but without success.[43]

CONCLUSION

In retrospect, we can see that the relationship of steel and the government in wartime price-fixing was a developmental process whose course was shaped by a complex interplay of a variety of forces. Given the great economic power of big steel, one could reasonably predict that the industry would have a large voice in any arrangement ultimately settled upon, but there was nothing predictable about the precise nature and timing of the process as it evolved.

It is significant that the case of steel price-fixing contains elements of both

[40] Brookings to J. A. Campbell, October 16, 1918, W.I.B. Records, File 21A–A3, Box 163. The oft-professed belief by both industry and federal officials that excess profits would be recovered by a discretionary tax proved, in the end, unsound. Although the War Revenue Act of 1918 established rates as high as 70 percent, governmental inexperience with collection and chaos over accounting procedures failed to hold down profits to desirable levels. During the war years, U.S. Steel had after-tax profits of over a half-billion dollars, and averaged over 15 percent return on investment, well above the proposed limit of 12 percent. Bethlehem and the other companies did even better, averaging 24 percent return on investment after taxes. See Federal Trade Commission, *Report . . . on War-Time Profits and Costs of the Steel Industry* (Washington, 1925), *passim.*

[41] Brookings to W. M. Wells (of the FTC), October 28, 1918, W.I.B. Records, File 21B–A3, Box 163; and Brookings to John A. Topping, October 16, 1918, *ibid.*

[42] John A. Topping to Brookings, November 11, 1918; Brookings to Baruch, November 13, 1918, and to John A. Topping, November 15, 1918; and to Elbert Gary, November 15, 1918, all in *ibid.*

[43] "Minutes of Special Meeting with Committee Representing the American Iron and Steel Institute with Members of the War Industries Board for the Purpose of Discussing Means of Stabilizing the Industry During the Transition Period Following the Signing of the Armistice, November 13, 1918," enclosed in H. P. Ingels to Baruch, January 3, 1919, Baruch MSS, Series 2, vol. 14. Also see Robert F. Himmelberg," "Business, Antitrust Policy, and the Industrial Board of the Department of Commerce, 1919," *Business History Review,* XLII (Spring, 1968), 13–14.

conflict and cooperation and that one cannot be wholly understood without the other. The nature and the timing of the ultimate cooperative arrangement was a product in part of the conflict that preceded it. Similarly, the conflict that marked the early months becomes less important when one analyzes the actual working relationships that followed. There were many sources of conflict, but foremost among them were the legacies of peacetime hostilities, the clash of unsympathetic personalities, organizational and administrative fragmentation, and divergent conceptions as to the responsibilities of business corporations in a national crisis. Only as these factors sorted themselves out could anything like meaningful harmony be achieved.

In regard to the development of an accommodation between the industry and the government, one cannot underestimate the importance of the September agreement itself. It surprised the industry by its mildness after all the harsh words of the previous months, including an emotional presidential intervention. Gary could see that the price-fixing agreement offered a fine opportunity to shape the sympathetic entente with the federal government for which he had searched so long in the pre-war years. But he saw this only after the implications of the September 21st meeting became clearer, and only after he was faced with an array of inimical proposals ranging from nationalization to the Pomerene Bill.

Robert Brookings shared the central values of his big business colleague and encouraged him in the direction of an entente and long-range economic stability. This goal was not without its opponents, of course, and an essential feature of steel price-fixing under the Price Fixing Committee was the way in which Gary and Brookings united against small steel producers and government purchasers who wished to modify the steel schedule. The Price Fixing Committee provided public legitimacy for the price structure while the AISI and Gary took on the practical responsibilities for enforcement and administration.

The Administration consistently avoided the more radical recommendations on steel price fixing, although it made good use of them to push industry in the direction of a more moderate compromise. It must be remembered that the Administration simply did not possess the organization or the administrative capacity to handle a complicated price-fixing strategy or to take over the steel industry. Its own options, therefore, were severely limited. And yet it probably could have secured passage of the Pomerene Bill had it wanted to, and thereby obtained a source of clear legal power for steel price fixing. Wilson and his business advisors, however, shared an ideology which held that America could and should wage war without wholly sacrificing private for public power. They wanted to preserve the basic nature of the American capitalist system. While they expected to advise and coordinate private economic decision-making, they did not really wish to supplant it. They wanted to prove that America could respond to national crisis without a public bureaucracy and the subversion of private enterprise. They wanted to prove that the genius of America in crisis lay in a peculiar combination of private and public power united in search of the national interest. While they succeeded in avoiding a federal takeover, they also avoided coming to grips with the problem of defining the public welfare in times of grave, national crisis.

9

JOHN DEWEY: TOWARD DOMESTIC RECONSTRUCTION 1915–1920

Alan Cywar

John Dewey's impact on American philosophy and education was massive and his influence in other fields considerable. Though his social views can be characterized as typical of American Progressivism in that he attacked intellectual absolutes and called for the enlargement of the concept of freedom beyond the mere absence of external restraints, he went far beyond most Progressives in demanding a basic reconstruction of American life. During World War I Progressives were bitterly divided about the war and the kind of world they hoped to see emerge from the conflict. John Dewey was a genuine American radical, who rejected the moral rigidity of Wilson as he rejected the doctrinaire rigidity of Marx. By examining Dewey's social views during this period, Alan Cywar adds to our understanding of both John Dewey and the impact of World War I on American thought. It is an appropriate conclusion to this section on the first two decades of twentieth-century American history.

Alan Cywar recently completed his Ph.D. at the University of Rochester. This article is his first published work. It is part of his dissertation, a study of John Dewey's political and social thought.

American progressivism, as a movement vitally preoccupied with domestic reform, was not brought to a halt by the emotionalism aroused in the United States by the war in Europe in the years 1914–1916.[1] A considerable portion of its

[1] Richard Hofstadter, *The Age of Reform: From Bryan to F.D.R.* (New York, 1955), 3, 6, 270, 273; "The Child and the World," *Daedalus,* (XCI, 1962),

Source: *Journal of the History of Ideas,* Vol. 30, No. 3 (1969), pp. 385–400. Reprinted by permission of *Journal of the History of Ideas, Inc.,* Philadelphia, Pennsylvania.

forces refused to retreat before government propaganda and patriotic hysteria after the United States entered the conflict militarily in April, 1917.[2] Insofar as it was embodied in John Dewey, and in the substantial segment of American radicalism which he represented, constructive progressivism persisted through the war and into the twenties.[3] During the period of the war it did not arrive at a culmination, but suggested a program for reconstruction which has yet to be realized.[4]

World War I definitely affected Deweyan progressivism. The movement, however, was neither so weakened by confrontation with the conditions of the war, nor did it so ineffectually respond to them, as usually has been thought. For Dewey the battle in Europe served to clarify the character and immediacy of the social and moral crisis which the modern world faced. He perceived that the crisis was essentially the product of the interaction of two social deficiencies. One of them was the continued existence of the ancient problem of hierarchical class structure accompanied by maldistribution of wealth. The other was the modern failure of improvement in the methodology of social direction to keep pace with the development of the techniques of applied physical science. The principal consequence of the disproportionately slow evolution of social science, in relation to "natural" science, was the swollen inflammation of the discontent caused by inequalities among persons and among nations. He maintained that the necessary response to this social illness was the increase by men of ameliorative control over their human environment, in order that inequalities of wealth, status, and power finally could be redressed.[5] The remaining dilemma concerned

---

502–504. In *The Age of Reform* Hofstadter contends that the progressive movement at home was killed by the outbreak of World War I. He excludes "advanced speculation" from the material dealt with in the *Age . . .* , but "The Child and the World," treating Dewey's educational theory, is in part an effort to assimilate Dewey into Hofstadter's over-all view of the progressive movement. In any case, the materials I use here from Dewey frequently contain advanced ideas, but they by no means constitute speculation.

[2] David W. Noble, "The New Republic and the Idea of Progress, 1914–1920," *Mississippi Valley Historical Review* (XXXVIII, 1951), 398. Noble shows that in the face of the combination of propaganda and patriotism, editors Croly, Lippmann, and Weyl gave up their advocacy of domestic reform, turning all their attention and hope upon support for Wilson's pursuit of a new international order. In 1919, of course, they condemned Wilson.

[3] Lewis S. Feuer, "John Dewey and the Back to the People Movement in American Thought," *J.H.I.*, XX (1959), 545; Sidney Kaplan, "Social Engineers as Saviors: Effects of World War I on Some American Liberals," *J.H.I.*, XVII (1956), 369. Alfred Kazin, *On Native Grounds: An Interpretation of Modern American Prose Literature* (New York, 1942), 142. Feuer shows that Dewey was already a political radical in the nineties. Both Kaplan and Kazin, though highly critical of Dewey, regard him as a representative and leading figure, with a considerable following. Kaplan attests to the consistency of Dewey's thought during and after the war.

[4] Arthur S. Link, "What Happened to the Progressive Movement in the 1920's?" *American Historical Review* (LXIV, 1959), 840. Link contends that progressivism endured through the war and, in an attenuated form, into the twenties; but by 1920, having achieved its major goals prior to and during the war, it was in need of a new platform. However, the aims of Deweyan progressives were clearly not achieved by 1920.

[5] John Dewey, "The Need for Social Psychology," *Characters and Events*, Joseph Ratner, ed. (New York, 1929), II, 719. This was originally an address delivered

the degree to which democracy would have to be sacrificed to centrism in achieving the cure. Dewey arrived at a formula only after experiencing the impact of the War Industries Board and the Committee on Public Information.

In the course of the period 1915–1920, especially after the declaration of war with Germany, Dewey was concerned with both the international and the domestic aspects of the crisis. This paper will be confined to describing the development of his viewpoint in respect to some of the problems which confronted American society at home. The evolution of his domestic thought in this period divided itself into two parts. In 1915–1916 the devastations on the Continent convinced him of the necessity of grappling concretely with the outstanding troubles facing American society, and he produced an unprecedented deluge of relatively popular articles and speeches printed mainly in *The New Republic*, *The Dial*, and a number of educational journals.

In these years Dewey defined a technique of social reconstruction which, discarding a traditional primary reliance upon the efficacy of the voluntary association, stressed education, individual responsibility, and limited central organization on the level of the state governments. He did not believe that significant centralization of intelligence on the national plane, for the purpose of contriving answers to social problems, would be achieved for a long while to come. His attitude toward the unmitigated advantage of national centrism was ambivalent, though he knew that centralization was necessary if social control was to be attained. At best he expected that intermediate organization in the present, especially in the educational sphere, would prepare the populace to cope with more extensive centrist rationalization in the future.

While the battle in Europe occasioned intense thought, the prevailing prognosis of the rate of social change remained a leisurely one.[6] Once Congress had fulfilled Woodrow Wilson's request for a proclamation of overt belligerence, time became compressed. For Dewey and for American society 1917 was a transitional year; by 1918 the socio-economic structure had become transformed, and Dewey's intellectual position had to absorb the change. Following formal entrance into the war, social direction was centralized in government hands to a degree, and with a rapidity, hardly imaginable before the event took place. It was with reconstructing a community which owned highly advanced techniques of social control, which in turn required control, that Dewey was concerned in 1918–1920. In 1917 he was forced to abandon his stress on education, and to concern himself mainly with the consequences of warfare for government, industry, and labor. What remained continuous in his thought were his reformism and his increasing radicalism.

---

before the American Psychological Association, Dec. 28, 1916. A brilliant, more philosophically oriented treatment of the class problem and its relation to morals in an industrialized world was Dewey's pre-war "Intelligence and Morals," *The Influence of Darwin on Philosophy and Other Essays* (New York, 1910), 46–76.

[6] I devote considerable space to the 1915–1916 period, in part because the materials for it, while readily accessible, are less available than the later articles, most of which were collected by Joseph Ratner in *Characters and Events*. But also, it is necessary for educational progressivism to be accorded the importance it deserves as a central factor in the movement for reconstruction. Historians generally have failed to recognize its integral role in progressivism, though Alfred Kazin stressed it as early as 1942 (see note #3 above). A valuable account of the development of educational thought in the United States is Rush Welter, *Popular Education and Democratic Thought in America*, (1962).

Classical democratic theory, as it had been applied in the United States, relied upon the leadership of the voluntary association for the solution of public problems. From the movement which culminated in the anti-imperial revolution of 1776, and the agitation against slavery in the first half of the nineteenth century, to the advocacy of woman suffrage and the opposition to child labor, Americans had depended upon self-constituted, unofficial organizations to initiate reform. While the war would force Dewey to surrender his faith in the instrumental efficacy of the voluntary association, the democratic preference which stood behind that faith remained among the values most influential in conditioning his thought. He felt that a democratic socialism, a stress, in part, upon "the common mind, the common intention . . . ," was implicit in American national life.[7] Americans, he said,

> *proceed most easily and most effectively along lines of cooperation and voluntary effort; that it is possible for us to develop leadership in these things, and that upon the whole the people are fairly responsive—and responsiveness is a large element in responsibility—to leadership which depends upon using educational methods rather than upon the prestige and authority of official position.*[8]

The traditional, non-governmental voluntary organization (Women's Christian Temperance Union, American Association of University Professors, etc.) was an organization of private individuals who perceived in common a particular social deficiency and joined together to cope with it collectively. It worked to channel public opinion at large in support of desired reforms. When effective, by means of specialized investigations revealed in skillful publicity, it was able to initiate and guide relevant public action. According to the theory then prevalent, the voluntary association arose out of a classless society in response to a community need. The members of the organization might be thought to possess special skills, if not superior capacities and virtue, presumably derived from an egalitarian context.

With naive idealism, no theoretical provision for the repugnant idea of a vertical hierarchy of classes was made. If obedient to theory, the association, having arisen out of a classless community, and addressing itself to a public which was, therefore, incapable of comprehending the idea of class divisions, could neither work effectually to eliminate a hierarchical structure, nor identify itself as representing the viewpoint of a particular class. By 1915 Dewey realized the insufficiency of the voluntary association as a primary means for accomplishing reconstruction, and he undertook a search for more highly formal and regularized instrumentalities for social control. Regarded as the foremost tool for advancing national development, the voluntary organization was the vestige of an earlier, more sparsely populated unindustrialized, less complicated America. The technique which it embodied was incapable of solving, for a modern society with progressive goals, the problems highlighted by the horror in Europe.

If one deficiency of the reform methodology of voluntary association was its inability to come to terms with the extant social stratification, another was its frequent failure to operate satisfactorily in areas for which its perception was

[7] Dewey, "Organization in American Education," *Teachers College Record* (XVII, 1916), 134.

[8] *Ibid.*, 137.

adequate. However accurate might be its appraisal of a problem, and recommendation of action, an association lacked the executive power to compel the necessary public response. It was unable to insure that its work would count in positive social consequences, and often its efforts were to no avail. But worse, in many cases no association rose up to attempt to deal with a community ill. In these instances insufficient communal responsibility existed among the citizenry to bring forth volunteers. Dewey knew that where, for lack of strength or for selfishness, public opinion was ineffective, community affairs remained under the jurisdiction of established, private interests, whose aim was to perpetuate the *status quo*.[9] For this reason he was concerned to bring about official organizations of intelligence which would serve to implement comprehensive reconstruction. Dewey sought reform in all social spheres, but before American entrance into the war it was principally in the realm of primary and secondary education that he labored to have rationalization partially applied. Reconstructed education would be the leading factor in remaking the social order, through the youths whose minds were formed by it. It would also serve as a paradigm of the use of organized intelligence.

Dewey was convinced that the United States had arrived at a crucial stage in its development:

> *We are reaching—have reached—a turning point, a critical point; . . . whatever may have been said in the past in favor of letting things drift and grow along their own lines in their own way, we have now reached a point where we have to take more conscious and deliberate thought respecting these matters. . . .*[10]

Up until that time, American history had evolved of its own accord. The complexities and dangers of the twentieth-century world did not leave room for the risks involved in what had been, except for occasions of spasmodic reform, largely an involuntary social life. Subsequent development would have to be a matter of conscious intent. But as much as planning was needed, Dewey knew that it was necessary to reconcile any efforts to organize with a long tradition of localism. With the localist tradition he was far from unsympathetic:

> *These little school houses dotted all over our land represent the fact that the parents took the initiative; they did not wait for any government, any state government, much less national government to force an education upon them.*[11]

Further, the need to cultivate individual responsibility, and the objective fact of variant local conditions, made it necessary to allow for a substantial measure of indigenous initiative.[12] However, industrialism issued in problems much more intricate than those which the frontier had yielded. The advantages of organization and expertise were too great to disregard. In 1916 Dewey proposed the official organization of intelligence on the level of the state governments, for the

[9] *Ibid.*, 134.
[10] *Ibid.*, 135.
[11] John Dewey, "Federal Aid to Elementary Education," *Child Labor Bulletin* (VI, 1917), 62.
[12] Dewey, "American Association . . . ," 149–150.

service of municipal education.[13] Dewey did not leave unmentioned the possibility of a nationally-centered educational program, but he stressed state government as the most plausible locus for a centralized system:

> *I think we can develop, for example, in New York State, a department of education which shall command the most expert educational capacity that there is in the whole state, and which shall put it at the disposal of every community that wants it, and of every community that needs it, whether it wants it or not.*[14]

There was an undeniable commitment to official compulsion, though of a moderate degree, in the program he outlined. It was essential that reform be assured in those situations where it was most needed and least likely to be undertaken. On the other hand, Dewey was careful to point out that the reform technique which he proposed would not work through executive fiat, but would function through direct, interpersonal communication. There would be "a staff of individuals, advisory experts, actually going out into the communities and staying there . . ." until they had placed their skills and knowledge at the command of the community.[15] The experts would remain in a given municipality until they had persuaded the local authorities to employ modern methods, and until they had seen their advice transformed into practice. Because the advisors accomplished their task by means of personal contact, without using legal coercion, this approach "would supply a kind of expert service which is in line with our traditions."[16] Dewey did not confine his vision of the application of specialized knowledge to the educational sphere alone. He approved of a program for county agricultural experts, and called for the development of an extensive system in which social scientists from a central bureau would carry out a "continuous investigation of both local schools and industries, and who should influence public opinion, make suggestions, and institute experiments."[17]

While looking ahead to the application of specialized skill to all regions of community life, in this earlier period of the war Dewey's thought focused upon education. The purpose of education was to develop in the individual socialized responsibility. It was an industrial age in which innovations in communications and transportation had brought to the fore the interaction, rather than the separateness, of persons and groups. The main faults of the American character were its excessive bias toward individualism and its lack of a community ethic: "We are overstimulated in matters of personal success and enjoyment; we have little that teaches subordination to the public good or that secures effective capacity to work in its behalf."[18] The weakness to which Dewey referred was epitomized in the excessive riches gained by fortunate entrepreneurs during the Gilded Age, and in their excessive abuse of the wealth they had obtained. The trait continued to be reflected in economic and political practice and thought that

[13] Dewey, "State or City Control of Schools?" *The New Republic* (II, 1915), 179–180.
[14] Dewey, "Organization . . . ," 136.
[15] *Ibid.*
[16] *Ibid.*
[17] Dewey, "Industrial Education—A Wrong Kind," *The New Republic* (II, 1915), 71.
[18] Dewey, "Universal Service as Education," *Characters and Events,* II, 469.

stressed the private interest over the public. Dewey believed that this social and intellectual environment could be replaced by a radically improved one, through educating youth to an alternative understanding of the nature of society, and the role of the individual in it. He found the fundamental social unit to be not the "rugged" individual, but rather the individual in his social context.

When, by 1918, his educational thought had matured, he expressed his aim succinctly. It was necessary, he said, to build

> *an education which will develop that kind of individuality which is intelligently alive to the common life and sensitively loyal to its common maintenance. It is not an antithesis of social control and individual development which our education requires. We want that kind of education which will discover and form the kind of individual who is the intelligent carrier of a social democracy—social indeed, but still a democracy.*[19]

Dewey desired to socialize America by transforming the psychology of its populace. Because his aim was to improve democracy, and not to destroy it, he sought to make the individual responsible for the welfare of the community. His goal was not to subordinate the individual to the whole, but to cause him to recognize ethically his participation in it. In order to bring about beneficent social control, greater official organization and stronger government would be necessary. The greatest reliance for the creation and sustenance of the new society, though, would be placed upon a change which had been made to take place in the minds of men, when they were children.

If intellectual ideals were ideally transformable into social realities, the structure of American collective life could have been reconstituted within, say, twenty-five years. If most of the generation born in 1916 had been educated in the new values, and if, twenty years later, they had been able to persuade the skeptics and opponents among their elders to espouse the new vision of community, by 1941 life in the United States could have been reconstructed. But Dewey understood the tenacity with which obsolete habits, governing institutions and ideas, were conserved.[20] On this account, a chief preoccupation of Deweyan progressives was with the issue of industrial education. By means of affording a radical education for future laborers, they expected to confront directly what they regarded as one of the most important causes behind the maldistribution of wealth, power, and status which plagued the United States. They worked to correct the failure of workers to understand the character of contemporary society, and to recognize the role they could play in transforming it. Dewey justified his position by invoking the historical argument of the passing of the era of the frontier. "The schools," he maintained, "have now to make up to the disinherited masses by conscious instruction, by the development of personal power, skill, ability, and initiative, for the loss of external opportunities consequent on the passing of our pioneer days."[21] Because business interests favored the institution of trade training programs, the problem of the progressive was not primarily to advocate their introduction. His task was to insure that they were planned in order to serve

[19] "Education and Social Direction," *The Dial,* (LXIV, 1918), 334–335.

[20] *Human Nature and Conduct: An Introduction to Social Psychology* (New York, 1922), 108.

[21] "Nationalizing Education," *National Education Association* (1916), 187–188.

progressive ends, rather than to perpetuate and solidify socio-economic stratification.

Dewey declared at the National Education Association in 1916;

> *Opportunities can be equalized only as the schools make it their active serious business to enable all alike to become masters of their own industrial fate. That growing movement which is called industrial or vocational education now hangs in the scales.*[22]

The choice of the direction in which vocational education would develop was an aspect of the moral crisis with which Americans were immediately confronted. The organization of the new schools probably would turn out to be along the lines of one of two opposed patterns. If the schools were confined to providing the children of laborers with narrow trade training, they would "be ineffective for every industrial end except setting up a congested labor market in the skilled trades and a better grade of labor—at public expense—for employers to exploit. . . ."[23] To forestall such an outcome, which could work to make hierarchical social segregation permanent, Dewey urged that vocational education programs be so constituted that students would be unable to complete them before they were eighteen or twenty years old. Minimally, the extended scheme would serve to eliminate from the labor market exploitable children with less than high school educations. More importantly, the additional time in school could be employed to provide the students with knowledge that would enable them to be not only skilled workers, but capable and responsible citizens. They would be introduced to such social (moral) studies as history and civics, which would not serve, in the conventional way, to "emphasize duties to the established order and a blind patriotism which accounts it a great privilege to defend things in which the workers themselves have little or no share."[24] The social studies would stress, rather, the fact that the struggle between the rich and poor was the orthodoxy of all previous ages; the battle for fundamental human liberty had yet to be won, and it was the duty of the laborer to participate actively in the conflict.[25]

At stake was the American dream. The dissonant notes sounded by the industrial education issue echoed the deep discord which pervaded the entire nation. If the radical course was not chosen, Dewey warned,

> *power is likely to pass more and more into the hands of the wealthy, and we shall end with this same alliance between intellectual and artistic culture and economic power due to riches which has been the curse of every civilization in the past, and which our fathers in their democratic idealism thought this nation was to put an end to.*[26]

With hierarchical, imperial Germany before his eyes, as well as the numerous

[22] *Ibid.*, 187.
[23] "Splitting Up the School System," *The New Republic* (II, 1915), 284.
[24] "Education vs. Trade Training," *The New Republic* (II, 1915), 42. This was a communication in reply to a letter by David Snedden to the *New Republic*, criticizing Dewey's position.
[25] "Learning to Earn: The Place of Vocational Education in a Comprehensive Scheme of Public Education," *School and Society* (V, 1917), 333.
[26] "Nationalizing Education," 187.

examples tendered by world history, it was the development of a permanently ineradicable class structure that Dewey feared most. The majority of Americans lived in circumstances of poverty, indignity, subjection, and intellectual inertia. Stratification was hardening, and soon the possibility of democratic socialism would be obliterated. Dewey understood that industrial workers could act to increase their share in the social order only when their power became manifest, and they became aware of the strength which they possessed. Marx had predicted that violent proletarian revolution would result from an increased solidification of class lines and the intolerable worsening of the lot of the worker. Though he disagreed with Marx, Dewey did not believe a violent revolution in America incredible. He knew that when the injury done affected men's psychological welfare, even more than it touched their material circumstances, aggravated alienation might be transmuted into bloody warfare. He told educators, simply, that unless all schools, industrial and academic, taught the supremacy of the community interest over the private interest, "class and sectional ideas and feelings will become dominant, and our democracy will fall to pieces."[27] From the outbreak of the war in August 1914, until the armistice of November 1918, a predominant image in discussions of social reconstruction was the autocratic, but efficiently organized German state. Although Germany lost the war, it fought so effectively, against enormous odds, that Americans were forced to accept its internal arrangements as representative of a viable structural alternative. To Dewey's mind Germany stood for the extreme of systemization of community life. It was emblematic of the direction in which the United States needed to move, but not the goal which it sought to attain. American history afforded a spectacle in which the factor of chaotic growth was far more evident than that of thoughtful planning. This disproportion required correction, but in remedying it care had to be taken to avoid erecting a state that was either mechanical or autocratic. Dewey could conceive of no way of reconciling a social order so comprehensively organized as Germany's with provisions for individual liberty.[28] It appeared to him, prior to American military participation in the war, that the preponderant individualistic aspect of the national character would obstruct the attainment of a high degree of efficient organization well into the future:

> *I do not believe, at least for a long time to come, we can have a high degree of centralized authority in the way of educational bureaus in this country without their doing quite as many mischievous and harmful things as good ones. . . .*[29]

National centralization, rapidly attained, would bring in its wake the congenital inefficiency of bureaucracies.

As we have seen, Dewey looked to his education program, to central organization on the level of the state governments, for a solution to the problem posed by the opposition of individualism to centrism. Before 1917–1918 his emphasis was less upon the outward plan than upon a change educationally induced in the American social psychology. But experience with the external apparatus of local state centrism was expected to contribute also to the achievement of a "vigilant,

[27] *Ibid.*, 184.
[28] "Organization . . . ," 135.
[29] "Splitting Up . . . ," 284.

enlightened, cooperative spirit in the community,"[30] which in time would make national centralization safe and effective. Soon, however, Dewey's thought would decisively stress, instead of psychology, the objective implements of social power and direction. For Americans were not permitted the time in which to acquire gradually the skills which would enable them to use fruitfully, and not be overwhelmed by, an intricate and power-laden systemization of social machinery. Addressing the Child Labor Conference in the spring of 1917, Dewey told of the introduction, on the final day of the Congressional session just terminated, of a bill proposing federal aid to elementary education. As far as its economic provisions were concerned, the program was such a one as Dewey desired. Financial assistance would be made available only to communities and states which had initiated, of their own accord, acceptable schemes of educational improvement. The passage of the bill did not appear unlikely, for it had been preceded by laws instituting federal aid for agricultural education (Smith-Lever Act) and federal aid for industrial education (Smith-Hughes Act). Dewey observed, though, that the introduction of the bill probably had gone unnoticed by almost everyone, for the day was "so crowded with other things. . . ."[31] The bill to which Dewey referred was never enacted by Congress. The educational progressivism which reached its peak in 1916–1917, a civilized reply to the European catastrophe, was subordinated to American mobilization. While Dewey did not cease to be concerned with education, his perception of the drastic social changes wrought by mobilization forced him to center his attention now upon problems of macro-institutional structure on the national level.

Dewey explained, in December 1918, that there had already existed a high degree of industrial centralization before the declaration of war. Nothing more had happened than that the exigencies of war had necessitated "explicit governmental sanction" of this organized power. The recognition accorded it by the government had been essentially all that was requisite for the achievement of consolidated central direction. For the most part there had been no significant change in the managing personnel. "The economists and business men called to the industrial front accomplished more in a few months to demonstrate the practicable possibilities of governmental regulation of private business than professional Socialists had effected in a generation."[32] Although Dewey was far from uncritical of the war directorate, he found awesome both their accomplishment and the promise it might hold for the post-war future. The most important fruits of the organization which the war had engendered were the development of the custom of organizing physical and social scientists to serve community ends, and the establishment of the precedents of subordinating profit to production and private property rights to public needs. No matter what had been the intentions of the governors of the domestic war effort, and even if the arrangements they had articulated were substantially dissolved with the arrival of peace, its consequences were, on the whole, positive. "Peoples who have learned that billions are available for public needs when the occasion presses will not forget the lesson. . . ."[33] There had been abuses, but the populace had been shown that reconstruction was technically and financially feasible.

[30] "Organization. . . ," 141.
[31] "Federal Aid. . . ," 62.
[32] "The New Paternalism," *Characters and Events,* II, 517.
[33] "What Are We Fighting For?" *ibid.,* II, 552, 555, 557.

If the huge governmental apparatus was not retained after the war, Dewey knew, it would be revived at a later date to deal with some other crisis. A decision had to be made respecting the manner and purpose according to which the administrative structure would be organized and operated. In June 1918 Dewey believed that the trend of events was in the direction of what he designated as "state capitalism." State capitalism, as he defined it, involved the nationalization of the mechanisms of production and distribution and the substitution of a bureaucracy of government officials for the corporate managers.[34] As Dewey later realized, the corporate directorate had not been supplanted by an official bureaucracy, but was itself absorbed into the government.[35] This latter process better deserved the name of "state capitalism" than did the former, which has come to be regarded as typical of socialism. Whatever their labels, Dewey approved of neither of these techniques of state organization, for both encouraged the excessive aggrandizement of the central authority. The intense consolidation of authority at a central point, whether by capitalists or by conventional socialists, denied recognition to what, in his view, was the principal requirement of the democratic society. Deweyan progressives were convinced that a widespread distribution of power and responsibility was necessary in a valid social democracy. They understood the need for an efficient central administration, but they desired to have the bulk of executive authority diffused from it to numerous local centers. To accomplish this end, they sought to have the controlling voice in industry (for most decisions) become that of the laborers in each plant.

Dewey saw that it would not be possible immediately to achieve decentralization and industrial democracy, either after the war, given the retention of the wartime structure, or on the occasion of a later revival. He prescribed a transitional arrangement to afford an intermediate step between the wartime agencies and the reconstructed state. This organization would not

> *involve absolute state ownership and absolute state control, but rather a kind of conjoined supervision and regulation, with supervisors and arbiters, as it were, to look after the public interests, the interests of the consumer, the interests of the population as a whole, others to represent those who have their capital immediately invested, and others to represent those who have their lives (in the form of work) immediately invested.*[36]

According to this plan, the representatives of the society as a whole, who would look after the interests of consumers and of the government, would also serve as mediators between capital and labor. Presumably the representatives of the stockholders would be the corporate managers, except in those cases where the functions of ownership and management remained combined. Most importantly, representatives of labor would have equal standing with the managerial-capitalist establishment. Dewey did not want to eliminate as a class those who operated the industrial plant. He greatly admired, and recognized the necessity of effectively employing, the skills possessed by the members of the technocracy. One crucial question for the American future was whether the skills of the mem-

[34] "The New Paternalism," 517; "What Are We Fighting For?" 558.
[35] *Ibid.*, II, 517.
[36] "Internal Social Reorganization after the War," *ibid.*, II, 758.

bership of the technocracy would be (as they had been in the past) "chiefly used in secret and irresponsible ways for personal power and advantage, or whether they are gradually sublimated by being put to public use in behalf of a public interest."[37] The corporate experts were almost indispensable to that aspect of reconstruction which would consist in the organization of intelligence to contribute to rational direction of community affairs. In order for them to become useful servants of society, the industrial managers would have to apprehend an ethics which assigned primacy to the community interest, rather than to that of the individual corporation.

As Dewey understood the brief history of the War Industries Board and its compatriot agencies, rapid wartime centralization had proved possible because a high degree of organization had been already achieved by businessmen. The assertion of explicit governmental control in only three critical areas had been sufficient to insure "public" management of the entire productive process. By administering transportation, the distribution of credit, and the labor market (by means of conscription), proficient businessmen were able to make the American economy subordinate private goals to public interest, insofar as that interest was defined in terms of the war effort. Beyond the achievement of the public direction of industry, if the war had lasted longer, "with sufficient experience to make methods of taxation scientific enough to control profiteering, the simplicity of some form of state capitalism (generally called state socialism) would have been demonstrated."[38] The cessation of fighting prevented the attainment of even "state capitalism," though, except as a temporary intermediate stage, this form of central control deviated far from Dewey's description of the way in which the American productive apparatus should be structured.

He would have continued a high degree of central direction only until the "transfer of power from the more or less rapacious groups now in control had been securely effected." Once the more noxious elements among the industrial élite had been displaced, and the remainder had been persuaded to place their skills at the service of their community, the government would surrender its ruling authority in all areas except, perhaps, such special ones as railways and fuel production. The outcome would be "a federation of self-governing industries . . . ," towards which the government would act "as adjuster and arbiter. . . ." By a self-directed industry, Dewey meant one from which the investors had been purged and in which ultimate managerial authority rested with the workers themselves. The significance of industrial federalism and worker control would be the "socialization of the services of the land. . . ."[39]

Dewey's demand for industrial federalism stemmed from prior intellectual commitments, and from the impact upon him of wartime centralization. While he long had desired to attain a condition of less chaos and more coherence in American society, he also had sought to conserve its characteristic plurality. If loyal to its more valuable traditions, a unified American community would be one "where the unity does not destroy the many, but maintains each constituent factor in full vigor."[40] Yet Dewey wrote, in respect to the psychological effect

[37] "The League of Nations and the New Diplomacy," *ibid.*, II, 609.
[38] "The New Paternalism," 517.
[39] "What Are We Fighting For?" 559.
[40] "America in the World," *ibid.*, II, 643.

of the war, that "men felt dwarfed, shrivelled in the face of the vastness of economic and political conditions."[41] He perceived the threat which the great assumption of power by the central government posed to individuality. The individual, instead of dealing morally with his environment, was left debilitated by it, lacking the strength of will and the desire to assume social responsibility. The success of the Committee on Public Information exemplified what a central authority, aided by powers of censorship and coercion, could do to fix political attitudes and stimulate patriotic hysteria, instead of fostering an informed and critical political consciousness. Solidarity achieved at the expense of freedom of thought and of individual dissent was grossly inefficient, for it denied useful employment to the intellectual resources of the nation.[42] When the armistice came, Dewey noticed that the voices which were most raised in favor of dissolution of national paternalism in finance, manufacturing, and transportation[43] were the same ones which urged its continuation in the area of news:

> *Heresy is proverbially a contagious disease. To learn anything about the Bolsheviki except their excesses would corrupt an otherwise staid and respectable America.*[44]

Dewey's opposition to excessive centralization and his hatred of the abuse of power, especially in respect to the government's "solicitude to safeguard against private initiative in belief . . . ,"[45] led him to espouse the cause of labor more stridently than ever before.

In the course of the war Dewey's thought regarding labor became increasingly radical. In 1916 he described in general terms those occasions when an extralegal strike was socially justified. Such a strike was legitimate, he argued, when it would serve to obtain socially beneficial ends which could not be attained by working within the established economic and legal forms.[46] Most significant about his formula was its elevation of the workingman, as an actively influential intellectual and political agent, to equal status with other citizens. It assigned to him responsibility for distinguishing goals which were valuable to the society as a whole from goals which were as selfish as those sought by his employer; and ethically it required him to seek ends of communal worth. The industrial education program advocated by Dewey was intended to develop in members of the working class this same character trait of social responsibility wedded to the capacity to understand social problems. With the onset of American belligerence, and its repressive domestic consequences, he was concerned increasingly with the acquisition by laborers of social power. Only in a much lesser degree did his earlier discussions focus upon the issue of power, and during the years 1918–1920 Dewey never divorced his emphasis on strength from his insistence that it had

[41] "The New Paternalism," 517.

[42] "Conscription of Thought," *Characters and Events*, II, 569; "The Discrediting of Idealism," 634; "What America Will Fight For," 563.

[43] Robert F. Himmelberg, "The War Industries Board and the Anti-trust Question in November, 1918," *Journal of American History* (LII, 1965), 59–74. Himmelberg shows that a considerable number of businessmen desired to have the authority of the WIB continue in effect well after the fighting ceased. Their motives were far from selfless, for they sought to have the WIB support prices and act to bring about the debilitation of anti-trust legislation.

[44] "The New Paternalism," 521.

[45] *Ibid.*, 521.

[46] "Force and Coercion," *ibid.*, II, 785.

to be accompanied by social responsibility. But he contended that the self-conscious possession of power was a necessary prerequisite to social action. When laborers realized that they were the most important factor in the productive process, then they would be able to demand to control it.

The patriotic consensus imposed by the government, right after the declaration of war, served to stifle the labor movement. In 1918 Dewey observed pessimistically that at present there was insufficient labor organization in the country to overcome the power of organized capital and management. He pointed out that labor's "centralization is hampered by a fixed habit of thinking and acting in terms of immediate wages and hours of labor instead of in terms of control of economic conditions."[47] On the other hand, to labor's benefit, Dewey made the shrewd and accurate point that, in the contest of organization, labor leaders suffered the disadvantage of working with complex human materials, while capital operated in the mechanical terms of finance. The recognition of this fact did not relieve Dewey's anxiety; and his forecast for the post-war period, given the continuation of present tendencies, was dismal:

> *Our constitution will presumably be again in force after the war. To see the property-less man in the saddle under such conditions requires a peculiarly exuberant imagination.*[48]

Deweyan progressives held that the United States had been founded, and had continued to exist, in accord with a Lockean world-view, which made property rights the prerequisite of social influence, while assuming that they were necessarily the possessions of the few. A plenitude of inexpensive land combined with a shortage of labor had served for a time to soften the necessarily inequitable consequences of the theory. However, the social extremes provoked by industrialization, coupled with rapid demographic increase through reproduction and immigration, confirmed the theory and revealed its full meaning. Growing numbers came to be without substantial property in any form, and therefore, under the Lockean assumptions, without political significance. For reconstruction to be accomplished in America, the Lockean viewpoint had to be abandoned for a more communally efficient and humane understanding of socio-economy.

From 1919 to 1920, while participating in the rising radicalism and enduring the reaction to it, Dewey articulated a clearly anti-Lockean view of the future of labor. Writing in criticism of the position expounded by Herbert Hoover, he noted that Hoover, a liberal, had conceded that the present socio-economic arrangement was unjust and the source of the current proletarian disturbances. Hoover believed that the only solution was a fairer distribution of wealth. Beyond an egalitarian adjustment in the allotment of material products, however, he saw no possibility of maintaining an industrial system without the extant capital-labor, management-worker hierarchy. Dewey was unable to accept Hoover's opinion. He maintained, instead, that redistribution of wealth, unaccompanied by other reform, would be at best a first step. If not followed by further and more fundamental amelioration, class hostility and conflict would increase.[49] The essence of the problem, he pointed out, was that

> *it is a mischievous mistake to suppose that wage earners are differently*

[47] "The New Social Science," *ibid.*, II, 734.
[48] *Ibid.*, 734.
[49] "Freedom of Thought and Work," *ibid.*, II, 522.

> *made. Not idealism but human psychology proclaims the fact that man does not live by wages alone. What men need is an outlet for what is human in them.*[50]

Because effective influence and responsibility were values to which American culture and western civilization accorded the highest esteem, economic peace would not be achieved until the laborer became the ultimate governor of the productive machinery which he presently served. Until the wage-earner exercised a directive influence upon the society in which he lived, until democracy was more fully realized, he would exhibit no durable commitment to the community in which he subsisted, but did not share.

Dubious about the possibility of the central government's taking the initiative to elevate the worker to full citizenship, Dewey looked for the "democratization of industry from within. . . ."[51] It could be achieved because the war had clarified the workers' "strategic position in modern social organization. . . ."[52] The fear exhibited by conservative groups in the course of their reaction attested to their new awareness of the importance and power of labor, and belied the idea that revolution would proceed out of the deepest misery of a proletariat intolerably oppressed. The possession of self-conscious strength was necessary if workers were to obtain for themselves their rightful position in the economy and the society; "the war gave labor precisely this accession of strength."[53]

During the period 1915–1920, excepting a brief lapse in 1917 following the declaration of war, Deweyan progressivism, as exemplified in the writings of Dewey himself, consistently pursued domestic reconstruction. Prior to April 1917, and after turning away from the traditional reform technique of the voluntary association, Dewey emphasized education as the means of remaking society, and in ensuing years he never lost sight of its importance. From 1918 to 1920, as the United States suffered from governmentally organized persuasion and coercion, his thought became more radical and more political. He perceived the utility of a strong central government as an instrumentality for the accomplishment of reconstruction, yet saw that it had to be offset and reduced by a diffusion of power to local centers. By enjoining the task of assuming decentralized power in industry upon organized labor, Dewey sought at once to strike a telling blow against hierarchical class structure, while ensuring the limitation of the central authority. Industrial democracy, in fact, involved the translation of the obsolescent concept of voluntary association into workers' unions which would become institutionalized within the industrial structure itself. Thus, Dewey gathered together the values of democracy, socialism, and conscious organization.

John Dewey has long been recognized as one of the intellectual leaders of the progressive movement. The character and content of his response to World War I, frequently viewed as the moment of truth for progressivism, reveal a tenacity and radicalism in the American mind of that era for which a careful examination of most of the relevant historical literature would leave the student unprepared. A broad reappraisal of the quality and nature of the mainstream of American thought in this critical period is clearly demanded.

[50] *Ibid.,* 523.
[51] "What Are We Fighting For?" 559.
[52] "The New Social Science," 734.
[53] "How Reaction Helps," *Characters and Events,* II, 819.

SHEBAS AND SHIEKS
1929 STOCK MARKET CRASH
NRA
WE DO OUR PART
ROW, ROW, ROW, WITH ROOSEVELT
The GREAT GATSBY
BY F. SCOTT FITZGERALD
HOLLYWOOD

PART TWO

1920-1940

The two decades following World War I present a study in contrasts: of prosperity and depression, of reaction and reform, of isolation and global involvement. As the following essays will indicate, the 1920's, too often depicted as simply an abnormal attempt to return to a pre-1900 normalcy, were in reality part of an historical continuum that links the Progressive era with the New Deal. There were continuing efforts to reshape old patterns to meet the exigencies of American life, and in some instances these efforts met with success. This colorful and exciting decade was also a difficult and confusing time for millions of Americans who thought they yearned for a lost simplicity but nevertheless had to live in a business civilization that necessitated a more highly organized social order than had previously prevailed. By 1930, it was evident to most Americans that more than the stock market had failed in October 1929.

Whereas in the 1920's big business, at times assisted by the government, created many of the patterns and standards prevailing in American life, in the 1930's the federal government set the guidelines and played a more direct role in numerous aspects of American life. Yet big government did not directly interfere with either production or the accumulation of profits. In fact, in the interest of recovery, it encouraged both. This period of two decades shows a further decline in the significance of rural life, while organized labor, at a nadir in the 1920's, became a powerful force in the 1930's.

Disillusioned with Wilsonian efforts at remaking the world, most Americans wanted their government to withdraw from meaningful and active participation in world affairs. Overseas events still, however, intruded upon the ever-evolving currents of human affairs in the United States. Until 1940 they did not predominate, but they presented challenges throughout the 1930's to the prevailing and pervasive isolationist sentiment.

These two decades, like the first two of the twentieth century, each in its separate way, sought but failed to reconcile the challenging and competing demands of security and freedom within the context of an urbanized and industrialized nation. The thirteen essays in this section illustrate some of the basic issues of concern. Six of the essays focus on the 1920's, six examine aspects of American life in the 1930's, while one reviews American isolation from the perspective of military policy for the first four decades of the twentieth century, with an emphasis on the New Deal period.

The essays that deal with the 1920's generally stress the continuation of Progressive themes in a period of reaction at the national level. It is a decade in which for the first time women everywhere had the vote. These newly enfranchised women exerted greater influence in keeping alive the Progressive tradition than they have generally been given credit for by historians of the period. J. Stanley Lemons provides a specific example in relating the passage of the Sheppard-Towner Act to the successful lobbying efforts of women over strong opposition, and Anne Firor Scott presents a picture of women organizing and working within the political system in the South.

The farmer, a minority figure in American society by 1920, became in this decade more integrated within the mechanization of a society dominated by big business, as Reynold Wik's article on Henry Ford's tractors points out. Another persistent minority issue that the Progressives had failed to deal with was that of the American black. David Tucker, in examining a basic theme of the 1920's—business history, but from the viewpoint of the black businessman—provides a much needed insight into an often neglected or misinterpreted area of entrepreneurial history.

In contrast to these hopeful signs of continuing Progressive thought and action, at the same time the 1920's made a mockery out of American idealism by racially and ethnically biased immigration laws and, most dramatically, by the resurgence of the Ku Klux Klan movement. Charles Alexander analyzes the impact of this organization on Texas politics, viewing it in an urban as well as a rural setting. A final appraisal of the American dream as the decade comes to a close with the general economic collapse is given by Arthur Ekirch, Jr., in "The Crisis in the American Dream."

New hope for the realization of that dream was given with the coming of the New Deal in 1933. Even more determinedly than before, America turned its back on the rest of the world while it wrestled with the problems of depression, labor organization, and regional and racial diversity in the early years of the Roosevelt administration. J. Chal Vinson, in his examination of the Johnson Act of 1934, emphasizes this overall isolationist sentiment, while Fred Greene delineates it from the military point of view.

A struggle for power between the executive and judiciary branches is illuminated by William Leuchtenburg's careful study of the Humphrey's Executor case. The impact of the New Deal on an entire region and the reaction of the intellectual spokesmen of that region to its effect is examined by Edward Shapiro in "The Southern Agrarians and the Tennessee Valley Authority.

Critics of the New Deal charged the federal government with direct interference into every aspect of American life, but in spite of rather sweeping labor legislation and some official encouragement given to blacks for racial advancement, Donald Sofchalk's article on "The Chicago Memorial Day Incident" and Lawrence Wittner's on "The National Negro Congress" give needed emphasis to a lesson that both labor and the blacks had to learn from bitter experience, that even in these years of reform, it was necessary for the exploited to take direct action themselves to ameliorate their social and economic conditions.

Finally, we close this section with James Patterson's study of the impact of the New Deal on state governments, and the equally important impact of state governments on the New Deal. Historians have only recently begun to examine this question. Washington might propose and attempt to administer reform legislation, but the execution of policy had to occur on the state level. American federalism was—and still is—a very real fact of our political and social life.

10

THE SHEPPARD-TOWNER ACT: PROGRESSIVISM IN THE 1920s

J. Stanley Lemons

This essay, by emphasizing the persistence of Progressivism in the 1920's, illustrates a changing interpretation of that decade by recent scholars stressing the continuity of themes in the first half of the twentieth century. It is also significant to note that the legislation discussed by Professor Lemons was introduced by legislators representing rural America, where throughout the 1920's Progressivism continued to find strength in Congress among spokesmen for the "farm bloc." This bill, concerned with the welfare of women and children, had been an issue of primary interest to urban Progressives during the previous period, but it now had powerful allies in the rural areas and among newly enfranchised women. This essay points up the necessity of examining both continuities and differences in historical periods. By stressing differences alone, historians have tended to overemphasize the uniqueness of the 1920's, missing the significance of this decade as a link between Progressivism and the New Deal.

J. Stanley Lemons teaches American social and intellectual history at Rhode Island College and has published several articles.

The first venture of the federal government into social security legislation—the Sheppard-Towner maternity and infancy protection act of 1921—has been generally ignored in discussions about the persistence of progressivism in the 1920s.[1]

[1] General treatments of the 1920s fail to mention the Sheppard-Towner Act: Eric Goldman, *Rendezvous with Destiny: A History of Modern American Reform* (New York, 1952); John D. Hicks, *Republican Ascendancy, 1921–1933* (New York, 1960); William E. Leuchtenburg, *The Perils of Prosperity, 1914–1932* (Chicago, 1958); Arthur M. Schlesinger, Jr., *The Crisis of the Old Order: 1919–1933* (Boston, 1957); Richard Hofstadter, *Age of Reform: From Bryan to F.D.R.* (New

Source: *Journal of American History,* Vol. 55, No. 4 (March 1969), pp. 776–786. Reprinted by permission of the author and the Organization of American Historians.

The maternity bill was a link in a chain of ideas and actions from Roosevelt to Roosevelt, which began with the White House Conference on Child Welfare Standards in 1909 and ended with the Social Security Act of 1935. In addition, the Sheppard-Towner Act was the first major dividend of the full enfranchisement of women. Women's organizations helped to force the enactment of the bill and later fought to preserve it from repeal. Although passed in the first year of the Harding administration, it was a product of the progressive movement.

The United States Children's Bureau developed from the White House Conference in 1909, and the Bureau's first major investigations were into the causes of infant and maternal mortality. The studies revealed that the nation had unusually high rates. For example, in 1918 it ranked seventeenth in maternal and eleventh in infant mortality. The Bureau found a correlation between poverty and the mortality rate. For families earning less than $450 annually, one baby in six died within the first year; for the income range of $650–$850 annually, the rate was one in ten; and for those earning about $1,250 annually, the rate was one in sixteen. Even the latter rate compared unfavorably to the average of a nation like New Zealand, which had a thorough program of care and an infant death rate of one in twenty-one. The studies found that 80 percent of America's expectant mothers received no advice or trained care.[2] To remedy this situation, Jeannette Rankin, who was the first woman to serve in Congress, introduced in 1918 a measure which was to provide public protection of maternity and infancy. It had been sponsored by Julia Lathrop, chief of the Children's Bureau. Democratic Senator Morris Sheppard of Texas and Republican Congressman Horace Towner of Iowa reintroduced the bill in the Sixty-sixth Congress. Little progress was made toward its passage until the full enfranchisement of women in 1920.

The National League of Women Voters, the direct offspring of the leading woman suffrage association, urged the national parties to approve of the maternity bill in their 1920 platforms. The Democratic, Socialist, Prohibition, and Farmer-Labor parties endorsed the proposal; the Republican platform ignored it, but Warren G. Harding came out squarely for it in his Social Justice Day speech on October 1, 1920.

Harding called a special session to begin the Sixty-seventh Congress, but reformers feared that the Sheppard-Towner bill might be ignored in the press to deal with tariff and budget matters. They urged the President to single out the bill for passage in his message to Congress, but Harding responded with a one-sentence endorsement: "I assume the maternity bill, already strongly approved, will be enacted promptly, thus adding to our manifestation of human interest."[3]

York, 1955). More specialized studies have almost neglected the measure: Clarke A. Chambers, *Seedtime of Reform: American Social Service and Social Action, 1918–1933* (Minneapolis, 1963); Roy Lubove, *The Struggle for Social Security in America, 1900–1935* (Cambridge, 1968). The most extensive treatment is in James G. Burrow, *AMA: Voice of American Medicine* (Baltimore, 1963), 161–64.

[2] *Senate Report*, 66 Cong., 2 Sess., No. 650, pp. 7–8; *Reports of the Dept. of Labor, 1918, Report of the Secretary of Labor and Reports of the Bureaus* (Washington, 1919), 183–88; *Reports of the Dept. of Labor, 1920, Report of the Secretary of Labor and Reports of the Bureaus* (Washington, 1921), 177–79; Sylvia Hardy, "The Children's Year," *Life and Labor*, VIII (July 1918), 139–40; Mary Sumner Boyd, "Let's Stop, Now, the Casualties of Motherhood," *Good Housekeeping*, LXXI (Dec. 1920), 43.

[3] Women's Committee on Sheppard-Towner Bill to Warren G. Harding, March

Sheppard and Towner resubmitted the bill in April; it passed the Senate on July 22, 1921, by a vote of 63 to 7. But the measure seemed destined to perish in the House Committee on Interstate and Foreign Commerce, whose chairman, Samuel Winslow, was an ardent anti-suffragist. For months he refused even to hold hearings; and only after women who were influential in the Republican party, such as Harriet Taylor Upton, vice-chairman of the Republican National Committee, warned Harding that the delay was alienating women did the President prod Winslow into action.[4] Harding's endorsement of this bill was important because many members of Congress not only opposed this "new fad appropriation" but also feared the unknown power of the women's vote. And members evaded the protests of the aroused medical profession by saying: "I am an organization republican and await instructions."[5] When the House finally voted, the bill passed easily 279 to 39. Ironically, the only woman member in Congress, the anti-suffragist Alice Robertson, voted against it. Harding signed the measure on November 23, 1921.

A principal force moving Congress was fear of being punished at the polls. The women's vote was an unknown quantity at the time. For years, the suffragists had promised to clean house when they got the vote, and they claimed that women would be issue oriented rather than party oriented. Politicians feared that women voters would cast a bloc vote or remain aloof from the regular parties. The leaders of the major women's organizations hoped to mobilize the female vote for reform. Passage of the maternity bill was the first goal of the newly enfranchised women, and it took precedence over all other efforts. In 1920, the League of Women Voters helped to create the Women's Joint Congressional Committee (WJCC), which coordinated lobbying activities in Washington for nearly two dozen national women's organizations and claimed to speak for 20,000,000 members. The WJCC lobbied vigorously, while the constituent organizations drummed up grass roots support and deluged Congress with a torrent of letters, telegrams, and personal delegations. If a woman read any of the mass circulation women's magazines—*Good Housekeeping, Pictorial Review, McCall's, Woman's Home Companion,* or *Delineator*—she was exposed to many articles which favored the Sheppard-Towner bill.

Florence Kelley, executive secretary of the National Consumers' League, chaired the subcommittee of the WJCC which worked for the enactment of the measure. She later said: "Of all the activities in which I have shared during more than forty years of striving, none is, I am convinced, of such fundamental importance as the Sheppard-Towner Act."[6] Testifying before Congress, she suggested that if Congress refused to pass the bill it would, like King Herod, con-

---

5, 1921, Box 157, folder 117–1; Address to Congress, April 13, 1921, Box 773, folder 1921, Warren G. Harding Papers (Ohio Historical Society, Columbus, Ohio).

[4] Harriet Taylor Upton to George B. Christian, May 31, 1921; Upton to Harding, June 18, 1821; Upton to Harding, July 30, 1921; Harlean James to Harding, May 17, 1921; James to Christian, May 30, 1921, Box 157, folder 117–1, *ibid.*

[5] "The Senate Discusses the 'Maternity Bill,'" *Capital Eye*, I (Oct. 1921), 4; "News Notes of the Fortnight," *Woman Citizen*, VI (July 30, 1921), 6; Clipping from *Ilinois Medical Journal* (Sept. 1921), enclosed in E. Forrest Herdien, M.D., to Harding, Sept. 9, 1921, Box 157, folder 117–1, Harding Papers.

[6] Quoted in Josephine Goldmark, *Impatient Crusader: Florence Kelley's Life Story* (Urbana, 1953), 93.

demn infants to death. "What answer can be given to the women in a myriad of organizations, who are marveling and asking, 'Why does Congress wish women and children to die?"[7] Pressing for passage of the bill, her subcommittee interviewed congressmen at the rate of fifty per day. The result was a handsome margin and full credit from friends and foes alike. The *Journal of the American Medical Association,* which had strongly opposed the bill, stated that the lobby for the measure was "one of the strongest lobbies that has ever been seen in Washington." Congressmen reported that they were told that if they voted against the measure every woman in their district would vote against them in the next election. "Members of Congress of years' experience say that the lobby in favor of the bill was the most powerful and persistent that had ever invaded Washington."[8] Senator William S. Kenyon, a supporter of the bill, confirmed the effectiveness of the lobby: "If the members could have voted on that measure secretly in their cloak rooms it would have been killed as emphatically as it was finally passed in the open under the pressure of the Joint Congressional Committee of Women."[9]

Although the Children's Bureau had revealed high maternal and infant death rates and despite the modest character of the Sheppard-Towner bill, the measure was assailed as a threat to the very institutions of the nation. Because suffragists favored the bill, anti-suffragists opposed it. Extreme conservatives condemned the plan as part of a Bolshevist conspiracy against America. States rights advocates alleged that it threatened the integrity of the states. Finally, the bill was caught in the cross fire between the American Medical Association and a collection of quack medical cultists. Sheppard-Towner was one of the first pieces of federal legislation to catch the brunt of the AMA's new fear of state medicine. The arguments advanced by the opponents at the time of the original debate and passage of the measure were repeated when the proposal came up for renewal in 1926 and in 1929.

The principal advocates of the theory that the Sheppard-Towner bill was a communist invention were the National Association Opposed to Woman Suffrage and its legacy, the Woman Patriots. For years, they had maintained that feminism and woman suffrage were the same as socialism and communism. Mary Kilbreth, a leading anti-suffragist, wrote Harding a six-page letter which condemned his signing of the bill. "It is not brought forward by the combined wisdom of all Americans, but by the propaganda of a self-interested bureau associated with the Feminist Bloc." "There are many loyal American men and women," she warned, "who believe that this bill, inspired by foreign experiments in Communism, and backed by the radical forces in this country, strikes at the heart of our American civilization. . . ."[10] The Woman's Municipal League of

[7] House, *Public Protection of Maternity and Infancy,* Hearings on H. R. 10925 before the Committee on Interstate and Foreign Commerce, 66 Cong., 3 Sess. (Dec. 20–29, 1920), 29.

[8] *Journal of the American Medical Association,* 77 (Dec. 10, 1921), 1913–14; *ibid.,* 78 (Feb. 11, 1922), 434.

[9] Quoted by Charles A. Selden, "The Most Powerful Lobby in Washington," *Ladies' Home Journal,* XXXIX (April 1922), 95.

[10] Mary G. Kilbreth to Harding, Nov. 25, 1921, Box 157, folder 117–1, Harding Papers; Senate, *Protection of Maternity,* Hearings on S. 1039 before the Committee on Education and Labor, 67 Cong., 1 Sess., No. 61, pp. 7–13.

Boston, the American Constitutional League, the Constitutional Liberty League of Massachusetts, and the Massachusetts Public Interests League agreed. Senator James Reed of Missouri echoed Kilbreth's words when he charged that the bill was communist inspired and that the standards drawn up by the Children's Bureau were made by crackpots.[11]

Certain "medical liberty" organizations (they opposed any state regulation in medicine: vaccination, quarantine, the Wasserman test, licensing of doctors, hospitals, and medical schools) viewed the Sheppard-Towner Act as another brick in the wall being erected by the regular medical profession to eliminate all but orthodox practices.[12] But the most significant opposition to the bill came from physicians who expressed themselves through the American Medical Association. The AMA had marched within the broad ranks of progressivism from 1900 to World War I and vigorously campaigned for pure food and drugs, protection of the public from medical quackery, a federal department of health, and the elevation of standards in medical practice and education.[13] Nevertheless, the AMA had always been silent on other great health problems: slums and tenements, factory hazards, child labor, and the exploitation of women in sweatshops and dangerous trades.

The AMA first broke away from progressivism over the issue of compulsory health insurance; and after its house of delegates condemned health insurance in 1920, the association came to see the Sheppard-Towner Act as only another form of the same thing.[14] State medical societies in Massachusetts, New York, Illinois, Ohio, and Indiana spearheaded the opposition to health insurance and the Sheppard-Towner proposal. In its attack on the Sheppard-Towner bill and other public health measures, the *Illinois Medical Journal*, official organ of the Illinois State Medical Society, declared: "Today Washington, D. C., is a hotbed of Bolshevism. . . . Where will it all end? We know where it ended in ruined Russia. . . . Can the people of America set up Bureaucratic Autocracy in Washington without a resulting industrial slavery?"[15] The *Journal of the American Medical Association* launched its campaign against Sheppard-Towner on February 5, 1921, and it continued to oppose the act until it was repealed.[16] The 1922 AMA house of delegates condemned Sheppard-Towner as an "imported socialistic scheme."[17]

In the 1920s the AMA did not speak for the whole medical profession. The Mayo brothers and other prominent medical figures from hospitals and universities endorsed Sheppard-Towner. The Medical Woman's National Association was a steadfast proponent of the program throughout the 1920s. This association

[11] *Cong. Record*, 67 Cong., 1 Sess., Appendix, lxi, 8759–69.

[12] Such groups included the Citizens Medical Reference Bureau, the American Drugless Association, the American Medical Liberty League, Inc., and the New York Anti-Vivisectionist Society. "The Lobby Discusses the 'Maternity Bill,'" *Capital Eye*, I (Oct. 1921), 6–8; Grace Cole to Harding, May 16, 1921; Lenora B. Simpkins to Harding, May 18, 1921, Box 157, folder 117–1, Harding Papers.

[13] Burrow, *AMA*, 65–67, 105, 157–58.

[14] *Ibid.*, 157–58.

[15] *Illinois Medical Journal* (May 1920), quoted in Citizens Medical Reference Bureau, *Bulletin No.* 33 (May 30, 1920), Box 157, folder 117–1, Harding Papers.

[16] *Journal of the American Medical Association*, 76 (Feb. 5, 1921), 383.

[17] *Ibid.*, 78 (June 3, 1922), 1709.

called for federal aid to maternity in 1917, joined the WJCC in 1920, and promoted Sheppard-Towner in its own journal throughout the decade.[18] The *Medical Woman's Journal* hailed Dr. Josephine Baker as one of the world's great citizens for her work in reducing by 50 percent the infant death rate in New York City.[19] Baker testified repeatedly for Sheppard-Towner, was a constant ally of the National Consumers' League and the League of Women Voters, and became president of the Medical Woman's National Association in the early 1930s. While the AMA lamented its failure to prevent the passage of the Sheppard-Towner Act, the women physicians spoke of the fine work being done.[20]

In retrospect, this pioneering bill seems pitifully small. The act authorized an appropriation of $1,480,000 for fiscal 1921–1922 and $1,240,000 for the next five years ending June 30, 1927. Of this sum, $5,000 would go to each state outright; $5,000 more would go to each state if matching funds were provided; and the rest would be allocated on a population percentage and matching basis. The cost of administering the program could not exceed $50,000, and the money was channeled by the Children's Bureau through the state child welfare or health divisions. Before a federal grant would be made, a state had to pass enabling legislation, provide a satisfactory plan for implementing the program, and vote matching funds. Both the state and the individual retained the right to reject aid. The law expressly denied agents or representatives of either state or federal government the power to enter a home uninvited or to take charge of a child without legal consent. It provided for instruction in hygiene of maternity and infancy through public health nurses, visiting nurses, consultation centers, child care conferences, and literature distribution.

By and large, the Sheppard-Towner Act was well received by the state authorities. Forty-one states joined in 1922; and eventually, only Connecticut, Illinois, and Massachusetts remained aloof. In New Jersey, the legislature passed the enabling act over the governor's veto in 1922. In Washington, the governor was unalterably opposed, and only the election of a new chief executive allowed the state to join the program. Louisiana waited until 1924 to enter the program, and Vermont joined in 1926. Unexpected opposition kept Rhode Island out until 1925, and Maine and Kansas finally accepted in 1927.

In New York, Governor Nathan Miller, who had upset Alfred E. Smith in the Harding sweep of 1920, told the opening session of the 1922 legislature that he would veto any bill which would accept Sheppard-Towner. Twenty-eight women's organizations formed the Association for the Sheppard-Towner Act and

[18] Kate C. Mead, "Is Infant Mortality an Index to Social Welfare? Scandinavia's Reply," *Woman's Medical Journal,* XXVII (Jan. 1917), 10–15; Esther Lovejoy, "Democracy and Health," *ibid.,* XXIX (June 1919), 116–24; Lauara L. Mearns to Editor, *Medical Woman's Journal,* XXVII (Feb. 1920), 62; "The Sheppard-Towner Bill," *ibid.,* XXVIII (Jan. 1921), 13–14; Editorial, *ibid.,* 22.

[19] "One of the World's Great Citizens," *Medical Woman's Journal,* XXIX (Aug. 1922), 180–82.

[20] "What Legislators are Doing for Mothers and Babies," *ibid.,* XXVIII (July 1921), 189; Frances Sage Bradley, "The Sheppard-Towner Bill as It Is Worked Out by Arkansas Women," *ibid.,* XXIX (Aug. 1922), 196–97; Mary Riggs Noble, "Prenatal Work in Pennsylvania," *ibid.,* XXXI (March 1924), 69–70; Ellen Stadtmuller, "Promotion of Maternal and Infant Welfare in California," *ibid.,* 66–67; Frances Sage Bradley, "What Is Hoped and Planned in Arkansas," *ibid.,* 67–68; William H. Peters, "Cincinnati's Participation in Sheppard-Towner Work," *ibid.,* 72–73.

worked to have New York appropriate $75,000 for the program. The Association circulated petitions, but Miller declared that he would not be influenced if every woman in the state signed. "The people . . . have no business to interfere with men in office." In keeping with Miller's mood, the legislature formally rejected the Sheppard-Towner Act. While deploring the financial drain of a maternity program, Miller signed a bill which appropriated $125,000 for a hog barn on the state fair grounds; and he approved of a twin barn for 1923. Kelley remarked: "It does not improve the outlook of a candidate for the governorship of New York to have 28 organizations of women experienced in working together know that swine shelters appeal to him more strongly than dying mothers and babies." Miller lost the next election to Al Smith, who pushed the Sheppard-Towner plan through the legislature in 1923. Smith credited the New York League of Women Voters for the passage of the bill.[21]

The Connecticut legislature rejected the Sheppard-Towner money on the grounds that it infringed on the rights of the state. The state appropriations committee declared that it was time to stop the federal aid process. This reason seemed hollow to Sheppard-Towner advocates when the same committee voted to accept a new federal aid program for an airplane squadron. Nevertheless, the legislature established a state program for maternity and infancy protection with an appropriation of $55,000. This sum was $12,000 less than would have been made available to the state under Sheppard-Towner. Furthermore, the appropriation was offset by a $30,720 cut in the funds for the Bureau of Child Welfare. This bureau, the major achievement of the Connecticut League of Women Voters in the 1921 legislature, was partially sacrificed to the states rights cause.[22]

From the outset, Massachusetts spawned most of the organized effort against the Sheppard-Towner plan. A state proposal for maternity and infancy protection had failed to pass three consecutive years, 1919, 1920, and 1921—the last time it received only two positive votes in the legislature. The opposition of the medical profession had been particularly vigorous. One group of critics labelled the measure "The *beginning of Communism in Medicine*. A very unjust, unwise, iniquitous & socialistic bill." "Vicious, un-American, paternal." "It is a step toward Sovietism."[23] When the legislature began consideration of an enabling act for Sheppard-Towner in 1922, the attorney general (an anti-suffragist who had ruled women off the ballot and out of the jury box in Massachusetts) issued an opinion that the Sheppard-Towner Act would misuse the tax money of Massachusetts and was unconstitutional because it violated the reserved rights of the states. The state filed a suit with the United States Supreme Court on behalf of its taxpayers to enjoin the law. Fearing that a state was ineligible to file a taxpayer's suit, Harriet Frothingham, president of the Woman Patriots, filed another suit in the Supreme Court of the District of Columbia. When this court dismissed her case and the United States Court of Appeals concurred, she ap-

21 Nathan Miller quoted in letter to Editor from Harriet W. Laidlaw, March 10, 1922, folder 27, Harriet W. Laidlaw Papers (Schlesinger Library, Radcliffe); Florence Kelley, "The Children's Amendment," *Good Housekeeping*, LXXVI (Feb. 1923), 170; Alfred E. Smith, "Safeguarding Our Assets—the Children," *Ladies' Home Journal*, XLVI (Oct. 1929), 304.

22 *Woman Voter's Bulletin* [Connecticut League of Women Voters], III (May 3, 1923), 2; *ibid.*, III (July 1923), 1–2.

23 "Why Physicians Are Opposing Maternity Bill," sent to Harding by the Massachusetts Civic Alliance, Box 157, folder 117–1, Harding Papers.

pealed to the United States Supreme Court. United States Solictor General James Beck considered the Sheppard-Towner Act to be unconstitutional and encouraged Massachusetts to pursue the case.[24]

These suits seriously threatened the whole range of federal programs which provided either direct aid or matching grants. Ironically, at the very time that Massachusetts was challenging Sheppard-Towner for violating the Tenth Amendment, the state was accepting money under twenty-two other federal programs which extended from soil surveys, county agents, highway building, and state militia to the eradication of the white-pine rust and the European corn borer. Ten states and the Association of Land Grant Colleges filed counter-briefs. On June 5, 1923, the Supreme Court dismissed both suits for want of jurisdiction and without ruling on the constitutionality of the act.[25]

Sheppard-Towner was considered a permanent law, but its appropriation was scheduled to cease automatically on June 30, 1927. Confident that the program was a success, its proponents moved in 1926 to have the authorization extended. The House of Representatives quickly voted a two-year extension by the healthy margin of 218 to 44, but opponents mobilized to stop the bill in the Senate. The foes included the American Medical Association, Woman Patriots, Massachusetts Public Interests League, Sentinels of the Republic, and the Daughters of the American Revolution. (In 1921, as a member of the WJCC, the DAR had supported the measure, but it was no longer espousing progressive causes.) The opposition was fresh from having recently beaten another progressive proposal—the federal child labor amendment.[26] They echoed the usual cries: "socializing medicine," "nationalizing the children," and introducing "Bolshevism."[27]

Senator Thomas A. Bayard of Delaware read into the *Congressional Record* a thirty-six page petition and letter from the Woman Patriots. It purported to show the Bolshevist origins of the entire progressive program for children, which included the Sheppard-Towner Act, the Children's Bureau, child labor laws, and the child labor amendment. The petition traced an intricate web which joined the national women's organizations together in a conspiracy to sovietize the United States. It was a feminist-socialist-communist plot under the leadership of Florence Kelley Wishnieweski. She was described as "the ablest legislative general Communism has produced." The petition also denounced Jane Addams, Julia Lathrop, the women on both the Republican and Democratic National Committees, the constituent organizations of the WJCC (such as the Parent-

[24] Upton to Harding, Dec. 2, 1922, Box 157, folder 117–1, Harding Papers; Marian Parkhurst to Cornelia Bryce Pinchot, Dec. 7, 1922, Box 24, Cornelia Bryce Pinchot Papers (Manuscript Division, Library of Congress).

[25] *Reports of the Dept. of Labor, 1923, Report of the Secretary of Labor and Reports of the Bureaus* (Washington, 1924), 117–20.

[26] Richard B. Sherman, "The Rejection of the Child Labor Amendment," *Mid-America*, XLV (Jan. 1963), 3–17; J. Stanley Lemons, "The New Woman in the New Era: The Woman Movement from the Great War to the Great Depression" (doctoral dissertation, University of Missouri, 1967), 319–24.

[27] *Journal of the American Medical Association*, 86 (Feb. 6, 1926), 421; *ibid.*, 87 (Nov. 27, 1926), 1833–34; "Sentinels Appeal for Rejection of Maternity Act," *Woman Patriot*, X (Feb. 15, 1926), 32; William C. Woodward, "Further Fallacies of Sheppard-Towner Act," *ibid.*, X (Dec. 1, 1926), 178–80. Burrow, *AMA*, 161, sees the AMA's opposition as based on its distrust of federal subsidization and the granting of benefits without clearly defined guidelines.

Teachers Association, the League of Women Voters, and the Women's Christian Temperance Union), the Women's Bureau, the Children's Bureau, and the United States Department of Labor. Bayard mailed copies of this petition under his frank to all state officers of the DAR; after which, the president-general of the organization urged the defeat of Sheppard-Towner.[28]

The bill was blocked in the Senate for nearly eight months, and proponents were forced to accept a compromise which extended the appropriations for two more years but repealed the law itself automatically on June 30, 1929. Supporters of the act hoped that a more progressive political climate would exist by 1929 and that the law would be restored. Efforts to preserve the maternity program were resumed in 1928. The WJCC and other organizations rallied behind a bill which was more liberal than Sheppard-Towner. It specified that the money would be spent in cooperation with the states, but did not require either acceptance by the state legislatures or matching funds. The American Medical Association, the Woman Patriots, and the Sentinels of the Republic led the opposition again. By now, the politicians were less concerned about a woman's voting bloc, and the conservative propensities of Congress had freer play. Although progressive women still lobbied for the bill, it languished in Congress. This time the President would not help. Herbert Hoover issued perfunctory formal statements which urged its enactment; and refusing to press the matter, he allowed the first federal social security law to lapse.

In reviewing the work under Sheppard-Towner, the Children's Bureau reported for the seven years that it conducted 183,252 health conferences and established 2,978 permanent centers of prenatal care. Visiting nurses made 3,131,996 home visits, and 22,020,489 pieces of literature had been distributed. In the final four years, more than 4,000,000 infants and 700,000 expectant mothers had been reached. The infant death rate in 1921 was seventy-five per thousand live births, and the years under Sheppard-Towner saw it fall to sixty-four per thousand. The maternal death rate was reduced from sixty-seven and three-tenths per thousand in 1921 to sixty-two and three-tenths in 1927, despite the fact that the general death rate of all people had risen slightly for the same period. Obviously, much more needed to be done; New Zealand had an infant death rate of thirty-five per thousand. The Medical Woman's National Association noted that Great Britain's maternal death rate was 50 percent that of the United States; and Britain spent $3,800,000 at the same time the United States was spending only $1,240,000.[29]

The end of the act did not leave a complete void: forty-five states had participated directly after 1926, and Illinois and Connecticut had their own programs. Most states had the apparatus and the awareness of the problem to continue maternity and infancy aid on their own. The removal of federal funds, however, restricted the programs. Only sixteen states appropriated enough money

[28] *Cong. Record,* 69 Cong., 1 Sess., 12918–52 (July 3, 1926); *ibid.,* 69 Cong., 2 Sess., 1280–81 (Jan. 8, 1927).

[29] United States Dept. of Labor, Children's Bureau, Publication No. 203, *The Promotion of the Welfare and Hygiene of Maternity and Infancy* (Washington, 1931), 26–37; Dorothy Kirchwey Brown, Speech at Chicago Forum [Winter 1928–1929], Dorothy Kirchwey Brown Papers (Schlesinger Library, Radcliffe); Rosina Wistein, "Maternal Mortality: A Comparative Study," *Medical Woman's Journal,* XXXIV (Feb. 1932), 28–32.

to exceed or equal the previous total. Although some states, at first, greatly increased their efforts, as the depression deepened, the plan suffered badly in the fiscal pinch. Several states dropped it altogether.[30] An attempt to revive the federal part in 1931 failed when Senators David Walsh, Millard Tydings, and Elbert Thomas filibustered against it. Consideration of maternity and infancy protection was merged with the broader development of social security legislation within the New Deal. Restoration came with the Social Security Act of 1935. Protection of maternity and infancy was embodied in Title V of the comprehensive measure. Opponents were shocked at the provisions which authorized appropriations for the Children's Bureau of $5,820,000 for maternity and infancy protection, $3,870,000 for crippled children, and $24,750,000 for aid to dependent children.

The Sheppard-Towner Act was both an example of the persistence of progressivism in the 1920s and a link between the progressive period and the New Deal. Its travail demonstrated no lack of effort because progressivism secured its passage in 1921, expanded it to include Hawaii in 1924, renewed its appropriations in 1926, and obtained its acceptance in forty-five states. Even though conservative forces were able to eliminate it on the eve of the depression, advocates of the idea finally triumphed during the New Deal.

[30] United States Dept. of Labor, *The Promotion of the Welfare and Hygiene of Maternity and Infancy*, 38–39; Katherine P. Lenroot to Carrie Chapman Catt, Aug. 1, 1932, Box 1, Carrie Chapman Catt Papers (New York Public Library).

11

AFTER SUFFRAGE: SOUTHERN WOMEN IN THE TWENTIES

Anne Firor Scott

The adoption of the Nineteenth Amendment in 1920, granting woman suffrage, was the last of the four so-called Progressive amendments that were added to the Constitution between 1913 and 1920. This amendment culminated nearly a century of struggle by women to achieve political equality. As the preceding article indicates, male politicians were unsure of what impact the female vote would have on national elections and party structure, just as politicians in 1972 were unsure of the impact of the youth vote. The first reaction, then as now, was to give the new voters what they wanted, which in great part explains the passage of the Sheppard-Towner bill against powerful forces of opposition. But both women and men were quickly to discover that the mere extension of suffrage was not enough to guarantee fundamental reforms in the system. Women, if they were to affect the political process, would have to organize and work, particularly at the local level. This article gives needed emphasis to women's political efforts at the grass-roots level, and in an area where they had the most difficult struggle against traditional views of "woman in the home" and "woman on the pedestal."

Anne Firor Scott is professor of history at Duke University. Her major historical interest is in the evolution of the status of women, particularly in the South. She has edited a compilation of articles entitled The American Woman: Who Was She? *(Englewood Cliffs, N.J., 1971), and she is the author of* The Southern Lady *(Chicago, 1970). This article forms the basis of a chapter of that book.*

In few parts of the country was the Nineteenth Amendment awaited with higher expectations than among an earnest group of Southern women. Not unlike the present-day Southern liberal who yearns for a federal civil rights bill because the

Source: *Journal of Southern History,* Vol. 30, No. 3 (August 1964), pp. 298–318.

road to state and local legislation is so long and rocky, Southern women who had labored for state suffrage and for social reform against an opposing tide looked to the federal amendment for help. For them the vote had also become a symbol of something much larger—the image of the "new woman." Long constrained by Southern tradition about women's place in Southern life, they saw the amendment as a grant of freedom and a new measure of independence.

One of these women remarked in a private letter in 1920 that she was planning a trip to Europe because "once we *really* get into politics (i.e., once the suffrage amendment is ratified) I will never be able to get away."[1]

Another, in North Carolina, thought "the advent of women into political life" would mean "the loosening of a great moral force which will modify and soften the relentlessly selfish economic forces of trade and industry in their relation to government. The ideals of democracy and of social and human welfare will undoubtedly receive a great impetus."[2] For many years these earnest women had organized themselves, talked to legislators, worked for or against congressmen in their home districts, testified at hearings, haunted the polls on election day, cajoled money, written newspaper articles, watched the progress of more advanced Northern and Western women—and now, at last, had the federal help that promised to open the way to substantial achievement.

By 1920 Southern women had come to exert increasing influence in public affairs, but many of the problems that concerned them were still unsolved: the dislocations caused by industrialization, the conditions of work for women and children, the inadequacies of the educational system, the lack of opportunity for many children, prison conditions, the ravages of alcohol and disease, injustice to Negro citizens. To all such problems, and some new ones they would discover along the way, the newly enfranchised women now addressed themselves with renewed hope. Their successes as well as their failures have tended to vanish—in Vann Woodward's phrase—in that twilight zone between living memory and written history. An examination of what they tried to do, of the goals reached, the obstacles encountered, the failures endured, throws new light on the South in the twenties and upon the springs and motives behind the emancipation of Southern women.

What this record shows will depend upon the questions we ask. If we ask whether woman suffrage led to progress in social reform in the Southern states and to a more active political life for women, the answer is clearly that it did. If we ask in addition whether the broader hope, the dream of a new life for Southern women in which their independence, their right to think for themselves, to work for the things they believed in, to be respected as individuals regardless of sex, was accomplished in the twenties, the answer must be much more qualified.

It may be worth recalling at the outset that early in the nineteenth century the South had adopted a more rigid definition of the role of women than any other part of the country and had elevated that definition to the position of a myth. There were inherent contradictions in the elements of a women's role as the culture defined it: women were supposed to be beautiful, gentle, efficient,

[1] Madeline McDowell Breckinridge to Allie S. Dickson, March 20, 1920, in Breckinridge Family Papers (Manuscript Division, Library of Congress).

[2] Notes for speech in Mary O. Cowper Papers (Mrs. Cowper, Durham, N. C.).

morally superior, and, at the same time, ready to accept without question the doctrine of male superiority and authority. On matters not domestic they were to be seen and not heard, while in the domestic sphere it was taken for granted that a woman would rule. For those without inherited means, marriage was the only road to economic security (as for inherited wealth, its control passed at marriage into the hands of the husband). For those who did not marry, the only acceptable pattern was to become the pensioner—and often *de facto* servant—of some male relative. Hints that some women felt the contradictory nature of these expectations, and resented them, appeared from time to time before the Civil War. After the war, changes which seemed likely to alter the culture pattern appeared on all sides; but, as part of the comforting glorification of the past with which the South tended to evade present problems, the image of the Southern Lady—whatever the reality—survived relatively unchanged.[3] The force of this cultural image was so strong that Southern women had to follow a more devious road to emancipation than those elsewhere. It was only after long apprenticeship in such outwardly safe organizations as church societies and the Woman's Christian Temperance Union that they began to venture into women's clubs and suffrage organizations.[4]

From this process a few women emerged as recognized leaders. These few had in common impressive social standing and family background, intelligence, courage, and a degree of inner security that permitted them to survive criticism. Such were Madeline Breckinridge in Kentucky, Mary Munford in Virginia, Nellie Somerville in Mississippi, Sallie Cotten in North Carolina, Pattie Jacobs in Alabama—each highly respected in her own state by men as well as women.[5] Now, with the power of the ballot and the new freedom it symbolized, they hoped not only to be more effective in public life but also to modify significantly Southern thought about the proper role of women.[6]

[3] W. J. Cash goes so far as to argue that woman's role was more rigidly defined after Appomattox and emancipation than before. *The Mind of the South* (New York, 1941), 131. He cites no evidence; and, on the basis of much reading in diaries, letters, newspapers, and church and organization records, I think he overstates his case.

[4] Anne Firor Scott, "The 'New Woman' in the New South," *South Atlantic Quarterly*, LXI (Autumn 1962), 473–83.

[5] The obituaries upon Madeline Breckinridge's untimely death in 1920 suggest she was Kentucky's leading citizen as well as its leading woman. Certainly she had a hand in almost every reform movement in that state for twenty years; and, by way of the Lexington, Ky., *Herald*, her voice was widely heard. A close study of her biography reveals all the elements that created the Southern "woman movement." See Sophronisba Preston Breckinridge, *Madeline McDowell Breckinridge, a Leader in the New South* (Chicago, 1921), and Breckinridge Family Papers.

[6] Madeline Breckinridge, for example, regularly advised every woman to read Margaret Fuller, John Stuart Mill, and Olive Shreiner. The private papers of the women upon whom this study is centered reveal their vision of an ideal woman, educated and fully developed and free to undertake the work that interested her most. They were so often criticized for wanting to "be like men" that it is worth pointing out that their ideal human being was not a man but some other woman (Jane Addams, Anna Howard Shaw, Frances Willard, for example) and that they did not think men were doing a very good job with politics and government or in shaping society generally. What they aimed for was not freedom to be like men but freedom to be themselves. Economic independence loomed large in the minds of the pioneers—they had nothing against marriage, and most were married, but they objected to it as an economic necessity. It is interesting to find exactly the same arguments in

They were well aware that the older image of the Southern Lady, although undergoing modification in a number of ways, was still very much alive in 1920. The image was, of course, made up of a number of components, some external: beauty, gentleness, winning ways. Other components related to appropriate behavior: modesty, domesticity, chastity, and submission to male opinions. It was a lovely image that could be maintained with a minimum of strain whenever the woman in question was lucky enough to be well endowed with the outward qualities (the proportionate number so endowed was doubtless about the same in 1920 as in 1820). But it was the definition of appropriate behavior that women were most anxious to modify. In earlier years the effective leaders of the movement had had to conform behavior to the image. As a Virginia woman remarked in 1918, "the wise suffrage leaders here have realized . . . that success depends upon showing their cause to be compatible with the essentials of the Virginia tradition of womanliness, and both instinct and judgment have prevented the adoption here of the more aggressive forms of campaigning."[7]

In the twenties, maintaining the ladylike image was still considered to be good politics, but the active women continued to alter behavior remarkably. A few of the more radical wanted to dispense, once and for all, with what they called the "chivalric nonsense" that put woman on a pedestal in order to keep her out of the affairs of the real world. A young North Carolina woman, for example, reflected:

> *Last year I travelled from one end of our State to another. I saw thousands of women, old and young, mothers and little girls, working in stores and factories ten or eleven or twelve hours a day; or worse, working in the factory all night, and taking care of their homes by day. And I asked, where is this chivalry that so protects women? And I saw working in the fields, hoeing cotton and corn and doing all kinds of hard labor, women and children, white as well as black. And again I asked, whom does chivalry protect? In the last session of the legislature, I heard arguments about a bill which would have raised the amount allowed from the estate to a widow and her children for the first year of widowhood. And many were the jokes made and the slurs slung about mothers who would spend the amount for silk stockings instead of on the care of children. Respect for motherhood, reverence for womanhood, was not the ruling thought when the bill was considered, for it was voted down. It was not the political rights nor any of the deeds of the "new woman" who took the working women from their homes and made them labor as if there was no such thing as chivalry and pedestals. . . . Genesis says that after the Lord had created male and female, he gave them dominion over the earth and then he rested. The two were created to work out welfare for all on earth. Why not go on with the work and stop babbling about chivalry when there is*

the most recent comprehensive work on the subject, Simone de Beauvoir, *The Second Sex*, H. M. Parshley, trans. and ed. (New York, 1953). Mary Johnston and Ellen Glasgow were active suffrage women, and their novels are rich in oblique attacks on the existing system. See especially Glasgow, *Virginia* (New York, 1913) and Johnston, *Hagar* (Boston, 1913). Both novels will repay careful reading for anyone interested in the inner springs of the woman movement.

[7] Orie Latham Hatcher, "The Virginia Man and the New Era for Women," *Nation*, CVI (June 1, 1918), 651.

no chivalry except for the small class whose financial conditions prevent their needing it.[8]

The older ideal of the Southern Lady cropped up in another way when the opponents of reforms for which women worked used it as a weapon. It was hardly politic to argue in public that one believed in child labor or enjoyed the profits that stemmed from women laboring long hours into the night, but—given the Southern frame of reference—it was quite possible to attack the proponents of reform on the ground that they were "unwomanly" and thus to discredit the cause for which they fought. This was done repeatedly, and the cry was often echoed, of course, by other men who feared for their own domestic comforts.

Even before the Nineteenth Amendment was ratified state suffrage organizations began to turn themselves into leagues of women voters with the announced purpose of educating newly enfranchised citizens and working for "needed legislation." Leaders gathered in Chicago for intensive training, organized by a political scientist from the University of Chicago, and went home with instructions to pass along all they had learned. "Citizenship schools" blossomed over the Southern landscape, and courses with reading lists worthy of graduate instruction in political science were found side by side with mundane classes in election law, registration procedures, and How to Mark a Ballot. The troops were receiving basic training.[9]

At the same time every state had its legislative council in which women's groups of the most diverse kinds joined together to work for legislation. The Alabama council was typical: it was made up of sixteen organizations, ranging from the Women's Trade Union League to the Methodist Home Missionary Council. Despite their diverse origins the organized women were in surprising accord on legislative goals.

Whether the goal was a social reform such as the abolition of child labor, or a political one such as the reorganization of the state government, veterans of the suffrage movement were political realists and skilled lobbyists. Their lobbying technique, developed before they had any votes to deliver, was based upon tact and superior information rather than upon threats. Though they were trying to throw off the shackles of chivalry, women voters were not above appealing for chivalric responses in a good cause.

An example of typical methods may be seen in a letter from a Virginia lady of the old school describing her efforts to persuade Congress to adopt a child labor amendment:

I got busy about the child labor amendment and stirred up the Virginia Federation of Labor and the Ministerial Union of Richmond which means all the Protestant clergymen of the city . . . the Federation of Labor sent official communications to all senators and all congressmen and our papers have given us good notices. . . . I carried your summary of the situation to

[8] Mary O. Cowper, "That Pedestal Again," North Carolina League of Women Voters, *Monthly News*, November 1927. See also the very interesting series of articles by Nell Battle Lewis in Raleigh, N. C., *News and Observer*, May 1926, in which she discusses the question thoroughly and perceptively.

[9] Charles E. Merriam, "The Chicago Citizenship School," *Journal of Social Forces*, I (September 1923), 600.

our leading morning paper and he promised to use it and comment on it editorially.[10]

A favorite device was the publication of complete lists of legislators with their views on various issues presented for the voters' information. Indeed, education of the electorate was a basic technique, and there was always an effort to develop support for their programs among "the people back home." The experience of the suffrage campaign came into play at every turn.

The ideological milieu of the twenties was nowhere conducive to social reform. The Red Scare had affected every part of the country, and programs considered mild in 1912 were now labeled Bolshevik.[11] The reform-minded women in the South were little disturbed at the outset by the fact that many of the causes in which they had long been interested were now termed radical. The president of the Tennessee League of Women Voters remarked mildly,

> *Some good souls are pleased to call our ideas socialistic. They are indeed uncomfortable often for some folk. Some timid souls of both sexes are only half converted to the new order . . .* [yet] *every clear thinking, right feeling and high minded man and woman should consecrate his best talents to the gradual re-organization of society, national and international.*[12]

The ink was scarcely dry upon the suffrage amendment before legislatures began to realize that women now expected more respectful attention than in the past. "The men were scared to death of what the women might do," one North Carolina woman recalled.[13] In that state, as a measure of insurance against reprisal for having rejected the suffrage amendment, the governor and legislature agreed to appoint the president of the Federated Clubs as commissioner of charities and public welfare, one legislator being overheard to remark that she was

[10] Kate Pleasants Minor to Mrs. John J. O'Connor, April 18, 1924, in League of Women Voters of the United States Papers (Manuscript Division, Library of Congress), Virginia file.

[11] Note, for example, the comment of the foremost woman progressive of the day: "Social progress during the decade from 1919 to 1929 was conditioned at every turn by the fact that we were living in the midst of postwar psychology. . . . Any proposed change was suspect, even those efforts that had been considered praiseworthy before the war. To advance new ideas was to be radical, or even a bolshevik. . . . Throughout the decade this fear of change, this tendency to play safe was registered most conspicuously in the fields of politics, but it spread over into other fields as well." Jane Addams, *The Second Twenty Years at Hull House, September 1909 to September 1929, with a Record of a Growing World Consciousness* (New York, 1930), 153. Or this characterization from the center of Southern liberalism: "Besides there is mighty little freedom of opinion anywhere in the old South as you know. . . ." E. C. Branson to R. W. Hogan, Chapel Hill, N. C., December 17, 1922, in Eugene Cunningham Branson Papers (Southern Historical Collection, University of North Carolina Library).

[12] Report of the President, Tennessee League of Women Voters, January 1923, in League of Women Voters Papers, Tennesse file.

[13] Interview with Mrs. Kate Burr Johnson of Raleigh, N. C., November 1, 1963. See also comment of the Georgia women who drew up a bill in 1921 to remove the civil disabilities of women: "These legislators were so courteous and obliging the women could scarcely believe it was the Georgia Legislature. They gave everything asked for and asked 'is there anything more we can do for you?' " Elizabeth Cady Stanton and others (eds.), *The History of Woman Suffrage* (6 vols., New York, 1881–1922), VI, 142.

"pretty, anyway, and won't give us any trouble." The insurance turned out to be inadequate, for in short order North Carolina women, abetted behind the scenes by the same pretty welfare commissioner, were demanding that the Woman's Bureau of the United States Department of Labor be invited to survey the working conditions of women in North Carolina textile mills.

Textile manufacturing was a major economic interest in the state, and working conditions in the mills were frequently bad, wages were low, and many children were employed. The millowners reacted strongly. The women were accused of being unwomanly to mix in things about which they knew nothing, of being dangerous radicals or at the very least dupes of Northern manufacturers bent on spoiling the competitive advantage that child labor and cheap female labor gave the South. The YWCA, one of the groups joining in the request for a survey, was threatened with a loss of contributions. The state president of the League of Women Voters was hailed before a self-constituted jury of millmen and lectured severely. The suggestion reached her that her husband's sales of mill machinery would diminish rapidly if she and the league continued their interest in women's working conditions. Families divided as wives argued with husbands about the survey. Textile men brought pressure upon the governor and upon agencies of the state government. In 1926 the governor, while standing firm against allowing "outsiders" to meddle in North Carolina's business, agreed to order his own Child Welfare Department to make the study—but nothing happened. In 1929 when the Gastonia strike became a national issue, the North Carolina League of Women Voters, in publishing an explanation of the strikers' side of the argument, remarked that if the women's request for a survey of working conditions had been granted the problems that had led to a bloody strike might have been ameliorated.[14]

North Carolina women were more successful in their efforts to bring about stronger state child labor laws.[15] In every Southern state, in fact, women worked strenuously against the use of child labor. Many of them supported the federal child labor amendment that Congress adopted in 1924 and then went on to work for its ratification by their state legislatures. In the meantime, an intensive effort to establish broad programs of child welfare took shape. In Virginia, for example, the women urged the legislature to set up a Children's Code Commission and, having secured it, persuaded the governor to appoint five of their number to it. When the commission brought in twenty-four recommendations for new laws, ranging from a statewide juvenile court system to compulsory education, the women turned their attention once more to the legislature, and as a result of their unceasing toil eighteen of the twenty-four recommendations became law in the 1922 session.[16]

14 The story of the long fight between millmen and North Carolina women's groups is covered in detail in Mary O. Cowper Papers. Mrs. Cowper was executive secretary of the North Carolina League of Women Voters. The outlines as given here are confirmed by Mrs. Kate Burr Johnson, who was commissioner of welfare during the 1920's and was working behind the scenes with the women's groups. For contemporary analysis, see Nell Battle Lewis, "The University of North Carolina Gets Its Orders," *Nation*, CXXII (February 3, 1926), 114–15. Nora Houston of Virginia who was active in the effort to improve working conditions was also a painter and left at her death a dramatic painting of the Gastonia strike.

15 North Carolina League of Women Voters, *Monthly News*, 1922–1926.

16 Adele Clark Papers (Miss Clark, Richmond). Miss Clark helped organize the

That same year a combination of women's groups in Georgia secured the passage of a children's code, a child-placement bill, and a training school bill but failed when they joined forces with the Federation of Labor for a legislative limitation on hours of work for women. The hearing on this last proposal brought out "every cotton mill man in Georgia," and, while the eloquent testimony of Mrs. Elliott Cheatham persuaded the committee to report the bill, the millowners' influence in the legislature prevented it from being brought to a vote. Two years later efforts to secure ratification of the federal child labor amendment also failed in the Georgia legislature, and women in the state then turned to efforts to strengthen state laws.[17]

Similar issues, all of them demonstrating the increasing influence of women, appeared in the other Southern states. In Arkansas, where as early as 1919 the suffrage organization had come out for minimum wages and maximum hours in all cotton mills, the federal child labor amendment was ratified by the legislature. Credit was given jointly to a woman legislator, the Arkansas Federation of Labor, and the women's organizations. The wife of the man who had led the floor fight against the amendment was reported to be delighted that he had failed; of her it was said, "she expressed the spirit of Arkansas women in politics."[18]

One result of the growing movement against the exploitation of women and children in the mills was an increasingly close association between Southern women and the labor movement. Lucy Randolph Mason, bluest of Virginia bluebloods, who was to become an organizer for the CIO, noted in 1930: "For a number of years many of us southern women have been concerned over the lack of social control in the development of southern industry. Vast numbers of southern women are becoming more acutely conscious of the need of safeguards, which have already been supplied by most of the states. . . ."[19] Association with labor unions actually had begun during the fight for suffrage when trade unions, along with the Farmers Alliances, were virtually the only male organizations to support woman suffrage. As early as 1910 the Georgia Suffrage Association reported holding its convention in the halls of "the Federation of Labor, *its true friend*."[20] Now, in the twenties, women's interests were in line with labor concerns, and they not only found a good press in liberal journals such as the *New Republic* but also co-operated with labor unions.[21]

Particularly important in deepening woman's concern for industrial labor was the work of the YWCA. Even before the first World War, the YWCA had undertaken to bring college students in touch with the facts of industrial life, and in the twenties a student-industrial movement flourished. Its legislative pro-

campaign. See also Eudora Ramsay Richardson, "Liberals in Richmond," *Plain Talk*, VI (February 1930), 213–19.

[17] Mrs. E. B. Chamberlain to Mrs. Solon Jacobs, October 25, 1922, and Report to Director of Southeastern Region, January 10, 1924, in League of Women Voters Papers, Georgia file.

[18] Miss Earl Chambers to Marguerite Owen, October 2, 1924, *ibid.*, Arkansas file.

[19] Lucy R. Mason to Henry P. Kendall, December 31, 1930, in Lucy Randolph Mason Papers (Manuscripts Collection, Duke University Library, Durham, N. C.).

[20] Stanton and others (eds.), *History of Woman Suffrage*, VI, 125.

[21] There is ample evidence for this in League of Women Voters Papers, state files, and Mary O. Cowper Papers. Common interests made inevitably for co-operation.

gram included the abatement of poverty, abolition of child labor, a living wage as a minimum in every industry, an eight-hour day, and protection of workers from the hardships of continued unemployment. Through the YWCA, students at Randolph Macon were studying the problems of coal miners, while those at Converse delved into social legislation, and at Westhampton, unemployment. Girls from these and other colleges served on a regional committee for student-industrial co-operation, seeking, as they put it, to Christianize the social order.[22] Part of this program included a series of summer institutes for factory girls that by 1927 had evolved into the Southern Summer School for Women Workers in Industry, directed and financed by Southern women. The school grew steadily through the twenties and early thirties. The nature of its sympathies was evident in 1928 when strikers from the Marion Manufacturing Company were invited to the campus to tell their story and were afterward joined by students and faculty in a march through Marion. It was the opinion of the *Nation* that "This small group of women . . . are playing an important part in the fight against economic slavery in the South."[23]

When unionization became a genuine possibility during the New Deal, a large proportion of the women graduates of the Summer School became active organizers. There is something appealing in the picture of a group of well-to-do Southern women, of ladylike mien, busy training labor organizers. Nor is there the least doubt, from the record, that they knew what they were doing. They were not innocent philanthropists taken in by hardbitten radicals.[24]

The Southern Council on Women and Children in Industry, organized in 1931 to bring about a shorter working day and an end to night work in all the textile states, was another joint effort growing out of the experience of women in their separate states. The council hired Lucy Mason to organize their campaign. Calling to the colors a few progressive-minded millmen who agreed with her objectives, she then set out to convert some of those who did not agree, recognizing clearly that pressure on the legislatures could not succeed without the support of some of the millowners.[25]

From a national point of view the concern for child welfare was reflected in the passage in 1921, largely due to the work of women over the nation, of the Sheppard-Towner Act for maternal and infant health. Nineteen of twenty-six Southern senators voted for the bill. In the House, 91 of the 279 votes in support of the bill came from the South and only 9 of 39 votes against it.[26] This support for a federal welfare program from Southern members of Congress is less impressive than the enormous amount of follow-up work that Southern women undertook to secure appropriation of the required matching funds from state legislatures and then to report on the actual results of the public health work thus instituted. It is not too much to say that the co-operative state work within

22 Gladys Bryson, student secretary, YWCA, to Lucy Somerville, March 23, 1923, in Somerville Family Papers (Woman's Archives, Radcliffe College Library, Cambridge, Mass.).

23 Marion Bonner, "Behind the Southern Textile Strikes," *Nation,* CXXIX (October 2, 1929), 352.

24 See Lucy P. Garner, "An Education Opportunity for Industrial Girls," *Journal of Social Forces,* I (September 1923), 612–13, and Alice M. Baldwin Papers (Manuscripts Collection, Duke University Library).

25 Lucy Randolph Mason Papers, box 1.

26 *Congressional Record,* 67 Cong., 1 Sess., 4216, 8036–37.

the framework of the Sheppard-Towner Act brought about a revolution in maternal and infant health.[27]

In some ways the most intriguing of all the public activities of Southern women in the twenties was their racial work. The roots went back at least to 1901 when Miss Belle Bennett encouraged the Woman's Board of Home Missions of the Methodist Episcopal Church, South, to undertake work among Negro girls and offered a personal contribution to that end. From that year forward the board annually appropriated money in behalf of work among Negroes. In 1910 another Methodist, Mary DeBardelben of Alabama, volunteered for missionary service, not in far-off lands but among Southern Negroes. In 1915 yet another Southern Methodist, Mrs. Lily H. Hammond, published a pathbreaking book in which she pleaded for a permanent burial of the "old Negro mammy" and some sensible attention to the needs of Mammy's daughters.[28]

The real breakthrough came in 1920 at an extraordinary meeting of Southern churchwomen in Memphis at which four Negro women spoke forthrightly of the needs of Southern Negroes. One of them told of having been forcibly removed by twelve white men from a Pullman car while on her way to Memphis. In the emotional stir of the moment, the ninety-odd white women, representing a number of churches, agreed that talk was not enough and constituted themselves the Woman's Department of the Commission on Inter-racial Cooperation. Headed by Mrs. Luke Johnson of Griffin, Georgia, and supported by leading women in every state, units of this organization set up interracial committees to attack common social and economic problems.

When the National League of Women Voters decided in 1924 to establish a Committee on Negro Problems with membership from every state that had more than fifteen per cent Negro population, members from eight Southern states accepted appointment. Many of these women had been active in their local interracial committees, of which there were eventually some eight hundred functioning in the South. In Tennessee white women organized a special citizenship school for Negro women. Many of the committeewomen took personal responsibility for their Negro fellow citizens, as did Mary Cooke Branch Munford of Richmond, who made a room of her house permanently available to Negroes for public meetings, or a busy doctor's wife in Alabama who waged a one-woman campaign for better Negro education. When the Richmond city council considered a segregation statute in 1929, it was Lucy Randolph Mason, almost singlehandedly, who brought about its defeat.[29]

The most spectacular work in this field began in the thirties. It started with the organization in 1930, under the imaginative leadership of Jessie Daniel

[27] This story is reflected in detail in League of Women Voters Papers, state files. See especially all the state-by-state reports on the operation of the law and the collection of letters from Texas women who benefited from it. Reports of the Children's Bureau also contain details of the actual workings of the law.

[28] Noreen Dunn Tatum, *A Crown of Service: A Story of Woman's Work in the Methodist Episcopal Church, South, from 1878–1940* (Nashville, 1960), 32, 65, 234; Lily Hardy Hammond, *In Black and White: An Interpretation of Southern Life* (New York, 1914). See also Wilma Dykeman and James Stokely, *Seeds of Southern Change: The Life of Will Alexander* (Chicago, 1961), 82–96.

[29] Norfolk *Journal and Guide*, February 2, 1929. See also Katherine Du Pre Lumpkin, *The Making of a Southerner* (New York, 1947), for evidence of the significance of the YWCA in breaking through traditional racial barriers.

Ames, a Texas woman who had been active in a dozen reform movements, of the Association of Southern Women for the Prevention of Lynching. At its peak this organization had 40,000 small-town and rural churchwomen enrolled in an effort to put an end to the most spectacularly disgraceful aspect of the Southern race problem. While the federal antilynching law was blocked in the United States Senate, this band of Southern women took upon themselves the sometimes heroic responsibility of opposing any specific threat of a lynching in their own towns or counties.

The crusade against lynching was the most dramatic aspect of women's interracial work. Less visible, but of great significance, was the way in which groups of white and Negro women in the twenties were sitting down together to tackle common problems in an atmosphere of forthright discussion. Though a few Negro women were careful publicly to eschew any desire for social equality, most of them hammered away on equal rights in court, an end to segregation and discrimination in transportation, the Negro's need for the ballot, and every other sensitive issue that stood between whites and blacks in the South during this period of the resurgent Ku Klux Klan.[30]

Although women's interests tended to center upon measures that had a humanitarian element, especially those affecting disadvantaged groups and children, they devoted much time to more strictly political questions. After learning the mechanics of government, they turned their efforts to the improvement of governmental organizations. Studies of local and state governmental structure were published and used in schools and by other organizations. In Virginia in 1922 women's groups worked for an executive budget and improved election laws. A year later the state legislative chairman of the Virginia League of Women Voters reported that she was in daily attendance at budget hearings.[31] In 1924 her organization concentrated its attention on the improvement of tax administration and reported it had won an initial skirmish in the legislature by securing active consideration of the question despite orders from the Democratic machine that the subject was not to be raised. In the same legislature Virginia women voters worked for a bill to create a uniform fiscal year and were successful in their effort.[32] The League had also supported bills, that failed to pass, for civil service, creation of a conservation department, county government reform, and reforms in the state educational machinery.

Similar interests and similar campaigns developed in other states. Women in Georgia and Tennessee, after initial forays into the question of more efficient government, became convinced that the supreme obstacle lay in outmoded state constitutions; and in both states campaigns for constitutional reform were launched in the twenties and were eventually successful.[33] Kentucky women in 1927 began to work for home rule for cities, improvements in local charters, and the adoption of city manager government.

30 The story of women's interracial work is in Jessie Daniel Ames Papers (Mrs. Ames, Tryon, N. C.). Mrs. Ames pioneered the antilynching group and was for twelve years executive secretary of the Woman's Department of the Inter-Racial Commission. What is given here is a mere glimpse into a complex and fascinating story that deserves a chapter or a book all to itself.

31 Nora Houston to Maud Wood Park, December 12, 1923, in League of Women Voters Papers, Virginia file.

32 Miss M. E. Pidgeon to Belle Sherwin, 1924, *ibid.*

33 *Ibid.*, Georgia and Tennessee files.

To an interest in the structure of government was added a concern for making government more democratic. Because of their long exclusion from politics, women were sensitive to the implications of "consent of the governed." It was they who invented the now commonplace idea of "getting out the vote." In some places women's work led to spectacular increases in the percentage of qualified voters going to the polls. In Alabama 54.4 percent of the qualified voters went to the polls in 1924 after women sponsored a get-out-the-vote campaign, compared to less than 30 percent in 1920. One county, where the women had been particularly active, got out 84.1 percent of its qualified voters.[34] Florida in the same year reported a 65.9 percent increase over 1920 in the qualified voters going to the polls.[35]

The poll tax was the subject of dual concern. Women's groups opposed the tax, but in the meantime they set out to collect money for the payment of poll taxes in order to increase the number of qualified voters. In 1925 Louisiana women collected $30,000 to this end. The work of North Carolina women for the Australian ballot, that finally succeeded in 1929, was part of the same interest in making the operation of government more democratic.

Close to home, yet a long way from women's traditional concerns, were two other political issues that developed strength in Southern women's groups in the twenties: government ownership of Muscle Shoals and the regulation of utility rates. Interest in both these questions developed from studies of the cost of living, and women in Alabama and Tennessee became enthusiastic supporters of what was to become the Tennessee Valley Authority. On these as on other questions the politically active women seem to have taken a pragmatic view without much concern for traditional free enterprise arguments.

In all their enterprises, political or social, women knew that the main road to influence lay through political parties. Interest in partisan politics antedated suffrage, and unofficially some women had long taken an interest in party fortunes. It had been the accepted doctrine that the national suffrage organization should be nonpartisan since it hoped to get support from both parties for the national amendment. That this principle was occasionally honored in the breach is made clear when we find Jane Addams trying to recruit Jean Gordon of Louisiana for the Progressive party in 1912 or discover Mrs. Breckinridge on a speaking tour for the Democrats in 1916. A keen interest in party methods and organization had been one of the by-products of the highly organized national suffrage campaign.[36] Carrie Chapman Catt, the commanding general of the final suffrage drive, was intent that women should find their way not to the outskirts but to the center of power in the political parties. At the Victory Convention in Chicago in 1920 she had told them:

> *The next battle is going to be inside the parties, and we are not going to stay outside and let all the reactionaries have their way on the inside! Within every party there is a struggle between progressive and reactionary*

[34] Report on the Get Out the Vote Campaign, November 29, 1924, *ibid.*, Alabama file.

[35] Mrs. J. B. O'Hara to Ann Webster, September 2, 1924, *ibid.*, Florida file.

[36] See Carrie Chapman Catt and Nettie Rogers Shuler, *Woman Suffrage and Politics: The Inner Story of the Suffrage Movement* (New York, 1924) and Maud Wood Park, *Front Door Lobby*, Edna Lamprey Stantial, ed. (Boston, 1960).

elements. Candidates are a compromise between these extremes. You will be disillusioned, you will find yourselves in the political penumbra where most of the men are. They will be glad to see you, you will be flattered. But if you stay long enough you will discover a little denser thing which is the umbra of the political party—the people who are picking the candidates, doing the real work that you and the men sanction at the polls. You won't be welcome, but there is the place to go. You will see the real thing in the center with the door locked tight. You will have a hard fight before you get inside . . . but you must move right up to the center.[37]

At the outset, a considerable number of Southern women set out to become active in party politics. Party organizations welcomed them, if not with enthusiasm at least with a realistic appreciation of their potential voting power. Some states began at once the custom that has since become standard of appointing a woman as vice-chairman of the state party committee. A considerable number of Southern women showed interest in running for elective office; and, though numerous obstacles lay between almost any woman and nomination, enough persisted so that by 1930 only Louisiana had yet to have women in the state legislature. But only a few, a very few, Southern women seem to have made their way to that mysterious center of power to which Mrs. Catt had directed them.

One of these was Mrs. Nellie Nugent Somerville of Greenville, Mississippi, whose political influence preceded the Nineteenth Amendment. As soon as it was legal to do so she ran for the state legislature in a campaign that was a model of thorough organization and was elected. She had been observing party organization long enough to know the ropes, and she hoped the newly enfranchised women would be similarly observant. She advised them to be certain they had a hand in choosing county committees and reminded them: "It now becomes the duty of women voters to take lively interests in the details of political machinery. When any meeting or election is ordered by your political party be sure you take part in it."[38]

The chief obstacle to following such advice was the unwillingness of male politicians to promote women of independent mind and political skill. They preferred more amenable females, and hence the forthright and well-trained suffrage veterans often found themselves at odds with the entrenched politicians.[39] Mrs. Somerville herself managed to surmount the obstacles, and in 1924 Mississippi Democrats were divided into Somerville and Percy factions. At the showdown, hers won. She also served as a member of the committee on permanent organization of the 1924 Democratic National Convention and marshaled William G. McAdoo supporters in imposing array.[40] Her record in the legislature suggests that she understood the effective use of political power. When a bill

37 Mary Gray Peck, *Carrie Chapman Catt, a Biography* (New York, 1944), 325–26.

38 Article in Jackson, Miss., *Woman Voter*, November 19, 1923. For the details of Mrs. Somerville's campaign, see letters of her daughter, September 1923, in Somerville Family Papers.

39 See analysis of first woman vice-chairman of the Democratic National Committee, Emily Newell Blair, "Women in the Political Parties," American Academy of Political and Social Science, *Annals*, CXLIII (May 1929), 217–29.

40 Clippings and note in Somerville Family Papers.

she had initiated failed to pass, the fact was reported as news—as a rule anything she offered did pass—and her colleagues were frequently in praise of her hard work and effectiveness as a lawmaker.[41]

Another politically minded woman who reached a position of genuine power in the party was Sue Shelton White of Tennessee, an independent court reporter, secretary to members of the Tennessee Supreme Court, and from 1920 to 1926 secretary to Senator Kenneth McKellar. In 1915 she drafted the first mother's pension law to be presented to the Tennessee legislature, finally passed in 1920. She went from Senator McKellar's office to practice law in Jackson, Tennessee, and was sufficiently effective in Democratic politics to be invited to work for the Democratic National Committee. With Nellie Davis (Tayloe) Ross she helped lay the groundwork for the extensive women's program of the party during the early Franklin D. Roosevelt years. A fellow lawyer, who was general counsel of the Federal Social Security Board, said at her death:

> *Sue knew politics from the inside and from the outside. Politics were more than a game to her, though I think she relished the intricacies of the game. She used her political acumen as an instrument for the promotion of the general welfare. And she wielded the instrument with a grace and effectiveness that delighted the wise and distressed the stupid.*[42]

Mrs. Somerville and Miss White were exceptional rather than typical, but women in politics ranged from those who were effective politicians in their own right to those who blamed the men for not permitting them to gain nomination. The success stories make good reading, but the overall picture of women's efforts to exercise real influence in the political parties, South or North, was not one to gladden Mrs. Catt's heart. Sue White analyzed the Southern situation in 1928 in a letter to Mary Dewson of the Democratic National Committee:

> *Women have been discouraged by the rank and file of the party organization. . . . We still have the old anti-suffrage attitude in the south, women have been indifferent, and their indifference has been preached to them, aided, abetted and encouraged. They have viewed politics as something they should stay away from. They have been told so and have believed it and the few feminists who have tried to push in have been slapped in the face. . . . And the few women who have been artificially reared up as leaders are not leaders of women and have been reared not to lead women but to fool them.*[43]

Miss White's analysis was confirmed by Emily Newell Blair, the national vice-chairman of the Democratic party in the twenties. In Mrs. Blair's view, at the very beginning, competent women—the genuine leaders—had essayed party politics, but when they showed themselves unwilling to be rubber stamps they were replaced by women more willing to be led. These were the artificial leaders to whom Miss White referred.[44]

[41] *Ibid.*, clippings. She had the additional distinction of providing the state with another successful woman politician, her daughter Lucy who followed her in the legislature in the 1930's and ultimately became a federal judge.

[42] Jack Tate in Sue Shelton White Papers (Woman's Archives, Radcliffe College Library).

[43] Sue Shelton White to Mary Dewson, November 23, 1928, *ibid.*

[44] Blair, "Women in the Political Parties."

An increasing number of Southern women did undertake simple party work of the doorbell-ringing and envelope-stuffing variety—a trend that still continues. And whether they helped make policy or not, women voters as voters affected the outcome of elections. Women claimed to have defeated James E. Ferguson and elected William P. Hobby governor of Texas in 1920. In Mississippi Henry L. Whitfield, former president of Mississippi State College for Women, was elected governor in 1923, largely through the efforts of alumnae of the college. South Carolina women thought they had a large hand in the defeat of Cole Blease. One South Carolina woman who worked through the whole campaign remarked innocently, "We made no partisan stand, we merely got out the vote." Tennessee Democrats, perhaps looking for a scapegoat, blamed the women for the Republican victory in Tennessee in the 1920 election. The women themselves claimed credit for the return of Cordell Hull to Congress three years later.[45]

Evidence of the increasing effectiveness of women voters may be deduced from the vituperative attacks leveled at them. In addition to the accusations that they were being used by Northern manufacturers, they were accused of being radical, unfeminine, of organizing Negro women, and of using "illegitimate pressure" to put across the measures of a "feminist bloc." David Clark, perhaps the South's bitterest enemy of child labor regulation, went so far as to claim that more babies died after the Sheppard-Towner Act was in operation than before. His *Textile Bulletin* attacked women harshly. The Associated Industries of Kentucky circulated a condemnation of "political women" reprinted from the Dearborn, Michigan, *Independent*. The Louisville *Herald* suggested the reason: "As we have said, the woman voter is making herself felt in ways not chartered for her. We will not go to the length of saying she is always welcome in these channels, but there are times when one may gauge the need for one's activity and curiosity by the ungracious manner of one's reception."[46]

Many of the women who undertook a more active role in Southern politics in the twenties had encountered this ungracious reception. But their motivation was deeply rooted. Those who had been trained during the two or three decades before suffrage were eager to move into a more active and effective political role in 1920. By then their general goals had been formulated. Their underlying motivation is complex, but at least two main drives seem clear: first, the drive to assert themselves as individual human beings with minds and capacities that could be used; and, second, the drive to improve the world in which they lived. The balance of these motives varied from person to person. Some, like Lucy Mason, were primarily interested in social reform:

> *When I was fourteen, a missionary's sermon made me want to be a missionary myself. Later I recognized that religion can be put to work right in one's own community. It was this belief that took me into the Equal Suffrage League, and later the League of Women Voters, both of which were interested in labor and social legislation.*[47]

[45] These claims appear in letters and reports to the National Office of the League of Women Voters in League of Women Voters Papers. The information about Governor Whitfield is contained in Lucy Somerville Howorth to author, February 5, 1964.

[46] Louisville, Ky., *Herald*, May 9, 1923.

[47] Lucy Randolph Mason, *To Win These Rights: A Personal Story of the CIO in the South* (New York, 1952), 4.

Others thoroughly enjoyed the game of politics and the feeling of power that might occasionally go with it. Nearly all felt that significant reforms would be more easily achieved with women's help.

The Nineteenth Amendment changed a good many things, but it brought only a partial modification in the Southern culture pattern, and the difficulties in the way of women's full participation in public life were considerable. One major obstacle, in addition to the demands of home and family, was the flat opposition of many men. Equally important was the unwillingness of many women to assume and carry through large responsibilities. From the record it seems that numbers of women had a vague desire to "do something" but needed leadership in finding what to do and how to do it, and the leaders were never sufficiently numerous to tap all the potential resources. A good example, no doubt an extreme one, was a Virginia town of which it was reported that when a certain Miss Terry was at home the town was jumping with women's political activities but when she went to Europe all was quiet.

Around the handful of leaders there gathered a slowly growing number of supporters and workers, and when this support was effectively channeled specific goals were achieved. In almost every instance groups of men were working to the same ends, and frequently there was co-operation. It is impossible to say what would have happened without the women's efforts, but it does seem clear that in the two areas of race relations and factory regulation much less would have been accomplished without them.

Through it all the outward aspect of the Southern Lady was normally maintained as the necessary precondition of securing a hearing. For some women, this was a perfectly compatible role, so long as they could change its behavioral aspects. Others impatiently called for an end to pedestals, but even they found it more effective to operate within the ladylike tradition. The other side of the coin was that the image of the proper Southern Lady was used effectively as a weapon by those who objected to the substantive goals for which women were working, hoping thus to discredit the goals themselves.

No one would argue that the Southern states became a progressive paradise in the twenties, but it is impossible to study the history of the welfare movements of the time without being surprised by the degree to which the spirit of progressivism was still in flower, and the amount of hopeful optimism about the future of reform that animated women in the face of the general spirit of reaction which is said to have permeated political life. Professor George B. Tindall has adumbrated the "business progressivism" of Southern state governments in the twenties.[48] To the picture he drew must now be added the decided growth through the decade of the conception of state responsibility for public welfare, not in the old custodial sense, but in the newer sense of ameliorating the underlying conditions that created serious human problems. To the growth of this idea and its application in law, Southern women made a considerable contribution.

When all this has been said we are left with the most troublesome questions still unanswered. In spite of the impressive record of accomplishment, the high expectations of the women who had led the suffrage movement did not come

[48] George B. Tindall, "Business Progressivism: Southern Politics in the Twenties," *South Atlantic Quarterly*, LXII (Winter 1963), 92–106.

to pass. What happened to the verve and enthusiasm with which the suffrage veterans set about to reorganize society? That it did not all vanish is evident from the Southern scene today, but that it did not lead to a clear-cut image of a New Woman to replace the Southern Lady is also evident. The numbers of women in public life, in proportion to the population, are probably no more today than in 1925. While the number of women in labor force climbs—some say alarmingly—the number of women in responsible jobs of leadership, policy-making, or in the professions is still not large. To these difficult and intriguing questions historians of women must now begin to turn their attention.

12

HENRY FORD'S TRACTORS AND AMERICAN AGRICULTURE

Reynold M. Wik

As steam power in the form of tractors was introduced into American agriculture, the farmer experienced, first, affluence during the Wilson years, and then serious economic crisis during the 1920's. The introduction of the tractor helped him to expand his operations and then played a part in creating the huge surpluses that were central to his dilemma. This essay tells the story of Henry Ford's entry into the tractor business and his attempts to utilize the same techniques of mass production, relatively low prices, and installment purchasing that he had developed in the production of the automobile and that had made his name a household word in the years just prior to World War I. Although Ford's early efforts in tractor production were not as successful as they had been in auto production, he pointed the way for the mass production of the tractor. The tractor and the "flivver" profoundly affected many phases of American life. Together they drove the horse from the highways and the fields, wrecked a $50,000,000 carriage and wagon industry, and along with electricity brought the farmer back into the main currents of American life.

Reynold M. Wik is the May Treat Morrison Professor of American History at Mills College. His book Steam Power on the American Farm *won the American Historical Association's coveted Beveridge Award. His scholarly work focuses on the theme of the application of power to American agriculture. See, for example, his* Henry Ford and Grassroots America *(Ann Arbor, 1972).*

Henry Ford greatly influenced farm life in the United States during the first half of the twentieth century. As father of the Model T he shared with 1,400 other automobile companies in the demise of the horse in rural America. From 1908

Source: *Agricultural History*, Vol. 38, No. 2 (1964), pp. 79–86. Reprinted by permission of the author and the Agricultural History Society.

to 1927 fifteen million Flivvers demonstrated the feasibility of motor transport in agricultural regions. These ubiquitous contraptions plowed through mud roads, crept along fence lines and rattled into farm yards with persistent fortitude. Observers claimed the Tin Lizzy put America on wheels and Ford among the billionaries and that this feat surpassed in sociological significance the impact of the first World War.[1] Will Rogers said Ford changed the habits of more people than Caesar, Mussolini, Charles Chaplain, Clara Bow, Xerxes, Amos n' Andy and Bernard Shaw.[2]

Yet, this fantastic automotive achievement has often obscured Ford's efforts to aid the American farmer in a more direct manner by providing mechanical power in the form of tractors.[3]

For many years Ford kept insisting that American agriculture should be made more mechanized by substituting mechanical power for animal power on the farm. He disapproved of horses and mules because they devoured too much hay and oats while tractors were superior to horse flesh in efficiency, in ease of handling and in the cost per unit of work produced.

The "Motor King's" efforts to encourage power farming were genuine, not merely a wealthy man's hobby reflecting nostalgia for the bucolic life. As a boy he thought about simplifying farm work when he saw a self-propelled Nichols and Shepard steam traction engine puff down a country road. Later he called this experience one of the most important in his early life because it led him to speculate about replacing horses with machines.[4] In fact, he attempted to make a farm tractor before he turned his attention to automobiles, for in 1883 he built a crude steam engine to be used for plowing.[5] Although the machine proved impractical, his initial intentions were apparent. Charles E. Sorenson, production manager of the River Rouge plant, insisted that Ford's first efforts were directed to tractor building but since people were more interested in automobiles, he began designing internal combustion engines for transportation.[6]

[1] Denis W. Brogan, "Unnoticed Changes in America," *Harper's Magazine*, February, 1957, p. 29.

[2] Will Rogers, *Wit and Philosophy from Radio Talks of Will Rogers* (New York, 1930), p. 33.

[3] As yet, there is no sound, comprehensive history of the farm tractor in American agriculture. However, certain aspects of the subject may be found in Fred R. Jones, *Farm Gas Engines and Tractors* (New York: McGraw-Hill, 1963); R. B. Gray, *Development of the Agricultural Tractor in the United States up to 1919*, Part I, United States Department of Agriculture, Information Series No. 107 (Beltsville, Maryland, June, 1954); Reynold M. Wik, *Steam Power on the American Farm* (Philadelphia: University of Pennsylvania Press, 1953), Chapter IX.

The word "tractor" was first used by George H. Edwards of Chicago on his patent No. 425,600 in 1890. Later, W. H. Williams, sales manager of the Hart-Parr Company of Charles City, Iowa, popularized the word in 1906 because he thought "gasoline traction engine" was an awkward expression.

[4] Henry Ford and Samuel Crowther, *My Life and Work* (New York: Doubleday Page and Co., 1922), p. 22.

[5] The Ford Motor Company Archives, Central Office Building, Dearborn, Michigan, Henry Ford Fair Lane Papers, Accession 1, Box 4, catalog *Fordson the Universal Tractor*, introduction by Henry Ford (Dearborn: Ford Motor Company, 1918), p. 10. This source will be referred to in subsequent citations, *Henry Ford Papers*.

[6] *Ibid.*, Accession 380, Box 25, memorandum, Charles E. Sorenson to R. B. Darragh, July 10, 1938.

Lord Alfred C. Northcliffe of England concurred saying the tractor had always been Ford's dream.[7]

The first tractors built by the Ford Motor Company were experimental, reflecting all the mechanical absurdities associated with the birth of this industry. In the summer of 1908, Henry Ford told Joseph Galamb and C. J. Smith to make a tractor in three days by attaching drive wheels to a Model B Ford car chassis. Galamb, who helped design the Model T automobile, placed wagon wheels in front and grain binder wheels in the rear with a gas tank in front of the radiator. This tractor pulled a binder in the wheat fields on the Ford farms near Dearborn, but since the 24 horsepower engine lacked power and the radiator over-heated, the monstrosity had limited value. Similar efforts were made in 1913 to convert a Model T chassis into a tractor by using a heavier frame and a worm gear transmission. Although several of these hybrid machines were built, they lacked durability and finesse.[8] Philip S. Rose of the agricultural engineering department of North Dakota State College, in 1915 claimed they drank 15 gallons of water daily, the steering devices needed frequent adjustments, and the engine bearings required tightening every two weeks.[9] The editor of *Gas Review* insisted Ford had not invented anything new by merely putting larger wheels on his Tin Lizzy. It was another Ford joke, probably gotten up like other Ford jokes for cheap publicity.[10]

However, Ford took a serious view of the farm tractor. He visited the spectacular plowing contest held near Winnipeg, Manitoba, in 1910 where he became convinced of the superiority of gasoline tractors over the steam traction engines. When stockholders opposed the manufacture of tractors in the Highland Park plant, he joined with Edsel to incorporate a separate tractor division in 1915 and put Charles E. Sorenson in charge of the experimental work. This action reflected little novelty because approximately 200 different companies had already manufactured the 51,000 tractors in use on American farms before the Ford Motor Company produced its first Fordson tractor in October, 1917.[11]

Since the tractors and automobiles both depended on the invention and development of internal combustion engines, their early history followed parallel lines. In fact, the first tractors appeared in the United States in 1892, the year

[7] *London Times*, October 22, 1917, p. 9.

[8] *Henry Ford Papers*, Accession 23, Box 7, C. J. Smith, *Oral History Interviews*, p. 16. See also Joseph Galamb, *Oral History Interviews*, pp. 61–63.

[9] Philip S. Rose, "Analysis of the Tractor Industry," manuscript 20 pp., 1915, p. 5.

[10] *Gas Review* (Madison, Wisconsin, November, 1915), p. 17.

[11] Martin R. Cooper, Glen T. Barton and Albert P. Brodell, *Progress of Farm Mechanization*, USDA, Miscellaneous Publication No. 630 (Washington, D. C., October, 1946), p. 85. Figures taken from the Reports of the Census of Agriculture. The number of tractors on farms were:

1910,	1,000	1914,	17,000	1918,	85,000	1922,	372,000
1911,	4,000	1915,	25,000	1919,	158,000	1923,	428,000
1912,	8,000	1916,	37,000	1920,	246,000	1924,	496,000
1913,	14,000	1917,	51,000	1921,	343,000	1925,	549,000

The number of tractors manufactured in the United States naturally exceeded the numbers in use at any given time. Tractor production figures are given in R. B. Gray, *Development of the Agricultural Tractor in the United States up to 1919*, Part I, USDA Information Series, No. 107, Agricultural Research Service (Beltsville, Maryland, June, 1954), pp. 2–26. In 1917 more than 200 tractor companies manufactured 62,742 tractors. In 1918, 132,000 tractors were manufactured.

Charles Duryea built his famous auto buggy. At the same time, John Froehlich of Iowa and William Patterson of the J. L. Case Company of Racine, Wisconsin, built tractors which performed some farm work.[12] Before 1900 farmers had purchased gas tractors from various firms such as the Waterloo Gas Traction Engine Company, Huber Manufacturing Company, Winona Manufacturing Company, Kinnard and Sons and the Best Company. However, the Hart-Parr engines produced in Charles City, Iowa, in 1901 became the first tractors to be manufactured and sold on a large scale. By 1907, two hundred, or one third of the tractors operating in this country, were of this origin.[13]

Unfortunately, the designing engineers imitated the construction of the lumbering steam traction engines which had been used for threshing and plowing for almost a half century before the advent of the gasoline tractor. The steam engines were powerful leviathans, but clumsy to operate and too heavy to handle on rough terrain. In wet fields the engines needed all their power to move themselves. Six hundred pounds of iron and steel per horsepower delivered on the drawbar was the best ratio that manufacturers could achieve.[14]

Since most of the early tractors were made by steam engine companies, the manufacturers merely substituted gasoline engines to replace steam boilers. As a result, most tractors prior to 1912 weighed from 20,000 to 50,000 pounds. The flywheels on some weighed a ton. The Emerson-Brantingham, for example had drive wheels eight feet in diameter and gas tanks holding 77 gallons. Some of these monsters were so hard to start that owners let them run all night rather than face this baffling problem in the morning. Faulty construction led to broken crankshafts, warped clutches, broken gears, dead magnetos and burned out bearings. Some farmers spent $1,500 for repairs in one year, while bankers often refused credit to men bent on spending several thousands of dollars for a new tractor.[15] The unreliability of large tractors coupled with an over extension of credit by manufacturers led to a collapse in the business in 1912 with many companies going into receivership.

Meanwhile, farmers demanded smaller tractors which would be less costly, easier to drive, and which could replace horses pulling farm implements. In harvest time light tractors would relieve horses from the 100 degree heat of the harvest fields. The *Kansas Farmer* reported in 1915 that the need for more power

[12] *Ibid.*, p. 13. According to R. B. Gray, the Charter Gas Engine Company built six gasoline tractors in 1889, but these machines were more stationary than self-propelled. "In 1892 John Froehlich, of Froehlich, Iowa, mounted a gasoline engine, built by the Van Duzen Gas and Gasoline Engine Company of Cincinnati on a Robinson running gear. This was probably the first gasoline tractor on record that was an operating success. It completed a 50-day threshing run belted to a 40 × 58 Case threshing machine. It pulled the thresher over difficult terrain and operated in temperatures from minus 3 to 100 degrees. The Froehlich was the forerunner of the Waterloo Boy and John Deere line of tractors. The Patterson engine developed ignition and carburetion troubles and was discarded after several years of experimentation.

[13] A. C. Seyforth, "Treatise on the History of the Tractor," unpublished manuscript written by an official of the International Harvester Company of Chicago, 21 pp., 1923.

[14] *American Thresherman and Farm Power* (Madison, Wisconsin, July, 1916), p. 28.

[15] Barton W. Currie, *The Tractor and Its Influence upon the Agricultural Implement Business* (Philadelphia, 1916), pp. 137–144.

on the farm justified the use of small tractors.[16] From 40,000 to 80,000 people attended tractor demonstrations in Midwestern cities in 1915 and 1916. As farmers watched 30 tractor companies exhibit their machines in field tests at Enid, Oklahoma, in 1915, hundreds of sales were made on the spot. Farmers pulled out their check books and dropped down on their knees in the plowed dirt to write their checks. A business man writing to Henry Ford on September 26, 1914, stated, "There are over two million farmers in the United States and Canada, every one of whom is a legitimate prospect for a small tractor. . . . You never saw the farmers so ripe for anything and plucking should not be long delayed."[17]

Anticipating this trend, the Bull Tractor Company of Minneapolis in 1913 introduced a 4,650 pound machine advertised as the "Bull with the Pull." Selling for only $645.00 the model was the forerunner of the small power units toward which virtually all of the tractor manufacturers were turning at the time.[18] The Wallis "Cub," the 7,000 pound Avery, the C.O.D. tractor, the Happy Farmer, the Kansas City Prairie Dog, the Bates Steel Mule and numerous other baby tractors soon followed. In 1915, Henry Ford announced his entrance into the light tractor field with an automotive system of mass production.

The Ford Motor Company's Fordson tractor was born in the fiery cauldron of World War I. The stalemate on the Western Front with its heavy losses on both sides indicated that victory would go to the side best prepared for total war. When German submarines accentuated the food crisis in Great Britain, the English people attempted to increase farm crops by making a rapid conversion to mechanized agriculture. On April 9, 1917, the day following America's entry into the war, Percival L. Perry, in charge of Ford affairs in England, called Edsel Ford to plead, "Would you be willing to send Sorenson and others with tractor drawings of everything necessary loaning them to British government so that the parts can be manufactured over here. . . . The matter is very urgent. . . . National necessity entirely dependent Mr. Ford's decision."[19] The following day, Henry Ford pledged full support to save Britain. He sent Charles E. Sorenson and a staff of experts to London to assist the British in the manufacture of Fordson tractors. However, a German air raid on London, July 23, 1917, caused British leaders to shift all their efforts to the manufacture of airplanes. Thus plans to build the Fordson in England were abandoned. Instead, Lord Milner, of the Minister of Munitions Board, urged that tractors be purchased from several American firms and imported into England. David Lloyd George, in November, announced his government had ordered 8,000 American tractors for breaking up estates, parks and lawns to convert them to agricultural purposes.[20] Under the pressures of war the first 15 Fordsons were built in October, 1917, and by the end of the year 254 had been shipped to beleaguered Britain.

[16] *Kansas Farmer*, September 12, 1914, p. 5.

[17] Letter written by an executive of the Minneapolis Steel and Machinery Company, Minneapolis, Minnesota, to Henry Ford, Dearborn, Michigan, September 26, 1914, in *Henry Ford Papers*.

[18] R. B. Gray, *op. cit.*, p. 22.

[19] *Henry Ford Papers*, Accession 54, Box 4, telegram from Percival Perry, London, to Edsel Ford, Dearborn, Michigan, April 7, 1917.

[20] *Ibid.*, Accession 266, Box 1, letter from David Lloyd George, 10 Downing Street, Whitehall S.W., First Lord of the Treasury, London, England, to Percival L. Perry, London, June 28, 1917. Lloyd George stated: "Owing to the changed condi-

However, in subsequent years there has been a tendency to exaggerate the Ford Motor Company's technical assistance to the British Isles during the war years. Henry Ford is often pictured as the hero with a heart of gold rushing off to save the starving Englishmen from the clutches of the marauding Huns. The mission accomplished, the benefactor received the undying gratitude of the terror stricken English populace.

Actually, many Englishmen disliked Ford in 1917 because of his Peace Ship venture two years earlier and for his opposition to the floating of a British loan in the United States. They recalled Ford's statement, "If I had my way I would tie a tin can on the joint Anglo-French Commission and chase it back to Europe."[21] They resented his pacifistic utterances labeling war as murder and that if the United States were involved and he were asked to produce munitions he would tear down his factories brick by brick with his own hands. In addition, certain businessmen in Britain opposed Ford's proposal to build a tractor plant at Cork, Ireland, because this would give a foreign manufacturer undue advantage in the local market. A malcontent writing to the *Times* on March 27, 1917 fumed,

> *What, I ask, is going to happen when the product of the Ford Cork factory is let loose on the British market? Are we to let them in free as Irish manufacturers, made in Detroit, U.S.A., and so ruin our own motor trade, or have all the fat in the fire over again when we attempt to collect customs duty. See the danger? It is positively criminal to create even a possibility of such an impasse.*[22]

Again, the British government's preference for Fordson tractors drew criticism on the grounds that the War Agricultural Committee had not recommended the Fordson for purchase because other American tractors had proved more successful in field tests. The editor of the *Implement and Machinery Review* accused the Minister of Munitions Board of failing to purchase tractors already on the market and instead waiting six months for Fordsons to leave the factory at Dearborn.[23] Some justification for this criticism resides in the fact that only 3,600 Fordsons reached Britain by March 1, 1918 and the entire consignment of 6,000 did not arrive until the war was almost over.[24] The newspaper

---

tions here, I very much regret that I have found it impossible to proceed with the manufacture of M.O.M. tractors in this country. I understand that you are about to proceed to America in order to make arrangements for the production of these tractors in the United States and I know that I may rely on you to do everything in your power to ensure the production of the greatest number of tractors for use in the United Kingdom. I regret very much that plans for the production of these machines have been altered, but I am certain that even under these circumstances I am able to count on Mr. Ford and yourself to do your utmost to assist us in order that the food production of this country may not suffer." The Lloyd George announcement to the public occurred on November 10, 1917, and was reported in *The Implement Machinery Review* (London, December, 1917), p. 95.

21 *London Times*, September 28, 1915, p. 9.

22 *Ibid.*, March 27, 1917, p. 7.

23 *The Implement and Machinery Review* (London, July 1, 1917), p. 293.

24 *Henry Ford Papers*, cablegram, Henry Ford to Lord Northcliffe, February 28, 1918, stated: "We have shipped to date 1800 assembled tractors and parts for another 1800 knocked down. Only ten per cent of this has been loaded aboard ship." *Ibid.*, Accession 268, Box 1, C. F. Elmer, Head of the Accounting Department of

files in the British archives and the farm journals in the Whitehall Library in London reflect the hostility of large numbers of Britons toward Ford and the tractor transactions.[25]

Meanwhile, in the United States the Fordson publicity became widespread. People conditioned to heatless Mondays, meatless Tuesdays and wheatless Wednesdays were told that food would win the war and the "Man with the Hoe" must go. The *New York Times* on April 22, 1917 ran the banner, "A Girl on a Tractor is Worth Two Men Behind the Plow and Two Horses in Front of It." The *Bridgeport Standard* admonished, "Buy Tractors and Win the War," while the *Newark Star-Eagle* predicted, "Detroit will Defeat Essen, Ford Will Triumph Over Krupp."

As might be expected, Ford himself had plenty to say on the subject. His press release on March 25, 1918 hailed motorized farming as solving the food problem because one tractor would produce 50 times its weight in food annually. One ship carrying tractors to Europe would equal 50 ships carrying food the next fall. Fifteen thousand men in his factories could produce one thousand tractors a day. Bookkeeping in the cities would not produce more food, but better machinery on the farm would do the job. The *Denver Post* quoted Ford as saying he would make a million tractors and sell them for ten cents a pound. "I am going to make a Ford car, truck and tractor and sell them all for $600.00," he boasted, "I'm going to do it, if I don't croak first."[26]

As a token of friendship, Ford on April 23, 1918 donated the first Fordson manufactured for domestic use to Luther Burbank. When the engine rambled into his yard at Santa Rosa, California, the botanist exclaimed, "Just like Ford, all motor and no frame."[27] Thomas Edison received the number two Fordson. Production increased at the River Rouge Tractor Plant until 26,187 tractors had left the assembly lines by Armistice Day, and 91,346 by the end of 1919.

To advertise the new engines, Ford dealers conducted plowing demonstrations in many sections of the country. Several thousand people witnessed a Fordson exhibition in East Oakland, California, on October 6, 1918, where a local scribe explained, "They came, saw, and were convinced. The horse is now the most extravagant motor known."[28] Special training courses were held to teach women the fundamentals of tractor operations. One farmerette stated she began the training with reservations not knowing if she could stand the monotony of driving a tractor six days a week for three months. Yet, after the harvest season she asserted, "To work out in the open air on a farm, knowing that we are having a direct part in supplying food for our fellowmen, was one of the most satisfying things I have ever experienced."[29]

Since tractors were scarce during the war years, the Ford Motor Company announced in March, 1918, that Fordsons would be distributed to American farmers

---

the River Rouge Plant, "Fordson Tractor Production Figures." This data shows that the first 3,078 Fordsons were not completed until April, 1918. The Cork factory in Ireland did not go into production until July, 1919.

25 *London Times*, August 24, 1917, p. 3, and passim August 27, 1917, p. 4.

26 *Denver Post*, August 1, 1916, p. 1.

27 *Santa Rosa Republican* (California, April 24, 1918), p. 1.

28 *Oakland Tribune* (California, October 6, 1918), p. 4.

29 *Henry Ford Papers*, Ford Ferguson File, Number 45632, "Tractor Driving a Farmerette's Way," July 6, 1918. An unsigned letter written by a farm girl attending the Berry School near Rome, Georgia.

through permits granted by County War Boards. To secure a permit, farmers must promise to keep the tractor working on the land, while the county agents were to see that the machines were given maximum use. The cost was $750.00 f.o.b. Detroit, but no profits were to go to middlemen as distributors. Most of the leading agricultural states were given a quota of 1,000 tractors.[30]

As with most ration programs, complaints arose on all sides. Some farmers begged for tractors, but were denied permits for their purchase. Dealers of farm implements accused Ford of a clever scheme to unload his tractors on war boards under the guise of patriotism. Thus civilian agencies in the states distributed millions of dollars' worth of Fordsons while the dealers received nothing for their work in making deliveries. Ford got the cash and the others the exercise. The *Farm Machinery Power* magazine in August, 1918, claimed Ford had promised to sell his tractors for $250.00 hence farmers withheld their purchases from other firms waiting for the Fordsons to appear on the market. When they finally arrived, they were priced at $750.00 indicating Ford's publicity department out ran his cost department.[31] In addition, Ford left the impression he sold his engines at cost as his contribution to the war effort. Yet, his business records show that the total cost of manufacturing a Fordson in 1918 was $567.14, thus leaving a tidy profit of $182.86 on each unit.[32] Again business managed to make a healthy profit during the war in spite of all flag waving to the contrary.

Following the war, the Fordsons infested the land like locusts for mass production techniques turned out 350 tractors daily in 1921 and 750 a day in 1924. It took only 30 hours and 40 minutes to convert raw materials into the 4,000 parts going into the tractor assembly. Some wags said they reached the farmers before they had cooled from the furnace heat. Others suggested facetiously that since Ford threw nothing away, he would probably utilize the heat from fever-stricken patients in his hospital to help dry the paint on his tractors. At any rate, the Fordson production figures reached 486,822 in 1925 and 650,000 by May, 1927. Officials of the company boasted they had manufactured more than half of all tractors built in the United States up to this time, with sales made in most foreign countries. Ten thousand Fordsons had been shipped to the Soviet Union by January 27, 1926.[33]

The original Fordson manufactured from 1917 to 1927, like its predecessor

[30] *Detroit Journal*, March 13, 1918, p. 1.

[31] *Farm Machinery Power* (St. Louis, Missouri, August 12, 1918), p. 5.

[32] *Ford Papers*, Accession 268, Box 1, C. F. Elmer, Head of the Accounting Department of the River Rouge Plant, "Fordson Production Figures." In 1921 the Fordson price dropped to $625.00 with production costs dropped to $534.00 leaving a profit of $91.00 per tractor.

[33] *New York Times*, January 27, 1926, p. 11. Ford officials explained that sales to Russia called for 75 per cent in cash and ten months' credit on the remaining 25 per cent. Shipment was made by rail to Seattle and by boat to Vladivostock.

For production figures of the Fordson see *Henry Ford Papers*, Accession 268, Box 1, C. F. Elmer, Head of the Accounting Department of the River Rouge Plant, "Fordson Production Figures," 1926. This data shows:

Number of Fordson tractors manufactured from 1917 to 1926.

1917,	239	1922,	57,759
1918,	33,926	1923,	101,938
1919,	58,410	1924,	78,635
1920,	34,115	1925,	96,463
1921,	25,107	Total.	486,822 tractors.

the Model T car, featured compactness and simplicity of design. A 20 horsepower four-cylinder motor was bolted directly to a cast iron transmission housing thus eliminating the steel frame common to most other tractors of the day.[34] The machine weighed only 2,500 pounds, was less than five feet high, had a wheel base of 63 inches and would turn in a 21-foot circle. Like the Model T, the electricity came off a low-tension magneto attached to the flywheel, while a thermo-syphon system cooled the motor. All gears ran in an oil bath, with the three forward speeds ranging from 2¾ to 6¾ miles per hour. Like many of its contemporaries, the engine burned either kerosene or gasoline, an economy feature which appealed to farmers most of whom thought gasoline prices were inordinately high.[35]

Although the Fordson had large sales, it never duplicated the success of the fabulous Model T because it possessed several disadvantages. In the first place it arrived too late. Had it appeared ten years earlier, it doubtless would have swept the farming communities like a winter blizzard, but by 1917, scores of other companies were already in the light tractor field to diminish the Fordson's claim to uniqueness. Secondly, the tractor was too light and impotent to meet the power needs on large farms where the minimum requirements were three and four plow engines. Therefore it became more of an auxiliary tractor used for lighter work instead of becoming the basic power unit on the farm. In the third place, the Fordson incorporated weaknesses which mitigated against its popularity. The small 45-inch wheels permitted the engine to mire down readily in muddy soil. Farmers complained this lowness let corn stalks punch holes in the radiator. The inefficient ignition system made it difficult to start, while the absence of a water pump caused the motor to overheat. An erratic governor permitted too great fluctuations in the speed of the motor, and on some the shifting lever failed to stay in position. The worm gear differential created friction causing the driver's seat to heat up in unbearable fashion.

However, its most negative feature lay in its tendency to rear up in front and flip over backwards if sudden resistance on the drawbar created excessive torque in the transmission. One Indiana farmer believed such a dangerous machine should be banned by law. The editor of *The Eastern Implement Dealer* claimed Fordsons killed 36 drivers in 1918, while *Pipp's Weekly* insisted the tractor had snuffed out the lives of 136 men prior to August, 1922.[36] These publications ran headlines screaming "Fordson Tractor Proved Man Killer," "Fordson Tractor Is Bad Medicine for Farmer's Ills," and "Fordson's are Huns of the Field." Irate

[34] *Henry Ford Papers*, Interviews of Eugene J. Farkas, Oral History Project, Vol. I, p. 73. Farkas worked as an engineer in designing the Fordson. He recalls that Henry Ford did not believe a tractor could be constructed successfully without a steel frame. "Mr. Ford had the idea that it had to have a frame. By that time I convinced Sorenson that it didn't have to have one. He could design the castings so they would be strong enough to support the entire tractor."

[35] *The Nebraska Farmer*, December 1, 1915, p. 1176. The editor stated in an editorial that gasoline had risen five to seven cents a gallon over the last few weeks. It had been selling at ten cents a gallon. By May, 1916, gasoline sold in many places for 26 cents a gallon.

[36] *The Eastern Implement Dealer* (Philadelphia, April 26, 1922), p. 6, and passim June 21, 1939, p. 1. See also *Pipp's Weekly* (Dearborn, Michigan, July 22, 1922), III, pp. 2–3; and *Farm Machinery-Farm Power* (St. Louis, Missouri, September 15, 1918), p. 4.

journalists insisted that press agents had made Henry Ford a benefactor, while in reality he was a public nuisance. When the Ratcliffe Brothers invented an attachment to cut off the ignition when the tractor began to rear, one editor thought they should be given the Carnegie Medal for saving human life and making the Fordson as docile as a suckling lamb and as safe to consort with as a depth bombed submarine.

In reply, Ford spokesmen maintained the accidents resulted from inexperienced and ignorant drivers who had no more knowledge of tractors than reading Chinese laundry checks. Any tractor could be dangerous if improperly handled. Those printing unsupported accusations were guilty of libel.

On the other hand, satisfied Ford customers praised the Fordson saying it made farm work easier, it performed ideally in orchards and on truck farms, it helped keep the boys on the farm and it was so versatile it could do everything except milk a cow or climb a tree. A Mississippi farmer in 1921 testified it defeated all competition in that region and would do anything any sensible man or fool wanted done. Some expressed their admiration for the iron horse in poetic lines:

The Fordson on the farm arose
Before the dawn at four.
It drove the cows and washed the clothes
And finished every chore.
Then forth it went into the fields
Just at the break of day
It reaped and threshed the golden yield
And hauled it all away.

or

I've worked mules and horses on the farm,
And yoke of oxen too;
But a Fordson tractor beats them all
By forcing the farm work through.
It seldom balks, or kicks or squeals
And never succumbs to heat
I tell you now my farmer friend
The Fordson's hard to beat.

or

Come here old mule, I've news for you
Here's a Fordson
It's come to make our lives anew
Here's a Fordson
It's come to change our work to play
It's come to turn our night to day
Oh yes old mule it's come to stay
For it's a Fordson.

Although this outburst of sentimentality may not reflect the greatest poetry ever to gush from the brain of man, perhaps the only thing unusual about it is that it appeared at all. One would look far to find similar odes dedicated to tractors assembled by International Harvester, Caterpillar, Advance Rumley, Flour City, Aultman Taylor, Tom Thumb, Emerson Brantingham or the Dayton-Dick Company of Quincy, Illinois.

In spite of reasonable success, the Fordson faced tough opposition in the 1920's. The agricultural depression of 1920 to 1923 created sales resistance and dealers reported farmers lacked money to buy machinery. When the Ford Motor Company had difficulty in disposing of their tractor production in 1924, sales managers blamed the local dealers for being more interested in selling automobiles than farm machinery. Charles E. Sorenson later insisted that the obligation to sell both cars and tractors had proved too much for the dealers.[37]

Meanwhile, the International Harvester Company increased competition by producing the highly successful McCormick Deering 10–20 and 15–30 tractors in the early twenties. Likewise the introduction of the Farmall in 1924 with its ability to farm row crops made the Fordson more obsolete. Then too, the success of other companies such as J. I. Case, John Deere and Minneapolis encouraged Ford officials in 1927 to discontinue the manufacture of the Fordson in the United States. The company continued tractor production at plants in Cork, Ireland and Dagenham, England. Not until the late 1930's did Ford again begin manufacture of tractors in the United States.

In retrospect, one could conclude that the Fordson failed to revolutionize American agriculture for it seems clear the mechanization of farming was inevitable regardless of the part played by the Ford organization. Other manufacturers built tractors before the birth of the Fordson and continued to do so after its demise in 1927.

However, the significance of this particular machine lay in the fact that it gave Henry Ford an excellent opportunity to propagandize the crusade for power farming in the United States. Certainly the Fordson proved that small versatile tractors could replace horses in work in which they had been thought to be indispensable. While this model was no better or worse than its contemporaries, the Fordson provided its sire with a sounding board. Now Henry Ford could point to his 7,000 acre farms in Michigan in 1921 to demonstrate that tractors did all the field work in 21 days of the year without the assistance of a single horse. Naturally, he suggested others could simplify their work in similar fashion. Since Ford was a prominent national figure, as well known as Pike's Peak, the Statue of Liberty or Niagara Falls, many looked to him as a seer, the Great White Father of Fair Lane whose dedication to improved farm machinery carried conviction. Henry A. Wallace believed Ford possessed profound insights in these matters, while the Governor of North Dakota wanted Ford to apply mass production methods to the construction of all farm implements.[38]

In addition the Ford Motor Company encouraged power farming by donating tractors to agricultural colleges, experiment stations and vocational and industrial schools. The tractor school in Dearborn, organized in 1919, provided instruction for both foreign and domestic students. Later the Farm Youth Organization assisted farm boys to make more intelligent use of power machinery.

[37] Charles E. Sorenson, *My Forty Years with Ford,* p. 240.

[38] *Henry Ford Papers,* Ford-Ferguson File, Number 03332, Henry A. Wallace, Des Moines, Iowa, to Henry Ford, December 20, 1921; also R. A. Nestos, Governor of North Dakota, Bismarck, North Dakota, to Henry Ford, Dearborn, Michigan, April 3, 1924.

Henry Ford consistently preached the doctrine of faith in the machine. He often said, "Man minus the machine is a slave. Man plus the machine is a free man." He believed machinery spoke a likely language and that technology led to progress. Tractors, trucks and automobiles would change rural life by easing the burden of labor. Needless to say he marched in the movement to eliminate drudgery from farm work. Although mechanization failed to solve the problem of agriculture surpluses in this country, his efforts did remove much of the misery formerly associated with producing them. Since the American farmer today represents the most technologically advanced agriculturalists in the world, Ford helped provide some of the impetus for this significant achievement.

13

BLACK PRIDE AND NEGRO BUSINESS IN THE 1920'S: GEORGE WASHINGTON LEE OF MEMPHIS

David M. Tucker

Although the decade of the 1920's has been characterized as "A Business Civilization," and President Calvin Coolidge declared that "the business of America is business," almost no attention has been devoted by scholars to small business. Large corporations and statistics of economic growth have been carefully examined and these data have been used to interpret the period which, with few exceptions, registered tremendous gains. Business consolidation, mass production, advertising, installment buying, excess profits, and undue speculation are themes fully covered. But small business, and particularly black-owned business during this decade, is rarely examined. Thus the significance of this path-breaking essay, which also provides a valuable corrective to the frequent interpretation of the black businessman as a tool of white capitalism and an exploiter of his less fortunate black brothers. As Professor Tucker perceptively states, "Negroes who went into business generally did so because few other white collar positions gave them as much freedom for independent thought and action."

David M. Tucker is a young scholar teaching at Memphis State University where he specializes in recent American and black history. He has published several articles and Lieutenant Lee of Beale Street *(Nashville, 1971), of which this essay is a part.*

Black business stands second only to the Negro church as the most maligned and caricatured of Negro institutions. Though at one time the universal hope of the race, black capitalism suffered a drastic loss of prestige in the 1930's when the

Source: *Business History Review*, Vol. 43, No. 4 (1969), pp. 435–451.

economic depression led the race intellectuals to initiate an anti-business tradition which has continued into the present.[1] According to this radical criticism, black business had ruthlessly exploited the race for the benefit of only a pitifully small Negro middle class; and since the black masses were, and would continue to be laborers, social reform and not black capitalism, it was said, should be the goal of the race. To be sure, there is much economic truth in this old leftist position; but as a perspective on history, it creates a certain distortion by dismissing the black businessman without ever really considering that as a racial leader, he might have been worth what he cost the race in higher prices. In the urban South, certainly black capitalists appear to have provided the most aggressive local leadership, and nowhere was this more true than in Memphis, Tennessee, where the positive role of black business was exemplified by the life of George W. Lee, one of the city's shrewdest and most articulate Negro insurance executives.

George Washington Lee had been born on a Mississippi cotton patch in 1894 but moved into town at an early age when his mother, the daughter of house servants rather than field hands, took the first opportunity to escape the sharecrop for town life in Indianola, Mississippi. As it happened, this small town in the heart of the Yazoo-Mississippi Delta was one of the nation's most thriving centers of black business; and there, Wayne Cox, the owner of the race bank and an insurance company, provided a model of black success for the young George Lee. Because Cox had graduated from Mississippi's Alcorn Agricultural and Mechanical College, George Lee enrolled at Alcorn, earning his way by working summers as a bellhop in the Memphis Gayoso Hotel. After completing his junior year at Alcorn in 1917, when America entered World War I, George Lee was among the few southern Negroes to be accepted by the Army's officer candidate school and serve in France as a second lieutenant with the 368th Negro Division. After the war, Lieutenant Lee, as he liked to be known thereafter, returned to make his fame and fortune in Memphis, the commercial capital of the mid-South with a population of 101,000 whites and 61,000 blacks.

The Beale Street to which Lieutenant Lee returned gave promise of becoming the business center of the Negro middle class. Black customers had deposited $1,000,000 in their Solvent Savings Bank, $500,000 in their Fraternal Savings, and purchased stock in the new business corporations organized on the street. The war-time Liberty Bond drives had convinced Negroes that investments other than real estate were safe, and Beale Street entrepreneurs financed a new era of business enterprise by selling securities to the black community. The new departure in black capitalism began with Bert M. Roddy's Citizens' Cooperative Stores. Roddy, cashier of Solvent Savings Bank and president of the National Negro Bankers Association, advertised his dream of the race's largest chain-store grocery business, sold his shares of stock to 9,000 small investors, and opened fifteen stores. Fraternal Savings bankers, not to be outdone by Roddy's success, drew up plans for Beale Street's first modern department store, incorporated the Citizens' Mercantile Company, and placed $100,000 worth of stock on the market. Then Wayman Wilkerson and other wealthy Memphians launched a $200,000 manu-

[1] The position of the economic left is stated by: Abram L. Harris, *The Negro as Capitalist: A Study of Banking and Business Among American Negroes* (Philadelphia, 1936), and Ralph Bunche in Gunnar Myrdal, *An American Dilemma* (New York, 1944), 804; E. Franklin Frazier's *Black Bourgeoisie* (Glencoe, 1957) continues the caricature of Negro businessmen.

facturing business, the Tri-State Casket & Coffin Company, with a main factory and outlet in Memphis and assembling plants in St. Louis, Indianapolis, Chicago, Dallas, and New Orleans.[2]

Negro Memphians acquired their largest business enterprise, a life insurance company, from Indianola, Mississippi, where it had been organized by Wayne Cox, the Indianola banker, in 1909. At that time, a young Negro physician, Dr. W. A. Attaway, had convinced Cox that mutual aid societies and fraternal orders were rapidly being replaced by more efficient commercial insurance enterprises; and if the race failed to offer an alternative to fraternal policies by organizing its own life insurance companies, the white-owned Prudential Insurance and Metropolitan Life would eventually get all the race business. Wayne Cox was thus persuaded to organize Mississippi Life with a capital of $25,000, and then, in 1910, to increase its capital to $100,000, making it the first Negro corporation to be chartered as a legal reserve company qualified to write every variety of insurance from the industrial to the endowment policy.[3]

In the beginning, Mississippi Life had struggled under poorly trained and sometimes dishonest officials until two Alcorn University graduates, Merah Steven Stuart and Dr. Joseph Edison Walker, took over the management of the company. Once Stuart became general manager in 1914, having had previous experience as an investigator for a fraternal insurance firm, and Walker, an Indianola physician and charter member of the Company, moved up, in 1916, to become president, Mississippi Life expanded rapidly into Tennessee, Arkansas, and Alabama; the office staff grew to thirty, the field agents to 400, and the annual income passed $500,000.[4] By 1919 the company had grown too large for the small Mississippi town, and Mississippi Life decided to move its home office to Memphis. It now seemed to Beale Street residents that Memphis was well on its way to becoming the center of Negro business.

Memphis was not free from racial prejudice, but Negroes did vote freely, and while white Memphis excluded blacks from any political positions which they felt would put a black man on a social par with a white, race relations were not so bad as to deter George Lee from his plans to make his future in Memphis. In fact, he found the city more concerned with keeping its black citizens than ever before in its history. The war-time migration of Negroes to Chicago and Detroit had created a serious labor problem, so serious in fact that the Memphis Chamber of Commerce had established a committee, the Industrial Welfare Committee, "to keep its Negroes in Memphis."[5] A white banker, S. W. Williamson, announced that colored people were one of Memphis' greatest assets and "anything therefore that will make our colored people more contented and happy, will necessarily be of great advantage to us in the future."[6] A commercial feed company president, J. T. Morgan, agreed; "the business men of Memphis should help make Memphis the best town in this country for our negro population, and make it so

[2] Memphis *Commercial Appeal*, June 3, July 4, August 1, 15, November 24, 1920.

[3] M. S. Stuart, *An Economic Detour: A History of Insurance in the Lives of American Negroes* (New York, 1940), 284; W. J. Trent, Jr., "Development of Negro Life Insurance Enterprises" (unpublished M.B.A. thesis, University of Pennsylvania, 1932), 39.

[4] Stuart, *An Economic Detour*, 179–182, 170–174, 288; Memphis *Chamber of Commerce Journal*, III (March 1920), 51–52.

[5] *Chamber of Commerce Journal*, II (December 1919), 263; *Commercial Appeal*, October 6, 1919.

[6] *Commercial Appeal*, March 26, 1919.

much better for them to live in that they will not want to migrate to better places."[7] If Memphians did not do more to keep their Negroes, George R. James, chairman of the Industrial Welfare Committee, warned, "business interests would languish, large and small property owners alike would suffer, and the city would disintegrate."[8]

Hence, while Chicago suffered from race riots, Memphis enjoyed a new era of interracial cooperation. Discussions between the white power elite and the Negro religious and civil leaders, initiated as they may have been by selfish white interests, nevertheless resulted in contributions of thousands of dollars of equipment for Plymouth Community House, the Market House Community Center, and Dr. Sutton E. Griggs' Tabernacle Baptist Church. As a result of interracial cooperation, the city administration began enforcing the sanitation and housing codes, and worked on improving Negro playgrounds and schools. The city even purchased the private Robert R. Church Park, for the price of $85,000, and turned it into another public recreation spot for the race.[9]

In so commercially oriented a city, it was not at all surprising that George Lee would decide to become a businessman. America, as he saw it, was essentially a business nation, a land whose folk heroes were leaders of industry and captains of enterprise. In Indianola, he had seen the wealthy Wayne Cox boss the Negro community; and he knew that in Memphis, another Negro businessman, Robert R. Church, Sr., for many years the kingpin of Beale Street, had grown so powerful he could whip white neighbor boys when he caught them throwing rocks at his prize peacocks. In American society, the young veteran felt, one thing was certain: business meant money, and money meant power. So it was that George Lee decided to sell life insurance. What he wanted was a chance to work his way up the economic ladder, an opportunity to build a business career. Life insurance showed promise of becoming the race's most lucrative business, and Mississippi Life was certainly the Negroes' foremost mid-South firm. When George Lee took a ten-dollar-a-week selling job with Mississippi Life, he was betting on the future of insurance and on his own ability as a salesman.[10]

Negro insurance was built on nickel-and-dime contracts called "industrial life" policies, designed to be sold to the working class. The business had been called "industrial" ever since 1849, when an English company, Industrial and General Life, developed the idea of selling insurance to the masses. Previously, ordinary life had been sold only to the middle and upper classes, but then Industrial and General decided to offer small policies on which the premiums would be collected weekly by an agent who visited the house of the insured. In 1875, after the English industrial classes had demonstrated their willingness to buy insurance policies and avoid the embarrassment of pauper burials, an American company, Prudential Insurance, began selling industrial policies in the United States where working families were also ready to pay for the promise of a decent burial.[11]

If a policy could be had for no more than a nickel or a dime a week, Negro

[7] *Ibid.*, March 28, 1919.
[8] *Ibid.*, July 7, 1920.
[9] *Chamber of Commerce Journal*, IV (May 1921), 11; *Commercial Appeal*, April 6, August 30, October 26, 1919, May 12, 1921.
[10] Interview with George Lee, February 13, 1967.
[11] Frederick L. Hoffman, *History of the Prudential Insurance Company of America* (Prudential Press, 1900), 1–4; Morton Keller, *The Life Insurance Enterprise, 1885–1910* (Cambridge, 1963), 1–11.

families would readily buy from the door-to-door salesman, especially if he were a brown-skinned lieutenant who spoke an educated, gentleman's English. A dime policy would do much more than pay for a big $104 funeral, Lee told his prospective buyers; it would also be helping Negro business to grow, and this in turn would prove that the Negro could successfully maintain his own financial enterprises. Negro families, the salesman insisted, owed it to themselves and to their race to buy a policy from Mississippi Life. By promising that his insurance would "increase happiness, stabilize the future home and make poorhouses a relic of the past," George Lee sold hundreds of policies to the masses, if very few to the Negro professional class which continued to buy from white companies like Metropolitan.[12]

After only a few weeks in the Memphis agency, George Lee had moved from salesman to manager, recruiting new agents whom he taught how not "to run away when the going got tough" or to "let door knobs turn into ghosts." By 1920 his Memphis agency had sold more insurance than any other company office, earning for George Lee a promotion to a vice-presidency. As a vice-president, Lee was asked to represent his firm at the annual meeting of the National Negro Business League. He expected the insurance division of the Philadelphia convention to be dominated by the large profit-making companies like Atlanta Life, North Carolina Mutual, Standard Life, and Mississippi Life; yet the old benevolent orders, which operated insurance programs for their members, controlled the meetings instead. Outraged that the Negro Business League had ignored the major firms in favor of non-profit insurance groups, George Lee returned to Memphis and made his objections known. The following year, the insurance men created their own National Negro Insurance Association in Durham, North Carolina, a trade organization initiated by George Lee for his own field of black capitalism.[13]

George Lee had worked with Mississippi Life for four productive years, watching his salary skyrocket to $6,500 a year, and looking ahead to an even greater future with the company, when in 1923 the firm was virtually destroyed. It was then that Mrs. Wayne Cox and her son-in-law sold their controlling interest to Heman Perry, an Atlanta Negro with a sixth-grade education, who had organized one of the race's most dynamic insurance companies. Perry went into business with Standard Life in 1913 and then expanded from Georgia into ten other states; but not content with the management of a single enterprise, Perry began to speculate in Atlanta banking, real estate, construction, printing, laundries, and drug stores until financial troubles forced him to borrow heavily from a white insurance company. By 1923, with debts of $500,000, and on the edge of bankruptcy, he made a desperate attempt to avoid catastrophe by buying controlling interest in Mississippi Life for $106,000, skimming more than that from the cash reserves within a matter of months, and then selling the company to a white firm, Southern Life, for $240,000.[14]

The circumstances of this tragedy were more than George Lee could ever accept. Having pointed with pride to Mississippi Life as proof of the Negro's ability to succeed in business, he could never admit that a Negro had intentionally ruined the company and sold it away from the race. Always overly sensitive to the hos-

[12] George W. Lee, "Insurance—Its Necessity and Value: Its Problems and its Future," *Messenger*, IX (March 1927), 77.

[13] Stuart, *An Economic Detour*, 323.

[14] *Ibid.*, 306–311; Trent, "Development of Negro Life Insurance Enterprises," 41.

tility of white society, and never able fully to admit to Negro failure, George Lee at once concluded that Mississippi Life had fallen victim to a conspiracy of the Ku Klux Klan to destroy the new power of the urban Negro; indeed he never lost his conviction that the Georgia Klan, alarmed by black prosperity, had made Heman Perry an unwitting dupe in their scheme to sap the black man's economic strength.[15]

Enraged by a conspiracy bred by his own imagination, George Lee determined to make a militant stand for the race. He entered the courts for an injunction to prevent the white Southern Life Insurance Company from collecting premiums on the old Mississippi Life policies, and he organized the sales managers of three states for a protest audience with the officers of Southern Life on March 4, 1924. George Lee spoke for the group:[16]

> *These managers who stand before you white men cannot assist you in carrying out your plans to take over the Mississippi Life without sinking into the basest ingratitude and handing their names down to posterity to be linked with Benedict Arnold and Judas as the arch traitors of their time. We cannot for any consideration continue in your employ if you win in the courts. . . . The Negroes everywhere are believing that this is a well-founded plan on the part of the white men of the South to exterminate the Negro in an economic way.*
>
> *You have told us time and time again that we should live here in the South by your side and develop our own institutions without interference. And now, when we build an institution, that is a credit to the race, you conspire to take it by sheer force and influence. Shall I interpret these actions to mean that you no longer want among you the thrifty and intelligent group of Negroes who are able by their own shoulder straps to lift themselves to the highest plane of self-determination? Shall I interpret this to mean that you want only the headscratching and Sambo Negro, who has no ambitions save to serve you and whose ambitions don't extend beyond being your body servant and your wood chopper, to live here in the South?*

Lee's group carried through their threatened walk-out of the old Mississippi Life Company, rendering the old business worthless to Southern Life without agents to collect the weekly premiums. Officials of the white firm sought to appease George Lee with an attractive offer of a $7,000 yearly salary and 2 per cent of all the premiums collected, but he turned it down and assured the company he would never help the white organization take over a business built by his race.[17]

Here, then, seemed an opportunity for George Lee to promote a company of his own, but Lee seemed to have little of the entrepreneurial drive demonstrated by men like Dr. J. E. Walker. Walker, who had resigned his presidency before the Mississippi Life disaster, organized another Memphis insurance company, Universal Life, in 1923, which was rapidly growing into one of the race's top ten insurance corporations. More cautious handling money than words, Lee had

[15] George W. Lee, *Beale Street: Where the Blues Began* (New York, 1934), 186–190.
[16] Pittsburg *Courier*, March 8, 1924.
[17] Interview with George Lee, November 14, 1966.

the less adventurous spirit of a managerial capitalist who wanted a guaranteed salary from an established firm; and so he turned to Alonzo Herndon of Atlanta Life, which had been watching the Memphis market, eager to move in and open an agency. Born into slavery, Herndon had become one of the leading entrepreneurs of the race. After the Civil War he had picked up an old pair of scissors and a straight-edged razor and gone into business cutting hair, and by 1905 he owned a string of barber shops, among them the finest in Atlanta.

Herndon saw the opportunity to move into insurance when a local mutual aid association went up for sale because it could not comply with the Georgia statute requiring a $5,000 reserve deposit. He bought the business for $160, and then reinsured the policy holders with his own stock company, Atlanta Life, which he built into the second largest Negro-owned business in the nation.[18] Upon learning of George Lee's refusal to work for white business, Herndon opened an office of Atlanta Life in Memphis and made Lee its manager. Lee was able to bring with him a majority of his thirty-five agents and most of the old customers, as well as the enthusiasm which had made his earlier agency the best in Memphis. Delighted by the arrangement, the home office in Atlanta predicted that in the years to come, Negroes would "bow in pride to George W. Lee as one of the men who had the moral courage to stand by his race."[19]

Successful Negro businessmen generally considered themselves the real leaders of the race. The development of Negro business had been the black man's main hope for progress at least as far back as the Fourth Atlanta University Conference in 1898, and the merits of capitalism as the means of racial advancement were vigorously impressed upon the black population by the Negro Business League and the Negro press. Typical of their educational effort was an editorial in the Memphis *Triangle*:[20]

> *The new Negro is the optimistic Negro. He believes in himself and, therefore, in others of his race. He believes in Negro business and gives it his full support. He believes in Negro institutions and lends his cooperation in building them up. He believes in Negro leaders and willingly joins the ranks as a follower. He believes in the future.*
>
> *The old Negro is the pessimistic Negro. He does not believe in himself or any other Negro. He does not believe in Negro business and hence does not trade at Negro stores or put his money in Negro banks. He does not believe in Negro insurance companies, and therefore takes his insurance with the other fellow. He believes the case of his race is hopeless unless someone else guides its destiny.*

The philosophy of the optimistic Negro businessman like George Lee became identified with the Harlem "New Negro" intellectual movement, which promoted the spiritual emancipation of the race by praising all things black, both the art and music of the folk, and even the business successes of the black bourgeoisie. E. Franklin Frazier, for example, a new Negro who later soured on the black middle class, told his people: "No longer can men say that the Negro is lazy and shiftless and a consumer. He has gone to work. He is a producer. He is respecta-

[18] Stuart, *An Economic Detour*, 118–120.
[19] E. M. Martin to George W. Lee, May 8, 1924, George W. Lee Papers.
[20] Memphis *Triangle*, June 1, 1927.

ble. He has a middle class."[21] Like Frazier, George Lee felt that racial chauvinism would emancipate the Negro from that terrible sense of inferiority bequeathed to him by a heritage of enslavement; and more than this, Lee was well aware that black pride would be awfully good for the growth of Atlanta Life. For as it was, Negroes were purchasing only 10 per cent of their insurance from Negro insurance companies; if they could be persuaded to put their confidence and money into their race's own firms, Lee's business would certainly profit.

As a bachelor, who lived with his mother, George Lee was free to use his leisure hours reading and reflecting about the Negro's position in the American social order. From the militant Negro monthlies, the *Crisis* and the *Messenger*, he learned the latest in protest thought, became acquainted with the literature read by every race intellectual, and deepened his faith in the future of Negro business. It was during this period that George Lee found a mentor in Robert R. Church, Jr., Memphis' wealthiest Negro realtor and member of the board of directors of both the National Association for the Advancement of Colored People and the Association for the Study of Negro Life and Culture. Church was well acquainted with all the leading Negro minds, and was ready to disagree with even the greatest of them. He listened sympathetically to the excited young lieutenant and spoke with a sense of authority on all racial questions. Robert Church became George Lee's personal contact with the Negro intellectuals and also introduced him to the Elks, the most prestigious Negro fraternal order. While the local Negro Masons and Odd Fellows were largely working class, the Improved Benevolent and Protective Order of Elks of the World drew its members from the city's businessmen, NAACP leaders, and Republican politicians. The Elks offered not only social status, but put a man in contact with the most progressive members of the race. The national fraternal order supported a Department of Civil Rights and a Department of Education which, in 1926, inaugurated annual oratorical contests to inform the Negro masses by having school children declaim their constitutional rights. The local champions of the Elk competitions went on to district, state, regional, and national contests, and were awarded college scholarships as encouragement to become spokesmen for their people.[22]

George Lee moved into the mainstream of American Negro thought guided by his connections with Robert Church, the Elks, race periodicals, and Negro business. If businessmen are not generally thought of as intellectuals today, the Negro businessman of the 1920's was often an exception. Indeed, Negroes who went into business generally did so precisely because few other white collar positions gave them as much, if any, freedom for independent thought and action. No insurance salesman was ever fired for militancy, and working, as he did, to develop racial pride for its psychic and economic profits, he was often regarded as among the race's most progressive leaders.

George Lee articulated, as a writer and orator, the need of developing black business and black pride as a detour toward full equality. To cure the black man's deep rooted sense of inferiority, the race must do what other persecuted ethnic groups had done; as the Jews had told themselves that they were God's chosen people, and as the Irish had preserved their identity by a stubborn pride in what

[21] E. Franklin Frazier, "Durham: Capitol of the Black Middle Class," in Alain Locke (ed.) *The New Negro: An Interpretation* (New York, 1925), 333.

[22] Charles H. Wesley, *History of the Improved Benevolent and Protective Order of Elks of the World* (Washington, 1955), 192–196.

made them different from the English, the Negro must learn to appreciate his unique contributions to society. Developing race consciousness by accentuating and applauding things Negro would create a line of defense against white racist propaganda. Racial pride would promote the growth of race business which, within the century, would liberate the race from poverty and prejudice. "America is a commercial country," George Lee said. "Its aristocracy is built upon the dollar. He that has the most dollars is prince."[23]

Thinking along these lines, George Lee had little use for the solutions offered by the Negro Memphis ministers and their Inter-Racial League. The all black Inter-Racial League had been organized in Memphis by Reverend T. O. Fuller, a dependable minister who had earned the approval of white businessmen and was able to enlist their support for his efforts to secure civic improvements and better treatment for black people. Fuller worked industriously to secure playgrounds for Negro children. He wrote letters to the *Commercial Appeal,* asking editor E. P. J. Mooney to "consider the advisability of eliminating the following terms when writing about Negroes: 'Darkey, nigger, coon, negress, the black.' "[24] But George Lee feared the Reverend and his League conceded too much in seeking white sympathy. Fuller was the minister who cooperated with the embarrassed white city fathers when Memphis became the murder capital of the world with sixty-seven murders for every 100,000 persons (as compared with six for every 100,000 in New York City). With the city's approval, the ministers' Inter-Racial League led a city-wide campaign among Memphis Negroes for "upholding the law, discouraging idleness, letting whisky alone, staying away from bad company and halting the custom of carrying dangerous weapons." Anti-crime orators spoke in the churches, schools, theaters, and on the street corners. There was even a Negro parade with a placard showing pictures of lethal weapons and bearing the slogans: "Don't shoot! Don't kill! Crime hurts our race. Crime hurts Memphis. Our murder record must be reduced. Fifty-seven men and women died at our own hands last year. Crime must be checked."[25]

George Lee was repulsed by these tactics, which stressed the race's worst characteristics, and most of all by the philosophy of one member of the League, Reverend Sutton E. Griggs. In particular, the Reverend Griggs had become convinced of the inferiority of Negroes after extensive reading in racist anthropology and suffering the traumatic disillusionment of a writer whose books go unread by the public. Originally a believer in racial equality, Griggs had composed a militant novel entitled *Imperium in Imperio* (1899), in the hope that the race would adopt the book as their text and endorse his leadership. But when he sent copies to twenty national Negro leaders for their reviews and endorsements, 80 per cent of them failed to reply, the masses showed no interest in buying the novel, and the author sustained a financial failure. Reluctant to draw hasty conclusions about his race, Griggs wrote another four novels, *Overshadowed* (1901), *Unfettered* (1902), *The Hindered Hand* (1905), and *Pointing the Way* (1908), all of which failed to attract a paying audience. Disillusioned by his people, Sutton E.

[23] George W. Lee, "Group Tactics and Ideals," *Messenger,* Lee Scrapbooks.
[24] T. O. Fuller to *Commercial Appeal,* October 31, 1925, reprinted in *Interracial Blue Book 1925–26* (Memphis, 1926).
[25] *Commercial Appeal,* January 29, 1924, February 1, 6, 1925.

Griggs lifted the blame from himself and "sorrowfully laid it at the door" of his race.[26]

So Sutton E. Griggs changed from a militant novelist concerned with Negro rights to an accommodating black minister soliciting white philanthropy. He used his Tabernacle Baptist Church for a home economics class and taught Negro women to be better cooks for white folks. He used his pulpit as a forum for helping his people accept white domination by preaching that the day of Negro militancy must end; that the race must abandon the northern Republican party, and make its peace with the white man in the South. To keep white Memphians fully informed of his efforts both to uplift his people and eliminate racial friction, Sutton E. Griggs took every opportunity to exploit the city's white press, submitting pamphlets, letters, and weekly reports of his activities.

From the teachings of white anthropologists, Reverend Griggs accepted the Social Darwinist position that Negroes had lagged behind other races in their social evolution and therefore were, in fact, inferior. Black men had developed more slowly, Griggs explained, because they had a deficiency or lack of certain racial traits; the Anglo-Saxon traits of honesty, reliability, tolerance, patience, courtesy, tact, and self-control, were either absent from the mental make-up of many Negroes or were present only in negligible amounts. Griggs was, nevertheless, essentially optimistic in his prognosis for the black man. He believed that a significant alteration of traits could be achieved, and to explain how, wrote a half dozen books expounding his "science of collective efficiency." Griggs' writings, with their detailed descriptions of trait deficiencies and the means of eliminating them, were intended to give the race the hope for improving its standing in the eyes of the world.

To promote his ideas, Sutton E. Griggs canvassed white businessmen for their financial support and organized the Public Welfare League. The League became an organ for disseminating his literature, and under its auspices Griggs delivered lectures and organized neighborhood improvement societies. Some Negroes complained bitterly that Griggs taught race children "to bow low and look up to the southern white man as something of a Jesus, and consider himself fortunate even to be living," but Griggs had the cooperation of the white city school superintendent and saw that his theories became required reading in the local Negro high school.[27] When the city superintendent invited Griggs to explain to the colored teachers that the Anglo-Saxon system of education was inadequate for a race which needed "socialization" rather than intellectual training, cooperative students and teachers at Booker T. Washington High School formed a socialization club, which resolved to repudiate "quarrels, brawls, and homicides," and develop the right instincts so that they might "gradually and eventually be moulded into a compact, sincere, loving and indissolvable whole similar to the other races of the nation."[28]

Lee's outrage at the Reverend Griggs' undermining of racial pride was compounded by his resentment of the special coverage the white press gave the

[26] Sutton E. Griggs, *The Story of My Struggles* (Memphis, 1914), 1–11; Robert A. Bone, *The Negro Novel in America* (New Haven, 1965), 32–35.

[27] Robert R. Church to Walter White, May 21, 1919, Box G–199, NAACP Papers, Library of Congress, Manuscript Division.

[28] *Commercial Appeal*, May 18, 1927.

Reverends Griggs and T. O. Fuller, while ignoring black militants like Lee and Robert Church. The city papers suggested that the race would prosper and advance "if the Negroes had more leaders with the vision of Sutton Griggs and T. O. Fuller." "Sutton Griggs," the *Commercial Appeal* declared, "is a thrifty, intelligent, self-respecting Negro, who possesses the faculty of looking facts squarely in the face: and we think he is an eminently safe leader of his people." The press could be even more generous: "Students of psychology say he is one of the profoundest thinkers of modern times, and agree almost unanimously that the movement he is now promoting, if put into practice, will by subconscious thought and action tend to eradicate undesirable traits of character."[29]

Never one to miss an opportunity to push his own ideas, Sutton E. Griggs attended the National Negro Insurance Association when it met in Memphis, and proposed that the insurance men send speakers to the Negro churches to lecture the congregations on their race's criminal behavior. The motion was no sooner introduced than George Lee got the floor and denounced the plan as utterly "repulsive" since it would surely persuade the Negro that he belonged to a race of criminals. Naturally, Lee stood for law, order, and middle-class respectability, and wanted to lower the Memphis homicide rate; and he was fully aware that the Beale Street Negro, fresh from the cotton patch and saw-mill of Mississippi, was highly susceptible to vice and violence when confronted by the sudden freedom of the city. Yet for all this, he could not endorse any program which would deepen the Negro's sense of inferiority. Indeed, Negro leaders might do well to consider instead that whites as well as Negroes committed murder, that the whites denied Negroes the privilege of serving on the police force and of helping to ward off crime, that the whites failed to give the Negro adequate recreation facilities which might deter the formation of criminal behavior among the young. White Memphians, in short, as well as the Negroes, were responsible for the city's murder rate, and they could be asked to do their share in this matter of crime prevention. Pursuing his argument relentlessly, George Lee eventually talked the entire assembly into disavowing the Griggs proposal.[30]

The Griggs-Lee controversy spilled over into the press, with Sutton E. Griggs accusing the Lieutenant of obstructing the socialization of the race, and with George Lee countering with the charge that Griggs sought only to win white funds and friends. While Griggs advocated an impractical theory of racial adjustment, George Lee charged, the National Negro Insurance Association taught racial pride and helped the masses to achieve full equality. The only means of winning the approval of the white community and advancing the cause of the race was "an intelligent exercise of citizenship rights, buying homes, buying farms, building businesses, and producing wealth."[31] If these problem-solvers and inter-racial exponents would leave Negro businessmen alone, then the race could develop its own community and help to "make the south blossom like a rose."

But even as George Lee praised the merits of black capitalism, banking institutions on Beale Street were tottering under a ruinous shortage of $500,000, incurred by manipulation, criminal negligence, and bad loans. Roddy's Citizens' Cooperative Stores, for example, had received $100,000 from Solvent Savings and

[29] *Ibid.*, August 17, 1925, March 13, 1921, March 30, 1924.
[30] Memphis *Triangle*, June 1, 1927.
[31] *Commercial Appeal*, May 29, June 5, 1927.

then failed in 1922, repaying none of its debt to the bank. Five years later, in a desperate attempt at survival, the rival banks, Solvent Savings and Fraternal Savings, merged, only to be ruined when customers made withdrawals for their Christmas shopping. On December 29, 1927, after rumors of the impending disaster and a run on the bank by its 28,000 depositors, Fraternal and Solvent Savings Bank, the South's largest Negro bank, fell into the hands of the state bank examiners. Never had Negro Memphians suffered a failure of such proportions; six bank personnel were jailed, from cashiers who had pilfered as little as $5,000 to President A. F. Ward who had fraudulently appropriated $170,000; and as former officials and directors of the ruined bank, a majority of Beale Street's most successful businessmen sustained great personal embarrassment.[32] In the wake of the disaster, Wayman Wilkerson, chairman of the bank directors, president of the Tri-State Casket Company, and husband of the local NAACP president, committed suicide. Before firing the pistol, the businessman attached a note and a clipping to his coat lapel:[33]

> *I am now 56 years old, spirit crushed—nerves shattered—ambition gone —health failing—the attached clipping tells the tale.*
>
> *If satisfaction in life hinges on one thing more than another, it is on the idea that today is better than yesterday and that tomorrow will be better than today.*
>
> *When that idea falls out of the picture—when people are on the downgrade and know it—when they have to live on memories and reminiscences —without any hope that they can do as well—much less better than they have—life loses its thrill.*

If others were disillusioned with black capitalism, one thirty-four year old insurance executive was not: Lieutenant George Lee picked up his pen to urge the race to keep the faith. Only race business could provide honorable employment for the youth and liberate the black man from poverty and prejudice. Could Memphis Negroes, the most advanced in the South, turn back? Never. "We must step forward and build upon the ashes of the ruins," George Lee urged. "To turn back means distintegration and economic slavery." The only road to the "Promised Land" ran "across the Red Sea of disappointment and sorrow" to the building of a new bank. The black man must do as the white, send his criminals to jail and then build anew. "Crookedness is not a racial trait," George Lee insisted. "Main Street has been sending her white crooks to the penitentiary for years. Beale Street must do the same and then march on with confidence in our race and in our God."[34]

Sutton E. Griggs could take comfort from white condolences for the race's banking disaster, and he could even find encouragement in the fact that there had been "no rejoicing anywhere in the white race over our calamity."[35] But George Lee drew little satisfaction from patronizing white generosity. He simply grew more militant in his attacks on interracial "back door diplomats" and "pussyfoots" like Griggs, whom he clearly blamed for the weaknesses of the race's

32 *Ibid.*, December 30, 1927, February 7, May 22, June 2, 1928.
33 *Ibid.*, July 2, 1928.
34 George W. Lee, "The Negro's Next Step," Memphis *Triangle*, January 28, 1928.
35 *Commercial Appeal*, January 5, 1928.

economic and social position. "We've got too many apostles of peace at any price," George Lee cried, "too many preaching about the glories of the other world and too few pointing out the hell of the world in which we now live."[36] The professional race adjusters were "flying about the South crying patience and peace" while Negroes were "ostracized like lepers" and segregated in the back alleys of civilization to be brow beaten and spit upon. "So long as this condition exists," George Lee said, "I for one, shall love confusion and despise peace." Only an aggressive, fighting leadership could establish the group consciousness in economics and politics necessary to win freedom for the race; yet the race was burdened with 40,000 accommodating ministers. More than $90,000,000 was being spent to teach the Negro to depend on God, while little if anything was being done to teach the Negro to depend on himself.

The progress of the race would come only through the black man's own efforts, George Lee believed, for certainly he could never count on the white man. In fact, the ministers' interracial cooperation had met with active resistance from the white community when they tried to build Howe-Roger Williams College for Negroes in Memphis. Half a million northern dollars had become available in 1928, for building this college on South Parkway, but white civic clubs quickly banded together and vigorously protested its construction. Such a Negro college, their newspaper advertisements pointed out, would bring in educated black and their belief in social equality from Nashville, Chicago, and St. Louis.[37] The city government capitulated to white racism, driving the college from Memphis, and illustrating that interracial cooperation had failed just as completely as black business.

Negro businessmen have been accused of betraying and ruthlessly exploiting the black masses, but certainly the Negro capitalists of the 1920's did much more than seek personal gain; providing, as they did, the real cutting edge of Negro protest. In Memphis, the businessmen challenged the accommodating attitudes of the ministers, contributed the most aggressive local leadership, and provided a militant philosophy of black pride. The business community had produced Lieutenant Lee, who never permitted his interests to be consumed by the practical business of selling and promoting insurance, but devoted much of his energy to the self-imposed role of race leader. Had he been nothing more than a money-maker, the Negro community would never have felt they needed to have him in Memphis; but as it was, when he was offered a position in Atlanta, the Memphis *Triangle*, speaking for its readers, declared: "Memphis Can't Lose Lieut. George W. Lee."[38] Black capitalism had not given Negro Memphians their freedom, but it did give them an eloquent protest leader.

[36] Baltimore *Afro-American*, June 8, 1929.

[37] *Commercial Appeal*, March 27, 1928.

[38] Memphis *Triangle*, January 25, 1930; George Lee became a vice-president of Atlanta Life in 1939 but remained head of the Memphis agency until his retirement in 1967; in politics he became the last black Republican patronage boss until he went down in defeat at the Goldwater convention in 1964; and in literature he published three books, two of which were written in the protest tradition.

14

SECRECY BIDS FOR POWER: THE KU KLUX KLAN IN TEXAS POLITICS IN THE 1920's

Charles C. Alexander

The dark side of Progressivism is further emphasized in this article on the rise of the modern Ku Klux Klan in the 1920's, which, like the racists in the first decade of the century, used the issue of prohibition to gain political power in the South and Midwest. The revived Ku Klux Klan had little in common with the original organization created in the post-Civil War period to resist the Radical Reconstruction policies. The new organization borrowed the name and some of the methods of the original Klan, but it was not confined to the South nor was it exclusively concerned with the Negro. The anti-alien, anti-Catholic aspects of its platform manifested an intolerance that had its counterpart in previous periods of American history and was to be reflected in the racially biased immigration acts that were passed in this decade. This article stresses the impact of the Klan upon state political organizations.

Charles C. Alexander specializes in both recent American social, cultural, and intellectual history and the history of American science and technology. He has published The Ku Klux Klan in the Southwest *(Lexington, 1965),* Nationalism in American Thought, 1930–1945 *(Chicago, 1969), and co-authored a history of Project Mercury, published by the Government Printing Office in 1966. This article is the basis of a chapter in his first book. Mr. Alexander is a professor of history at Ohio University.*

Several years ago the writer listened to an address by the founder of "Freedom in Action," a secret ultrapatriotic organization then enjoying some vogue in the southwestern states, in which the speaker described F I A's plans for "grass roots"

Source: *Mid-America*, Vol. 46, No. 1 (1964), pp. 3–28. Reprinted by permission of the publisher.

political activity to control nominations and elections and thus ensure the placing of "the right men" in office. F I A never received much publicity outside of Texas, where a few prominent figures were identified with the movement. In the past two years public attention has turned to the mysterious John Birch Society, also secret, also ultrapatriotic, and possibly the successor to F I A throughout the nation as well as in the Southwest. As a result of the voluminous publicity given the Birch Society, the prospect of a disciplined, purposeful group of unknown numbers and resources carrying on secret political maneuverings has reached the consciousness of most Americans.[1]

Some people, however, remember another nativist organization from earlier in the century, a white-robed secret fraternal order which boasted an active membership of perhaps five million and which commanded political power on a scale unprecedented in the history of secret political organizations in America—the Knights of the Ku Klux Klan of the 1920's. The Klan's territory of operations, called the "Invisible Empire," included every state of the Union, and everywhere Klan chapters existed Klansmen had political ambitions. They had some notable successes, too. At the Democratic national convention of 1924 the Klan and its sympathizers were strong enough to prevent the presidential nomination of Alfred E. Smith of New York and a denunciation of the Klan in the party platform. In Indiana the order enjoyed almost complete control of the state government for a brief period. In Oregon the Klan elected its favorite to the governorship, while in Georgia it turned out a hostile governor and elected its own man to replace him. In Oklahoma Klansmen and their allies brought about the impeachment and removal of the colorful John C. Walton from the governorship.[2] The Klan was a potent element in politics elsewhere, but there was no state where the hooded fraternity's political ventures were more spectacular, more widely-publicized, or, everything considered, more successful than Texas, the fourth most populous state in the nation in 1920.

A fair-sized amount of information is available regarding the operations of the Klan in Texas, particularly in state politics. A survey of the order's political career in Texas, its techniques and difficulties, successes and failures, throws

[1] On Freedom in Action see *The Texas Observer* (Austin, Texas), October 9, October 30, November 6, and December 4, 1959. From March, 1961, through October, 1963, national periodicals carried some seventy stormy articles on the John Birch Society, the great majority in the first eighteen months of that time. The articles and the many newspaper accounts attacked the secrecy and radical nature of the Society. In the present dwindling publicity the Society denies it is a secret society.

[2] On the power of the Klan in Oregon, Indiana, Georgia, and Oklahoma, see Waldo Roberts, "The Ku-Kluxing of Oregon," *Outlook*, CXXXIII (March 14, 1923), 490–491; "Klan Victories in Oregon and Texas," *Literary Digest*, LXXV (November 25, 1922), 12; Robert L. Duffus, "The Ku Klux Klan in the Middle West," *World's Work*, XLVI (August, 1923), 363–372; Morton Harrison, "Gentlemen from Indiana," *Atlantic Monthly*, CXLI (May, 1928), 676–686; Norman F. Weaver, "The Knights of the Ku Klux Klan in Wisconsin, Indiana, Ohio, and Michigan," Unpublished Ph. D. dissertation, University of Wisconsin, 1954, chapters IV, V; Arnold S. Rice, *The Ku Klux Klan in American Politics*, Washington, 1962, 58–64; Charles C. Alexander, "Invisible Empire in the Southwest: the Ku Klux Klan in Texas, Louisiana, Oklahoma, and Arkansas," Unpublished Ph. D. dissertation, University of Texas, 1962, chapters VI, VII, VIII, and IX.

light into a hitherto hidden corner of the history of the state and helps to clarify the whole problem of the Klan as a political force in the twenties. It also makes for an interesting case study of how secret nativist and vigilante societies get into politics and the methods they employ, and perhaps suggests why they fail.

The twentieth-century Ku Klux Klan had its beginning in October, 1915, when a visionary fraternal organizer and ex-Methodist preacher named William Joseph Simmons established the first Klan chapter in Atlanta, Georgia. With an initial membership of thirty-four, Simmons' Klan was chartered under the laws of Georgia as the "Invisible Empire, Knights of the Ku Klux Klan, Inc." Its founder intended the new fraternal order as a "living memorial" to the earlier Ku Klux Klan, the secret organization most Southerners credited with saving white supremacy and virtuous womanhood during the Reconstruction period; as a harmless patriotic society; and as a scheme for selling mutual benefit insurance. Simmons proclaimed himself "Imperial Wizard" of the new Klan and sallied forth to make his "Invisible Empire" national in scope, but from 1915 to 1920 the Klan enlisted a maximum 6,000 members and had chapters only in Atlanta, Birmingham, Mobile, and a few other places in Georgia and Alabama.[3]

The Klan languished in obscurity until the summer of 1920, when the inept Simmons formed a business partnership with Edward Young Clarke and Mrs. Elizabeth Tyler, two poor but talented Atlanta publicity agents. Clarke, a bespectacled, bushy-haired little man in his late thirties, and Mrs. Tyler, a rugged, rotund widow, agreed to "sell" the Klan to Americans in exchange for a generous cut of the ten-dollar initiation fees or "klectokens" paid by new members. The two publicity agents proceeded to change the fuzzy ideological framework of the Klan, as it operated under Simmons, into an aggressive statement of white supremacy and racial and religious nativism. They were shrewd enough to realize that by wrapping their product, the Klan, in a package of prejudices and hatreds—anti-Catholic, anti-Semitic, anti-radical, anti-foreign, anti-Negro—they could take advantage of the disillusionment and the accumulated animosity toward everything not "100 percent American" which prevailed in the immediate post-World War I years.[4]

Under Clarke and Mrs. Tyler the growth of the Klan was phenomenal. The "Kleagles," or organizers for the Klan, found rich fields for their solicitations,

[3] Among the best items on the founding and early history of the Klan are Robert L. Duffus, "Salesman of Hate: the Ku Klux Klan," *World's Work*, XLVI (May, 1923), 31–38; William G. Shepherd, "How I Put Over the Klan," *Collier's*, LXXII (July 14, 1928), 10–11; Shepherd, "Ku-Klux Koin," *Ibid.*, (July 21, 1928), 8–9; Walter F. White, "Reviving the Ku Klux Klan," *Forum*, LXV (April, 1921), 424–434; Emerson H. Loucks, *The Ku Klux Klan in Pennsylvania: a Study in Nativism*, Harrisburg, 1936, chapter II; Rice, *Klan in American Politics*, 1–12.

[4] Many writers have attempted to fathom the "mind of the Klan." Among the most informative items in the interpretive literature on the order are John Higham, *Strangers in the Land: Patterns of American Nativism, 1860–1925*, New Brunswick, 1955, 234–299; John M. Mecklin, *The Ku Klux Klan: a Study of the American Mind*, New York, 1924; Frank Tannenbaum, *Darker Phases of the South*, New York, 1924, chapter I; Frank Bohn, "The Ku Klux Klan Interpreted," *American Journal of Sociology*, XXX (January, 1925), 385–407; Guy B. Johnson, "A Sociological Interpretation of the New Ku Klux Movement," *Social Forces*, I (May, 1923), 440–445; Weaver, "Klan in Wisconsin, Indiana, Ohio, and Michigan," chapter II; Rice, *Klan in American Politics*, chapter II.

and by the end of 1920 Imperial Wizard Simmons commanded tens of thou sands of subjects in Georgia, Alabama, Florida, Tennessee, Mississippi, Louisiana, and Texas. In 1921 the Klan moved north and west, established itself firmly in Oklahoma, Indiana, Ohio, Pennsylvania, and on the Pacific Coast, and even reached into that mecca of wickedness and un-Americanism (in Klan thinking), New York City.[5]

The initial postwar growth of the Klan was most striking in Texas. Entering the state quietly in October of 1920, with the installation of a chapter in Houston, the order within little more than a year planted local Klans in practically every part of the vast state and inducted perhaps 80,000 Texans into the Invisible Empire.[6] Texas was the star Klan state and Dallas was the star Klan city, although Houston, Fort Worth, Waco, Austin, Wichita Falls, and Beaumont also became strongholds of the hooded organization.

There was little of the element of politics in this burgeoning of Klan membership in Texas, except that numerous local and state politicians joined the order to protect their political futures in Klan-dominated communities, counties, and districts. The primary motivation behind the spread of the Klan over Texas, it seems, was not so much a nativist impulse, as in the northern states, or even racial antagonism, as in the Deep South. Rather it was fear that the established system of law enforcement could not cope with the postwar crime wave sweeping the Southwest, especially violation of the prohibition laws, and anxiety over the purported breakdown of orthodox standards of morality, chastity, and propriety in Texas and the rest of the nation. Thus in its original form in Texas the Klan was principally an extralegal law enforcement and moral reform body, a vigilante organization, an instrument of masked terrorism which sent threatening letters to miscreants and whipped, tarred, and feathered persons suspected of objectionable behavior.[7]

By 1921 there were enough Klan members in Texas to make the order a genuine political force. But there were only a few municipal elections held in the state that year, and consequently Texas Klansmen occupied themselves with staging parades and initiations, visiting Protestant churches in their role as defenders of Protestant Americanism, and proscribing, usually by violent means, the conduct of errant "aliens," people outside the Invisible Empire. Then, too, political activity required organization and money, and the Klan in Texas, and elsewhere, had little of either in 1921. The "Realm," or state organization, for Texas was not perfected until early 1922, and before that time nearly all the

[5] The early expansion of the Klan benefited greatly from the publicity afforded by a well "ballyhooed" but inconclusive investigation of the order undertaken by the Rules Committee of the United States House of Representatives in the fall of 1921. See *The Ku Klux Klan, Hearings before the Committee on Rules, House of Representatives*, 67th Congress, 1st Session (1921); William J. Simmons' testimony is on pp. 67–185. For a running account of the hearings see the *New York Times*, October 2–18, 1921.

[6] In an interview in Dallas Edward Y. Clarke, visiting the city as "Imperial Wizard Pro Tem," estimated that 75,000 to 90,000 men belonged to the Klan in Texas. *Dallas Morning News*, January 23, 1922.

[7] For an analysis of the factors behind the growth of the Klan in Texas see Charles C. Alexander, *Crusade for Conformity: the Ku Klux Klan in Texas, 1920–1930*, Texas Gulf Coast Historical Association Publication Series, VI, August, 1962, 5–13.

money the Kleagles collected from initiates and that Klansmen paid after they became members went to Imperial headquarters at Atlanta. Finally, the people who headed the Klan before 1922, Simmons, Clarke, Mrs. Tyler, "King Kleagle" George B. Kimbo of Texas, were interested mainly in enriching themselves by enlisting as many members of whatever caliber as quickly as possible, not in carrying out any political program.

The Simmons-Clarke regime was not ambitious enough to suit a growing number of Klansmen in the strongest Klan states: Texas, Oklahoma, Arkansas, Louisiana, Georgia. There were also dissatisfied Klansmen in Indiana, where the Klan was just beginning its expansion. These "insurgent" Knights in various states saw the potentialities of the Klan as a political organization and regarded the woolgathering Simmons and the cynical Clarke as millstones impeding the order's fulfillment. They also distrusted the financial practices of the Atlantic coterie, which collected millions of dollars and never bothered to report its receipts and disbursements.[8] The leader of the insurgent group, the political-minded Klansmen, was Hiram Wesley Evans, a pudgy, blue-eyed dentist and the first "Exalted Cyclops" (chapter leader) of the powerful Dallas Klan No. 66.[9]

During January, 1922, Imperial headquarters constituted the "Realm" organization for Texas. At the head of the state hierarchy was a "Grand Dragon" appointed by Imperial Wizard Simmons; the Realm was divided into five "Provinces," or districts, headed by "Great Titans."[10] Hiram W. Evans became Great Titan of Province No. 2, with offices in Dallas. A few weeks later Simmons, partly because he wanted an efficient assistant in the Imperial hierarchy and partly, it seems, to quiet the demands of the disgruntled Texas Klansmen for representation in Atlanta, brought Evans to national headquarters as "Imperial Kligrapp" (national secretary). From the standpoint of loyalty Simmons picked the wrong man. Evans immediately began working to transform the Klan into, in his words, "a great militant political organization" which, operating within the two major parties but never on its own, could control nominations and elections over the nation. This achievement, as Evans conceived it, necessitated the elimination of Simmons, Clarke, and their followers as powers in

[8] Hiram W. Evans' assumption of the leadership of the Klan late in 1922 was supposed to bring a regularization of the order's finances. There was probably less open embezzlement under the Evans regime, but Evans continued the Clarke-Simmons policy of refusing to report the receipts and disbursements of national headquarters. The Evans administration frequently faced charges of corrupt financial practices from unhappy Klansmen. For Evans' fullest statement of the Klan's assets and liabilities, see *Proceedings of the Second Imperial Klonvocation, Held in Kansas City, Missouri, September 23–26, 1924*, Atlanta, 1924, 87, 90–91, 183–185.

[9] Others in the insurgent faction included Nathan Bedford Forrest, Jr., of Georgia, son of the legendary Confederate general and alleged "Grand Wizard" of the original Klan, David S. Stephenson and Walter F. Bossert of Indiana, H. Kyle Ramsey of Louisiana, James A. Comer of Arkansas, Edwin DeBarr of Oklahoma, and H. C. McCall, Brown Harwood, and Z. E. Marvin of Texas; Alexander, "Invisible Empire in the Southwest," chapter VI. On Stephenson, who became political boss of Indiana and the most powerful man in the Klan besides Evans, see Harrison, "Gentlemen from Indiana"; Weaver, "Klan in Wisconsin, Indiana, Ohio, and Michigan," chapter IV; Isabel Leighton (ed.), *The Aspirin Age, 1919–1941*, New York, 1949, 105–129.

[10] *Constitution and Laws of the Knights of the Ku Klux Klan*, Atlanta, 1921, Article XVI, Section 1.

the Klan, the regularization of the order's finances, and the conversion of the Klan into a "movement" rather than a terrorist organization or a lodge.[11]

Evans was remarkably successful in carrying out his personal program for the Klan. During 1922, under his leadership and with the acquiescence of Clarke and the ineffectual Simmons, the Klan entered local and state political contests in various parts of the country and scored several victories. In November, fortified by the triumphs of the Klan in politics, Evans' followers "persuaded" Simmons to relinquish the Imperial Wizardship and accept the specially-created but powerless office of "Emperor." As the result of a well-engineered *coup* Evans was elected Wizard by the delegates to the first "Imperial Klonvocation," or national convention, in Atlanta. "They thrust the Wizard job on me," was the way Evans later described his ascension to the most powerful office in Klandom. One of his first official acts was to cancel Edward Y. Clarke's contract with the Klan for propagation work. "As long as I wasn't responsible for Clarke, I was satisfied," recalled Evans. "But as soon as I became Wizard I didn't dare take the responsibility of permitting Clarke to make so much money."[12]

The removal of Simmons from the Wizardship and the severance of the Klan's relations with Clarke marked the beginning of a process by which the original rulers of the Klan were driven from the order. In 1923 Simmons' efforts to organize a secret women's organization precipitated a long, involved power struggle with Evans, fought out in the courts and within the ranks of the Klan. By the end of 1923 the Evans regime had liquidated the influence of the Simmons-Clarke faction, and in the early part of the next year the Imperial Wizard "banished" (suspended from membership for life) the founder of the order and its chief salesman.[13] By that time Evans had also put an end to most of the Klan's vigilante activities and had seen the organization, under his direction, become essentially a political machine.

Yet one suspects that the Klan would probably have evolved into an instrument for gaining political power if Hiram W. Evans had never joined the order. The character of the Klan, with its unified membership and revivalistic spirit, bred political ambitions and made the entrance of the organization into politics seemingly inescapable. The Klan had in mind a rather definite "program for America," which included protecting the country from Roman Catholics dominated by a foreign pope, wily Jews scheming to control the nation's finances, "undesirable" foreigners contaminating the native American stock, both physically and ideologically, and "uppity" Negroes trying to rise economically and socially. Klansmen were also much concerned about "good government" in their communities and states, meaning honesty, rigid economy, and strict enforcement

[11] William G. Shepherd, "Fiery Double Cross," *Collier's* LXXII (July 28, 1928), 8–9; testimony of Robert L. Henry, *Senator from Texas, Hearings before a Subcommittee of the Committee of Privileges and Elections, United States Senate,* 68th Congress, 1st and 2nd Sessions (1924), 46.

[12] Shepherd, "Fiery Double Cross," *loc. cit.*, 48.

[13] *New York Times*, September 16, p. 23, November 6, pp. 1, 5, November 7, p. 15, 1923; January 3, p. 3, January 12, p. 1, February 13, p. 5, February 25, p. 17, 1924; "The Clash in the Klan," *Literary Digest*, LXXVII (April 1, 1923), 13; Loucks, *Klan in Pennsyvania*, chapter X; *Minutes of the Imperial Kloncilium, Knights of the Ku Klux Klan, Meeting of May 1 and 2, 1923 . . .*, Atlanta, 1924, *passim.* Mrs. Elizabeth Tyler left the Klan early in 1923 and married a wealthy Atlantan. She died the next year; Rice, *Klan in American Politics,* 10.

of ordinances and laws against bootlegging, gambling, and prostitution. Realization of the Klan's objectives—the preservation of the American Way and the "reform" of government and society—could come about only if the Klan took to politics, or so the overwhelming majority of Klansmen came to believe.[14]

By the Spring of 1922 Klansmen in various states, but particularly in Texas, were looking toward politics and preparing to make their bid for power. The Klan's quest for new members was always acute, but local Klans in the Realm of Texas now stepped up their membership drives, abandoning what few reservations they had had about admitting "aliens" to the Invisible Empire. As a former member of Corsicana Klan No. 55, in northern Texas, recalled, "they just throwed the doors open, and every man that had the money, they took him in to get his vote, . . . and if he did not have any money, they took his note payable in the fall, and the thing then was to get his vote."[15] Such methods brought the membership of the Texas Klan to perhaps 100,000, a unified minority which sent Klansmen to the state legislature, elected sheriffs, attorneys, and judges at the local and district level, and won one of the most important victories in the history of the order, the election of Earle B. Mayfield to the United States Senate. During 1922, and for the next two years, the Klan furnished the chief element of controversy in the political affairs of Texas, a state where the voters, experiencing the apathy of the postwar years, needed issues. The Klan created the issues and brought people back to the polls.

While Klansmen were organizing to nominate Klan tickets in their county Democratic primaries and thus ensure their election in Texas, virtually a one-party state in the twenties, they were interested mainly in the statewide races. The governor, Pat Morris Neff, was not a Klan member, but the order did regard him as something of a "friendly neutral"; besides, in Texas an incumbent governor can usually win renomination and reelection if he chooses to run for a second term. Consequently the obvious target for the Klan was the United States Senate seat of Charles A. Culberson, who in 1922 was seeking reelection after serving four terms. Culberson was sixty-seven years old and in failing health, and his vote against the national prohibition amendment had alienated most Texas drys. He further angered Klan members when he issued a statement early in the campaign criticizing the methods of the order and calling for its destruction.[16]

Three Klansmen entered the campaign for the Democratic senatorial nomination, Sterling P. Strong, an attorney who was a member of Dallas Klan No. 66, former Congressman Robert L. Henry of Waco, a member of Waco Klan No. 33, and Earle B. Mayfield, a member of the Texas Railroad Commission, who

[14] The most comprehensive exposition of the Klan's objectives is to be found in the writings of Hiram W. Evans himself. See the following items, all published under the authorship of the Imperial Wizard: *The Menace of Modern Immigration*, Dallas, 1923; *The Public School Problem in America*, Atlanta, 1924; "The Klan: Defender of Americanism," *Forum*, LXXIV (December, 1925), 801–814; "The Klan's Fight for Americanism," *North American Review*, CCXXIII (March, 1926), 33–63; "For New Marriage Laws," *Forum*, LXXVII (May, 1927), 730–739; "The Catholic Question as Viewed by the Ku Klux Klan," *Current History*, XXVI (July, 1927), 563–568; "Ballots behind the Ku Klux Klan," *World's Work*, LV (January, 1928), 243–252.

[15] Testimony of W. H. Castles, *Senator from Texas, Hearings*, 992.

[16] James W. Madden, *Charles Allen Culberson* . . . , Austin, 1920, 245–246; *Houston Post*, April 2, 1922.

joined Capital City Klan No. 81 of Austin but stopped paying his dues in February of 1922, early in the senatorial race. Strong, Henry, and Mayfield began a three-cornered competition for the 100,000 and more votes the Klan represented in Texas, and for several weeks Klansmen in the state watched the contest with perplexity. They saw Henry and Strong openly praise the Klan in a bold solicitation of their votes, while Mayfield avoided discussing the issue, stating simply that it was "a matter over which the United States Senate has no jurisdiction."[17] Since the Realm hierarchy had shown no preference among the three Klan candidates, it appeared that the Klan vote would be fatally divided at the summer Democratic primary.

In late March the five Great Titans of the Realm, Brown Harwood of Fort Worth, Hiram W. Evans of Dallas, H. C. McCall of Houston, Erwin J. Clark of Waco, and Ralph Cameron of San Antonio, met at the Raleigh Hotel in Waco to decide which of the three Klansmen in the senatorial race, Henry, Strong, or Mayfield, would receive the full support of the Texas Klan. At one point in the discussion Evans turned to Erwin J. Clark, a booster of Henry, and said:

> *Erwin, I have a dead one in Dallas* [Strong] *and you have a dead one here in Waco* [Henry]. *Mayfield is the man. Now, they are all three Klansmen, and Strong and Henry are both good fellows, and we do not want to hurt their feelings. Let them ride for awhile and at the proper time we will ditch them and concentrate on Mayfield.*

The Great Titans talked for hours but were unable to agree, and the meeting broke up with the understanding that all three candidates would have an equal chance to win Klan votes. This understanding came to be known as the "Waco agreement."[18]

After Evans was called to Atlanta by Simmons and made Imperial Kligrapp, he set out to solidify the Texas Klan behind Mayfield. Edward Y. Clarke, acting as Imperial Wizard while Simmons, now either drunk or ill most of the time, was absent, gave Evans a free hand in the Texas enterprise. On May 21, 1922, Evans returned to Dallas and met with Henry, Mayfield, Z. E. Marvin, Evans' successor as Great Titan of the Dallas Province, and George K. Butcher, secretary of the Dallas Klan. Evans and Mayfield implored Henry to drop out of the senatorial contest so Mayfield could become the only Klan candidate. In answer Henry recited the "Waco agreement" and pulled out a telegram signed by Evans and Edward Y. Clarke authorizing him to make the race. Evans ignored the telegram and replied that he only meant "to make a stalking horse" of Henry, "although Mr. Mayfield has been intended as our candidate all the time." After several hours of indecisive háranguing Henry left the meeting, much disenchanted but still determined to make the race.[19]

The ex-Congressman continued to make speeches and plea for the votes of Texas Klansmen, while Imperial Kligrapp Evans spent most of his time in the state trying to sidetrack Henry. At one meeting of Dallas Klan No. 66, held at the Fair Grounds Coliseum in Dallas, Evans introduced Earle B. Mayfield as "a good Klansman and the next senator," after which Mayfield made a short talk

[17] *Dallas Morning News*, April 6 and 22, 1922; *Austin American*, April 16, 1922; *Waco Times-Herald*, April 22, 1922; *Houston Post*, May 31, 1922.

[18] Testimony of Erwin J. Clark, *Senator from Texas, Hearings*, 65–68.

[19] Testimony of Edward Y. Clarke and Robert L. Henry, *ibid.*, 55, 423–426.

"along Klan lines."[20] In June, after a brief stay in Atlanta, Evans came back to Texas and called still another meeting of Klan politicos, this one for the Driskill Hotel in Austin. Henry was not even informed of this gathering, but his friend Erwin J. Clark, the Great Titan from Waco, was there to represent his interests. Mayfield, Marvin, Butcher, Harwood, McCall, Cameron, and Evans were on hand to denounce Henry and to try to persuade Clark that Mayfield should be the Klan candidate. Finally Z. E. Marvin jumped up from his chair and told the Waco Titan that he was going back to Dallas and organize Klan No. 66 solidly for Mayfield.[21]

Marvin, with Evans' blessing, made good on his promise. The Dallas Klan, by far the largest chapter in Texas, conducted an "elimination primary," or poll of the members, to choose among the senatorial aspirants. Mayfield received about 1,400 preferential votes to 700 for Henry and 400 for Sterling P. Strong. Two other Evansites, Brown Harwood and Exalted Cyclops Dudley Kent, conducted a similar poll among the membership of Fort Worth Klan No. 101, and again Mayfield received a majority. It is doubtful whether other Texas Klans held their own elimination primaries, but it is beyond question that practically every Klansmen in the state, including the membership of Henry's own chapter, Waco Klan No. 33, was aware of the actions of the Dallas and Fort Worth Klans and had accepted Mayfield as the "official" Klan candidate by July 22, the day of the First Democratic primary.[22]

Sterling Strong quietly accepted his fate and withdrew from the senatorial contest in June. But Henry stubbornly refused to withdraw and remained in the race after being completely abandoned by most of his sheeted brethren. The Waco Klansmen toured the state denouncing the "Klan politicians" who had tried to "fix and eliminate" him (and had succeeded). Although Henry attracted only a handful of Klan votes and finished last in the Democratic primary, his public excoriations of Evans and his cohorts did much to air the political machinations of the order in Texas.[23]

By the date of the Democratic primary the Evans clique had united about 100,000 Texas Klansmen behind Mayfield, an advantage that enabled the railroad commissioner to lead five opponents in the senatorial race. Elderly Charles A. Culberson finished a poor third and would thus see his long public career come to an end the next March, when Congress adjourned. Billie Mayfield of Houston (no relation to Earle), editor of a weekly Klan newspaper and a candidate for lieutenant governor; George D. Garrett of Dallas, candidate for state treasurer; and Ed R. Bentley of McAllen, running for state superintendent of public instruction, all three Klansmen, survived the first primary and entered the runoff campaign.[24]

In the senatorial runoff Earle B. Mayfield faced one of the most controversial

[20] Testimony of L. M. Ballowe, *ibid.*, 327.

[21] Testimony of Erwin J. Clark, *ibid.*, 65.

[22] Testimony of Dave C. McCord, *ibid.*, 377, 569–570; interview of the writer with two former Klansmen who asked to remain anonymous, Dallas, May 18, 1959.

[23] Testimony of H. M. Keeling, *Senator from Texas, Hearings*, 463; *Dallas Morning News*, July 29, 1922.

[24] Alexander Heard and Donald S. Strong, *Southern Primaries and Elections, 1920–1949*, University, Alabama, 1950, 133; *Dallas Morning News*, August 6, 1922. On the Klan membership of Billie Mayfield, Bentley, and Garrett, see the testimony of Brown Harwood, *Senator from Texas, Hearings*, 558–559.

figures in Texas political history, James E. Ferguson, ex-governor, banker, and gentleman farmer from Temple in Bell County. Ferguson, a demagogic, ruthless politician, was making a comeback after his impeachment and ouster from the governorship in 1917 and a bootless candidacy for president on his own "American Party" ticket in 1920.[25] "Farmer Jim," as Ferguson liked to call himself, was the oracle of the white tenant farmers and day laborers, who together with the anti-prohibitionists, comprised what Ferguson's opponents termed his "pocket vote." In the runoff campaign Ferguson locked horns with Mayfield in one of the fiercest fights of an especially vitriolic era in the history of the state. While Ferguson found little wrong with the Klan except its political ambitions, he denounced the white-robed organization and its candidate in the crude but effective fashion for which he had become famous. Among other choice epithets, he referred to Mayfield as a "drunkard," "the crown prince of the Klan," and a "Klandidate." The railroad commissioner continued to bypass the Klan issue, and concentrated instead on the ex-governor's dubious public record and his well-known moistness on the liquor question.[26]

In Atlanta Imperial Kligrapp Evans grew increasingly excited over the prospects of victory in Texas. He probably did not divert any of the Imperial funds to be spent in Mayfield's behalf, but he worried a great deal about the contest and remarked at various times that the campaign between Mayfield and Ferguson was a "Klan fight" and that the Klan had to win. The other statewide races also centered on the Klan issue, and to make sure that all Klansmen knew the "right men" to support, Brown Harwood of Fort Worth, by now the Grand Dragon, mailed statements through the Great Titans' offices to each of the Realm's 240 local Klans, calling on the faithful to vote solidly for Earle B. Mayfield for senator, Billie Mayfield for lieutenant governor, Ed R. Bentley for state school superintendent, and George D. Garrett for state treasurer.[27]

When the runoff primary returns were all in Mayfield had won the Democratic nomination over Ferguson by a margin of 44,607 votes. The Klan had nominated a United States Senator, although the order's choices for lieutenant governor, state treasurer, and state school superintendent, Billie Mayfield, Garrett, and Bentley, were defeated by their non-Klan opponents. But a large majority of Klan-endorsed candidates in Harris (Houston), Dallas, McLennan (Waco), Jefferson (Beaumont), Tarrant (Fort Worth), Wichita (Wichita Falls), and many less populous counties were nominated.[28] Hiram W. Evans was jubilant. He had good reason to be happy, for his supporters in Texas had done an excellent job of organizing the rank and file, not only behind Mayfield, but

[25] Rupert N. Richardson, *Texas, the Lone Star State,* Englewood Cliffs, N. J., 1958, 292–293; Seth S. McKay, *Texas Politics, 1916–1944, with Special Reference to the German Counties,* Lubbock, 1954, chapter III.

[26] *Dallas Morning News,* August 16 and 26, 1922; McKay, *Texas Politics,* 118; Ralph W. Steen, "A Political History of Texas, 1900–1930," in Frank C. Adams (ed.), *Texas Democracy . . . ,* 4 vols., Austin 1937, I, 427; Ouida Ferguson Nalle, *The Fergusons of Texas,* San Antonio, 1946, 162–164.

[27] Testimony of E. J. Jones and Brown Harwood, *Senator from Texas, Hearings,* 364, 558–559.

[28] Heard and Strong, *Southern Primaries and Elections,* 133; *Dallas Morning News,* September 3, 1922; testimony of Jesse Martin, *Fort Worth Grain and Elevator Co. v. Alliance Insurance Co.* (No. 1068) (United States District Court, Fort Worth, Texas) reported in *Fort Worth Star-Telegram,* January 2, 1924.

behind numerous local candidates. In Dallas, for example, Klansmen set up precinct organizations outside the regular Democratic party machinery, conducted fund-raising drives for local Klan politicians, spent about $700 a week during the three months before the primaries, and perhaps gave money to Mayfield's state headquarters, which were located in Dallas. The Fort Worth Klan made its members pledge to vote for the Klan ticket in the county primaries and "banished" two Knights who refused to support the entire slate.[29]

Klansmen and sympathizers controlled the state Democratic convention, held in San Antonio the first week in September, and shouted down all attempts to incorporate an anti-Klan plank in the state party platform.[30] After the convention angry Fergusonites and other Klan-haters, calling themselves "Independent Democrats," bolted the party, fused with the Texas Republican party, which had gone on record against the Klan, and chose George E. B. Peddy, the young assistant district attorney of Harris County, to oppose Earle B. Mayfield in the general election campaign.[31]

Peddy's campaign against Mayfield in the fall, while less blustering than Ferguson's of the previous summer, was just as vigorous, but his chances were doomed from the outset. The votes of Klansmen and their allies, the prohibitionists, remained solid for Mayfield; the primary pledge worked against the Houstonian; and the secretary of state refused to certify Peddy's name for the general election ballot because he had voted in the Democratic primaries. Peddy's supporters, facing the nearly impossible task of electing their candidate by write-in, charged Mayfield with excessive campaign expenditures and with being the instrument of a "political conspiracy" on the part of the leaders of the Klan. They began legal proceedings to bar his name from the November ballot. After a bewildering round of litigation the state supreme court certified the Democratic nominee's name, and at the general election on November 5, Mayfield triumphed with 264,260 votes to 130,744 write-in votes for Peddy.[32] Just before the election Hiram W. Evans, worried that Mayfield's name might be left off the ballot, was said to have given a delegation of Texas Klan officials $25,000 to use in instructing Klansmen over the state how to write the Klan favorite's name on the ballot.[33]

Overwhelmed by Mayfield's vote in the general election, Peddy refused to give up. He carried his charges against Mayfield and the Klan before the United

[29] Testimony of Dave C. McCord, J. F. Collier, H. M. Keeling, and F. G. Van Valkenburg, *Senator from Texas, Hearings,* 373–375, 380, 382, 399–402, 466–477, 533–535; testimony of Jesse Martin and T. H. Mills, *Fort Worth Grain and Elevator Co.* v. *Alliance Insurance Co.*, reported in *Fort Worth Star-Telegram,* January 2, 1924. Hiram W. Evans was generally correct in his estimate of the importance of the Klan vote in nominating Mayfield, but he ignored the fact that thousands of people who did not like the Klan voted for Mayfield because they could not stomach Jim Ferguson. For typical prohibitionist but anti-Klan sentiments see Thomas B. Love to William Gibbs McAdoo, August 9, 1922, Love to Zach L. Cobb, August 18, 1922, Thomas B. Love Papers, Archives of the Dallas Historical Society, Dallas.

[30] *San Antonio Express,* September 7, 1922.

[31] *Dallas Morning News,* September 18, 1922.

[32] Heard and Strong, *Southern Primaries and Elections,* 167–169; *Fort Worth Star-Telegram,* September 26, 1922; *Austin American,* September 29, October 28, and November 5, 1922; *Dallas Morning News,* October 3, 1922.

[33] Testimony of J. Q. Jett, *Senator from Texas, Hearings,* 193.

State Senate's Committee on Privileges and Elections, a subcommittee of which conducted an extended inquiry into the 1922 campaign in Texas, the Klan's part in the election of Mayfield, and the expenses of the senator-elect. The subcommittee, after interviewing several Klansmen and discovering abundant evidence of Mayfield's Klan backing, finally submitted a negative report and recommended his confirmation by the senate. On February 3, 1925, nearly two and a half years after his election, the senate voted unanimously to seat Mayfield.[34]

The election of Earle B. Mayfield to the United States Senate was a striking victory for the Klan, one of the best-known and most spectacular of its numerous conquests in the 1920's. Yet this was only one of many Klan successes during 1922. The order had elected county and state officials in Oregon, Oklahoma, Arkansas, Georgia, Louisiana, and elsewhere.[35] The Klan almost certainly had a majority in the house of representatives of the 38th Texas Legislature, which met in January of 1923. In county after county in the eastern two-thirds of the state the Klan's dominance was unquestioned. In 1923, a political off year in Texas, the Klan lost in the city elections in San Antonio and El Paso, but won control of the governments of Dallas, Fort Worth, and Wichita Falls.[36] Lone Star Klansmen could boast of the fact that Texas was the number one Klan state politically, and could look forward to even greater conquests in 1924, a presidential election year.

By 1924 Hiram W. Evans had taken over the Imperial Wizardship, consolidated his power as a theoretically supreme ruler of the Invisible Empire, and installed a highly political-minded regime in Atlanta. Now, with the membership of the Klan climbing toward five million, he was even looking beyond governorships and senatorships and had acquired a few notions about presidential politics. Nationally, the Klan's objectives in 1924 were three-fold: (1) to block either major political party from condemning the Klan *by name* in its party platform; (2) to help win the Democratic presidential nomination for William Gibbs McAdoo; (3) failing to nominate McAdoo, to prevent the nomination of Alfred E. Smith, the Catholic, anti-prohibitionist governor of New York, or Oscar W. Underwood, the anti-Klan United States Senator from Alabama. The Klan achieved the first and third objectives but failed with regard to the second. Neither party mentioned the Klan in its platform, both Republicans and Democrats adopting ambiguous affirmations of racial and religious tolerance. McAdoo, perhaps hurt more than helped by the Klan's endorsement of him, could not muster the necessary two-thirds majority at the marathon Democratic national

[34] *Dallas Morning News,* February 4, 1925; *Congressional Record,* 68th Congress, 2nd Session (1925), 2929–2930.

[35] See Roberts, "Ku-Kluxing of Oregon"; "Klan Victories in Oregon and Texas"; Rice, *Klan in American Politics,* 58–64; Alexander, "Invisible Empire in the Southwest," chapters VI, VII.

[36] *Austin Statesman,* February 25, 1923; *American Citizen,* Fort Worth, Texas, April 13, 1923. Despite the Klan's strength in the 38th Legislature, only one bill that could be attributed to Klan influence was introduced in the 1923 session. This was a bill proposed in the house of representatives to prohibit teaching the theory of evolution in the public schools of the state. The measure passed the house but died in the senate and was not revived in later special sessions. Thirty-eighth Texas Legislature, *House Journal,* Regular Session (1923), 49, 163, 185, 655, 1313, 1459; *Senate Journal,* 1064–1066, 1149.

convention in New York, but neither could Smith nor Underwood; and Klan and anti-Klan, prohibitionist and anti-prohibitionist Democrats finally compromised on John W. Davis, who was nominated on the 103rd ballot.[37]

The delegation Texas sent to the Democratic convention contained a preponderance of Klansmen and Klanswomen, organized by the Klan as a companion women's order.[38] In Texas the McAdoo movement, fostered to a considerable extent by the Klan, was extremely well-organized; and the Klan probably reached the zenith of its political power in the state during the contest for the state's forty votes at the national convention. The Klan and its allies easily controlled an overwhelming number of the poorly-attended precinct conventions in Texas, and thus the conventions in most of the 252 counties in the state. After the precinct meetings Underwood's supporters realized that they had lost the Texas delegation. W. E. Lea of Orange, Underwood's campaign manager in Texas, charged that the Klan was responsible for McAdoo's victory in the precincts, and that the order went so far as to distribute handbills in the local gatherings instructing those who attended to vote for a McAdoo delegation to the county convention.[39]

The Klan was the dominant element at the state Democratic convention, held in Waco late in May. Perhaps two-thirds of the delegates at the state meeting were Klansmen, Klanswomen, and Klan sympathizers. Prior to the convention the Democratic State Executive Committee first voted 25 to 3 to endorse Governor Pat M. Neff for the presidential nomination, then reversed itself and endorsed McAdoo. A large majority at the convention voted to send an instructed McAdoo delegation to New York.[40] The delegation included such prominent Texas Klansmen as Earle B. Mayfield, Mike T. Lively of Dallas, Marvin A. Childers of San Antonio, and W. L. Thornton of Dallas. At New York the Texas group, bound by the unit rule, cast its forty votes against naming the

[37] Democratic National Committee, *Official Report of the Proceedings of the Democratic National Convention Held in Madison Square Garden, New York City, June 24, 25, 26, 27, 28, 30, July 1, 2, 3, 4, 5, 7, 8, and 9, 1924*, Indianapolis, 1924, 102, 279–309, 338–979. Some of McAdoo's staunchest supporters, like Democratic national committeeman Thomas B. Love of Dallas, pointed to "the parochialness and bigotry of that organization [the Klan]" and urged him to "disassociate your name from alleged adhesion to the K. K. K. . . ." But McAdoo acquiesced in the Klan's adoption of him, accepted the support of the order, and never publicly took a stand against it; see Thomas B. Love to William Gibbs McAdoo, October 23, 1923, Love Papers. A good summary of the McAdoo movement is Lee N. Allen, "The McAdoo Campaign for the Presidential Nomination in 1924," *Journal of Southern History*, XXIX (May, 1963), 211–228. On the Klan's role in national politics in 1924 see Rice, *Klan in American Politics*, chapter VI.

[38] The best discussion this writer has seen of the career of the Women of the Ku Klux Klan, established by national Klan headquarters in June, 1923, is in Loucks, *Klan in Pennsylvania*, chapter X. The women's order in Texas apparently never attained the size that it did in some of the northern and eastern states; see Alexander, *Crusade for Conformity*, 38–39.

[39] *Dallas Morning News*, May 4 and 6, 1924.

[40] There is a copy of the minutes of the first meeting of the Democratic State Executive Committee, including the vote on the endorsement of Neff, in the Love Papers. A useful account of the non-Klan drive for McAdoo in Texas is Lee N. Allen, "The Democratic Presidential Primary Election of 1924 in Texas," *Southwestern Historical Quarterly*, LXI (April, 1958), 474–493.

Klan in the party platform and, like most of the other delegations in which Klan influence was high, voted for McAdoo until he released his delegates after the 100th ballot.[41]

Mastery of the state delegation at the Democratic national convention demonstrated that, by the spring of 1924, the Texas Klan was a well-organized, efficient political minority. Working quietly and mysteriously, the hooded crusaders were on the verge of dominating state politics. Perhaps 400,000 Texans had joined the Klan at one time or another. The membership of the order in Texas was quite fluid, as it was everywhere else, but in 1924 there were between 97,000 and 170,000 paid-up Klansmen in the Lone Star State.[42] Observers of Texas politics agreed that the Klan would have a candidate for governor in 1924, and the secret organization seemed well-prepared for its all-out drive to put a Klansman in the governor's mansion. Yet the Klan was experiencing internal difficulties in Texas.

Early in the year dissension broke out in the Realm over the order's selection of a gubernatorial candidate. In Houston Billie Mayfield, an ex-colonel in the Texas National Guard and the unsuccessful Klan candidate for the lieutenant governorship in 1922, published a weekly newspaper marked by a combination of xenophobia and crude moralism. In the first weeks of 1924 he began exhorting Texas Klansmen through his newspaper to unify behind Dallas attorney V. A. Collins as the Klansman to carry "100 per cent Americanism" and moral reform into the coming gubernatorial race.[43] Collins, an active member of Dallas Klan No. 66, had served in the state senate during the First World War. He had been an ardent advocate of the statewide prohibition legislation passed during the war and a member of the senate committee that wrote the verdict removing Jim Ferguson from the governorship. Collins had never met Billie Mayfield or even read an issue of his newspaper before he received the endorsement of *Colonel Mayfield's Weekly*. Yet Mayfield, probably trying to build a large personal following in the Realm, boomed Collins as if they were old friends.[44]

Mayfield quickly discovered that he actually had little influence in Texas Klan circles, or least among the Realm officials, the men who controlled Klan affairs in the state. He soon learned that the Collins boom conflicted with the wishes of Z. E. "Zeke" Marvin of Dallas, the head of the state organization. Marvin, a transplant from Indiana, had acquired a chain of drug stores and extensive real estate holdings in Dallas. During the past two years he had worked his way up the Texas Klan hierarchy to the office of Grand Dragon. He was a good friend of Hiram W. Evans and one of the leading disciples of the Imperial

[41] *Dallas Morning News*, May 27, June 26 and 30, 1924; *Forth Worth Star-Telegram*, June 26, 1924. For the balloting on the platform and the presidential nomination, see *Proceedings of the Democratic National Convention*, 279–334, 338–979.

[42] *Washington Post*, November 2, 1930, Sec. I, p. 4; *New York Times*, February 21, 1926, Sec. VIII, p. 1; Duffus, "Klan in the Middle West," 354. Since the membership rolls of the Klan were never opened to the public, all figures on the size of the order in a particular place or time must represent rather broad estimates. It seems to be the consensus of observers who estimated Klan membership in the 1920's that the organization reached its peak during 1924 with about five million members.

[43] *Colonel Mayfield's Weekly* (Houston, Texas), January 19, 1924.

[44] V. A. Collins to writer, February 24, 1962, in the writer's possession.

Wizard in the Southwest. As Grand Dragon, and with Evans and the Dallas Klan, about 13,000 strong, behind him, Marvin ran matters virtually as he pleased in the Realm. He had his own candidate in mind for the governorship—District Judge Felix D. Robertson of Dallas, a charter member of the Klan in that city and, like V. A. Collins, a zealous prohibitionist. In late January Marvin announced from Realm headquarters in Dallas that Robertson would be the official candidate of the Klan in the coming Democratic gubernatorial primary.[45]

Marvin's decree infuriated Billie Mayfield. "I am not ready, and the Klan is not ready," exploded the Houston moralist, "to accept as its governor the call boy of an individual man in Texas no matter what exalted position he holds within the Klan."[46] Mayfield began trading editorial volleys with editor J. D. Hutt of the *Texas 100 Per Cent American*, a weekly published by the Dallas Klan and thus the organ of the Grand Dragon. Mayfield's fulminations apparently created enough commotion to worry Marvin, for the Realm leader visited the local Klans in Waco, Fort Worth, Houston, and San Antonio to explain Robertson's selection. According to the Grand Dragon the whole process had been very democratic and proper; Robertson was the nominee of the executive committee of the Realm, comprised of seven officials from each of the five Provinces in Texas, plus five additional Klansmen from each Province, making a total of sixty. The "Klorero," or state convention, of October, 1923, had stipulated the makeup of the executive committee. Marvin's explanation sounded simple enough, but he neglected to add that as Grand Dragon he exercised direct or indirect appointive power over every member of the executive committee and over all of those attending the Klorero.[47] His control of the individuals who chose Robertson suggested that the judge's nomination hardly expressed the voice of the rank and file.

Members of the Fort Worth and Waco Klans endorsed the choice of the state leader, but the Klansmen in Houston and San Antonio rebelled against Marvin and refused to approve Robertson's candidacy. Billie Mayfield, buttressed by growing evidence of dissension, stepped up his attacks on Marvin and demanded a Realm-wide elimination primary, similar to the polls held by the Dallas and Fort Worth Klans two years earlier. Finally, yielding to the din raised by Mayfield and other disgruntled Knights, Marvin decreed that each of the 300 or more local Klans in the state could hold its own elimination primary to decide between Robertson and V. A. Collins. Mayfield, while continuing to push Collins' candidacy, congratulated himself on his successful fight for democracy in the Realm and announced that all was well in Texas Klandom. "I am sorry that I was naughty," wrote the Houston Klansman. "Gimme your hand, old klansman, and forgive your little erring brother. Slip me your hand, Zeke, it's all over now. We are going into the battle together, and the fighting can't start any too soon for me."[48]

Klansmen over Texas, perhaps fearful that the Evans-Marvin-Dallas faction

[45] Interview of the writer with an ex-Klansman, Dallas, May 18, 1959. The figure 13,000 as the size of the Dallas Klan was given by Z. E. Marvin in the *New York Times*, February 21, 1926, Sec. VIII, p. 1.

[46] *Colonel Mayfield's Weekly*, February 2, 1924.

[47] *Texas 100 Per Cent American* (Dallas), February 15, 1924; *Constitution and Laws of the Klan*, Article 18, Section 7.

[48] *Colonel Mayfield's Weekly*, February 16 and 23, March 1, 1924.

would bolt the Klan if they did not abide by the wishes of the Grand Dragon, endorsed Robertson by a heavy majority when the standing votes were taken in the chapter primaries in March. Zeke Marvin and his friends in Dallas, although relieved, were still not sure that Mayfield could be trusted despite his protestations of harmony. They brought the Klan editor to Dallas for a conference. Mayfield spent the better part of a day talking with Marvin and J. D. Van Winkle, Exalted Cyclops of the Dallas Klan. After the conference Mayfield saw V. A. Collins and reported that Marvin and Van Winkle had presented a "great inducement" if the Houstonian would cease supporting Collins and swing to Robertson in his editorial policy.[49]

Collins was bitterly disappointed at his rejection by the Klan and the defection of Mayfield. In April he took to the hustings to tell the voters of Texas how "a tyrannical conspiracy" had betrayed his candidacy. Back in Houston Mayfield executed an editorial about-face, condemning Collins for trying to promote a strife and assuring his readers that he would not follow the Dallas attorney in a bolt.[50] Throughout the spring, in speech after speech, Collins recounted the story of his elimination by the Grand Dragon and his cronies. He admitted that he had belonged to the Klan for three years and that he had no quarrel with the tenets of the order. His only offense, he remarked acidly, was announcing for the governorship without the consent of the Realm hierarchy, and after his announcement Marvin began a campaign of vilification within the Klan, throttled his protests in the chapter meetings, and finally had him suspended from membership in the order.[51] Collins was determined, but his candidacy was doomed and he seemed to know it. He made fewer and fewer appearances as the campaign moved into the summer months. Collins still contends that he "had never sought the Klan support or asked any member of the Klan to support me, but . . . was just running as a private citizen on my merit."[52] His fate in 1924 was to be the same as that of Robert L. Henry two years earlier.

The organization of the Texas Klan in the face of disunity on the part of its opponents had made possible its victories at the precinct, county, and state conventions in the spring. This condition persisted at the first Democratic primary in July and enabled Felix D. Robertson to lead eight candidates for the governorship with 193,508 votes. His nearest opponent polled about 47,000 fewer votes, but this was enough to put Mrs. Miriam Amanda "Ma" Ferguson, the wife of Jim Ferguson, in the runoff against Robertson.[53]

Although he was barred from running for state office because of his impeachment and removal from the governorship in 1917, Jim Ferguson had vowed a fight to the death with the Klan and had entered the gubernatorial race through his wife. From the beginning of the race Jim, doing most of his wife's campaigning, neglected all other issues to concentrate his choice invective on the Klan. The runoff campaign between Robertson and Mrs. Ferguson featured four

[49] *Ibid.*, March 22, 1924; V. A. Collins to writer, February 24, 1962.

[50] *Colonel Mayfield's Weekly*, March 22, 1924.

[51] *Forth Worth Star-Telegram*, March 19, 1924; *Dallas Morning News*, April 11, 1924; V. A. Collins to writer, February 24, 1962.

[52] *Ibid.*

[53] Heard and Strong, *Southern Primaries and Elections*, 136–138; *Dallas Morning News*, July 29, 1924; Nalle, *Fergusons of Texas*, 168–180.

weeks of the worst vituperation in Texas political history. Ferguson used such delicate phrases as "the great grand gizzard mouthpiece of the Grand Dragon" to describe Robertson, who called the ex-governor a "whiskey-throated politician," a "thief," and a "liar." In the runoff all the defeated gubernatorial candidates of the first primary, including the brooding V. A. Collins, threw their support to Mrs. Ferguson, as well as most of the daily newspapers in the cities, hitherto neutral in the political fights over the Klan, and such prominent Texans as former governor Oscar B. Colquitt, former United States Senator Joseph W. Bailey, and Alvin Owsley, national commander of the American Legion.[54] By August 23, the day of the second primary, Robertson and the Klan faced a heterogeneous but effective coalition of loyal Fergusonites, principally "wets," tenant farmers, small farmers, and day laborers, businessmen who thought that the unsettled conditions fostered by the Klan were "bad for business," persons who sincerely opposed the hooded order on moral and ideological grounds, and nervous politicians who wanted to end the Klan's disruptive influence in state politics.[55]

The combination was too much for the Klan. Mrs. Ferguson's vote totaled 413,751 to 316,019 for Klansman Robertson, a difference of 97,732. The crusading spirit of the anti-Klan coalition also gave Barry Miller of Dallas, a bitter foe of the Klan, the nomination for lieutenant governor over Will C. Edwards, generally backed by the order. District Attorney Dan Moody of Travis and Williamson counties, who had sent a Klansman to prison for flogging, won the nomination for attorney general over Edward B. Ward of Corpus Christi who ran with Klan support.[56] After the runoff primary Dallas and Tarrant counties were the only major counties in Texas still under the dominance of the Klan, as voters in Wichita, Harris, and many other counties over the state nominated anti-Klan slates.[57]

The final setback of the summer for the white-robed order came at the state Democratic convention, held in Austin early in September. With forces hostile to the Klan controlling about 90 per cent of the county delegations, the convention endorsed the nomination of Mrs. Ferguson, denounced the Klan as "un-American, un-Christian, and un-Democratic," and demanded the public registration of secret organizations and an anti-mask law.[58]

[54] *Forth Worth Star-Telegram*, August 22, 1924; *Waco Times-Herald*, August 14, 1924; *Dallas Morning News*, August 20, 1924; Sam H. Acheson, *Joe Bailey, the Last Democrat*, New York, 1932, 394; V. A. Collins to writer, February 24, 1962; see also Reinhard Luthin, *American Demagogues: Twentieth Century*, Boston, 1954, 153–181.

[55] On the nature of the anti-Klan forces in the 1924 gubernatorial runoff, see Charles W. Ferguson, "James E. Ferguson," *Southwest Review*, X (October, 1924), 26–39.

[56] For a Klan ticket circulated by the Abilene, Texas, Klan endorsing Felix D. Robertson for governor, Will C. Edwards for lieutenant governor, and Edward B. Ward for attorney general, see *Congressional Record*, 68th Congress, 2nd Session, 94.

[57] Heard and Strong, *Southern Primaries and Elections*, 136–138; *Austin Statesman*, August 25, 1924; *Fort Worth Star-Telegram*, August 31, 1924.

[58] *Austin Statesman*, September 3 and 4, 1924; C. V. Terrell to Oscar B. Colquitt, August 28, 1924, Oscar B. Colquitt Papers, University of Texas Archives, Austin. In 1925 the Texas Legislature, showing many new members over the Klan-oriented 38th Legislature, enacted a law prohibiting the wearing of masks in public places,

In the general election campaign thousands of Texas Democrats who could not accept "Fergusonism" and "government by proxy" deserted the dominant party and supported the Republican gubernatorial candidate, Dr. George C. Butte, dean of the University of Texas School of Law. The only group which formally bolted the Democracy was an organization headed by erstwhile Wilsonian progressive and present Democratic national committeeman Thomas B. Love of Dallas, called the "Good Government Democratic League."[59] But most Klansmen, it appears, also voted for Butte, who polled almost three times as many votes as any Republican candidate for governor had ever received in the state. Butte displayed his greatest strength in such Klan hotbeds—and Democratic strongholds—as Dallas, Harris (Houston), Tarrant (Fort Worth), Wichita (Wichita Falls), Jefferson (Beaumont), McLennan (Waco), Grayson (Sherman), Potter (Amarillo), and Smith (Tyler) counties. The massive, if unofficial, support the Klan evidently gave the Republican candidate represented a last desperate try at stopping the hated Fergusons. Klansmen had little to gain in the way of political advantage by bolting the Democratic party, for the Republicans of Texas had gone on record against the Klan in both their 1922 and 1924 state platforms. Klan influence in a Republican state administration would have been negligible. Yet even the negative satisfaction of frustrating the Fergusons was no longer within the grasp of Klansmen. There were enough irreconcilable Klan-haters and ever loyal Democrats left in the state to give Mrs. Ferguson 422,558 votes to 294,970 for Butte.[60]

Thus the Klan failed to win the Democratic nomination for Felix D. Robertson, then failed to block the arch enemies of the order, "Ma" and "Pa" Ferguson, in the general election. Yet this was not the extent of the disaster of 1924 for the Klan. The organization lost nearly all the counties it had formerly controlled, and a predominantly anti-Klan legislature was elected. These developments signaled the passing of the Klan as a force in Texas politics. "It was all over," recalled a former Klansman. "After Robertson was beaten the prominent men left the Klan. The Klan's standing went with them."[61] By the end of 1924 Texas, once the most cherished prize of Hiram W. Evans and the men who ran the Invisible Empire, was no longer the number one state in Klandom. Other states, such as Indiana, Oklahoma, or Alabama, became more important than Texas in Klan affairs, but within a brief period the Klan also fell apart in those states.[62]

Within two years after Robertson's defeat and the other Klan reverses of 1924

---

thus placing Texas with Oklahoma, Louisiana, and New York, where laws to regulate the Klan had been passed earlier. Thirty-ninth Texas Legislature, *House Journal,* Regular Session (1925), 146, 906–907; *General Laws of the State of Texas,* Regular Session, 39th Legislature (1925), 213–214.

[59] The folder headed "Good Government Democratic League" in the Thomas B. Love Papers contains material on the anti-Ferguson movement.

[60] Heard and Strong, *Southern Primaries and Elections,* 136–138; *Dallas Morning News,* November 9 and 18, 1924. For a more extended explanation of Butte's vote in the general election, see Alexander, *Crusade for Conformity,* 67–68.

[61] Interview of the writer with an ex-Klansman, Dallas, May 18, 1959.

[62] See Weaver, "Klan in Wisconsin, Indiana, Ohio, and Michigan," chapter IV; Alexander, "Invisible Empire in the Southwest," chapter XI; R. A. Patton, "A Ku Klux Klan Reign of Terror," *Current History* XXVIII (April, 1928), 51–55; Rice, *Klan in American Politics,* 87–90.

membership in the Realm of Texas had dropped to about half its former size. The once-mighty Dallas Klan's enrollment dwindled from 13,000 to 1,200. One of the Dallasites who left the Invisible Empire was Zeke Marvin, who resigned from the office of Grand Dragon in late 1924 and was "banished" by the Dallas chapter the next year.[63] In 1926 Dan Moody challenged the Fergusons in the Democratic primaries and beat them by a lopsided margin. Most of the remaining Klansmen probably voted for Moody, an enemy of the Klan though an ardent prohibitionist, but their votes were not nearly as important as the fact that Mrs. Ferguson again benefited from her husband's "pocket vote."[64]

Two years later Herbert Hoover and the Republican party won the electoral voters of Texas from Al Smith, the Democratic candidate, thus emphasizing that the fears and prejudices which had given rise to the Klan in the first place had by no means disappeared from the state. But the foremost manipulator of those fears and prejudices, the Klan, was almost gone. That same year Earle B. Mayfield, trying for a second term in the United States Senate but running without the powerful Klan organization that had elected him, met defeat at the hands of Congressman Tom Connally. By the end of the decade Klansmen in Texas were numbered in the hundreds rather than in thousands and tens of thousands.[65] Still the many Texans who had joined the Klan in the early twenties could look back on the career of the order in the state as featuring a combination of violence and political power unsurpassed anywhere.

The Klan's career in politics was meteoric, lasting no more than seven years in any state. For the duration of its ventures in politics, however, the Klan shared certain characteristics with other secret political societies, such as the various groups comprising the Know-Nothing movement of the 1840's and 1850's and the American Protective Association of the 1890's. Perhaps the history of the Klan also points up some things to expect from succeeding superpatriotic organizations like the John Birch Society.

However much its leaders disclaimed political intentions, in almost every state the Klan sooner or later found its way into politics. In most communities and counties and in all states the active membership of the Klan constituted a minority. Consequently the best hope for success in politics was to operate within the two established parties. The Klan worked within the Democratic party in the southern states and Texas, usually within the Republican party in the north, and within both parties in border states like Oklahoma and on the national level. Division of voting strength or indecisiveness in choosing a candidate, either in the party primaries or the general elections, was usually fatal to

[63] *New York Times*, February 21, 1926, Sec. VIII, p. 1; *Forth Worth Star-Telegram*, December 18, 1924; *Dallas Morning News*, October 11, 1925.

[64] Rice, *Klan in American Politics*, 72–73; *Austin American*, July 4, 1926; *Dallas Morning News*, August 14, 1926; Heard and Strong, *Southern Primaries and Elections*, 138–141.

[65] The *Washington Post*, November 2, 1930, Sec. I, p. 4, gave the following figures on Klan membership in Texas in the 1920's:

1920–1925	450,000 (cumulative)
1926	79,878
1927	11,891
1928	2,487
1929	1,620
1930	780

the Klan's chances.[66] Yet this necessity to concentrate on one candidate led to autocratic methods on the part of the Klan's leaders and dissension among subordinates and the rank and file Klansmen. This was the case in Texas in 1922, when Hiram W. Evans overrode all opposition to the naming of Earle B. Mayfield as the Klan senatorial candidate, and in 1924, when Grand Dragon Z. E. Marvin virtually dictated the Klan's endorsement of Felix D. Robertson for the governorship, to the dissatisfaction of many Klansmen.[67]

The presence of the Klan as a disciplined yet indeterminable minority upset the prevailing political equilibrium and gave an air of uncertainty to local, state, and even national politics. Thus the secret order inspired hostility among many of the professional politicians, who did not know whether to make their peace with the organization or abjure it. It is highly significant that in the 1924 runoff campaign between Robertson and Mrs. Ferguson all of the eliminated gubernatorial hopefuls supported Mrs. Ferguson. This was a critical factor in Mrs. Ferguson's victory in the runoff primary over the Klan favorite, whom she had trailed in the first primary. Finally, when the Klan met defeat in politics its decline was precipitate; within a year after a major failure the order could usually be discounted as a political element. The emotional intensity, the crusading fervor with which the Klan went at politics, together with the hazards of telling Klan members how to vote, precluded much of a rebound. Defeat meant disintegration for an organization like the Klan, which thrived on crisis, real or imagined, and demanded success in order to survive.

[66] In 1924, in the Democratic primary contest for United States Senator in Oklahoma, N. Clay Jewett, the Grand Dragon, kept switching the Klan's endorsement from one candidate to another, thus dividing the vote of the order and making possible the nomination of Klan-hater John C. Walton, ousted from the governorship by the legislature the previous fall. In Arkansas many Klansmen revolted against the Klan candidate for governor dictated to them by Grand Dragon James A. Comer, with the result that the Klan vote was split and a non-Klan candidate was nominated. See Alexander, "Invisible Empire in the Southwest," chapter X.

[67] Two former Klansmen interviewed by the writer remarked that Felix D. Robertson was not a fit candidate, that he was unknown in many parts of the state, and that he was the tool of Hiram W. Evans, Z. E. Marvin, and George K. Butcher, Kligrapp (secretary) of the Dallas Klan. Then why did Robertson receive the united support of Texas Klansmen? "We had no choice but to accept him" was the reason given by one of the Klansmen. "If we hadn't, the Klan would have been split and Ma Ferguson would be elected. That would have been the end of the Klan in Texas." Interview of the writer with two ex-Klansmen, Dallas, May 18, 1959.

15

THE CRISIS IN THE AMERICAN DREAM

Arthur A. Ekirch, Jr.

When Herbert Hoover was inaugurated as the thirty-first president in March 1929, the future appeared bright for a prosperous America. Hoover confidently predicted that by continuing the policies of his Republican predecessors in the 1920's the nation could abolish poverty and spread the blessings of prosperity throughout the land. By the end of his first year in office, industrial production was declining, trade and commerce were faltering, agriculture was more depressed than ever before, and millions were unemployed. Optimism gave way to despair as more and more Americans questioned the gospel of success propounded by leaders in all fields during the 1920's. It is this mounting pessimism that Arthur Ekirch examines in the essay presented here. This serves as an appropriate concluding statement on the decade of the 1920's. As all of the intellectuals of the period with whom he deals seem to be saying, it was clearly a time for a reevaluation of the American dream, for a new deal in American thought and action.

Arthur A. Ekirch, Jr., is an intellectual historian. The essay published here is the first chapter of Ideologies and Utopias: The Impact of the New Deal on American Thought *(Chicago, 1969). He is professor of history at the State University of New York at Albany. Much of his recent writing focuses on twentieth-century themes. Among his other books are* The Decline of American Liberalism *(New York, 1955),* The Civilian and the Military *(New York, 1956),* Ideas, Ideals and American Diplomacy *(New York, 1963), and* Man and Nature in America *(New York, 1963).*

Two years after the fateful stock market crash of October 1929, in the midst of the deepening economic depression, a distinguished American historian published one of the most widely read books of the 1930's. The overriding question posed

Source: "Arthur A. Ekirch, Jr., *Ideologies and Utopias* (Chicago: Quadrangle Books, Inc., 1969) pp. 3–35. Copyright © 1969 by Arthur A. Ekirch, Jr. Reprinted by permission of the publisher.

by James Truslow Adams in his work, to which he gave the title *The Epic of America*, was what the fate of the American dream, as he called it, would be. . . .

The concept of the American dream, which many disillusioned and bewildered Americans in the darkest days of the depression were ready to dismiss as beyond recall, played an important role in American history. To the early discoverers, and to the settlers who had fled the political and religious strife of the Old World, the virgin North American continent was a New Eden or El Dorado, rich in the promise of unsurpassed material and spiritual rewards. Building their Bible Commonwealth in the wilderness, the New England Puritans, like the ancient Hebrews, considered themselves to be God's chosen people. And in the Thirteen Colonies this same sense of grandeur and uniqueness was reinforced and fulfilled by the glorious triumph of the American Revolution. Confident of their manifest destiny and of the inevitability of their progress, the American people believed they had a mission to educate the rest of the world in the virtues of republican government and free institutions.

Americans were optimistic because within their own lifetime they could see tangible results: they had spanned a continent and tamed the wilderness. Already by the close of the nineteenth century the United States, despite the trauma of its Civil War, was the premier industrial and agricultural nation of the world. And at the dawn of the new century, American fighting men crossed the oceans to plant the American flag on distant shores, thus adding new worldwide dimensions to the American dream. . . .

A mixture of romance and reality, of idealism and practical common sense, the American dream was not a logical idea. "Like every great thought that has stirred and advanced humanity, it was a religious emotion, a great act of faith, a courageous leap into the dark unknown." Yet, until the depression of the thirties, following hard upon the disillusionment over American entrance into the First World War, the American dream stood largely unquestioned in the minds of the American people as a valid philosophy and article of popular belief. In the nineteenth century, for example, Americans, though occupied with the conquest of a continent and the building of a civilization, never lost the vision of something nobler. "If we hastened after the pot of gold, we also saw the rainbow itself, and felt that it promised, as of old, a hope for mankind." In its material achievements alone, Adams believed, America "would have made no distinctive and unique gift to mankind. But there has been also the *American dream*, that dream of a land in which life should be better and richer and fuller for every man, with opportunity for each according to his ability or achievement."[1]

A stockbroker before he turned author and wrote a Pulitzer prize-winning history of the founding of New England, James Truslow Adams passed severe judgment on his own postwar generation. What he called "Our Business Civilization" and "The Tempo of Modern Life" he found equally wanting. The country in its rush to forget Europe and the war had succumbed to the Red Scare of 1919. "The whole state of mind of the nation, including many elements in it which should have kept their heads, was disgraceful, but tended strongly to alienate us from Europe, with its Bolshevism and what was considered, somewhat

[1] James Truslow Adams, *The Epic of America* (Boston: Little, Brown, 1931), pp. 198, 403–404.

vaguely, its sources of infection for Socialism and Communism." The sudden end of the war, Adams suggested, left the American people emotionally unsatisfied. Urged to build up a great fighting machine, and encouraged by propaganda to concentrate all their energies upon the war, the mob element and mass psychology in the population "demanded sacrificial victims and found them in all who differed in any way from the conservative and the stereotyped."[2]

Even the prosperity of the twenties was, in Adams' eyes, a troubled achievement. It entailed a heavy expense in goods and services which encouraged materialism and standardization and damaged intellectual life and moral values. As compared with England and Europe, Adams argued that America's business civilization exacted a high degree of social conformity with an accompanying decline in the art of living in favor of piling up material goods and "things." With business and money-making and material improvement accepted in themselves as ultimate goals, they took on the qualities of moral virtues, while serious criticism was regarded as obstructive and dangerous. "The one liberty that is still valued is the liberty to exploit and to acquire. That liberty will be defended to the death, but other liberties, such as freedom of thought and speech, have become pale and unreal ghosts, academic questions of no interest to the practical man." Meanwhile, the demand for more money to meet the high cost of postwar living put a premium on speculation at the expense of traditional values of hard work and thrift. "The old desire to control the great corporations in the interests of the American dream became changed into a desire to see their stocks go up. . . ." Eventually, however, the law of diminishing returns was bound to affect even the optimism of Wall Street.[3]

Fortunate in his unusual combination of the talents and insights of financier and historian, Adams was one of the prescient few who were not caught in the collapse of the stock market. His belief "in laws and precedents, and merely following history, declining to believe in a 'new era,'" he later wrote, "enabled me to scuttle out of every stock before the crash." He selfishly welcomed the 1929 panic which, he declared, he "would be glad to see go further." He predicted in November "a long slow decline," noting that it was silly "to say that the slump can't hurt business for there have been only 'paper losses.'" Although the end of the bull market had been foreseen by some of the saner financial heads in Europe and America, "In no case," Adams pointed out, "could the nation, or whatever party might have been in power, have avoided the inevitable, but," he added, "the country need not have been advised to crowd on every rag of extra sail as it headed into the hurricane." Disillusioned by the Great Crusade for peace and democracy, the American people had been urged to place their destiny in the hands of practical businessmen and realistic politicians. ". . . Having surrendered idealism for the sake of prosperity, the 'practical men' bankrupted us on both of them."[4]

Studying the collapse of the American dream from the vantage point of the depression, Adams contended that it had been a mistake to consider man merely

[2] *Ibid.*, p. 391.

[3] Adams, *Epic of America*, pp. 395–396, 405–406; Adams, *The Tempo of Modern Life* (New York: Boni, 1931), p. 42; Adams, *Our Business Civilization* (New York: Boni, 1929), Chap. 2.

[4] Adams to Wilbur L. Cross, July 19, 1932; Adams to Mark A. De W. Howe, November 1, 1929, Adams Papers; Adams, *Epic of America*, p. 400.

as a producer and consumer. Material plenty, though it seemed now to count more than ever, was not the foundation of the dream, and any future restoration would require a greater concern for human and aesthetic values. In the modern industrial state an economic base was essential, and Adams found "no reason why wealth, which is a social product, should not be more equitably controlled and distributed in the interest of society." But, if the American dream was to come true and again be a reality, "those on top, financially, intellectually, or otherwise, have got to devote themselves to the 'Great Society,' and those who are below in the scale have got to rise, not merely economically, but culturally. We cannot become a great democracy by giving ourselves up as individuals to selfishness, physical comfort, and cheap amusements. The very foundation of the American dream of a better and richer life for all is that all, in varying degrees, shall be capable of wanting to share in it." Adams was certain that neither business nor political leaders could guarantee the American people a "good life" in the old Greek sense, and he feared that "just so long as wealth and power are our sole badges of success, so long will ambitious men strive to attain them." The prospect, he concluded, was discouraging but not hopeless.

> *We have a long and arduous road to travel if we are to realize our American dream in the life of our nation, but if we fail, there is nothing left but the old eternal round. The alternative is the failure of self-government, the failure of the common man to rise to full stature, the failure of all that the American dream has held of hope and promise for mankind.*[5]

A modern conservative, or an old-fashioned classical liberal, Adams stood somewhere between the New Humanists and the Old Progressives of 1912. Like the Humanists, he feared the implications of mass production and doubted most of the claims of modern science. But he also followed some of the Progressives in questioning the wisdom of tying the economic welfare of the nation to the policies and credo of a businessman's government. In the golden glow of the twenties, the Republican party had staked its claim for political support on the argument of presidential prosperity. Under the leadership and ideas of Secretary of the Treasury Mellon and Secretary of Commerce Hoover, Adams wrote, "we are asked to envisage and experiment with a wholly new conception of the Business-State, a Business-State under Capitalism much as the Soviet government is a Business-State under Communism." Caught in the trap of their own optimistic political and financial philosophy, President Hoover and his associates continued to predict the return of normal business conditions in the months after the stock market crash. Noting the statement of Governor Roy Young of the Federal Reserve Bank in May 1930 that the country was now in "what appears to be a business depression," Adams penned a sarcastic epitaph for the reigning Republican theory of engineering permanent prosperity: "If we were not also in a Republican administration, there would be less doubt among our present leaders as to whether we were in 'what *appears* to be a business depression.' "[6]

The crash and ensuing depression were climactic blows in the series of buf-

[5] Adams, *Epic of America*, pp. 410–411, 415–416.

[6] Adams, *Tempo of Modern Life*, pp. 277, 295. See also the statements of Republican leaders compiled in Edward Angly, *Oh Yeah?* (New York: Viking, 1931), *passim*.

fetings which had beset the American dream in the decades before and after the First World War. In his *Epic of America,* Adams put into historical perspective the increasingly troubled concern and sense of malaise shared by so many of the intellectuals of the twenties. At bottom, one sensed, was a disillusionment not only with the late war and the cult of prosperity, but also, and even more importantly, with democracy and the whole philosophy of progressive reform as it had developed in the early 1900's.[7]

One of the first to prepare a formal statement of liberal disenchantment was Harold Stearns, who wrote in the tradition of Randolph Bourne's indictment of the pragmatist-progressives for their support of the war and the administration that had waged it. Stearns in his own career fulfilled the popular stereotype of the sensitive, young literary radical who was part of the postwar Lost Generation. An alumnus of Harvard and Greenwich Village, where he mixed journalism and the gayer side of life, Stearns left the United States after the war to join the growing number of American expatriates in Paris. His *Liberalism in America: Its Origins, Its Temporary Collapse, Its Future,* published in 1919, was his first critical salvo. Three years later he added a postscript, editing a symposium in which some thirty well-known writers analyzed the defects in American civilization.[8] In between these works, Stearns also composed his *America and the Young Intellectual.*

Convinced that a decent respect for the dignity and worth of the individual had vanished since 1914, Stearns noted bitterly: "Everywhere we turn it is the same story—coercion, force, force to the utmost without stint or limit." The war had failed to achieve its liberal ends partly because the leaders themselves were not liberal; they had been content, with the intellectuals, to become the hired dupes of the military machine. The charm of being a big-shot in Washington had occasioned such a flood of eager personnel and energy that the "war itself was forgotten in the intensity of waging it," while President Wilson, the most conspicuous exemplar of "The Technique of Liberal Failure," showed "to what extremes of cruelty and intolerance and injustice the idealist in politics can go." With the intellectuals and educated leaders of the country more hysterical and wrong-headed even than the masses, Stearns concluded that disillusionment was inevitable. The American people no longer believed Wilson's pious phrases.[9]

Among the thousands of young men who came back from France after the Great War, one of the most promising was Walter Lippmann. A youthful Harvard radical and journalist like Stearns, Lippmann had left his post with the *New Republic* magazine to help fight the war in Washington and then had joined the large group of experts who accompanied President Wilson and Colonel House to the Paris Peace Conference. Like his fellow editors on the *New Republic,* Lippmann was affronted by the harsh peace terms he found in the Treaty of Versailles and by the grave weaknesses of the League of Nations. "In my opinion," he declared privately in midsummer of 1919, "the Treaty is not only illiberal and in bad faith, it is in the highest degree imprudent. It is a far worse job, I think, than

[7] See Henry F. May, *The End of American Innocence: A Study of the First Years of Our Own Time, 1912–1917* (New York: Knopf, 1959), Introduction and *passim.*

[8] Harold Stearns, *Civilization in the United States* (New York: Harcourt, Brace, 1922).

[9] Stearns, *Liberalism in America* (New York: Boni and Liveright, 1919), pp. 5, 102–103, 143.

the Treaty of Vienna a hundred years ago. . . . I am certain that the present League is in structure and function and ideal the enemy of a real League of Nations, and the greatest danger is that its failure, like that of the Holy Alliance before it, will disillusionize a whole generation."[10] Lippmann was . . . disturbed, even more, by the dismal prospects for democracy at home. In a frank and anguished correspondence with his old friend and wartime boss, Secretary of War Newton D. Baker, early in 1920, he made clear the bases of his despair: "You know what hopes were put in this administration, how loudly and insistently it proclaimed its loyalty to the cause of freedom. Well it was possible to fail in these hopes. It was credible that the wisdom and the strength to realize them would be lacking. But it is forever incredible," Lippmann continued, "that an administration announcing the most spacious ideals in our history should have done more to endanger fundamental American liberties than any group of men for a hundred years." Citing the political sentences, deportations, censorship, and new sedition legislation advocated by the Justice Department, he concluded: "These are dreadful things and they have dreadful consequences. They have instituted a reign of terror in which honest thought is impossible, in which moderation is discountenanced, in which panic supplants reason." Instead of carrying out its "solemn duty to allay fear and restore sanity," the Wilson administration had "done everything humanly possible to add fresh excitement to an overexcited community."[11]

In reply to his younger correspondent, Baker sadly indicted his own generation. At the same time he tried to explain to Lippmann his deep personal sense of hopes unfulfilled:

> *I have no fears about America; the excesses and hysteria to which you refer are clearly passing phases which trouble the surface after a deep disturbance; but I have a grief which time may modify but can not cure, and that is that at the very crossing of the ways, when the supreme moment for America had arrived, we poured our liberal spirit through a sieve, each of us became particularists and formalists and so lost the opportunity to seize and hold the spiritual leadership of the world.*[12]

As he looked back upon America's wartime experience from the background of the early twenties, Lippmann wondered whether democratic self-government, in the historic sense of the American dream, was still possible. . . . Very early in his life, as a young man fresh from a brief postgraduate course in government as an assistant to the muckraking Lincoln Steffens, Lippmann had published *A Preface to Politics* (1913). In this precocious work, its author, scorning moral absolutes and traditional values, set forth an ambitious psychological analysis and theory of progressive politics. Years later, on the eve of the Great Depression, Lippmann wrote a companion piece to his earlier work which he entitled *A Preface to Morals* (1929). The first book had celebrated America's coming emancipation from conservative modes of thinking. But now Lippmann, surveying "the dissolution of the ancestral order," in which "whirl is king," sought a principle of authority, some certainty in the midst of "the genius of modernity" to which "the moralist in an

[10] Lippmann to Fosdick, August 15, 1919, in *Letters on the League of Nations, From the Files of Raymond B. Fosdick* (Princeton: Princeton University Press, 1966), pp. 10–12.

[11] Lippmann to Baker, January 17, July 23, 1920, Newton D. Baker Papers, Box 12.

[12] Baker to Lippmann, January 20, 1920, Baker Papers, Box 12.

unbelieving world" could cling. ". . . The modern man who has ceased to believe, without ceasing to be credulous, hangs, as it were," he wrote, "between heaven and earth, and is at rest nowhere." Coerced no longer by moral authority, but compelled nevertheless by the force of events, the modern man was conquered but unconvinced. "In the old order the compulsions were often painful, but there was sense in the pain inflicted by the will of an all-knowing God. In the new order the compulsions are painful and, as it were, accidental, unnecessary, wanton, and full of mockery."[13]

What Lippmann said with scholarly restraint and a certain piety, H. L. Mencken, whom Lippmann called "the most powerful personal influence on this whole generation of educated people,"[14] spread flamboyantly across the pages of the *American Mercury* magazine. More savage than the New Humanists in his indictment of the materialism and conformity of the great mass of his fellows, Mencken joined the growing company of intellectuals who despaired of the future of democracy. More faith than reason, democracy, in Mencken's view, was always in need of elevating new leaders to prevent its degenerating into a mob.

In his *Notes on Democracy*, published in 1926, Mencken argued that fear and envy were the two main characteristics of democracy and "of its twin, Puritanism." Evidence of fear he saw in the United States' tendency to chase monsters, from the time of the British Redcoats to the Bolsheviks in the Red Scare of 1919. In a democracy motivated by such hysteria, "The statesman becomes, in the last analysis, a mere witch-hunter, a glorified smeller and snooper. . . ." The Department of Justice he attacked as misnamed and as the chief violator of the Bill of Rights it was supposed to defend. Nine-tenth of American Presidents, he pointed out, had reached office by making promises that were basically immoral. Yet, after election day, the President was criticized not for making the promises but for his failure to keep them. "No man," he wrote, "would want to be President of the United States in strict accordance with the Constitution. There is no sense of power in merely executing the laws; it comes from evading or augmenting them."[15]

An individualist rather than a Progressive, Mencken's liberalism was personal rather than social in scope. Like so many intellectuals in the twenties, he saw little hope in political action. The Progressives' old hero, Theodore Roosevelt, he likened to the German Kaiser as an exponent of authoritarian reform from the top, while Woodrow Wilson was "the self-bamboozled Presbyterian, the right-thinker, the great moral statesman, the perfect model of the Christian cad." Mencken denounced the regal concept of the citizen's duty to the state, race, or nation, as a synonym for docile obedience: "For the man who differs from this inert and well-regimented mass, however slightly, there are no duties *per se*. . . . Human progress," he contended, "is further, not by conformity, but by aberration. The very concept of duty is thus a function of inferiority; it belongs naturally only to timorous and incompetent men."[16]

[13] Lippmann, *A Preface to Morals* (New York: Macmillan, 1929), pp. 3–4, 9–10, 314. See also Joseph Wood Krutch, *The Modern Temper* (New York: Harcourt, Brace, 1929), Chaps. 2, 8.

[14] Lippmann, *Men of Destiny* (New York: Macmillan, 1927), p. 61.

[15] H. L. Mencken, *Notes on Democracy* (New York: Knopf, 1926), pp. 22ff., 38, 181ff.

[16] Mencken, *Prejudices, Second Series* (New York: Knopf, 1920), pp. 102, 111–112; *Prejudices, Third Series* (New York: Knopf, 1922), p. 314.

Under the new businesslike interpretation of the American dream during the 1920's, the alienation of the intellectuals was perhaps inevitable. The widespread demand for conformity in politics and morals and the all-pervading emphasis on material prosperity seemed accurate measures of the enormous decline from the idealism of the war and the Progressive era. Like certain of the Jacksonian Democrats after the defeat of their party in 1840, many of the older liberals and Progressives of 1912 lost confidence in the virtue and intelligence of the people. Harding's triumph, followed four years later by La Follette's disappointing showing as presidential candidate of a renewed Progressive party, cast doubt on the traditional liberal assumption that the average citizen wanted government to be an instrument of reform and progress. The severe judgments of a Lippmann or a Mencken on the possibility of an informed public opinion or mass democracy appeared to be confirmed all too well by the election returns. . . .

The postwar dilemma of the liberal democrat and reformer was well illustrated in the writings of J. Allen Smith and Vernon L. Parrington. Close friends and colleagues at the University of Washington, both men were scholars who also exercised a wide intellectual influence. Smith's first book, *The Spirit of American Government*, published in 1907, attracted the attention of Progressives—including Theodore Roosevelt and Robert M. La Follette—by anticipating in part Charles Beard's celebrated thesis on the economic origins of the Constitution. Overlooked, however, by most Progressives was Smith's insistence on the need for strengthening local government—the theme of his now almost forgotten work, *The Growth and Decadence of Constitutional Government*, which he completed in the early twenties. The late war, with its encouragement of centralized power, showed Smith the undemocratic, illiberal side of government. There was a wide discrepancy between the theory and practice of democracy, while the growth of the suffrage and the acceptance of majority rule were no guarantees of individual liberty. Such political democracy, by removing the main ground for the people's distrust of governmental authority, merely concealed the steady rise of state supremacy over the citizen under the guise of popular sovereignty. Centralization, accompanied by militarism and imperialism, Smith believed, was a direct threat to popular rule. "Democracy, in any sense of the term," he concluded, "is possible only when there is the largest practicable measure of local self-government."[17]

Smith's book, with an introduction by Parrington, was generally ignored when it was published posthumously at the outset of the depression. In contrast, Parrington's *Main Currents in American Thought* was an outstanding critical and popular success. Yet *Main Currents*, with its rich historical details about American literature, reflected also much of Smith's pessimistic point of view. Reread today for the insight it provides into Parrington's own beliefs, *Main Currents* is an impressive monument to its author's lamentations over a declining liberalism and a failure to realize the American dream. "We must have a political state powerful enough to deal with corporate wealth," he wrote to a friend a few months before his own death in 1929, "but how," he asked, "are we going to keep that state with its augmenting power from being captured by the force we want it to control?" Power, Parrington recognized, resulted always in a struggle to dominate its use.

[17] J. Allen Smith, *The Growth and Decadence of Constitutional Government* (New York: Holt, 1930), p. 197.

> *When one controls the political state, whatever one wants can be done under cover of the law and with the sanction of the courts. Have you been able to convince yourself that the corporate wealth of America will permit that centralized political state to pass out of its control and become an agent to regulate or thwart its plans?*[18]

Parrington's query, posed in the final year of prosperity, on the eve of the stock market crash and his own death, lay at the heart of the liberals' difficulties. Neither Parrington nor most of his contemporaries could foresee, of course, that the depression would go far to destroy the political influence of big business and to restore to the people the political power they appeared to have lost in the twenties. Both Parrington and Smith were pessimistic idealists whose vision of the American dream carried them a century into the past, back to the era of Jeffersonian liberalism and a simpler, agrarian type of society. Neither as sophisticated nor as cynical as Lippmann or Mencken, they were also not as sanguine as, for example, Charles Beard and John Dewey, who retained their belief that the American dream might still be realized through the great vistas being opened up to the common man by science and education.

In *The Rise of American Civilization*, the magisterial historical synthesis which he wrote with his wife and published in the same years as Parrington's volumes, Beard called attention to the coincidence, and even probable causal relationship, between scientific progress and the rise of democracy in the United States as well as in Europe in the second quarter of the nineteenth century. It was science, the Beards wrote, which

> *pointed the way to progressive democracy in its warfare against starvation, poverty, disease, and ignorance, indicating how classes and nations long engaged in strife among themselves might unite to wring from nature the secret of security and the good life. It was science, not paper declarations relating to the idea of progress, that at last made patent the practical methods by which democracy could raise the standard of living for the great masses of the people.*[19]

That confidence in the efficacy of science which the Beards traced back one hundred years to the age of Jackson they also invoked to resolve some of their own doubts concerning the preemption of industrial society by the conservative political and business forces of their day. . . .

Like Beard, John Dewey, who had once described democracy as an ethical ideal, now believed it was even more a social experience, "a mode of associated living, of conjoint communicated experience." Not just a form of government or the product of political forces, democracy represented "the convergence of a great number of social movements," and in this sense it had to be born anew in every generation with education serving as its midwife. But the democratic public was "still largely inchoate and unorganized," apathetic to false issues stirred up by the "hired promoters of opinion called publicity agents."[20]

[18] Parrington to Professor Ross L. Finney, January 23, 1929, quoted in Eric F. Goldman, "J. Allen Smith," *Pacific Northwest Quarterly*, XXXV (July 1944), 209.

[19] Charles and Mary Beard, *The Rise of American Civilization* (New York: Macmillan, 1927), I, 737.

[20] John Dewey, "The Ethics of Democracy," *University of Michigan Philosophical*

To Dewey the major question was when the Great Society, fashioned in the last century by the discoveries and use of steam and electricity and by technology in general, would become the Great Community. The traditional individuality of the Western European civilization, which was threatened by American mass culture, had been a very limited boon in which the peasantry and proletariat had hardly participated. In America, many of the attributes of rural community life, which had formerly given focus and direction to personality, were being lost, and as a consequence the individual found himself bewildered. Thus insecurity with unemployment was often a feature of modern industrial civilization. But it was also true, Dewey wrote, that "Evils which are uncritically laid at the door of industrialism and democracy might, with greater intelligence, be referred to the dislocation and unsettlement of local communities." American democracy, which had developed out of small community life and been taken over from English political institutions, now was in the process of evolving into a public or democratic socialism. Yet Dewey also believed that "Democracy must begin at home, and its home is the neighborly community." The problem, therefore, was somehow to preserve the individualistic values of the older community and transmit them into the newer social or collective democracy that Dewey called "corporateness."[21]

Convinced of the need for a thorough political and social reformation, and dissatisfied with the business civilization of the twenties, liberal thinkers nevertheless differed widely in their prescriptions for the realization of the American dream. Individualism, socialism, science, education, and democracy were all accordingly subjected to searching analysis and considerable reinterpretation by the scholars and journalists of the postwar decade. Yet few of them discerned any immediate crisis until the detonations in Wall Street heralded the end of an era and the onset of a major economic depression.

However much intellectuals decried its crassness and lack of culture, the economic structure of business enterprise was able to win their general, if grudging, acceptance in the years before its 1929 collapse. Like science and machinery, big business was conceded to be a part of the price of modern civilization, and, at least in an economic sense, the system admittedly seemed to work. "In 1929 business, particularly big business," writes historian Thomas C. Cochran, "enjoyed a degree of public approval unique in American history." Walter Lippmann, for example, found the chief cause of widespread political indifference in the mid-twenties in the rising standard of living under the New Capitalism. The American people simply believed that "the opportunities to make money were so ample that it was a waste of time to think about politics." In an urbanized, industrial society, American business had moved ahead faster than its socialist critics, so that "The more or less unconscious and unplanned activities of businessmen are for once more novel, more daring, and in a sense more revolutionary, than the theories of the progressives."[22]

Papers (Ann Arbor: Andrews, 1888), p. 28; Dewey, *Democracy and Education* (New York: Macmillan, 1916), pp. 100–101. Dewey, *The Public and Its Problems* (New York: Holt, 1927), pp. 109, 168–169.

[21] Dewey, *Public and Its Problems,* pp. 212–213; Dewey, *Individualism Old and New* (New York: Minton, Balch, 1930), pp. 28, 35ff.

[22] T. C. Cochran, *The American Business System* (Cambridge, Mass.: Harvard University Press, 1957), p. 140; Lippmann, *Men of Destiny*, pp. 23–26. See also

As Arthur Schlesinger, Jr., has pointed out in *The Crisis of the Old Order*, the suspicion grew by 1929, "even among liberals, that the theorists of the New Era might be right—that business leadership was not only stronger but wiser than ever before, that the next step might really be, as Mr. Hoover had promised, the abolition of poverty." Lincoln Steffens, who at the beginning of the twenties had been impressed by both the Russian Revolution and Benito Mussolini, who "took the method, the spirit, the stuff, of Bolshevism and used it to go—right," was moved to reconsider. Russia and the United States each emphasized mass production and mass consumption, while the best of American businessmen, like Henry Ford, had a plan. Wasn't it possible, Steffens wondered, "that these two young peoples, the Russians and the Americans, are driving the one consciously, the other unwittingly, toward the same end?" Perhaps "the unconscious experiment this country is making in civilization and culture is equal to that of Soviet Russia. The race is saved," he concluded, "one way or the other and, I think, both ways."[23]

Like Steffens and Lippmann, the Beards in the concluding pages of their *Rise of American Civilization*, published in 1927 at the high noon of the Coolidge prosperity, were inclined toward a hopeful appraisal of what they called the Machine Age. . . . Seeing dangers only in war or in some Malthusian crisis of overpopulation, the Beards concluded that "there was no doubt about the nature of the future in America. The most common note of assurance was belief in unlimited progress. . . . Concretely it meant an invulnerable faith in democracy, . . . a faith in the efficacy of that new and mysterious instrument of the modern mind, 'the invention of invention,' moving from one technological triumph to another, overcoming the exhaustion of crude natural resources and energies, effecting an ever wider distribution of the blessings of civilization—health, security, material goods, knowledge, leisure, and aesthetic appreciation. . . ."[24]

The leading journals of liberal opinion, in their comments on the American business system in the months of its transition from prosperity to depression, shared on the whole the Beards' optimism. The major emphasis of the *Nation* and the *New Republic* at this time was upon foreign affairs. . . .

Especially interesting in view of his later eminence as a popular writer on economics, and because his articles were obviously written before the Great Crash, was the series in the *Nation* by Stuart Chase entitled "Prosperity—Believe It or Not." On Wednesday, October 23, the first day in a week of catastrophic breaks on the New York Stock Exchange, Chase's initial essay, subtitled "What Is Prosperity?," appeared with ill-fated precision. Through the next three months, into the following January, the series continued with Chase doggedly analyzing the effects of prosperity upon America's different social classes and income groups. In common with the prevailing progressive thought of the twenties, Chase pointed to the many Americans who did not enjoy the prosperity of their fellows. He gave no indication, however, of any premonitions of the crash.[25]

Henry F. May, "Shifting Perspectives on the 1920's," *Mississippi Valley Historical Review*, XLIII (December 1956), 405–427.

[23] Arthur M. Schlesinger, Jr., *The Crisis of the Old Order* (Boston: Houghton Mifflin, 1957), p. 142; *The Autobiography of Lincoln Steffens* (New York: Harcourt, Brace, 1931), pp. 851ff., 865ff.; Steffens to Jo Davidson, February 18, 1929, in Ella Winter and Granville Hicks, ed., *The Letters of Lincoln Steffens* (New York: Harcourt, Brace, 1938), II, 829–830.

[24] Beard and Beard, *Rise of American Civilization*, II, 719–720, 800.

[25] *Nation*, CXXIX (October 23, 1929), 460–462, and seqq.

Editorially the *Nation* viewed "Wall Street's Crisis" as a healthy, though costly, reaction to overpriced stocks and excessive speculation. It found fault chiefly with the Federal Reserve Bank's easy money policies, established in 1927 to help resolve the financial difficulties of Europe. Dissenting still at the end of November from the blame being heaped on Wall Street, the *Nation* contended that the stock market was only a reflection of business conditions. Surprisingly, in the light of this comment, the editors responded negatively to their own question: "Is the country headed for calamity, with the stock market carrying the flag?" After some relative stagnation, a slow recovery was expected. And, in tune with most statesmen and financiers, the *Nation* affirmed solemnly: "The great task of the next few months is the restoration of confidence. . . ."[26]

The *New Republic*, like the *Nation*, was cautiously optimistic about economic conditions, although its editors preferred some form of economic planning. Praising President Hoover for calling a conference of leaders from trade and industry, agriculture and labor, the editors nevertheless declared that they did not want merely another report from a conclave of experts. Instead, "We must begin to experiment with a governor for our engine. We must frankly recognize that the wild play of individualistic forces out for private gain does not automatically result in a desirable economic equilibrium. . . . Fortunately," the editors concluded at the end of November, "the present breakdown is not likely to be serious in any case." Two months later, after exploring the connection between automobile production and prosperity, the *New Republic* expressed the view that prospects were not at all bright. "We shall have to look for our stimulus elsewhere. Can it be aviation, television, motor-boating? Or what?" As the decline in key industries continued through the spring of 1930, the editors decided that fundamental readjustments were necessary and that "such a prosperous era as we have recently experienced cannot again arrive without being preceded by a deeper depression than we have yet had—accompanied, of course, by a general increase in the efficiency of production which will make possible a higher average of incomes with a lower average of retail prices." . . .[27]

The hopeful and expectant mood of watchful waiting in which intellectuals observed the aftermath of the Great Crash could not survive the evidence of growing depression. Whereas previous economic slumps had affected the agricultural or industrial population, now in the 1930's all classes and all sectors of the economy were hurt in some way. The middle class, traditionally the bulwark of American society, succumbed to the mounting unemployment and drastically reduced incomes of its white-collar workers and professional people. As stock prices tumbled to ever lower levels, doctors, lawyers, teachers, clerks and skilled laborers, writers and artists, all felt the reality of the depression and the pangs of poverty. Authors and publishers especially found a declining market for their wares. John Steinbeck, for example, recalled later that, being without a job during the first years of the depression, he kept on writing—"books, essays, short stories. Regularly they went out and just as regularly came back. Even if they had been

[26] *Nation*, CXXIX (November 6, 13, 27, 1929), 511, 539–540, 614.

[27] *New Republic*, LXI (November 27, 1929), 4–6; *ibid.*, LXI (January 29, 1930), 263–264; *ibid.*, LXIII (May 21, 1930), 4–5.

good, they would have come back because publishers were hardest hit of all. When people are broke, the first things they give up are books." . . .[28]

Formal education also suffered severely from the effects of the depression. Public schools were affected by the sharp decline in tax revenues, and in Chicago a combination of tax delinquency and bad government forced teachers to go unpaid for the school year 1932–1933. Across the country budget cuts meant shorter school terms, ill-paid teachers, and fewer classrooms. By 1933 the United States Office of Education estimated that fifteen hundred colleges and commercial institutions devoted to vocational or professional education had closed their doors. College enrollments, despite an increase in the graduate schools, fell by approximately 250,000 students from pre-depression totals.[29]

Students, worried by their own frequent lack of funds and the dismal prospects of pursuing the careers for which they had prepared, also showed the shock of the depression. Alternately accused of being aloof and cynical, with no concern for politics except in presidential years, and of being too radical in their protests and demands, college youth shared the intellectual confusions of their time. According to William Allen White, who defended their actions against conservative criticism, increasing student riots were evidence of a healthy intellectual growth. "Youth should be radical," White urged.

> *Youth should demand change in the world. Youth should not accept the old order if the world is to move on. But the old orders should not be moved easily—certainly not at the mere whim or behest of youth. There must be clash and if youth hasn't enough force or fervor to produce the clash the world grows stale and stagnant and sour in decay.*
>
> *If our colleges and universities do not breed men who riot, who rebel, who attack life with all the youthful vim and vigor, then there is something wrong with our colleges. The more riots that come on college campuses, the better world for tomorrow.*[30]

As the economy continued its rapid descent into the darker labyrinths of the depression, confidence in the automatic fulfillment of the American dream all but vanished. No one was able to see the ravages of the hard times more closely than the social workers and journalists in America's large cities. They knew the facts of poverty. In the slums of New York, Lillian Wald, for years director of the Henry Street settlement house, commented darkly upon "the long-unemployed breadlines which are a disgrace to this so-called civilization of ours. I don't know what civilization is," she wrote in the early 1930's, "but whatever its concept, it isn't insufficient food and relinquishment of bathrooms for cheaper houses or breadlines, however 'unworthy' the men in the line may be. . . . Have you ever heard a

[28] Quoted in Don Congdon, ed., *The Thirties: A Time to Remember* (New York: Simon and Schuster, 1962), p. 24.

[29] C. J. Enzler, *Some Social Aspects of the Depression* (Washington: Catholic University of America Press, 1939), Chap. 5.

[30] W. H. Hale, "A Dirge for College Liberalism," *New Republic*, LXVI (May 13, 1931), 348–350; Harold J. Laski, "Why Don't Your Young Men Care?" *Harper's Magazine*, CLXII (July 1931), 130–136; William Allen White, *Emporia Gazette*, April 8, 1932, in R. H. Fitzgibbon, ed., *Forty Years on Main Street* (New York: Farrar and Rinehart, 1937), p. 331.

hungry child cry? Have you seen the uncontrollable trembling of parents who have gone half starved themselves for weeks so that the children may have food?" Summing things up, the *Nation* commented that the year 1931 was one "of suffering, bitterness, and increasing disillusionment." Americans, confident that prosperity would be "our vassal for all time," had shown an astonishing self-control in the general lack of riots and disorder. Clearly, however, the republic was in jeopardy—even though the *Nation's* editors also affirmed that "we have not lost faith that it can be rescued and set upon the right paths through the instrumentality of the present form of government, adequately altered to meet the needs of the situation."[31]

From his vantage point in London, to which he now made more frequent retreats, James Truslow Adams continued to question some of the false business values and perverted democratic ideals which, he felt, prevented the realization of the American dream. His correspondents in the United States were, however, too concerned by business failures and political futility at home to join Adams in philosophizing on the general state of civilization and culture. From these literary friends Adams therefore received a most gloomy picture of affairs. A few weeks after the crash, the newspaperman and historian Claude Bowers noted already that "The conditions here are bad. The press generally is lying outrageously, heroically trying to prevent depression. The cancellation of Xmas orders has been unprecedented. In every nook and corner are the victims of the market—ruined." Denouncing Hoover and his Republican predecessors, Bowers feared that the Democrats would win the next election by default. "The Republicans are utterly demoralized and if there were a militant, constructive, united Democratic Party it could sweep the country in three years."[32]

Allan Nevins, who had recently left his editorial position on the *New York World* to become professor of history at Columbia University, was an old Adams friend and frequent correspondent. "Times are hard here," Nevins reported in 1930 following the November elections. "Merely in walking the streets one sees many distressing sights. At every corner unemployed men are selling boxes of apples at 5 cents each; they make $1.75 a box, and thus keep alive. Beggars are numerous, and I understand that the suffering among the white-collar class is really appalling. The election showed how the people feel about the Hoover administration, and most Republicans think they were lucky to get off so easily." In the new year Nevins, upon returning from the regular annual meeting of his fellow historians, passed on to Adams the pessimistic mood of the nation's scholars:

> *This country remains pretty low down in the trough of depression. There are just two bright aspects of the whole affair: it has brought the Hoover Administration and the Republican party into an unpopularity which on other accounts it richly deserves, and it has reduced retail prices of all kinds. . . . I might add that it has taken from America an arrogant cockiness that was growing very offensive. . . . However, it is depressing to hear con-*

[31] Quoted in R. L. Duffus, *Lillian Wald* (New York: Macmillan, 1938), pp. 287, 349; *Nation*, CXXIV (January 6, 1932), 4. See also Clarke Chambers, *Seedtime of Reform: American Social Service and Social Action, 1918–1933* (Minneapolis: University of Minnesota Press, 1963), Chap. 8.

[32] Claude Bowers to Adams, November 27, 1929, Adams Papers.

stantly of bitter personal hardships, and to see the long bread lines that gather nightly in Columbus Circle and Times Square.[33]

. . . In 1931 Lincoln Steffens, like Adams, published an important book—his famous *Autobiography*, which vied with Adams' *Epic* as one of the most popular works of serious nonfiction in the early 1930's. A veteran journalist who had first captured attention in the Theodore Roosevelt era, Steffens had gone on to report at firsthand the revolutions and wars in Mexico and Europe. Always managing somehow to be at the scene of the latest dramatic moment in world history, Steffens was able to achieve some of the same rapport in interviewing European dictators that he had enjoyed in his earlier personal contacts with American political bosses. Though it was therefore no doubt true that the experienced Steffens had long since lost any youthful illusions he may have had about politics, the *Autobiography*—at once hailed as a classic—managed to convey that sense of disenchanted idealism which was so tremendously appealing to the new depression generation of the 1930's.[34]

Back home in the United States, after a decade of wandering in Europe where he had watched the developing political crisis with a growing admiration for the Soviet way of life, Steffens, after the crash of '29, largely lost his earlier notion that America and Russia were headed in the same fundamental direction. If the depression killed the remnants of his lingering faith in the reform possibilities of the new business capitalism, it did not destroy his belief in the efficacy of technocracy and mass production as harbingers of a socialist society. "We can be free, or democratic, or safe, but not by wishing; only by economic arrangement of the circumstances of life. . . . We have to get rid of our old moral culture and learn the new culture. . . . No more thinking, nothing but theorizing and experimenting. . . . American business is nearer right than American ideals."[35]

During the thirties, until his death in 1936, Steffens continued to comment vigorously on the severity of the depression and the breakdown of capitalism. Although he refused to accept membership in the Communist party, out of his conviction that ex-liberals were not suited for leadership and action, his conception of the American dream and his hopes for the future all pointed toward Moscow. Noting in June of 1932 that the depression was growing worse and worse, with stocks "down almost to their real value" and his neighbors complaining of a cut to one-third of their incomes, Steffens wrote: "It looks as if we might not have to have a bolshevik revolution at all. We are getting there by the swift process of evolution which is not so slow and gradual as the optimists predicted. It is, as a matter of fact, very, very funny." "I am elated over the world news," he told Theodore Dreiser later that year. "You bulls don't understand us bears. I'm selling capitalism short; and morality, too; and . . . liberalism and culture, so I can sit in the sun, watch my neighbors read Technocracy and feel no drive to run the world down and the minds of men up."[36]

Throughout America the prevailing mood in the last two years of the Hoover

33 Allan Nevins to Adams, November 27, 1930; January 31, 1931, Adams Papers.

34 See Christopher Lasch, *The New Radicalism in America* (New York: Knopf, 1965), Chap. 8.

35 Steffens to Alfred Harcourt, April 24, 1930, *Letters*, II, 870.

36 Steffens to Sam Darcy, April 28, 1934; Steffens to Jo Davidson, June 3, 1932, *Letters*, II, 982–983, 923; Steffens to Dreiser, December 16, 1932. Lincoln Steffens Papers.

administration was one of profound pessimism. With people dazed and bewildered by the turn of events since 1929 and national morale growing weaker, the country's leading spokesmen and men of affairs rose to render their solemn verdict on an economic catastrophe unprecedented in its severity. "Among the fatalities of the depression were the capitalists and the intellectuals," Gilbert Seldes noted in his contemporary *Years of the Locust*, and after the first months of the economic crash "hardly an authoritative word was spoken in defense of the capitalist system. . . ." Yet it was also true that, as Edmund Wilson observed of the writers and artists of his generation "who had grown up in the Big Business era and had always resented its barbarism, its crowding-out of everything they cared about, these years were not depressing but stimulating. One couldn't help being exhilarated at the sudden unexpected collapse of that stupid gigantic fraud. It gave us a new sense of freedom; and it gave us a new sense of power. . . ."[37]

In this spirit, with the intellectuals in the van, the American people engaged in a desperate search for salvation, hoping to discover in the darkest days of the depression the means by which they could recover the lost hopes of the American dream.

[37] Gilbert Seldes, *The Years of the Locust* (Boston: Little, Brown, 1933), p. 331; Edmund Wilson, "The Literary Consequences of the Crash" (1932), in *The Shores of Light: A Literary Chronicle of the Twenties and Thirties* (New York: Farrar, Straus and Young, 1952), p. 498. See also Matthew Josephson, *Infidel in the Temple: A Memoir of the Nineteen-Thirties* (New York: Knopf, 1967), pp. xi, 155ff.

16

WAR DEBTS AND PEACE LEGISLATION: THE JOHNSON ACT OF 1934

J. Chal Vinson

During the first years of the decade of the 1930's, America's concerns were primarily domestic. As the economic depression deepened, Franklin Roosevelt in his first inaugural promised a New Deal, but it was to be a new deal at home. Neither he nor the American people gave much thought to foreign affairs, and many were quite ready to retreat even further into the isolationism that had marked the administrations of Harding and Coolidge. Isolationism has deep roots in the American past. Related in part to the continental insularity of the United States and to deeply ingrained American attitudes toward Europe, it has continually expressed itself in a policy of "no entangling alliances." This policy was originally based upon several premises involving the security, prosperity, and possibly even the existence of the new nation. Though the foundations of American isolationism had been steadily undermined as the nation became a world power, the popularity of the policy was unimpaired, thereby creating a tension that provoked a crisis over American neutrality in the 1930's. This article examines the shaping of a basic prop of American isolationism during this decade. It also picks up a theme dealt with in the article by Professor Lowitt (Selection 7)—the question of who was to control American foreign policy, the president or Congress. In 1934, Roosevelt, in the interest of obtaining needed domestic legislation and tariff reform, was willing to yield to Congress a determination of policy that he would later feel obliged to take back.

J. Chal Vinson is a professor of American diplomatic history at the University of Georgia. His publications include The Parchment Peace: The United States Senate and the Washington Conference, 1921–1922 *(Athens, Ga., 1955) and* William E. Borah and the Outlawry of War *(Athens, Ga., 1957). This article extends his research on American isolationism into the decade of the 1930's.*

Source: *Mid-America*, Vol. 50, No. 3 (1968), pp. 206–222. Reprinted by permission of the publisher.

The Johnson Act was described, at the conclusion of the Second World War, as the climax of Senate isolationism in the pre-war period, a prime cause of the conflict: They "had the last say after all, by writing the Johnson Act. . . . And the cost was little enough; only a Second World War."[1] Certainly its embargo on lending to governments in default on debts to the United States government ended any lingering hope that the war debts controversy could be amicably settled. It was also the first in the series of neutrality laws through which Congress virtually arrogated control of foreign policy and dedicated it to peace. Nevertheless, the Johnson Act has been largely overlooked even in studies of the 1930's. This neglect is understandable. Gerald Nye's sensational munitions investigations and the more spectacular neutrality laws that incorporated and expanded its provisions have overshadowed it.

The Act, and in particular its evolution in reaching final form, have much to tell about the processes of American diplomacy in the early years of the decade before the war. When introduced in February, 1932, the Act had nothing to do with directing foreign policy, establishing neutrality or attempting to force collection of war debts, its eventual purposes.[2] It was one of three laws Hiram Johnson of California proposed to protect private American investors from the sale of unstable Latin American bonds. More than a billion in bonds issued by Brazil, Chile, Ecuador, and El Salvador were bought by private investors in the United States during the 1920's only to become virtually worthless by 1932. Johnson, aroused by this shameful spectacle promoted by "American financiers to make outrageously high profits," called for an investigation to ascertain the facts and recommend needed legislation. The investigation began in December, 1931, when Johnson in a long and detailed address to the Senate asserted: "The story of our foreign loans is a sordid tale, at once grotesque and tragic." Tragedy lay in stark statistics showing American citizens' investments during the 1920's in Latin American bonds, sold through American banks, had dropped in value from $1,600,000,000 to only $422,000,000.[3]

Johnson chose an opportune time to attack banks. In addition to the failure of bank-sponsored bonds, banks themselves were failing at an unprecedented rate —500 in the third quarter of 1931, more than twice that number in the fourth quarter. Each failure intensified the discontent of a public already disillusioned in its hope, so strong in the 1920's, that full government cooperation with business would bring prosperity for all.

As Johnson probed the South American bond default scandal, the chief cul-

[1] Charles A. Beard, *American Foreign Policy in the Making, 1932–1940: A Study in Responsibilities*, New Haven, 1946, 6, quoting "Washington Notes," *New Republic* (June 18, 1945).

[2] Senate Committee on Foreign Relations, National Archives, Senate 76 A-F9 (138) 1939–1940, Key Pittman Papers, National Archives. (The bulk of Pittman's papers are in the Manuscript Division of the Library of Congress, but many documents relating to his work as Chairman of the Senate Committee are in State Department files in the Archives.) This document, dated Apr. 28, 1934, was sent by Franklin Roosevelt to Pittman Oct. 2, 1939, under the title, "Conference on the Johnson Bill." *Congressional Record*, (*C.R.* hereafter) 72 Cong. 1 sess., 213–4 *Senate Reports*, (*S.R.*), 19. *Foreign Relations*, I, 1934, 525, 529. Ernest K. Lindley, *Half Way With Roosevelt*, New York, 1935, 297.

[3] Harry Bernard, *Independent Man: The Life of James Couzens*, New York, 1958, 205.

prit, he quickly discovered, was the international banker. He invariably disposed of large foreign bond issues at a sure profit by compelling small banks to buy them for resale to the public. Even if the bond became worthless, the international banker without assuming any risk had his commission amounting to millions. But the little man who bought these securities with his hard-earned savings saw his equity vanish. Thus aroused against the international banker, Johnson's investigation of private financiers led him into their connection with the war debt question brought to the fore by the Senate debate on the Hoover Moratorium. Johnson had opposed the moratorium from the start and his investigation satisfied him that this ill advised program was instigated by international bankers to bring about cancellation of the debts. Could it be a coincidence, he asked the Senate, that the German government, relieved of $246 million in governmental debts in 1931 by the moratorium, repaid short term credits to private American bankers to the amount of $230 million?

Two years ahead of Nye, Johnson's committee investigated the J. P. Morgan Company and charged that it profited directly from the American policy of scaling down inter-allied debts. In one example the United States government readjusted the Italian war debt at 23 cents on the dollar with interest of .012 percent. This low rate enabled them to pay 7 percent interest when, almost immediately, the Morgan company lent the Italian government $100 million. Hoover's policies, the Senator asserted, "placed a priority upon the claims of the international bankers subordinating the public claims to the interests of a privileged few." Evidence that the wealthy international banker had a Midas touch in every transaction could not fail to impress millions of depression ridden citizens. Again and again in his grandiloquent but repetitious speeches Johnson condemned international bankers, with evidence presented to his committee, for making "outrageous profits," in both public and private loans at the direct expense of the American taxpayer.[4]

By January 28, 1932, Johnson's investigation proved so productive that his committee was ready to propose three laws to protect the small investor. The first required publicity on certain foreign loans and was subsequently sponsored by Senator Duncan Fletcher for the Banking Committee. The second provided "more effective supervision" of foreign commercial transactions and was eventually sponsored by Senator McCarran for the Judiciary Committee. A few days later Johnson introduced a third bill, S. 3587, making it unlawful to loan money or to purchase or sell bonds or other obligations of any foreign government in default on its obligations to the United States. The California senator reintroduced this bill, March, 1933, as S. 682. It was altered to read, in place of "obligations to the United States," "obligations to the United States government, citizens and corporations." Over a year later, April, 1934, it became, with some very significant amendments, the Johnson Act.[5]

[4] *C.R.*, 72:1, 539, 6053.

[5] *Ibid.*, 213–4 (S.R. 19), Dec. 10, 1931; *Ibid.*, 72:2, 3571 (S.R. 3587). The other bills submitted Jan. 28, 1932 were (S. 3350) requiring publicity of certain foreign loan transactions; (S. 3351) providing more effective supervision of foreign commercial transactions. On Mar. 22, 1933, (S. 3587) was reintroduced as (S. 682); (S. 3350) as (S. 681); (S. 3351) as (S. 683). Later (S. 882) protecting United States citizens from the sale of foreign securities under circumstances where those securities could not be sold in the United States was added.

Johnson could not in February, 1932, have applied his bill to war debts for there were no defaulters at that time. Congress was engaged, when he began his investigation in December, 1931, in debating formal consent to the Hoover Moratorium. Proof of the frequently made charge that Europeans would not pay was not established in fact until December of 1932 and June of 1933.

The Senator did foreshadow his later concentration on war debts by strongly opposing the Hoover Moratorium. Europeans, he argued with information he gained from his investigation of the bond scandal, could pay their debts—their huge armaments budgets were proof. England, France, and Italy spent $424,637,565 on armament in 1931 while postponing, through the moratorium, payment on $244,227,125 due on debts.[6] The moratorium was nothing more than a device to prepare the way for cancellation of the debts. These debts ought never to be cancelled, Johnson declared. Cancellation would relieve Europeans of the odium of dishonesty and make debt default appear respectable. Johnson wanted any failure to settle the debts at one hundred cents on the dollar branded as default. Obviously the United States would not collect any more money by default than it would by cancellation, but forcing Europeans to acknowledge default would shock the American people. This shock would be profound enough, Johnson hoped, to arouse the American people out of their dangerous 15 year stupor of internationalism and drive them back to the safety of traditional non-intervention and non-entanglement. Americanism alone, Johnson declared, offered hope for the future. Speaking in favor of the Congressional amendment to prevent further reductions in debt liability, he asserted: "Today we are standing at the crossroads of destiny of the United States of America. . . . For the love of God let's take the American road!"[7]

In Senate speeches, Johnson attacked, on an ever widening front, foreign bond sales, international bankers, the administration's foreign policy in general and the role of the State Department in supervising bond issues in particular. He had found, he charged on March 15, 1932, that the Department investigated proposed sales of foreign bond issues only when a political question was clearly involved. In other cases, and these included most of the bond issues then in default, the Department did not investigate and registered its neutrality with the misleading formula, "the Department of State offers no objection." Private investors assumed that "no objection" was a stamp of approval. They were not enlightened by the bankers.[8]

Johnson also raised the issue of Presidential versus Congressional authority in foreign affairs, so important in the League of Nations debates over a decade earlier and destined to be the nub of the controversy over neutrality laws later in the 1930's. Hoover, Johnson maintained, should have called Congress into special session in June to consider the moratorium rather than gaining approval of individual members by telegraph.[9]

6 *Ibid.*, 998.

7 *Time* (Jan. 4, 1932), 7.

8 *C.R.*, 72:2, 6052. The Democrats featured this issue in the 1932 Presidential race (see note 13 *infra*). The state department in 1929 had changed its statement to read "the State Department is not interested." This it was hoped would clear the confusion about granting approval; Herbert Feis, *The Diplomacy of the Dollar, 1919–1932*, New York, 1966, 13.

9 *C.R.* 72:2, 998, 1077–80, 6052–8. Representative Louis T. McFadden said that Hoover's methods "savored more of the ways of an oriental potentate drunk with power than a United States President." *Time* (Dec. 28, 1931), 7.

In keeping with a growing public sentiment, Johnson's concern was collecting debts, not with attempting to use debt remission diplomatically as a reward to encourage Europeans to reduce armament or renegotiate the Versailles treaty.[10] All attempts at negotiation had failed to bring results; no further concessions were justified. Patience must give way to pressure. The need was for resolute application of enough force to bring these rich, obstinate, and untrustworthy nations to pay their just debts. Nations that refused to yield to pressure, Johnson continued to insist, ought publicly to be branded as defaulters and cut off from all future borrowing in the United States until their obligations were met in full. These stern measures were justified, especially in time of American depression, because war debts could not be cancelled. The loans had been floated by the sale of war bonds to American citizens. If Europeans failed to meet them, these obligations still remained and would have to be met by "overburdened American citizens."[11]

Prospects for war debt collection were dealt a series of blows in 1932, and conversely Johnson's proposal to punish debt delinquents gained support with the emphasis shifting from Latin American to European offenders. The first blow came with the convocation of the often postponed Lausanne Conference on German reparations. Hoover, declaring that "our hands were tied by Congress," declined to send a representative. Thus, there was no opportunity to discuss the American position—reparations and war debts were separate issues. When Europeans scaled down the German reparations from $33 billion to $700 million, it appeared that they expected the United States to reduce inter-allied war debts on a similar scale. A second blow fell when the moratorium ended June 30, 1932. Then it became evident that European nations would resume payment only on a limited scale if at all. The point was underscored when Britain and France announced, July 14, a "solid front" on war debts. Some European statesmen insisted that the moratorium was to remain in force until Germany resumed its reparations payments.[12]

American concern with the debt issue subsided somewhat with the adjournment of Congress and was not revived by the 1932 Presidential campaign. Evidently guided by political considerations, Hoover ignored debts entirely until after the election; Roosevelt also evaded the debt problem. Only Senator William E. Borah, described by one critic as still being in session even though Congress was not, made any attempt to gain a clarification of American opinion on the debt issue at this time. In one of his headline-catching speeches, he called once again for American renegotiation of debts in exchange for an European pledge

[10] *C.R.* 72:2, 1118. Howell's resolution to this end was voted down 63–16, *Ibid.*, 213–7. The Canadian author Stephen Leacock facetiously proposed that the Congo be given the U.S. in lieu of debts. Senator Borah replied that Leacock "had the wrong end of the horse." The United States ought to get the debtors to take the American colonies, the Philippines, Puerto Rico, *et al.* W. Y. Elliott, Professor of Government at Harvard, suggested to Hall that the West Indian Islands be taken in exchange for debts provided they voted to accept United States control; Hull Papers, Box 57, W. Y. Elliott to Hull, Jan. 1, 1933. Elliott also proposed a "consultative pact" for France in exchange for disarmament.

[11] *Ibid.*, 1272. Roosevelt in a message to Congress, June 1, 1934 confirmed this view. The United States government in the absence of debt payment would be compelled to raise the shortage "by general taxation of its own people. . . ." *For. Rel.*, I, 1934, 556.

[12] *For. Rel.*, I, 1934, 585. Pierre Laval of France stated that the moratorium was in effect until Germany resumed payments of reparations to France and that this plan had been ratified by Congress.

to disarm.[13] The lull was ended abruptly when default by some nations and only token payments from most of the others marked the December, 1932, due date. Congressmen vied with each other to be loudest in the chorus of condemnation. While ostensibly debating the Hoover banking bill in January, 1933, the Senate devoted most of its time to the debt problem.

Johnson renewed his proposals to cut off future credit to nations defaulting on war debts. As early as January 4, 1933, he proposed to put this idea into a law as soon as possible. Rather than draft a new bill the Senator later decided to expand his pending measure on debt default of Latin American governments to include war debts. This measure, Johnson asserted, would force war debt payment. Even if it did not, it would clearly mark European powers as defaulters. This object lesson in the dishonesty of European governments would teach American voters the futility of any further cooperation. "For twelve to fifteen years," the Senator lamented, "we have been looking beyond the sea," and participating in the "drunken European orgy." Clear-cut default on debts would show Americans "just where we stand. . . . Then we shall go back to the old American rule and the old American tradition."[14] Here the importance of the bill in promoting peace through reasserting American neutrality was established.

Proposals to cut off credit to debt delinquents was, as Johnson himself pointed out, not new. He traced his own interest in the plan back to the World War Debt Funding Commission, authorized by Congress in 1922. When the Commission failed to get cooperation from debtor nations, it announced in 1925 that it would withhold all types of credit from nations failing to make, or seeking to make, adjustment in their war debts: "National interest," the Commission explained, "demands that our resources be not permitted to flow into countries that do not honor their obligations to American citizens."[15] The threat apparently served its purpose, for thirteen nations adjusted their debts before the end of 1926. The policy remained in effect until the Hoover Moratorium suspended it. Johnson explained to the Senate that the suggestion to reinstitute this policy was passed on to him from a Senate colleague who, in turn, had gotten it from a prominent American living abroad. Although Johnson did not mention it, Senator Howell of Nebraska had made essentially the same proposal in December, 1931.[16]

[13] Borah Scrapbook, undated & unnamed news item, Borah Papers, Library of Congress. The Democratic platform charged that the State Department had failed to warn American investors against questionable bonds and had given "implied approval" for their sale. F. D. R. reiterated to this governmental shortcoming in a campaign speech at Columbus, Ohio, in August, 1932; Feis, *Diplomacy of the Dollar*, 14. Johnson, of course, had made this specific charge earlier in the year; note 8, *supra*.

[14] *C.R.*, 72:1, 1081–2. Feis, *Diplomacy of the Dollar*, 25, says Americans had fallen into the vague and idealistic notion that the dollar could somehow settle all international problems. Johnson thought the impact of default would shock the public into never taking sides again.

[15] *Ibid.*, 72:2, 1273.

[16] *Time* (Dec. 21, 1931), 12. "Repudiation would be better for the cause of peace because European nations then would never be able to borrow another dime from the United States for future wars." The State Department throughout the intrawar period "vigorously applied" a rule of no loan to debt delinquent nations. This policy was the "precursor to the Johnson Act," Feis, *Diplomacy of the Dollar*, 20. No doubt Johnson knew of the policy but he attributed his plan to the Debt Commission, an agency of Congress, rather than the State Department, an Executive agency.

While Johnson was taking this step early in 1933 there was much discussion and conjecture in the Senate as to President-elect Franklin Roosevelt's views on the debt issue, for he already had asserted his belief in strong, independent Presidential power in foreign policy formulation—quite in contrast to Johnson's proclamation of Senate supremacy. When news reports on January 21 described the President-elect as determined to get debt reduction for Great Britain, even if he had to oppose Congress, Arthur R. Robinson of Indiana joined forces with Johnson to lead an attack on Presidential "usurpation of [Senate] authority" and denounced any relaxation of American financial claims on European nations. Joe Robinson of Arkansas, soon to be Roosevelt's right hand man in the Senate, initiated a vitriolic exchange of opinion by upholding the President's right and duty to direct foreign policy.[17]

Standing apart from this argument over prerogative for the moment, Johnson concentrated on the perfidy of European governments, their fiscal irresponsibility, and the absurdity of their claims that they could not pay. This sorry spectacle of faithlessness and fraud, he argued, justified the case for American nationalism as opposed to internationalism. For a time he hoped to get his resolution, in committee since its introduction in February, 1932, brought before the Senate and enacted immediately.[18] Apparently getting no encouragement from Hoover, he decided to hold his fire until Roosevelt came to power. Things would change, Johnson predicted, when there was a man in the White House who would look out for his country with "the eye of an American" and would "do his duty by America."[19] A part of Roosevelt's duty would be to avoid cancellation or reduction of the debts. It was beneath the dignity of the United States to assume the role of "a drunken fishwife or a whispering pawnbroker" and "meet with any people to determine whether we take 5 percent or 6 percent or a 7 percent . . . of an obligation due us."[20]

Shortly after Roosevelt took office, Johnson reintroduced his bill.[21] This time the Judiciary Committee, after only two weeks deliberation, returned the bill to the Senate. Senator Henry F. Ashurst, in reporting the bill, explained that it now applied to war debts. Investigation in early 1932, he reminded the Senate, made clear the need to end a traffic in worthless bonds and securities that amounted to "little less than a fraud upon the American people." However, since the original measure was introduced, failure by certain foreign governments "well able to pay but which nevertheless repudiate their written engagements" to pay their war debts had made the application of the Johnson Bill to the war debt problem a logical and "laudable" effort to achieve "simple justice for the protection of the American investor and the American people generally."[22] Ashurst regarded this as a major shift in emphasis.

While the language of the bill was neither clear nor specific in its definitions, the bill was well on the way to its final interpretation, the emphasis on neutrality. This it would achieve in two ways. First, the threat of no credit would make

[17] *C.R.*, 72:2, 2471. This draft of the memo proposed that for the next two years, while discussion was underway, the British be required to pay the principle but not the interest on the debt; Herbert Feis to Hull, Mar. 3, 1933, Hull Papers.
[18] *C.R.*, 72:2, 1271.
[19] *Ibid.*, 1278.
[20] *Ibid.*, 2472.
[21] *Ibid.*, 705 (S. 682); *For. Rel.*, I, 1934, 525.
[22] *S.R.*, 73:1, (no. 9769) Cal. 21, Rept. No. 20.

Europeans think twice before going to war; second, it would be extremely difficult to finance a future conflict without American credit. If Europeans did go to war despite this deterrent, America would not be drawn into the conflict, as Johnson was convinced had been the case in 1917, in order to save the obligations of the big financial interests.

After Ashurst presented the bill with these explanations there was still no debate on the measure in the Senate and no action was taken. Certainly it was not, from the Executive point of view, an opportune time to discuss war debts. Passage or even debate on such a bill could not fail to stir trouble at the World Economic Conference scheduled to convene in London in two months. The British tenaciously insisted, over American protest, that agreement to negotiate on war debts (scale them down or cancel them) must be achieved at London before there could be any progress in other economic matters. Secretary of State Cordell Hull hoped to use debt remission as an inducement for Britain to support trade agreements. The Johnson Act's blunt demand for payment in full would have disrupted such Anglo-American amity as existed and wrecked the conference before it began. For these and other reasons both the state and treasury departments strongly opposed the Johnson proposal.[23]

Why Johnson did not press for his measure despite opposition is not clear. If pressure was used by the administration to silence him, it did not take a form that offended him. Roosevelt had demonstrated his determination, even during the Presidential campaign, to keep at almost any cost the goodwill of this leading progressive. After the election Roosevelt offered Johnson the post of Secretary of Interior.[24] The Senator could have been a delegate to the London Conference, with the privilege of disagreeing with any proposals it made.[25] In view of the extremely mild nature of Roosevelt's opposition to the Johnson Act when it was passed early in 1934, there is at least room for speculation, and it is only speculation, that the President got Johnson to defer action by means of a confidential pledge not to oppose the legislation after the London Conference was over.

Whatever the cause, Johnson, during May and June, was strictly on his good behavior and said nothing about debts. Even Roosevelt's June 16, 1933, ruling that nations making token payments were not in default brought no comment from the Senator, although he had much to say against this interpretation later. However, a number of other Congressmen, led in particular by Arthur Robinson of Indiana, were sharply critical of this decision in June.[26] Failure of the London Conference later in the year was attributed by the American public to European obduracy, not to Roosevelt's celebrated "bombshell." As a consequence, public demand for protection from the "Shylocks" of Europe through war debt legislation, such as Johnson's, was increased.

Either because of a previous agreement or for lack of a way to stop him, the administration did not attempt to halt Johnson when he announced, at the beginning of the 1934 session, that he would make his debt bill the first item on the calendar. The Senator still stood so well with the administration that it

[23] James M. Burns, *Roosevelt, the Lion and the Fox*, New York, 1956, 249.

[24] *Ibid.*, 149. Johnson supported Harold Ickes for Secretary of the Interior; Hull Papers, Box 57, Huston Thompson to Hull, Feb. 21, 1933.

[25] *Time*, (May 29, 1933), 7; (June 12, 1933), 15; Arthur M. Schlesinger, Jr., *The Age of Roosevelt: The Coming of the New Deal*, Boston, 1965, 208.

[26] *C.R.*, 72:1, 2020.

was rumored he could become a justice as soon as there was a vacancy on the Supreme Court bench.[27] The measure was brought up January 8; it took the Senate only three days to pass a bill that could not get out of committee just two years earlier.

At this point the Department of State somewhat belatedly launched a counter attack. Administration Senate leader Joe Robinson, who was not present when the bill passed, gained agreement, shortly after the vote had been taken, to have it reconsidered. With this period of grace assured, Under-Secretary of State, R. Walton Moore, January 19, urged Roosevelt to see Johnson and attempt to persuade "him to abandon any effort to pass the Bill." Apparently Roosevelt did not make such an attempt but both Moore and William C. Bullitt made unsuccessful efforts.[28] It seemed certain that the bill would pass when it came to a second vote.

Moore, in a rear guard action, listed for Roosevelt a number of specific objections to the bill that should be eliminated or modified by amendments: it would irritate many governments, especially in Latin America; it would prevent many desirable transactions; it would raise many difficult legal questions of interpretations; and it would accomplish no useful purpose.[29] Some agreement must have been reached for later the same day, January 31, Moore wrote Robinson that Roosevelt was most anxious to confine the bill's scope to obligations owed the Federal government and delete the provision eliminating his power to accept token payments. Hull also saw Roosevelt, and in a long conference drew up a list of amendments for Robinson's use when the bill came to a second vote.[30] The most important of these proposed changes reserved to the President, rather than to Congress, the right to discharge all of the bill's provisions.[31] This was one of the President's favorite techniques in dealing with legislative acts that he opposed but could not block. It had proved effective, for example, in curbing the extreme demands of Senate inflationists even though the Thomas Bill of 1933 was adopted.

When the Johnson Act came to a vote February 2 for reconsideration, Robinson failed to get for Roosevelt authority to administer the act or the power to rule that token payments did not constitute default. In still another blow at the Executive, the Senate refused to exempt Russia, just then attempting to capitalize on its newly won recognition by borrowing American money to finance trade, from the provision of the act.[32] In fact, the final version was more specific in denying this possibility than the earlier versions. It specifically prohibited loans to governments in default, while earlier versions were limited to making it unlawful to "purchase or sell . . . bonds, securities or other obligations."

While much was taken much remained, for the administration did succeed

[27] *Time* (Jan. 1, 1934), 5: Bernard, *Couzens*, 296, suggested that continued support of the New Deal by Senators Couzens, Johnson, La Follette, Jr., and Norris appeared a threat to the Republican Party itself. No peacetime President had ever so candidly asked that opponents of his program be defeated in congressional elections as did Roosevelt in 1934. His purpose was personal government by general consent; *Literary Digest* (Feb. 10, 1934), 6 and (Feb. 17, 1934), 11.

[28] R. Walton Moore Papers, Franklin Roosevelt Library, Hyde Park, Box 8, Moore to Robinson, Jan. 27 and Jan. 31, 1934.

[29] *For. Rel.*, I, 1934, 526.

[30] Moore Papers, Box 8, Moore, Memo for Hull, Jan. 19, 1934.

[31] *C.R.*, 72:2, 1923.

[32] *For. Rel.*, I, 1934, 525.

in limiting the measure to debts due the Federal government. The sweeping provisions of the earlier versions also applied to debts owed "to any citizen of the United States or to any corporation organized in the United States."[33] These obligations were almost exclusively with Latin American states, while European states owed the bulk of Federal debt. Thus the administration's amendment was far reaching in its implications, in view of its determination to get the Trade Agreements Act adopted before the end of the Congressional session. Johnson's provision to include individual and corporation debts certainly would have clouded relations with the Latin American governments whose sharply depreciated bonds had prompted the Senator's investigation. Roosevelt, forced to choose between undesirable alternatives, decided that hemispheric solidarity was more important than trans-Atlantic ties.[34]

The odds were strongly against the administration. Roosevelt had little opportunity for maneuver and was forced to salvage what he could. The bill was acclaimed by the public as a blow at bankers, the corrupt money power that had brought on the depression. Congress, by 1934, was so antagonistic to the financial community in general that financial expert Shepard Morgan of the Chase National Bank in New York, who thought the measure most ill advised, was convinced it would be worse than useless to object.[35] Roosevelt was further handicapped because the Republican progressives led the pro-Johnson forces and he was determined not to offend them. So anxious was he to hold progressive leader Hiram Johnson's support that political chieftain Jim Farley, as spokesman for him, ignored Democratic hopefuls in California and gave full endorsement to Johnson in his bid for reelection to the Senate while the Congressional debate on the debt bill was going on, although it was months until the campaign.[36] After February 2 the President, while officially against the measure, quietly dropped all opposition to the Johnson Act for the next two months while it went to the House and back to the Senate for final confirmation.

There is ample evidence of this hands off policy. Sir Ronald Lindsay, the British ambassador, sought without success to get information about the bill from Hull and assurance that the administration would seek to prevent passage. Hull stressed Congressional responsibility for the legislation and added, for the edification of his British listener: "Congress is a coordinate and independent branch of the government and has an equal right to express its attitude on debts. It would be most difficult for the Executive branch of the government to influence Congress." The Secretary pointed out that after its initial passage in

33 Senate Committee on Foreign Relations, Sen. 76 A-F9 (138).

34 Hull's correspondence, especially with ambassador to Mexico, Josephus Daniels, reflects a great concern in Mexico and other Latin American nations that debt collection not be a subject at the Montivideo Conference. It was not included on the agenda, but a proposal for a five-year moratorium was introduced by Mexico. Professor Samuel Guy Inman, a State Department advisor on Latin American affairs, wrote Hull that his preconference assurances to Latin American nations that debt collection would not be pressed contributed greatly to the harmony that assured success of the meeting; Hull Papers.

35 Moore Papers, Memo, conversation with Shepherd Morgan of the Chase Manhattan Bank.

36 *Time* (Feb. 5, 1934), 18. In the future the battle line would not be along party line but Rooseveltians and anti-Rooseveltians. To promote his dream of a "realignment of parties" Roosevelt "Buttered up Hiram Johnson at every opportunity." Schlesinger, *The Coming of the New Deal,* 504–5.

the Senate, the act had been reconsidered and held on the calendar for two weeks. During that time no complaint had been made by any representative of any debtor government. Congress, added Hull, ever careful to emphasize the legislative branch's responsibility, then concluded that foreign nations must not have been much concerned about passage of the act.[37] The British could have drawn little encouragement from the Secretary's lesson in American political science.[38]

In the State Department the bill's opponents, by the end of February, had to help prepare its path to passage in the House. Johnson wrote Moore, February 28, instructing him to get the bill out of the House Judiciary Committee where it had been lodged for over three weeks and put it under the Foreign Affairs Committee. The Senator predicted passage as soon as the bill could be brought before the House. Moore, carrying out his orders efficiently, urged the Chairman to give the bill quick and favorable consideration. In less than a week it was voted out.[39] Johnson now had Roosevelt's support for the bill but the President was most anxious not to publicize the fact if it could be avoided. At his insistence, Moore got Johnson's agreement to "be careful not unnecessarily to quote" the President in support of the bill in testimony before the House Committee on Foreign Relations. The Chairman, Moore assured Johnson, already understood Roosevelt's attitude.[40]

Unlike House officials, the British Ambassador did not know Roosevelt's attitude but suspected it was not in accord with what Britain wished. In a second effort to find out more than Hull had told him, Ambassador Lindsay went to Moore and bluntly demanded a clear statement of the President's position on the Johnson Act. The Under-Secretary parried with "No Comment," thinking, as he explained later, that it was "best not to bring the President into the picture." When Sir Ronald continued to probe, Moore insisted that Roosevelt probably had not reached any conclusion at all. The British Ambassador was left to sift rumors.[41]

Roosevelt's public support for the act was not needed to assure passage. Moore wrote Phillips, March 21, 1934: "While it is a fact that the President favors the legislation, that was not stated in the Senate, nor was it stated in the hearing before the House Committee, nor does it seem probable that there will be any need to state it when the bill, as now expected, is put upon its passage in the House . . . April 2."[42] In fact, Roosevelt was a thousand miles away on a vacation in Florida, when the act came up for final vote.[43] As ex-

[37] *For. Rel.*, I, 1934, 527, Memo by Hull, Feb. 5, 1934.

[38] Cordell Hull, *The Memoirs of Cordell Hull.* 2 vols., New York, 1948, I, 382.

[39] Moore Papers, Box 8, Johnson to Moore, Feb. 28, 1934.

[40] *Ibid.*, Moore to Johnson, March 7, 1934. Hull, still seeking a solution, proposed to Roosevelt short term bonds to pay war debts. F. D. R., who received this plan March 14, returned it May 30, with no comment. Hull to F. D. R., Mar. 14, 1934, Hull Papers, Box 67A.

[41] Moore Papers, Box 8, Phillips, Memo of Moore's conversation with the British Ambassador, Mar. 20, 1934.

[42] *Ibid.*, Moore to Phillips, Mar. 21, 1934.

[43] *Time* (Apr. 23, 1934), 13. *Time* saw a certain irony in members of Congress, 230 of them, meeting the President's train when they had, during his absence, overridden his veto of the Pension Bill, threatened to remonetize silver, and taken the teeth from his Stock Exchange Bill.

pected the Johnson Act passed April 13, 1934. It was now illegal for any person to purchase or sell bonds, securities, or other obligations of "any foreign government or political subdivision thereof or any organization or association, issued after the passage of this act or to make any loan to any government or political subdivision thereof or any organization or association thereof except renewal or adjustment of existing loans, while such government is in default in its obligations or any part thereof."[44]

As Moore had predicted, the bill raised a number of difficult questions that kept State Department lawyers busy for the next two months. Johnson was sure that the bill would bring, at the next due date in December, a full payment of the $662,000,000 due the United States. Opponents were equally confident that it would not prevent default but would engender a harvest of ill will. As evidence of the bill's faulty logic, they pointed out that Japan, an unfriendly nation, was still free to borrow from the United States while our British and European friends could not.[45]

Predictably, the British who had made token payments on the last two due dates were much displeased with the act's provisions. Equally predictable was Roosevelt's attempt to smooth things over. He told British Ambassador Lindsay, May 8, that nothing could be done so long as Congress was in session, but "possibly after adjournment something can be worked out."[46] These vague assurances did not placate Lindsay who warned Roosevelt of "repercussions which will occur." If nothing could be done about the act as a whole, the Ambassador insisted that the word default not be applied to Britain's debt policy. Roosevelt, of course, could not comply but he did suggest that there might be at some future date conversations on the debt question either at London or Washington. "Sir Ronald," Phillips recorded in his memo of the meeting, "did not seem to receive the President's suggestion in a very happy spirit."[47]

Roosevelt no longer had authority to rule as to whether token payments constituted default or not. Johnson, in explaining the purposes of his bill, declared that only Congress could alter the terms of indebtedness and thus specifically stripped the President of authority to accept token payment. Henceforth, any nation not paying in full was in default unless Congress chose to modify its debt agreement.[48]

Roosevelt accepted a law that seriously hampered his authority in foreign affairs and put the debt question beyond his reach partly at least in order to achieve his immediate foreign policy objective for 1934—passage of the Trade Agreements Act. To this end plans to press for World Court membership also were ruled out for the rest of the session. Already Hull's pet project was a year late, sacrificed in the first session of 1933 to the urgent political and domestic necessity for getting the Economy Act passed. Subsequent failures in conferences at London and Geneva and final default on war debts had so increased the fury

44 *New York Times,* Apr. 14, 1934.

45 *Foreign Policy Bulletin,* XIII, No. 24 (Apr. 13, 1934).

46 *For. Rel.,* I, 1934, Phillips, Memo, May 8, 535.

47 *Ibid.,* May 11, 535–6; May 22, 541. Norman Davis reported that certain groups of Tories in Parliament resented the Johnson Resolution, but that even that group would not in a showdown oppose us; Norman Davis to Hull, Nov. 6, 1934, Hull Papers, Box 37.

48 *Ibid.,* May 11, 535.

of the "isolationist cyclone" in the United States as to put the tariff program in grave danger of destruction.[49] The House passed it with only two Republican votes.[50] Chances for Senate approval appeared so slight that *The Baltimore Sun* predicted: "All other opposition . . . will seem pale by comparison with the desperate resistance with which a tariff cut will be opposed.[51] Roosevelt's political sagacity in allowing the Johnson Bill to pass paid dividends. Contrary to the dire predictions in the press, the Trade Agreements Act not only swept through Congress but also proved to be both a popular success and a political triumph. Through it the President appealed to liberals without outraging conservatives. As such it was a good example of his "something for everybody" technique of political management designed to promote continued political unity.

Roosevelt's general political strategy, as previously noted, ruled against a show-down with the progressive Republicans—strongly back of the Johnson Act. Intense cultivation coaxed these leading insurgent senators close enough, by early 1934, "to be under his wing."[52] There the President had to keep them to help assure success in the Congressional election of 1934, support for future New Deal measures and, possibly, the formation of a new political party of liberals from both Democratic and Republican camps.[53]

Tariff policy and domestic politics were good reasons for not opposing Johnson or his bill but the choice, nevertheless, was to have fateful consequences. Probably there was little chance for a satisfactory settlement of the war debt problem before the act passed, but there was none afterwards.[54] The Johnson Act as Ernest K. Lindley explained in 1935, was "an official rebuke to our war debtors," but its "main purpose" was the maintenance of American neutrality in the next European war: "It severed America's historical position as a supply base for Europe" and "narrowed by an inch or two the channels to financing another war by loans."[55] Because of the Johnson Act, predicted diplomatic historian Samuel F. Bemis in 1936, "it is unlikely that any defaulting country will ever be able to borrow money on this side of the water from private sources even to save its life."[56] As Bemis pointed out in later editions of his *Diplomatic History of the United States*, the Lend Lease Bill of March, 1941, had to be written to evade the Johnson Act. It was left standing even though it was declared inoperative, February, 1942, when the United States was at war.

In its blunt rebuke for war debt defaulters and its prescription for a Congressionally directed policy of neutrality, the Johnson Act in its two year period of evolution accurately reflected the changing mood of the American people—

[49] Alfred L. Burt, "Foreign Problems Under Roosevelt, 1933–1935," in Allan Nevins and Louis M. Hacker, *United States in World Affairs, 1918–1943*, 381. Hull in a memo to F. D. R. said that "almost any temporary expedient is better than deficit" and in twenty-seven pages explored all other possible methods for dealing with the debt question, including his own short term bond plan proposed earlier; Hull Memo for F. D. R., May 22, 1934, Hull Papers, Box 90.

[50] William E. Leuchtenburg, *Franklin Roosevelt and the New Deal*, New York, 1963, 204.

[51] *Literary Digest* (Mar. 10, 1934), 8.

[52] *Ibid.*, 13.

[53] Bernard, *Couzens*, 296.

[54] Hull, *Memoirs*, I, 382.

[55] Ernest K. Lindley, *Half Way With Roosevelt*, New York, 1936, 297.

[56] Samuel F. Bemis, *Diplomatic History of the United States*, 1st Ed., New York, 1935, 723.

a mood of frustration at home and disillusionment with the foreign policy of the 1920's that opened the way for a headlong flight back to "traditional" American foreign policies.[57]

[57] Selig Adler, *The Isolationist Impulse: Its Twentieth Century Reaction,* New York, 1961, 222, has asserted: "Perhaps no other single result of the depression bred more isolationists than the repudiation of the war debts."

17

THE MILITARY VIEW OF AMERICAN NATIONAL POLICY, 1904–1940

Fred Greene

It is difficult for students of the present generation to realize how pervasive the doctrines of isolationism and antimilitarism were in the 1930's. Having lived their entire lives in a period of time when the military has received over two thirds of the national budget, they will find the following essay a fascinating and unreal glimpse into the past. It deals with military planning in an age of isolation when the services, starved for funds, were calling for retreat from the Far East. The transition from pacificism to militarism came abruptly in 1940, after the fall of France. Franklin Roosevelt was to bombard Congress with a series of messages calling for increased funds to expand, fully equip, and modernize the armed forces. The immediate appropriations amounted to $13 billion; within a year they reached $37 billion, more than the cost of American participation in World War I. "At this time, when the world—and the world includes our own American hemisphere—is threatened by forces of destruction," Roosevelt informed the American people, "it is my resolve and yours to build up our armed defenses. We shall build them to whatever heights the future may require." But while the methods and scope of warfare were changing the administration's thinking, military leaders, as Professor Greene's essay reveals, responded slowly to these changes with the result that the top echelons of military leadership in 1940 were at first unable to grasp fully the implications of Roosevelt's messages concerning the possibilities of global warfare.

Fred Greene is a political scientist specializing in American relations with the Far East. He is the author of two books The Far East *(New York, 1957) and* U. S. Policy and the Security of Asia *(New York, 1968). Professor Greene teaches at Williams College.*

Source: *American Historical Review,* Vol. 66, No. 2 (1961), pp. 354–377. Reprinted by permission of the author.

In the decades before 1940, the army and navy repeatedly complained about the lack of guidance they received from the White House or the State Department concerning American national policy. The absence of over-all directives and the failure to establish a formal coordinating agency during this time compelled the military planners to fall back on their own resources in defining our national policy, national interests, and position in international affairs. This they felt compelled to do in order to plan for the country's military security within a meaningful frame of reference.[1] Hence their studies of strategy, reorganization of forces, alterations in security arrangements and disposition of troops, and preparations for international conferences were all prefaced by estimates of American national policy.[2]

A study of the conception of American foreign policy held by the military planners indicates that they made a painstaking effort to gain a clear understanding of national policy. They then shaped plans and programs in accordance with the position of the United States as they understood it. To a considerable extent, these broad analyses were responses to such specific, current problems as the shape of war plans, a disarmament conference, retrenchment in the army, or Philippine independence. Hence any one paper would be colored by the immediate issue, but the over-all background study sought to identify American national interests objectively. In this manner the services gradually developed their interpretations of national policy over several decades. When confronted with a new problem at any given point, they tended, perhaps unconsciously, to consider these views as the position of the United States government.

At the time the country became a world power the nature of American foreign policy was a source of confusion. An isolationist nation undertaking potentially serious commitments in the Western Pacific while remaining isolationist, despite a world war, in the Atlantic created an enormous strain on planners in search of basic guidance. It is not surprising that this ambivalent American attitude led to uncertainty or to divergent views between the army and the navy. Changes in technology and the international political scene also subjected the positions held by the two services to constant modifications. With the rise of the Axis powers, the relationship between "national" and "military" policy became most intimate, and a unified position in the Joint Board of the Army and the Navy was soon established. Finally, there was a continued effort, without much success, to align our commitments and objectives with American capabilities—immediate or even projected.

[1] The agency in charge of planning was the Joint Board of the Army and the Navy (JB), established in 1903. It was the highest interservice military agency in the government until the Second World War. It was succeeded by the Joint Chiefs of Staff. After 1918 the Joint Board comprised the Army Chief of Staff and the Chief of Naval Operations, their deputies, and the heads of the two services' War Plans Divisions (WPD). In 1919 the Joint Board was given an effective staff—the Joint Planning Committee (JPC)—which had at least three representatives from each service's WPD. The JPC and WPD comprised the highest-level strategic planning agencies in the armed forces during this period.

[2] See Mark S. Watson, *Chief of Staff: Prewar Plans and Preparations* (Washington, D. C., 1950). Chapters I–VI deal with the interplay of strategic planning with foreign policy and domestic pressures. For the pre-1940 development of planning organizations and concepts, see Chapters II and III of Ray S. Cline, *Washington Command Post: The Operations Division* (Washington, D. C., 1951).

Military planners considered the causes of war to be rooted in a nation's security and foreign policy, and viewed military policy as subordinate to these affairs of statecraft.[3] They also recognized that the nation's over-all military posture had to be determined by the government. As expressed by the Chief of Staff, General Charles Summerall, it was "based upon international relations, especially our obligations as a World Power, internal order, past experience and financial limitations."[4] When the need arose to build up the country's armed forces against the Axis threat to the New World, the army stressed its obligation to provide for hemisphere defense. It observed that "the War Department has no thought of aggression, nor does it desire to build up and maintain [in time of peace] the military forces that might be required to win a war."[5]

The kind of subordinate position accepted by the military leadership was reflected in a conversation in 1936 between Dr. Stanley Hornbeck of the State Department and Lieutenant Colonel L. T. Gerow. Responding to the army's evident desire to remove its forces from the Far East, the State Department representative inquired why it did not seek to have America's policy in that region changed. This, Hornbeck added, was more logical than requesting the removal of the military forces supporting that policy. Gerow reported,

> *I told him that the War Department was not the State policy making agency, that being a State Department responsibility. But that the War Department was responsible for the military aspects of any policy adopted and that it was a duty of the War Department to point out the extent to which we might become involved through military commitments and make recommendations accordingly.*[6]

The sense of being responsible for this type of professional advice weighed heavily upon the strategic planners and led them to stress the importance of prudence. In considering the relationship between national and military policy in the grim atmosphere of 1939, a joint planning paper observed that the military's task did not include the responsibility to establish or amend national policy. Instead the overriding requirement was for army and navy actions so planned as to make effective the national policy as defined by the executive and Congress.

The planning paper went on to caution that, when we commit the furtherance of national policy to military and naval action, we alter the conditions under which it can operate. Military operations in turn may unavoidably change national policy in a manner unforeseen by the civilian officials who resorted to armed force or by the military and naval executors of the action. In Clausewitzian terms, the Joint Planning Committee (JPC), the Joint Board's staff agency, added that to some extent every military decision in war threw to fate a hostage of uncertain value as to the future of the nation. It was therefore an

[3] Presentation by General Tasker Bliss before the Joint Board, June 10, 1904, JB 305. Pre-1918 Joint Board records are located at the World War II Branch of the War Records Division of the National Archives, GSA, in Alexandria, Virginia.

[4] Memo, Chief of Staff (C of S) to the five divisions of the General Staff, Aug. 8, 1929, sub: Survey of the Military Establishment, War Plans Division (WPD) 3345. Post-1918 WPD records are also located in Alexandria; see n. 3.

[5] Memo, Assistant Chief of Staff (AC of S) to Deputy Chief of Staff (DC of S), Feb. 2, 1939, sub: Need for Five Divisions, WPD 3674–13.

[6] Nov. 24, 1936, WPD 3533–8.

ethical responsibility of the military and naval authorities to choose courses of action most surely adapted to advance the national policy and not to change it. The professional experience of the military and naval officers, the JPC concluded, was therefore to serve the high purpose of enabling them to advise whether a certain course of military action would advance or harm the national interest involved.

Military planners had to develop their views under the handicap of two types of isolation. The country as a whole appeared satisfied with its traditional diplomacy of isolation from Europe during this period and looked upon the events of 1917–1919 as a mistaken departure in policy. The other isolation was administrative: the planners were kept apart from the civilian directors of policy. The absence of any permanent coordinating agency often prevented them from explaining important military aspects and consequences of a foreign policy on which they felt obliged to tender advice and recommendations.[7]

As early as 1908 the Joint Board complained that it had difficulty in deciding where to concentrate the fleet because the government did not clarify its major policies and areas of greatest interest.[8] Repeated proposals between 1912 and 1922 for an agency to coordinate national and military policy brought no results. The most determined effort was a proposal to Secretary of State Hughes in 1921 that members of his department sit with the Joint Board and the Joint Planning Committee to consider questions of national policy. The JPC, which initiated this suggestion in 1919, felt that national policy had to be formulated first, as the foundation of any war plan, and that this was primarily a State Department responsibility.[9] Hughes rejected the offer because he feared that it would lead to military intervention in matters of foreign policy. It was not until 1938 that a regular coordinating agency was formed.[10]

The State Department did agree to joint deliberations on specific problems suitable to such efforts, with highly beneficial results. Three examples of fruitful cooperation and continual exchanges of views were the fields of arms limitations in both the naval aspects and the more general discussions at Geneva, relations with Latin America during the 1920's when the country shifted its policy to one of nonintervention, and the clarification of our position and military forces in the Far East.[11] But this did not satisfy the JPC, which echoed a lament of twenty years' standing in 1939.

> *Frequently in joint planning tasks, the Joint Planning Committee has had to work in the dark with respect to what national policy is with respect to*

[7] Letter from Captain H. W. Yarnell to Lieutenant Colonel J. W. Gulick, Oct. 28, 1919, sub: National Policy and War Plans, JB Ser. Miscell, 18.

[8] JB Copy Book, Feb. 21, 1908, 325–27.

[9] Letter from Secretaries of War and Navy to Secretary of State, Dec. 7, 1921, sub: Coordination of War and Navy with State Department, JB 301, Ser. 147.

[10] For a study of this problem based on State Department files, see Ernest May, "The Development of Political-Military Consultation in the United States," *Political Science Quarterly*, LXX (June 1955), 163 ff.

[11] On the difficulties and complexities of military-diplomatic coordination, see Louis Morton, "National Policy and Military Strategy," *Virginia Quarterly Review*, XXXVI (Winter 1960), esp. 4–7. See also his study of United States ground forces in China, withdrawn in 1938, in "Army and Marines on the China Station: A Study in Military and Political Rivalry," *Pacific Historical Review*, XXIX (Feb. 1960).

a specific problem, or what it may be expected to be. The Joint Planning Committee has not always been in a position to seek authoritative expressions of fact or opinion from representatives of other Executive Departments, in particular the State Department.[12]

The effect of the national posture of isolationism was more far-reaching. To a considerable extent, it limited the sphere of military thought and preparation to the defense of the homeland. Thus the two war plans dealing with a maximum national effort were couched in terms of the defense of the United States. These plans in turn played a major role in influencing the army viewpoint regarding other strategic considerations as well as questions of personnel, logistics, and weapons.[13] When Congress passed the National Defense Act of 1920, it incorporated many organizational reforms on the basis of recent experience, but these too were geared toward the efficient mobilization of economic strength and of the three echelons of manpower—the regular army, the National Guard, and the organized reserve—for continental defense.[14] Even the capacity for action under this minimal arrangement was drastically curtailed by budgetary economies which Congress adopted after 1920.[15] The economies also had a devastating effect on the development of new weapons, since outlays for research were very modest. As a consequence, it became difficult to evaluate the full impact of new weapons, or attain that vital degree of momentum in which technological change spawns combat innovations and gives rise to further change.[16]

The importance of an isolationist context and tight budgets is mirrored in the army's force levels. Though Congress authorized a regular army of 280,000 in 1920, it immediately reduced this number to 175,000 over a presidential veto. This was followed by a debate to reduce the force to 150,000 enlisted men, during which Senator John S. Williams of Mississippi expressed the prevailing viewpoint:

. . . to my mind it seems obvious that there are two theories with regard to a military establishment. . . . One would be to establish an Army to whip anybody and everybody that might by remote possibility make any attack upon us. In order to do that we would need about 2,000,000 men on a peace establishment, or a million, at any rate. [Author's note: *Chief of Staff Peyton March determined on 508,000 in his 1920 recommendation with just such an objective in mind.*] *Then everybody of a timid character and temperament who is always scared to death about somebody*

[12] WPD memo, July 22, 1939, sub: College of National Defense, WPD 2500–6.

[13] See, for example, WPD memo, based on war plan operations, WPD to G-3, Mar. 13, 1936, sub: Organization of the Army, WPD 3662–2. Navy requirements, however, were estimated in light of another plan, War Plan ORANGE, after 1921. See n. 26.

[14] See, for example, House Committee on Military Affairs, 66 Cong., 1 sess., Hearings on H.R. 8287 (Sept. 3–Nov. 12, 1919), for the army's original position, and General Order 31 (July 18, 1921), summarizing the meaning of the legislation passed on June 4, 1920.

[15] The army's requirements in materiel are discussed in Chapter VI of R. Elberton Smith, *The Army and Economic Mobilization* (Washington, D. C., 1959).

[16] See Constance Green, Harry C. Thomson, and Peter C. Roots, *The Ordnance Department* (Washington, D. C., 1955). Chapters II and VII discuss the slow rate of research and development before 1940.

whipping us would feel safe. The other is to pursue our traditional policy of conserving the financial resources of the people during times of peace and, when war comes, submit ourselves to the immense strain necessary, with the extravagance of expenditure of blood and capital both necessary, but having accomplished the purpose of keeping the people free during peace times from the burdens of war.

This war has shown . . . that . . . you can meet the most efficient . . . military force that the world ever dreamed of . . . but if in the meantime you had kept your people burdened all those 50 years, they could not have done it, they would have had neither the spirit nor the financial ability nor the morale to do it.[17]

Congress reached its lowest level of authorization, 125,000 enlisted men, in 1924. Actual strengths were fixed by appropriations at 118,750 for 1924–1926, but even lower than that, hitting 109,356 in 1926 and 110,940 in 1927 before being raised to 118,000 in 1928.[18] Meanwhile the army worked out a series of developmental projects, including a stillborn ten-year ordnance plan, and Major Army Project Number 1 to raise the regular force to 165,010 men.[19] The most caustic appraisal of this plan and related projects came from Major General William Snow, who felt it was idle to talk of 165,000 men.

With the nation at the height of financial prosperity the military establishment year after year has suffered cuts in appropriations. It would be a foolish optimist who could see any prospect for better treatment in the immediate future or who, in the event of a decline in our present prosperity, failed to count upon further severe slashes in army appropriations. . . . The basic consideration which must govern the strength of the Army in time of peace is the Budget.[20]

In fact, the Secretary of War told the Chief of Staff in 1927 not to seek an increase, for Congress felt that it had been generous in raising existing strengths from their depressed levels to 118,000.[21] And it was to be a full decade before the army approached a strength of 165,000.

Force deficiencies were of great strategic significance to the army. It felt the 1920 law itself was barely adequate for the limited task of continental defense, comparing "with foreign types as the rough forging of a finished tool. Nevertheless, circumstanced as we are, it is an instrument adequate for our security." The regular army had the task of absorbing the first shock of any aggression, but, given our favorable location, a moderate force was considered adequate to deny a base in or near the United States to an enemy. Under the 1920 act the

[17] *Congressional Record,* 66 Cong., 3 sess. (Jan. 13, 1921), 1349–50.

[18] Memo, G-4 to C of S June 24, 1927, AG [Adjutant General] 320–22 (6–18–26), and memo, G-3 to C of S, Jan. 10, 1927, sub: Hearings before Military Affairs Committee, AG 011 (12–29–26), (1) Sec. 1. These and other AG files are in the National Archives, Washington, D. C.

[19] *Ibid.* See also Comprehensive Report on Present State of National Defense, 1929, WPD 3311.

[20] Comments submitted by Chief of Field Artillery, Jan. 4, 1927, sub: Major Army Project No. 1, AG 011 (12–29–26) (1) Sec. 1.

[21] *Ibid.,* Conference of C of S and Branch Chiefs, Jan. 19, 1927.

regulars were to have nine infantry and two cavalry divisions. In 1927, however, only eighty thousand troops were in the United States, and over half of these were committed to specific assignments. This left a strategic force of just three divisions, totaling nineteen thousand men, and six reinforced bridgades totaling thirteen thousand, as well as 5,700 cavalry. The army concluded that "the condition of our emergency force . . . is the cause of our gravest concern" because it would be hard pressed to carry out the initial mobile defensive assignments in the major war plans.[22]

In 1939, when America's perspective widened to include hemisphere defense against the Axis, the same picture emerged on a slightly broader canvas. Though naval and air power were being augmented, the army had but four divisions and five brigades, in various stages of completion, to meet or deter an Axis threat in South America. To guarantee hemispheric security, through control of vital bases, the army requested that its forces be raised to five complete divisions.[23]

The navy, too, experienced economies in force. These were effected by a combination of disarmament treaties and congressional budgetary pressure.[24] Since Congress was determined to curtail expenses, the navy bowed to the inevitable and accepted a naval holiday in 1922. The navy did, however, express a desire for a 10:10:5 ratio and successfully opposed the Japanese request for a 10:10:7 arrangement in capital ships. It reluctantly accepted the 10:10:6 settlement finally agreed upon.[25] More important was its success in having the Anglo-Japanese alliance terminated, thus ending even the remote possibility of a coalition of these naval powers. In the London Treaty of 1930, however, it had to go along with a 10:10:7 settlement in cruisers. It is known that Japan built up to its treaty line while the United States, even with some construction during the depression, was still below its alloted levels when the treaty lapsed in 1936.

The prime naval concern before 1914 centered in the Caribbean, but with the defeat of Germany, attention shifted to the Pacific. There the combination of a "natural enemy" and a very distant Philippine possession presented a difficult situation. Defense of the Western Pacific was a strategic problem for the navy, much as continental defense was for the army.[26] Also, both services were sorely taxed by other obligations, in addition to their major assignments. They were, therefore, alert to any change in world conditions and highly sensitive to proposals that might affect their precarious positions. They realized how profoundly the naval disarmament treaties had weakened America's strategic position in the

22 Statement prepared for C of S by Colonel Stanley D. Embick for presentation to the House Committee on Military Affairs, Hearings on the National Defense Act, 1927, AG 011 (12–29–26) (1) Sec. 1. Similar concern is expressed in memo, WPD to G-4, June 9, 1925, sub: Reduction of Military Activities, WPD 2189; and WPD memo, July 5, 1934, sub: Readiness of Army to Carry Out Missions, WPD 3828.

23 WPD 3674, cited in n. 5.

24 On congressional voting patterns, see George L. Grassmuck, *Sectional Biases in Congress on Foreign Policy* (Baltimore, 1951), esp. Chap. II.

25 General Board to Secretary of the Navy, Nov. 21, 1921, added to the important General Board study, sub: Naval Recommendations on the Coming International Conference, Sept. 21, 1921, GB 438, Ser. 1088, in WPD file, sub: Limitations of Armaments Conference, WPD 375–14.

26 The complexity of planning for both the Philippines and a general war with Japan are detailed in Louis Morton, "War Plan ORANGE: Evolution of a Strategy," *World Politics*, XI (Jan. 1959), 221–50.

Western Pacific and were quick to oppose any further proposals to dismantle existing fortifications or limit our full liberty of action in the Canal Zone or Hawaii.[27] The requirement to defend these three overseas territories was always a major conditioning factor in their policy considerations.

The commitment to the Philippines would inevitably be challenged in this era of isolationism and inadequate continental defense. By common consent Hawaii and the Canal Zone were essential bastions which had to be maintained, but the Philippines were an unrewarding burden, which threatened to involve us in a war after 1930 with Japan. Early manifestations of the great tide of Asian nationalism further complicated the issue. For in 1934 the Filipinos were promised their freedom after a decade of transitional rule. The Philippine question, with its strands of nationalism, Axis aggression, and American obligations, forced the United States into major diplomatic and military considerations beyond the bounds of isolation. But it took the rise of German power to shatter the narrow isolationist framework to which the Philippine issue was an anomalous appendage. Gradually and painfully, continental defense expanded to hemispheric and eventually global commitments.

It is difficult to recapture the novelty of that step toward hemispheric defense in 1938–1939. The fact that it was of great significance to the armed forces indicates how powerful the pressure of isolationism had been. In a critical review of past policies, the army in 1939 noted that the peace-pacifism-economy pressures of twenty years had compelled it to adopt a completely passive mission of defending the continental United States and its overseas possessions, a mission held consonant only with "the stonewall defense of complete isolation."[28]

The insular nature of the American political environment left the armed forces ill prepared to think in terms of transatlantic operations. When General Tasker Bliss, a leading army intellectual, sought to establish a basis for joint war planning in 1904, he began with the essentials of United States foreign policy: the enforcement of the Monroe Doctrine, efforts to extend trade, and intervention in a Latin American state to maintain order.[29] He considered the first to be the basic one, the second to be the root cause of aggression. That is, we had but one policy for three generations, the Monroe Doctrine, and would respond in its name to an act of aggression, undertaken for extension of trade. With 1898 in mind, Bliss noted that one policy led to war, causing other policies to be adopted and so, perhaps, to other wars. The Monroe Doctrine, a precept that stemmed from a desire for isolation from Europe, led to war with Spain, and "the unanticipated acquisition of an immense empire in the remote waters of the Pacific." Thus we sustained our isolation in one direction and found it "completely destroyed in the other."[30]

The guides for army planners were the Monroe Doctrine, isolation from Europe, an economic determinist interpretation of the causes of war with par-

[27] Letter from Secretary of War to Secretary of State, Sept. 22, 1921, WPD 77; memo, AC of S WPD to C of S, Apr. 27, 1927, sub: Three Power Naval Conference at Geneva, WPD 2938.

[28] Memo, AC of S WPD to C of S, Nov. 1, 1939, sub: War Department Concept of Military Mission of National Defense Prior to Adoption of Policy of Hemisphere Defense, WPD 4175–2.

[29] Presentation, June 10, 1904, JB 305.

[30] *Ibid.*

ticular emphasis on foreign trade, and a distracting possession, the Philippine colony. Bliss felt that the Philippines' tie to Oriental trade might lead to war. More likely the colony would become the target of a European enemy in a war growing out of the Monroe Doctrine and would be the real objective of such a war ostensibly undertaken for other causes.

A decade later the army still viewed the Monroe Doctrine and the avoidance of entangling alliances as the two "underlying and abiding national policies" whose maintenance was "as necessary as our national life."[31] It recognized that in the Far East new policies might evolve as a result of international relations regarding trade conditions, similar to the Open Door in China. The European war brought the claim that America traditionally asserted its own rights and respected others, seeking right to prevail over lawlessness.

But, the army added, changing conditions required more than a passive defense. It cited the "increasing facility with which armies and navies can be transported"; the rise in importance of trade and industry the world over, especially in the United States with the end of its continental expansion; and the added responsibilities in the Pacific. By 1920 it was even more evident that America was a world power. Its industry "is or will be advanced as to make the security of her commerce and markets vital to her economic life." The old policies had to be enforced, as new ones were framed, in relation to a military force whose size "is measured by the degree of need which is behind our Foreign Policy."[32] After the First World War the army view continued to stress the Monroe Doctrine, which enjoyed "tacit general recognition" throughout the world, and the isolationist strand of thought, but it recognized that we had vast Pacific commitments and growing world interests, particularly economic needs.[33]

The navy's analysis of American foreign policy revealed a similar spectrum of concepts but it laid greater emphasis on the new elements of world trade needs and the Pacific, both of which converged upon the target of Japan. This focus on a specific opponent was also a consequence of the navy's duty to meet any attack while the army mobilized its full strength behind this shield. The joint planners therefore came to consider the protection and security of the United States fleet as one of America's vital interests. Naval plans were developed in the early years with regard to a likely opponent, selected on the basis of his foreign policy objectives and naval power. Thus the navy shifted its major interest from Britain to Germany to Japan during the generation after 1890. Isolation in the naval sense had the more limited meaning of not seeking a war or initiating aggressive actions in waters distant from the New World.

In 1904 Rear Admiral Henry Taylor, in discussing the basis for joint war plans, explained that by the turn of the century Germany had replaced Britain as the main opponent in our naval plans. He stressed that one can best determine the alignment for war by studying the development of great nations and comparing

[31] Memo, War College Division (WCD) to Secretary of War, Sept. 11, 1915, sub: A Proper Military Policy for the United States, WCD 9053–90. WCD file materials dating before 1918 are generally in the National Archives, Washington, D. C.

[32] Memo, AC of S WPD to C of S, Sept. 22, 1921, sub: Policies and Influences Determining the Development of Armaments of the Great Powers, WPD 80.

[33] On the persisting importance of the Monroe Doctrine and the nonaggressive attitude of the United States in Latin America, see memo, AC of S to C of S, Aug. 31, 1926, sub: Possible Menace to Panama Canal, WPD 1162–21.

the general international situation with the past. In the case of both European powers, the Monroe Doctrine was at the root of his reasoning and the Caribbean was the most sensitive and vital theater. But even at this early date he pointed to American commercial interests in Asia and the complication aroused by our possession of the Philippines. To him the present moment was "one of rapidly changing conditions, international and military," requiring a change in the basis of our plans because of "the increasing prominence assumed by the situation in Northeast Asia."[34] In advancing the then very popular argument that America's industrial development had a vital and dependent connection with the great populations of East Asia, Taylor concluded, "We may expect in the future to find the sacredness of the Monroe Doctrine drop to second in the national mind, and our trade relations with Eastern Asia assume first place, and become the principal cause of war."

It should be noted that at the time the Joint Board addressed itself to the immediate problem at hand. It drafted instructions for the preparation of a complete plan for war, "the cause and origin of which should be the infringement of the Monroe Doctrine, and which should consist of an attack by a European nation upon the territory of South or Central America or adjacent islands."[35]

In 1912 the General Board justified its shipbuilding program as support for our well-established policies of no entangling alliances, the Monroe Doctrine, the Open Door, Asiatic exclusion, and exclusive military control of the Panama Canal and contiguous waters. In its view, the size of the navy was not primarily related to the development of further American objectives. Rather, to what extent was America willing to support and defend existing national policies most threatened by Germany in the Atlantic and Japan in the Pacific?[36]

The navy also held that the maintenance of national sovereignty and independence required a "closed cycle of industry," encompassing agriculture, mining, manufacturing, and transport and cable services among the different elements. All the territory necessary for this cycle did not have to be under the American flag, as long as we had friendly relations with the foreign lands concerned and possessed a navy able to control the trade routes to them. To the navy this meant an ability to deny control of Latin America to a major enemy as far south as the mouth of the Amazon and an offensive capability against the ocean trade routes of any aggressive power.[37] This naval view was at variance with the army's opinion that America could satisfy its economic needs at home. On the other hand, the army recognized that the market problem for our manufactures abroad involved a vital interest.[38]

In preparing for the Washington Conference of 1921–1922, the navy studied the fundamental policies of the great powers and expressed its own view of international relations.[39] The four main American policies were no entangling alli-

[34] Revised draft of presentation made by Rear Admiral Taylor before the Joint Board, May 31, 1904, JB 325.

[35] JB Copy Book, June 10, 1904, 75–76.

[36] Memo, General Board to Secretary of the Navy, Sept. 25, 1912, sub: Building Program Outlined since 1903, in GB 438, Ser. 1088.

[37] General Board memo, Aug. 1920, *ibid.* This memo cited a General Board letter of 1901 which emphasized the navy's ability to hold the Caribbean but doubted if the Monroe Doctrine could be enforced below the mouth of the Orinoco River.

[38] WPD 80, cited in n. 32.

[39] The following is from the long study GB 438, Ser. 1088.

ances, the Monroe Doctrine, the Open Door, and the recently developed exclusion of Asiatics. The Open Door was understood to include China's territorial and political integrity and equal commercial and industrial opportunities there for all nations. The navy held that the Monroe Doctrine and the Open Door had a vital feature in common—respect for national sovereignty. On the other hand, alien exclusion was justified on the grounds that internal development "free from any discordant foreign element is a supreme right," completely distinct from the Open Door.

The navy categorized the major external problems as controversies between states of similar governments and ideals and issues between states of dissimilar foundations and ideals or different racial viewpoints and traditions. Disputes of the first type, essentially economic in character, were of increasing importance because nations came to depend on unmolested channels of trade and accessibility for their high living standards. Their very existence becomes involved as the tendency toward specialization increases. It was the task of governments to prevent commercial rivalries from finding expression on foreign soils and to resolve harmoniously the struggle for commercial control of world markets. Difficulties with Britain were considered amenable to settlement by arbitration, treaty, and commercial agreement if a spirit of harmony could be preserved. In arguing for permanent naval equality with Britain, however, the General Board observed that no war between two peoples or nations was "unthinkable."[40]

Issues between fundamentally dissimilar states, according to the navy, arose from policies of exploitation, conquest, or alliance. The last, a thinly veiled reference to the Anglo-Japanese alliance, was not considered as durable as friendly relations between democratic states, even when such connections were loose and informal. The issue of exploitation was applied specifically to Japan's ambitions in China, which were firmly denounced. Japan's claim of an Asian Monroe Doctrine was branded a spurious argument. Controversies in this category did not appear to be permanently adjustable, and it seemed that any settlement would have to be maintained by force.

Finally, the navy discussed sea power in the service of a democracy's foreign policy. A strategically isolated America could influence world affairs only by way of the sea, and so needed naval strength commensurate with its world position. It argued that the "silent pressure of sea power" could support diplomacy firmly and rapidly, adding that this was primarily a defensive weapon, serving aggressive purposes only when used to sustain a dominant commercial position or to exploit weaker peoples overseas. The development of both large land forces and great sea power, by contrast, was deemed evidence of aggressive interest. Finally, the study observed that, in time of war between great nations, naval power would play an important role because economic pressure and blockades were vital weapons in such a struggle.

After the First World War, the nation's isolationist attitude toward Europe was faithfully reflected in the thoughts and plans of the military strategists, though they were keenly aware of the extent to which the balance of power and America's security had hinged upon events across the Atlantic. As General Sum-

[40] General Board memo, July 15, 1921, *ibid.* It noted that the war of 1861 was not foreseen in 1830 and concluded that blood relations count for little. Otherwise the United States would have been exempt from wars with all nations it fought except Mexico.

merall observed, "Had it not been for the British Navy and the Allied Army, the impression of the war that exists in America would be quite different."[41] Similarly, the navy recognized that had the German navy been equal to Britain's, the results of the war might have been reversed with all Europe "dominated by Prussian ideals . . . and eventually America might have fallen."[42] But it was also realized that France after 1918 wanted "American support in her European policies, which, if accorded, might involve us in an embarrassing situation."[43] Army planning ruled out the possibility of armed American intervention in Europe;[44] and in 1933 it could be categorically stated, "We have no plans for the invasion of any of these [great power] countries."[45] The intervention of 1917–1918 was treated as an accident, as were the eighteen months we had to prepare ourselves before facing German armies. The National Defense Act of 1920 was justified as applicable to "more normal circumstances, those in which we would have to depend upon ourselves. . . ."[46]

Toward the end of the 1920's, under the pressure of new budget cuts, the army intensified its quest for efficient organization.[47] It studied the causes of war, the international situation, and the policies of the United States, to determine their effect on the army's mission and size. General George Simonds, director of WPD, also ordered a review of our major national policies—neutral maritime rights, the Monroe Doctrine, the Platt Amendment, the Open Door in China, and the Japanese immigration issue. WPD followed the traditional view in tracing the causes of war to conflicts of national policy arising from questions affecting vital interests. National policies themselves were rooted in experience, growing out of the "moral, economic, and political influences in the lives of countries and peoples."[48] Causes for conflict were categorized as political, economic, racial, and moral.

The Simonds study noted that political wars often had economic influences, such as expansion due to population pressure, as underlying causes. War could also result from problems concerning racial minorities or be deliberately started by a weak government seeking internal unity. Such wars were described as aggressive and imperialistic, of a kind not undertaken by the United States, an isolated state which did not suffer from such tensions. Our rise to world power, however, created new rivalries abroad and increased our concern regarding economic and moral causes of war. "Economic questions have been in the past the fundamental

[41] Memo, C of S to DC of S, Aug. 3, 1929, sub: Study of Value of Coast Defense, WPD 3345.

[42] Naval study of Sept. 12, 1921, GB 438, Ser. 1088, cited in n. 25.

[43] *Ibid.*

[44] For an early exposition of the defensive cast of our planning, see two WPD studies of 1922: National Defense in Readiness, WPD 598; National Position of Readiness, WPD 670.

[45] Memo, WPD to the Special Committee of the General Council, Sept. 15, 1933, sub: Summary of Plans Submitted by the Chief of the Air Corps for the Defense of the U. S. with Comments on Selected Points, WPD 888–75.

[46] In statement prepared by Colonel Embick for C of S in 1927, AG 011 (12–29–26) (1) Sec. 1.

[47] See WPD 3311, cited in n. 19, and WPD study, July, Aug. 1929, sub: Survey of the Military Establishment, WPD 3345.

[48] The following discussion is based on WPD 3311 Sec. IV, General World Outlook.

cause of much of the strife that has gone on in the world."[49] WPD noted, however, that economic questions tended to be settled by other means than war. With the world so interdependent, a solution by war was considered less likely to benefit either side, as the world war showed.

But, the Simonds study continued, certain principles of human existence matter more than economic gain in the history of every people who have become a great nation. For these they will fight bitterly and make great sacrifices. Our people, it was argued, were more likely to go to war over moral outrage than for economic causes, especially since moral issues are so difficult to settle by agreement, compromise, or outside arbitration. "No great moral issue has ever been definitely settled except through the method of war, the last resort when all else fails."[50] Our own wars were classified as moral and economic (the Revolutionary War, the War of 1812, the Spanish-American War, the world war); racial and economic (the Indian and Mexican Wars); moral (the Civil War).

National policies then were not arbitrary mandates directed aggressively at others but were lines of conduct pursued as a nation's best interest. Violation of and violence to these policies created the greatest likelihood of war and so WPD turned to our own foreign policies for guidance. The vital historical issues were grouped into five major categories: (1) Maritime rights of neutrals were fundamental in the struggle of the 1790's, 1812, and the world war. In light of the great development of foreign trade and our aloofness from alliances, these principles were "a cause of war of constantly increasing likelihood. . . . Failure to settle the question constitutes the crux of the problem of our present rivalry with the world's other great naval powers." (2) The Monroe Doctrine, called wholly defensive in character, embodied the principles determined upon to safeguard American national interests with relation to the Eastern as well as the Western Hemisphere. The danger of war with a European power on this count was evident in 1863, 1895, and 1902. Its major contemporary importance was focused on the Panama and proposed Nicaraguan Canals, whose purpose was to strengthen our defenses and extend advantageous trade routes to South America. (3) The Open Door in China gave rise to a serious problem of defense in sustaining existing state policy. Related to this was the quiescent Japanese immigration issue which might again be raised when the United States became embarrassed by other critical international involvements. Our Philippine base was vulnerable, but with "potentiality as an outpost of trade at the gateway to the great underdeveloped resources and trade possibilities of eastern Asia." (4) Foreign debt and trade rivalries comprised the most important issue after these three specific ones. First, debtor states presented a united front against the United States. More significantly, the debt was symptomatic of our growth in wealth and industry, placing us ahead of all others in the expansion of our foreign trade.[51] Historically, "ascendancy in world trade, coupled as it must be with a growth in sea power for its maintenance, has always been a great potential cause of war." (5) The press

49 *Ibid.*

50 *Ibid.*

51 In plans drawn up in the late 1920's these economic factors were given prime importance as the likely cause of war. American encroachments on the foreign trade of other maritime powers, threatening standards of living and potential economic ruin, are cited as the causes of war in these plans.

and public opinion, when inflamed, formed a potential cause of unexpected war even though the government was seeking a settlement.

Studies in the late 1920's concluded that the situation was then calm, with no issue calling for immediate military preparation. But since the United States had clearly defined national policies conflicting with those of other countries, the chance of war still existed.

During the 1920's and the first half of the 1930's, the power of the airplane did not have a major impact on strategic thinking about national policy. The planners felt that the flying range and carrying capacity of even the latest aircraft did not create special problems or opportunities. Regarding continental defense, the army believed that the weapon could be handled primarily within the framework of the major war plans. Planners made allowance for the destructive capabilities of existing aircraft, including carrier-borne types, both in developing war plans and organizing harbor and coastal defenses.[52] They concentrated, however, upon protection against combined-arms attacks, rather than a sudden air assault alone. WPD and the Air Corps vigorously disputed this point as well as the deployment and use of air components to meet major attacks. But the entire argument was couched in terms of an isolationist America defending itself against aggression.[53]

The major administrative disputes of the period were over the boundary line between army and navy jurisdictions in continental defense and the degree of autonomy to be enjoyed by the Air Service, reorganized as the Air Corps in 1927, within the army. Basically, the navy enjoyed primary jurisdiction over the oceans; within the army, the Air Corps was enjoined from formulating basic policies of its own, though it had representation on General Staff planning agencies.[54] Again the relatively primitive level of technology played a powerful role, but these administrative decisions aided in slowing the rate of development still more. The old restrictions did not disappear until the late 1930's, when the B-17 prototype effected a strategic breakthrough in flying range and carrying capacity, and so in planning concepts.

Events of the 1930's destroyed the calm atmosphere of normalcy. Japan's rise sharply revealed the gap between our interests and commitments in light of the forces and policies we had fashioned to sustain them. With troops in China and the Philippines, an Asiatic fleet, a war plan against Japan, and an entire Pacific strategy at stake, the army and the navy reexamined basic American policies. They had to bear in mind such political questions as the Open Door and the future of the new Philippine Commonwealth, and relate them to the world situation and

[52] See, for example, memos, AC of S WPD to C of S, Mar. 8, 1928, and the reply, DC of S to AC of S WPD, Mar. 9, 1923, sub: Harbor Defenses, WPD 1105; and memo, Major General Andrew Hero, CAC [Coast Artillery Corps] to AG, Mar. 18, 1929, sub: Antiaircraft Defense, AG 381 (2–16–26).

[53] See WPD 888–75, cited in n. 45.

[54] The files on these administrative disputes are voluminous. See, for example, the WPD 888 files, and, regarding the Joint Army and Navy Aeronautical Board, AG 334.3 and 580.1. For a summary of the interservice dispute, see memo, WPD to Assistant Secretary of War, Aug. 27, 1937, sub: Relations between the Army and the Navy, WPD 3740–1, Appendix C. For a general discussion of this problem, see Major Lawrence J. Legere, "Unification of the Armed Forces" (doctoral dissertation, Harvard University, 1950).

American obligations elsewhere. The result was a sharp disagreement between the services in defining American interests and future policies.[55]

On November 26, 1935, the JPC noted that our policy toward Japan had weakened over the past two decades. It added that the current policy could force America into an unsuccessful war.[56] In the split over what to do, the army emerged with an isolationist doctrine. It wanted to leave China and drop the burden of the Philippines, for it did not consider the Western Pacific a vital area in terms of American interests. The navy sought to continue our commitments there, maintaining that the area was worth fighting for and that the basic strategic plan was sound and feasible. A strongly worded army draft statement put the issue squarely.[57] Starting in a manner reminiscent of General Bliss in 1904, Colonel Walter Krueger stressed the accidental nature of our acquisition of the Philippines. The premise behind our policy was that the Philippines were of great economic and strategic importance to us. This view Krueger challenged, holding that the economic value never materialized. In fact, he called the policy of 1898 a sharp divergence from the obvious and natural path along which our future lay, adding "that this departure might and in all probability would produce a clash with a power into whose natural domain of expansion we had accidentally strayed." He felt that phrases like the "open door," "American interests," and "trade expansion" had become mere repetition and dogma which guided our policy.

The immediate issue at hand, whether to retain a naval base in the Philippines, raised the question of the purpose of such bases. Generally, bases were required for the operation of naval forces in light of strategic requirements. Krueger held that of the two essentials of sea power, the merchant marine and the fleet, the former was the real source of power, relying on the latter for protection. Bases in turn served the fleet. "But a fleet and naval bases without a merchant marine become an anachronism." Britain, with world trade routes and bases, needed a fleet of equal proportions, but America was a continental power whose vital lines of communication were practically confined to the Western Hemisphere. Therefore a base in the far Pacific, given our small merchant marine and the low vulnerability of its essential lines of communication, could only serve an offensive mission. He called the argument of the "greater navy advocates" that our fleet was primarily our first line of defense "an expensive delusion." This function was incidental to the main task of gaining and maintaining command of the seas and communication lines vital to the homeland. A fleet larger than one required for this purpose, he concluded, became an expensive luxury and a tool that might serve an aggressive purpose.[58]

He described our strategic position as very strong since we enjoyed potential hegemony in the New World. Then, in tones remarkably similar to Charles Beard's contemporary study *The Idea of the National Interest*, Krueger stated,

[55] The following discussion is based upon the study made in 1935–1936, Military (including Naval) Position in the Far East, JB 305, Ser. 573, as well as the accompanying JPC Development File.

[56] Memo, JPC to JB, *ibid.*, Development File.

[57] *Ibid.*, WPD draft prepared by Colonel Walter Krueger, Oct. 28, 1935, sub: Our Policy in the Philippines.

[58] *Ibid.*

> *Properly directed, the energies of our people can be fully absorbed in that hemisphere for many generations to come. It is practically self-supporting and could be assailed from overseas with the greatest difficulty only. Granted reasonable naval and military preparedness on our part, it is virtually invulnerable.*

He depicted Japan as anxious to avoid a war unless goaded, adding, "War on the Atlantic side is even more unlikely, unless again we leave the sphere in which our future virtually lies." To Krueger the decision to free the Filipinos enabled us to attain a perfect solution by "washing our hands of the Philippines once they become independent, and not to retain even a coaling station, to say nothing of a naval base there."[59]

He later broadened his argument to include the whole Far East where America's position, never very strong against Japan, had become so progressively weakened since 1920 as to be untenable.[60] We might have successfully challenged Japan's quest for hegemony at one time, but it was now too late to do so. Since none of our interests in the Far East were vital, Krueger felt that war in their defense could not be justified. The forces we had in the Philippine Islands were too weak to resist serious attack, and the small garrison in China had only irritant value. He therefore called for total withdrawal from the Philippines even before independence was granted. Larger state policies naturally governed in China, but he warned that the State Department should clearly realize that its policy of keeping a garrison there would probably lead to war.

General Stanley Embick was another leading army planner who, with Krueger, played a dominant role in WPD during the interwar period. He too reflected the prevailing American mood of isolationism and looked upon any postindependence commitment to the Philippines as a retention of a hazardous front-line trench against Tokyo's southward advance.[61] And he too saw no vital American stake here, and warned against being maneuvered by interested European nations into bearing the brunt of the first resistance to a Japanese assault. Embick regarded American national policy as standing for peace and the avoidance of entanglements that might lead to war. A military commitment to the Philippines was therefore the gravest threat to that policy, and the decision to grant freedom was a graceful way out. Britain, he argued, had an artificially created empire, dependent upon a colonial structure. It had to remain at Singapore and fight to defend that key base. The American position, that of the most self-contained nation in the world with inconsequential interests in the Far East, was exactly the reverse. "Our vital interests continue to lie in the continental United States. This fact must be the fundamental premise in the formulation of our military (including Naval) policy." With a peacetime frontier in the Pacific along the Alaska-Hawaii-Panama line "our vital interests will be invulnerable."[62] This paper was submitted

[59] *Ibid.*

[60] WPD memo, Dec. 5, 1935, sub: Reexamination of Our Military (including Naval) Position in the Far East, JB 305, Ser. 573, JPC Development File. See also n. 65.

[61] WPD memo, Dec. 2, 1935, sub: Military Aspects of the Situation That Would Result from the Retention by the United States of a Military (including Naval) Commitment in the Philippine Islands, JB 305, Ser. 573, JPC Development File.

[62] *Ibid.*, Appendix A, Defense of the Philippine Islands by the United States. He favored a multilateral treaty of neutralization of the Philippines and a local defense

to the President and, on April 16, 1936, Embick added that "the conclusion contained therein has been concurred in without qualification by the following, viz: Generals [Malin] Craig, [George] Simonds, [Dennis] Nolan, Fox Connor, [Paul] Malone, [George] Mosely, [Preston] Brown and [Herbert] Brees."[63] It thus served as an authoritative summary of the army's position during the inconclusive discussions held that year.

A third army planner, Colonel Sherman Miles, arrived at similar conclusions by an empirical analysis of American foreign policy.[64] Recognizing that military policy must be subordinate to national policy, he sought to determine what that was in Asia. Our desires seemed to include the integrity of China, the Open Door, the development of Filipino nationalism and independence, the protection of American lives and interests, and a general support of the *status quo* south of Siberia. We were, however, willing to employ only diplomatic means to attain these goals. Miles wryly observed that we sought, at times quixotically, to be friends of China and Japan, and cooperated with European powers in Asia to a far greater extent than was our custom. But we would not use force to advance our objectives, apart from protecting American lives. As Japan rose in power and the requirement to use force correspondingly mounted, our unwillingness became more evident. All our Far Eastern objectives were therefore jeopardized because, though the United States grew in potential military power, it was "not as a kinetic force in the Far East."[65] To Miles it was clear that our objectives were incompatible with their implementation.

> *We cannot indefinitely sustain and protect our objectives against an aggressive imperialism based on force without the use of force. But our unwillingness to use force is as much a part of our national policy as is our desire to sustain and protect our objectives. Ultimately, therefore, a choice must be made between the two incompatible parts of our national policy. . . . There can be little doubt that the nation now feels that we have no interests in the Far East, except the lives of our people, worth a war, and that we have no intention of bringing on such a war.*

This he considered to be our true policy, the one to which our military policy should be geared. A complete withdrawal from the Western Pacific was therefore in order, unless we reversed a national policy of several decades, decided to use force, and sent adequate military formations to that area. All of this Miles believed to be highly unlikely.

The army position can be traced to several factors. Sensitive to the surrounding intellectual and political environment, the planners responded to the strongly isolationist current of the time. This found reflection in the hypotheses that the

---

force geared to maintain internal order only. This plan was detailed in Appendix B, Military System for the Philippine State.

63 JB 305, Ser. 573, JPC Development File.

64 WPD memo, probably mid-Dec. 1935, sub: U. S. Military Position in the Far East, JB 305, Ser. 573, JPC Development File.

65 Miles cited the Lansing-Ishii notes following the Twenty-One Demands, our rejection of the League of Nations in good part because of the military commitments it implied, the 1922 treaties, the Kellogg-Briand Pact, the Stimson notes, our self-limitation to naval reservation and fueling stations after the Philippines became free, and the total lack of interest to stand firm against more recent threats to China's integrity.

New World was the universe of our national interest and that there literally were no other interests vital enough to fight over. A second conditioning element was the fact that only War Plan ORANGE against Japan was in effect at that particular moment. To stress this plan to the exclusion or deemphasis of other considerations disturbed the army on two counts. It meant a reorientation of budgetary allocations and force structures in favor of a navy-dominated Pacific effort at a time when funds were extremely scarce. And, there appeared to be something dangerous about carrying a war immediately across the Pacific, as the plan provided.[66] The army felt that obligations toward the Philippines were forcing controlling political considerations into a vital military question.

The army wished our strength to be deployed in a balanced fashion, prepared for any critical emergency involving our vital interests. If we were ready in the Atlantic and the Eastern Pacific as the crisis developed, we could be free to concentrate in either area, depending on the turn of events. As the Axis danger mounted during 1936–1938, the threat to the New World gave more credence to this outlook.

In 1935, however, the navy's appraisal of American foreign policy objectives led it to a series of opposite conclusions. The General Board traditionally regarded our outlying main and secondary bases as vital supports of existing American policies.[67] These remained: the Open Door, the territorial integrity of China, the protection of American nationals and economic rights, and the protection of the Philippines regardless of its eventual status. To give up a base in the Western Pacific, the navy felt, meant a decision not to support these policies or remain a factor in that area's development.[68] The President's view in 1935 that a base in an independent Philippine state would be a liability led the navy WPD to undertake a broad study to justify its stand.[69]

Like the army members of the JPC, the navy planners considered our national policies to be the governing factors.[70] In the Far East and the Pacific they were enumerated as follows:

Policy	*Purpose*
Participation in the Pacific	To maintain the *status quo* and preserve the general peace and balance of power in the Pacific.
Integrity of China	To maintain the rights, interests, and territorial integrity of China.
Open Door in China	To promote intercourse between China and other powers on the basis of equal opportunity.

[66] Appendix A, Study by General Embick, cited in n. 59.

[67] General Board to Secretary of the Navy, GB 404, Ser. 1683, Apr. 16, 1935, in JB 305, Ser. 573, JPC Development File.

[68] Secretary Claude Swanson to the President, Op—12B—CTB 4/18 (SC) A 16/GH (Pacific), Apr. 22, 1935, in JB 305, Ser. 573, JPC Development File.

[69] *Ibid.*, President to Secretary Swanson, May 3, 1935. See accompanying memo by Captain George Meyers to the General Board, stressing the need for a complete statement of arguments in favor of retaining a naval base.

[70] Commander Arthur Carpender for the JPC, Op—12B—CTB, Dec. 17, 1935, sub: Examination of U. S. Military (including Naval) Position in the Far East, JB 305, Ser. 573, JPC Development File.

Policy	*Purpose*
League of Nations mandates	To protect the rights of the United States regarding joint rights in mandates; to prevent the assumption of sovereignty by states holding mandates.
Limitations of armaments	To eliminate naval competition and further peace by an equitable ratio and removal of friction and fear.
Freedom of the seas	To safeguard our rights at sea in accordance with existing international law.
Neutrality	To preserve the rights of the neutral under existing international law.
Political isolation	To prevent entangling alliances.

The navy held the task of military policy to be the study of forces needed to support national policies. It justified using existing declaratory policy as its point of departure, holding that if "the national policy in the Far East is clouded the necessary military steps must be taken which will support that policy, regardless what it is or may turn out to be."[71] It recognized that serious conflict existed with Japan on the first five points and that there was dissention within the United States regarding the last three items. It asked for a clear-cut decision to withdraw or to maintain our strength in the Far East. Above all, the navy sought to avoid a middle course, the path of the greatest danger. It stood firmly against withdrawal and opposed yielding a geographic barrier against what it termed the yellow race's usurpation of the white man's place in the Far East, with the consequent desertion of the European and Commonwealth powers there.[72] A return to isolation would, the navy contended, leave Britain to play a lone hand against Japan, leave China to its fate, abandon the Philippines in their experiment at self-government, deny our commercial interests encouragement and support in the Orient trade, encourage Japan to extend and accelerate its domination of the Far East and world markets, and, finally, weaken our international standing and influence in Europe and Latin America.

The navy held that such a policy ran counter to the interests and wishes of the people, who, moreover,

> *will never throw the Philippines to the lions. . . . It is believed and assumed that our existing national policies in the Far East and in the Pacific must and will be maintained; that our diplomacy must be directed towards that end on the fundamentally sound basis of right; that force must be used if and when diplomacy fails.*[73]

The navy also defended the strategy of carrying the fight to the Western Pacific and forcing a decision there.

> *Many people simply attempt to visualize what effect the retention of our*

[71] *Ibid.*
[72] *Ibid.*
[73] Op—12B—CTB, Navy draft, Jan. 14, 1936, JB 305, Ser. 573, JPC Development File.

> *existing national policies would have as a provocation of war; a defeatist attitude pure and simple, in which the national prestige is subordinated to the insane desire to avoid war at any cost. . . . [This attitude is] an affront to the diplomat and military man, who know full well that our policies are sound and that our power to enforce them exists.*[74]

A split paper submitted to the Joint Board by the JPC with two sets of conclusions and recommendations was the final result. The army asked for the withdrawal of our forces from the Philippines upon independence and an exit from China as soon as possible. The navy agreed that any element not needed in China could be withdrawn, but proposed that no decision affecting our dispositions in the Philippines after independence be made at this time. The paper was filed, its arguments soon overtaken by the rise of a German-Japanese menace to the New World.

With the rise of the Fascist powers in Europe, the more prudent Asian position advocated by the army gradually prevailed. By 1938, planning emphasized the contingency of a threat stemming from either ocean, or a simultaneous challenge from both directions. The resultant study was a highly competent and thorough analysis of this problem in which the JPC again presented a unified view. After the Munich crisis, the planners saw the possibility of German-Italian penetration of the New World while Britain and France remained neutral. Since our forces were not prepared to protect the entire Western Hemisphere and our Pacific possessions simultaneously, an order of priority had to be established. The ultimate threat to American security was believed to be the establishment of Axis bases in South America, followed by extension of military control over certain developed areas of that continent. Compared to this challenge, the loss of Guam or the Philippines was not a surrender of our vital interests, although admittedly a great blow to our prestige and an indication of failure in our sovereign responsibilities.

It was also evident that such losses in the Pacific, if permanent, would deprive us of a base for action, signify an end to any physical support for the Open Door in China, and limit our share of the China trade to remnants, at Japan's convenience. But, it was added, since our people had continually placed our Far Eastern interests at the mercy of Japanese good faith since 1922, they could not have considered these interests as vital. Further proof was evident in our refusal to fortify the Philippines and Guam after Japan denounced the naval treaties in 1935. These expressions of national policy, it was noted, overrode such military and naval opinion which was allowed to be expressed.

By 1940, following the fall of France, our general national interest came to be identified to an unprecedented extent in military security terms. Since our armed power was increasing, the planners began to think more hopefully of taking a stand in both oceans. The JPC identified our national objectives in December 1940 as the preservation of the territorial, economic, and ideological integrity of the United States and of the remainder of the Western Hemisphere; prevention of the disruption of the British Empire and the consequences of such an eventuality; and opposition to the extension of Japanese rule over additional territory, while protecting our economic and political interests in the Far East.

[74] *Ibid.*

The relative importance of these objectives was reflected in this order of presentation. Isolationism and the popular notion that the oceans themselves were adequate protective moats died hard and continued to influence the political debate over the substance of our national policy. Meanwhile, to the extent that our military power and international position permitted, our planners endeavored to attain these three major goals.

18

THE CASE OF THE CONTENTIOUS COMMISSIONER: HUMPHREY'S EXECUTOR v. U.S.

William E. Leuchtenburg

The Supreme Court case discussed in the following essay pertains to the president's power to remove members of the so-called independent commissions; it is another illustration of a struggle for power between the executive and the legislative branches, although in this instance, it was the Supreme Court that was championing a legislative power that Congress had not sought. This case also gives evidence of the powerful opposition manifested toward the New Deal which Roosevelt and his allies had to battle on many fronts. The opposition sought legal redress of their grievances, with the result that the courts became a major battleground, in which the New Deal was on the losing side in almost every instance prior to the president's proposal to enlarge the Supreme Court in 1937. Though Roosevelt lost the battle of court reorganization, he won the war, so that as the New Deal waned in the legislative arena in the late 1930's, it won important and lasting victories in the judicial arena.

William E. Leuchtenburg is a prominent historian in the field of recent American history and a professor of history at Columbia University. Two of his books, The Perils of Prosperity, 1914–1932 *(Chicago, 1958) and* Franklin D. Roosevelt and the New Deal, 1932–40 *(New York, 1963), are widely used as texts in contemporary American history courses. More recently he has revised and brought up to date the classic Samuel Eliot Morison and Henry Steele Commager textbook,* The Growth of the American Republic. *Currently, he is preparing a full study of the fight between Franklin D. Roosevelt and the Supreme Court. This essay, which is related to that conflict, appeared in a volume by former graduate students honoring Henry Steele Commager.*

Source: Harold M. Hyman and Leonard W. Levy, eds., *Freedom and Reform: Essays in Honor of Henry Steele Commager* (New York: Harper & Row, Publishers, 1967) pp. 276–312.

Of the many cases which come before the United States Supreme Court, some are born to fame and some to obscurity. On Black Monday, May 27, 1935, the Supreme Court delivered an opinion about some sick chickens which won immediate acclaim as one of the most significant decisions since the Dred Scott case.[1] A few minutes earlier, the Court had ruled on a suit filed by the estate of one William E. Humphrey, late of the Federal Trade Commission. The Humphrey decision was overshadowed by the Schechter opinion at the time, and only a few commentators have accorded it the attention it deserves since. Poor Humphrey, so jealous of his reputation, has had the unhappy fate of having gone down in more than one work of history, when history noticed him at all, as "Humphries."[2] Yet the case of *Humphrey's Executor* v. *U.S.* raised important questions about the prerogatives of the President and the doctrine of separation of powers, and it had consequences more far-reaching than its humble reputation would suggest.[3]

Born on March 31, 1862, on a farm near Alamo, Indiana, William Ewart Humphrey was destined to carry into the era of the New Deal the values and aspirations of a Hoosier farmboy. After attending Wabash College, Humphrey began law practice in the college town of Crawfordsville. When the Panic of 1893 struck, he decided to seek his fortune in the Pacific Northwest. In Seattle, he rose quickly in the ranks of the Republican Party; by 1898 he was corporation counsel of the city. Four years later, he won election to the U.S. House of Representatives.

From 1903 to 1917 Humphrey faithfully represented the economic interests of his state. In these years, no more ardent member of the Republican Old Guard could be found anywhere in the country. He was a shrill standpatter and a fierce partisan. "If a Democrat is elected," he warned in 1912, "a panic will commence in this country within twenty-four hours after that news is flashed throughout the world."[4] Instead of the good-natured guile thought essential for a successful politician, Humphrey's manner was outspoken to the point of rudeness. He wrote one constituent:

> *I am in receipt of your letter in regard to the establishment of an office at Concrete. I will consider it a personal favor if you will write to the people who wrote to you concerning the matter and tell them that they are making a great nuisance of themselves and doing their cause no good by having people all over this state write me about this matter.*[5]

[1] *A. L. A. Schechter Poultry Corp. et al.* v. *United States*, 295 U.S. 553; Dred Scott v. Sandford, 19 How. 393 (1857).

[2] See, for example, C. Perry Patterson, *Presidential Government in the United States* (Chapel Hill: University of North Carolina Press, 1947), 153.

[3] I am happy to acknowledge my indebtedness to an outstanding paper on the Humphrey and Myers cases, "Two Against the President," prepared for my graduate colloquium on the American political process by John W. Chambers.

[4] W. E. Humphrey to C. B. Bagley, February 3, 1912, Bagley MSS, University of Washington Libraries, Seattle, Wash. The letters in these and other collections at the University of Washington were kindly made available to me on microfilm by Richard C. Berner and Robert E. Burke.

[5] Humphrey to E. G. Eames [sic], October 29, 1906, Edwin G. Ames MSS, University of Washington.

In 1916 Humphrey made a bid for a U.S. Senate seat and met defeat. Never shy about demanding political favors as a matter of right, he now called on his former associates to find him a job as a lobbyist. Senator Wesley Jones actively solicited business interests in the Northwest to obtain remunerative employment for him.[6] To one such inquiry the shipping magnate, Robert Dollar, replied: "I feel confident that a fund will be raised immediately to employ Mr. Humphrey to look after the Pacific Coast Ship Owners interests."[7] But Humphrey's friends were embarrassed when the Tacoma *Times* learned of these overtures and published an account of them. Humphrey, the *Times* stated, had been "a noisy, ill-mannered, narrowly-partisan, always-carping critic of the Wilson administration. He was the pet G.O.P. baiter of Wilson, Wilson's policies, Wilson's appointees and Wilson's acts, in Congress and out. It became with him a mania."[8] Some of the groups Jones approached decided not to employ him, but Humphrey was too undeviating a supporter of business interests and had too much influence in Washington to be unconnected for long. Shortly after his term in Congress expired, he became a lobbyist for Northwestern lumber interests.

Humphrey, who always had his eye on the main chance, did not propose to spend the rest of his days as a lobbyist. He played an active role in national Republican politics; in the 1922 Congressional elections, he served as chairman of the Speakers Bureau of the Republican National Committee. He remained a forthright champion of the Grand Old Party and a vocal viewer-with-alarm. After the war, Humphrey had stated: "I think that our country today is facing a much more serious condition, so far as the perpetuity of our institutions is concerned, than it has at any time since the close of the Civil War."[9] His years in Washington, he said on another occasion, had given him "a profound distrust of the reformer."[10] Humphrey, in short, offered precisely that combination of economic orthodoxy and party loyalty that should have commended him to Republican administrations in Washington. Yet, for some years, although he was aggressive about calling attention to his services, he was passed by. Not until 1925 did his search for preferment end. That year, President Calvin Coolidge, who wanted just such a man as Humphrey, named him to the five-member Federal Trade Commission.

Coolidge's decision was a deliberate attempt to force this "independent" agency into line with the Administration's policies. The appointment of Humphrey proved to be the most important single event in the history of the FTC. By placing on the Commission an aggressive defender of business interests, it gave conservatives a 3–2 majority. Progressives were appalled. The effect of Humphrey's appointment, said Senator George Norris, was "to set the country back more than twenty-five years."[11]

Humphrey quickly transformed the FTC into an agency that served not as an overseer but a partner of business. Only three weeks after he took office, the

[6] See, for example, Jones to Joshua Green, April 10, 1917, Wesley Jones MSS, University of Washington.
[7] Dollar to Jones, April 12, 1917, Jones MSS.
[8] Tacoma *Times*, May 4, 1917, clipping, Jones MSS.
[9] Humphrey to E. G. Ames, October 27, 1919, Ames MSS.
[10] G. Cullom Davis, "The Transformation of the Federal Trade Commission, 1914–1929," *Mississippi Valley Historical Review*, XLIX (December, 1962), 447.
[11] *Ibid.*, 447–48.

Commission voted new rules of practice and procedure. Under the new rules, cases were settled informally with little investigation or publicity. As Humphrey explained: "So far as I can prevent it, the Federal Trade Commission is not going to be used as a publicity bureau to spread socialistic propaganda." *Outlook* observed: "Business has always hated and has steadily determined to throttle the Commission. Because of the change in control due to the appointment of Commissioner Humphrey, it is proceeding rapidly. . . ."[12]

Humphrey boasted of his own role in the alteration. "I certainly did make a revolutionary change in the method and policies of the commission," he was quoted as stating. "If it was going east before, it is going west now." Nor was he shy about admitting that he had stacked the FTC's board of review. "What of it?" he asked. "Do you think I would have a body of men working here under me that did not share my ideas about these matters? Not on your life. I would not hesitate a minute to cut their heads off if they disagreed with me. What in hell do you think I am here for?" Humphrey recognized that some disapproved of what he had done, but he dismissed these critics as "the vocal and beatific fringe, the pink edges that border both of the old parties." "No longer" would FTC serve "as a means of gratifying demagogues."[13]

A bald, round-faced man with a bushy mustache and beard, Humphrey was a pugnacious autocrat who seemed to be forever embroiled in controversy. He quarreled not only with his critics in Congress but with his fellow commissioners, Abram F. Myers and Charles W. Hunt. When Myers said that at some point a federal licensing law for corporations would be needed, Humphrey commented: "It would be hard to imagine a more socialistic proposal than this."[14] In the fall of 1927 Humphrey wrote President Coolidge to object to a statement by Myers and to state that he hoped the next appointment to the FTC would be one "in keeping with that of the rational and conservative business element in this country."[15]

Humphrey's solicitousness toward the "conservative business element" brought him into some steamy brawls with progressives of both parties. Early in 1928 Gifford Pinchot wrote him that he thought it was "hopeless" to expect an adequate investigation by the FTC of abuses in the utilities industry, "because of long personal experience with you as a bitter enemy of the Roosevelt Conservation policy, an opponent of Federal action and a lobbyist of lumbermen." Humphrey replied: "Your letter of regurgitated filth received. For your own famished sake, and for the infinite relief of the country, have your keeper lead you to a thistle patch." Then, characteristically, Humphrey released both letters to the press.[16]

Under Humphrey, the functions of the FTC atrophied, in part as a consequence of court decisions, but also because of Humphrey's policies.[17] Early in

[12] Thomas C. Blaisdell, Jr., *The Federal Trade Commission* (New York: Columbia University Press, 1932), 82.

[13] G. Cullom Davis, "Transformation of FTC," 448–51.

[14] Mimeographed statements, William E. Humphrey MSS, Library of Congress, Box 2.

[15] Humphrey to Coolidge, October 10, 1927, Humphrey MSS, Box 1.

[16] Pinchot to Humphrey, February 22, 1928; Humphrey to Pinchot, n.d., Humphrey MSS, Box 1.

[17] For the role of the courts, see Myron W. Watkins, "An Appraisal of the

1928 he wrote Senator Arthur Robinson that he objected to "fantastic fishing expeditions" by the Commission which were "doing the administration great harm with the business interests."[18] Subsequently, he opposed appropriations for FTC investigations of unfair business practices in a number of industries. Disgusted by the way in which Humphrey was frustrating the original intent of Congress in creating the Commission, Senators in both parties proposed to abolish the FTC. When President Herbert Hoover nominated Humphrey for another six-year term in 1931, the new Senator from Louisiana, Huey Long, made his maiden speech in opposition to confirmation, and twenty-eight Senators voted not to confirm. By the time Franklin D. Roosevelt had won election in 1932, Humphrey had become a symbol of all that progressives abhorred in the Old Order. In January, 1933, Congressman Wright Patman of Texas sounded a popular note when he voiced the hope that when Roosevelt entered the White House he would "certainly change the policy of the Federal Trade Commission and put it back to its original function or intent."[19]

As soon as the Hundred Days Congress concluded its historic session, President Roosevelt turned toward the task of manning the agencies that had been created that spring or which had had new assignments bestowed on them. The Federal Trade Commission had been designated by the National Industrial Recovery Act as a court of appeals in trade practices litigation. Even more important, the draftsmen of the Securities Act of 1933 had decided, surprisingly, to vest authority for administering the new law in the FTC. As James M. Landis, one of the draftsmen, later explained: "Its reputation as an effective regulatory agency during the Harding–Coolidge–Hoover era had admittedly not been of the highest, but we understood that the administration intended to restaff and reinvigorate it."[20]

As he thought about the new role of the FTC, Roosevelt scrawled his ideas about personnel on a White House paid:

Fed. Trade Comm 10,000
Humphrey—out F. Murphy?
La Follette?
March, Minn. ok
McCulloch—dead Perk?
Fergusson ok
Hunt retired[21]

Of the five positions on the Commission, two were vacant. Not only Edward A. McCulloch, a Democrat, but the Republican, Charles W. Hunt, listed by

Work of the Federal Trade Commission," *Columbia Law Review*, XXXII (February, 1932), 278.

[18] Humphrey to Robinson, January 27, 1928, Humphrey MSS, Box 1.

[19] Robert E. Cushman, *The Independent Regulatory Commissions* (New York: Oxford University Press, 1941), 226.

[20] James M. Landis, "The Legislative History of the Securities Act of 1933," *George Washington Law Review*, XXVIII (October, 1959), 34.

[21] Memorandum, Franklin D. Roosevelt Library, Hyde Park, N.Y. (henceforth FDRL), Official File (henceforth OF) 100, Box 1. Roosevelt misspelled Ferguson's name.

Roosevelt as "retired," had died recently. To these vacancies Roosevelt decided to name Erwin L. Davis of Tennessee and Raymond B. Stevens of New Hampshire, one of the authors of the original FTC Act of 1914 and a former special counsel to the Commission. The three remaining members were Humphrey, whose term would expire in 1937; C. H. March, a liberal Republican from Minnesota whose term ran until 1936; and Garland S. Ferguson, a North Carolina Democrat whose term was about to run out. Roosevelt resolved to reappoint Ferguson, to leave March undisturbed, but, as his note on the memo pad indicated, to oust Humphrey and to name someone like Detroit's Democratic mayor, Frank Murphy, or Philip La Follette, the progressive Republican from Wisconsin, in his place.

Toward the end of the second week in July, 1933, rumors began to circulate about the President's intentions. By July 13, they had reached as far as Myrtle Beach, South Carolina, where Senator E. D. "Cotton Ed" Smith wrote Roosevelt to ask him to defer action until they could confer.[22] Sometime in the next few days, Will Humphrey got wind of the disturbing news. On July 19, he wrote the President:

> *Information comes to me that you are going to ask my resignation. For what reason I do not know.*
>
> *Senator Dill, who is more responsible for my being in this position and more interested personally and politically in my retaining it, is away and cannot be reached. His return is expected within a few days.*
>
> *If final action cannot be delayed until his return, then in behalf of the Senator as well as myself, I feel that I should ask for a personal interview. If I have neglected my duty, done anything dishonorable, or discreditable; or have been guilty of disloyalty, it is not necessary for you to ask my resignation. Certainly it seems to me that it is not necessary to involve mutual friends in this matter.*
>
> *For the greater part of forty years, I have been in the public service. I am not aware of anything discreditable in my record, or of any act that I would blot out. If that long service is ended by forced resignation, it would be to some extent a reflection on my career and would greatly injure me in my profession if I should again take up the practice of law.*[23]

For half a century Humphrey had been playing the political game of favors and rewards. In his memory, he kept a ledger of good turns he had done for which he expected payment in full.[24] On July 25, he sent a typically blunt letter to Senator C. C. Dill, a Democrat from his own state of Washington:

> *I was amazed and shocked at what you said yesterday. If I had known what you told me a few weeks ago, it would have been entirely different, and I could easily have made other satisfactory arrangements.*

[22] E. D. Smith to FDR, July 13, 1933, FDRL OF 100, Box 2.

[23] Humphrey to FDR, July 19, 1933, FDRL OF 100, Box 2.

[24] For Humphrey's conception of loyalty, see Pendleton Herring, "The Federal Trade Commissioners," *George Washington Law Review*, VIII (January–February, 1940), 353. As early as 1912 he had telegraphed: "In view of attitude of Star and the rest of outfit of Anarchists can you not persuade Dovall to stop fighting me for judgeship. I feel that I have a right to ask my friends to protect my reputation." Humphrey to E. G. Ames, January 15, 1912, Ames MS.

Naturally, after I left you I got in touch with several of my friends, including Senators and other prominent people, who know about affairs of this kind. Each one said that the President would do whatever you desired in the matter, that he would not ask my resignation unless you acquiesced. This opinion I could not and cannot change. They did not think it advisable for them to attempt to do anything further, as they had been depending on your active assistance. . . .

I cannot believe, as I have been informed, and as you seem to believe, that the President is going to ask my resignation without giving me an opportunity to be heard. If it is done in this manner, as you well know, it will smirch my record and greatly handicap me in my profession. I think if he contemplates this, I have the right to insist that you protest such action and that you will arrange an interview with you and myself. . . .

I shall only add that I have carefully reviewed our many years of friendship, extending from the time you left the House of Representatives—a friendship of which I have been proud—and in all of those years I remember gratefully the many favors that I have received. Of those given, I shall not mention—only to say that they were given gladly, either when they were political or personal, without regard to the effect on me, and I have found nothing in all those years which I feel does not justify me in thinking I have the right to expect that you will be pleased to comply with the request I have made—and that you will do everything in your power to carry it out. And so I do believe. Nothing but your failure to do so will ever make me believe that you will not.[25]

Dill, who may already have interceded for Humphrey, was quick to oblige the Commissioner. On July 28 he wrote Roosevelt that he had heard a rumor, he hoped unfounded, that the President was planning to replace Humphrey with a "Progressive Republican." He pointed out that he had served in Congress with Humphrey; both had been members of the Committee on Rivers and Harbors. He reminded Roosevelt that when the IWW had incited hostile response to Secretary Josephus Daniels during World War I, Humphrey had leapt to Daniels' defense, and that Humphrey had displayed "disinterested kindness" to one of the President's wartime subordinates. "While Bill Humphrey is an ardent partisan in politics," Dill wrote, "I believe he has been equally as loyal in his public service to you as he was to your predecessors."[26]

Even before Dill wrote, Roosevelt had informed Humphrey that he would not grant him an interview. He continued:

Without any reflection at all upon you personally or upon the service you have rendered in your present capacity, I find it necessary to ask for your resignation as a member of the Federal Trade Commission. I do this because I feel that the aims and purpose of the Administration with respect to the work of the Commission can be carried out most effectively with personnel of my own selection.

May I take this opportunity to tell you that at the earnest request of

[25] Humphrey to Dill, July 25, 1933, Humphrey MSS, Box 1.
[26] Dill to FDR, July 28, 1933, Humphrey MSS, Box 1.

Senator Dill, I have been withholding this action for some time but have now reached a definite decision to proceed along the lines I have in mind.[27] . . .

It was altogether out of character for so combative a man as Humphrey to accept being driven out of office this meekly. Sometime in the first two weeks of August, he sought legal advice; he was told that there were strong grounds for doubting that the President had the authority to remove him. As he later explained: "While I started out with the belief that the President had the power to remove for any cause he saw fit, fuller examination of the authorities convinces me beyond reasonable doubt that he can remove me only for the reasons specified in the statute, and after hearing." He had employed "two of the best Democratic lawyers," and they had confirmed the opinions of counsel he had consulted earlier.[28]

On August 11, Humphrey, in a letter to Roosevelt, denied that he had tendered his resignation. Nor, indeed, did he intend to resign. To do so would be interpreted as an admission that he was guilty of one or more of the failings that would, by statute, justify the President in removing him: "inefficiency, neglect of duty, or malfeasance in office." Moreover, if he were to quit in order to permit the President to have his way, the independence of all regulatory commissions would be placed in jeopardy.[29] . . .

If there had ever been a time when Dill might have dissuaded Roosevelt from acting—and that is highly improbable—that time had now passed.[30] As soon as Roosevelt had received Humphrey's letter of August 11, he had recognized that the Commissioner might refuse to resign, and he had initiated steps to build a case against him. On August 14 he sent a confidential memorandum to Attorney General Homer Cummings requesting him to look into the allegation that Humphrey had favored a cut in funds for the FTC's investigation of utilities in 1932. He also asked his new commissioner, Raymond Stevens, to examine a charge by Samuel I. Rosenman, one of the original Brain Trusters, that Humphrey had acted improperly in a rayon trust case. On August 17 Roosevelt received word that Stevens had reported that the "matter you asked him to investigate has reached a very critical stage. Anxious to talk with you as soon as possible."[31]

In the last two weeks in August reports reached the White House from the Department of Justice and from Stevens, who took advantage of his official position to comb the FTC files for evidence of wrongdoing by Humphrey. Some of the leads failed to prove out. It developed that Humphrey had not advocated a cut in FTC appropriations for the utilities probe, and his relation to the rayon affair was not clear-cut. Yet there was ample evidence that he had

[27] FDR to Humphrey, July 25, 1933, FDRL OF 100, Box 2.

[28] Humphrey to C. C. Dill, August 28, 1933, Humphrey MSS, Box 1.

[29] Humphrey to FDR, August 11, 1933, Humphrey MSS, Box 1.

[30] Moreover, by now, Dill, understandably, was miffed. He replied to Humphrey: "I assure you I never for one moment thought our friendship was strained. I have done more for you than I ever did for any republican in this country." C. C. Dill to Humphrey, September 1, 1933, Humphrey MSS, Box 1.

[31] FDR to Marvin H. McIntyre, August 18, 1933; Stephen T. Early to FDR, August 17, 1933, FDRL OF 100, Box 1.

opposed FTC investigations, that he had belittled the work of the Commission, and that he had been guilty of using "intemperate and abusive language."[32]

Bolstered by the reports he had received from Stevens and others, the President was now ready to move once more. On August 31 Roosevelt, in a firm but tactful manner, requested Humphrey's resignation and asked that he have it in the next week. He stated: "You will, I know, realize that I do not feel that your mind and my mind go along together on either the policies or the administering of the Federal Trade Commission, and frankly, I think it is best for the people of this country that I should have full confidence."[33]

Even the unmistakably final tone of this letter did not convince Humphrey that Roosevelt truly meant to fire him. Once again he badgered Dill to wire the President to undertake an investigation. . . . The President refused to see Humphrey, but he did ask Charles H. McCarthy, who had served as Roosevelt's secretary during his tenure as Assistant Secretary of the Navy, to telephone Humphrey. McCarthy explained that the President did not believe that Humphrey agreed with him either on FTC policy or on administration of the Securities Act, and that he wished to name a securities expert to the FTC. Quite apart from "the legal aspect of the matter," Humphrey would be well-advised to resign and avoid being humiliated, McCarthy said.[34] That very day Associated Press tickers reported news of the impending ouster. The A.P. story, Humphrey wrote Roosevelt ten days later, had confirmed him in his determination not to resign.[35]

Once Roosevelt accepted the fact that he could not persuade Humphrey to resign, he proceeded with plans to fire him and to appoint a successor. Since Philip La Follette either was unavailable or seemed an inadvisable choice, the President began negotiations with another progressive Republican from Wisconsin, George Mathews, formerly Wisconsin Public Utilities Commissioner and currently a rate expert for the receivers of the Insull empire. Mathews first sought assurance that he would not be involved in litigation with Humphrey. His fears were assuaged, and on October 3 the President learned that Mathews would accept an appointment to succeed Humphrey, if such an offer were made.[36] The White House then arranged to have a wire appointing Mathews sent on the same day, October 7, 1933, that a brisk note was delivered to Humphrey, stating: "Effective as of this date you are hereby removed from the office of Commissioner of the Federal Trade Commission."[37] . . .

Humphrey was too much of a scrapper to give up the fight now. He retained William J. Donovan, former assistant to the Attorney General, as his lawyer, and carried his battle into the courts. On advice of counsel, he acted out a

[32] William Stanley to Stephen T. Early, August 19, 1933; R. F. to Early, August 22, 1933; Raymond Stevens to FDR, August 26, 1933; Stevens to Cummings, August 26, 1933; Memorandum, probably from Stevens, n.d., FDRL OF 100, Box 2.

[33] FDR to Humphrey, August 31, 1933, Humphrey MSS, Box 1.

[34] Humphrey to McCarthy, September 17, 1933; McCarthy to FDR, September 18, 1933, FDRL OF 100, Box 2.

[35] Omaha *World Herald*, n.d., clipping; Humphrey to FDR, September 27, 1933, Humphrey MSS, Box 1.

[36] Mathews to M. H. McIntyre, October 3, 1933, and McIntyre's notations, FDRL OF 100, Box 2.

[37] FDR to Mathews, October 7, 1933, FDRL OF 100, Box 1; FDR to Humphrey, October 7, 1933, Humphrey MSS, Box 1.

charade of pretending still to be the Commissioner.[38] On October 9 he wrote Mathews:

> *You are hereby notified that your appointment as Federal Trade Commissioner is invalid, because there was no vacancy to which you could be appointed, and you are notified that I am still a Member of the Federal Trade Commission, filling the term for which you are supposed to be appointed, and that I claim and shall claim the emoluments of the said office to the expiration of my present term.*[39]

That same day, when the FTC held its regularly scheduled meeting, Humphrey turned up to hand the Commission a statement disputing the validity of his removal and to sit in silence for two hours while the Commission conducted its business. The commissioners, however, voted to accept the validity of Humphrey's removal and of Mathews' appointment.[40] Humphrey also filed periodic claims for back pay with the disbursing officer of the FTC, but these claims were turned down, and the Acting Comptroller General ruled that Mathews' appointment was valid.[41]

The legal niceties having been attended to, Humphrey was ready to press his case. On October 20, he wrote Colonel Donovan that he thought "action should be taken soon." Predictably, he disagreed with his attorney's interpretation of legal precedents in the case.[42] On December 28, Humphrey filed suit in the U.S. Court of Claims contesting his removal and demanding $1,251.39 in back salary. (Eventually, the sum was raised to $3,043.06 with interest.)

Since Humphrey had been confirmed by the Senate for a full six-year term, he believed that Congress would resent Roosevelt's actions as an infringement on its prerogatives and that he could count on aid from that quarter. On January 18, 1934, Humphrey, once more exploiting his influence with Dill, secured an invitation to appear before the Senate Interstate Commerce Committee, of which Dill was chairman, to challenge the confirmation of Mathews. The Committee even postponed the hearing in order to accommodate Humphrey, who had been ill. Yet Humphrey expressed disappointment about one matter. "I doubt if we are going to have any Senator make a speech on our side of the case when the matter of Mr. Mathews' confirmation comes up for consideration," he wrote Colonel Donovan.[43] Silence in the Senate, Humphrey feared, would give the Court the impression that Congress was willing to waive its rights.

Humphrey's concern proved generally well-founded. The Senate, after brief

[38] A memorandum from "M.B.H.," undated but penciled "September," stated: "I hope Mr. H. will preserve his inchoate right to accruing salary by appearing regularly at each regular session, even though it be but to acquiesce in the action of the Commission in excluding him and bowing himself out." Humphrey MSS, Box 1.

[39] Humphrey to Mathews, October 9, 1933, Humphrey MSS, Box 1.

[40] Humphrey to FTC, FTC to Humphrey, October 9, 1933; Press release, FTC, October 9, 1933, Humphrey MSS, Box 1; *New York Times*, October 10, 1933.

[41] Humphrey to Rudolph Schwickardi, October 9, October 17, 1933; Humphrey to Otis Johnson, *et al.*, November 2, 1933; R. L. Golze to R. B. Schwickardi, November 11, 1933, Humphrey MSS, Box 1.

[42] Humphrey to Donovan, October 20, 1933, Humphrey MSS, Box 1.

[43] Humphrey to Donovan, January 19, 1934, Humphrey MSS, Box 1.

speeches criticizing the President's action by two Old Guard Republicans, Simeon Fess of Ohio and Daniel O. Hastings of Delaware, confirmed the nomination of George C. Mathews unanimously.[44] . . .

On February 14, 1934, four weeks after his testimony before Dill's committee, Humphrey suffered a stroke and died at the age of seventy-one. Yet this did not terminate his suit. The executor of Humphrey's estate, Samuel Rathbun, assumed the role of plaintiff, and the case henceforth bore two names: Rathbun v. U.S., and Humphrey's Executor v. U.S.[45] So the struggle went on. A barefisted brawler all his life, Humphrey continued to provide the occasion for a fight even after his death.

Early in 1935, President Roosevelt named Stanley Reed the new Solicitor General. When Reed took office, Attorney General Cummings called him in and solicitously suggested that he pick out a certain victory for the first case he would argue before the U.S. Supreme Court. Reed looked over the list of pending litigation with this in mind, and hit upon a sure winner: the Humphrey case.[46]

Reed's confidence stemmed from an opinion delivered by the Supreme Court in response to a suit filed by another federal official; like Humphrey, he was from the Pacific Northwest, quarrelsome, and had died before the Court ruled. The postmaster of Portland, Oregon, Frank S. Myers, appointed by President Woodrow Wilson to a four-year term with the advice and consent of the Senate, had been removed by Wilson in February, 1920, without the consent of the Senate, before his term had expired. He filed suit in the Court of Claims for back salary on the grounds that the President needed Senate consent to fire him, since an act of 1876 had stipulated: "Postmasters of the first, second and third classes shall be appointed and may be removed by the President by and with the advice and consent of the Senate, and may hold their offices for four years unless sooner removed or suspended according to law."[47] The Court of Claims ruled against Myers, and the case was appealed to the Supreme Court by Myers' widow.

Until the Myers case reached it, the Supreme Court had been circumspect about ruling on the President's removal power. The Court appeared to be willing to accept the precedent set by the so-called "Legislative Decision of 1789," when the First Congress, somewhat ambiguously, had recognized the right of the President to remove the Secretary of Foreign Affairs without its consent. Moreover, it was understandably reluctant to meddle in so "political" a question. On the few occasions the Court had spoken, it had construed liberally the President's removal power. In the Shurtleff case, in upholding President William McKinley's ouster of a minor official, the Court had stated: "The right of removal would exist if the statute had not contained a word upon the subject. It does not exist by virtue of the grant, but it inheres in the right to appoint, unless limited by Constitution or statute." Yet the Shurtleff opinion was open

44 *Congressional Record*, 73rd Cong., 2nd Sess., 1679–84.

45 The actual docket title was *Rathbun, Executor v. United States*. Some commentators refer to it as the Rathbun case, but it is more generally known as *Humphrey's Executor v. U.S.*

46 Wesley McCune, *The Nine Young Men* (New York: Harper, 1947), 61.

47 19 Stat. 80, 81 (1876), U.S. Comp. Stat. (1916) 7190.

to more than one interpretation, and the Court had still not defined the exact scope of the removal power.[48]

The Myers case, however, came to a court led by William Howard Taft, a Chief Justice who had no hesitation about intervening in matters that some previous courts would have shied away from. Stung by the many barbs flung at him by insurgent Congressmen during his term as president, Taft seized on this suit as a way to strike a blow for the authority of the Chief Executive. He quickly found that a majority of the justices shared his belief that Myers' ouster was a legitimate exercise of the President's power. But he was not content to confine himself to the issue at hand; he wished to define the widest possible latitude for the removal power. To this end, he called a rump meeting of the justices who supported him, and, to meet their objections, worked and reworked the draft of his opinion.[49] Not until a year and a half after arguments had been completed was Taft ready with his opinion. "I agree with you that we have not had a case in two generations of more importance," he told Justice Harlan Fiske Stone.[50]

On October 25, 1926, almost seven years after Myers had been ousted, the Court finally ruled on *Myers v. United States*. For a Court divided 6–3, Taft, in a sixty-one page opinion, sustained the decision of the Court of Claims. He ruled that the section of the act of 1876 requiring Senate concurrence in the removal of a postmaster was unconstitutional. Devoting almost half of his opinion to the "Legislative Decision of 1789," the Chief Justice claimed that there was ample historical precedent to support the view that the President's removal power was illimitable. Furthermore, he stated that the President's exclusive power of removal derived from his power to appoint and his obligation to execute the laws. Even more far-reaching was Taft's contention that this power was an inherent part of the executive power granted by Article II of the Constitution, and could not be circumscribed by Congress. All "executive officers of the United States" were subject to removal by the President at will.

Not content with enunciating this sweeping doctrine, the Chief Justice went out of his way to offer a brief obiter dictum which claimed that the President's removal power extended even to members of independent regulatory commissions. Taft stated:

> *There may be duties of a quasi-judicial character imposed on executive officers and members of executive tribunals whose decisions after hearing affect interests of individuals, the discharge of which the President cannot in a particular case properly influence or control. But even in such a*

[48] *Shurtleff* v. *United States*, 189 U.S. 311, 316–317 (1902). See, too, Ex parte Hennen, 13 Pet. 230, 258 (1839); *Parsons* v. *U.S.* 167 U.S. 324, 339 (1897); Carl Russell Fish, "Removal of Officials by the Presidents of the United States," *Annual Report of the American Historical Association: The Year 1899* (2 vols., Washington: Government Printing Office, 1900), I, 67–86.

[49] Alpheus Thomas Mason, *Harlan Fiske Stone* (New York: Viking, 1956), 222–31; Mason, *William Howard Taft: Chief Justice* (New York: Simon and Schuster, 1965), 225–55; Henry F. Pringle, *The Life and Times of William Howard Taft* (2 vols., Hamden, Conn.: Archon Books, 1964), II, 1023–27; Taft to Stone, n.d., Stone MSS, LC, Box 54.

[50] Taft to Stone, December 26, 1925, Stone MSS, Box 54.

case, he may consider the decision after its rendition as a reason for removing the officer, on the ground that the discretion regularly entrusted to that officer by statute has not been on the whole intelligently or wisely exercised. Otherwise, he does not discharge his own constitutional duty of seeing that the laws be faithfully executed.[51]

Taft, who prided himself on his ability to mass the Court, suffered the embarrassment of three separate dissents. Justice Oliver Wendell Holmes required only three paragraphs to state his disapproval of the "spiders' webs" the Chief Justice had woven. Affirming his belief in the authority of Congress, Holmes stated: "We have to deal with an office that owes its existence to Congress and that Congress may abolish tomorrow. Its duration and the pay attached to it while it lasts depend on Congress alone. . . ."[52]

The irascible Justice James C. McReynolds prepared a dissent which ran to sixty-two pages. Instead of reading it, he delivered an acrid extemporaneous speech from the bench as he was later to do in the gold clause cases.[53] As Mark Sullivan of the New York *Herald-Tribune* caught his remarks, McReynolds said: "The decision of the majority of the court is revolutionary, and the sooner the thinking people of the country understand it the better. Yesterday we supposed we had a government of definitely limited and specified powers. Today no one knows what those powers are."[54]

The most powerful dissent came from Justice Louis D. Brandeis. James M. Landis, who was Brandeis's law clerk at the time, later called the dissent "as thorough a piece of historical research as you would find in the Supreme Court reports anywhere."[55] . . .

A detailed, learned statement of his objections to Taft's arguments, Brandeis' dissenting opinion ran fifty-six pages. Embarrassed by its length, Brandeis offered to pay the cost of printing it, but Taft would not hear of it, although he deeply resented the opinion.[56] In his dissent, Brandeis disputed Taft's claim that the removal power was an inherent aspect of the authority of the Executive. Such power, he argued, came from Congress, and the Founding Fathers had opposed granting the President unlimited removal power. "The conviction prevailed then that the people must look to representative assemblies for protection of their liberties," Brandeis asserted. "And protection of the individual, even if he be an official, from arbitrary or capricious exercise of power was then believed to be

[51] 272 U.S. 135 (1926). James M. Landis has noted: "Some efforts were made to remove this unnecessary dictum but Taft was adamant." Landis, "Mr. Justice Brandeis: A Law Clerk's View," *Publication of the American Jewish Historical Society*, XLVI (June, 1957), 472. Authorities differ on the number of pages consumed by each opinion; I have followed the pagination in the *U.S. Reports*.

[52] 272 U.S. at 177.

[53] *Perry* v. *United States*, 294 U.S. 330 and other cases; an annotated version of his dissent in the gold clause cases may be found in the James McReynolds MSS, Alderman Library, University of Virginia, Charlottesville, Va. Taft wrote of McReynolds' performance in the Myers case: "His exhibition in the Court room was such as to disgust Holmes." Mason, *Taft*, 227.

[54] New York *Herald-Tribune*, October 26, 1926.

[55] James M. Landis, Columbia Oral History Collection, 37–39.

[56] Mason, *Taft*, 226. Taft observed: "Brandeis can not avoid writing an opinion in a way in which he wishes to spread himself, as if he were writing an article for the Harvard Law Review."

an essential of free government." Moreover, he pointed out, the principle of separation of powers had been adopted "not to promote efficiency, but to preclude the exercise of arbitrary power. The purpose was, not to avoid friction, but, by means of the inevitable friction incident to the distribution of the governmental powers among three departments, to save the people from autocracy."[57]

The Myers decision stirred up a storm. For the first time since the Insular Cases a quarter of a century earlier, a Supreme Court decision won front page coverage in the morning newspapers. Taft's opinion met a volley of criticism in the law reviews and from a political spectrum ranging from liberals like Robert M. La Follette, Jr., to conservatives such as George Wharton Pepper. Thomas Reed Powell found the logic "lame" the language "inconclusive," the history "far from compelling." Senator Hiram Johnson declared that the opinion gratified those who thought the country needed a Mussolini.[58]

So disturbed was the National Municipal League by the possible consequences of the Myers decision for local as well as national officials that it invited Edward S. Corwin, McCormick Professor of Jurisprudence at Princeton University, to write an analysis. Corwin's monograph, published in 1927, assailed Taft's logic and his handling of historical data. The Chief Justice's opinion, Corwin protested, "permits congress to vest duties in executive officers in the performance of which they are to exercise their own independent judgment; then it permits the president to guillotine such officers for exercising the very discretion which congress has the right to require of them!" The power of removal, Corwin concluded, should vary with the nature of the office.[59]

Such widespread criticism of the Myers opinion should have made Roosevelt more hesitant about ousting Humphrey. Apparently, Roosevelt never thought to get a legal opinion from Cummings. Yet it is also true that Cummings raised no objections. Moreover, Stevens, who had known the FTC from its infancy, advised that, on the basis of the Shurtleff and Myers opinions, Roosevelt could remove Humphrey for whatever reason he wished. He suggested to the President that, in removing Humphrey, he adopt the very language of McKinley's order dismissing Shurtleff, and the President's final order did follow closely the form of McKinley's edict.[60]

57 272 U.S. 240–295, especially at 293–295. The dissents, Stone wrote Taft, "have rather assumed that the people speak only through legislation, forgetting for the moment that the people spoke through the Constitution and the legislative branch, as well as other branches of the government, have only such powers as were conferred upon it by the Constitution." Stone to Taft, March 29, 1926, Stone MSS, Box 54.

58 Powell, "Spinning Out the Executive Power," *New Republic*, XLVIII (November 17, 1926), 369; *New York Times*, November 7, 16, 1926; Morton Keller, *In Defense of Yesterday* (New York: Coward-McCann, 1958), 181; George B. Galloway, "The Consequences of the Myers Decision," *American Law Review*, LXI (July–August, 1927), 481–508; James Hart, "Tenure of Office under the Constitution," *Johns Hopkins University Studies in Historical and Political Science*, Extra Volumes, New Series, No. 9 (Baltimore: The Johns Hopkins Press, 1930); George Wharton Pepper, *Family Quarrels* (New York: Baker, Voorhis, 1931), 124; Wilson K. Doyle, *Independent Commissions in the Federal Government* (Chapel Hill: University of North Carolina Press, 1939), 23–24.

59 Corwin, *The President's Removal Power under the Constitution* (New York: National Municipal League, 1927), 3.

60 Stevens to FDR, August 26, 1933, FDRL OF 100, Box 2.

There appeared to be good reason for Roosevelt, and for lieutenants like Stevens and Reed, to feel sanguine. If Taft's opinion had been raked over, it had also elicited considerable support.[61] Not only commentators who approved the opinion but some who deplored it stated that it was now the law of the land that FTC Commissioners were removable by the President at will.[62] A Chicago attorney, writing in the *American Political Science Review*, applauded the fact that the Court had recognized "the untrammeled control by the President of his subordinates, including . . . the Federal Trade Commission."[63] Furthermore, no amount of adverse commentary meant as much as the fact that only seven years had passed since a Chief Justice, supported by a majority of the justices, had offered such a drastic interpretation of the President's power and had, albeit in an obiter dictum, applied it to the specific problem at hand. . . .

On May 1, 1935, Solictor General Reed and Colonel Donovan came before the Supreme Court to argue the matter of Humphrey's claim. The case had been certified to the Supreme Court by the Court of Claims, which, instead of ruling, had posed two questions. Both centered on the provision of the FTC statute of 1914 which stipulated: "Any commissioner may be removed by the President for inefficiency, neglect of duty, or malfeasance in office."[64] The Court of Claims asked: Did this section limit the President's power to remove commissioners to one of these specific causes? If so, was such a limitation on the President's removal power constitutional?

The joust between Reed and Donovan took a predictable form. Reed claimed that the Myers and Shurtleff decisions offered sufficient precedent for the President's action. More than this, he reasoned that the duty to carry out faithfully such novel legislation as the Securities Act of 1933 "may presuppose wholehearted sympathy with the purposes and policy of the law, and energy and resourcefulness beyond that of the ordinarily efficient public servant. The President should be free to judge in what measure these qualities are possessed and to act upon that judgment." Donovan countered that *Shurtleff* was not relevant because it dealt with an official whose tenure had not been stipulated by statute, and that *Myers* was inapplicable because a postmaster belonged to a different category from a member of a regulatory commission, a type of agency whose independence must be safeguarded from executive domination.[65]

[61] Doyle, *Independent Commissions*, 24; *Illinois Law Review*, XXI (March, 1927), 733–36; *Oregon Law Review*, VI (February, 1927), 165–71; *Virginia Law Review*, XIII (December, 1926), 122–27; *Michigan Law Review*, XXV (January, 1927), 280–87. However, most of the commentators ignored Taft's dictum, and the *Michigan Law Review*, while supporting the Chief Justice's opinion, denied that members of the Federal Trade Commission were now "subject to the President's pleasures or caprice." *Loc. cit.*, at 287.

[62] *University of Cincinnati Law Review*, I (January, 1927), 74–79. Corwin, the chief critic of the decision, went so far as to state that laws like the FTC act were now "void." Corwin, *President's Removal Power*, 7. See, too, the discussion in Hart, "Tenure of Office," 369–73, taking off from *Springer et al.* v. *Philippine Islands*, 277 U.S. 189 (1928).

[63] Albert Langeluttig, " 'The Bearing of Myers v. United States Upon the Independence of Federal Administrative Tribunals'—A Criticism," *American Political Science Review*, XXIV (February, 1950), 65.

[64] Certificate from the Court of Claims, filed January 26, 1935, U.S. Briefs 1934, No. 405.

[65] Both arguments are printed in 295 U.S. 604–618 (1935).

On May 27, 1935, less than a month after argument, the Supreme Court gathered for the next to the last time in the old Senate chamber. That October it would reconvene in the marble edifice across the Capitol Plaza. Shortly after noon the nine black-robed justices filed in. Six of the nine judges who had taken part in the Myers case marched in the procession; in the interim, Charles Evans Hughes had replaced Chief Justice Taft; Owen Roberts had succeeded Edward Sanford; and Holmes's berth had been filled by Benjamin Cardozo. Without ceremony, they proceeded to read the day's decisions. First came Pierce Butler's opinion for the Court in an insignificant life insurance suit; as Butler read, spectators squirmed in their seats. They had come expecting more momentous events, and their boredom with this first opinion was unconcealed.[66]

Attention quickened as the Chief Justice nodded to Justice Sutherland, and Sutherland, in an indistinct murmur, began to read his fourteen-page opinion in the case of *Humphrey's Executor* v. *U.S.* For some minutes, as Sutherland recited the terms of the Federal Trade Commission Act, the thrust of his opinion was not apparent. In an orderly fashion, he dealt in turn with each of the questions posed by the Court of Claims. Did the FTC act restrict the power of a president to remove a commissioner except for cause? Of this, there could be little doubt. Nor was there any question at all that Roosevelt had not removed Humphrey for cause; instead of charging him with some dereliction like malfeasance, he had indiscreetly written that their minds had not gone along together.

The crucial question was the second one asked of the Court: Was the restriction on the President's removal power set forth in the FTC law valid? Here the Court came squarely up against the Myers precedent. Although Sutherland had joined in Taft's opinion, he now denied its relevance to the Humphrey matter. All that the Myers decision had settled, he said, was that a president could dismiss a postmaster, but "the office of a postmaster is so essentially unlike the office now involved that the decision in the Myers case cannot be accepted as controlling." But had not the Chief Justice said a good deal more than that in the Myers case? Sutherland stated blandly: "In the course of the opinion of the court, expressions occur which tend to sustain the government's contention, but these are beyond the point involved, and therefore, do not come within the rule of stare decisis. In so far as they are out of harmony with the views here set forth, these expressions are disapproved." Without ever joining issue with Taft directly, Sutherland noted that "dicta . . . may be followed if sufficiently persuasive but . . . are not controlling."

Sutherland then sought to explain how the office of a federal trade commissioner differed from that of a first-class postmaster. "A postmaster is an executive officer restricted to the performance of executive functions," Sutherland stated. "He is charged with no duty at all related to either legislative or judicial power." The Myers decision, he insisted, applied to "purely executive officers," not to "an officer who occupies no place in the executive department and who exercises no part of the executive power vested by the Constitution in the President."

Sutherland continued:

The Federal Trade Commission is an administrative body created by Con-

[66] Washington *Post*, May 28, 1935.

gress to carry into effect legislative policies. . . . Such a body cannot in any proper sense be characterized as an arm or eye of the executive. Its duties are performed without executive leave and . . . must be free from executive control. In administering the provisions of the statute . . . the commission acts in part quasi-legislatively and in part quasi-judicially. . . . To the extent that it exercises any executive function—as distinguished from executive power in the constitutional sense—it does so in the discharge and effectuation of its quasi-legislative or quasi-judicial powers, or as an agency of the legislative or judicial departments of the government.

After noting that if the President were conceded unlimited power to remove members of the FTC he would, in principle, be able to remove at will almost all civil officers, including judges of the Court of Claims, Sutherland declared:

We think it plain under the Constitution that illimitable power of removal is not possessed by the President in respect of officers of the character of those just named. The authority of Congress, in creating quasi-legislative or quasi-judicial agencies, to require them to act in discharge of their duties independently of executive control, cannot well be doubted; and that authority includes, as an appropriate incident, power to fix the period during which they shall continue, and to forbid their removal except for cause in the meantime.

The doctrine of illimitable power of removal, Sutherland contended, did violence to the principle of the separation of powers. "Its coercive influence," he observed, "threatens the independence of a commission, which is not only wholly disconnected from the executive department, but which . . . was created by Congress as a means of carrying into operation legislative and judicial powers, and as an agency of the legislative and judicial departments."

The President's power to remove, Sutherland concluded, hinged on the character of the office. The Myers decision, he reiterated, had been confined to "purely executive officers"; the decision in the pending case made clear that the President did not have unlimited power of removal over an officer like an FTC commissioner. He conceded that the Court might be leaving a "field of doubt" between the two rulings, but he added: "We leave such cases as may fall within it for future consideration and determination as they arise."[67]

Only when Sutherland ended his reading and no dissents were announced did the full import of the Court's decision become clear. By a unanimous 9–0 verdict, the Court had ruled that Roosevelt had exceeded his authority, and, by implication, it had instructed the Court of Claims to award Humphrey back pay. Sutherland had adroitly put together an opinion which caused a minimum of embarrassment for the Court, whatever other failings it might have had. There was not a suggestion in Sutherland's opinion that he, as well as three of his brethren—Van Devanter, Butler, and Stone—had gone along with Taft's sweeping opinion in the Myers case or that the President had grounds for believing that the Myers opinion represented the Court's view of the scope of his powers in 1933.[68] For Franklin Roosevelt, it was but the first of the rebuffs he would

[67] *Humphrey's Executor* v. *United States,* 295 U.S. 602 (1935).

[68] Joel Paschal, *Mr. Justice Sutherland* (Princeton: Princeton University Press, 1951), 184–85. It is possible that more than one of these men may have tried to

receive that afternoon. For Will Humphrey it was a posthumous triumph, the final victory the old warrior would ever win.

The "field of doubt" the Court had left was far more extensive than Sutherland suggested; no one has yet measured its metes and bounds. Even commentators who approved of the Humphrey decision found Sutherland's discussion of executive power confusing. Analysts familiar with the operation of the Federal Trade Commission were startled by his contention that an FTC Commissioner occupied "no place in the executive department." Nor could commissions like the FTC be categorized as "arms of Congress" in any meaningful sense, since they performed executive and judicial functions which Congress could not perform constitutionally. Moreover, as Robert E. Cushman has noted, "No task has been given to an independent regulatory commission which could not, with equal constitutional propriety, be given to an executive officer."[69]

E. S. Corwin, while generally in accord with the Humphrey verdict, has observed:

> *The truth is that some of Justice Sutherland's dicta are quite as extreme in one direction as some of Chief Justice Taft's dicta were in the opposite direction; and especially does he provoke wonderment by his assertion that a member of the Federal Trade Commission* "occupies no place in the executive department." . . . *The dictum seems to have been the product of hasty composition, for certainly it is not to be squared by any verbal legerdemain with more deliberate utterances of the same Justice. . . . Moreover, if a Federal Trade Commissioner is not in the executive department, where is he? In the legislative department; or is he, forsooth, in the uncomfortable halfway situation of Mahomet's coffin, suspended "'twixt Heaven and Earth?" . . . Nor is Justice Sutherland's endeavor to make out that* [*Federal Trade Commissioners*] *are any more "agents of Congress" than is a postmaster at all persuasive. Both officials get their powers—such as they are—from an exercise by Congress of its constitutionally delegated powers; there is no other possible source.*[70]

Subsequent decisions by the Court have failed to clarify Sutherland's distinction between an "executive officer" and one exercising "legislative or judicial power."[71] When, in 1938, Roosevelt fired Arthur E. Morgan, chairman of the Tennessee Valley Authority, the President was charged with exceeding his

---

persuade Taft to modify his opinion. Yet their objections were not strong enough for them to have filed a concurring opinion, let alone a dissent. The Court, it should be added, did not embrace the extreme view that the President's illimitable removal power is restricted to purely executive officers. McReynolds, who apparently believed the Court had not gone far enough, concurred in the Sutherland opinion but noted tersely that his dissent in Myers had stated "his views concerning the power of the President to remove appointees." 295 U.S. at 632.

[69] Cushman, *Independent Regulatory Commissions*, 450–51. See, too, *Columbia Law Review*, XXXV (June, 1935), 936–38; *Harvard Law Review*, XLIX (December, 1935), 330–31.

[70] Edward S. Corwin, *The President: Office and Powers 1787–1957* (New York: New York University Press, 1957), 93.

[71] Louis W. Koenig, *The Chief Executive* (New York: Harcourt, Brace & World, 1964), 159.

authority, since it was said that the TVA was not in the executive department.[72] The Circuit Court of Appeals, however, sustained the President in an opinion which held that the TVA was primarily an arm of the executive branch. The Supreme Court declined to hear the case.[73] On the other hand, when President Dwight D. Eisenhower removed a Truman appointee from the War Claims Commission, the Supreme Court ruled against the President and awarded back salary. It held that a president could not remove a member of a quasi-judicial agency without cause, even if Congress had not stipulated grounds for removal.[74]

The actual effect of the Humphrey doctrine has been much less than some commentators have implied. Although the Court has twice ordered restitution of back pay, it has never restored a man to his job. To attempt to do so might carry the Court farther into the "political" forest than it would like to venture.[75] Nor has the Court ever had occasion to inquire whether a president had sufficient grounds for removing a commissioner "for cause." What would happen if a president decided to get rid of a member of the FTC and, to avert another Humphrey decision, trumped up a cause of removal stipulated by statute? One commentator has stated that it was "almost certain" that the courts would not challenge a president's discretion in assigning causes of removal.[76] Another has agreed that terms like "inefficiency" were so vague that courts would acknowledge that a president had "considerable, if not complete" discretionary authority.[77] Should a president, in the future, decide to fire a commissioner, he will no doubt have learned from the Humphrey decision that he should be more subtle than Roosevelt was in going about it.

In ruling out any kind of role for the President in the functioning of independent commissions, Sutherland never troubled to look at the actual history of the FTC and similar tribunals. . . . Although Sutherland insisted that the FTC was a creature of Congress and must be kept independent of the Executive, Congress had, on more than one occasion, indicated its belief that the President had various kinds of authority over the commissions, and it had even scolded the President for their shortcomings. "In short," Cushman has written, "the commission was very definitely an agent of the executive branch and was recognized by Congress as being so." He summed up the situation at the time Roosevelt took office: "Throughout the discussions of this whole period there runs an underlying assumption that the commission's policy, if not actually directed from the White House, at least conforms to the President's wishes, that the President cannot escape responsibility for the commission's policy, and that an incoming

[72] For a statement of this view see Arthur Larson, "Has the President an Inherent Power of Removal of His Non-Executive Appointments?" *Tennessee Law Review*, XVI (March, 1940), 259–90.

[73] *Morgan* v. *Tennessee Valley Authority*, 115 F. 2d 990 (6th Circ. 1940); Cert. denied, 312 U.S. 701 (1941).

[74] *Wiener* v. *U.S.*, 357 U.S. 349 (1958); *George Washington Law Review*, XXVII (October, 1958), 129–32. The Court might have dealt with the removal power in the Lovett case, but it chose, instead, to invalidate the statute as a bill of attainder. *U.S.* v. *Lovett*, 328 U.S. 303 (1946). The Court has not yet found occasion to define the scope of the power of Congress to participate in removals, a matter that captured attention recently when some Congressmen threatened to compel Sargent Shriver to relinquish one of his two government posts.

[75] Corwin, *The President: Office and Powers*, 85–86.

[76] Patterson, *Presidential Government in the United States*, 153.

[77] Doyle, *Independent Commissions*, 30–31.

President objecting to such policy should change it, if not by the actual issuance of orders to the commission, at least by the making of suitable appointments." In removing Humphrey, Cushman concluded, "the President was apparently doing in this situation what Congress assumed that he would and should do."[78]

Although Congress was perceived to be one of the beneficiaries of the Humphrey ruling, it found the implications of the opinion perplexing. In 1938, when Congress faced the question of drafting legislation to regulate the aviation industry, Representative Clarence Lea explained the measure that he was sponsoring: "It is the belief of the committee that we have written a bill in harmony with the Humphrey decision. We limit the power of the President to remove the members of the authority. We leave him unlimited authority to remove the members of the safety board and the administrator, because those officers are manifestly executive officers, concerning whom the President has the right of removal." The new bill created within a single authority two executive agencies whose officers were subject to discretionary removal by the President while the authority itself remained independent of presidential control, although it could delegate some of its jurisdiction to an officer under presidential control. In this fashion, Congress believed it was abiding by Sutherland's distinctions. Yet, the matter remained confusing:

> MR. BOREN. *Under the Humphrey decision, the Federal Trade Commission is made an orphan child, so far as the three constitutional branches of the Government are concerned?*
>
> MR. HESTER. *That is correct.*[79]

Sutherland's conception of the separation of powers was mechanistic. He failed to recognize that there was no way in which the fused functions of the independent tribunals may easily be reconciled with the doctrine of the separation of powers. The Interstate Commerce Commission, for example, has been variously described as "an executive body," "wholly legislative," and "in essence a judicial tribunal."[80] Sutherland's opinion gave most comfort to those who thought of the three branches as warring sovereignties and who aligned themselves with Congress against the President. The Detroit *Free Press*, in criticizing the removal of Humphrey, had referred to Congress and "the rival establishment centered in the White House."[81] At no point did the Court consider how the branches actually work together to enable the government to function.

For those who believed that the commissions must be kept independent of "political control," the Humphrey decision was a thrilling triumph. One authority on the FTC wrote afterwards: "This signal victory brought incalculable prestige to the Commission."[82] In a confidential interview a month after the

[78] Cushman, *Independent Regulatory Commissions,* 222–26.

[79] *Ibid.,* 410–15. When the Humphrey opinion was delivered, Congress was in the process of enacting the Wagner labor bill. After the opinion, Congress modified the measure to stipulate that the National Labor Relations Board was to be an agent of Congress, not the President. *Ibid.,* 363–66.

[80] *Ibid.,* 418.

[81] *Congressional Record,* 73rd Cong., 2nd Sess., 1679.

[82] S. Chesterfield Oppenheim, "Federal Trade Commission Silver Anniversary Issue: Foreword," *George Washington Law Review,* VIII (January–February, 1940), 253.

decision, Brandeis, pleased by the outcome, warned that if such commissions could not exercise independent judgment, the country would be, in effect, a dictatorship. "What would happen to us if Huey Long were President and such a doctrine prevailed?" he asked.[83] "The real significance of the Humphrey doctrine," noted James M. Landis approvingly, lay "in its endorsement of administrative freedom of movement."[84] Yet others, equally devoted to democratic ideals, were dismayed by the decision. For those who wished modern government to be both effective and democratic, the clashing claims on behalf of independence on the one hand and party government and presidential leadership on the other raised some hard questions. It was these hard questions which Justice Sutherland and the Court never tried to answer.

Of the many misconceptions surrounding the Humphrey case, none is so striking as the misunderstanding of Franklin Roosevelt's aims. Many criticized the ouster as an attempt by the President to create another opportunity for patronage. Humphrey himself wrote Senator Dill: "The truth about it is that the action of the President is about the boldest act to restore the spoils system that has occurred since the days of Andrew Jackson."[85] Several weeks later, he protested to Senator Norris: "When I remember that during all the time I have been in this office, I have not written a political letter, or made a political speech, or made a political contribution . . . I feel exasperated that I should be removed for purely political reasons."[86] Humphrey's defenders repeatedly castigated Roosevelt for trying to "Tammanyize" the national government. "The deduction is a simple one, that Mr. Humphrey being a real Republican was therefore objectionable to the President," asserted Congressman Hooper. "If Mr. Hoover had removed a Democrat for *purely political reasons* from an office such as this, the country would have rung with denunciations."[87]

Those who attributed Roosevelt's removal of Humphrey to "political" motivations quite missed the point; the President fired Humphrey not because he was a Republican but because the obstreperous Commissioner might disrupt an important phase of the New Deal recovery program. At first glance, it appears surprising that Roosevelt would run the risk of ousting Humphrey when he already had enough vacancies on the FTC to control the agency. Yet Humphrey was an adamant conservative. When a friend, in jest, called him a "standpatter," he replied: "When I think of the 'brain trust,' the progressives and the other fanatics and reformers, I think the word 'standpatter' is a badge of distinction and honor."[88] It seemed highly likely that Humphrey, as the senior member of a commission which now had added duties under the National Industrial Recovery Act and the Securities Act, would create dissension within the government. To be sure, any new administration must tolerate the presence of holdovers in such tribunals. But Roosevelt's coming to power in the crisis of March, 1933, was no ordinary changing of the guard; if the New Deal did not

[83] A. T. Mason, *Brandeis: A Free Man's Life* (New York: Viking, 1946), 619.

[84] Landis, *The Administrative Process* (New Haven: Yale University Press, 1938), 115.

[85] Humphrey to C. C. Dill, August 18, 1933, Humphrey MSS, Box 1.

[86] Humphrey to Norris, October 4, 1933, *idem.*

[87] *Congressional Record,* 73d Cong., 2nd Sess., 1290–1291. Emphasis added.

[88] Humphrey to Jerry A. Mathews, September 22, 1933, Humphrey MSS, Box 1.

mark a "revolution" in American government, it did represent, in areas like regulation of Wall Street, a significant new departure. Roosevelt was unwilling to leave a man of the old order in charge of administering the legislation of the new order.

When the new President sought to rebuild the government to enable it to cope with the enormity of the Great Depression, he quickly recognized that the Federal Trade Commission cried for attention. If his administration was to have coherence, he could not permit the FTC to move in opposite directions from the National Recovery Administration in policies toward business. Furthermore, although it was no doubt a mistake to turn the administration of the Securities Act over to the FTC, once this had been done Roosevelt could not afford to maintain the fiction that the Commission was a tribunal which should be altogether "independent" of executive influence. . . .

The removal of Humphrey should be seen not as an isolated episode but as one encounter in Roosevelt's campaign to reshape the national government. When the President took office he found most of the commissions manned by men hostile to the New Deal. "We stood in the city of Washington on March 4th," Raymond Moley recalled, "like a handful of marauders in a hostile territory."[89] Pendleton Herring has explained:

> *When President Franklin D. Roosevelt embarked upon his plans for national recovery, he gathered into his hands every strand of authority that might lead toward his objectives. At the level of the presidential office, a greater degree of integration was introduced into the federal administrative organization than has ever been witnessed in peacetime experience. And the reach of the President did not falter before the independent commissions. The problems of these bodies were regarded as presidential responsibilities as well. The tasks of the Federal Trade Commission, the Tariff Commission, or the Interstate Commerce Commission could not be separated from the rehabilitation of trade and industry. Yet how could these establishments participate in a national recovery program and still remain administrative agencies? The President got around this difficulty in his characteristically adroit fashion. Placing his key men in the departments was a simple matter, but bringing the independent establishment within his control required more ingenuity. The judicial calm of the Interstate Commerce Commission was left undisturbed, but the most able and aggressive commissioner was created federal coordinator of transportation. The Tariff Commission was reduced to a harmless position through the passage of the reciprocal tariff act. The Radio Commission was abolished outright and a New Deal commission took its place. The President secured the resignation of Hoover's chairman of the Power Commission and added two appointees of his own.*[90]

The ouster of Humphrey represented only one step in this march of events.

For the rest of the decade, Roosevelt persisted in his determination to bring the independent regulatory tribunals under his control. As early as 1933, he had told Secretary of Commerce Daniel Roper: "I'd like to see all the independent

[89] Raymond Moley, *After Seven Years* (New York: Harper, 1939), 128.
[90] Herring, "Politics, Personalities and the Federal Trade Commission: II," 32–33.

commissions brought under the general supervision of Cabinet officers."[91] The multiplication of independent commissions, the Administration feared, would cripple the office of the president and seriously threaten the social objectives of the New Deal by making it harder to implement national policies. To deal with such problems, the President, early in 1936, set up a Committee on Administrative Management to prepare a plan for overhauling the machinery of the federal government. When it reported back Roosevelt expressed enthusiasm about most of its recommendations, but when he found that there was no concrete plan for the independent commissions, he inquired sourly: "Is that all you can say?"[92]

A month later he read a new draft, and this time he said, "I think that is grand."[93] In its report the Committee described tribunals like the FTC as constituting "a headless 'fourth branch' of the government, a haphazard deposit of irresponsible agencies and uncoordinated powers" which obstructed "effective over-all management of national administration." Noting the rapid proliferation of independent commissions, the Committee stated: "Every bit of executive and administrative authority which they enjoy means a relative weakening of the President, in whom, according to the Constitution, 'the executive Power shall be vested.' As they grow in number his stature is bound to diminish." To forestall this development the Committee proposed: "Any program to restore our constitutional idea of a fully coordinated Executive Branch responsible to the President must bring within the reach of that responsible control all work done by these independent commissions which is not judicial in nature."[94]

When the reorganization bill was introduced in Congress in 1937, it contained drastic provisions on the independent commissions. The measure authorized the President either to place these tribunals in a department or to abolish them outright. But Roosevelt's bill went down to defeat, in part because the independent commissions, as rival power centers, were able to rally opposition to it. The chairman of the Federal Trade Commission, for one, spoke out against permitting the President "to impair or thwart the functions of the Commission —perhaps even to render the Commission helpless."[95]

At the very same time that Roosevelt was attempting to push the reorganization bill through Congress in 1937, he was engaged in a not dissimilar struggle to win approval for his plan to "pack" the Supreme Court, a plan born in part out of his resentment at the Humphrey opinion.[96] Not only had the Court upheld the claim of Humphrey's estate for back pay, Rexford Tugwell has noted, but it "also—and this was the irritant—forbade future dismissals of the duly

[91] Richard Polenberg, *Reorganizing Roosevelt's Government* (Cambridge: Harvard University Press, 1966), 25.

[92] *Ibid.*, 20–21. The Humphrey decision proved to be a stumbling block for the reorganization plan, both during the drafting stage and in its subsequent travail in Congress. See Robert E. Cushman, "Independent Boards and Commissions and their Relation to the President," typescript, Charles Merriam MS., University of Chicago Library, Chicago, Illinois, Box 260; Memorandum from H. G. Moulton to Louis Brownlow, March 24, 1937, *idem.*

[93] *Ibid.*, 21.

[94] Corwin, *The President: Office and Powers*, 96–97.

[95] Polenberg, *Reorganizing Roosevelt's Government*, 44, 91. By 1938, the FTC was one of the agencies exempted from the provisions of the bill.

[96] For the relation of the two controversies, see the perceptive comments in Barry Karl, *Executive Reorganization and Reform in the New Deal* (Cambridge: Harvard University Press, 1963), 247–48.

appointed and confirmed members of such commissions. It seemed vital to Franklin that the executive powers extensively employed by these 'semi-judicial' agencies should not remain beyond presidential control."[97]

Roosevelt and his lieutenants believed that Sutherland had gone out of his way to chastise Roosevelt unfairly. Had the Court admitted that it was modifying the Myers opinion, and had it conceded that the President might have been acting in good faith in justifying his action by that earlier opinion, the Court's ruling in the Humphrey case would not have aroused so much animosity. Robert H. Jackson has written:

> *Within the Administration there was a profound feeling that the opinion of the Court was written with a design to give the impression that the President had flouted the Constitution, rather than that the Court had simply changed its mind within the past ten years. The decision could easily have forestalled this by recognizing the President's reliance on an opinion of Chief Justice Taft. But the decision contained no such gracious acknowledgment. What the Court had before declared to be a constitutional duty of the President had become in Mr. Roosevelt a constitutional offense.*

The Roosevelt circle thought that "the Court was applying to President Roosevelt rules different from those it had applied to his predecessors" and that there was a "touch of malice" in Sutherland's opinion.[98]

Of Roosevelt's anger at the opinion there could be no doubt. Secretary of the Interior Harold Ickes reported on the Cabinet meeting of June 4, 1935: "The President said he had made a mistake in not preferring charges. He had actual proof of malfeasance in office, but he didn't want to file such charges against Humphreys, believing as he did that he could get rid of him by milder methods."[99] Sutherland's objection to presidential supremacy in 1935 when he had accepted Taft's opinion in 1926 raised the suspicion that the main difference in the two cases lay less in their nature than in the fact that FDR was now in the White House. The Humphrey case helped persuade the President that, sooner or later, he would have to take bold action against a Court which, out of personal animus toward him, was determined to embarrass him and to destroy his program.[100] Jackson commented later: "I really think the decision that made Roosevelt madder at the Court than any other decision was that damn little case of *Humphrey's Executor* v. *United States*. The President thought they went out

[97] Rexford G. Tugwell, *The Democratic Roosevelt* (Garden City, New York: Doubleday, 1957), 393.

[98] Robert H. Jackson, *The Struggle for Judicial Supremacy* (New York: Alfred A. Knopf, 1941), 108–9. Not until Justice Felix Frankfurter's opinion in the Wiener case in 1958 did the Court admit that Roosevelt's assertion of authority had a basis in Taft's opinion. Walter F. Murphy, *Congress and the Court* (Chicago: University of Chicago Press, 1962), 279, n. 107.

[99] *The Secret Diary of Harold L. Ickes* (3 vols., New York: Simon and Schuster, 1954), I, 374. I have not attempted to correct the spelling of Humphrey's name in this and other quotations.

[100] Moley, *After Seven Years*, 301. Landis later observed: "In those early days of the New Deal, there were some decisions of the Supreme Court of the United States whose sole purpose was to embarrass the President of the United States." Landis, COHC, 39–41.

of their way to spite him personally and they were giving him a different kind of deal than they were giving Taft."[101]

Tugwell has suggested not only that Roosevelt's decision to curb the Court may have come from irritation at the Humphrey decision, but that it was Roosevelt's anger at that opinion which determined the character of the particular plan he submitted, a plan doomed to defeat. Tugwell observed:

> *If Franklin, who not only had a vivid sense of presidential prerogatives but who by election and reelection was the chosen leader of the American people, felt that the obstructions of the Court constituted an impertinent denial of his right to act as leader, there was certainly justification. It has been suggested that the Humphries case constituted an affront to the presidency. It may very well have been that case, even more than the other decisions of 1935, which provided the motive for the post-election attempt to humiliate the Court in turn; for of all the ways open to him, Franklin does seem to have chosen the one most upsetting to judicial dignity. And it was this more than anything else—more even than the attempt to reduce the judicial power—which created reaction of a violence he hardly anticipated. Most of those who wanted to eliminate the interferences of the Court with progress still had a deep concern for its dignity. Senators who were lawyers, particularly, found that in the end they could not condone such an affront as was proposed.*[102] . . .

When on February 5, 1937, Roosevelt precipitated the historic controversy over his plan to "pack" the Supreme Court, a number of his opponents traced the conflict back to the Humphrey decision. On the very next day, Representative Earl C. Michener, Michigan Republican, commented on Roosevelt's message:

> *The President used a lot of words and indulged in a lot of argument to tell Congress something the Congress already knew, to wit, that the President is convinced that if the mind of the Supreme Court, the mind of the Federal Trade Commission, as in the Humphrey case, or the mind of any other government agency does not run along with the President's mind, then the agency should be changed.*[103]

The following month Ray Lyman Wilbur, who had been Hoover's Secretary of the Interior, wrote a friend: "In my judgment you are quite right in going back to the Humphrey decision. That was the first knock-out blow from the Court and no doubt was an offense to the idea that the Tammany system could be made national."[104] To an audience in Washington that same month, Dr. Ed-

[101] Eugene C. Gerhart, *America's Advocate: Robert H. Jackson* (Indianapolis: Bobbs-Merrill, 1958), 99.

[102] Tugwell, *The Democratic Roosevelt,* 392. For an early statement by a leading constitutional historian in defense of the Court as the guardian of liberty, because of its decision in the Humphrey case, see *Chicago Tribune,* June 9, 1935, clipping, Andrews C. McLaughlin MS., University of Chicago.

[103] Flint (Mich.) *Journal,* February 7, 1937, clipping, Prentiss Brown Scrapbooks, St. Ignace, Michigan (privately held). I am indebted to Mr. Brown, formerly U.S. Senator from Michigan, for permitting me to borrow his scrapbooks and diaries.

[104] Ray Lyman Wilbur to Dr. Arthur Hill Daniels, March 15, 1937, Wilbur MSS, Stanford University, Stanford, California.

mund A. Walsh, S.J., Vice-President of Georgetown University, stated that future historians would trace the controversy between Roosevelt and the Court to the summary removal of Commissioner Humphrey. It was more important in triggering the dispute, he asserted, than the Schechter decision.[105]

Roosevelt, who had been frustrated by the Court in the Humphrey case and was to be rebuffed by Congress on the reorganization bill, met defeat on the Supreme Court measure, too. One reason for the setback was that many liberals who shared Roosevelt's annoyance at a Court which had invalidated so much social legislation did not agree with the President's conception of executive power, and as a consequence, they parted company with him in the Court fight. Tugwell has written:

> *They feared an indefinitely strengthened executive. They were highly sensitized to dictatorship by Hitler and Mussolini; and Franklin had shown signs, they thought, of suggestive impatience. Nevertheless, they . . . wanted . . . freedom for the legislative branch to regulate business in the interest of public welfare. They felt the same frustration that Franklin felt about the no man's land in which neither the federal nor the state governments could touch business enterprise. But they did not want, as Franklin did, to reconstitute the Court so that on no issue could it oppose the other branches. Decidedly, this was too much. They felt, for instance, that the Court was right in the matter of Humphries, which had so incensed Franklin.*[106]

From his first communication to Humphrey, Roosevelt had displayed that indifference to public sensitivity about unchecked presidential power that was to cause him so much grief in the court-packing scheme. If the President's critics were sanctimonious, Roosevelt himself was careless about quieting uneasiness about the vast power concentrated in his hands. The President's action in removing Humphrey was not an arbitrary deed but a rational attempt to enable the presidency to emerge as the central institution to cope with the problems of the twentieth-century world. But it did not seem to be—and that made all the difference.

105 Washington *Post*, March 6, 1937. One woman asked: "Is Mr. Roosevelt's venom due to the fact that the nine old men ruled against his injustice in dismissing William E. Humphrey?" Mrs. Barbour Walker to Hon. House of Congress, April 9, 1937, W. W. Ball MS., Duke University. See, too, Edward H. Neary to Josiah Bailey, n.d. [1937], Bailey MS., Supreme Court file, Duke University.

106 Tugwell, *The Democratic Roosevelt*, 400.

19

THE SOUTHERN AGRARIANS AND THE TENNESSEE VALLEY AUTHORITY

Edward Shapiro

The TVA is a major achievement of the New Deal. Created by Congress in 1933 to provide for the unified development of the entire Tennessee Valley, tangible results were soon evident in the construction of huge multipurpose dams on the Tennessee River and its tributaries, which joined the original dam at Muscle Shoals, Alabama, to provide for navigation, flood control, and power development. In addition the agency sought to further transform the valley by educating the farmers, reinvigorating the soil, and cooperating with other agencies in programs designed to improve the countryside. In most instances the agency and its work met with favorable response. Until the publication of the following article, it was generally assumed that the southern Agrarians, whose essays in I'll Take My Stand *bitterly denounced the ugliness of industrial society, were hostile to TVA. As Professor Shapiro reveals, this was not the case.*

Edward Shapiro teaches modern American and intellectual history at Seton Hall University. This article, which appeared in 1970, is his first publication.

Historians have generally misunderstood the attitude of the Southern Agrarians toward the Tennessee Valley Authority.[1] Donald Davidson, it is true, consistently

[1] Idus Newby, "The Southern Agrarians: A View After Thirty Years," *Agricultural History*, XXXVII (July 1963), 152–53; Thomas L. Connelly, "The Vanderbilt Agrarians: Time and Place in Southern Tradition," *Tennessee Historical Quarterly*, XXII (Mar. 1963), 28–29, 33. Historians and literary critics have usually described the Agrarians as nostalgic reactionaries. See Christopher Lasch, *The New Radicalism in America, 1889–1963: The Intellectual as a Social Type* (New York, 1965),

Source: *American Quarterly*, Vol. 22, No. 4 (1970), pp. 791–806.

opposed the Authority from the late 1930s on, but the five other Agrarians who expressed an opinion were generally favorable to the project and two of them were highly enthusiastic.[2] John Gould Fletcher called the TVA a "success," and desired a similar project for his native Arkansas. Frank L. Owsley described it as "a great venture in unified public works, planning, and 'pump priming' on a regional development basis." Allen Tate, although dubious about some aspects of the TVA, nevertheless contended that it was "a good thing." Herman C. Nixon asserted that the Authority represented "the most sympathetic use of outside money . . . on a large scale the South has ever known. . . . It is making it possible for more people to live with a little more convenience, security, and happiness in 'God's Valley.' " The Authority, he argued, "may be fairly called the strongest card in the New Deal. . . . The nation needs a series of the grand projects of the TVA type . . . but it seems fortunate that the eroded South became the scene of the first experiment." Henry Blue Kline even worked for the Authority for several years, and during this period wrote an important study on the effect of discriminatory railroad rates on southern industial development. After leaving the TVA, Kline joined the staff of the St. Louis *Post-Dispatch* where he wrote several editorials defending the TVA and favoring a Missouri Valley Authority modeled on it.[3]

---

p. 297; John Lincoln Stewart, *The Burden of Time: The Fugitives and Agrarians* (Princeton, 1965), chaps. 3, 4; Charles Rosenberg, "Insurrection," *New Yorker*, XL (Mar. 14, 1964), 169; Gay Wilson Allen, "Criterions for Criticism," *Saturday Review*, XLIX (June 11, 1966), 64–68; George Steiner, "Thought in a Green Shade," *Reporter*, XXXI (Dec. 31, 1964), 36; Wallace W. Douglas, "Deliberate Exiles: The Social Sources of Agrarian Poetics," *Aspects of American Literature*, ed. Richard M. Ludwig (Columbus, Ohio, 1962), pp. 277–300; Robert Gorham Davis, "The New Criticism and the Democratic Tradition," *American Scholar*, XIX (Winter 1950), 9–19; Alexander Karanikas, *Tillers of a Myth: Southern Agrarians as Social and Literary Critics* (Madison, Wis., 1966), *passim*; I have sharply criticized Karanikas' work in *Southern Humanities Review*, I (Summer 1967), 199–201. The most extreme view of the Agrarians as political reactionaries is that of James L. McDonald, who asserts that they "wanted to abolish the twentieth century, called for a return to the life of the antebellum South, and opposed all attempts at modernization." McDonald, "Reactionary Rebels: Agrarians in Defense of the South," *Midwest Quarterly*, X (Jan. 1969), 160. I have shown in my Harvard dissertation, "The American Distributists and the New Deal" (1968), that the Agrarians can be more accurately described as radical Populists than as reactionaries, and that they were closer in political outlook to a Borah than to a Talmadge.

[2] I have been unable to find any written evaluation of the TVA by Lyle H. Lanier, John Donald Wade, Andrew Nelson Lytle, John Crowe Ransom, Stark Young and Robert Penn Warren. Warren told me that he supported the TVA. Interview with Warren, Apr. 19, 1965.

[3] Fletcher to Donald Davidson, July 27, 1933, Davidson Papers (Vanderbilt University); Fletcher, *Arkansas* (Chapel Hill, N.C., 1947), p. 399; Owsley to Davidson, Aug. 5, 1933; Davidson Papers; Owsley, "Mr. Daniels Discovers the South," *Southern Review*, IV (Spring 1939), 670; Owsley, Oliver P. Chitwood and Herman C. Nixon, *A Short History of the American People* (New York, 1948), II, 634–35. Owsley wrote the section on the New Deal in this textbook. Frank L. Owsley Jr. notes that his father "believed that TVA had given much to the prosperity of the area and helped all of the people. With some reservations, he thought the program did much more good than harm." Owsley Jr. to Edward S. Shapiro, June 11, 1965; Chattanooga *Times*, Nov. 4, 1936; Nixon, *Forty Acres and Steel Mule* (Chapel Hill, N.C., 1938), pp. 80–81; Nixon, *Possum Trot: Rural Community, South* (Norman,

This support for the TVA grew logically out of the Agrarians' social and political thought and their analysis of the causes of the 1929 depression. The essence of Agrarian social thought was their belief that a society, if it was to be free and prosperous, must have a majority of its people owning productive property. The Agrarians hated modern large-scale industrialization because it centralized the ownership of property among a small percentage of the population and created an insecure and subservient proletariat. They also maintained that the class consciousness and bitter social and economic conflict accompanying industrialization were due to the transformation of the stable, conservative and propertied middle class into coupon clippers and wage slaves.[4]

The Agrarians further claimed that the economic centralization occurring under industrialism led to political centralization and autocratic control of the government either by the wealthy or by radicals. They emphasized that both plutocracy and socialism favored economic consolidation, centralized planning and the dispossession of the middle class. Socialism simply carried out the implications of large-scale corporate ownership to their logical conclusion by having the economy controlled by one gigantic public corporation instead of a few private leviathans. As Allen Tate wrote to Malcolm Cowley, "From my point of view . . . you and the other Marxians are not revolutionary enough: you want to keep capitalism with the capitalism left out." Only a program which looked to a return to the widespread ownership of property had a chance to overthrow capitalism and "create a decent society in terms of American history."[5]

Okla., 1941), pp. 152–53; Professor Don K. Price of Harvard's political science department worked with Kline in the TVA and believes that he was "a thorough convert to the TVA approach." Price to Shapiro, Apr. 7, 1965.

[4] John Crowe Ransom, "What Does the South Want?" *Who Owns America? A New Declaration of Independence*, eds. Herbert Agar and Allen Tate (Boston, 1936), pp. 83–84; Donald Davidson, "Agrarianism and Politics," *Review of Politics*, I (Apr. 1939), 121–23; Twelve Southerners, "Introduction; A Statement of Principles," *I'll Take My Stand: The South and the Agrarian Tradition* (New York, 1930), pp. xxii-xxv; Tate, "The Problem of the Unemployed: A Modest Proposal," *American Review*, I (May 1933), 143, 149; Tate, "Notes on Liberty and Property," *Who Owns America?*, pp. 80–93; Tate, "What Is a Traditional Society?" *American Review*, VII (Sept. 1936), 386–87. The Agrarians believed that Henry Ford, because of his assembly line and the regimentation of his employees, personified large-scale industrialization. See, for example, Donald Davidson's comments in John Tyree Fain, ed., *The Spyglass: Views and Reviews, 1924–1930* (Nashville, Tenn., 1963), pp. 235–38.

[5] Tate quoted by Daniel Aaron, *Writers on the Left: Episodes in American Literary Communism* (New York, 1961), pp. 352–53, 458; Davidson, "The Agrarians Today," *Shenandoah*, III (Autumn 1952), 17–18; Andrew Nelson Lytle, "The Backwoods Progression," *American Review*, I (Sept. 1933), 434; Owsley, "The Foundations of Democracy," *Who Owns America?*, p. 67; Henry Blue Kline, "Loophole for Monopoly," St. Louis *Post-Dispatch*, Jan. 25, 1946; Ransom, "Shall the South Follow the East and Go Industrial?" Institute for Citizenship, Emory University, *Proceedings of Fourth Annual Session*, Feb. 10–13, 1931 (Atlanta, Ga., 1931), p. 51; the Agrarians believed the liberal attempt to reform large-scale industrialism without extensive socialism was impossible. Government bureaucrats, according to John Crowe Ransom, would be unable to stop at a minimum of direction but "will call for regulations, . . . And the grand finale of regulation, the millennium itself of regulated industrialism, is Russian communism." Ransom quoted by Davidson, *Southern Writers in the Modern World* (Athens, Ga., 1958), p. 49. The Agrarians were so concerned over the threat of industrial communism that they almost entitled their 1930 symposium "Tracts Against Com-

The Agrarians blamed the 1929 depression on a gap between production and consumption resulting from the holding down of wages by monopoly capitalists and from the pro-big business policies of the government during the 1920s, especially the high protective tariff. Low wages and the tariff, they argued, had reduced the purchasing power of the working class, had forced the consumer to pay artificially high prices and had deprived farmers of foreign markets for their surplus products. This gap had been temporarily bridged in the 1920s by advertising which, according to Donald Davidson, by "persuading the people always to spend more than they have, and to want more than they get," offered "precisely the same temptations that Satan offered Christ." The 1929 depression was due, then, to economic imbalances caused by large-scale industrialism and its control of the government—an imbalance between workers and owners, an imbalance between agriculture and industry, and an imbalance between the rural South and West and the industrial Northeast.[6]

The struggle between the Northeast, the center of large-scale capitalism, and the decentralized and propertied societies of the West and South was, according to the Agrarians, the key to understanding America's post-revolutionary history. They praised Frederick Jackson Turner's emphasis on sectionalism, and they agreed with him that the most fundamental fissures in American life were along regional, rather than class, lines. The conflicts between Jefferson and Hamilton, Jackson and Biddle, the North and the South during the Civil War, and Bryan and McKinley were all aspects of this basic antagonism between the industrial and financial Northeast and the South and West with their farmers and small businessmen. "There is no other nation in the Western world," Davidson wrote, "in which sectional alignment on major questions so often occurs." Walter P. Webb's book *Divided We Stand: The Crisis of a Frontierless Democracy*, a work highly praised by the Agrarians, confirmed for them the importance of sectionalism. Webb dedicated the book to the "small businessmen of America" who were being slowly crushed by giant corporations. Webb argued that these corporations were the advance guard of an imperialistic and plutocratic northeastern capitalism determined to control the economies of the South and West and to destroy the "traditional principles of American democracy" which were dependent upon the widespread distribution of property. Wherever one went in the South and West, he would find "people in chains and paying tribute to someone in the North."[7]

---

munism." Rob Roy Purdy, ed., *Fugitives Reunion: Conversations at Vanderbilt, May 3–5, 1956* (Nashville, Tenn., 1959), p. 207.

[6] Fain, ed., *The Spyglass*, p. 238; Ransom, *God Without Thunder: An Unorthodox Defense of Orthodoxy* (New York, 1930), pp. 194–95; Ransom, "The State and the Land," *New Republic*, LXX (Feb. 17, 1932), 8–10; Lanier, "Big Business in the Property State," *Who Owns America?*, p. 22; Owsley, Chitwood, Nixon, *Short History . . .*, II, 605–7. For the emphasis which New Deal thought placed upon this concept of "imbalance," see William E. Leuchtenburg, *Franklin D. Roosevelt and the New Deal: 1932–1940* (New York, 1963), p. 35.

[7] Davidson, *The Attack on Leviathan: Regionalism and Nationalism in the United States* (Chapel Hill, N.C., 1938), pp. 24–25; Owsley, "The Foundations of Democracy," pp. 53–54; Lytle, "John Taylor and the Political Economy of Agriculture," *American Review*, III (Sept. 1934), 432; Lanier, "Mr. Dollard and Scientific Method," *Southern Review*, III (Spring 1938), 669–71; Fletcher, *The Two Frontiers: A Study in Historical Psychology* (New York, 1930), pp. 247–48; Robert Penn Warren, "The Second American Revolution," *Virginia Quarterly Re-*

As Southerners, the Agrarians were especially sensitive to the imperialistic and exploitative character of large-scale industrialism. The idea that the South was in economic thralldom to the capitalistic North was a staple of southern social thought and southern political rhetoric during the 1930s. For Davidson and the other Agrarians, the nature of the Northeast was "to devour, to exploit, to imperialize," to "walk in silk and satin," while the West and South went in "shoddy." They pointed to the taking over of southern banks, factories and national resources by Yankee capitalists during the late 19th century as illustrating the aggrandizing character of northern capitalism. They claimed that the New South movement, which had encouraged this invasion of northern capitalists, had merely benefited the northern worker and capitalist, while the South had been left impoverished and sucking at the "hind tit."[8]

The dominance of the financial-industrial plutocracy, the Agrarians believed, could be traced back to the southern defeat during the Civil War. They accepted the Beardian interpretation of the war as a struggle between an agrarian, conservative South and an industrial, imperialistic North which destroyed the last major barrier to the complete victory of large-scale capitalism. Fletcher wrote of Reconstruction as

> . . . the hour
> When Grant and Wall Street linked, began their work
> Which has not ended yet. . .

After 1865, the Northeast reduced the South and West to "the position of complaisant accomplices and servile dependents," and through the Republican Party enacted a program fostering big business, the centralization of finance, the proletarianization of the middle class and the destruction of agriculture. The Agrarians cited the protective tariff, the Supreme Court's interpretations of the Fifth and Fourteenth Amendments, and discriminatory railroad rates as examples of advantages acquired by northern capitalists because of their control of the national government. They blamed these subsidies and privileges for the postbellum growth of big business and high finance and the creation of "an economic fascism which threatens the essential democratic institutions of America." The Agrarians argued that the only way to check the economic imperialism of the Northeast was through a revival of regional sentiment in the South and West resulting in sectional economic self-determination.[9]

---

view, VII (Apr. 1931), 282–88; John Donald Wade, "Old Wine In a New Bottle," *Virginia Quarterly Review*, XI (Apr. 1935), 246; Webb, *Divided We Stand, The Crisis of a Frontierless Democracy* (New York, 1937), *passim*; for a typical Agrarian response to Webb's book, see Ransom, "The Unequal Sections," *Saturday Review of Literature*, XVII (Dec. 18, 1937), 6–7.

[8] George B. Tindall, "The 'Colonial Economy' and the Growth Psychology: The South in the 1930's," *South Atlantic Quarterly*, LXIV (Autumn 1965), 465–77; Davidson, *Attack on Leviathan*, pp. 110–15, 126, 262–92; Fletcher, *Life Is My Song* (New York, 1937), p. 374; Lytle, "The Hind Tit," *I'll Take My Stand*, pp. 202–3; Ransom, "Reconstructed But Unregenerate," *ibid.*, pp. 22–23.

[9] Fletcher, *South Star* (New York, 1941), p. 42; Lytle, "Principles of Secession," *Hound and Horn*, V (July–Sept. 1932), 688: Davidson, *Attack on Leviathan*, pp. 110–15; Davidson wrote in his history of the Tennessee River that during the Civil War hunting in the Tennessee Valley had greatly decreased and not since pioneer days had there been such a feast of "wild turkey, quail, deer, and fish of the river. This is the only undebatably 'good result' of the Civil War that any historian has

The urbanization of the United States dismayed the Agrarians as much as did industrialization. The anonymity, alienation, loneliness and regimentation of the modern American city contrasted sharply, they believed, with rural values and the rural way of life. In addition, they attributed the urban popularity of radical, anti-democratic political movements to the city's large proletariat and its lack of a large property-owning middle class. Davidson's poem "The Long Street" perhaps best reveals the Agrarian attitude toward the modern city.

> It was different, once, for Orestes Brown. He lived
> In the hill country where the bluegrass turns
> To upland fallows and tobacco barns,
> A land of no strangers. Orestes Brown had known
> Man, woman, child, both white and black, and called
> Folks by their first names from the Cumberland on
> To his own hearthside. But all that was before
> The family trouble that besets our race
> Drove him to wander through a kinless world
> Till he became a function and a number—
> Motorman Seventeen, on the company rolls—
> For whom, by singular principles of bondage,
> Man, woman, child, both white and black, we were turned
> To strangers all, who dropped their seven cents
> Into the cash-box, so becoming fares,
> Then sat or stood, nameless, till they got off.
> But he, Orestes Brown, was not content
> That people should go back and forth without
> The pleasure of a name between themselves
> And him; and in the fullness of his heart
> He broke the rules—he talked to sulky boys
> After the school and movies, or old men
> With hound-dog weariness in their eyes, or forms
> That had a country slouch about the shoulders.
> These last would sometimes talk; the rest, not often.
> . . . .
> But I knew how the Lord said long ago:

recorded." Davidson, *The Tennessee* (New York, 1948), II, 107–17; Warren, *The Legacy of the Civil War: Meditations on the Centennial* (New York, 1961), pp. 13, 42; Lanier, "Big Business in the Property State," p. 18; Kline, *Regional Freight Rates: Barrier to National Productiveness,* U. S. House of Representatives Document No. 137 (Washington: U. S. Government Printing Office, 1943); Owsley, "The Irrepressible Conflict," *I'll Take My Stand,* pp. 85–89; Fletcher, "Cultural Aspects of Regionalism," *Round Table on Regionalism,* Institute of Public Affairs, University of Virginia, July 9, 1931 (mimeographed, 1931), pp. 6–7; Tate to Seward Collins, Dec. 23, 1933, in Seward Collins Papers (Beinecke Library, Yale University). Indicative of the failure to understand the Agrarians is the comment of Thomas J. Pressley that the Agrarians were "individuals of quite conservative political and economic views" who could be contrasted with the followers of Beard and Parrington who "vigorously criticized the 'New South' spirit and program and insisted that the South's economic difficulties were due primarily to its status as an exploited 'colony' of Northeastern business interests." Pressley, *Americans Interpret Their Civil War* (Princeton, 1954), p. 241.

I have set my face against this city for evil!
And the Lord said: *It shall be given*
To the King of Babylon to burn with fire;
And desolate is Zion's mount where the foxes run![10]

The Agrarians pointed to the city's flashy and cosmopolitan artists as proof of its estrangement from traditional American culture. Truly American art, they proclaimed, could be produced only by artists rooted in a provincial and conservative society, such as the South, and not by deracinated and bohemian urbanites who prefer "sophistication over wisdom; experiment over tradition; technique over style; emancipation over morals." New York, "an island of transplanted Europeans anchored off the Atlantic coast," "a spectacular cosmopolitan city of borrowed culture," which attracted "all the celebrities and semi-celebrities of Europe into its orbit," exemplified the metropolis' alienation from the American hinterland.[11]

The Agrarians' emphasis on regionalism was not unique during the 1920s and 1930s. The art of Thomas Hart Benton, the regional sociology of Howard Odum and Rupert Vance at the University of North Carolina, and the establishment of regional historical journals such as the *New England Quarterly* (1928), the *Pacific Historical Review* (1932), the *Journal of Southern History* (1935) and the *Bulletin* of the American Association for State and Local History (1941) also reflected the increasing importance of regionalism during this period.

The return of America to a propertied, small town, rural society depended, the Agrarians asserted, upon a political coalition between the West and South. Only if these two sections put aside their differences dating from the Civil War and realized that their common enemy was now the Northeast could industrialism, urbanization and high finance be turned back. As John Crowe Ransom put it, both sections "desire to defend home, stability of life, the practice of leisure, and the natural enemy of both is the insidious industrial system." With

[10] Wade, "Of the Mean and Sure Estate," *Who Owns America?*, pp. 254–60; Ransom, *God Without Thunder: An Unorthodox Defense of Orthodoxy* (New York, 1930), p. 125; Davidson, *The Long Street: Poems* (Nashville, Tenn., 1961), pp. 64–66; see also Fletcher's poem "Twentieth Century" which described the modern metropolis with its "Pinnacles steeper than all Babels of the Past" and "wreathed with Manhattan mobs that will not rest." *Alcestis,* I (Apr. 1935), n.p.

[11] Davidson, *Attack on Leviathan*, pp. 68–100; Fletcher, *Life Is My Song*, p. 299; Fletcher, "Regionalism and Folk Art," *Southwest Review*, XIX (July 1934), 432–34; Fletcher, "The Stieglitz Spoof," *American Review*, IV (Mar. 1935), 589 ff.; Richard Crowder, "John Gould Fletcher as Cassandra," *South Atlantic Quarterly*, LII (Jan. 1953), 89–91; Tate, "A View of the Whole South," *American Review*, II (Feb. 1934), 416; Tate, "What Is a Traditional Society?" pp. 384–85; Warren, "Literature as a Symptom," *Who Owns America?*, pp. 264–79; Stark Young, "History and Mystery," *New Republic*, LXX (Feb. 28, 1932), 46. Davidson and Fletcher believed the Jew, particularly the New York Jew, embodied the materialism, commercialism, radicalism, deracination and cosmopolitanism characteristic of the city dweller. This led both to espouse a mild form of cultural anti-Semitism. Davidson to Seward Collins, Oct. 10, 1934, Collins Papers; Fletcher to Collins, Dec. 10, 1934; Jan. 18, 1935, Collins Papers; Fletcher to Frank L. Owsley, Dec. 12, 1933, in Owsley Papers (in possession of Mrs. Frank L. Owsley, Nashville, Tenn.); Shapiro, "American Distributists and the New Deal," pp. 66–68, 72–77.

the overthrow of the urban industrial-financial plutocracy, the nation's attention could then turn to the plight of the small businessman and the farmer.[12]

The condition of agriculture, particularly southern agriculture, greatly interested the Agrarians. Contrary to what Henry Steele Commager and others have written, most of the Agrarians did not idealize ante-bellum plantation life. Rather, they saw the small southern farmers as uniquely possessing such desirable agrarian virtues as economic independence, strong family ties and religious sentiment. The Agrarians were fully aware of the perilous condition of most small southern farmers. Widespread tenant farming and absentee-landlordism, they argued, had led to economic dependence, dispossession, extreme poverty, political demagoguery and a general atmosphere of hopelessness and degradation. They feared that, if something was not done immediately, the entire South would soon come to resemble one vast Tobacco Road. Davidson, politically the most "conservative" of all the Agrarians, bitterly complained of "Southern lands eroded and worn-out," "the devilish one-crop system and the tenant system," the "illiterate and diseased population" and "the fierce despair" and "terrifying apathy" found throughout the South.[13]

The belief that economic and political collectivism, urbanization and the decay of agriculture were not inevitable, and that the United States could once again become a nation dominated by small proprietors and farmers determined the Agrarians' approach to the problems of the 1930s. They claimed that the trend toward economic and demographic concentration, which had been artificially stimulated through political subsidies, could be reversed by means of electricity. Electricity, in contrast to steam power, could be transported cheaply over great distances, thereby enabling industry to move out of the metropolis and into rural areas. In addition, electricity could easily be adapted to small-scale manufacturing and agriculture, which would allow industry to decentralize and would improve the condition of farming. An intelligent use of electricity, the Agrarians contended, could foster a widespread distribution of property and help rectify the economic imbalance between the South and the West and the Northeast. The considerations uppermost in the minds of the Agrarians when they evaluated the electrification program and other aspects of the Tennessee Valley Authority were: would it inhibit the growth of large-scale industry and aid small business; would it help the South in its struggle with the industrial-

12 Ransom, "The South Defends Its Heritage," *Harper's Magazine*, CLIX (June 1929), 117; Lytle, "Hind Tit," p. 224.

13 See the essays by Lytle, "The Hind Tit," Wade, "The Life and Death of Cousin Lucius," and Kline, "William Remington: A Study in Individualism" in *I'll Take My Stand*; Nixon, *Forty Acres . . .*, pp. 17–27, 38–49; Fletcher, *Arkansas*, pp. 338–50; Davidson, *Attack on Leviathan*, p. 113. Owsley has been largely responsible for altering the image of the ante-bellum South as a land of slaves, planter aristocrats and poor whites. Using social science techniques, Owsley conclusively demonstrated that the social structure of the Old South was based upon "a massive body of plain folk . . . neither rich nor very poor," who were mostly small, independent farmers. Owsley, *Plain Folk of the Old South* (Baton Rouge, La., 1949), pp. vii, ix, 7. For a differing interpretation of the Agrarians which emphasizes their admiration for an aristocratic, stratified society, see Anne Ward Amacher, "Myths and Consequences: Calhoun and Some Nashville Agrarians," *South Atlantic Quarterly*, LIX (Spring 1960), 251–64, and Amacher, "Myths and Consequences: Allen Tate's and Some Other Vanderbilt Traditionalists' Images of Class and Race in the Old South" (Ph.D. diss., New York University, 1956).

financial oligarchy of the Northeast; would it encourage the decentralization of the metropolis; and would it improve the status of the southern farmer?[14]

The TVA, the Agrarians predicted, by providing "the means for a decentralization of productive wealth," would be "a solid contribution to the economic life of the Valley." They anticipated that the TVA's hydroelectric plants would enable the South to industrialize slowly without repeating the mistakes of northern industrialization. Because the South now had a source of power which could be used by small-scale, rural factories, there was no reason why southern industrialization need be accompanied by the urbanization, political centralization and proletarianization which had occurred in the North. And because southern manufacturing could remain small-scale, southern industrialists could probably secure necessary capital from southern sources without having to go to New York banks. Control of southern industries would remain in southern hands, industrial profits would stay in the South and could finance further economic development, and the South could begin to free herself from the grip of northern colonialism. Writing in 1943, Henry Blue Kline argued that the TVA had been "a very significant landmark" in the crusade for economic decentralization, and had fulfilled the expectations of the Agrarians.[15]

Herman C. Nixon was especially impressed by the activities of the TVA's Industrial Division in behalf of economic decentralization. This division encouraged small-scale manufacturing by inventing and demonstrating machines and methods of manufacturing suitable for small factories, by taking surveys and engaging in other research looking toward local production, and by teaching how the manufacture of goods could be domesticated. The TVA's creation of a series of navigable lakes and rivers and the establishment of several parks also encouraged Nixon. He reasoned that the future growth in the economy would be largely in service-oriented enterprises, such as recreation, rather than goods-producing industries, and that the TVA's rivers, lakes and parks, combined with the area's mild climate, could transform the Tennessee Valley into a prime tourist attraction. The growth of tourism would result in the establishment of countless small businesses, such as hotels and restaurants, and this would mean, in turn, an increase in the number of independent businessmen and a diffusion of property ownership.[16]

The Agrarians hoped that the TVA's electricity would also destroy the control of northern holding companies over the southern utility industry. These companies, they contended, had exploited the South through a policy of high prices and low consumption. Not only had the South been paying high electricity bills with the profits flowing north into Wall Street, but many areas of the rural South were without electricity because it had not been immediately

[14] Nixon, *Forty Acres . . .*, pp. 72, 77–78; Chattanooga *Times*, Nov. 4, 1936; Davidson, Review of *This Ugly Civilization*, by Ralph Borsodi, *American Review*, I (May 1933), 240–41.

[15] Chattanooga *Times*, Nov. 4, 1936; Nixon, "The South After the War," *Virginia Quarterly Review*, XX (Summer 1944), 323; Nixon, *Lower Piedmont Country* (New York, 1946), pp. 153–55; Owsley, Chitwood, Nixon, *Short History . . .*, II, 630–32; Kline, *Regional Freight Rates*, pp. 43–44.

[16] Nixon, *Possum Trot*, pp. 118, 152–53; Nixon, *The Tennessee Valley: A Recreation Domain*, Papers of the Institute of Research and Training in the Social Sciences, Vanderbilt University, Paper No. 9 (Nashville, Tenn., 1945), *passim*; Nixon, *Lower Piedmont Country*, pp. 228–29.

profitable to service them. Allen Tate, for one, held that southern economic independence from northern capitalistic control was absolutely dependent upon alternative sources of electrical power. The Agrarians' recognition of the effect of the northern holding companies upon southern economic development resulted in their support for the Public Utility Company Act of 1935, which aimed at breaking up the utility holding company empires. They anticipated that this act, by striking at northern control of southern power, would further encourage economic decentralization and promote southern economic independence.[17]

Kline's efforts while employed by the TVA to change the national railroad freight rate schedule reflected this emphasis on the need for regional economic independence. He believed these rates had discriminated in favor of the Northeast and against the South and West. Discriminatory freight rates, Kline stressed, hampered the industrialization of the South and West, forced these regions to concentrate on extractive industries and to neglect the more profitable fabricating industries, resulted in artificial economic concentration, and, by destroying free competition, inhibited national productivity.[18]

The TVA's electricity, the Agrarians predicted, would benefit the Valley's agriculture as well as its industry. They foresaw electrification of the southern farm lessening much of the monotony, drudgery and long hours of farm labor, thereby helping stem the rural migration to the city by making farming a more attractive occupation. The ownership of machinery by the individual farmer made possible by electrification would increase his standard of living and his economic independence. The farmer would now have the means to process many of his own crops, thus freeing him from dependence on exploitative middlemen. Electrification would also partially end the cultural isolation of farm life by enabling the farmer to enjoy the radio and to read by electric lights. Other aspects of the TVA which Nixon pointed to as beneficial to farmers were the resettling of farmers on more desirable land created as a result of irrigation projects, the establishing of demonstration farms to bring the latest farming techniques to Valley residents, the producing of cheap fertilizers, the developing of inexpensive farm machinery, the teaching of new methods of processing farm products, the investigating of new crops suitable for the Southeast, and the organizing of soil conservation programs. The TVA, Nixon wrote in 1938, "is the greatest movement in the South for modernizing agriculture, conserving rural manhood, and facilitating village development. It should prove a godsend to hill-

[17] Chattanooga *Times*, Nov. 4, 1936; interview with Warren, Apr. 19, 1965; Kline, "Utilities vs. Southwest," St. Louis *Post-Dispatch*, June 2, 1946; Kline, "Upholding Public Power Policy," *ibid.*, Aug. 25, 1949; Nixon, *Possum Trot*, pp. 152–53; Owsley, Chitwood, Nixon, *Short History . . .*, II, 626.

[18] Kline, *Regional Freight Rates, passim*; Kline, *Freight Rates: The Interregional Tariff Issue*, Papers of the Institute of Research and Training in the Social Sciences, Vanderbilt University, Paper No. 3 (Nashville, Tenn., 1942); Kline and Alvin W. Vogtle, *Freight Rates and the South*, *ibid.*, Paper No. 5 (1943); Kline, "As to Southern-Western Revolt," St. Louis *Post-Dispatch*, Dec. 1, 1946; for Nixon's support of the TVA's work in this area, see "The New Deal and the South," *Virginia Quarterly Review*, XIX (Summer 1943), 331; for a general study of the freight-rate issue, see Robert A. Lively, "The South and Freight Rates: Political Settlement of an Economic Argument," *Journal of Southern History*, XIV (Aug. 1948), 357–84.

billies." The Agrarians, as might be expected, also strongly supported the Rural Electrification Administration which aided farmers in establishing nonprofit electrical cooperatives in order to build power lines. The REA, they believed, would enhance the farmer's economic position and broaden his cultural outlook, and, by encouraging the decentralization of industry, would help restore economic balance to the nation.[19]

The major misgivings of the Agrarians regarding the TVA were sociological rather than economic. Some Agrarians suspected the TVA of endeavoring to uplift and modernize the inhabitants of the Valley. Allen Tate, for instance, although strongly in favor of the economic impact which the TVA was having in the Valley, nevertheless attacked it for its reformist spirit. "When the TVA tries to go into the mountains and change ways of living followed by the mountaineers for 150 years," he stated, "it is all wrong. It tries to make them play the radio instead of pitching horeshoes. They've been pitching horseshoes for 150 years and they ought to go right on pitching horseshoes." There were also fears that the TVA's newly created lakes were unnecessarily displacing large numbers of subsistence farmers. Nixon attempted to quiet such fears by claiming that the displacement of farmers had been done in such a manner as to disrupt life least, and that only "a small proportion" of the displaced families had been left stranded, dissatisfied and unadjusted. Both Nixon and Kline emphasized that the efforts of the TVA to work closely with the people of the Valley and through their local institutions indicated a democratic and decentralist orientation. For Kline, the TVA was an "experiment in applied democracy."[20]

Donald Davidson registered the only major dissent among the Agrarians regarding the TVA. Because Davidson wrote more about the TVA and over a longer period of time than the other Agrarians, historians have naturally assumed that his views were typical. Even Davidson, however, initially welcomed the TVA, and it wasn't until the mid-1930s, and especially after 1940, that he became critical. In 1940, he accepted a commission to write a two-volume history of the Tennessee River for the Rinehart Rivers of America series, and his work on these volumes deepened and clarified his earlier apprehensions.

In 1934, Davidson claimed that the TVA was an "ideal regional undertaking. It seems to promise a controlled and reasoned development of ways of life and institutions that are adapted to the soil wherein they grow. In principle, it is statesmanlike and highly imagined, and it naturally excites the interest and wins the support of most thinking Southerners." Despite this, Davidson feared the TVA might degenerate into an abstract attempt to reform the South. He warned there was a possibility of the South becoming a laboratory for the social experimentation of TVA bureaucrats and New Deal brain-trusters. He wished to know whether the TVA was "to continue indefinitely under the paternal wing of the

[19] Nixon to George Fort Milton, Aug. 2, 1934, Milton Papers (Library of Congress); Nixon, *Forty Acres . . .*, pp. 74, 80–81; Nixon, *Possum Trot*, pp. 112, 152–53; Ransom, "What Does the South Want?" p. 189; Kline, "Utilities Rampant Again," St. Louis *Post-Dispatch*, July 6, 1946.

[20] Chattanooga *Times*, Nov. 4, 1936; for a criticism of the TVA similar to Tate's by a friend of the Agrarians, see Richmond Croom Beatty, "Mountaineers Are Shakespearean," *Kenyon Review*, III (Winter 1941), 130; Nixon, *Possum Trot*, pp. 152–53; Nixon, "New Deal and the South," p. 322; Kline, "TVA's for Everybody Else?"; Kline, "Wrong Standard, Right Man," St. Louis *Post-Dispatch*, Oct. 29, 1946.

federal government, like some gigantic Berea College which distributed humanitarian benefits, but in an external missionary way; or whether it is finally to be integrated with the section of which it is a natural part." Although the heads of the TVA were capable, most of them were not Southerners, and this gave "color to the charge, already current, that the TVA is another Yankee raid into Southern territory." Despite these early misgivings, Davidson believed the TVA to be one of the more hopeful ventures of the New Deal.[21]

By 1936, however, Davidson's attitude toward the TVA had become decidedly negative. Although continuing to believe the TVA manifested a New Deal recognition of the reality of regionalism, he now argued that it was a regionalism which ignored the wishes of the South. The TVA was a foreign body, foisted upon an unwilling South by a distant political bureaucracy. As presently constituted, it was "an irresponsible projection of a planned, functional society into the midst of one of the most thoroughly democratic parts of the United States. It therefore does not guide us very far in our search for the right kind of regionalism." He proposed reforming the Authority so that the South would have effective control over it and could escape the manipulation of its "resources and population by a paternal . . . agency."[22]

Davidson, furthermore, predicted that the TVA would lead neither to the decentralization of property, nor to an increase in southern-owned businesses. The TVA was, in reality, a subsidy "to any migrating manufacturers who want to set up shop in the Tennessee Valley, and above all to the great monopolistic northern corporations which have a great many articles to sell to the Tennessee Valley people." There was nothing in the purpose or the operations of the Authority which insured that decentralized and southern-owned industries would be fostered. On the contrary, the TVA intended to open up the Valley "to a rush of Northern industry much as the old Indian Territory of Oklahoma was opened up . . . to rushing land speculators and homesteaders."[23]

The ultimate goals of the TVA were thus completely alien to the rural culture of the Tennessee Valley. The Authority, Davidson asserted, wished to replace an agrarian economy with industrialism. While industrialists and urbanites would benefit, most of the region's population would soon feel "the impact of an exploitative system." Davidson claimed that the TVA, properly understood, was simply another in the long line of subsidies handed out to northern industrialists since the Civil War. Evidence of this was the Authority's failure to do something about the South's colonial relationship with the North.[24]

The second volume of Davidson's history of the Tennessee River, published in 1948, brought these scattered criticisms together into an extremely bitter critique of the TVA. He declared that when Congress established the Authority in 1933 it had in mind such traditional governmental concerns as flood control and navigation; there was no thought of even having the TVA engage in com-

21 Davidson, "Where Regionalism and Sectionalism Meet," *Social Forces*, XIII (Oct. 1934), 25–27.

22 Davidson, "That This Nation May Endure: The Need for Political Regionalism," *Who Owns America?*, pp. 124–25; Davidson, "Regionalism as Social Science," *Southern Review*, III (Autumn 1937), 219–20.

23 Davidson, "On Being in Hock to the North," *Free America*, III (May 1939), 4.

24 Davidson, "Political Regionalism and Administrative Regionalism," *Annals of the American Academy of Political and Social Science*, CCVII (Jan. 1940), 138–43.

petition with private power companies. Nevertheless, the independence granted the Authority enabled TVA bureaucrats to transform it into an instrument for paternalistic uplift by utopian social scientists. It became another attempt to "civilize" the South, following in the footsteps of the Scopes trial and the Scottsboro case. If these bureaucrats "achieved good," Davidson remarked, "it would be the good that they and their staff of experts had pondered and blueprinted, not the good that might emerge from the various assemblies, nonexpert, discursively democratic, of the people of the valley."[25]

The displacement of farmers by the lakes created by the TVA exemplified the Authority's paternalistic outlook. Despite the extinguishing of hearth fires, the vanishing of old landmarks and the obliteration of old graveyards, the TVA juggernaut marched on. "There would be tears, and gnashing of teeth, and lawsuits," Davidson wrote. "There might even be feuds and bloodshed. Yet these harms . . . weighed less in the TVA scales than the benefits that would accrue, in terms of industrial and social engineering, to the nearby or the distant majority who sacrificed only tax money."[26]

Davidson believed there was a basic and irreconcilable conflict between the TVA's engineers and the farmers of the Valley. If the engineers had their way, the Valley farmer would soon become a cattle raiser, "enslaved to the aching compulsive teats of a herd of cows and to the trucks and price scale of Borden, Pet, Carnation," or he might become "a forester, a mountain guide, an operator of tourist homes and hot-dog stands, a tipped purveyor, and professional friend to tippling fishermen, hunters of ducks unlimited, abstracting artists, tired neurotics, and vacation seekers of all sorts." Davidson blamed the TVA's anti-agrarian bias for the decline of subsistence farming in the Valley and the transformation of many farmers into urban slum dwellers.[27]

Davidson's view of the TVA, despite what some historians have written, was not typical of the Agrarians. This failure to understand the politics of the Agrarians arises out of a belief that reform and liberalism since the 1930s have been a monopoly of the collectivistic left. When collectivistic and urban-oriented historians read that the Agrarians favored the widespread distribution of prop-

[25] Davidson, *The Tennessee*, II, 217–24. Davidson believed that David E. Lilienthal, one of the three TVA directors, was the prime example of a God-playing bureaucrat. For Henry Blue Kline, Herman C. Nixon and most students of the TVA, Lilienthal has been the symbol of the decentralist and democratic impulses within the Authority. Robert Drake wrote that when Davidson mentioned Lilienthal's name he made it sound "like it was one of the vilest words in the English language" ("Donald Davidson and the Ancient Mariner," *Vanderbilt Alumnus*, XLIX [Jan.–Feb. 1954], 21). Davidson fully agreed with President Eisenhower's comment that the TVA was "creeping socialism" ("Regionalism," *Collier's 1954 Year Book*, ed. William T. Couch [New York, 1954], 509); see also Davidson, Review of *Regionalism in America*, ed. Merrill Jensen, *American Literature*, XXIV (Mar. 1952), 95–96.

[26] Davidson, *Tennessee*, II, 236–38, 313.

[27] Davidson, *Tennessee*, II, 289–305; Davidson, "The Agrarians Today," *Shenandoah*, III (Autumn 1952), 20; Drake wrote that it broke Davidson's heart "to think a lot of scientists and sociologists were going to come in and try to make the Valley over again and 'improve it'—people that didn't give a damn about Andrew Jackson or anybody else." Drake, "Davidson and Ancient Mariner," p. 21; see also Louise Davis, "He Clings to Enduring Values," *Vanderbilt Alumnus*, XXXV (Oct.–Nov. 1949), 9.

erty, aid for rural America and the destruction of economic, political and demographic centralization, they immediately conclude that Agrarianism was, at best, "conservative," or, at worst an American version of lower-middle-class fascism. In truth, the Agrarians were anti-fascist as well as radical critics of the New Deal. When they criticized the New Deal it was for failing to move more vigorously against high finance and big business, and for neglecting the small businessman and the small farmer.[28]

For many American intellectuals the aspirations of rural and small-town America are irrelevant and atavistic. They praise cosmopolitanism and sophistication, and maintain that political and economic centralization and urbanization are inevitable tendencies from which stem the most important and valuable aspects of American culture. The danger of such beliefs is that they alienate the intellectual from the great majority of Americans who do not share his glorification of urbanization and collectivism, and from an America which is not destined to resemble New York, Chicago, Boston and San Francisco. When seen in these terms, the failure to understand the Agrarians, much less appreciate them, reflects the alienation of much of the American intellectual community from the values of their nation.[29]

[28] For Agrarian opposition to fascism, see Tate, "Fascism and the Southern Agrarians," *New Republic*, LXXXVII (May 27, 1936), 75; Davidson to Tate, May 27, 1936, Tate Papers (Princeton University); and Arthur M. Schlesinger Jr., *The Politics of Upheaval* (Boston, 1960), pp. 70–71. For Agrarian criticism of the New Deal for not being radical enough, see Nixon, *Forty Acres . . .* , pp. 56–60; Owsley, Chitwood, Nixon, *Short History . . .* , II, pp. 663–66; Davidson, "Mr. Babbitt at Philadelphia," *Southern Review*, VI (Spring 1941), 700; Tate, "How Are They Voting: IV," *New Republic*, LXXXVIII (Oct. 21, 1936), 304–5, and Review of *Pursuit of Happiness*, by Herbert Agar, *Free America*, II (Oct. 1938), 16–18; Warren, "Robert Penn Warren," *Twentieth Century Authors*, eds. Stanley Kunitz and Howard Haycraft (New York, 1942), p. 1477; Kline, "Mr. Harriman's Idea," St. Louis *Post-Dispatch*, Jan. 11, 1947; Lanier to Tate, Dec. 7, 1936, Tate Papers.

[29] For the overwhelming preference of Americans for small-town and farm life and their corresponding distaste for cities, see the report of a Gallup Poll in the *New York Times*, Feb. 19, 1970; for the refusal of America to become urbanized, see Daniel J. Elazar, "Are We a Nation of Cities?" *Public Interest*, No. 4 (Summer 1966), pp. 42–58.

20

THE CHICAGO MEMORIAL DAY INCIDENT: AN EPISODE OF MASS ACTION

Donald G. Sofchalk

The New Deal had a greater effect on American labor than on any other segment of the national economy. In March 1933 fewer than 3,000,000 workers belonged to labor unions; a decade later there were more than 12,000,000 organized workers, and their influence, which was almost nil in 1933, now was considerable. Even more important, workers in the great mass-production industries with considerable travail had been organized for the first time. And the new industrial unions, combined in the CIO, were forging ahead of the more traditional craft unions in the AF of L. Violence occurred as union organizers sought to recruit workers in mass-production industries. In the steel and automobile industries they tackled some of the largest and most powerful corporations in the nation. In the steel workers' attempt to organize a group collectively known as "Little Steel" (Bethlehem, Youngstown Sheet and Tube, Inland, and Republic) occurred the bloody clash in south Chicago on Memorial Day in 1937 described in this article.

Donald G. Sofchalk is a specialist in American labor history who has published several important articles in this field. He teaches at Mankato State College.

The 1930s was one of the most turbulent and sanguine periods in the history of American labor. Stirred to action by the depression, encouraged by the New Deal labor policy, and mobilized by the CIO, industrial workers and organizers pursued their struggle for collective bargaining rights with a new *élan*. In a widening series of organizing drives and strikes directed primarily toward union recognition,

Source: *Labor History*, Vol. 6, No. 1 (1965), pp. 3–43. Reprinted by permission of the author and publisher.

American unions utilized aggressive new tactics as well as the traditional ones. The sit-down strike, the stay-in, the flying squadron,[1] and the mass picket line came into use, often spontaneously, as expedients to soften up obdurate anti-union employers. Soon these daring devices were pragmatically adopted by many workers as normal weapons in labor's arsenal.

The dubious legality of such tactics, the risk of violence inherent in them, and the possibility of their arousing a hostile public reaction, did not deter the CIO from continuing to use them. On the contrary, by enlisting Communists and other radicals as cadre in organizing drives and strikes, the top leaders of the CIO tacitly approved the militancy of the rank and file. And many organizers were quite ready to promote forceful methods. One CIO firebrand, who tried to develop "strike strategy" into something akin to military strategy, declared that ". . . mass picketing is the surest road to victory." Even when it was not necessary to combat strikebreakers, he believed mass picketing was useful to sustain the strikers' morale. Another former organizer has recalled how he and his colleagues sometimes went to extremes, condoning the use of guns and "Molotov cocktails" by embattled strikers. (Such methods seemed justifiable when employers used guards who were thugs and criminals and who had few qualms about shooting workers.)[2] The older, more responsible CIO leaders were reluctant to call a halt to radicalism, for a more cautious approach might have lessened the enthusiasm and dynamism which were so important to the hectic organizing campaigns of the '30s. The consideration uppermost in the minds of the CIO leaders and their followers was that these tactics were successful.[3] . . .

The formative period of the CIO offers numerous examples of strikes and organizing campaigns won largely by virtue of militancy on the part of aroused workers. In the coal and coke region of southwestern Pennsylvania, thousands of striking miners, armed with pick handles roamed the countryside, attacking strikebreakers and barricading roads to make sure no coal was mined. In the face of this pressure and the refusal of Governor Pinchot to intervene, H. C. Frick Coke Company, a "captive" concern which had never before dealt with unions, recognized the United Mine Workers.[4] The efficacy of the sit-down technique was forcefully demonstrated during the famous General Motors strikes in the winter of 1936–37. Meanwhile, rubber, steel, and electrical workers engaged in mass picketing to extract concessions from their employers. It took throngs of parading strikers and their families only thirty-six hours to win exclusive bargaining rights for their new union from Jones and Laughlin Steel Corporation.[5] By 1937 mass

[1] A roving contingent available on short notice to bolster picket lines or combat strikebreakers. Used for a long time by Pennsylvania and West Virginia miners, it became popular among strikers generally for the first time in the 1930s.

[2] "The Industrial War," *Fortune*, XVI (November, 1937), p. 105; John Steuben, *Strike Strategy* (New York: 1950), pp. 101, 129, 130.

[3] Walter Galenson, *The CIO Challenge to the AFL, A History of the American Labor Movement, 1935–1941* (Cambridge: 1960), pp. 111, 157, 201–202; J. G. Rayback, *A History of American Labor* (New York: 1959), pp. 366–367; Louis Adamic, *My America, 1928–1938* (New York: 1938), pp. 409, 413, 424; *Nation's Business*, XXV, No. 4 (April, 1937), p. 125.

[4] Muriel S. Sheppard, *Closed by Day, The Story of Coal and Coke People* (Chapel Hill, 1947), pp. 122–148; M. Nelson McGeary, *Gifford Pinchot, Forester-Politician* (Princeton: 1960), pp. 378–381.

[5] Galenson, *op. cit.*, pp. 134 ff., 246, 269–277; Robert R. Brooks, *As Steel Goes . . . Unionism in a Basic Industry* (New Haven, 1940), *passim*. Mary H. Vorse

action in conjunction with able leadership had breached several of the strongest bastions of anti-unionism.

Although the mass picketing which became common in the '30s was often orderly and peaceful, it sometimes erupted into wild scenes of disorder and bloodshed. In some cases, the main responsibility lay with local CIO organizers, who were either unable or unwilling to keep strikers in check; in others, tension and strife resulted from the actions of employers intent upon resisting union demands whatever the consequences. Such employers, either failing to recognize the popular fervor behind the CIO movement or in open defiance of it, usually invoked the whole gamut of traditional strikebreaking techniques. This determination to meet force with force precipitated many of the outbursts of industrial violence which punctuated the labor scene of the decade. One of the most serious and disastrous of these outbursts, the Memorial Day "massacre," as it was popularly known, occurred during the Little Steel strike of 1937.

Refusal of the Little Steel companies—Bethlehem, Republic, Youngstown Sheet and Tube, and Inland—to sign a written contract with the Steel Workers Organizing Committee (SWOC) was, at least superficially, the cause of the strike.[6] Underlying this issue, however, were more basic considerations. For the Little Steel bloc, the strike seemed to afford an opportunity to stem the onrushing tide of industrial unionism, propelled by the successful General Motors strike and the contract between Big Steel and the CIO earlier in the year. To the CIO, the strike presented the first real challenge to its compaign of unionizing the entire steel industry, an aim crucial for the success of the drive to organize unorganized workers throughout the mass production and heavy industrial sectors of the economy. As the strike progressed, with the stakes high on both sides, neither displayed much disposition to compromise its original position.

On management's side, the commanding figure was Tom M. Girdler, the tenacious, outspoken chairman of Republic Steel. A long-time opponent of unions who had assumed the mantle of anti-union leadership recently discarded by the hierarchy of U. S. Steel, Girdler was quite willing to invoke all known strikebreaking devices in order to defeat the new steelworkers' union and, as he hoped, to smash the entire CIO. While Youngstown and Inland closed all of their plants when the walkout began in late May, Republic adopted a more aggressive strategy. Claiming that only a minority of its employees actually supported the strike, the corporation maintained several plants in partial or token operation. Provisions were made for housing nonstriking workers inside the mills, and large numbers of well-armed guards appeared at the gates. Republic officials also prevailed upon local law enforcement agencies to police picket lines stringently and to protect nonstrikers. The purpose of all these measures was to destroy the morale of the strikers and convince the public that the situation was not a strike at all, but rather a

---

wrote in the *New Republic*, LXXXXI (June 2, 1937), p. 91, that the UAW "achieved its success through some of the most remarkable demonstrations of mass action that this country has ever seen."

[6] For a more detailed history of the strike see the writer's unpublished dissertation, "The Little Steel Strike of 1937" (The Ohio State University, 1961). Galenson, *op. cit.*, pp. 97–109, has a good summary of the strike. Contemporary accounts are in Levinson, *Labor on the March* (New York, 1938); R. J. Walsh, *CIO, Industrial Unionism in Action* (New York: 1937); and U.S. Senate, *Labor Policies of Employers' Associations, Report No. 151*, 77 Cong., 1 sess., Part 4 (Washington: 1941), hereafter cited as *Senate Report No. 151*.

conspiracy by a small minority of troublemakers and "outside" union agitators to foist the "radical" and "irresponsible" CIO on the workers. Whatever justification there may have been for these actions, they were scarcely calculated to promote peace and good will on the picket lines. Indeed, there is some evidence that they were largely intended to antagonize the strikers and provoke violence.

In most of the affected steel communities, the strike began peacefully enough. In Youngstown, Ohio, one of the major centers of the walkout, there was even a kind of amiability between pickets and some plant guards in the first days of the strike; certainly, there were no significant disturbances. At Indiana Harbor, in East Chicago, the focal point of the strike in the Chicago area, workers voiced their intention of keeping the mill closed until they received a contract. They frequently engaged in mass picketing, but it was generally routine and orderly. East Chicago police did not interfere with the picket lines.

But at the South Chicago mill of the Republic Steel Corporation the situation was drastically different. There the management announced that since there were enough nonstriking employees to operate several departments the mill would not be closed. While estimates of the number of nonstrikers varied, at least one-third of the 2,500 workers normally employed did not join the walkout. Because of the vulnerability of their position, the strikers and their leaders were anxious to establish a strong picket line in order to prevent nonstrikers from entering the plant and to persuade those inside to come out. But from the beginning the plan was frustrated by the determination of Republic officials and the Chicago police to render the picketing ineffective.[7]

A few days before the strike several police officers had visited the plant and been informed by company officials of an impending walkout. The police did not bother to consult with any union officials before the strike. When on the afternoon of May 26 it became clear that a strike was going to occur, a large detachment of about fifty police, under a captain and several other officers, was rushed to the Republic plant with orders to "preserve the peace and protect life and property." The police set up temporary headquarters just inside the single plant gate, which they proceeded to guard.[8]

During the evening of the twenty-sixth a confused situation developed at the Republic plant. Although the walkout was not formally slated to begin until 11:00 P.M., many workers jumped the gun. By dusk a crowd of several hundred strikers and sympathizers was milling in the street in front of the gate. From time to time small groups of employees walked out the gate and joined the crowd. Meanwhile, a local SWOC official arrived and organized a regular picket line. Then some of the strikers, apparently aroused by the presence of police in the mill, began to jeer, calling them scabs and strikebreakers. At that point, a squad of police emerged from the gate, broke up the picket line, chased the crowd away, and arrested a score of people—including two minor union officials—on charges of unlawful assembly and disorderly conduct. Shortly thereafter a permanent detail of ninety-six police

[7] U.S. Senate Committee on Education and Labor, *Violations of Free Speech and Rights of Labor, Hearings*, 75 Cong., 1 sess., Part 14 (Washington: 1937), p. 4879, hereafter cited as LFC, with appropriate part; *The New York Times*, May 27, 1937, p. 2, hereafter cited as NYT; Chicago *Daily News*, May 27, 1937, p. 1.

[8] *Report of the Citizens Joint Commission of Inquiry on the South Chicago Memorial Day Incident* (Chicago: August 31, 1957), p. 4–5; LFC, Part 14, 4641, 4668, 4683, 5159.

was assigned to guard the plant.[9] Thus by the time the strike was originally supposed to begin, the picket line had been dispersed, the local leaders jailed, and the company assured of enough strikebreakers within its plant to maintain at least token production.

The next day, Thursday, police allowed a dozen strikers to picket some distance from the Republic gate. At strike headquarters hastily set up in Sam's Place—an abandoned tavern a half mile from the plant—about three hundred strikers assembled. Having read in the press that Mayor Edward Kelly approved of peaceful picketing, they decided to bolster the small picket force. But when the group advanced within two blocks of the plant, it was intercepted and turned back by the police who announced that mass picketing would not be tolerated.[10]

Thus the immediate cause of the trouble at the strikebound Republic plant was the question of what constituted permissible picketing.[11] . . . Each side had its own idea of a peaceful picket line. The Chicago police department, the agency immediately responsible for maintaining order, lacked a consistent policy. Shortly before the strike, the Corporation Counsel of Chicago had advised the department to "take no action to interfere with picketing when such picketing is conducted in a peaceable manner. If . . . relief is necessary, the action indicated is an appeal to the courts rather than to the Police Department, except if there is disorder or *clear* probability of disorder."[12] Presumably, then, it was not the function of the police to decide whether mass picketing as such was permissible or not. In accordance with this advice, Police Commissioner James P. Allman took the position that there was no necessity to limit the number of pickets as long as they were peaceful. But his immediate subordinate, the chief of the uniformed police, was of the opinion that there should be no more than one hundred pickets. Actually, these officials' opinions had little effect, for the legal number of pickets was determined by lesser police officers at the scene.[13]

Nor did niceties of law especially bother the strikers. As they saw it, peaceful picketing meant the right to have as many pickets as they felt the situation warranted. Lacking the cautious restraint of conservative or experienced unionists, they apparently saw nothing wrong in swarming onto picket lines. Moreover, there were compelling reasons for doing so. As the only Little Steel installation in

[9] LFC, Part 14, 4686–87, 4726, 4867, 4879–81, 5012; Chicago *Daily News*, May 27, 1937, p. 1; NYT, May 27, 1937, p. 2. Pierce Williams to Harry L. Hopkins, Memorandum on the Chicago Steel Strike, Selected Materials from the Papers of President Franklin D. Roosevelt Concerning Administration Policy toward Labor in the Steel Industry, 1933–38; hereafter cited as FDR Papers. Williams claimed Republic deliberately precipitated the walkout in order to disrupt union plans and to establish a force of nonstrikers inside the plant before the picketing could become effective. Although this view is plausible and consistent with the company's policy elsewhere, it is contradicted by other evidence which strongly suggests that the workers themselves made the strike premature Whatever caused it, the situation was promptly exploited by Republic. Cf. Citizens Commission of Inquiry, 5; affidavit of Emil Koch, Memorial Day File, SWOC District 31.

[10] LFC, Part 14, 4687, 4876, 4882; Chicago *Daily News*, May 27, 1937, p. 1, May 28, 1937, p. 10.

[11] Barbara Newell, *Chicago and the Labor Movement: Metropolitan Unionism in the 1930's* (Urbana: 1961), p. 139.

[12] LFC, Part 14, 5006, writer's italics.

[13] LFC, Part 14, 4643, 4669 ff., 4686, 4863, 4867; Chicago *Daily News*, May 29, 1937, p. 1; NYT, May 28, 1937, p. 10.

the Chicago area still operating, and as part of a firm known for its hostility to the CIO, Republic's South Chicago plant was the symbol of a singular defiance of the strike. Therefore the strikers and workers from other steel firms in the area were anxious to demonstrate their solidarity *vis à vis* Girdler's intransigence and make the strike complete by closing the plant. Mass picketing, then a common practice, offered the only immediate hope of achieving this.[14] Any qualms about such action were probably dispelled by the feeling that, after all, it was no more drastic than the sit-down strike which, though roundly condemned by many, seemingly had been approved by the President.[15]

The SWOC leaders' attitude toward mass action also had an important bearing on the behavior of the strikers. Neither the local rank-and-file leaders of the Republic lodge nor the officials of the Chicago Regional Office acted to discourage it, although they repeatedly urged the strikers to conduct themselves in a peaceful and orderly manner. By this policy the leadership averred that mass picketing was justified, charging that police interference was a denial of the right to strike and picket. As soon as he had learned of the pickets' dispersal by police on Wednesday evening, Van A. Bittner, the top SWOC official in the Chicago area, had wired President Roosevelt, charging "collusion" and "conspiracy" between Republic and the police to defeat the strike and demanding an investigation of the situation by the federal government.[16] . . .

By this time, some Chicago liberals, aroused by the police interference with picketing, were protesting to local and national officials in an effort to draw public attention to the strikers' situation. In an open letter of May 29, 1937, to Mayor Kelly, the Chicago Civil Liberties Committee accused the police of deliberately violating the strikers' rights to assemble and to picket. The Chicago chapter of the National Lawyers Guild, composed for the most part of young liberals, had quietly conducted a "preliminary investigation" of police policy toward picketing, and issued a report alleging that the police were "actively cooperating" with Republic in a strikebreaking campaign. Specifically, the report charged that:

> *The police under Captain Mooney . . . have imposed such arbitrary restrictions on the right to picket peacefully that this legal right has been virtually denied. . . . The police have been guilty of illegal and discriminating arrests of union members and sympathizers, and have accompanied the arrests with brutality. . . . The police* [*in the incidents of May 26 and 28*] *willfully used violence although no violence was necessary.* [*In conclusion*], *the lawlessness of the police in this case seems clearly to constitute not only a gross violation of Illinois constitutional and statutory rights but also a concerted attack upon rights granted by the National Labor Relations Act and the United States Constitution.*[17]

It is pertinent to note that since the attorneys involved in the investigation were

[14] LFC, Part 14, 4881, 4885; Chicago *Daily News*, May 29, 1937, p. 1; *Washington Post*, May 29, 1937, p. 1.

[15] Levinson, *op. cit.*, p. 183.

[16] LFC, Part 14, 4880 ff., 4917–18; NYT, May 28, 1937, p. 10; May 29, 1937, p. 1; May 30, 1937, p. 3.

[17] Chicago Civil Liberties Committee, Press Release, May 29, 1937; National Lawyers Guild, Chicago Chapter, Report of Sub-Committee on Activities of Law Enforcement Officers in Labor Disputes; The Chicago Police and the Republic Steel Strike.

not associated with the labor movement the Guild action was independent of the SWOC protests. The report was hurriedly drafted on Saturday afternoon, and copies were sent to the White House, the NLRB, the La Follette Committee, Mayor Kelly, and Van Bittner's office. Covering letters, signed by Alfred Kamin, Secretary of the Chicago Chapter, were dated May 30, 1937.[18]

Memorial Day, 1937, was a typical bright and warm Sunday in late spring. Approximately 1,500 people attended the meeting which was held in a field outside strike headquarters. On the whole, the crowd was a cross section of the industrial working population of South and East Chicago, which included many Slavs, Italians, Jews, and some Mexicans. In addition to Republic employees, there were a couple of hundred striking steelworkers from Indiana Harbor, a few sympathizers from the Carnegie-Illinois mills, and several unemployed workers. Also mingled in the crowd were a score or two of the steelworkers' wives and older children. A large proportion of the men were dressed up for the holiday, but many of them removed their coats as they stood in the sun listening to the speakers.

At 3:00 P.M. the meeting was called to order by Joe Weber, a young organizer who introduced the main speakers: Leo Krzycki, a veteran Amalgamated Clothing Workers leader with a Socialist background on loan to SWOC, and Nicholas Fontecchio, chief SWOC organizer for the Calumet district. Later there were to be sharp differences of opinion as to the exact tenor of the speakers' remarks—whether they were inflammatory or just the usual sort of thing that one might expect to hear at a CIO rally. According to several more or less neutral observers, the speakers—using a truck as a platform—extolled the CIO, denounced Republic's position, and castigated the Chicago police for interfering with picketing. In the course of his speech, Fontecchio contrasted the South Chicago situation with that in Indiana Harbor where, he pointed out, picketing was not restricted by the municipal authorities. When he finished, resolutions of protest addressed to the Governor of Illinois and the La Follette Civil Liberties Committee were adopted.[19]

Then, just as the meeting was about to break up, a man standing in the crowd moved that the strikers proceed to the Republic plant for a mass picketing demonstration. As soon as the motion was acknowledged by Weber and generally approved, several strikers with flags and placards took a position on the edge of the prairie which lay between Sam's Place and the plant. Gradually, over a period of ten to fifteen minutes, most of those who had attended the meeting, including several of the women and children, fell in behind the flag bearers to form an irregular column. That the march was not an entirely spontaneous affair was evidenced by the efficiency with which it was organized and the presence of a couple dozen

[18] Alfred Kamin to Van A. Bittner, May 30, 1937, enclosing Report of Subcommittee on Activities of Law Enforcement Officers . . . , General File, 1936–37, SWOC District 31; Professor Alfred A. Kamin to the writer, November 14, 1964.

[19] LFC, Part 14, 4852, *passim;* Part 15-D, 6853, 6913; Newell, *op. cit.*, p. 140; Milton Derber and Edwin Young, *Labor and the New Deal* (Madison: 1957), p. 104; NYT, May 31, 1937, p. 5; Meyer Levin, "Slaughter in Chicago," *Nation*, CXLIV, No. 24 (June 12, 1937), p. 670; affidavits of O. Bachman, C. Rock, F. Thompson, Memorial day File, SWOC District 31. A former SWOC officer who was at the Memorial Day affair has identified Joe Weber as a Communist; my informant has also maintained that Weber had no part in instigating violence. Philip Taft (*Organized Labor in American History* [New York: 1964], p. 620) assigns Weber a "provocative role in the Memorial Day Riot . . ." Cf. LFC, Part 14, 4917–20; Weber was on the SWOC payroll on May 30, 1937.

painted signs attached to boards. Yet such effusions and manifestations of union spirit were quite common at the time, and there would seem to have been nothing sinister or unusual about a demonstration, whether prearranged or otherwise, following a mass protest meeting.[20]

In the meantime, three hundred Chicago police were preparing to meet the marchers. According to the police officer in charge, Captain Mooney, they were under orders to prevent the strikers from breaking into the plant, the assumption being that this was the main objective of the march. The police were apparently instructed to thwart the anticipated assault without resort to their guns, unless absolutely necessary to defend themselves.[21] . . .

At the head of the procession, as it entered the prairie, two flag bearers marched. Behind them stretched a column of two or three hundred strikers, marching six to eight abreast, many of them carrying signs charging Republic with violations of the Wagner Act and urging the nonstrikers to "come out" and join the strike. Toward the rear and to both sides of the column sprawled a nondescript mass of several hundred people. Walking along without any semblance of order, they gave the formation a haphazard appearance. Many of them had come simply to be a part of the excitement or out of curiosity. Also scattered in the crowd were several persons not directly involved in the strike: a Hull House social worker, a novelist, an attorney from the Council for Social Action of the Congregational Churches, a minister, and four or five divinity students. But there were "others . . . strikers, who did not have a casual appearance at all." Some of these, perhaps fifty or one hundred, had picked up stones, tree branches, and pieces of scrap metal lying in the field. The majority of the marchers, however, either carried signs or walked empty-handed. As they moved across the prairie some of them sang a union song; others started to chant: CIO! CIO![22]

The leading strikers continued marching until they were within a yard or two of the police line which blocked their way. There they stopped, three hundred yards short of their destination. Many of the people to their rear now fanned out and moved up as close as possible to the police in order to better observe the situation. Thus the two groups—the police holding a line two and three deep, the demonstrators massed in a crowd—confronted each other along a two hundred foot front across the corner of the field.[23]

For a tense five or six minutes, two police captains, addressing themselves to the front ranks of the crowd, commanded it to disperse. But their voices were probably submerged in the terrific roar of hundreds of shouting strikers. The only intelligible sounds were piercing shouts of "picket, picket." There was no violence up to this point. Then, suddenly, from somewhere back in the crowd a club and several stones came hurtling through the air aimed at the right side of the police formation. At the same moment, even while the missiles were in the air, a policeman fired his revolver into the air and others threw two tear gas bombs. One of these landed in the left flank of the crowd, which immediately turned and began

[20] Levin, *loc. cit.*; LFC, Part 14, 4852, 4893, 4921; Part 15-D, 6853; the chairman of the strike committee claimed that it had "no part in organizing" the march, Memorial Day File, SWOC District 31.

[21] The testimony later given by police was so vague and contradictory that it is difficult to determine exactly what orders were issued.

[22] LFC, Part 14, *passim;* Part 15-D, pp. 6735–40; Levin, *loc. cit.*

[23] LFC, Part 14, pp. 4704–05, 4857, 5141, 5150–52.

to retreat. Many of the demonstrators on the right also turned as if to take flight. But before they could get away there was a sudden burst of police revolvers. Although it lasted only ten or fifteen seconds, the fusillade of police bullets mowed down several people in the front tier of marchers as well as many further back in the crowd. Five of them fell dead, and scores of wounded crumpled to the ground.[24]

The rest of the crowd, panicked by the blood, confusion and the billowing clouds of tear gas, tried to escape the scene as quickly as possible. By running back toward strike headquarters, most of them were able to evade the charging police—who had now substituted their clubs for revolvers. Some of the strikers, however, found all avenues of escape blocked—either by groups of converging police or by the heaps of dead and injured. Many of the police savagely attacked not only these strikers, but in several instances persons who had already been knocked to the ground.[25] One such attack was later described by a Congregational minister who witnessed the scene from the sidelines:

> *Trying to get across a ditch, the young man fleeing the police stumbled, falling on the other side, and in a moment both policemen were standing over him, taking turns at slugging him with their clubs as hard as they could. I did not count how many times they struck him, but it must have been at least six or eight times. . . . I was close enough to hear the terrible impact of each blow as it landed on his head.*[26]

Photographs testify to several similar attacks by the police, while their superior officers stood by calmly watching.

The treatment of the injured was, in general, no less frightful than the carnage itself. Although union members took care of some of the seriously wounded, the police took charge of the majority. These were dragged or carried to patrol wagons into which they were dumped indiscriminately along with the less seriously injured and about twenty uninjured persons rounded up by the police. It is fairly clear that one striker—shot in the leg—bled to death because of such treatment.[27]

As a direct result of the Memorial Day incident ten of the demonstrators died—six at the site of the encounter, four later in hospitals. The coroner's report

[24] LFC, Part 14, pp. 4858, 4890, 5133, 5137, 5140; Part 15-D, p. 6854; St. Louis *Post-Dispatch*, June 20, 1937, p. 3-C; Paramount Newsreel: "Conflict Between Police and Strikers Near the South Chicago Plant of the Republic Steel Corporation, Memorial Day, 1937," Copyright, 1937, National Archives; hereafter cited as Paramount Newsreel. The writer is indebted to the Motion Picture Branch of the National Archives for making their newsreel available. It is the best single item of evidence of the event. As it happened, however, the camera man was changing lens during the instant the conflict broke out, making it impossible to determine beyond reasonable doubt whether the police or the marchers precipitated the violence.

[25] LFC, Part 14, pp. 4858–60, 4926, 5134, 5142, 5154; Paramount Newsreel.

[26] St. Louis *Post-Dispatch*, June 20, 1937, p. 3-C; cf. LFC, Part 14, p. 4899. Howard Fast, in an account slightly garnished with fiction, relates that as they went about their deadly work "the cops squealed with excitement." Howard Fast, "An Occurrence at Republic Steel," Isabel Leighton (ed.), *The Aspirin Age 1919–1941* (New York: 1949).

[27] LFC, Part 14, pp. 4722, 5138, 5144; St. Louis *Post-Dispatch*, June 20, 1937, p. 3-C; Paramount Newsreel. It should be pointed out that a few of the police patrolmen rendered humane assistance to the wounded.

indicated that six had been shot in the back and one had been hit by four bullets. Thirty persons, including two women and an eleven-year-old boy, received nonfatal gunshot wounds, and twenty-eight others were hospitalized, mostly for head injuries. Sixteen policemen were injured, three seriously enough to require hospital treatment. The accident report on one of the latter revealed that "while dispatching reserve men to scene of riot, left leg was caught in middle upright of main gate."[28]

In trying to account for the brutal and unrestrained conduct of the police, it is pertinent to recall the record of strained relations between the workers and the radicals, on the one hand, and the Chicago police department, on the other, during the depression decade. In the early '30s, trouble usually accompanied demonstrations by the unemployed and the dispossessed, frequently led by Communist organizers who missed few chances to stir up strife. Such demonstrations and meetings "inevitably led to police intervention, swinging billies, and bleeding heads."[29] By 1933–34, as organized labor in Chicago became more active, there were also clashes between the police and trade unionists. Picket lines were broken up, sit-down strikers driven from the plants they had occupied, and charges of brutality and murder hurled back and forth by police and union leaders. An attorney representing the CIO later swore that, from the inception of the steel organizing drive in Chicago, strikers, pickets, and organizers had been subjected to "continual harassment" by the police. Whatever the validity of such specific charges, there is evidence enough to conclude that by 1937 many members of the Chicago police department believed it was open season on strikers and union organizers.[30] . . .

Thus the police attitude toward the strikers was a composite of hostility and fear. Given this attitude, plus the incompetency of their immediate superiors and the militancy of the strikers, it is not difficult to explain why the police acted as they did. Confronted by the milling, noisy demonstration, they were tense and uneasy. When a few of the more impetuous strikers resorted to minor violence, many of the police panicked, lost all sense of judgment, and without waiting for the tear gas to take effect, attacked the crowd with every weapon at their command.

The "Memorial Day" massacre, as the CIO immediately dubbed it, stirred up a furor in the Chicago area. SWOC leaders hurled serious accusations at the police and the city administration; the Kelly machine and the prosecuting attorney's office responded with countercharges against the union leadership. While the Chicago press praised the police department for crushing the "murderous mob" and stemming the "revolutionary" tide, liberal, labor, and church groups organized to demand an investigation of police conduct.[31]

The day after the clash in South Chicago, five thousand CIO strikers and sympathizers met at Indiana Harbor. Placards calling for industrial democracy and inscribed "In memory of Our Fallen Heroes of the Republic Steel Picket Line"

[28] LFC, Part 14, pp. 4998, 5092 ff.; Part 15-D, p. 6757 ff.

[29] Irving Bernstein, *The Lean Years, A History of the American Worker 1920–1933* (Boston: 1960), pp. 426–428.

[30] Newell, *op. cit.*, pp. 47, 51, 150; LFC, Part 14, p. 4821; Part 15-D, pp. 6750–51.

[31] Chicago *Daily Tribune*, June 1, 1937, p. 12; Chicago *Daily News*, June 2, 1937, p. 18; LFC, Part 15-D, pp. 6858, 6928–36.

were prominently displayed. Van A. Bittner, standing coatless alongside several bandaged strikers, eulogized the dead and wounded Memorial Day marchers as martyrs to the cause of labor and demanded indictment of the police for "first degree murder."[32]

At a conference called that evening by the Governor, Republic reiterated its refusal to sign a contract, even if an NLRB election showed a SWOC majority, and Bittner reaffirmed the union's determination to hold out indefinitely. The singular achievement of the conference was an informal—and rather belated—agreement by which Bittner assured that there would be no more trouble in South Chicago and the police commissioner promised to allow the strikers an unlimited number of pickets. But the following day the commissioner assigned additional men to duty—making a grand total of 900 policemen in the shift.[33]

Over the next few days Bittner and his aides maintained constant pressure on the Kelly administration. Among other things, they stepped up their campaign to enlist public sympathy for the dead and wounded strikers as "defenseless" victims of a conspiracy between a conscienceless management and a ruthless police department. . . . By June 2 a team of CIO attorneys, rushed to Chicago by the UMW, was busy gathering evidence as a basis for "demanding criminal prosecution of the guilty police."[34] Meanwhile, SWOC officers in the Chicago area were laying plans for an even more impressive project: a mass funeral and demonstration for some of the Memorial Day dead.

Although obviously staged by SWOC with the aid of several other CIO affiliates in Chicago, the mass funeral seems to have been a genuine display of working-class support for the striking Republic Steel employees. Two first-rate reporters—F. Raymond Daniell of *The New York Times* and E. A. Lahey of the Chicago *Daily News*—recorded the pathetic tableau. All day long "a single file of spectators shuffled past the five modest caskets" in the union hall. Most of those in attendance were workers. "They came in dusty overalls from the mills, and in clean overalls on their way to the mills, squat Croatians, sallow-skinned Poles, awed Negroes, bustling Nordics and phlegmatic Mexicans. Spacing them were tradesmen in shirt sleeves and housewives in summer prints." During the service, conducted in the afternoon, the "bodies of the dead were visible in the open coffins" to about 1,800 persons inside the hall. "An Ave Maria was sung by a contralto, and hymns were sung between the speeches. . . ." Bittner took occasion to castigate Republic officials and the police, likening them to Judas, for the "wanton murder" of the Memorial Day "martyrs." Outside in the street, which had been cordoned off by police, loudspeakers carried the service and speeches to several thousand mourners. Moving through the crowd were Communist activists hawking a special black-bordered edition of the Chicago *Daily Worker*.[35]

[32] NYT, June 1, 1937, p. 9; Chicago *Daily Tribune*, June 1, 1937, p. 1.

[33] NYT, June 1, 1937, p. 9; June 2, 1937, p. 10; Chicago *Daily News*, June 1, 1937, p. 1; June 2, 1937, p. 4; Chicago *Daily Tribune*, June 1, 1937, p. 1; LFC, Part 14, pp. 4673, 5165.

[34] Chicago *Daily News*, June 3, 1937, p. 4; NYT, June 2, 1937, p. 10; Chicago *Daily Tribune*, June 3, 1937, p. 4. On June 2, Philip Murray had wired Bittner expressing "almost indescribable horror" over the incident and pledging support from the national office for legal action against the police department. NYT, June 3, 1937, p. 16.

[35] NYT, June 2, 1937, p. 1; June 3, 1937, p. 16; June 4, 1937, p. 15; Chicago *Daily News*, June 3, 1937, pp. 9, 34.

Whether this union-sponsored demonstration aroused any general public concern about the "massacre" of the steelworkers is problematical; but a favorable reaction was clearly evidenced at a huge meeting in the Civic Opera House on the evening of June 8. It was called to consider the circumstances of the Memorial Day incident and the "breakdown of democratic processes in Chicago." Although leaders of organized labor were of course present, the primary impetus came from liberal and church groups interested in the rights of Chicago labor generally. Involved were the Citizens' Rights Committee (affiliated with the American Civil Liberties Union), the Citizens' Emergency Committee on Industrial Relations, the Chicago Church Federation (representing 1,000 churches), and the local chapter of the National Lawyers Guild. Also present were Paul Douglas, Carl Sandburg, Robert Morse Lovett, A. Philip Randolph—men who struggled to protect basic liberties in a city which, on the whole, did not value such things very highly. After hearing speeches (including one by the doughty Bittner), and eyewitness accounts from some of the strikers, the meeting adopted resolutions attributing the "murder" of the workers to "the unfitness of the police," urging the La Follette Committee to look into the Memorial Day incident, and establishing a Citizens' Joint Commission of Inquiry to investigate the "connection between the Chicago police and the Republic Steel Corporation."[36]

At the same time, inquiries of a different nature were undertaken by the police department and the state attorney's office, where a frantic effort was being made to build up a case that would completely absolve the police of all legal and moral responsibility for the Memorial Day killings. The crux of this case is that a bloodthirsty mob, whipped into wild fury by "outside" agitators and "Communists," had attacked the police, thus justifying their stringent action. In their attempt to create such a picture, the police received yeoman aid from the Chicago press, especially the *Daily Tribune*. . . . The *Daily News* was also certain that there would be no "difficulty in fixing the responsibility" for, after all, the strikers had been the assailants, the police the defenders, of the law.[37]

In the end, neither the accusations of the CIO nor the counteraccusations and indictments of the press and the municipal authorities proved very helpful in accurately assigning responsibility for the bloodshed. Certainly they accomplished little in the way of clarifying the immediate issues for the public. The charges assiduously built up by CIO attorneys to make the police department appear culpable were ultimately dropped; and the CIO vendetta with the Kelly machine soon began to subside, though not before the union forces obtained a *quid pro quo*. Signs of this appeared as early as June 6, when the Mayor, acting on grounds of a violation of a municipal ordinance, ordered Republic to stop housing nonstrikers in its South Chicago plant. Within a year of the Memorial Day affair the CIO supported Kelly in the Democratic primary in return for a promise of police neutrality. As for the question of whether the police were responsible for the Memorial Day deaths, a coroner's jury found, in July 1937, that the killing of ten marchers was an act of "justifiable homicide."[38]

[36] NYT, June 9, 1937, p. 1; Chicago *Daily News*, June 9, 1937, p. 3; *Senate Report No. 151;* Newell, *op. cit.*, p. 147; Robert M. Miller, *American Protestantism and Social Issues, 1919-1939* (Chapel Hill; 1958), p. 279.

[37] June 2, 1937, p. 18.

[38] NYT, June 7, 1937, p. 1; Newell, *op. cit.*, pp. 224–225; LFC, Part 14, p. 5166; Part 15-D, p. 6371 ff.

Nor were the assertions of the municipal authorities substantiated or sustained. In retrospect, the charge that the march was maliciously contrived by Communists and CIO troublemakers in order to disarm the police and take the mill, along with the argument that the police fired upon the strikers only in the line of duty and in self-defense, appear thoroughly transparent, if not patently absurd.

The insinuation that the march was inspired, organized, and led by Communists is simply not borne out by available facts. That some Communists were among the strikers, as was the case in many strikes of the 1930s, and that the party used the incident to smear the "capitalist exploiters" there can be little doubt. Yet close scrutiny of the records shows that of the fifteen marchers who the police claimed were Communists or closely associated with the party no more than five were actually party members or sympathizers. A case in point is George Patterson. Arrested as an agitator and branded by both police and the press as a Communist, he was, in fact, a long-time trade unionist, a registered Democrat, and a respected citizen. He has been reliably characterized as "a church deacon, Sunday school superintendent, and scout master . . . an upstanding member of his community." Finally, even granting that there were some radicals involved, there is no evidence that any of them were in a position to determine SWOC policy in Chicago or to influence substantially the nature of the Memorial Day demonstration.[39]

Similarly, charges that the strikers used firearms are contradicted by a number of facts and circumstances. For example, although sixty of the marchers were taken into custody and the field was combed by police after the encounter, no firearms were found. The fairly complete pictorial history of the incident also fails to show any of the marchers with firearms, although it does clearly show several policemen with revolvers in hand. This may account for the fact that no strikers were indicted for carrying concealed weapons or assault with a deadly weapon. When their cases finally came to trial in December 1937, fifty of the demonstrators were fined $10 each. All conspiracy charges were nol-prossed.[40] . . .

Before the La Follette Committee or any other reasonably objective investigatory body had had time to examine the details of Memorial Day, the press and the public generally had already reached their own conclusions. Some papers put all the blame for the incident squarely and exclusively on the strikers and their leaders. The Pittsburgh *Post-Gazette*, for example, had no doubt that the police "were simply discharging a fundamental duty of law. . . . In such cases the responsibility for bloodshed rests with those who started acting in a disorderly manner. By no stretch of the imagination can a mob armed with clubs and brickbats be accepted as peaceful picketing."[41] A more widely-held view was that, though the Chicago police might well have used more discretion and restraint, the strikers after all had challenged law and order and therefore had only themselves to blame for the death of their colleagues and the injury to their cause. The opinion of the Washington *Post* was typical. Granted that the attitudes and actions of Republic gave the strikers some provocation, "Violence is no cure for arbitrary conduct. . . . This ill-advised resort to force has put the union in an even more indefensible position than that assumed by the company."[42] A few influential editors did not comment

[39] LFC, Part 14, 4927–33, 5010; Newell, *op. cit.*, pp. 126–128.

[40] LFC, Part 14, pp. 4648, 4927–31, 5065–66; Part 15-D, pp. 6940–46.

[41] June 26, 1937, p. 6.

[42] Washington *Post*, June 1, 1937, p. 8; Cleveland *Plain Dealer*, June 1, 1937, p. 10; Youngstown *Vindicator*, June 1, 1937, p. 8.

specifically on the Chicago outbreak, but reserved their remarks for a sweeping denunciation of the "illegal methods" and "terroristic" tactics of the CIO in strikes and labor disputes generally. They further charged that at bottom the Roosevelt Administration was at fault, for while consciously increasing labor's powers, it was neglecting "to develop a sense of responsibility commensurate with these greater powers."[43]

Some editors refrained from trying to pass immediate judgment. The *Christian Century* felt that, in view of the fact that only strikers were shot, "apparently all the firearms were in the hands of the police, but it is not equally evident that a thousand strikers with clubs were intent solely upon parading to maintain their own morale." The *Commonweal* was not interested in assigning blame for the events in Chicago; rather it viewed the incident as symptomatic of a broader problem—the threat of general "class war." The opinion of this group of editors was best summed up by the *Christian Science Monitor* when that paper pointed out that "what happened at Chicago . . . may never be satisfactorily known," but that in any case the use of force rather than the provisions of the Wagner Act by either side was to be deplored.[44]

Not too surprisingly, the *New Republic* and the *Nation* rallied to the defense of the Memorial Day marchers. Writing in the former, George Soule found the police "criminally reckless" at the very least, and "T. R. B." called the incident a "massacre . . . as bloody and unforgivable as anything that happened in Ethiopia, or is happening in Spain." An editorial concluded that it was precisely the sort of result that could be expected from Tom Girdler's ruthless policy. The *Nation* was even less restrained in castigating Girdler—"a glorified company cop"—and the police—agents of "wanton brutality." It also accused him of violating the Byrnes Act, and suggested that "to put him in jail for two years would greatly improve industrial relations." At the same time that they held management culpable for the strife, these two liberal journals forthrightly approved of CIO militancy. The *New Republic* maintained that, while it would behoove labor to refrain from pointless acts of violence, mass-picket demonstrations were legitimate in order to display worker solidarity. The *Nation* observed that CIO leaders could force employers like Republic Steel to terms "only by economic action in the field —organization, education, strikes." As for the Wagner Act, it gave industrial workers a "fighting chance" for the first time, but in order to make something of that chance they would have to be ready to "fight."[45]

This defense of the militant approach to industrial organization contrasted with majority press opinion, which censured the CIO for aggressive policies and irresponsible actions. For no more than a handful of the leading newspapers and journals made a real defense of the Chicago steel strikers in the two weeks following their ill-fated march.

It was also indicative of the general trend of opinion that neither President Roosevelt nor the AFL leadership spoke out in defense of the strikers. In an effort

[43] New York *Herald Tribune*, June 7, 1937, p. 14; June 9, 1937, p. 20; NYT, June 9, 1937, p. 24.

[44] *Christian Century*, LIV, No. 24 (June 16, 1937), p. 763; *Christian Science Monitor*, June 4, 1937, p. 14; *Commonweal*, XXVI, No. 7 (June 11, 1937), p. 171.

[45] *New Republic*, LXXXXII, No. 1177 (June 23, 1937), pp. 176, 187; No. 1178 (June 30, 1937), p. 207; *Nation*, CXLIV, No. 23 (June 5, 1937), p. 634; No. 24 (June 12, 1937), p. 665; No. 25 (June 19, 1937), p. 692.

to get the President's support, CIO leaders cited the Chicago "massacre" as graphic proof of the need for administration intervention to offset the "high-handed" policy of Little Steel and prevent a recurrence of "wholesale murder." Fulminating against Republic and the "armed killers" of the Chicago police force, John L. Lewis insisted that "somewhere in this nation should be a force strong enough to bring these uniformed killers and their co-conspirators to justice."[46] Meanwhile, the White House was deluged with telegrams from SWOC locals in the Chicago area protesting the police attack and urging the President to force the companies to sign contracts. Studiously avoiding public comment on these appeals, Roosevelt simply referred them to Secretary Perkins and the National Labor Relations Board.[47] Nor was his first public utterance on the strike calculated to assure the strikers of presidential compassion. While expressing his belief that it was "just plain common sense" to put a wage agreement in writing—which the companies still steadfastly refused to do—Roosevelt did not show any intent to intervene on the strikers' behalf.[48] By this time CIO leaders could no longer avoid the distasteful conclusion that the President did not want to become personally involved, either by expressing sympathy for the Memorial Day dead or by taking more direct action.

The AFL's attitude reflected its traditional aversion to giving aid or comfort to striking industrial workers and the mounting bitterness between its top leaders and the CIO's. The rank and file of the Chicago Federation of Labor demanded that it support the struggling steelworkers and aid in the investigation of the police conduct, but John Fitzpatrick, head of the Federation, quickly squelched this. His action was all the more surprising since several AFL locals in Chicago had cooperated with the general plan of the CIO for organizing steel and packing-house workers into industrial unions.[49] As for William Green and the more conservative members of the executive council, apparently neither alarmed by the ability of labor's foes to attack workers with impunity nor moved by sympathy for the Memorial Day victims, they maintained a significant silence. Indeed, only a few days after the Chicago incident the executive council ordered the expulsion of all CIO members and locals from the Chicago Federation of Labor and the Central Trades Councils of Illinois. Later in June, when Green did express himself on industrial workers' strife, it was to put the blame for violence squarely on their leaders. "The riots, the reprisals, the violence and the deaths," Green declared, could be attributed to a single "evil influence . . . the C.I.O. leadership."[50]

In Congress, the general reaction to the steel strike and the Memorial Day

[46] *Steel Labor,* II, No. 10 (June 5, 1937); p. 1; Cleveland *Plain Dealer,* June 4, 1937, p. 1.

[47] U.S. Labor Department folder "Conciliation-Steel" in the National Archives, SWOC Lodge, Harvey, Illinois to White House; M. H. McIntyre to Secretary of Labor, Frances Perkins; SWOC Lodge, Chicago Heights to White House; NYT, June 7, 1937, p. 1; June 8, 1937, p. 1; Chicago *Daily News,* June 7, 1937, p. 3; *Christian Science Monitor,* June 8, 1937, p. 1.

[48] *The Public Papers and Addresses of Franklin D. Roosevelt, 1937 Volume, The Constitution Prevails,* ed. Samuel I. Rosenman (New York: 1941), 264; NYT, June 16, 1937, p. 1.

[49] Newell, *op. cit.,* pp. 184–185. That considerable local sympathy for the Memorial Day marchers existed was borne out by the formal denunciation of the police action by the annual meeting of the Illinois State Federation of Labor in the fall of 1937.

[50] *Ibid.; AFL Weekly News Service,* XXVII, No. 25 (June 19, 1937), p. 1; XXVII, No. 26 (June 26, 1937), p. 1.

incident was not unlike Green's, except for a strong inclination to put the ultimate blame on Franklin Roosevelt and Secretary of Labor Perkins. Southern Democrats were especially aroused by alleged "cringing" of the administration in the face of labor lawlessness. But conservatives of both parties were highly critical of the CIO's conduct of the strike and Roosevelt's hands-off policy. Increasingly, they made good use of these issues in what was fast shaping up as a full-scale assault on the whole range of New Deal domestic policies.

Many liberal politicians simply refrained from questioning the CIO's mass action strategy, while a few openly justified it. But even among those who had always sympathized with the CIO movement there were few explicit expressions of support for the Memorial Day marchers in the immediate aftermath of the event. To be sure, from the first a handful of liberals sided with the strikers. Senator La Follette's civil liberties subcommittee began looking into the circumstances of the clash as early as June 15, but formal hearings did not begin until the last day of the month. . . .

Public opinion, then, turned against the Chicago steel strikers. They—and especially their CIO leaders—were held largely responsible for the violence. As for the deaths and injuries, these occasioned surprisingly little concern or outrage. Nor was there much interest in looking beyond the strikers' overt action for possible underlying motives. The marchers were viewed not so much as ordinary workers with real grievances, but as unreasonable radicals bent upon forcing acceptance of their demands. Some editors felt that perhaps they were the dupes of CIO agitation. But it was generally agreed that, however unfortunate the injuries and loss of life among the rioters, such after all were the perils of resorting to mass militancy and defiance against lawful authority. Thus, although the CIO's attempt to make the Memorial Day dead martyrs to the cause of industrial democracy succeeded with Chicago liberals, it failed to touch a responsive chord in the nation at large. The decade's most spectacular single occurrence of industrial warfare—unsurpassed for its awesome circumstances and gruesome outcome—did not provoke any important indignation about the violation of workers' rights.

Such a reaction, at a time when the trend of opinion had been running in favor of labor, appears inexplicable. Yet there were several reasons for public apathy. For one, in the days following the incident the news media, for the most part, did not present a balanced account of what actually happened. Initial press reports featured the police version of the clash. Anyone reading the first Associated Press accounts, which appeared in papers across the country, could only have concluded that the rioters had started the melee by attacking a police line drawn up to keep the mob from breaking into the mill.[51] Several articles in *The New York Times* were of a similar tenor. For example, a "special" report of May 31, 1937, made the points that:

> *The strikers said they were going to march through the main gate entrance in an effort to force closing of the mill. . . .*
>
> *The union demonstrators were armed with clubs, slingshots, cranks and gearshift levers . . . bricks, steel bolts and other missiles. Police charged that some of them also carried firearms.*
>
> *The police said they stood their ground but made no effort to harm the*

[51] p. 1; Akron *Beacon Journal*, May 31, 1937, p. 1; NYT, May 31, 1937, p. 5.

> *invaders until showered with bricks and bolts. The police then used tear gas. When the rioters resorted to firearms, the police said, they were forced to draw their revolvers to protect themselves. Even then, the police declared, they fired into the air as a final warning.*[52]

The implication is clear: the police, in command of the situation throughout, merely resorted to progressively sterner measures to quell the rioters as they became increasingly aggressive.

A contrary version of the story was played up in the mass circulation press after mid-June. It first came to public notice after the Paramount newsreel of the Memorial Day clash—in disregard for the free flow of news—had been suppressed. This startling documentary—which recreates most of the encounter and provides incontrovertible proof of police culpability—was withheld from public viewing on grounds that it was too strong for ordinary audiences and might touch off "riotous demonstrations in theatres." Within a few days, however, the La Follette Committee learned of the film, subpoenaed a copy of it, and viewed it behind closed doors about June 10. At that point the public had still not seen the film.[53]

Then, on June 16, the St. Louis *Post-Dispatch* carried an article by reporter Paul Anderson, who had entree to the Committee, giving a vivid, detailed description of the newsreel. Anderson's account speaks for itself:

> *Without apparent warning, there is a terrific roar of pistol shots, and men in the front ranks of the marchers go down like grass before a scythe. . . . Instantly the police charge on the marchers. . . .*
>
> *Although . . . the mass of the marchers are in precipitate flight . . . a number of individuals . . . have remained behind, caught in the midst of the charging police.*
>
> *In a manner which is appallingly businesslike, groups of policemen close in on these isolated individuals. . . .*
>
> *In several instances, from two to four policemen are seen beating one man. One strikes him horizontally across the face, using his club as he would a baseball bat. Another crashes it down on top of his head, and still another is hitting him across the back. . . .*
>
> *The scene shifts to the patrol wagons in the rear. Men with bloody heads, bloody faces, bloody shirts, are being loaded in. . . .*
>
> *There is continuous talking, but it is difficult to distinguish anything with one exception—out of the babble there arises this clear and distinct ejaculation: God Almighty.*

[52] May 31, 1937, p. 1.

[53] Paul H. Douglas was instrumental in bringing the film to the attention of the La Follette Committee. Learning of the film's existence, he urged Paramount Pictures, Inc. to release it. The film's editor replied: "Our pictures depict a tense and nerve-racking episode which in certain sections of the country might well incite local riot and perhaps riotous demonstrations in theatres, leading to further casualties. For these reasons . . . the pictures are shelved and so far as we are concerned will stay shelved. We act under editorial rights of withholding from the screen pictures not fit to be seen." NYT, June 8, 1937, p. 8; *Time Magazine*, XXIX, No. 26 (June 28, 1937), p. 13.

The scene shifts back to the central scene. . . . A policeman, somewhat disheveled, his coat open, a scowl on his face, approaches another who is standing in front of the camera. He is sweaty and tired. He says something indistinguishable. Then his face breaks into a sudden grin, he makes motions dusting off his hands and strides away. The film ends.[54]

The failure of such a version to gain currency immediately after the event, and of Paramount to release its newsreel, helped shape hostile public opinion. So did other events of the steel strike which diverted public attention. Strife erupted in several steel towns during the first half of June. At Republic's Warren, Ohio, plant, which had been sealed off by a cordon of picket posts, irate strikers fired at company planes flying in food for nonstrikers. In nearby Youngstown, strikers rioted as steel companies ran food through picket lines. On June 10, at a small Republic installation in Monroe, Michigan, deputies and vigilantes broke up the picket line and manhandled strikers; CIO auto and glass workers from Michigan and Ohio staged a huge protest rally outside the besieged city. Beginning on June 14, Johnstown, Pennsylvania, also experienced violence, as Bethlehem strikers and nonstrikers clashed in the streets. When the mayor and a citizens' committee organized a back-to-work drive, John L. Lewis countered by shutting down several captive mines, and miners from nearby coal towns threatened to invade the city en masse to bolster the steelworkers' picket lines. Although none of these incidents were as serious as Memorial Day, they were given just as much press coverage. The Monroe situation, for example, was featured as front page, headline news in papers across the country.[55] In part this publicity was the result of a subtly-executed campaign by Republic Steel. But it also reflected an unmistakable trend of public opinion.

Appearing first as a kind of malaise at the time of the General Motors sit-down strikes in the winter of 1936–37, public concern about the labor scene mounted during the spring and came to a climax in the summer of the Little Steel strike. It manifested itself most clearly as increasing hostility toward the great CIO organizing drives and apprehension over the accompanying strikes—which soon reached a record peak. For those who had vehemently opposed industrial unionism all along, the situation seemed to bear out their warnings that the CIO offensive would have the direst consequences. Of greatest significance, however, was the more widely-held view that industrial workers and CIO trade unionists had displayed an utter lack of responsibility by their abuse of the rights and opportunities provided them by the Wagner Act. While Arthur Krock likened CIO picketing to "banditry" and Congressman Claire Hoffman (Michigan) castigated Lewis and his "lawless creatures of revolution" for fomenting communism in Detroit, the *Christian Science Monitor* expressed the essence of moderate opinion in an editorial of June 11, 1937:

"That's not right. Those fellows are going too far." Many times in the last

[54] Cf. NYT, July 3, 1937, p. 5; see also the St. Louis *Post-Dispatch*, Sunday, June 20, 1937, in which an entire section was given over to an account of Memorial Day based on the film and theretofore unpublicized eye-witness accounts.

[55] For detailed accounts of these incidents see Sofchalk, op. *cit.*, pp. 155, 190, 208–222, 233–234, 245, 262; *Senate Report No. 151*, *passim*; even the outbreaks in Michigan and Ohio were reported in great detail by *The New York Times* and other metropolitan papers.

few days news from the labor front has provoked that spontaneous judgment from laymen. Such comments are coming from men who have had much sympathy with the general effort of American workers to win better conditions and a larger share of the national income. But they have revolted against the recent excesses and arrogances of union labor.

From other information that comes to us, including some reflecting similar attitude gathered by agencies which poll popular opinion, we believe . . . the American public is reaching decisions which unions may well take into account. . . . the volunteering of citizens at Monroe . . . and the wide public disapproval of the Post Office refusal to deliver food to workers . . . are only two of the most recent indications that the people will put limits on the power of organized labor.

Militancy and mass action—the sit-down strikes, the wildcat walkouts, the unruly picket lines, the besieged steel plants, the invasions of industrial towns, the disregard for the rights of nonstrikers, resulting in vigilantism and bloodshed—all these, it was felt, were the consequence of a governmental labor policy which had permitted labor to overstep the bounds of legal procedure and peaceful protest in seeking more than was rightfully due it. The initial reports of the Memorial Day strife and news of other steel strike incidents seemed to confirm the current estimate of the CIO, the alleged recklessness of its leadership, and the responsibility of the rank and file for industrial warfare.[56] . . .

And it was shared by the President, for Roosevelt, whom many had supposed to be a champion of industrial labor, revealed a surprising lack of enthusiasm for labor's cause. It was in reference to the Little Steel situation—which seriously threatened to immobilize the CIO movement—that he made his famous "a plague on both your houses" remark, castigating both management *and labor*. Hardly inadvertent, this reference indicated the President's disenchantment with the CIO high command, a disenchantment caused in part by public concern and congressional uproar over administration labor policy.[57] Ironically, then, the very methods to which the exasperated steelworkers resorted (a similar approach had brought victory to the auto workers) reinforced a trend of public opinion which seriously damaged their cause and threatened to stop the momentum of the entire CIO campaign. What had promised to be a successful display of militant solidarity turned out to be a costly mistake.

It remains yet to comment on the investigations of Memorial Day by the La Follette Committee and the Chicago Citizens Commission. Of the two the former, because of its comprehensive nature, was by far the more significant.

Senator La Follette's probe began June 30, exactly one month after the clash. A host of CIO witnesses, some of them still bandaged, told of their harrowing experiences. Two reporters and several other persons who had witnessed the march

[56] NYT, June 13, 1937, p. E-7; June 15, 1937, p. 22; New York *Herald Tribune*, June 8, 1937, p. 24; June 16, 1937, p. 20; *Literary Digest*, June 26, 1937, p. 6; Chicago *Daily News*, June 16, 1937, p. 20; Washington *Post*, June 6, 1937, p. 6; June 17, 1937, p. 8; Cleveland *Plain Dealer*, June 11, 1937, p. 8; June 16, 1937, p. 8; Pittsburgh *Post-Gazette*, June 1, 1937, p. 8; Youngstown *Vindicator*, June 10, 1937, p. 6; Akron *Beacon Journal*, June 8, 1937, p. 4; Canton (Ohio) *Repository*, June 10, 1937, p. 4; *Congressional Record*, Vol. 81, pp. 825, 2379, 2472, 2915, 5736–37.

[57] NYT, June 30, 1937, p. 1.

testified that the crowd seemed bent mainly on reaching the plant in order to picket, and that at the first show of force by the police most of the marchers had begun to retreat. A doctor testified that the majority of those killed or wounded by gunfire had been shot in the back. The hearings came to a climax on July 2 when an expectant throng of congressmen, reporters, and witnesses filled the Senate caucus room to view the Committee's most conclusive item of evidence, the suppressed Paramount newsreel. As the film ended, Maury Maverick rushed back to the House to give his reaction. "This was one of the most uncommonly brutal things I have ever seen in my life. It showed an attack made entirely by the police. It will always be known as the shame of Chicago . . . , and one of the most shameful occurrences in the history of any civilized country." Maverick may have been somewhat overwrought, but few persons who saw the film could deny that it portrayed industrial strife at its worst and reflected scant credit upon the Chicago police.[58]

Against such evidence the police offered vacillating, contradictory testimony, some of it verging on the ridiculous. Captains James Mooney and Thomas Kilroy, who had been directly in charge of the police detail, were somewhat reluctant to reiterate their earlier statements, given freely and unequivocally to the press, that the mob had fired into the police ranks. In reply to questioning by La Follette, Mooney said he had heard some shots a few seconds after the riot began. La Follette went on to ask: "You could not tell from your own knowledge whether they came from the police or from the crowd?" Mr. Mooney: "No, sir; I do not know." Mooney also swore that the only police he had seen firing were those who shot at their assailants in self-defense, which created a mystery as to how several marchers had been shot in the back. But Captain Kilroy was quick to explain that their fellow strikers probably shot them while firing at the police.[59]

As if they had not already weakened their defense enough, Mooney and his colleagues went on to testify that the crowd had been extremely hostile toward the police—this in the face of their earlier assertions that the strikers had been victimized by radical agitators. They "acted like wild people," said Mooney. "I never saw such people in all the years of my experience." A patrolman provided the key explanation of the mob's behavior. Many of the marchers, he testified, "had a [strange] monotonous chant 'C. I. O., C. I. O.' " which indicated they were under the influence of "marihuana and liquor." The police counsel added that in any event the crowd must have consisted largely of agitators, outsiders, and malcontents, because it was unthinkable that the "average American workingman" would act as the marchers had.[60]

The Committee's report, released only three weeks after the hearings closed, generally vindicated the strikers' account of the march. Dismissing as sheer fantasy the police argument that the aim of the march was to seize the plant, the report found that the "sole objective . . . was to picket in mass at the plant gate." It further concluded that, assuming it was desirable to break up the demonstration, the police had used far more drastic action than was necessary.[61] . . .

58 LFC, Part 14, *passim; Congressional Record*, Vol. 81, p. 6162; NYT, July 1, 1937, p. 5; July 3, 1937, p. 5.

59 LFC, Part 14, pp. 4641, 4663, 4710–12, 4719–20, 4738, 4999, 5025–52; NYT, July 1, 1937, p. 5.

60 LFC, Part 14, pp. 4707, 4821, 4849; NYT, July 2, 1937, p. 3.

61 U.S. Senate Committee on Education and Labor, *The Chicago Memorial Day Incident, Report No. 46*, 75 Cong., 1 sess. Part 2 (Washington: 1937), pp. 39–41.

Meanwhile, Chicago liberals—among them, Malcolm Sharp, Alfred Kamin, and Paul H. Douglas—were conducting their own investigation. They had the support of the Chicago Church Federation and the assistance of the local chapter of the National Lawyers Guild. Their report, which relied rather heavily on evidence turned up by La Follette, made the point that, considering the Republic plant was more than adequately defended by armed men while the marchers were unarmed, it was "preposterous" to maintain—as the police did—that the crowd had any purpose other than "to establish temporary or more or less permanent mass picketing." And according to a brief submitted by Arthur J. Goldberg, then a young liberal lawyer, mass picketing was permissible under Illinois law. As for the behavior of the police, the report asserted that they had acted in a wholly irresponsible and improper manner under the direction of prejudiced, incompetent leadership. "No one familiar with the facts can suppose there was any good reason for shooting anyone," the report concluded.[62]

Yet these investigations did not really alter the main trend of opinion about Memorial Day. By the time they brought to light evidence that the strikers were perhaps not entirely blameworthy, public concern over the industrial warfare in steel was on the wane. Energetic strikebreaking activity and lack of New Deal support had, by mid-summer, demoralized the strike effort; and once it became clear that the CIO would make only a token attempt to prolong the walkout, which now rarely produced outbreaks of violence, the public began to lose interest in it.[63] The front-page coverage which the steel strike had received was now devoted to other domestic matters and to the Japanese invasion of China.[64]

But if many Americans were quite willing to let the turbulence of the steel strike pass into history, the CIO's detractors were of a different mind about the matter. Citing the steel strike as a prime example of the labor extremism which John L. Lewis had unleashed and the New Deal had foolishly tolerated, they placed all the blame for the violence of the 1937 labor crisis squarely on the CIO and Roosevelt. Thus CIO "irresponsibility" and "terrorism" became the *raison d'être* of the anti-Lewis forces, as they attacked on several fronts. Employers like Girdler, Weir, and Ford eagerly anticipated the moment, which they believed was close at hand, when they could deliver the *coup de grâce* to the CIO on the picket lines and in the shops. Politicians and editors vied with each other in propounding ingenious means of putting some backbone into the administration and of curbing the CIO brand of unionism.[65] Sensing a good chance to hasten the demise of its rival, the AFL also joined the attack. William Green solemnly declared that "no hostile employer in America has done the cause of organized labor more harm than those who formulated, executed and administered the policies of the . . . CIO." Chiding the CIO for its "ill-advised and untimely" steel strike, Green announced that the steel-

[62] *Report of the Citizens Joint Commission of Inquiry on the South Chicago Memorial Day Incident* (Chicago, August 31, 1937). Miller, *American Protestantism*, p. 279.

[63] Sofchalk, *op. cit.*, Chapter X.

[64] See the NYT, especially the first half of July, 1937.

[65] New York *Herald Tribune*, June 12, 1937, p. 14; June 19, 1937, p. 10; June 22, 1937, p. 18; NYT, June 11, 1937, p. 22; June 18, 1937, p. 20; July 4, 1937, p. E-3; Chicago *Daily News*, June 24, 1937, p. 19; *Atlantic Monthly*, CLX, No. 3 (September, 1937), p. 314; Levinson, *op. cit.*, pp. 210 ff.; *Literary Digest*, June 26, 1937, p. 6; *Congressional Record*, Vol. 81, pp. 5749–51, 5894.

workers, led astray and then betrayed by SWOC, would now be organized by a federally-chartered AFL union.[66] . . .

More significant was the situation in Congress, where the furor reached new heights of intensity at the very time the La Follette Committee was conducting its hearings. While some critics contented themselves with demands for "remedial" labor legislation, the more vociferous among them seemed determined to settle for nothing short of the political scalps of the Secretary of Labor and the President.[67] Representative White of Ohio urged action to protect the "right to work" and to make the "use of weapons of destruction by agents either of industrial concerns or labor" a federal offense. Senator Allen Ellender, reflecting on the CIO's purposes, warned that their realization well might result in the "destruction of the sacred rights of free government." Representative E. E. Cox of Georgia fired what was perhaps the most telling fusillade. He belabored the New Deal for "shameful cringing" in the face of "labor despotism," and accused the CIO of utter ruthlessness—the sit-down strikes, "armed picketing," and obstructing the mails were cited—in its "efforts to terrorize industry" and force acceptance of the "closed shop." Many House members responded heartily, cheering and applauding Cox for his bitter attack on the CIO and its supporters.[68]

As the congressional clamor reached its peak, the administration again acted to disassociate itself from CIO policies. On July 3, Frances Perkins issued a letter insisting that contrary to the general belief the Labor Department had never considered the sit-down strike as "either lawful, desirable, or appropriate."[69] . . .

Historical assessments of the Memorial Day incident are mixed. Several writers believe that the "ghastly violence," as Max Lerner called it, so shocked the general public as to engender considerable sympathy for the steel strikers.[70] Others find that the incident failed to stir such sentiment, which is borne out by the conclusions of this paper.[71] Still others contend that it prefigured the futility of efforts to crack Little Steel, and the strikers should have realized it; and indeed one student of the Chicago labor movement concludes that the debacle there "demoralized" the entire strike.[72] The circumstances of the strike as a whole hardly seem to justify such sweeping conclusions. The crucial center of the walkout was in Ohio, where the main citadel of Little Steel was located in the Youngstown-Warren complex. Here the Chicago defeat did not seriously affect the strikers' morale. Far from daunting them, it probably strengthened their will to win. They evidenced no disposition to forego mass action, and some of the most savage

[66] NYT, July 9, 1937, p. 1; July 13, 1937, p. 4; Youngstown *Vindicator*, July 14, 1937, p. 15.

[67] NYT, July 2, 1937, p. 2; July 4, 1937, p. E-3.

[68] NYT, July 1, 1937, p. 2; July 2, 1937, p. 1; *Congressional Record*, Vol. 81, 5894, 6058.

[69] NYT, July 4, 1937, p. 6.

[70] Max Lerner, *America as a Civilization* (New York: 1957), p. 321; Foster Rhea Dulles, *Labor in America, A History* (New York: 1960), p. 301; Rayback, *op. cit.*, p. 352; Leighton, *op. cit.*, p. 387; Walsh, *op. cit.*, pp. 13–14.

[71] John D. Hicks, *The American Nation* (Cambridge: 1955), p. 580; O. T. Barck, Jr. and N. M. Blake, *Since 1900, A History Of the United States in Our Times* (New York: 1952), p. 532; Harvey Wish, *Contemporary America* (New York: 1955), p. 496.

[72] Derber and Young, *op. cit.*, p. 21; Dumas Malone and Basil Rauch, *Empire for Liberty* (New York: 1960), II, pp. 597–598; Newell, *op. cit.*, p. 141.

picket-line battles of the '30s occurred in Ohio after Memorial Day.[73] The strike was finally broken by a combination of hostile public opinion, successful back-to-work drives, and the activity of the National Guard, but it was in the steel region of Ohio rather than in Chicago that the CIO met its first major setback.

Of course this is not to say that the Memorial Day encounter had no significant bearing on the outcome. Along with the other instances of militancy and violence in the steel strike, it confirmed the belief of many Americans that the CIO had gotten out of hand. In turn, this widespread public disapproval of CIO militancy was the underlying reason for the collapse of the steel strike, for it caused Roosevelt to withdraw his support of the CIO at a crucial juncture in its drive to unionize the entire steel industry. Not only did Lewis and his colleagues face the task of rebuilding the union in Little Steel, they also confronted a "public outcry" so strong that it threatened to stop the momentum of the entire CIO movement.[74]

It did not take long for the upper echelon of the CIO leadership to absorb and act upon the lesson of the steel strike. Even before the strike had ended, SWOC purged some of its more militant organizers and tried generally to discourage militancy by impulsive rank and filers.[75] Furthermore, the union changed its approach in the campaign against Little Steel. Shifting the major emphasis from picket-line pressures to legal maneuvers, it now availed itself of the National Labor Relations Board's judicially-confirmed authority stemming from the Jones and Laughlin decision. Following the strike, SWOC pressed unfair labor complaints against all of the Little Steel firms; and the Board's decisions upheld the union demand for signed contracts and required the companies to rehire (with back pay) all employees who had been fired for strike activity. Then, using painstaking organizing drives and NLRB procedures (elections and cross checks) as alternatives to strike action, Murray and his colleagues by 1941 forced Little Steel to grant SWOC *de facto* recognition.[76]

So the same CIO leaders who had succeeded in creating the first really viable industrial union movement, precisely because they had recognized the potential of the mass unrest among American workers in the 1930s, quietly gave up reliance on mass action as a matter of policy. While there was no denying that it had been highly effective in the initial, heroic phase of the CIO, the policy of militancy was now abandoned, partly as a result of the NLRB's new efficacy but primarily because the Memorial Day affair and the steel strike generally had shown that it was a liability. Whatever usefulness the policy might still have retained by the summer of 1937 was outweighed by the problems it had raised.

Mass picketing, sit-down strikes, and other acts of mass militancy—and the victories won through their use—had stirred up fears and resentments which culminated in one of the most virulent anti-union campaigns in the nation's history. Not since the heyday of the I. W. W. and the "Red Scare" of 1919 had such a large number of Americans been so worried about labor aggressiveness and

[73] Sofchalk, *op. cit.*, Chapter VI, VII, IX, X; interview with John Mayo, Aug. 19, 1964.

[74] Louis Stark, "Are Lewis and the C.I.O. on the Downgrade?" NYT, July 4, 1937, p. E-3.

[75] NYT, July 4, 1937, p. 2; Youngstown *Vindicator*, July 3, 1937, pp. 1, 2; July 5, 1937, p. 2.

[76] *How Collective Bargaining Works*, ed. Harry A. Millis (New York: 1942), pp. 532–533; Galenson, *op. cit.*, pp. 109, 115–116.

the radicalism from which it allegedly sprang. Many of them feared that the increasing tempo of industrial strife might turn into full-scale class warfare. They failed to distinguish the inchoate, spontaneous radicalism, of which the CIO had much, from doctrinaire radicalism, of which it had relatively little. The working-class Chicagoans who marched across the prairie on that fateful Memorial Day were engaged in a disciplined assault on a capitalist rampart. Yet, however unintentional it may have been, their reaction was radical in nature, and a radical labor movement is something which middle-class America has not been willing to tolerate.

21

THE NATIONAL NEGRO CONGRESS: A REASSESSMENT

Lawrence S. Wittner

The Great Depression was a critical period in the history of the American Negro. Victimized more severely by the economic crisis than white Americans, black voters responded to the New Deal by shifting their political allegiance to Franklin D. Roosevelt and the Democratic party. During these years, there was no abatement in the patterns of black migration from the South to the North and from the country to the city, with the result that the political force latent in northern urban ghettos began to emerge. But black leaders were divided as to how they might best achieve their goals. Should they seek primarily civil and political rights, permitting blacks to vote and attend unsegregated schools, or should they stress human rights, maintaining an active concern for the plight of the poor whose incidence of disease, delinquency, and squalor made the blacks a threat both to themselves and to the general community? Some black leaders opposed reform within the system and sought more radical solutions to the plight of the blacks. The National Negro Congress was caught up in this controversy. It finally came under the strong influence of Communists and of white labor leaders who sought to use it for purposes other than those espoused by its early leader, A. Philip Randolph. In the process, these outside white forces killed the effectiveness of the congress. But as this essay points out, during the four years from 1936 to 1940, the congress accomplished a great deal at the local level. Above all, it sought to teach the American black a fundamental lesson, as expressed by Randolph at the 1940 Convention—if the Negro were to "save himself, he would have to depend on his own right arm!" The recent Black Caucus meeting in Gary, Indiana, in the spring of 1972, revealed the same divisions within the black community that existed in 1940, but Randolph's statement is as valid today as it was thirty years ago.

Lawrence S. Wittner teaches at Vassar College and has published Rebels Against War: The American Peace Movement, 1941–1960 *(New York, 1969). His interests also include black history.*

Source: *American Quarterly*, Vol. 22, No. 4 (1970), pp. 883–901.

In the three decades since its collapse in 1940,[1] the National Negro Congress has been subject to the burden of characterization as a "Communist front." Wilson Record's two books on Communist activity among black Americans have treated the Congress as little more than a Party exercise in manipulation.[2] Irving Howe and Lewis Coser, in their biting study of the history of American Communism, label the National Negro Congress as "the main front organization in the Negro community during the Popular Front period."[3] More recently, Harold Cruse has traced Communist domination of the National Negro Congress and blamed it for the "sellout of the black ghettoes."[4] The official imprimatur has been supplied by the Attorney General of the United States and by the House Committee on Un-American Activities, who have conveniently classified it for the benefit of patriots among "Communist" and "Communist front" organizations.[5]

Strangely, despite the unanimity of these critics, none has apparently bothered to study the activities of the National Negro Congress. Fascinated by the obvious Communist strength within the organization, and frequently devoted to exposing Communist machinations, they have neglected to delve into the work of the national office and the more than seventy local councils engaged in daily struggles for racial advancement—struggles that were often successful. Nor can their one-dimensional view of the National Negro Congress adequately explain the breadth of support it received. Among the prominent non-Communists who spoke at or sent messages of greeting to its meetings were Franklin Roosevelt, Eleanor Roosevelt, Fiorello LaGuardia, John L. Lewis, Norman Thomas, Walter Reuther, Philip Murray, Walter White, Ralph Bunche and A. Philip Randolph.[6] Finally, Communist perfidy does not provide a completely balanced explanation of the disastrous 1940 convention, which ended the effectiveness of the Congress. While it may be of some value to know that the Communist Party sought to, and did manage to, use the National Negro Congress to fulfill some of its objectives, this knowledge does not provide a sufficient basis for understanding the life and death of the organization.

[1] The National Negro Congress continued to exist until 1948, but most scholars agree that it ceased to play a significant role in racial affairs after its national convention of April 1940.

[2] Record, *The Negro and the Communist Party* (Chapel Hill, N.C., 1951) and *Race and Radicalism: The NAACP and the Communist Party in Conflict* (Ithaca, N.Y., 1964).

[3] Howe and Coser, *The American Communist Party: A Critical History, 1919–1957* (Boston, 1957), p. 356.

[4] Cruse, *The Crisis of the Negro Intellectual* (New York, 1967), pp. 171–80.

[5] U.S. House of Representatives, Committee on Un-American Activities, *Guide to Subversive Organizations and Publications* (Washington, D.C.: U.S. Gov't Printing Office, Jan. 2, 1957), pp. 64–65.

[6] Roosevelt to Randolph, Mar. 29, 1940, National Negro Congress manuscripts, Schomburg Collection, New York Public Library (NNC MSS), Box 20; Roosevelt to John P. Davis, Oct. 14, 1937, NNC MSS, Box 7; *New York Times*, Feb. 11, 1938, p. 16; LaGuardia to John P. Davis, Oct. 15, 1937, NNC MSS, Box 11; *Official Proceedings of the Second National Negro Congress, 1937* (Washington, D.C., 1937), NNC MSS, Box 11; *New York Times*, Oct. 17, 1937, p. 11; Walter White to John P. Davis, Sept. 14, 1937, NNC MSS, Box 15; Record, *Race and Radicalism*, p. 96.

The National Negro Congress developed out of a conference in May 1935 at Howard University on the economic status of the Negro. Sponsored jointly by the Social Science Division of the university and the Joint Committee on National Recovery, a short-lived coalition of twenty-two major Negro organizations which sought to secure nondiscriminatory treatment for Negroes under New Deal programs, the conference turned up telling evidence on the plight of the black community during the Great Depression. John P. Davis, the articulate young executive secretary of the Joint Committee, and Ralph Bunche, head of the Department of Political Science, impressed by the severity of the crisis, invited a select group of Negro leaders to Bunche's residence at the end of the conference to consider the possibility of calling together a National Negro Congress. At the meeting there was general agreement that the critical situation of blacks in America called for some degree of organizational coordination to exert maximum strength in the struggle for racial justice. Eventually, more than two hundred and fifty well known figures in various walks of life signed a call for the meeting of a National Negro Congress in February 1936, among them: Lester Granger and Elmer Carter, of the National Urban League; Dr. Alain Locke and Dr. Ralph Bunche, of Howard University; James W. Ford, of the Communist Party; A. Philip Randolph, President of the Brotherhood of Sleeping Car Porters; Bishops James A. Bray, R. A. Carter and W. J. Walls; and Langston Hughes. In the introduction to Davis' eloquent pamphlet, *Let Us Build a National Negro Congress*—50,000 of which were distributed across the country —A. Philip Randolph explained their purpose: "The magnitude, complexity and danger of the Negro's present condition demands the mobilization of overwhelming mass pressure and force, which can only be achieved through the agency of a National Negro Congress."[7]

The National Negro Congress that convened in Chicago on February 14, 1936 had many elements of success. At the opening of its first session, more than five thousand men and women jammed into the Eighth Regiment Armory, despite subzero weather and a threat by the Chicago "red squad" to close the building, and cheered speeches by Randolph and other prominent spokesmen until well after midnight; similar crowds thronged the meetings of the following two days. Among those in attendance were 817 delegates from 585 organizations

[7] Ralph J. Bunche, "The Programs, Ideologies, Tactics and Achievements of Negro Betterment and Interracial Organizations," pp. 319–20, prepared for the Carnegie-Myrdal study, June 7, 1940, transcript copy in Schomburg Collection; Gunnar Myrdal, *An American Dilemma: The Negro Problem and Modern Democracy* (2 vols; New York, 1944), II, 817; Eleanor Ryan, "Toward a National Negro Congress," *New Masses*, XV (June 4, 1935), 14; NAACP press release, May 25, 1934, NNC MSS, Box 1; "Statement of John P. Davis, executive secretary of the Joint Committee on National Recovery, before the Complaint Hearing of the National Recovery Administration, February 28, 1934," NNC MSS, Box 1; James W. Ford, "The National Negro Congress," *Communist*, XV (Apr. 1936), 322–23; Randolph to John P. Davis, May 3, 1935, NNC MSS, Box 3; Alain Locke to John P. Davis, Feb. 13, 1936, NNC MSS, Box 6; Langston Hughes, statement of Feb. 1, 1936, NNC MSS, Box 5; John P. Davis to T. Arnold Hill, Nov. 21, 1935, NNC MSS, Box 5; Horace R. Cayton and George S. Mitchell, *Black Workers and the New Unions* (Chapel Hill, N.C., 1939), p. 416; John P. Davis, *Let Us Build a National Negro Congress* (Washington, D.C., 1935), pp. 3–4, NNC MSS, Box 2.

—largely civic groups, trade unions, religious bodies, political parties and fraternal societies—with an estimated membership of 1,200,000 persons. According to Lester Granger, the crowd was an exceptionally diverse one, with widely divergent philosophies: "Old line Republican wheel horses and ambitious young Democrats exchanged arguments; Communists held heated altercations with proponents of the Forty-Ninth State Movement, and Garveyites signed the registration books immediately after Baha'ists." The delegates enthusiastically voted to establish a permanent body to coordinate the local activities of constituent organizations, and passed resolutions endorsing the organization of Negro labor, attacking lynching, supporting the Negro church, condemning the Italian invasion of Ethiopia and calling upon the black community to patronize Negro business.[8]

The heterogeneity of the convention and of its resolutions reflected the conviction of its organizers that the primary purpose of a National Negro Congress was not to promote a specific program or ideology, but to develop a united movement for racial progress. "The grave situation of the Negro population . . . demands united action," declared Davis in his call to Chicago; "only the unity of action of the widest masses . . . can solve the problems facing us today." Such unity, of course, necessitated submerging or ignoring divisions in the black community, in an effort to reach a compromise accord. Ralph Bunche recalled that the delegates had hoped to make the Congress "the medium for integrating the forces of Negro organizations" by "determining a minimum program of action upon which the . . . organizations could agree." In line with this approach, the convention not only constructed a diverse and at times inconsistent platform, but declared that the National Negro Congress would never be dominated by any political faction or party and would remain completely nonpartisan in political struggles. While the Communist Party stood in the forefront of those urging a nonsectarian policy in the days of the United Front, the program of united race action appealed to a much broader element than Party stalwarts, for it drew upon the submerged current of Negro nationalism. Thus, Randolph, who wrote Davis that "the united front of all Negro organizations" should be "the main principle" of the Congress, told the delegates in Chicago in his keynote address: "The Negro should not place his problems for solution . . . at the feet of his white sympathetic allies . . . for in the final analysis, the salvation of the Negro . . . must come from within." Therefore, despite the fact that the National Negro Congress contained a scattering of white organizations, its cornerstone was racial unity.[9]

[8] Granger, "The National Negro Congress—An Interpretation," *Opportunity*, XIV (May 1936), 151–52; "What Is the National Negro Congress?" (1936), NNC MSS, Box 2; Cayton and Mitchell, *Black Workers and the New Unions*, p. 417; Ford, "The National Negro Congress," p. 323; Richard Wright, "Two Million Black Voices," *New Masses*, XVIII (Feb. 25, 1936), 15; *Official Proceedings of the National Negro Congress, February 14, 15, 16, 1936* (Washington, D.C., 1936), NNC MSS, Box 2.

[9] Davis, *Let Us Build a National Negro Congress*, pp. 5–6, NNC MSS, Box 2; Bunche, "The Programs, Ideologies, Tactics," pp. 323, 339, 353–54; Randolph to Davis, Jan. 31, 1936, NNC MSS, Box 7; *Official Proceedings of the National Negro Congress, February 14, 15, 16, 1936*, NNC MSS, Box 2. In April 1935, when Davis had first broached the idea of a National Negro Congress, he suggested the

Randolph and Davis quickly emerged as the key leaders of the new organization. Elected the first president of the National Negro Congress, Randolph served as a handsome and inspiring symbol of Negro militancy. A Socialist newspaper editor and champion of labor for many years, the dynamic Randolph left journalism to organize the Brotherhood of Sleeping Car Porters. As the first president of the new union, which enrolled almost half the Negroes in the American labor movement, Randolph had little time to spare for his unsalaried position with the National Negro Congress. Thus, the real burden of Congress work fell on the capable shoulders of John P. Davis, secretary and chief staff member of the organization. Davis was a young graduate of Harvard Law School who, as an excellent speaker and writer, had gained the plaudits of the N.A.A.C.P. and other Negro organizations in his role as secretary of the Joint Committee on National Recovery. A waspish critic of the New Deal in its early years, Davis had been accused in the Negro press of being in the pay of the Republican Party. However, judging from his speeches, correspondence and subsequent activities in the National Negro Congress, it appears likely that his sympathies lay more with the Communists than with the Republicans.[10]

In the first years of its existence, the National Negro Congress performed some of its most effective work on the local level. Regional councils, composed of representatives of organizations affiliated with the Congress, were established in approximately seventy cities, and these coordinating bodies frequently waged spirited crusades. Although the "grass-roots" quality of the Congress later declined, its existence at the outset gave the organization a constituency far more solid than that of many radical groups. As late as 1939 and 1940, when Swedish sociologist Gunnar Myrdal traveled across the United States investigating racial conditions, he found that "the local councils of the National Negro Congress were the most important Negro organizations in some Western cities." Despite the consistent reluctance of the N.A.A.C.P. to provide more than token cooperation with the Congress—motivated both by fears of Communists and by simple organizational jealousy—the local councils of the National Negro Congress made a significant impact upon community affairs.[11]

In Chicago, for example, the local council carried on a vigorous campaign to improve employment opportunities, housing conditions and relief work in the black community. Through persistent efforts, the council obtained jobs for Negroes as motormen on city street cars—positions previously barred to them—

establishment of "a minimum program of action which would win the agreement of most organizations." Others, with a more sectarian view, deplored the heterogeneity of the resolutions of the first Congress, Davis to "Friend" of the Joint Committee on National Recovery, Apr. 18, 1935, NNC MSS, Box 1; "Toward Negro Unity," *Nation*, CXLII (Mar. 11, 1936), 302.

[10] Brailsford R. Brazeal, *The Brotherhood of Sleeping Car Porters: Its Origin and Development* (New York, 1946), pp. 16–19; *Souvenir Bulletin of the Southern Negro Youth Conference* (1937), NNC MSS, Box 2; news release of Apr. 23, 1934, NNC MSS, Box 2; John P. Davis, "A Black Inventory of the New Deal," *Crisis*, XLII (May 1935), 141–42; news release of July 31, 1934, NNC MSS, Box 3.

[11] John P. Davis, "Report of National Secretary, Cleveland, Ohio, June 19–20, 1936," p. 10, NNC MSS, Box 2; Bunche, "The Programs, Ideologies, Tactics," pp. 337, 348; "Tentative Draft of Outline of Organization for National Negro Congress" (1937?), NNC MSS, Box 10; Myrdal, *An American Dilemma*, II, 818; Record, *Race and Radicalism*, pp. 94–96.

and attacked discriminatory practices in other public utilities. Its South Side Tenants League conducted frequent rent strikes and protests against the policies of slum landlords, occasionally winning substantial reductions in rents or improvements in conditions. When a public housing project was blocked by an injunction secured by Chicago real estate interests, the Congress organized a mass meeting of ten thousand people on the site, and forced a reversal of the court order. Representatives from the local council also were active in several relief committees on Chicago's South Side which sought to improve the size of the appropriation and the method of distribution of state relief funds.[12]

In Boston, the local council engaged in a broad range of activities. Outraged by public school textbooks which insulted blacks, the Congress called a meeting in which a 12-year-old child read the offensive passages to seven hundred parents. The gathering appointed a delegation which protested to the school board and secured the removal of the books. When a survey of a public park in a Negro area of Boston revealed woeful conditions, the council organized the community and eventually obtained a $48,000 WPA grant to hire unemployed black males from the community to improve children's play facilities. The council sponsored another protest meeting when a black girl was excluded on racial grounds from entering the nurses training school at Whidden Memorial Hospital in Everett. Awakened by the furor, the Everett Board of Aldermen passed a unanimous resolution rebuking the management of the public hospital, which now found a place for the girl. Having entered the cultural realm in 1936, when it successfully protested the ouster of Negro singers from a WPA chorus, the Boston council moved on in 1937 to undertake a program at Boston Symphony Hall, which presented young black artists and their music. A member of the Congress later reported the event to Davis: "Symphony Hall was filled. . . . Boston's '400' were in regal style. . . . I simply wept tears of joy and pride, that our Congress could and did make it possible for a brown skinned colored girl to play a concert with Boston's Symphony Orchestra."[13]

The Washington, D.C. council of the National Negro Congress focused its activities upon the issues of police brutality and inadequate recreational facilities. In July 1938, the council sponsored a meeting on police brutality attended by delegates of more than fifty local organizations. It followed this with six radio broadcasts and four mass meetings, and within several months had secured twenty-four thousand signatures on petitions protesting assaults by law enforcement officers upon innocent blacks. Eventually, the Washington council forced

[12] St. Clair Drake and Horace R. Cayton, *Black Metropolis* (New York, 1945), pp. 737–38 note, 744; Charles W. Burton to Davis, May 18, 1936, NNC MSS, Box 4; Charles W. Burton to Davis, May 12, 1938, NNC MSS, Box 12; Davis to Marcus Goldman, Dec. 29, 1936, NNC MSS, Box 5; Davis, "Report of National Secretary" (1936), NNC MSS, Box 2; Davis to Max Bedacht, June 22, 1937, NNC MSS, Box 9; Davis to Ethel Clyde, Sept. 7, 1939, NNC MSS, Box 12; Charles W. Burton to Davis, Aug. 18, 1936, NNC MSS, Box 4.

[13] Davis to Morris Rodman, Mar. 1, 1938, NNC MSS, Box 14; Davis to Helen Bryan, Mar. 3, 1938, NNC MSS, Box 12; Davis to Marcus Goldman, Dec. 29, 1936, NNC MSS, Box 5; *Malden Press*, Oct. 16, 1936, clipping in NNC MSS, Box 7; Davis to Carl Murphy, July 22, 1936, NNC MSS, Box 6; Davis, "Report of National Secretary" (1936), NNC MSS, Box 7; Davis to Helen Bryan, Oct. 21, 1938, NNC MSS, Box 12; Mary E. Moore to Davis, June 22, 1937, NNC MSS, Box 11.

the establishment of a civilian trial board and the punishment of two officers who had killed Negroes without cause—the first such punishment in the history of Washington. In 1939, the Congress published a study entitled *Public Recreation: A Report on the Adequacy of Public Recreational Facilities for Negroes in the District of Columbia,* which highlighted the paucity of facilities open to blacks. By 1940, after a meeting with the Secretary of the Interior, the local council announced the opening of "17 new tennis courts to Negroes" and "an end to all restrictions against Negro use of baseball diamonds and park picnic areas." Thanks to the efforts of the Washington Congress, many federal recreational facilities in the nation's capital were opened for the first time to blacks.[14]

Across the country, the local councils of the National Negro Congress plunged into a wide variety of ventures. In Newark, the Congress picketed chain stores refusing to employ blacks in sales capacities, and won some minor victories. In Oakland, the council helped to end discriminatory practices at the state university dormitory, and sponsored a weekly radio program, "Negroes in the News." The Detroit council campaigned vigorously against the neo-fascist Black Legion, and scheduled a week of Negro cultural activities, with an art exhibit viewed by fifteen thousand people. In St. Louis, the local council picketed a theater in the black community which refused employment to Negro operators and ticket takers, and ended these practices. Omaha's council secured an agreement from city authorities to establish summer recreational facilities for the black community in a local school. In Baltimore, the Congress succeeded in obtaining two white-collar WPA projects for Negroes. Although the local councils would prove unstable and short-lived, perhaps because of the difficulties they encountered in overcoming divisions in the black community, they imparted a healthy "grassroots" flavor to the National Negro Congress in the first years of its existence.[15]

Throughout 1936 and 1937, the heyday of the local councils, the national staff members of the Congress found themselves preoccupied with "housekeeping" details and with laying plans for the second national gathering, held in 1937. Establishing local councils, sending out charters and publicizing the new organization through speeches and writing occupied much of Davis' time. Furthermore, chronic shortages of funds kept Davis on the run in a frantic effort to keep the administrative engine moving. "Unless we can receive $25.00 by Saturday," he told an associate in late 1936, "the office of the National Negro Congress must be closed. This is a final request. . . . There is nothing else that I can do or say." Davis did manage to organize an extremely successful Second

[14] Davis to Frank Horne, Dec. 12, 1938, NNC MSS, Box 19; "Tentative Draft of Outline of Organization for National Negro Congress" (1937?), NNC MSS, Box 10; Davis to Alfred Baker Lewis, Oct. 21, 1938, NNC MSS, Box 13; Davis to Vito Marcantonio *et al.,* June 10, 1939, NNC MSS, Box 17; news release, July 31 (?), 1938, NNC MSS, Box 11; *Public Recreation: A Report . . . ,* NNC MSS, Box 17; *National Negro Congress News,* Vol. I, No. 1 (July–Aug. 1940), NNC MSS, Box 22; Speech of John P. Davis to Third National Negro Congress, Apr. 27, 1940, NNC MSS, Box 21.

[15] Davis to A. R. Mayo, July 2, 1940, NNC MSS, Box 19; Davis to Alfred Baker Lewis, Oct. 21, 1938, NNC MSS, Box 13; Davis to Helen Bryan, Oct. 21, 1938, NNC MSS, Box 12; Davis to J. Westbrook McPhearson, Apr. 20, 1938, NNC MSS, Box 11; Davis to Carl Murphy, July 22, 1936, NNC MSS, Box 6; Ishmael Flory to Davis, May 24, 1937, NNC MSS, Box 10; Davis to Ethel Clyde, Sept. 7, 1939, NNC MSS, Box 12; Davis, "Report of National Secretary" (1936), NNC MSS, Box 7; unidentified newspaper clipping, NNC MSS, Box 11.

National Negro Congress in Philadelphia in October 1937, which brought many prominent figures such as Walter White to speak to a record number of delegates. Nonetheless, there can be little doubt that the achievements of the local councils eclipsed those of the national office in the first two years.[16]

After 1938, however, although the local councils declined, the national office exhibited increasing strength, mobilizing support for bills in Congress and garnering votes for "progressive" politicians. In 1938, the national office organized dozens of demonstrations across the country in behalf of the Wagner-Van Nuys antilynching bill, sponsored a meeting in Washington of more than one hundred organizations in its behalf, and brought large delegations to the nation's capital to influence wavering legislators. Similarly, it waged campaigns in support of the Roosevelt Administration's court reform bill, the Fair Labor Standards Act and housing and education bills, and sought to amend the Social Security Act to include domestic and agricultural workers. Perhaps because liberals supported some of its aims, perhaps because Communists and their adherents had warmed up to the New Deal, or perhaps simply because of a taste for partisan politics, the national office of the National Negro Congress moved increasingly into electoral action. It urged Negro voters to support the liberal Maury Maverick in his successful campaign for mayor of San Antonio, and gave its endorsement to the Ohio State Democratic Party when it sought to install New Dealers in the governor's chair and in Congress in 1938. "We are doing everything possible to rally the Negro voters to the support of progressive candidates," Davis declared in 1938. That such partisanship violated the principles upon which the Congress had been founded in 1936 seems to have given Davis few qualms. He told Harold Ickes with some pride in 1938 that the organization had "consistently supported the policies of the Roosevelt Administration, both foreign and domestic."[17]

Another reason for the growing partisanship of the Congress lay in the alliance it had forged with the C.I.O. during the great steel organizing drive of the late 1930s. From its inception, the Congress had been strongly pro-labor, and committed to bringing black workers into trade unions. "At the very heart of the program of the National Negro Congress will be the question of organization of the hundreds of thousands of unorganized Negro workers," Davis had promised labor unions in 1935. "We feel the necessity of throwing the whole influence of the Negro population . . . solidly behind organized labor." The

[16] Davis to Henry Johnson, Oct. 5, 1936, NNC MSS, Box 6; Bunche, "The Programs, Ideologies, Tactics," p. 352; Davis to Karl Gerber, Mar. 1, 1938, NNC MSS, Box 13; *Official Proceedings of the Second National Negro Congress, 1937*, NNC MSS, Box 11.

[17] A. Philip Randolph to Davis, Mar. 12, 1938, NNC MSS, Box 14; Davis to Randolph, Apr. 7, 1938, NNC MSS, Box 14; Davis to DeWitt Alcorn, Apr. 15, 1938, NNC MSS, Box 12; Charles W. Burton to Davis, Mar. 8, 1938, NNC MSS, Box 12; *New York Times*, Apr. 3, 1938, p. 24; National Negro Congress press release, Mar. 19, 1938, NNC MSS, Box 90; Davis to Frank Scott, Apr. 18, 1938, NNC MSS, Box 15; Davis to Max Bedacht, June 22, 1937, NNC MSS, Box 9; Davis to Karl Gerber, Mar. 1, 1938, NNC MSS, Box 13; Davis to Lillian Jones, Mar. 29, 1939, NNC MSS, Box 16; Davis to Gardner Jackson, May 23, 1939, NNC MSS, Box 16; Davis to Ethel Clyde, Sept. 7, 1939, NNC, MSS, Box 12; Davis to Bedacht, Mar. 17, 1939, Box 12; Ray C. Sutliff to Davis, Sept. 20, 1938, NNC MSS, Box 13; Davis to Joseph Albright, Oct. 22, 1938, NNC MSS, Box 12; Davis to Ickes, Sept. 15, 1938, NNC MSS, Box 13.

founding convention of the Congress had voted to support the A.F. of L. and the C.I.O. in organizing Negro workers, and its trade union subsection was the best attended and most hotly discussed of the meetings. With a strong commitment to organized labor, and with its president the leading spokesman for black unionism, the National Negro Congress was poised and ready to act when the C.I.O. began its dramatic drive to unionize the steel industry.[18]

The battleground of the bloody Homestead strike of 1892 and of the great steel strike of 1919, the steel industry stood as a seemingly impregnable symbol of company strength in 1936, when the C.I.O., revolting against the caution of the A.F. of L., launched a determined campaign to unionize it. In June, the Steel Workers Organizing Committee (S.W.O.C.), under the direction of Philip Murray, set up headquarters in Pittsburgh and sent four hundred organizers into the steel towns of Pennsylvania, Ohio, Illinois and Alabama to rally the more than one-half million steelworkers. The steel industry met this challenge with a massive anti-union publicity barrage, assuring its employees that the companies had their interest at heart and that the C.I.O. was a Communist organization. "Let him who will, be he economic tyrant or sordid mercenary," thundered John L. Lewis in reply, "pit his strength against this mighty upsurge of human sentiment . . . in the hearts of thirty million workers who clamor for the establishment of industrial democracy." The fortunes of the C.I.O. and of organized labor in America hung in the balance as the battle raged for the loyalty of the steelworkers.[19]

Blacks had a crucial position in the emerging struggle, as well as a vital stake in it. In 1936, there were perhaps as many as 85,000 Negro steelworkers—20 per cent of the laborers and 6 per cent of the operators in the industry. Restricted to the worst jobs, with intense heat and noxious gases, they also encountered a wide network of racially discriminatory social practices. Their wages—based on a racially discriminatory differential—averaged $3.60 per day. Bethlehem Steel's black workers at Sparrows Point, Maryland, for example, endured hazardous and degrading employment for $16 to $18 a week. Keen students of these conditions, the leaders of the National Negro Congress were determined to bring black workers into the steel union. "There is no effort in which the National Negro Congress could possibly engage at this time more helpful to large numbers of Negro workers . . . than the organization of Negro steel workers," wrote Davis. Like Lewis, he looked beyond the steel campaign to its hoped-for ramifications: "85,000 Negro steel workers with union cards will signal the beginning of the organization of all Negro workers." It would "mark a start toward the liberation of hundreds of thousands of Negro sharecroppers" and "Negro women sweating away their lives as domestics." Davis saw the steel campaign as a chance to "write a Magna Charta for black labor."[20]

[18] Davis to the officers and members of all trade unions affiliated with the A.F. of L. and to the Railroad Brotherhoods (1936?), NNC MSS, Box 5; Davis, *Let Us Build a National Negro Congress*, NNC MSS, Box 2; *Official Proceedings of the National Negro Congress, February 14, 15, 16, 1936*, pp. 20–22, NNC MSS, Box 2; Granger, "The National Negro Congress," p. 152.

[19] Foster Rhea Dulles, *Labor in America: A History* (New York, 1967), pp. 293–300; Walter Galenson, *The CIO Challenge to the AFL: A History of the American Labor Movement, 1935–41* (Cambridge, Mass., 1960), pp. 75–96; Walter Galenson, "The Unionization of the American Steel Industry," *International Review of Social History*, I (1956), 8–27.

[20] Davis, " 'Plan Eleven'—Jim Crow in Steel," *Crisis*, XLIII (Sept. 1936), 262–

With this object in mind, the National Negro Congress threw its energies into the struggle to organize the steel industry. In talks with John L. Lewis, Philip Murray, John Brophy and regional directors of the S.W.O.C., Davis recommended and secured the appointment of a dozen Negro organizers, many of them leaders of the local councils. Wherever councils existed in steel areas, they contributed volunteer organizers and served as the nerve centers of the campaign to unionize black steelworkers, distributing more than a quarter of a million pro-union leaflets in the black communities of the nation. "We colored workers must join hands with our white brothers . . . to establish an organization . . . which shall deliver us from the clutches of the steel barons," declared one circular; "we appeal to all colored workers in the steel mills to join the union." Another, entitled "National Negro Congress Supports the Steel Workers Organizing Committee," maintained that the C.I.O. union was "the only guarantee for full rights to all workers, Negro or White." As secretary of the Congress, Davis spent months in the field in steel communities, speaking and creating citizens' committees in support of the organizing drive.[21]

In dozens of cities and towns, the National Negro Congress carried the campaign deep into the black community. Davis told a S.W.O.C. official that five out of six black steelworkers in Baltimore would see a Congress leaflet or a reprint of it in the Baltimore *Afro-American*, and that he was making a series of talks from a loud-speaker truck and on the local radio. The Pittsburgh Council distributed twenty to thirty thousand leaflets in Allegheny County and had two of its leaders hired as organizers by the S.W.O.C. On February 6, 1937, in cooperation with the S.W.O.C., the Congress sponsored a conference in Pittsburgh attended by approximately 350 black union delegates on methods of organizing black steelworkers. A favorite tactic of the Congress organizers would be to gather a corps of sympathizers in the unorganized community who would then pressure their local churches, clubs and organizations to sponsor mass meetings encouraging blacks to join the steelworkers union. A Congress organizer in the Gary area who employed this strategy reported "a very successful open air meeting," replete with speeches and a performance of *Waiting for Lefty*. In Chicago, another organizer wrote Davis that "we have been able to get practically everything in the *Defender* that we want. . . . There is an editorial on the steel question this week, and also pictures of . . . the Negro organizers."[22]

The organizing work undertaken by the National Negro Congress proved to be of considerable significance for the union. Despite their traditional estrangement from the labor movement, blacks joined the S.W.O.C. in most areas in

63, 276; Cayton and Mitchell, *Black Workers and the New Unions*, pp. 17–42; Davis to Charles W. Burton, July 22, 1936, NNC MSS, Box 4.

[21] Davis to Carl Murphy, July 22, 1936, NNC MSS, Box 6; Philip Murray to Davis, Nov. 10, 1936, NNC MSS, Box 6; Davis to Van A. Bittner, Aug. 7, 1936, NNC MSS, Box 4; Clinton Golden to Davis, Aug. 19, 1936, NNC MSS, Box 5; Davis to Marcus Goldman, Dec. 29, 1936, NNC MSS, Box 5; Davis to Arthur H. Fauset, July 22, 1936, NNC MSS, Box 5; Davis to C. C. Spaulding, Aug. 24, 1936, NNC MSS, Box 7; *Official Proceedings of the Second National Negro Congress, 1937*, NNC MSS, Box 11; "Steel Drive Moves Colored People into Action!" NNC MSS, Box 20; "National Negro Congress Supports the Steel Workers Organizing Committee," NNC MSS, Box 20.

[22] Davis to Clinton Golden, Aug. 11, 1936, NNC MSS, Box 5; Davis to Bertram M. Gross, Apr. 29, 1938, NNC MSS, Box 13; Cayton and Mitchell, *Black Workers and the New Unions*, p. 205; Henry Johnson to Davis, Sept. 10, 1936, NNC MSS, Box 6; Eleanor Rye to Davis, Aug. 27, 1936, NNC MSS, Box 7.

about the same proportion as did whites; indeed, in some areas of Pittsburgh and Chicago, they signed up in even greater proportions. Sociologists Horace Cayton and George Mitchell, in their excellent study of black workers and the C.I.O., conclude that "the importance of the Negro organizers in winning Negro union members for the S.W.O.C. can hardly be overestimated." Moreover, the pro-union campaign by the Congress did much to counteract the long-term antilabor sentiment in the black community, and even to rechannel it into strong support for the C.I.O. Henry Johnson, a Congress leader employed by the S.W.O.C. in Gary, reported that after his speech in a local black church, the minister arose and announced:

> *I have always been against the A.F. of L. and organized labor, but I am convinced that this C.I.O. move is the only thing for my people. I want every steel worker of my church to sign up for this Union. And . . . I want you to . . . sign up every steel worker you come into contact with in Chicago Heights. If anybody asks you what you are doing, tell them Rev. Pinkett told you to sign them up and he has God and the people with him.*

Cayton and Mitchell maintain that "the National Negro Congress . . . did much in the way of creating a friendly public opinion in the Negro community," and that "the S.W.O.C. was fortunate" that the Congress was "in a position to challenge the leadership in the Negro community of the more conservative element."[23]

Similarly, there can be little doubt that black steelworkers gained through their membership in the union. By the end of 1937, when the S.W.O.C. was bargaining for 550,000 employees, it had raised wages by a third and put an end to the Jim Crow practices in much of the steel industry. Blacks often played leadership roles in local S.W.O.C. lodges, even in the South, and frequently represented their lodges at S.W.O.C. national conventions in the late 1930s; at one conference, there were an estimated fifty to one hundred black delegates. Inside the union racial prejudices softened and declined in communities where intense hostility had previously prevailed. One black steelworker somewhat optimistically claimed that the C.I.O. was "doing away with this color question." Although the 85,000 Negro steelworkers continued to lead rugged lives, their situation had vastly improved.[24]

The steel campaign, however, represented only the most dramatic instance of cooperation between the National Negro Congress and organized labor. In Richmond, the Congress organized several thousand Negro tobacco workers, led the first strikes in the tobacco industry since 1905, and created seven locals, which it turned over to the C.I.O. The Chicago council of the Congress entered into an agreement with the International Ladies Garment Workers Union to

[23] Cayton and Mitchell, *Black Workers and the New Unions*, pp. 202–6; Henry Johnson to Ben Careathers, Feb. 25, 1937, NNC MSS, Box 10; Davis, who attended countless rallies and gatherings during this period, described one as follows: "I spoke last night at a meeting in Baltimore attended by 700 steel workers. After my talk more than one hundred signed a card asking trade union organizers to visit them at their homes." Davis to Arthur H. Fauset, Aug. 14, 1936, NNC MSS, Box 5.

[24] Cayton and Mitchell, *Black Workers and the New Unions*, pp. 196, 207–9, 218–20; Herbert R. Northrup, "Organized Labor and Negro Workers," *Journal of Political Economy*, LI (June 1943), 217–19.

assist in organizing three thousand black women in clothing plants on the South Side. In Washington, the Congress mobilized support among black hotel workers for the hotel and restaurant workers union, which thereafter won collective bargaining elections in twelve out of thirteen hotels; "the credit for these victories belongs to the National Negro Congress," the union's vice-president declared. The Congress aided striking maritime workers on both the East and West coasts, and played an active role in the auto and textile organizing drives. In Los Angeles, Philadelphia, Houston, New York, Washington and Chicago, the Congress attempted to organize Negro domestics and to provide them with a free employment service and adult education classes. By 1940, the Congress had distributed more than a million pieces of literature to industrial workers, and had played an active part in unionizing a wide variety of black workers, ranging from miners to government white-collar employees.[25]

As part of its attempt to bring blacks into the labor movement, the Congress became a leading force for ending the racial restrictions on membership in many unions. In 1934, A. Philip Randolph had urged delegates at the American Federation of Labor convention to order "the elimination of the color clause and pledge from the constitution and rituals of all trade and industrial unions" and the expulsion of all unions which maintained "said color bar." Continuing to introduce this resolution at A.F. of L. conventions well into the postwar period, Randolph witnessed its consistent rejection by the leaders of organized labor.[26] Nonetheless, the National Negro Congress took up the "Randolph Resolution" and persistently pressed for its enactment. In Cleveland, for example, the Congress secured its endorsement by the Cleveland Metal Trades Council, the District Council of Painters and eventually by the Cleveland Federation of Labor. The Machinists Union of that city, which had barred blacks for forty years, voted after a meeting with local Congress leaders to abolish its racial restrictions and to begin an active compaign to organize black machinists. Through the efforts of the Congress, the "Randolph Resolution" was adopted by the Ohio State Federation of Labor, the Philadelphia Central Trades and Labor Council, the Buffalo Central Labor Union and the Maritime Federation of the Pacific Coast. In Chicago, although the Congress failed to have the resolution endorsed

[25] Davis to John Brophy, May 18, 1937, NNC MSS, Box 9; Esther McNeill to Joe Cook, Nov. 22, 1937, NNC MSS, Box 9; Davis to Francis A. Hanson, Sept. 17, 1937, NNC MSS, Box 10; Davis to E. M. Hutchinson, June 15, 1937, NNC MSS, Box 10; Davis to Charles Lakey, June 15, 1937, NNC MSS, Box 11; Davis to Carl Murphy, July 22, 1936, NNC MSS, Box 6; Davis to William Green, May 29, 1939, NNC MSS, Box 16; William Gaulden to Davis and Abram Flaxer, July 13, 1940, NNC MSS, Box 20; Davis to Max Bedacht, June 22, 1937, NNC MSS, Box 9; Davis to Walter Hardin, Oct. 6, 1937, NNC MSS, Box 10; Davis to Marcus Goldman, Dec. 29, 1936, NNC MSS, Box 5; Davis to Heva Ryan, Sept. 2, 1936, NNC MSS, Box 7; Davis to Michael Quill, Jan. 26, 1940, NNC MSS, Box 14; *Official Proceedings of the Second National Negro Congress, 1937*, NNC MSS, Box 11; W. A. Hunton to Clarence Johnson, Dec. 21, 1938, NNC MSS, Box 10.

[26] Randolph became such a gadfly at labor federation conventions that in 1959 President George Meany lost his temper, pounded the rostrum, and roared at him: "Who the hell appointed you as guardian of all the Negroes in America?" Marc Karson and Ronald Radosh, "The American Federation of Labor and the Negro Worker," *The Negro and the American Labor Movement*, ed. Julius Jacobson (Garden City, N.Y., 1968), pp. 163–87; Herbert Hill, "The Racial Practices of Organized Labor: The Contemporary Record," ibid., p. 288.

by the city's labor federation, it distributed ten thousand leaflets to white union members in its behalf. The Congress was also active at the A.F. of L.'s Tampa convention of 1936, where it led the unsuccessful fight for an end to the color bar.[27]

Like its efforts in the steel campaign, the work of the National Negro Congress in bringing large numbers of Negroes into the labor movement greatly aided the unions and won their support. Organized labor, which had exhibited only the mildest of interest in the National Negro Congress at the time of its formation, became a strong partisan of the black organization in the late 1930s. Endorsements poured forth from top C.I.O. officials, including: John L. Lewis, chairman of the C.I.O.; Philip Murray, chairman of the S.W.O.C.; John Brophy, director of the C.I.O.; Thomas Kennedy, secretary-treasurer of the United Mine Workers; E. L. Oliver, executive vice-president of Labor's Non-Partisan League; and Maurice Sugar, counsel for the United Auto Workers. Despite a much cooler attitude on the part of the A.F. of L. hierarchy, President William Green sent the Congress a letter of congratulations and a contribution. Once the victim of perpetual budgetary crises, the National Negro Congress began to receive sizable amounts of money from the C.I.O. and its affiliated unions. Six large C.I.O. unions, as well as a number of A.F. of L. organizations, endorsed the 1940 convention of the Congress, including the S.W.O.C., the Transport Workers Union, the Construction Workers Organizing Committee, the United Rubber Workers of America, and the American Federation of Teachers.[28]

Negroes, too, gained substantially from the labor organizing drive of the Congress. Before its establishment in 1936, barely one hundred thousand Negroes were members of American trade unions; by 1940, there were roughly half a million. Although the work of the Congress alone cannot account for this increase, there is little reason to doubt that it played a significant role in achieving it. If the steel drive and subsequent organizing campaigns did not result in salvation for black labor, they did produce higher incomes, better working conditions and some measure of job security for hundreds of thousands of black workers. Moreover, Negroes also secured a strategic vantage point in influencing labor's social policies. For example, the C.I.O., which enrolled the lion's share of black union members, took a consistently strong stand in behalf of racial equality throughout the 1930s, both in the factory and in political life. By contrast, it may be worth speculating on what policies toward blacks a lily-white labor federation would have supported in those days of economic crisis.[29]

[27] Davis, "Report of National Secretary" (1936), NNC MSS, Box 7; Davis to Carl Murphy, July 22, 1936, NNC MSS, Box 6; Davis to George Brown, June 9, 1936, NNC MSS, Box 4; Davis to Marcus Goldman, Dec. 29, 1936, NNC MSS, Box 5; Davis to Frank Morrison, Nov. 10, 1936, NNC MSS, Box 6.

[28] Davis to Officers and Members of International Unions, Central Labor Unions, State Federations of Labor and Local Unions (n.d.), NNC MSS, Box 90; John L. Lewis to National Negro Congress, Sept. 22, 1937, NNC MSS, Box 11; John Brophy to Davis, May 13, 1937, NNC MSS, Box 9; William Green to Davis, June 29, 1937, NNC MSS, Box 10; National Negro Congress press release, Mar. 15, 1940, NNC MSS, Box 89; Ralph Hetzel Jr. to Davis, Aug. 27, 1937, NNC MSS, Box 10; William Hargest to Davis, May 19, 1937, NNC MSS, Box 10; National Negro Congress press release, Apr. 20, 1940, NNC MSS, Box 89.

[29] Davis, "The Negro Vote and the New Deal" (1939), NNC MSS, Box 16; Sumner M. Rosen, "The CIO Era, 1935–1955," *The Negro and the American Labor Movement*, pp. 188–208; Cayton and Mitchell, *Black Workers and the New Unions*, pp. 211–12.

Yet the very success of the National Negro Congress in fostering a vigorous program in the late 1930s established the preconditions for its collapse at the 1940 convention. As the national office supported liberal legislation and politicians, the Congress began to lose its nonpartisan flavor. As the Congress concentrated upon drawing black workers into the C.I.O., it cemented a class rather than a racial alliance. Despite the broad program of action adopted at the founding convention in 1936, the Congress had drifted toward political partisanship and affiliation with organized labor by the late 1930s. This gradual movement away from its original principles of racial unity set the stage for the final transformation of the National Negro Congress in 1940 from a nationalist to a sectarian organization.

In 1940, the Communist Party added its strength to the forces pressing for this transformation. From the time of its founding in 1936, the Congress had won the fervent applause of the Party. Although the first convention of the Congress "did not adopt a Communist program," noted black Communist leader James W. Ford, "we Communists stand one hundred per cent behind it." In line with the "united front," the Party submerged its class emphasis to support broad racial unity. "Shall problems of the artisans, professionals and small business men suffering discrimination receive the attention of the Congress?" Ford asked his Party colleagues. "We hold the answer should undoubtedly be in the affirmative." Articles in the Party press continued throughout the late 1930s to oppose sectarianism and to support racial solidarity. As late as September 1939, Ford told Party members that "for the Negroes the central task is the promotion of unity." By 1940, however, after the Nazi-Soviet Pact, the Party's policy changed drastically. In line with "The Yanks Are Not Coming" campaign launched by the Party, a top official told the National Committee that it must build "the National Negro Congress as the broad expression of anti-war and anti-imperialist struggle." Racial unity was forgotten.[30]

The 1940 convention of the National Negro Congress brought both the long-term trends and the Party's short-term reversal to the surface. Symbolizing the new directions of the Congress by his presence, John L. Lewis addressed the opening session on April 26. In his speech, he attacked the Democratic Party for breaking its 1936 campaign pledges, demanded the enactment of antilynching legislation and the elimination of poll taxes, and urged America to avoid entanglement in the European war. But the most important part of his speech came at the end, when, hinting at the development of a new political force, he issued an invitation to the Congress "to affiliate with or to reach a working agreement with Labor's Non-Partisan League that our common purposes may better be attained." Here lay the culmination of the labor alliance so painstakingly forged by the Congress, as well as an ideal opportunity for Communists to reject the Roosevelt Administration without isolating themselves entirely

[30] James W. Ford, "Political Highlights of the National Negro Congress, *Communist*, XV (May 1936), 464; Ford and A. W. Berry, "The Coming National Negro Congress," *Communist*, XV (Feb. 1936), 141; Ford, "Build the National Negro Congress Movement," *Communist*, XV (June 1936), 552–61; Israel Amter, "May Day—In Peace or War?" *Communist*, XVII (Apr. 1938), 334–38; Ford, "The Struggle for the Building of the Modern Liberation Movement of the Negro People," *Communist*, XVIII (Sept. 1939), 826–27; Pat Toohey, "Greater Attention to the Problems of the Negro Masses!" *Communist*, XIX (Mar. 1940), 280; Record, *The Negro and the Communist Party*, pp. 191–93.

from other elements of the American Left. Lewis accordingly received tremendous applause.[31]

Sensing the drift of the Congress toward left-wing sectarianism, A. Philip Randolph fought back in behalf of its traditional aims of racial integrity and black unity. In a speech entitled "The World Crisis and the Negro People Today," he cautioned blacks against tying their interests to any American political party or to any foreign nation. He rejected Congress affiliation with both major parties, the Communist Party, the Socialist Party and with the Soviet Union; none, he noted, placed the interests of Negroes first. "The Communist party is not primarily, or fundamentally, concerned about the Negro . . . in America," he declared. Blacks did not "reject the Communist party because it is revolutionary or radical," but "because it is controlled . . . by a foreign State, whose policy may or may not be in the interests of . . . the Negro people." He attacked affiliation with American labor organizations, maintaining that if the Negro were to "save himself, he must depend upon his own right arm!" Appealing to the Congress, he asked for a leadership that would be "free from intimidation, manipulation or subordination . . . a leadership which is uncontrolled and responsible to no one but the Negro people." An article in the *Communist* later denounced Randolph for every conceivable crime, but rather accurately observed that he had struck a "nationalist note."[32]

Randolph's approach aroused great hostility among those present. Angry murmurs rose during his speech, and after about fifteen minutes the delegates began a stormy exodus from the room; at its conclusion, barely a third remained in their seats. John P. Davis followed with what was obviously a counterattack by the angry pro-Communist, pro-C.I.O. forces. "There is an increasing ground swell . . . saying, 'The Yanks Are Not Coming,' " he proclaimed. "The Negro people are saying: we shall not die in the war of American imperialism." He told of his visit to the Soviet Union, of "its many nations and people busy and working in amity, collaboration and peace"; he knew, he said, of "their deep friendship and aid to all oppressed peoples." Randolph's implicit rejection of C.I.O. affiliation struck him as particularly heinous. "Long has the Negro worker awaited the extended hand of organized labor," he declared. "Are there those who would have us turn our back upon the friendly offer made by John L. Lewis . . . last night? If there be such, we are doubtful of their loyalty to the cause of our people."[33]

It soon became apparent that Davis, rather than Randolph, had the ear of the convention. The composition of the delegate body explains much of this. Out of a total of 1,285 delegates, 464—the largest single group—represented trade unions, generally C.I.O. affiliates. By contrast, the two preceding conventions

[31] *New York Times*, Apr. 27, 1940; Speech of John L. Lewis to the Third National Negro Congress, Apr. 26, 1940, NNC MSS, Box 21; Bunche, "The Programs, Ideologies, Tactics," p. 357.

[32] A. Philip Randolph, "The World Crisis and the Negro People Today," NNC MSS, Box 21; *New York Times*, Apr. 28, 1940, p. 9; Bunche, "The Programs, Ideologies, Tactics," pp. 357–59; Theodore R. Bassett, "The Third National Negro Congress," *Communist*, XIX (June 1940), 548.

[33] Bunche, "The Programs, Ideologies, Tactics," pp. 357–58; Speech of John P. Davis to the Third National Negro Congress, Apr. 27, 1940, NNC MSS, Box 21; *New York Times*, Apr. 28, 1940, p. 9; Bassett, "The Third National Negro Congress," p. 547.

had drawn 83 and 219 labor delegates. Moreover, almost a third of the total delegate body in 1940 was white. Although this group frequently overlapped with the union representatives and the Communists, together all three had more than enough muscle to dominate the proceedings. Thus Randolph found himself in conflict with exactly those forces whom he correctly feared were undermining the Congress' traditional aim of racial unity. Over Randolph's objection that affiliation with Labor's Non-Partisan League would tie the Congress to "a partisan program" and split the "mass action" of the organization, the delegates voted to support such affiliation, as well as to condemn "involvement in this imperialistic war." A new constitution adopted made no mention of the organization's original nonpartisan principle. The new political trends and their constituency had clearly triumphed.[34]

These developments forced Randolph's withdrawal from a leadership role in the Congress. After the report of the resolutions committee was adopted, Randolph arose to announce that he was stepping down as president. "We have come to a point in the development of the organization where a departure from the principle of minimum demands is reached," he declared. He noted his dismay that the C.I.O. and the Communist Party had been funding the Congress, and stated his opinion that it "should be dependent on resources supplied by the Negro people alone." He did not "oppose domination of the Congress by the C.I.O. because I am opposed to the C.I.O.," he later observed; "I would be opposed to domination of the Congress by the A.F. of L. or any other white organization." Randolph had hoped that the "united front" would mean united racial action; by 1940, the Congress no longer answered that hope. "I quit the Congress because it is not truly a Negro Congress," he wrote. The large number of white delegates at the convention "made the Congress look like a joke. . . . Why should a Negro Congress have white people in it?" Criticizing the Congress for affording the Communist Party a position of control, Randolph continued to assert the nationalist viewpoint in which he had first assumed the presidency: "The American Negro will not long follow any organization which accepts dictation and control from any white organization."[35]

Thus, the 1940 convention of the Congress, which ushered in its rapid demise, did not simply represent the exercise in Communist control which a number of critics have alleged. To be sure, the Communist Party played a major role in deposing Randolph, but it did so by supporting a position to which many non-Communist delegates were already committed. According to Lester Granger, one of Randolph's adherents, "some of the opposition was no doubt ideologically inspired. . . . Some of the opposition, however, was thoughtful enough and

[34] "To the Delegates to the Third National Negro Congress" (May 7, 1940), NNC MSS, Box 18; Bassett, "The Third National Negro Congress," p. 544; Bunche, "The Programs, Ideologies, Tactics," pp. 355–56, 360–62; *New York Times*, Apr. 29, 1940, p. 17.

[35] Bunche, "The Programs, Ideologies, Tactics," pp. 366–68; *New York Times*, Apr. 29, 1940, p. 17; Randolph, "Why I Would Not Stand for Reelection as President of the National Negro Congress," *American Federationist*, XLVIII (July 1940), 24–25; Myrdal, *An American Dilemma*, II, 1401. Randolph was not, of course, anti-white. He observed: "While I oppose white members of the Negro Congress, I favor the Congress collaborating with nonpolitical white organizations." He merely wanted the Congress to represent blacks and their interests. Randolph, "Why I would Not Stand for Reelection," p. 25.

honestly arrived at, growing out of some delegates' conviction that the Congress has a job to do in the field of political and labor action." He believed, though, that the Congress should "drop all pretense at coordinating . . . national programs for improvement of the Negro population." This role, the original one of the Congress, Randolph sought to revive by creating the March on Washington Movement, which had the same broad scope and nonpartisan character as the early Congress. In one respect, however, it differed from its predecessor; this time, Randolph excluded whites.[36]

In a number of respects, then, the history of the National Negro Congress cannot be understood solely by reference to Communism. Its successes and its internal tensions did not pivot around Communist participation, but around other concerns in the black community. From 1936 to 1940, the period of its greatest activity, the Congress succeeded both on the local and on the national level in removing some of the barriers to black advancement in America. Ironically, however, many of its achievements, particularly within organized labor, undercut the broadly-based program upon which it had been founded. Political partisanship, alliances with the C.I.O. and narrower sectarian considerations gradually subverted the original nationalist emphasis of the organization and its local councils. The Communist Party assisted in the final reorientation of the Congress in 1940—as did whites and the C.I.O.—but it worked within an organization that had forsaken a nationalist approach for other types of alliance years before. By failing to see beyond the role of the Communist Party in the career of the National Negro Congress, American scholars have ignored much of the meaning of the past, while contributing to the paranoias of the present.[37]

[36] Lester B. Granger, "The Negro Congress—Its Future," *Opportunity*, XVIII (June 1940), 166; Myrdal, *An American Dilemma*, II, 818; Herbert Garfinkel, *When Negroes March: The March on Washington Movement in the Organizational Politics for FEPC* (Glencoe, Ill., 1959), pp. 47–53, 131–32.

[37] The preparation of this article was greatly facilitated by a grant from the National Endowment for the Humanities and by the research assistance of Miss Constance Messerly.

22
THE NEW DEAL AND THE STATES

James T. Patterson

The New Deal, in its efforts to cope with the economic crisis, had to deal with specific problems related to agriculture, unemployment, banking, and currency. In meeting this very large range of problems, agencies, boards, and at times government corporations were created with headquarters in Washington and with offices and administrators in central cities throughout the nation, and in some cases in every state as well. These programs helped to change American life along with the views and outlook of many citizens. Thus far, however, the New Deal has been examined largely from the vantage point of Washington, D.C. The political and legislative aspects have been carefully scrutinized. Administratively, scholars have rarely left the Washington scene. The author of this essay suggests that the full impact of the New Deal cannot be known and evaluated until the lower levels of administrative concern have been carefully examined.

James T. Patterson teaches recent American history at Brown University and is the author of two volumes on the New Deal, Congressional Conservatism and the New Deal *(Lexington, 1967) and* The New Deal and the States: Federalism in Transition *(Princeton, 1969), and a recent biography of Senator Robert A. Taft (Boston, 1972). This article presents an overall view, which is more fully developed in the second book on the New Deal.*

While a rough consensus may be developing concerning the aims and philosophy of the New Deal, only controversy surrounds the question of its effect on the states. One group speaks of the "new federalism" of Franklin D. Roosevelt—a potentially cooperative relationship enriched by matching grants and mutual advantage. Conservatives, however, have talked of a Leviathan state. "We are all beginning to look to Uncle Sam to be Santa Claus," one Democratic governor complained in 1935. "I think the toughest problem that we as Governors have is to stay away from it

Source: *American Historical Review*, Vol. 73, No. 1 (1967), pp. 70–84. Reprinted by permission of the author and the publisher.

if we can. . . ." And liberals, reflecting a third view, have maintained that the New Deal failed to pull the states out of an entrenched and miasmatic conservatism. "Since 1930," a critic has remarked, "state government has dismally failed to meet responsibilities and obligations in every field. . . . The federal government has not encroached on state government. State government has defaulted."[1]

Although scholars are only beginning to test these viewpoints, a wealth of evidence exists with which to attempt a synthesis. Two questions especially need more study. To what extent did state politics and services change from 1933 to 1945? To what extent were these changes or lack of changes the result of the New Deal?

In many ways state government appeared to change dramatically in the 1930's. States seemed willing to spend more for positive purposes, disbursing some $2,000,-000,000.00 in 1927 and between $2,800,000,000.00 and $3,400,000,000.00 annually from 1932 through 1934. When economic conditions improved after 1935, the rise in state spending was considerable—to $4,600,000,000.00 in 1938 and to $5,200,000,000.00 in 1940. State legislators, perhaps, were at last recognizing the need to provide costly services.[2] Much of this increased spending was for relief, a trend that seemed to reflect the diversion of public funds toward "other Americans." Many states developed central welfare agencies by removing both the financial responsibility for and administration of poor relief from the archaic local units that had monopolized the field. State spending for welfare purposes rose from thirty-five cents per capita in 1922 to seventy-seven cents per capita in 1932 and to four dollars per capita in 1942.[3]

Labor also seemed to benefit from state action in the 1930's. In 1933 alone fourteen states passed the child labor amendment, while only six had approved it between 1924 and 1932. Eight more did so from 1934 to 1938. By 1939 nineteen states had adopted laws modeled along lines of the Norris-La Guardia anti-injunction act of 1932, and twenty-five had enacted legislation providing for minimum wages for women and children. And five states passed so-called "Little Wagner

[1] For an account of a new federalism, see Jane P. Clark, *The Rise of a New Federalism* (New York, 1938). The Democratic governor was David Sholtz of Florida, quoted in *Proceedings of the Governors Conference, 1935* (Chicago, 1935), 37. The critic in 1949 was Robert S. Allen in *Our Sovereign State*, ed. *id.* (New York, 1949), xxix. For a more favorable view of state activity since the 1930's, see James A. Maxwell, *Financing State and Local Governments* (Washington, D. C., 1965), esp. 29.

[2] US Department of Commerce, Bureau of the Census, *Historical Statistics of the United States, Colonial Times to 1957* (Washington, D. C., 1961), 728. For other more detailed data, see *Federal, State, and Local Government Fiscal Relations*, 78th Cong., 1 sess., Senate Docs., No. 69 (Washington, D. C., 1943), esp. 358; James Maxwell, *The Fiscal Impact of Federalism in the United States* (Cambridge, Mass., 1946), 260 ff.; US Department of Commerce, Bureau of the Census, *Historical Statistics on State and Local Government Finances, 1902–1953* (Washington, D. C., 1955), 22; Council of State Governments, *State-Local Relations* (Chicago, 1946), 78–79.

[3] *Historical Statistics of the United States*, 728 (computed from population statistics on p. 7). Per capita welfare expenditures for state and local government were $1.00 in 1922, $3.50 in 1932, and $9.00 in 1942. For these figures, see *Historical Statistics on State and Local Government Finances*, 16, 22. For an exhaustive study of state welfare policies in the 1930's, see Josephine C. Brown, *Public Relief, 1929–1939* (New York, 1940), esp. 85–102, 171–91.

Acts" in 1937. Compared to the inaction or hostility of legislatures in the 1920's and 1950's, this flurry of progressive labor law was remarkable.[4]

Federal-state relations also appeared cooperative. Certainly, many federal officials sought to involve the states in New Deal programs. As one observer remarked in 1936, Washington agencies "are better organized, know better what they want, and are more insistent upon getting it than in any previous year. . . ."[5] The National Emergency Council employed officials to explain and report on federal efforts in the states and to coordinate the many new federal-state programs. Spurred by this activity, states passed an impressive amount of coordinating legislation. By 1937 forty-two states had facilitated administration of the Federal Housing Act, and thirty-two had acted to implement the lending activities of the Farm Credit Administration. In 1935 alone five hundred state laws cleared the path for Public Works Administration grants to localities.[6] Every state had created state planning agencies by 1937 (only fourteen such agencies had existed in 1933), and all states had assisted the Social Security Act within three years of its passage.[7]

A few states went beyond mere cooperation and enacted "Little New Deals." The 1937 legislative session in Georgia under Governor Eurith D. Rivers was, one observer said, the "bill passin'est session since Oglethorpe climbed out on Yamacraw Bluff."[8] Legislation included welfare reorganization, free school textbooks, state support of public schools for seven months, and larger appropriations for public health.[9] In Pennsylvania Governors Gifford Pinchot and George H. Earle transformed the Keystone State from one of the most reactionary into one of the most progressive. Earle followed national trends so closely that Pennsylvania legislation during his tenure appeared to pass "by ear."[10] Rhode Island and New York under Governors Theodore F. Green and Herbert H. Lehman were two other eastern states to enact sizable portions of New Deal legislation.[11]

[4] For developments in child labor legislation, see US Department of Labor, *Growth of Labor Law in the U. S.* (Washington, D. C., 1962), 42 ff. For minimum wage legislation, see *ibid.*, 191–223. See also Clara M. Beyer, "Major State Labor Legislation Enacted in 1937," *Labor Information Bulletin*, IV (Aug. 1937), 5–8; "Principal State Labor Laws Enacted in 1935," *ibid.*, II (Sept. 1935), 2–4.

[5] W. Brooke Graves, "The Future of the American States," *American Political Science Review*, XXX (Feb. 1936), 27.

[6] V. O. Key, Jr., "State Legislation Facilitative of Federal Action," *Annals of the American Academy of Political and Social Science*, CCVII (Jan. 1940), 7–13.

[7] National Resources Committee, "The Future of State Planning," Mar. 28, 1938, National Resources Planning Board (NRPB) Files, National Archives, 445.5, box 1070, 9. For information on the states and social security, see Abraham Epstein, "The Future of Social Security," *New Republic*, LXXXIX (Jan. 27, 1937), 373–76; Richard E. Dawson and James A. Robinson, "The Politics of Welfare," in *Politics in the American States: A Comparative Analysis*, ed. Herbert Jacob and Kenneth M. Vines (Boston, 1965), 371–410. This collection of excellent articles contains sophisticated comparative analyses of states by political scientists.

[8] Allen L. Henson, *Red Galluses: A Story of Georgia Politics* (Boston, 1945), 181.

[9] Roy E. Fossett, "The Impact of the New Deal on Georgia Politics, 1933–1941," doctoral dissertation, University of Florida, 1960, 220–46.

[10] Richard C. Keller, "Pennsylvania's Little New Deal," doctoral dissertation, Columbia University, 1960, 157.

[11] For Rhode Island, see Erwin L. Levine, *Theodore Francis Green: The Rhode Island Years, 1906–1936* (Providence, R. I., 1963), *passim;* for New York, see Allan Nevins, *Herbert H. Lehman and His Era* (New York, 1963), 170–72; Warren Moscow, *Politics in the Empire State* (New York, 1946), 166–68.

Liberal governors also appeared in other states. In Indiana Governor Paul V. McNutt anticipated much of the New Deal with a remarkable record in the legislative session of January 1933.[12] Culbert L. Olson, governor of California from 1939 to 1943, fought valiantly if unsuccessfully for liberal legislation, as did Governor Frank Murphy of Michigan from 1937 to 1939.[13] And Wisconsin under Philip La Follette and Minnesota under Floyd B. Olson tried to surpass the New Deal. The Wisconsin legislature, after some prodding, produced a "Little NRA," a state planning board, and a surtax on incomes, dividends, and utility companies in 1935; and a "Little TVA," a state reorganization act, and a "Little Wagner Act" in 1937.[14] Despite conservative legislative opposition, Olson succeeded in achieving a progressive income tax, the abolition of yellow-dog contracts, an anti-injunction statute, and a maximum work week of fifty hours for women.[15]

Given the activities of most states in the 1920's, these various developments were heartening to liberals. They suggested a resurgence of state progressivism, dormant for some years.[16] It also seemed that the New Deal was partly responsible for this resurgence, that there was indeed a new federalism, and that henceforth the national government would serve as the model for states to emulate.

There was also a gloomier side. States in the 1930's witnessed conflict as well as cooperation, conservatism as well as progressivism, reaction as well as reform.

State spending was far from revolutionary when considered in long-range terms. While it increased some 90 per cent from 1932 to 1942, it had increased some 100 per cent from 1922 to 1932 and would increase some 300 per cent from 1942 to 1952.[17] Given the depressed conditions and the increased federal spending of the

[12] See Robert R. Neff, "The Early Career and Governorship of Paul V. McNutt," doctoral dissertation, Indiana University, 1963, esp. 139–71. For an uncritical account, see I. George Blake, *Paul V. McNutt: Portrait of a Statesman* (Indianapolis, 1966).

[13] For California, see Robert E. Burke, *Olson's New Deal for California* (Berkeley, Calif., 1958); H. Brett Melendy and Benjamin F. Gilbert, *The Governors of California: Peter H. Burnett to Edmund G. Brown* (Georgetown, Calif., 1965), 395–411; Ronald E. Chinn, "Democratic Party Politics in California, 1920–1956," doctoral dissertation, University of California, Berkeley, 1958, *passim;* for Michigan, see Richard D. Lunt, *The High Ministry of Government: The Political Career of Frank Murphy* (Detroit, 1965), 123–62; James K. Pollock and Samuel J. Eldersfeld, "Michigan Politics in Transition," *Michigan Governmental Studies,* No. 10 (Ann Arbor, Mich., 1942).

[14] Charles H. Backstrom, "The Progressive Party of Wisconsin, 1934–1946," doctoral dissertation, University of Wisconsin, 1956, esp. 348–63.

[15] See the readable study by George H. Mayer, *The Political Career of Floyd B. Olson* (Minneapolis, 1951), esp. 122–40, 260–71.

[16] For other state studies that discuss the impact of the New Deal, see Rowland L. Mitchell, Jr., "Social Legislation in Connecticut, 1919–1939," doctoral dissertation, Yale University, 1954; John D. Minton, "The New Deal in Tennessee, 1932–1938," doctoral dissertation, Vanderbilt University, 1959, esp. 371; Allan P. Sindler, *Huey Long's Louisiana: State Politics, 1920–1956* (Baltimore, 1956); and Richard M. Judd, "A History of the New Deal in Vermont," doctoral dissertation, Harvard University, 1960, esp. 91–102, 120, 205, 268–70. John Gunther, touring the states in the mid-1940's, also commented upon the impact of the New Deal upon party attitudes. (See *Inside U.S.A.* [New York, 1947].)

[17] *Historical Statistics of the United States,* 728. The increase from 1902 to 1913 was 105 per cent; from 1913 to 1922, 350 per cent; and from 1952 to 1962, some $21,000,000,000.00, or 130 per cent.

1930's, the comparatively small increase in state expenditures is not surprising. It is nonetheless important to stress that in so far as spending is a guide positive state government was not a product of the 1930's but a fluctuating movement since the late nineteenth century.

Trends in state taxation during this period were even more revealing. At a time when some New Dealers were demanding steeper taxes upon the wealthy, many states were seeking revenue through increased levies on consumers. The result was a powerful sales tax movement. The first modern retail sales taxes did not become effective until 1932, yet by 1938 thirty-four states were depending on them. By 1942 general sales taxes accounted for 11 percent of all state revenue from state sources, and gasoline taxes for 18 percent more. Individual and corporate income taxes brought in only 9 percent.[18]

The remarkable aspect of these statistics is not that income taxes produced so little: many states looked hungrily in this direction, only to discover that the federal government had devoured this source of sustenance. Nor should it be surprising that states were seeking new revenue, for the desperate financial condition of local governments in the depression years forced states to finance formerly local functions. And it is not strange that states shied from deficit financing; so did most New Dealers. The total picture is nonetheless striking. While per capita state and local spending increased from $60.00 in 1927 to $69.00 in 1940, per capita state and local taxation rose considerably more—from $66.00 to $89.00. States and local subdivisions not only balanced their budgets; often they were able to retire past debts.[19] Far from revolutionary in spending policy, states in the 1930's were more regressive than in the past in raising revenue.

States were also penurious in relief spending. New Deal field agents were alternately astounded and embittered by the conservative and sometimes corrupt policy of state officials. New Jersey's relief administration, one agent noted, "is not a question of mal-administration and it is not altogether inefficient administration. I should say it is inept." An Arkansas agent was more blunt. "We have got to bear down on these local units of administration," he wrote the Federal Emergency Relief Administration head, Harry L. Hopkins. "I am convinced there is an enormous amount of crookedness going on in them." Governor Charles Bryan of Nebraska, brother of the Peerless Leader, received the most unflattering portrait of all. "His idea of social work," the FERA man wrote, "is that performed in cleaning up a political situation, with possibly some value in work done by ladies of the W.C.T.U. or the Elks in distributing Christmas baskets."[20]

18 *Ibid.*, 727. For state and local figures, see *Federal, State, and Local Government Fiscal Relations*, 345 ff., 431–32; Maxwell, *Fiscal Impact*, 293 ff. For the sales tax movement, see Neil H. Jacoby, *Retail Sales Taxation: An Analysis of Economic and Administrative Problems* (Chicago, 1938), 23–75, esp. table, 72.

19 The figures for spending and taxes are from *Historical Statistics on State and Local Government Finances*, 22. For state debts, see Maxwell, *Financing*, 179–200, and *Federal, State, and Local Government Fiscal Relations*, 359. Federal debt increased from $149.00 per capita in 1934 to $272.00 in 1940, but state per capita debt increased during the same period only from $14.00 to $15.00, and local per capita debt decreased from $100.00 to $97.00. (Figures, *ibid.*)

20 These letters are, in order, Arch Mandel to Hopkins, Dec. 17, 1934, Federal Emergency Relief Administration (FERA) Files, National Archives, 401.2–420, N.J.; Aubrey Williams to Hopkins, Aug. 9, 1933, *ibid.*, 401.1–406.2, box 16; Sherrard Ewing to Home Office, June 23, 1933, *ibid.*, 401–406.2, Neb., Box 173. Herbert Hoover's fieldmen had also been frustrated by the unwillingness of states to

If these agents were unhappy, Miss Lorena Hickok, Hopkins' perceptive roving observer, was dismayed. Denouncing Maine officials, she wrote that "to be a 'deserving case' in Maine, a family has got to measure up to the most rigid Nineteenth Century standards of cleanliness, physical and moral. . . . a woman who isn't a good housekeeper is apt to have a pretty rough time of it. And Heaven help the family in which there is any 'moral problem.' " The situation in Georgia was worse. "Oh, this *IS* the damnedest state!" she wrote. "I just itch to bring all the unemployed teachers and doctors and nurses and social workers in the North down here and put them to work! Which is, of course, no solution at all." By the time she reached Texas, she was approaching despair. Describing the factionalism that was impairing relief, she cried, "God help the unemployed." "If I were twenty years younger and weighed 75 pounds less," she added, "I think I'd start out to be the Joan of Arc of the Fascist movement in the United States." California was worst of all. "It's California politics, that's all, God damn it, and I think we ought to let Japan have this state. Maybe they could straighten it out."[21]

Most of these complaints were justified. Under the FERA federal money accounted for 71 per cent of all public relief spending in 1934 and 1935. Hopkins struggled constantly to persuade states to contribute their shares to the relief fund, but often only the threat of cutting off federal money coerced economy-conscious legislators. Hopkins had to federalize relief administration in six states rather than leave it in the hands of state and local officials, and had he not been anxious to avoid the appearance of federal dictation, he might have federalized many more.[22]

When the national government abandoned the task of aiding unemployables in 1935, the result was often disastrous for the destitute. Twelve states spent less than fifty cents per month for each recipient of direct poor relief in 1939; thirteen more contributed nothing at all, leaving poor relief in the hands of inefficient local officials.[23] The situation in too many states resembled that in Illinois in 1940 where "the administration of general assistance in Illinois, since the exit of the F.E.R.A., has been a retreat to the poor law."[24] Although relief administration improved in

appropriate adequate funds for relief. (See the files of President's Organization on Unemployment Relief [POUR], National Archives, file 501.)

21 These letters in the form of narrative reports to Hopkins are dated as follows: Sept. 30, 1933; Jan. 23, 1934; Apr. 11, 1934; and Aug. 1, 1934. All are in Harry L. Hopkins Papers, box 89, Franklin D. Roosevelt Library. These voluminous reports, while often harsh concerning state officials, are a remarkably complete and useful primary source. No other agent traveled so widely or reported so thoroughly.

22 Theodore E. Whiting, *Final Statistical Report of the F.E.R.A.* (Washington, D.C., 1942), *passim*. For Hopkins' problems in Colorado, see James F. Wickens, "Colorado in the Great Depression: A Study of New Deal Policies at the State Level," doctoral dissertation, University of Denver, 1964, 105–14. For Ohio problems, see David J. Maurer, "Public Relief Programs and Policies in Ohio, 1929–1939," doctoral dissertation, Ohio State University, 1963, 1–150. For "federalization" of relief, see Arthur H. Benedict, "Federal Centralization through Congressional Legislation, 1924–1939," doctoral dissertation, Ohio State University, 1948, 46 ff.

23 Brown, *Public Relief*, 336–40; Donald S. Howard, *The W.P.A. and Federal Relief Policy* (New York, 1943), 551.

24 Arthur P. Miles, "Relief in Illinois without Federal Aid," *Social Service Review*, XIV (June 1940), 300; see also Arthur Dunham, "Public Welfare and the Referendum in Michigan," *ibid.*, XII (Sept. 1938), 417–39; William Haber and Herman M. Somers, "The Administration of Public Assistance in Massachusetts," *ibid.*, 397–416.

some states, the picture was far from satisfactory, and states continued to lag far behind the federal government in distributing relief.

Labor's gains on the state level were also more apparent than real. Because the Supreme Court did not rule in favor of the Wagner Act and minimum wages until 1937, many states considered it folly to enact complementary statutes before that time. The sit-down strikes of 1937 then turned many moderates against organized labor. The conflict between the AFL and the CIO was also harmful; in Minnesota the AFL, fearing that a state labor board would favor the CIO, helped defeat a "Little Wagner Act."[25] Other states were reluctant to pass progressive labor laws that might hurt them in the competitive struggle to attract industry. Finally, state legislatures continued to be dominated by the same kinds of people who had ruled in more conservative times: lawyers, farmers, and businessmen. Few of these men encouraged unionism.[26]

For these reasons organized labor made few gains in the states after 1937. As the assistant director of the Division of Labor Standards wrote ruefully in 1939, "The legislatures, in almost every instance, are dominated by farmers and big business. Very little labor legislation will be enacted."[27] The Pennsylvania legislature amended its "Little Wagner Act" on behalf of business interests; Wisconsin legislators repealed theirs. Minimum-wage legislation received unsympathetic hearings, and only two new laws passed in 1939.[28] A federal agent reported that the "outstanding feature" of labor legislation in 1939 was the "tendency in several states to enact measures seriously restricting the rights of labor to organize and to bargain collectively."[29] Right-to-work laws in the early 1940's served to emphasize the accuracy of his remarks.

Federal-state relations were also far from smooth. Officials of the National Recovery Administration worked diligently to persuade states to create "Little NRA's" covering intrastate matters, but with disappointing results. One field agent wrote, "the hope we have is very slim. We find NRA and Codes decidedly unpopular in the rural regions and it is these regions that dominate our legislature. . . ." Another added, "there is a natural antagonism toward federal legislation in general and NRA in particular, existing in the minds of a great many legislators. . . . too many requests for legislation are coming from the various branches of the Federal Gov-

[25] Ivan H. Hinderaker, "Harold Stassen and Developments in the Republican Party in Minnesota, 1937–1943," doctoral dissertation, University of Minnesota, 1949, 93.

[26] Clement C. Young, *The Legislature of California: Its Membership, Procedure, and Work* (San Francisco, 1943), 18–19 *et passim*, contains considerable information regarding occupational backgrounds of legislators in California and elsewhere. See also Charles S. Hyneman, "Tenure and Turnover of the Indiana General Assembly," *American Political Science Review*, XXXII (Feb., Apr. 1938), 51–66, 311–31. For the unfriendly attitude toward organized labor of the supposedly radical Long machine in Louisiana, see Sindler, *Huey Long's Louisiana*, 105–6.

[27] Clara M. Beyer to Paul Sifton, Mar. 20, 1939, Division of Labor Standards Files, National Archives, box 59, 12-0-15-4.

[28] Sanford Cohen, *State Labor Legislation, 1937–1947: A Study of State Laws Affecting the Conduct and Organization of Labor Unions* (Columbus, Ohio, 1948), 50.

[29] Charles F. Sharkey, "State Legislation on Labor Relations," *Labor Information Bulletin*, VI (Sept. 1939), 10; "Progress of State Minimum Wage Legislation in 1939," *Monthly Labor Review*, L (Feb. 1940), 312–24.

ernment."[30] By 1935 when the Supreme Court invalidated the NRA, few states had cooperated earnestly.

Many liberals were equally dismayed by the failure of the planning movement, encouraged by some New Dealers to induce states to consider long-range solutions for their problems. As long as states received federal money to finance planning (they obtained some $1,800,000.00 in 1937), they were willing to cooperate superficially. They set up planning boards, conducted studies, and issued reports. But when the money declined, so did the boards. A careful survey in 1938 observed that "the boards have been groping, experimenting, feeling their way. . . . there exists confusion." Boards were "precarious" in one-third of the states and either "nonexistent or relatively inactive" in another one-third.[31] Neither the depression nor the New Deal was able to persuade state legislators to indulge in the frills of long-range planning.

Federal-state conflicts were common in the 1930's. Such friction was partly the result of the emergency situation: the New Deal enacted so many new laws calling for state implementation that some confusion was inevitable. New Dealers, moreover, were too often unable to clarify their intentions for state officials. One competent observer saw little "formal organization for handling the federal-state legislative relationship." New Dealers, he continued, were "unaware of the part that state legislation plays in departmental activity." The National Emergency Council, supposedly the coordinator, was merely a group of people who "assisted the President in gauging political winds."[32]

Hickok, surprised to find that many state officials had never heard of the NEC, was especially disillusioned. The NEC, she wrote, "hasn't even begun to live up to its possibilities. . . . And I think that one trouble is that the coordinating end of it has been 'nobody's baby.' Just a grand idea that nobody ever really did much about." State NEC agents, she advised, should have authority to " 'crack down' on the heads of the other government agencies in the state, or to interfere with policies laid down by the heads of those agencies in Washington." Urging more frequent meetings between state and federal officials, she concluded wisely, "There's nothing else in the world quite so effective as personal contact—hours of conversation over a highball—to break down this kind of thing."[33] The New Deal, far from autocratically imposing its programs upon the states, sometimes failed to impose them at all.

The fate of the "Little New Deals" also revealed the transitory nature of state progressivism in the 1930's. In Georgia, Rivers managed to win again in 1938, only to plunge into partisan warfare with conservative legislators. Soon the state had financial troubles, and Rivers' prestige disappeared. Of the three Democratic candidates in the 1940 gubernatorial primary, not one endorsed the New Deal, and

[30] E. J. Brennan to R. S. Beach, Mar. 16, 1935, Charles S. Ausley to Walter Hawkins, May 13, 1935, National Recovery Administration (NRA) Files, National Archives, Ser. 101, Mo. File, and box 7939.

[31] National Resources Committee, "The Future of State Planning," Mar. 28, 1938, NRPB Files, 445.5, box 1070, 9; see also Ralph B. Cooney, "Planning by the States," *New Republic*, XCV (July 20, 1938), 296–97.

[32] Ernest Engelbert and Kenneth Wernimont, "Administrative Aspects of the Federal-State Legislative Relationship," *Public Administration Review*, II (Spring 1942), 126–41.

[33] Hickok to Hopkins, May 27, 1935, Hopkins Papers, box 89.

former Governor Eugene Talmadge, a staunch foe of liberalism, swept to victory on an economy platform.[34]

Other progressive administrations failed to survive the 1938 elections. Harold Stassen defeated the Farmer-Labor administration in Minnesota; a conservative Republican replaced La Follette in Wisconsin; the Republican victor in Pennsylvania set out to make good his pledge to burn all three thousand pages of liberal legislation signed by Pinchot and Earle; and Murphy was defeated in Michigan, to be replaced after the death of his opponent by an eighty-year-old lieutenant governor who bragged, "I have a pipe-line to God," and whose friends referred modestly to themselves as "just a couple of fellows hanging on the public tit."[35] A few progressive governors remained after 1938, but none succeeded in enacting much of the New Deal, and in many states the liberal programs achieved in the mid-1930's remained on the defensive for the next two decades.

Various factors help explain the difficulties encountered by state progressivism in the 1930's. Perhaps the most obvious was the limited nature of positive state action prior to the depression. Scholars have rightly shown that states contributed materially to nineteenth-century economic development, that they preceded the national government in efforts to regulate corporations, and that they often served as laboratories of social reform.[36] But neither the states nor the federal government prior to the depression had been forced to think seriously of costly welfare legislation, deficit spending, or legislation beneficial to organized labor. Since these were the staples of the new progressivism of the 1930's, it was not strange that state leaders, like many New Dealers, were slow to adopt them.

Lack of funds provided a second problem. Even before the depression, real-estate and personal property taxes—until then the chief sources of state and local revenue—had proved burdensome, and states, faced with the enormously expensive task of road building in the 1920's, had been forced to turn to bond issues. When the depression descended so sharply, it caught many states in an unsound financial position, which they tried to escape first through drastic economies and then through regressive taxation.[37] Chastened by this experience, these states lacked faith in renewed deficit financing, and they therefore shunned costly progressive services.

Another difficulty was a peculiar one of timing. The reform impulse of the 1930's, unlike that of the progressive era, was federal in origin and limited in

[34] Fossett, "Impact of the New Deal," 261–314.

[35] Keller, "Pennsylvania's Little New Deal," 320–24; "The Republican Party; Up from the Grave," *Fortune*, XX (Aug. 1939), 100; see also Philip La Follette *et al.*, "Why We Lost," *Nation*, CXLVII (Dec. 3, 1938), 586–90.

[36] See Sidney Fine, *Laissez Faire and the General-Welfare State: A Study of Conflict in American Thought, 1865–1901* (Ann Arbor, Mich., 1956), 19 ff., 353 ff.; Daniel J. Elazar, *The American Partnership: Intergovernmental Cooperation in the 19th Century United States* (Chicago, 1962); Robert S. Maxwell, *La Follette and the Rise of the Progressives in Wisconsin* (Madison, Wis., 1956); Gerald D. Nash, *State Government and Economic Development: A History of Administrative Policies in California, 1849–1933* (Berkeley, Calif., 1964).

[37] State per capita debt rose from $7.70 in 1919 to $15.03 in 1930. (*State-Local Relations*, 79.) For state debts, see also "Going into the Red," *State Government*, V (Apr. 1932), 10–11; Edna Trull, "Two Decades of State Borrowing," *National Municipal Review*, XXVI (June 1937), 277–82, and "Resources and Debts of the Forty-Eight States," *ibid.*, XXVII (June 1938), 293–98.

duration. Pressed for funds in the early years of the depression, states awaited federal action. But since many key New Deal laws affecting states—social security, the Wagner Act, and fair labor standards—were passed in or after 1935, and since the Supreme Court did not sustain them until 1937 or later, many states were reluctant to enact "Little New Deals" before 1937. Then the conservative reaction of 1937–1938 descended, and the main chance was gone. While several states managed to accomplish much in 1935 or 1937, the great majority needed more time.

Institutional factors presented a fourth hurdle. Just as courts thwarted the New Deal, so they interfered with progressive state legislation. State constitutions imposed unrealistic obstacles to financing new services,[38] and state legislatures continued to be dominated by ill-trained, inexperienced, and poorly paid men, chosen according to systems of apportionment that were inequitable in forty-one state senates and thirty-six assemblies. In practically every case, this unfair apportionment favored rural areas; in such key urban states as Connecticut and Ohio this fact helped prevent comprehensive "Little New Deals."[39]

A more serious institutional problem was the incorrigible factionalism of state Democratic parties. This factionalism was sometimes selfish, sometimes the result of new, liberal elements challenging an existing organization, but it almost always blocked cohesive party policy. When Democratic National Chairman James A. Farley asked state politicians to voice their complaints, he received innumerable protests against selfish factions that were damaging the President's program. "The Democratic organization has fallen down," a Montana Democrat wrote. "I never went to a single county that factions did not exist. . . . The party has simply got to be reorganized from the bottom." An Ohio Democrat added in 1938:

> *Things are not as good in Ohio as they were two years ago. We have had too much discord among the leaders and the near-leaders in the party. We have been in office quite a while; we are well fed. This makes for unnecessary and unseemly ambition on the part of too many Democrats who are "hell-bent to be first in the kingdom."*[40]

Federal field agents concurred. One wrote to Hopkins: "legislation would be much simpler in Iowa if there was one good political boss. There is no leadership. The legislature is divided into numerous factions . . . and these factions are not split along party lines."[41] Hickok concluded:

[38] See B. U. Ratchford, "Constitutional Provisions Governing State Borrowing," *American Political Science Review*, XXXII (Aug. 1938), 694–717.

[39] For the quality of state legislatures, see Hyneman, "Tenure and Turnover"; Henry W. Toll, "The 48: A Smiling Comparison of Some Features of Our Legislators," *State Government*, III (May 1930), 3–11. For unfair apportionment, see Thomas R. Dye, "State Legislative Politics," in *Politics in the American States*, ed. Jacob and Vines, 160–64; David O. Walter, "Reapportionment and Urban Representation," *Annals of the American Academy of Political and Social Science*, CXCV (Jan. 1938), 11–20.

[40] James F. O'Connor to Arthur F. Lamey (Montana Democratic state chairman), Nov. 22, 1938, George H. Kemath to Farley, Oct. 28, 1938, Official File 300 [hereafter cited as OF 300], boxes 105, 106, Election Forecasts and Analyses, Roosevelt Library. This file is a major source of evidence of party factionalism in the 1930's.

[41] T. J. Edmunds to Hopkins, Feb. 2, 1934, FERA Files, Iowa, box 97.

> *in each of these states you have one or more of the boys trying to build up Tammany organizations overnight, with plenty of opposition from other Democrats, while the Republicans piously hold their noses! And the President, if he isn't actually dragged into it, is left without any organization, or any spokesman.*[42]

Democratic politicians, moving ambitiously to majority status, gathered like bees about the honey, and all too often the progressives fell to the ground.[43]

What could New Dealers have done to assure a deeper impact upon the states? Little. The limited nature of predepression state progressivism was not the fault of the New Deal, nor was the financial chaos of many states in the early 1930's. Indeed, federal aid to the states, which increased from $217,000,000.00 in 1932 to $2,000,000,000.00 in 1935, was indispensable in rehabilitating state finances.[44] Problems presented by state courts, unfair apportionment, and state constitutions were soluble by state action alone.

Federal coercion was not the answer. Men such as Farley and Hopkins realized only too well that state officials were easily offended and that to charge in, as Roosevelt did in the purge of 1938, was to invite defeat. As Hopkins said of a factional struggle in Delaware, "I am not disposed to do anything in this administrative jam. I think this is up to Delaware. I am disposed to let them stew in their own juice."[45] Farley was equally cautious. California Democrats besieged him with pleas in 1934 to halt the factionalism surrounding Upton Sinclair's "End Poverty in California" campaign. One correspondent complained: "The Democrats here are all fighting among themselves. . . . Frankly, you are the only one who could save the situation. These Democratic factions should unite and concentrate upon one good man, with your approval." Farley passed the letter to Louis McH. Howe, Roosevelt's friend and political adviser. Howe was no help. "You are running California," he cracked. "What will I tell this man?" Farley was at a loss: "I don't know what to say to you, Louis, except to pass the letter back to you and

[42] Hickok to Hopkins, Nov. 3, 1935, Hopkins Papers, box 89 [italics hers].

[43] Many secondary works document this factionalism in individual states or regions. These include V. O. Key, Jr., *Southern Politics in State and Nation* (New York, 1949); John H. Fenton, *Politics in the Border States: A Study of the Patterns of Organization and Political Change* (New Orleans, 1957); Sindler, *Huey Long's Louisiana;* Elmer L. Puryear, *Democratic Party Dissension in North Carolina, 1928–1936* (Chapel Hill, N.C., 1962); *Rocky Mountain Politics,* ed. Thomas Donnelly Albuquerque, N. Mex., 1940). Among state histories dealing with politics in the 1930's are Charles H. Ambler and Festus P. Summers, *West Virginia: The Mountain State* (Englewood Cliffs, N. J., 1958); Duane Meyer, *The Heritage of Missouri, A History* (St. Louis, 1965); Elwyn B. Robinson, *History of North Dakota* (Lincoln, Nebr., 1966); Carl Ubbelohde, *A Colorado History* (Boulder, Colo., 1965); T. A. Larson, *History of Wyoming* (Lincoln, Nebr., 1965); James C. Olson, *History of Nebraska* (Lincoln, Nebr., 1955); Warren A. Beck, *New Mexico: A History of Four Centuries* (Norman, Okla., 1962); Seth S. McKay and Odie B. Faulk, *Texas after Spindletop* (Austin, Texas, 1965); Edwin C. McReynolds, *Oklahoma, A History of the Sooner State* (Norman, Okla., 1954). Political patterns in these states were, to state it mildly, inauspicious for progressive reform.

[44] Henry J. Bittermann, *State and Federal Grants-in-Aid* (New York, 1938), 142. The latter sum included FERA and PWA funds.

[45] Hopkins telephone conversation, Apr. 19, 1934, Hopkins Papers, box 93.

write him and say you will call the matter to my attention. It is a terrible mess but how we are going to be able to do anything, I don't know."[46]

Patronage problems also revealed the dilemma faced by Roosevelt and his advisers. To many Republicans it seemed that only Democrats were receiving key administrative positions. As the decade advanced, charges that relief spending was "Farleyized" were especially loud, culminating in widespread attacks on the WPA in 1938.

In fact the opposite was often true, and Republicans managed to secure important federal jobs in many states. Early in the New Deal Farley approved a procedure whereby job seekers had to receive the endorsement of county chairmen, congressmen, or senators. The Democratic National Committee would then review the endorsements, filling jobs on the basis of ability and past support of Roosevelt. The system failed. For one thing, there were too many applicants—some 10 for each of the 150,000 jobs. Worse, it was easy to get endorsements from local politicians anxious to please hard-pressed constituents. "Endorsers," one observer commented, "are as undiscriminating as poppy girls at a Legion ball."[47] Distribution of New Deal patronage was far from centralized, and many appointees proved unsympathetic with the programs they were supposed to administer.

As if this situation were not troublesome enough, some New Dealers, notably Hopkins and Interior Secretary Harold L. Ickes, refused to allow Farley to interfere with their staffing procedures. The result was incessant complaining from disgruntled Democrats. "I do not want you to understand that I am desirous of making a political football out of the W.P.A.," an Illinois county chairman wrote, "but I certainly object to the W.P.A. being operated to the disadvantage of the Democratic Party."[48] A Michigan national committeeman added: "I would appreciate greatly anything you can do in Washington to encourage Harry Hopkins to go along with us in a [*sic*] effort to make this machinery balance up to the point of making it a nonpartisan picture. It is now and has been a 90% Republican picture."[49] Another complainer was Senator Harry S. Truman. Missouri, he told Farley, gave Roosevelt a large majority, but "when the patronage was handed out the people who control things in the party in this State were not recognized. . . . it is rather discouraging to say the least."[50] Even Hickok, ordinarily contemptuous of politicians who tried to control relief administration, was concerned over the number of conservative Republican appointees. She complained to Hopkins, "I can't see that leaving it [relief] all in the hands of the gang that handled it under Hoover—and who are about as popular out here as grasshoppers—was exactly smart. It hasn't 'taken' well, I can assure you. Yours for a REAL DICTATORSHIP."[51]

[46] H. R. Keefe to Roosevelt, June 22, 1934, Howe to Farley, June 29, 1934, Farley to Howe, July 2, 1934, OF 300, box 16.

[47] "The Democratic Party," *Fortune*, XI (Apr. 1935), 135.

[48] W. M. Burton to Farley, Dec. 12, 1938, OF 300, box 104.

[49] Horatio J. Abbott to Emil Hurja, Apr. 4, 1934, Emil Hurja Papers, Roosevelt Library. Hurja was Farley's aide; his papers contain letters concerning patronage problems.

[50] Truman to Farley, Aug. 28, 1936, Democratic National Committee Files, box 5, Missouri, Franklin D. Roosevelt Library. These files and those of the Women's Division of the Democratic National Committee under OF 300 also contain revealing political correspondence.

[51] Hickok to Hopkins, Nov. 9, 1933, Hopkins Papers, box 89.

Far from being controlled for the benefit of the Democratic party, relief administration was remarkably nonpartisan in the 1930's and often hostile to the New Deal. But what were Hopkins and Ickes to do? Had they chosen to make relief and public works the province of machine Democrats, relief standards might have been no better, and the critics of "Farleyization" would have been all the more vociferous. Federal restraint was the wisest policy.

The politics of America is state politics. The effect of the New Deal thus depended on the creation and sustenance of forty-eight strong liberal Democratic machines, and this the New Deal failed to do. One critic perceived this failure as early as 1935:

> *The Democratic machine of the early thirties is in no remarkable way distinguishable from the political machines, Republican or Democratic, which have preceded it. It is not, that is to say, a device upon which the United States Patent Office would look with interest. Aside from certain improvements in the timing gears . . . it is a dead ringer for earlier and too familiar models.*[52]

And a liberal columnist, commenting on Democratic defeats in 1938, warned that the election should "persuade Roosevelt that the local Democratic machines which have flourished under his Administration are liabilities, and that the work of spreading the gospel is not a proper mission for gorillas."[53] It is undeniable that Roosevelt, working with often unprogressive state and local Democratic parties, failed to construct a liberal Democratic apparatus in many states.

But his alternatives were restricted. New Dealers, especially in the busy first term, did not have much time to devote to political questions in nonelection years. It was simpler to work within the existing machinery, much of which functioned in city halls rather than statehouses, than to embark upon the difficult task of liberalizing state parties. And given the autonomy of state political organizations, it is doubtful that the strongest pressures would have succeeded. Had Roosevelt systematically sought to purge Democratic organizations of uncooperative elements at the height of his popularity in 1936, he might have made a start. But it is not at all certain that he would have succeeded, and politicians of all persuasions would have hotly resented the attempt.

Few historians would maintain that the New Deal left the states unchanged. States centralized services, applied new taxes, approved progressive labor laws, and increased relief spending. A host of ambitious federal agencies prodded state departments into new services. Without the depression and New Deal, the striking developments in state government of the 1940's and 1950's might not have come so quickly. The over-all picture, however, reveals almost as much continuity as change on the state level from the progressive period (excepting perhaps the 1920's) to the 1960's, and it suggests that historians would do well to revise nationalistic interpretations of the New Deal. The New Deal years witnessed neither federal dictation, a completely cooperative federalism, nor a dramatically new state progressivism. Moreover, many of the changes that did occur, notably in relief administration and taxation, were forced upon the states by the depression and not by the New Deal.

[52] "Democratic Party," 63.

[53] Paul Y. Anderson, "What the Election Means," *Nation*, CXLVII (Nov. 19, 1938), 527–29.

New Dealers must unquestionably accept some responsibility for this limited effect on the states. Some federal officials neglected state affairs; others appointed hostile personnel; still others were unnecessarily fearful of offending entrenched machines. The lack of coordination among various federal agencies was at times distressing. But the most striking feature of federal-state relations during the 1930's was not the failure of New Dealers but the limits in which they had to operate. Time was short, courts hostile, state institutions blocked change, and state parties were often divided, conservative, or concerned with patronage instead of policy. Roosevelt, by working with instead of against the *status quo* in the states, kept federal-state friction to a minimum and concentrated on achieving the national legislation that proved more important in assuring social change in twentieth-century America.

CIVIL RIGHTS
THE BEATLES
IT'S HOWDY DOODY TIME
ASK NOT WHAT YOUR COUNTRY...
"GI JOE"
"I HAVE A LIST"
SENATOR JOE McCarthy
FUTURE SHOCK

PART THREE

1940-1970

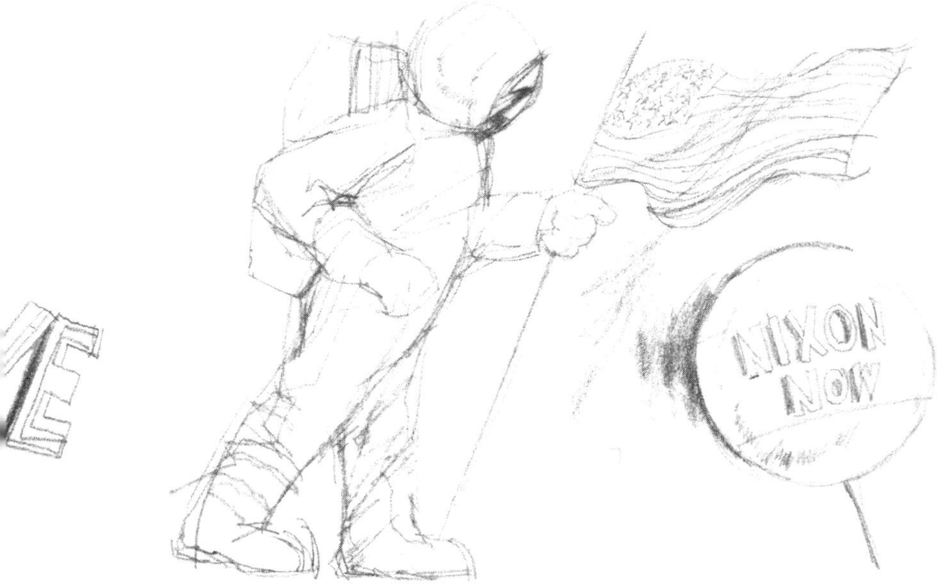

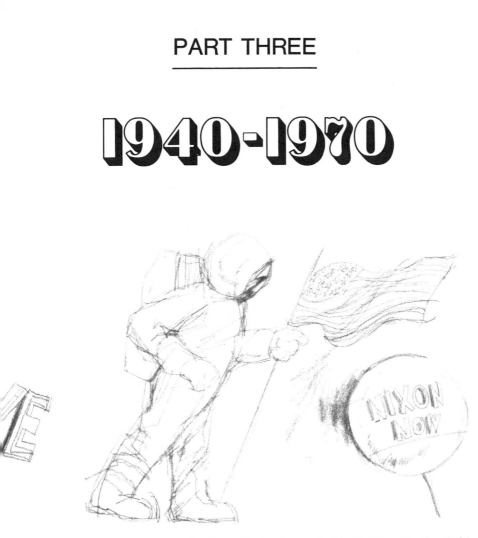

The three decades following the New Deal witnessed World War II, the Cold War, Korea, Vietnam, and domestic turmoil and conflict affecting all facets of American life from urban blight to rural decay, from conservation to racial violence. Indeed no aspect of American life was safe from scrutiny and challenge during these decades. In the 1940's the American people participated as partners in what Franklin D. Roosevelt called "the most tremendous undertaking in our American history" while their president played a prominent role as world leader. Upon his successor, Harry S Truman, however, fell the burden of leading the nation to ultimate victory in war and guiding it in the postwar years through the difficult period of demobilization and reconversion. At the same time, new international tensions involving the United States and the Soviet Union confused and embittered a war-weary people eager to enjoy material comforts and to resume the older and more familiar patterns of living. Mid-century found the United States involved in a "Cold War" that threatened to erupt into another global holocaust, but, in fact, continued to smolder in costly conflicts that kept American forces almost continually involved in East Asia. The problems of reconversion, the Cold War, and the attendant concern with Communism raised issues that harassed the American people throughout the decade of the fifties and brought the liberal New Deal legacy under sharp attack. The Democratic party remained the dominant party, but the Republicans, capitalizing on domestic discontents and divisions among the Democrats, were able to dominate the executive branch during the decade of the fifties and to return to power at the end of the sixties. Though there was growing general concern about poverty and race during these years, affluent but unkempt college youth aroused public indignation as they asked penetrating questions and rejected much that older Americans accepted or took for granted, from sexual mores to the value of a college education and military intervention abroad. On leaving office, President Eisenhower, warning against what he termed the military-industrial complex, observed, "the potential for the disastrous rise of misplaced power exists and will persist." This complex came in for much criticism, even though it was responsible for the American exploration of outer space and for placing men on the moon. The employment of power and the issue of misordered priorities were the primary sources of antagonisms and disruptions besetting American life at the end of the seventh decade of the twentieth century. Whether it was military might in Southeast Asia, a lack of economic power that deprived poor people of equal opportunity, or police power that assailed young Americans as they marched in protest, the resultant confusion, owing in part to a lack of responsive and responsible leadership, left many citizens wondering just what of the old values remained. Many voices were heard—and some of the more inspired were to be stilled by assassins' bullets—but none was able by the outset of the 1970's to win the confidence of a majority of the American people and dispel the contradictions and confusions that engulfed them.

The nine articles in this section examine developments during these three turbulent decades. The first article, by Kenneth Shewmaker, in part predates the period covered in this section, but it points up the fact, later lost sight of in the Cold War, that many of those who had had extensive experience in China—missionaries, doctors, and in this instance, a high-ranking marine officer—were sympathetic to the Chinese Communists and saw a new China emerging out of the agonies of internal divisions and the Japanese invasion. Sidney Fine's article, on the other hand, reveals a quite different American attitude toward the Asian, the sometimes latent but never dormant racial bias against the Japanese-American, which flared into open hostility following Pearl Harbor. The cruel irony of a nation fighting against the Nazi ideology of racial and religious bigotry while at the same time displaying racial discrimination at home is further emphasized by Richard Dalfiume's article, which examines the struggle of black Americans for equality and civil rights during the war years. This struggle, though temporarily frustrated, nevertheless established a beachhead from which the main thrust could be launched in the succeeding decades.

George Herring, by concentrating on an aspect of wartime diplomacy, the winding down of our lend-lease arrangements with the Soviet Union, anticipates the coming of the Cold War but at the same time effectively refutes the argument frequently made by the Russians and some American historians that lend-lease was simply "a weapon of aggressive American imperialism."

In June 1950, President Truman, under the aegis of, and with the support of, a large majority of the United Nations, sent American troops into South Korea to repel an invasion by North Korea. H. H. Wubben deals with an aspect of that conflict—the morale and behavior of American prisoners of war in Korea. He denies the charge of some critics that the response of these POW's was markedly different from that of American prisoners in previous conflicts and that their behavior revealed a deterioration of the American character attributable to the welfare philosophy of the New Deal and the softness of progressive education.

In turning to the domestic scene in these post-World War II years, F. S. O'Brien evaluates the effectiveness of the efforts of the major labor unions to purge themselves of Communist influences, and Don Hadwiger criticizes the ineffectiveness of even sympathetic administrations in alleviating rural poverty and racial discrimination by their agricultural programs.

As has been the case since the beginning of the Industrial Revolution, Western man, and particularly the American, once again demonstrates in this period his far greater talent to deal with scientific and technological problems than his ability to find solutions to social and economic questions. Loyd Swenson's article on "The 'Megamachine' behind the Mercury Spacecraft" examines in detail the successful cooperation between private industry and government to put man in outer space as the prelude to putting man on the moon, or as Lewis Mumford has expressed it, "securing, at an extravagant cost, a passage to Heaven for the favored few."

Finally, we conclude this section and the book with an essay-review by William Appleman Williams of Lyndon Baines Johnson's memoir, *The Vantage Point.* Mr. Williams, with wit, perception, and a great deal of sympathetic understanding, presents the tragedy of a president who did have a sincere vision of a Greater Society for all Americans than had ever been known before, but who was to be defeated by policies long operative and blinded by the hood of tradition, which he refused to remove.

The seventy years that are covered by the essays in this volume, a period which is a third of our history as an independent nation, reveal both the constancy and the change in man's historical record. In 1900, only a poetic, scientific spoofer like Jules Verne would envision man walking on the moon within seven decades. But also in 1900, only the most cynical pessimist, in that age of progressive optimism, would have believed that our cities were to become more dirty, more dangerous, more unmanageable in his grandchildren's time than in his own. In the lifetime of one man, mankind has taken giant steps forward scientifically and technologically. But man has crawled at a snail's pace through the social mire which the muckrakers of 1900 were so busily and hopefully stirring.

As we enter the last quarter of this violent century, all of the big issues that confronted the nation at the century's beginning are still with us. Only now perhaps we see more clearly than before that time is running out for all of us and "the securing of a passage to Heaven" for the favored few of us is not a salvation for any of us.

23

THE AMERICAN LIBERAL DREAM: EVANS F. CARLSON AND THE CHINESE COMMUNISTS, 1937–1947

Kenneth E. Shewmaker

America has always had a curious love-hate attitude toward China. We pitied it for its sprawling political ineptitude, but we officially discouraged any efforts at internal reform. We participated eagerly in its international humiliation in 1900, but we claimed we did so only for the preservation of its territorial integrity. We insisted on an Open Door into China while at the same time we closed our own doors to Chinese immigrants. We sent our missionaries to "Christianize and civilize the heathen Chinee," but we remained in awe of its rich, unparalleled culture. No event in the immediate post-World War II years upset us more than "the loss of China." The very phrase is revealing of our patronizing attitude toward a quarter of the world's population —as if China were ours to hold or to lose. And the efforts to find a simplistic explanation for this "loss" contributed more than anything else to the McCarthy anti-Communist hysteria of the early 1950's.

Now after twenty years when we are once again making an effort to establish a more normal relationship with China it is important to remember earlier attitudes toward the rise of Chinese Communism. Professor Shewmaker's article is most helpful in reminding us of that time when many American observers in China saw in Mao Tse Tung the leader whom China had been seeking throughout the twentieth century.

Kenneth E. Shewmaker teaches American diplomatic history at Dartmouth College. His chief interest is recent Sino-American relations.

Source: *Pacific Historical Review*, Vol. 38, No. 2 (1969), pp. 207–216.

In 1937 Captain Evans F. Carlson of the United States Marine Corps became the first foreign military observer to scrutinize at firsthand the operations of the Chinese Red Army. This historic encounter with Chinese Communists had significant consequences. It led to a harvest of publicity favorable to the Chinese Reds, to a dramatic resignation from the Marine Corps, to the formation of the famed Marine Raider battalions of the Second World War, and to Carlson's postwar activities as a spokesman for groups advocating the withdrawal of American support from the government of Chiang Kai-shek.

When Brigadier General Carlson died of a heart attack in 1947, he was eulogized in the editorial columns of the *New York Times* as a great marine and an individual "faithful to himself and to that which he believed."[1] Less than five years later, Senator Joseph R. McCarthy indicted Carlson as a hero of the international Communist movement and a "disciple" of the radical American journalist Agnes Smedley.[2] The *New York Times* had in mind primarily Carlson's leadership of the Marine Raiders during the Second World War. Senator McCarthy was more interested in Carlson's active participation in such organizations as the National Citizens Political Action Committee, the National Committee to Win the Peace, the Committee for a Democratic Far Eastern Policy, and the Progressive Citizens of America. Both the senator from Wisconsin and the New York newspaper were trying to comment, in their very different ways, on what remains an instructive topic—Evans Carlson's strong advocacy of the Chinese Communist movement.

Evans Carlson was a Bible-quoting New Englander in the American Puritan tradition.[3] The son of a Congregationalist minister, he never finished high school, but he found a place for himself in the United States Army. Carlson joined in 1912 and attained the rank of captain before resigning at the conclusion of the First World War. After giving civilian life an unsuccessful try, he enlisted as a private in the Marines in 1922. In 1930 he gained some valuable experience—and the Navy Cross—by fighting against Augustino Sandino's guerrillas in Nicaragua. From 1927 to 1929 and again from 1933 to 1935, Carlson served as an intelligence officer in China.[4] He was, then, a professional soldier who knew something about partisan warfare and who had spent a number of years in China prior to the outbreak of the Sino-Japanese War.

Although his career had been largely within the military establishment, Carlson did not fit many of the stereotypes ordinarily associated with the practitioners of his craft. Contemporaries were struck by Carlson's distinctive personality. One of his acquaintances characterized him as a "romantic," another as a principled moralist, and a third as a cultured military officer.[5] Carlson's biographer thought

[1] "Semper Fidelis," *New York Times*, May 28, 1947.

[2] Senator Joseph R. McCarthy, *America's Retreat From Victory: The Story of George Catlett Marshall* (New York, 1951), 68, 118.

[3] Samuel B. Griffith, II, *The Chinese People's Liberation Army* (New York, 1967), 255.

[4] Michael Blankfort, *The Big Yankee: The Life of Carlson of the Raiders* (Boston, 1947), 81, 97, 162–169.

[5] Freda Utley, *China at War* (New York, 1939), 211; Agnes Smedley, *Battle Hymn of China* (New York, 1943), 198–199; Haldore Hanson, *"Humane Endeavor": The Story of the China War* (New York, 1939), 242. For other contemporary appraisals of Carlson, see Ilona Ralf Sues, *Shark's Fins and Millet* (Boston, 1944), 302, and James M. Bertram, *Beneath the Shadow: A New Zealander in the Far East, 1939–46* (New York, 1947), 56.

the marine best could be described as a "kind of Christian socialist."[6] As these appraisals suggest, Evans Carlson was something more than a professional soldier who understood the business of war. Indeed, he was also a romantically-inclined idealist who espoused the Ten Commandments, the Declaration of Independence, and the brotherhood of man.

During his wanderings with the Red Army in North China, Carlson's companion was a pocket edition of the four gospels. He hoped to compare systematically the doctrines of Christianity with those espoused by the Chinese Communists.[7] Deeply religious, he was an avid reader of Ralph Waldo Emerson's *Essays* and the New Testament. If Carlson was anything, he was a man "drunk with democracy."[8] Egalitarian democracy and sacrificial selflessness were his pedestaled ideals.

Carlson was also an eminently gregarious and highly impressionable person who formed opinions of others quickly. Shortly after being introduced to Chu Teh, the commander-in-chief of the Chinese Red Army, Carlson recorded in his diary: "Immediately and intuitively I felt that I had found a warm and generous friend, and a man who was a true leader of men."[9] Carlson got along well with most people and numbered individuals from many walks of life among his friends. A partial listing of his more important acquaintances would include Edgar Snow, Ambassador Nelson T. Johnson, and President Franklin D. Roosevelt.

In 1935, Captain Carlson was appointed second-in-command of the President's military detachment at Warm Springs, Georgia. This fortuitous circumstance ultimately led to conversations between Roosevelt and Carlson in 1936, 1937, 1939, 1940, 1941, 1943, and 1944. One of the President's sons, James Roosevelt, served as Carlson's executive officer in the Second Marine Raider Battalion during World War II. The most significant product of Carlson's association with the President, however, consists of personal letters, many of them on the topic of China's Communists, which the marine wrote for the benefit of his commander-in-chief.[10]

[6] Michael Blankfort to the author, Oct. 19, 1964.

[7] Evans Fordyce Carlson, *Twin Stars of China: A Behind-the-Scenes Story of China's Valiant Struggle for Existence by a U.S. Marine Who Lived and Moved With the People* (New York, 1940), 176.

[8] Blankfort, *The Big Yankee*, 360.

[9] *Ibid.*, 108. The most valuable sections of Blankfort's biography are the lengthy citations from Carlson's diary and other private papers.

[10] This hitherto unexamined correspondence is on deposit at the Franklin D. Roosevelt Library in Hyde Park, New York. It is located in the President's Personal File (PPF), 4951, Evans F. Carlson. Like other materials which the writer has examined in the Roosevelt papers, this collection reveals almost nothing about the President's thinking, but the very fact that the Carlson correspondence exists is of some importance. Carlson wrote frequently and extensively of his encounters with Chinese Communists. His letters were not addressed directly to the President. They were channeled through the President's personal secretary, Miss Marguerite Le Hand. Nevertheless, they were intended for the eyes of Franklin D. Roosevelt. Miss Le Hand periodically acknowledged receipt of Carlson's reports, and she referred to the President's interest in them on several occasions. On November 27, 1937, after not hearing from Carlson in three weeks, Miss Le Hand wrote him expressing a desire to receive more information. In an undated memorandum to Miss Le Hand, probably written on April 26, 1938, Roosevelt requested that she write Carlson a cordial letter expressing his appreciation of the reports. Furthermore, Harold Ickes' account of a conversation with Roosevelt on March 4, 1938, clearly demonstrates that the President was reading Carlson's reports. See Harold L. Ickes, *The Secret Diary of Harold L. Ickes: The Inside Struggle, 1936–1939* (New York, 1954), II, 327–328.

On July 15, 1937, just prior to his departure for the Far East, Carlson had an appointment with the President. Roosevelt asked Carlson to write him privately about what was going on in China. The President proposed that they keep this correspondence confidential.[11] From 1937 on, Carlson regularly forwarded accounts of his experiences in China to the White House. As the President had requested, the marine kept these communications a closely guarded secret.[12]

While Carlson enjoyed his tour of duty at Warm Springs, he was also filled with nostalgia for the contemplative life of Peiping. As he wrote one of his friends: "I can think of nothing more interesting than to have access to a room full of dusty old records over which to pore and from which to glimpse here and there into the lives and thoughts of the men of ancient China."[13] In a subsequent letter to the same intimate, Carlson joyously gave notice that he would soon be returning to the Orient. He eagerly anticipated studying the language and customs of the Chinese people.[14] In August of 1937 Carlson was back in China. He did not, however, have time to gratify his scholarly appetite. China was at war. The United States government now placed a premium on military observers, not cultural anthropologists. Admiral Harry E. Yarnell appointed Carlson an intelligence officer with the task of gathering information on the Sino-Japanese conflict.

It was as an official observer for the United States Navy that Carlson went to Red China. The marine's curiosity had been aroused by Edgar Snow's characterizations of the Communists. Carlson read a manuscript copy of *Red Star over China*, discussed the subject with its author, and decided to have a look for himself. Snow obtained Mao Tse-tung's acquiescence, Carlson's superiors gave their consent, and Chiang Kai-shek put his stamp of approval on the proposed venture.[15] The ostensible purpose of the trip was to learn about Japanese methods of combating guerrilla warfare.[16] On November 19, 1937, Carlson left Shanghai bound for Sian.

Carlson made two extended tours of the Communist regions. On the first, he proceeded directly to the Eighth Route Army headquarters in Shansi. From December 1937 to February 1938, Carlson accompanied the Red guerrillas in their forays behind Japanese lines. In fifty-one days, he traveled a thousand miles in Shansi and Hopei. It was an exhilarating experience. Carlson returned to Hankow on February 28, 1938, "feeling like an Olympic athlete."[17] The second undertaking was even more ambitious, involving a survey of the entire area from Inner Mongolia to the Shantung peninsula. Carlson arrived in Yenan on May 5, 1938. Ten days and two lengthy conversations with Mao Tse-tung later, Carlson departed for the front. When he returned to Hankow on August 7, 1938, Carlson could boast that he had traveled "nearly fifteen hundred miles across north China, and thrice through the Japanese lines."[18] This expedition had taken the American observer into the provinces of Shensi, Suiyuan, Shansi, Hopei, and Shantung.

[11] Carlson to Marguerite Le Hand, Aug. 14, 1937, Franklin D. Roosevelt Papers.
[12] Carlson to Le Hand, Sept. 23, 1938, *ibid.*
[13] Carlson to Ambassador Nelson T. Johnson, Jan. 26, 1936, Nelson T. Johnson Papers, Library of Congress.
[14] Carlson to Johnson, Feb. 21, 1937, *ibid.*
[15] Edgar Snow, *Journey to the Beginning* (New York, 1958), 196; Carlson, *Twin Stars of China*, 33–58; Blankfort, *The Big Yankee*, 188–194.
[16] Carlson to Le Hand, Nov. 1, 1937, Roosevelt Papers.
[17] Carlson to Le Hand, March 4, 1938, *ibid.*
[18] Carlson, *Twin Stars of China*, 266.

After this three-month journey in North China, Carlson was so excited that he could not, as one newspaperman wrote, "keep what he had seen to himself."[19] He had been to Valhalla and wanted to tell the world about it. Carlson exceeded the limits of his diplomatic position by granting extensive interviews to the colony of American and European reporters who had congregated in Hankow. Unsparing in his praise of Communist military and political institutions, Carlson astonished the journalists by answering all the questions put to him and by allowing his name to be mentioned in their dispatches.[20]

On September 17, 1938, Carlson's superiors informed him that he would be held strictly accountable for these activities. Although Agnes Smedley and others urged Carlson to exercise more discretion, the talkative marine impulsively resigned from the Corps.[21] "I wished to be free to speak and write," Carlson explained, "in accordance with my convictions."[22] Toward the end of December 1938, he was back in the United States. Driven by his conscience, Carlson spoke and wrote "like a man possessed."[23]

The ex-marine delivered orations before public audiences, contributed articles to several magazines, and published two books. The first, *The Chinese Army*, was a mediocre technical treatise which went almost unnoticed in the general press.[24] Carlson's subsequent volume, *Twin Stars of China*, aroused a good deal of interest.[25] Several reviewers rated the work above all competitors when it came to an analysis of the military aspects of the Sino-Japanese conflict. They were even more impressed, however, at the spectacle of a leatherneck who spoke in ecstatic terms of a Red utopia in the remote hinterlands of China.[26] Their incredulity is understandable. Carlson's characterization of the Chinese Communist movement was, to say the least, striking.

Carlson's Communists were a remarkable breed. The United States marine could scarcely find words adequate to express his admiration for the soft-spoken commander of the Chinese Red Army, Chu Teh. He possessed, in Carlson's estimation, "the kindliness of a Robert E. Lee, the humility of an Abraham Lincoln, and the tenacity of a U. S. Grant."[27] Carlson's appraisal of the Eighth Route Army was no less enthusiastic. He was profoundly impressed by this un-

[19] I. Epstein, *The People's War* (London, 1939), 200.

[20] Anna Wang, *Ich Kämpfte für Mao: Eine deutsche Frau erlebt die chinesische Revolution* (Hamburg, Germany, 1964), 201–204.

[21] *Ibid.*, 203.

[22] Blankfort, *The Big Yankee*, 255. The quotation is from Carlson's diary entry of Sept. 19, 1938. See also Carlson to Le Hand, Sept. 23, 1938, Roosevelt Papers.

[23] Blankfort, *The Big Yankee*, 269.

[24] Carlson, *The Chinese Army: Its Organization and Military Efficiency* (New York, 1940).

[25] Carlson sent copies of his books and articles to the White House. On one occasion, the President forwarded a Carlson essay to Secretary of State Cordell Hull with the comment, "read and return." President Roosevelt, memorandum for the Secretary of State, Dec. 4, 1939, Roosevelt Papers.

[26] For example, see R. L. Duffus, "An American Marine Reports on China: After Wide Investigation He Expresses High Hope For Democracy There," *New York Times Book Review*, Sept. 22, 1940, pp. 4, 34; Rodney Gilbert, "When the Japanese Came," New York *Herald-Tribune: Books*, Oct. 27, 1940, p. 22; Maxwell S. Stewart, "Report From the Front," *The Nation*, CLI (Oct. 5, 1940), 307–308; Freda Utley, "Sir Galahad in China," *Saturday Review of Literature*, XXII (Oct. 5, 1940), 13.

[27] Carlson, *Twin Stars of China*, 66.

orthodox armed force and believed that the clue to its dynamism lay in what he ambiguously called "ethical indoctrination."

"Ethical indoctrination" was a phrase loosely employed by Carlson to designate a lethal combination of observed traits: political consciousness, high moral standards, democratic camaraderie between officers and men, and individual motivation dynamically coordinated with group cooperation.[28] Carlson detailed what he meant by his elusive terminology in a letter of December 24, 1937, to the White House. The marine emphasized that the Red Army's military style was novel. He contended that the Communists had been able to inculcate "the spirit of willing service" in their troops by establishing the simple principle that an individual behaves in an upright manner "because it is the right thing to do." Second, Carlson reasoned that, since Communist officers confided in their men and freely discussed strategy with them, "a strong bond of understanding" had been built up between the leaders and the led. This combination of voluntary motivation and mutual understanding, a kind of dialogue between the collective mass and the individual soul, eventuated in what Carlson judged to be a superior fighting machine endowed with a magnificent spirit—the Chinese Red Army.[29]

Carlson was so convinced of the viability of the Communist approach to the art of warfare that after being recommissioned in 1941 he patterned the Marine Raider battalions after the Chinese Red Army. The rallying cry of the Raiders was "*Gung Ho!*," an adaptation of the Chinese slogan for "working together." Like "ethical indoctrination," "*Gung Ho!*" implied cooperative comradeship and selfless personal dedication. The Raider actions at Makin Island and Guadalcanal in 1942 would seem to indicate that Colonel Carlson was successful in applying the knowledge he had accumulated from his observations of the Eighth Route Army.[30]

Carlson's military evaluations were as penetrating as his political judgments were naïve. To Carlson, Yenan incarnated the "spirit of liberalism" and representative government was the "backbone" of the Communist system. He was certain that the Communist system approximated a "pure democracy" and inferred that the Reds were advocating social and economic ideals which could be associated with the ethics of Christianity.[31] Carlson dismissed the possibility of China's "going Red" as "utterly ridiculous."[32] His observations convinced him that the doctrines of the Chinese Communists were "in their political aspects, representative government (democracy), in their economic aspect, the co-operative theory, and that only in their social application could they be called communistic, for

[28] *Ibid.*, 110–111, 121. See also *The Chinese Army*, 34–43.

[29] Carlson to Le Hand, Dec. 24, 1937, Roosevelt Papers.

[30] One can get a pretty good idea of what Carlson meant by "ethical indoctrination" by viewing the 1943 film "Gung Ho!" Carlson acted as technical advisor to Walter Wanger for this Hollywood version of the Makin raid. "Gung" and "Ho" are Chinese words for "to work" and "harmony." As suggested in the movie, the Raiders were to think for themselves but to help each other. They were to live in a democratic fashion with one another, as well as to be ready to die for democracy. Television's proclivity for subjecting the public to old westerns and war dramas makes it possible for today's addict to view such relics of the past as "Gung Ho!" The phrase, "Gung Ho!," which is listed in such standard dictionaries as Webster's, has become part of the English language.

[31] Carlson, *Twin Stars of China*, 176, 216–217, 231.

[32] Carlson, "America Faces Crisis in the Orient," *Amerasia*, III (Feb., 1940), 556.

emphasis is placed on social equality." Carlson's Communists, then, were an ill-defined species of utopian democrats whose teachings were closer to Christianity than to Leninism.[33]

Because of Carlson's political judgments, it is not surprising that Senator McCarthy associated him with the Communist conspiracy. To the senator, it seemed impossible that a loyal American could find anything good to say about Chinese Communists. But to accuse a man like Evans Carlson of being a Communist is presumptuous. He was anything but a Marxist. As the wife of an important Chinese Communist official observed, Carlson cannot even be called a revolutionary.[34] Rather, Carlson is quite explicable as a fairly conventional product of the American experience in China.

In the 1930's and early 1940's, there was nothing exceptional about Carlson's assessment of the Chinese situation. A surprisingly large number of Americans were disillusioned with Chinese Nationalists and enthusiastic about Chinese Communists. Like many other Americans, Carlson had difficulty relating to Nationalist officials on a personal basis. Two interviews with the Generalissimo in 1938 left the marine with one firm impression. Chiang Kai-shek, he wrote, had a face which "could be called inscrutable without exaggeration."[35] Carlson's personal contacts with Chinese Communist leaders like Chu Teh were invariably more satisfying.

Carlson was convinced that Chinese Communists had discarded old-fashioned Chinese customs, while Nationalists clung to them. Traditional Chinese cultural mores left the marine weary. Nationalist officials often subjected Carlson to the ordeal of *li*—sipping tea and exchanging platitudes. The Chinese Reds offered, from his point of view, a happy contrast. Carlson thought the Communists were more like Americans than any other group in Chinese society.[36] In a revealing statement, he suggested why the Reds had captured his sympathies. Among the Communists he found

> *a desire for directness in speech and action, a desire to avoid the superficial politeness which has been so much a part of Chinese official etiquette since the days of Confucius. No orthodox Chinese official, for example, would have come out to greet me in the spontaneous manner of Chu Teh. Instead I would have been received by ceremonious secretaries and ushered into the presence of the Great One with pompous unctuousness. There would have followed twenty minutes of tea sipping, as we sat stiffly on the edges of our chairs and exchanged meaningless platitudes. But here was an ease of manner and an absence of reserve which was refreshingly genuine.*[37]

Chinese Communists seemed more familiar to Carlson than Chinese Nationalists.

By late 1938, moreover, Carlson had become persuaded that China needed a purge. Although he considered Chiang Kai-shek to be personally honest and above reproach, he had no doubt whatever that the Nationalist bureaucracy and army

[33] Carlson, *Twin Stars of China*, 176, 299.
[34] Wang, *Ich Kämpfte für Mao*, 202.
[35] Carlson, *Twin Stars of China*, 131.
[36] Carlson to Le Hand, March 4, 1938, Roosevelt Papers.
[37] Carlson, *Twin Stars of China*, 68. See also Carlson to Le Hand, Dec. 24, 1937, Roosevelt Papers.

were filled with corrupt and self-serving officials. Chinese Communists, by contrast, he regarded as honest, dedicated, idealistic, equalitarian, and incorruptible. In Carlson's opinion, only the Reds were willing and able to cope efficiently with the inertia and corruption that handicapped the Chinese war effort.[38] Chinese Communists approximated, in sum, Carlson's conception of what could and should be.

Americans tend to view other societies in terms of their own self-image.[39] Carlson was standing firmly in the American tradition when he assessed Chinese developments in the light of what one scholar has called the American liberal dream.[40] That is, Carlson projected onto an Asian society Western conceptions of what is good and right. In so doing, he made a misjudgment that was especially commonplace in the era of the New Deal.[41] He confused Chinese Communist and American liberal values. As Carlson wrote to President Roosevelt, the so-called Chinese Communists were really a party of "Liberal Democrats" seeking only honest government and equality of opportunity.[42]

This confusion of values was facilitated by another American characteristic—a fundamental indifference to abstract philosophies. The fact that Carlson never followed through on his plan to make a systematic comparison between the doctrines of Christianity and those of Chinese Communism is symbolic. Carlson's religious convictions were less a matter of theology than of morality. His political standards also were essentially nonideological. Democracy was not so much a theory of government to Carlson as it was the absence of class distinctions in social intercourse.[43]

Evans Carlson simply did not think in structured ideological terms. His writings reflect an almost total lack of concern about Marxist or any other kind of dogma. It would be difficult to find fault with Agnes Smedley's evaluation of Carlson. The marine knew nothing, Miss Smedley sneered, "of the basic principles which motivate the Communists throughout the world, and which motivate the Eighth Route Army."[44] This criticism would apply with equal validity to many of the Americans who had firsthand encounters with Chinese Communists prior to the onset of the Cold War.

Evans F. Carlson's strong advocacy of the Chinese Communist movement, then, was the product of a particular American tradition at a particular time in history. The Chinese Reds were nearly all that he said they were. He has appraised their

[38] Carlson to Le Hand, Nov. 15, 1938, Roosevelt Papers.

[39] This idea is developed at length in Tang Tsou, "The American Political Tradition and the American Image of Chinese Communism," *Political Science Quarterly*, LXXVII (1962), 570–600, and *America's Failure in China, 1941–50* (Chicago, 1963), especially 219–230.

[40] John K. Fairbank, *China: The People's Middle Kingdom and the U. S. A.* (Cambridge, Mass., 1967), 51–52.

[41] Earl Latham, *The Communist Controversy in Washington: From the New Deal to McCarthy* (Cambridge, Mass., 1966), 359–360.

[42] Carlson to Le Hand, March 4, 1938, Roosevelt Papers.

[43] For example, see Carlson, *Twin Stars of China*, 72–74, and Carlson to Le Hand, Dec. 24, 1937, Roosevelt Papers.

[44] Agnes Smedley, *China Fights Back: An American Woman With the Eighth Route Army* (London, 1939), 253.

dynamism and potential strength realistically. But Chinese Communists were something more than Carlson imagined. They were also Communist revolutionaries committed to a Marxist-Leninist reorganization of their society. Carlson's inability to perceive the true nature of the Chinese Communist movement had nothing to do with a conspiracy. Rather, his partial myopia was born of an excessive confidence in American values and a massive inattention to alien ideologies. Instead of exemplifying an insidious conspiracy within our midst, Evans F. Carlson typifies the American tradition of nonideological pragmatism.

24

MR. JUSTICE MURPHY AND THE HIRABAYASHI CASE

Sidney Fine

As compared with World War I, civil liberties were more generally respected and protected in World War II. But this relatively better record in respect to pacifists, conscientious objectors, German-Americans, and socialists was offset by the grossest invasion of the rights of American citizens by the government in our history when President Roosevelt issued an executive order in February 1942 authorizing the exclusion of "any or all persons" from areas designated by local military commanders. Aimed at Japanese-Americans on the West Coast, this program established detention camps into which were herded over 100,000 American citizens of Japanese ancestry. The Supreme Court case testing the constitutionality of this order is the subject of the following article by Sidney Fine. It is presented from the point of view of Justice Frank Murphy, one of the most dedicated civil libertarians to serve on the Court. It is a rare revelation in constitutional history of a justice struggling with his own conscience and with the pressure from his brethren on the Court. That Justice Murphy should finally yield to his colleagues' desire for unanimity reveals how precarious is the protection of the Bill of Rights in moments of national emergency and public hysteria.

Sidney Fine is a professor of history at the University of Michigan. He is the author of many books and articles in the field of recent American history, including Laissez Faire and the General Welfare State *(Ann Arbor, 1956);* The Automobile Under the Blue Eagle *(Ann Arbor, 1963); and* Sit-Down: The General Motors Strike of 1936–1937 *(Ann Arbor, 1969). He is currently preparing a biography of Justice Frank Murphy.*

Source: *Pacific Historical Review,* Vol. 33, No. 2 (1964), pp. 195–209.

"The one discordant note in [Frank] Murphy's opposition to racism," to quote one of Mr. Justice Murphy's devoted law clerks, "was struck in his concurring vote and opinion in *Hirabayashi* v. *United States*."[1] Commentators on the case have recognized that Murphy concurred with considerable reluctance[2] and the recently available Frank Murphy Papers[3] have revealed that Justice Murphy really intended to dissent in the case, wrote a dissenting opinion, and circulated it among his brethren on the United States Supreme Court, but in the end was dissuaded from issuing it.

The legal troubles of George Hirabayashi, a native-born American of Japanese descent and a resident of Seattle, Washington, began on February 19, 1942, when President Franklin D. Roosevelt, by executive order, authorized the Secretary of War and such military commanders as he might designate to prescribe military areas from which any or all persons might be excluded and to impose such restrictions as these officials saw fit on the right of any person to enter, remain in, or leave such areas.[4] The stated purpose of the executive order was the protection of national defense resources from espionage and sabotage. On March 18, 1942, the President issued an executive order establishing the War Relocation Authority and authorizing its director to formulate and carry out a program for the removal and relocation of persons designated under the February 19 order. Three days later, Congress, in a statute described by Edward S. Corwin as "just about the most heartless measure ever enacted" by the national legislature,[5] provided that whoever knowingly entered, remained in, or left a prescribed military zone or committed therein an act contrary to the restrictions applicable to the area was to be deemed guilty of a misdemeanor.

On March 2, 1942, pursuant to the executive order of February 19, 1942, Lt. General J. L. DeWitt, Military Commander of the Western Defense Command, designated two military areas within his command and then on March 24 proclaimed a curfew applicable to all alien Japanese, Germans, and Italians and all persons of Japanese ancestry within Military Area No. 1, which included the city of Seattle. Subsequently, DeWitt issued a series of Civilian Exclusion Orders and a Public Proclamation excluding all persons of Japanese descent from portions of Military Area No. 1, instructing them to report to Civil Control Stations, and stating that it would be necessary to provide for their evacuation and resettlement. Hirabayashi, then a senior at the University of Washington, did not comply with the military orders applicable to him as an American of Japanese descent. He was indicted and tried for having failed both to observe the curfew order and to report

1 Eugene Gressman, "Mr. Justice Murphy—A Preliminary Appraisal," *Columbia Law Review*, L (Jan., 1950), 36; 320 U.S. 81 (1943).

2 John P. Frank, "Justice Murphy: The Goals Attempted," *Yale Law Journal*, LIX (Dec., 1949), 11; Alfred L. Scanlan, "The Passing of Justice Murphy—The Conscience of a Court," *Notre Dame Lawyer*, XXV (Fall, 1949), 23; Gressman, "Mr. Justice Murphy," 36; C. Herman Pritchett, *The Roosevelt Court: A Study in Judicial Politics and Values, 1937–1947* (New York, 1948), 121–122; Byron F. Lindsley, "Constitutional Liberties of Japanese-Americans as Affected by the War," *Georgetown Law Journal*, XXXII (Jan., 1944), 191.

3 The Frank Murphy Papers are located in the Michigan Historical Collections, Ann Arbor, Michigan.

4 The factual background of the case is conveniently summarized in *Hirabayashi* v. *United States*, 320 U.S. 81, pp. 85–89.

5 Corwin, *Total War and the Constitution* (New York, 1947), 98.

to the Civil Control Station in his area, was found guilty by jury trial of having violated the act of March 21, 1942, and was sentenced to three months' imprisonment for each of the two counts of the indictment, the sentences to run concurrently. His case was appealed to the United States Supreme Court, which heard arguments on May 10 and 11, 1943, and handed down its opinion on June 21, 1943. It was "the first important test of civil liberties" to reach the Supreme Court in World War II.[6]

Speaking for the Court, Chief Justice Harlan Fiske Stone argued that since Hirabayashi's sentences were to run concurrently, it was unnecessary for the Court to consider the questions raised by this conviction for failure to report to a Civil Control Station, an obvious preliminary to his exclusion from the Pacific Coast, provided that his conviction for violation of the curfew order could be sustained.[7] Although it would have been perfectly proper for the Supreme Court to have addressed itself to the validity of the exclusion order,[8] the Chief Justice chose to focus on the curfew order alone, which permitted the Court to "present a front of rather wary unanimity to the world."[9] The questions for the Court to decide, Stone contended, were whether the curfew order was promulgated by General DeWitt in the exercise of an unconstitutional delegation by Congress of its legislative powers and whether it unconstitutionally discriminated between persons of Japanese ancestry and of other ancestry in violation of the Fifth Amendment.

Since Stone thought the evidence indisputable that the act of March 21, 1942, had confirmed and ratified the executive order of February 19, 1942, he addressed himself to the issue of whether Congress and the Executive had the constitutional authority to impose the curfew restriction and to leave it to designated military commanders to appraise the relevant conditions and to decide that the order before the Court was an appropriate means of carrying out the executive order. Broadly defining the war power, in the words of Charles Evans Hughes, as "the power to wage war successfully" and as extending "to every matter and activity so related to war as substantially to affect its conduct and progress," Stone found both the executive order and the statute at issue to be legitimate exercises of the power to wage war conferred on the President and the Congress by the Constitution. He thought that it could not be doubted that "reasonably prudent men" had ample grounds for concluding that the United States at the time the curfew order was issued faced the danger of a Japanese invasion, that they had to take measures to cope with this possibility, and that in the selection of the appropriate means they had to take the internal situation of the country into account. Where conditions called for the exercise of judgment and discretion and the choice of means by those branches of the government on which the Constitution had conferred the war-making power, it was "not for any court to sit in review of the wisdom of this action or substitute its judgment for theirs."

Since the curfew order, however, applied only to those citizens who were of Japanese descent, the Court had to inquire "whether in the light of all the facts and circumstances there was any substantial basis for the conclusion" that the

[6] Washington *Star*, June 24, 1943.

[7] For Stone's opinion, see *Hirabayashi* v. *United States*, 320 U.S. 81, pp. 83–105.

[8] On this point, see Eugene V. Rostow, "The Japanese-American Cases—A Disaster," *Yale Law Journal*, LIV (June, 1945), 504.

[9] Jacobus ten Broeck *et al.*, *Prejudice, War and the Constitution* (Berkeley, 1954), 212.

particular curfew order before the Court was necessary to protect the Pacific Coast against espionage and sabotage. Arguing that espionage by persons sympathetic with the Japanese government had played a part in the attack on Pearl Harbor, Stone contended that at the time of the threatened invasion "the nature of our inhabitants' attachment to the Japanese enemy" was understandably "a matter of grave concern." He noted that most of the approximately 112,000 persons of Japanese descent residing on the Pacific Coast, about two-thirds of whom were American citizens, were concentrated in or near Seattle, Portland, and Los Angeles, all in Military Area No. 1. He maintained that there was "support" for the view that social, political, and economic conditions prevailing in the United States in the twentieth century had intensified the feeling of "solidarity" among the Japanese in America and had in large measure "prevented their assimilation as an integral part of the white population." He called attention to the large number of Japanese-American children sent outside regular public-school hours to Japanese-language schools, some of which were believed to be sources of "Japanese nationalistic propaganda," the ten thousand *Nisei* children sent to Japan for all or part of their education, the maintenance by the Japanese government of a system of dual citizenship, particularly with regard to persons of Japanese descent born abroad before December 1, 1924, the limited "social intercourse" between Japanese and whites on the Pacific Coast, and the irritating restrictions imposed on Japanese-Americans that had enhanced their sense of isolation and attachment to Japan. "Whatever views we may entertain regarding the loyalty to this country of the citizens of Japanese ancestry," Stone wrote, "we cannot reject as unfounded the judgment of the military authorities and of Congress that there were disloyal members of the population, whose number and strength could not be precisely and quickly ascertained" and who could not, in a critical hour, be dealt with separately.

Stone rejected the argument that the curfew order discriminated against citizens of Japanese ancestry in violation of the Fifth Amendment. He noted that although the amendment did not contain an equal protection clause, distinctions between citizens solely because of their ancestry were "odious" to a free people and legislative classification based on race alone had often been held to constitute a denial of equal protection. The danger of espionage and sabotage in time of war and of threatened invasion, however, required the military to consider all the facts bearing on the population in the danger zone. "Because racial discriminations are in most circumstances irrelevant and therefore prohibited, it by no means follows that, in dealing with the perils of war, Congress and the Executive are wholly precluded from taking into account those facts and circumstances which are relevant to measures for our national defense and for the successful prosecution of the war, and which may in fact place citizens of one ancestry in a different category from others."

Stone thought that the Court had presented "facts and circumstances" with respect to Japanese-Americans residing on the Pacific Coast that afforded grounds for the military to distinguish citizens of Japanese ancestry from other groups in the United States. The fact that the invasion was threatened by Japan automatically set Japanese-Americans apart from other citizens since it had been "demonstrated by experience" that residents having an ethnic affiliation with an invading enemy may be "a greater source of danger" to the imperiled nation than those of different ancestry. There was thus a "rational basis" for the decision that had been made, and it was irrelevant to consider whether the Court would have made a similar decision. Hirabayashi's conviction for violating the curfew order, Stone concluded, was "without constitutional infirmity."

It is agreed by most commentators on the Hirabayashi case that Stone reviewed in an altogether perfunctory manner the judgment of the military that the curfew order was necessary to effect the purposes of the executive order of February 19, 1942.[10] The Chief Justice, in effect, answered in the negative the question he had raised in the famous footnote 4 of his opinion in the Carolene Products Company case as to whether statutes directed at "national . . . or racial minorities" were "to be subjected to more exacting judicial scrutiny under the general prohibitions of the Fourteenth Amendment than are most other types of legislation" and whether "prejudice against discrete and insular minorities" might call for a "more searching judicial inquiry" than was normally required.[11] The test set forth in *Hirabayashi* was whether "in the light of all the facts and circumstances there was any substantial basis" for the judgment of the military, but the Court did not actually apply even this test in determining whether the curfew order before it was a necessary and appropriate means to prevent espionage and sabotage. The "facts" which it claimed it had presented with regard to Japanese-Americans and which it offered as affording a "rational basis" for the curfew order were not facts at all but simply the prejudiced racial opinions of a vocal minority on the Pacific Coast.[12] That General DeWitt shared these prejudices is revealed in his Final Recommendation of February 14, 1942, in which he asserted that "the Japanese race" was "an enemy race" and that although many citizens of Japanese descent had been " 'Americanized,' " the "racial strains" were "undiluted," and it therefore followed that "along the vital Pacific Coast over 112,000 potential enemies of Japanese extraction are at large today." To be sure, not a single act of sabotage had been committed up to that time by these "potential enemies," but this very fact, DeWitt incomprehensibly argued, was "a disturbing and confirming indication that such action will be taken."[13]

The Supreme Court also assumed that time had not been available to investigate

[10] Rostow, "The Japanese-American Cases," 503, 505, 507, 508, 531; ten Broeck *et al.*, *Prejudice, War and the Constitution*, 215–216, 308; Milton R. Konvitz, *The Alien and the Asiatic in American Law* (Ithaca, 1946), 253; Morton Grodzins, *Americans Betrayed: Politics and the Japanese Evacuation* (Chicago, 1949), 352–354; Nanette Dembitz, "Racial Discrimination and the Military Judgment: The Supreme Court's Korematsu and Endo Decisions," *Columbia Law Review*, XLV (March, 1945), 186–188. "At the suggestion of one of the war hawks [on the Court]," Stone, declares Alpheus Thomas Mason, "appears to have sanctioned shrinking judicial review of the war power almost to the vanishing point." Mason, *Harlan Fiske Stone* (New York, 1956), 675. It is not always possible in the works noted above to separate out criticism of the Court's standards of review in the Hirabayashi case from the standards later applied in *Korematsu* v. *U.S.*, 323 U.S. 214 (1944).

[11] *U.S.* v. *Carolene Products Co.*, 304 U.S. 144 (1938), pp. 152–153. For Stone's rejection of the standards of review considered in the footnote, see Wallace Mendelson, "A Note on a Famous Legal Footnote," *Journal of Politics*, XXV (May, 1963), 373–376.

[12] ten Broeck *et al.*, *Prejudice, War and the Constitution*, 96, 268–287, 309–310, 326; Rostow, "The Japanese-American Cases," 496–497, 505–507, 519–520; Grodzins, *Americans Betrayed*, 356; Harrop A. Freeman, "Genesis, Exodus, and Leviticus: Genealogy, Evacuation, and Law," *Cornell Law Quarterly*, XXVIII (June, 1943), 440–450.

[13] Cited in ten Broeck *et al.*, *Prejudice, War and the Constitution*, 110.

the loyalty of Americans of Japanese descent on an individual basis, but this too was a questionable conclusion. The curfew order had not been issued until three-and-one-half months after the attack on Pearl Harbor, and in the interim no effort had been made to weed out the disloyal from the loyal. Hawaii, under martial law, facing a greater threat than did the Pacific Coast and with a proportionately larger population of Japanese descent, had nevertheless treated both Japanese aliens and Hawaiians of Japanese descent on an individual basis, and this was the procedure Great Britain had followed in dealing with the enemy aliens in its midst.[14]

Considering the important place occupied by the Bill of Rights in his value system and his confidence in the nation's ability to assimilate peoples of varying backgrounds, colors, and creeds, it is not surprising that Frank Murphy should almost instinctively have taken exception to the failure of the Chief Justice to scrutinize the judgment of the military in a more searching manner and to his unsupported observations concerning the Japanese in America. Throughout his long public career, Murphy had been dedicated to the cause of civil liberties, and it was he who as Attorney General of the United States had created the Civil Liberties Unit in the Department of Justice in 1939 and had pledged the federal government "to protect civil liberties for . . . the people of all racial extractions in our midst."[15] As lawyer, judge, and mayor in Detroit and as governor of Michigan, Murphy had developed very close and affectionate ties with the ethnic groups in the city and the state, and he had come to look upon ethnic and cultural differences in the United States as a source of national strength rather than of national weakness.[16]

At the Supreme Court conference on the Hirabayashi case, on May 16, 1943, there seemed to be general agreement that the decision should deal only with Hirabayashi's violation of the curfew order. "I want it done on [the] narrowest possible points," declared Justice Hugo L. Black. In outlining the case, the Chief Justice concentrated on the two principal issues to which he later devoted his decision, namely, whether there had been an unconstitutional delegation of power and whether citizens of Japanese descent had been discriminated against in violation of the Constitution. "It is jarring to me that U.S. citizens were subjected to this treatment," Stone stated with regard to the discrimination question, but he did not regard the action taken as unreasonable under the circumstances. Justices Stanley F. Reed and Owen J. Roberts seem to have had at least some doubts concerning the application of the curfew order to "a certain type of citizen," but if this point was debated at great length, it is not evident in the notes that Murphy made of the conference deliberations.[17] Since Murphy's conference notes for this as for nearly all the other cases in which he participated contain no reference to what he himself might have contributed to the discussion, we do not know whether he objected on this occasion to the Chief Justice's line of reasoning.

Since Murphy, however, believed that the record disclosed neither "reasonable

14 Rostow, "The Japanese-American Cases," 494–495, 507–508.

15 Murphy, "Civil Liberties," Speech of March 27, 1939, Box 67, Murphy Papers. The name of the Civil Liberties Unit was later changed to "Civil Liberties Section" and, more recently, to "Civil Liberties Division."

16 See, for example, Detroit *News*, March 22, 1931.

17 Conference Notes on *Hirabayashi* v. *U.S.*, May 16, 1943, Box 132, Murphy Papers. Anticipating his *Korematsu* dissent, Justice Robert H. Jackson declared at the conference that he did not believe that military commanders were bound by due process of law.

grounds" for the military's action nor evidence of the " 'general disloyalty' " of Japanese-Americans,[18] he decided to dissent from Stone's opinion. Early in June at least some of his brethren had in their hands the draft of a powerful opinion in which Murphy argued that discrimination among citizens on the basis of their ancestry was "so utterly inconsistent with our ideas and traditions, and in my judgment so contrary to constitutional requirements, that I cannot lend my assent."[19]

Despite the extensive scope of the war power, it did not follow, Murphy wrote, that the broad guaranties of the Bill of Rights and other provisions of the Constitution protecting essential liberties were suspended by "the mere existence of a state of war." Had the progress of the war and the possibility of invasion justified the declaration of martial law and had martial law been proclaimed, Hirabayashi would have had "no legal ground for objection." But since the government had decided not to resort to martial law, it was necessarily subject to the constitutional limitations governing the exercise of the war power. The act of Congress of March 21, 1942, in Murphy's view, transgressed these limitations.

> *To vest the military authorities with uncontrolled discretion to establish military zones outside the actual theatre of military operations, in which constitutional guaranties may be suspended or disregarded and the civil authorities be subject to the order of military commanders, utterly subverts the security afforded to individuals by the Bill of Rights and amounts to a pure and unqualified delegation of legislative authority which is not justified by any previous decision of this Court.*

Murphy found the statute not only "unconstitutional in its broad aspects," but he thought the particular action taken under it was also "defective." "I would protect rights on the basis of ancestry," he wrote to Felix Frankfurter on June 5. "But I would never deny them."[20] The curfew order was "discriminatory" and hence did not conform to the requirement of due process of law contained in the Fifth Amendment. It was true that the amendment did not contain an equal protection clause, but it did not follow that "there may not be discrimination of such an injurious character in the application of laws as to amount to a denial of due process as that term is used in the Fifth Amendment. I think that point is reached when we have one law for the majority of our citizens and another for those of a particular racial heritage." Under the curfew order, at least seventy thousand American citizens had been

> *placed under a special ban and deprived of their liberty because of a particular racial inheritance. This is the first time, so far as I am aware, that a substantial restriction of the personal liberty of citizens based solely on the accident of race or ancestry has been upheld by this Court. The result is to permit the creation in this country of two classes of citizens for the purposes of the war—to sanction discrimination between groups of United States citizens on the basis of ancestry. This is in contravention of principles that have always been regarded as immutable and sacred to our way of life.*

[18] Murphy to John [Pickering], June 8, 1943, Box 132, Murphy Papers.

[19] The drafts of Murphy's proposed dissent are in *ibid*. The printed drafts are virtually identical. There is one typewritten draft that differs somewhat from the printed versions.

[20] Murphy to Frankfurter, June 5 or 6, 1943, *ibid*.

Although there is no indication that Murphy at this point had made a detailed study of the subject, he sensed, as the scholarship on the subject demonstrates beyond cavil, that the "facts" put forward by the military, and accepted by the Court, to justify the special treatment of Americans of Japanese descent were really nothing more than opinions based on prejudice and error. Evidence for the disloyalty of Japanese-Americans was singularly lacking, he observed, and "power," therefore, "should not be generated by the general considerations, applicable to many racial and cultural groups," that the Chief Justice had noted in his opinion.

Judging by a marginal comment he made on his copy of one of the drafts of Stone's opinion, Murphy wondered if Stone's remarks about Japanese-language schools were equally applicable to "Catholic and other church schools."[21] We have had foreign language schools in this country for generations, without considering their existence as grounds for racial discrimination," he observed in his dissent. The Michigan Justice found particularly galling the apparent belief of the military that "persons of Japanese descent had not been and could not be assimilated and that by and large they gave primary allegiance to the Empire of Japan." This view, Murphy thought, struck at the very basis of American democracy and was belied by his own experience in associating with a variety of ethnic groups. "To say that any racial or cultural group cannot be assimilated," he wrote, "is to admit that the great American experiment has failed, that our way of life has failed when confronted with the normal attachment of certain groups of people to other lands. . . . If people of Japanese extraction have shown an inclination to associate together and have not been fully assimilated, it is due largely to restrictions that have been placed upon them by law and social custom." No effort had been made "to isolate disloyal elements," but rather seventy thousand citizens had been set apart "because of the accident of ancestry." The nation had "not seen fit to do this to citizens of German and Italian ancestry. We have not done it to any other group of citizens."

Whereas Stone's opinion did not dispute the military judgment that the action taken against the Japanese-Americans was necessary to win the war, Murphy feared that what had been done might have baleful consequences both at home and abroad. The discrimination practiced was at variance with the principles for which the nation was fighting and might have "unfortunate repercussions among peoples in Asia and other parts of the East whose friendship and good-will we seek." He was appalled that what the United States had done bore "a melancholy resemblance to the treatment accorded to members of the Jewish race in Germany and other parts of Europe." It was, of course, necessary for the United States "to wage war to win, and to do it with all our might," but it would "avail us little to win the war on the battlefield and lose it at home. We do not win the war, on the contrary we lose it, if in the process of achieving military victory we destroy the constitutional safeguards and the best traditions of our country. What we want to do is win it on the field and also win it at home."

When it became evident to his brethren early in June that Murphy intended to dissent in the Hirabayashi case, one of the Justices, anxious that the Court present a united front in this troublesome case, sought to appeal to his colleague to withdraw his dissent. "Please Frank—," he wrote, "with your eagerness for the austere functions of the Court and your desire to do all that is humanly possible to main-

[21] Comment in Murphy's handwriting on draft of Stone opinion, *ibid.*

tain and enhance the *corporate* reputation of the Court, why don't you take the initiative with the Chief in getting him to take out everything that either offends you or that you would want to express more irenically."[22] Murphy does not appear to have followed this advice, but judging from the futile effort of Justice William O. Douglas to persuade Stone to omit from his opinion "any suggestion of racial discrimination" and to indicate that the "individual member of the group" should be given the "opportunity at some stage . . . to show that he has been improperly classified," it is unlikely that Murphy, whose objections to the Chief Justice's opinion were even stronger than those of Douglas, could have persuaded Stone to alter his draft in any substantial way. At one point, Stone, as a matter of fact, had added a reservation to his opinion in order to satisfy Douglas, but, in the end, to hold other members of the Court, he had decided "to stand by the substance of my opinion."[23]

When Murphy seemed intent on going ahead with his dissent, the Justice who had previously appealed to him now advised his colleague that he would no longer attempt to dissuade him from writing, "not because I do not think it highly unwise but because I think you are immovable." But obviously stung by the language of Murphy's proposed dissent, the Justice urged Murphy at least to soften the language of his opinion.

> *Do you* [he asked] *really think it is conducive to the things you care about, including the great reputation of this Court, to suggest that everybody is out of step except Johnny, and more particularly that the Chief Justice and seven other Justices of this Court are behaving like the enemy and thereby playing into the hands of the enemy? Compassion is, I believe, a virtue enjoined by Christ. Well, tolerance is a long, long way from compassion—and can't you write your own views with such expressed tolerance that you won't make people think that when eight others disagree with you, you think their view means that they want to destroy the liberties of the United Sates and "lose the war" at home?*[24]

These biting words seem to have had their effect on Murphy. He may also have been swayed by a question previously raised about his proposed dissent by Justice Reed, who had found Murphy's opinion "appealing" but who had nevertheless

[22] Note to Murphy [June 5, 1943], *ibid.*

[23] Mason, *Stone*, pp. 673–675. In the end, both Douglas and Wiley B. Rutledge wrote concurring opinions. In his concurrence, Douglas asserted that the Court was dealing with the problem of loyalty, not the problem of assimilation, that loyalty was not a matter of race, and that guilt was personal. The Court had decided only that the appellant could not test the validity of the orders applied to him by defying them. But, Douglas concluded, "Obedience to the military orders is one thing. Whether an individual member of a group must be afforded at some stage an opportunity to show that, being loyal, he should be reclassified is a wholly different question." Rutledge wished to take exception to Stone's suggestion, if it were so intended, that courts might not review the action a military officer chose to take regarding civilians in a military zone once he had found that an emergency had created the conditions justifying creation of the zone. The officer was entitled to wide discretion, "but it does not follow there may not be bounds beyond which he cannot go and, if he oversteps them, that the courts may not have power to protect the civilian citizen." *Hirabayashi* v. *U.S.*, 320 U.S. 81, pp. 105–109, 114.

[24] Letter to Murphy, June 10, 1943, Box 132, Murphy Papers.

remained "unconvinced." "If there were substantial evidence that citizens of Japanese ancestry were generally disloyal," Murphy had written, "or had generally so conducted themselves in this area as to constitute a special menace to defense installations and to measures being taken or planned for the defense of the area, or had otherwise by their behavior furnished reasonable ground for dealing with them in this manner as a distinct group, the curfew order and other restrictions imposed on them might be defended and upheld against legal attack in the light of the conditions and the military situation which then prevailed." Commenting on this statement, Reed had remarked, "If you admit this you give your case away. Military protection only needs reasonable grounds, which this record has. You cannot wait for an invasion to see if loyalty triumphs."[25] At first Murphy advised his law clerk to omit the language that had prompted Reed's observation, since it possibly conceded "too much,"[26] but shortly thereafter, apparently swayed by the views of his colleagues, Murphy abandoned altogether the idea of writing a dissent. "I congratulate you," the most critical of his brethren soon was able to write to him, "on the wisdom of having been able to reach a concurrence."[27]

But the concurring opinion that Murphy wrote bore a striking resemblance to the dissenting opinion he had intended to issue. The published concurrence contained the same language as the unpublished dissent with regard to the applicability of the Bill of Rights in wartime, Murphy's abhorrence of distinctions based on ancestry, his faith in the American melting pot and his lack of concern about ethnic differences in American society, and the relationship of the due process clause to discrimination based on racial heritage. Now, however, Murphy found that the curfew order went only to "the very brink of constitutional power," whereas previously he had held that it went over the brink, and he eliminated the stinging sentence, "Until today our laws have been just and equal." In his proposed dissent he had asserted that the point at which discrimination became a denial of due process of law was reached "when we have one law for the majority of our citizens and another for those of a particular racial heritage," but in his concurrence he maintained that the point had simply been "dangerously approached."

In his concurring opinion, Murphy omitted the judgment contained in the dissent that the action of the military had been based on the belief that persons of Japanese descent were unassimilable and gave their primary loyalty to Japan, and he eliminated his criticism of the treatment of the problem of loyalty on a group rather than an individual basis. In view of the critical situation on the Pacific Coast in the spring of 1942, military authorities, he now reluctantly conceded, could "not be required to conform to standards of regulatory action appropriate to normal times. . . . Modern war does not always wait for the observance of procedural requirements that are considered essential and appropriate under normal conditions." The military had made "an allowable judgment" at the time the restriction had been imposed, which was not to say that such a restriction would still be valid.

In the concluding paragraphs of his concurring opinion, Murphy revealed how limited was the degree of his assent with the Chief Justice's opinion and how difficult it had been for him to join with the Court in upholding the curfew order.

[25] Comment on draft of Murphy dissent, *ibid.*
[26] Murphy to Pickering, June 8, 1943, *ibid.*
[27] Undated note to Murphy, *ibid.*

> *In voting for affirmance of the judgment* [*he wrote*] *I do not wish to be understood as intimating that the military authorities in time of war are subject to no restraints whatsoever, or that they are free to impose any restrictions they may choose on the rights and liberties of individual citizens or groups of citizens in those places which may be designated as "military areas." While this Court sits, it has the inescapable duty of seeing that the mandates of the Constitution are obeyed. That duty exists in time of war as well as in time of peace, and in its performance we must not forget that few indeed have been the invasions upon essential liberties which have not been accompanied by pleas of urgent necessity advanced in good faith by responsible men. . . .*
>
> *Nor do I mean to intimate that citizens of a particular racial group whose freedom may be curtailed within an area threatened with attack should be generally prevented from leaving the area and going at large in other areas that are not in danger of attack and where special precautions are not needed. Their status as citizens, though subject to requirements of national security and military necessity, should at all times be accorded the fullest consideration and respect. When the danger is past, the restrictions imposed on them should be promptly removed and their freedom of action fully restored.*[28]

In the Hirabayashi case the Supreme Court had carefully avoided passing on the constitutionality of the exclusion of persons of Japanese ancestry from military areas on the west coast. When the matter was frontally presented to the Court in the Korematsu case, Justice Black, speaking for the majority and ignoring the guarded language of Stone's *Hirabayashi* opinion, cited the "principles we announced in the *Hirabayashi* case" as the basis for upholding the exclusion policy.[29] "Read this and perish!" Justice Murphy wrote to his law clerk. "The court has blown up on the Jap case—just [as] I expected it would."[30] If an effort was made by any of his brethren to persuade Justice Murphy to concur in the Korematsu case, the Murphy Papers provide no evidence of the fact. Such an attempt, we can be certain, would have been futile in any event. Murphy had concurred in *Hirabayashi* only with the greatest reluctance and, to a degree, against his better judgment. One senses from his *Korematsu* dissent that he welcomed the opportunity to write again on the Japanese-American question and to state, as he had wished to state with regard to the curfew order, that the exclusion policy "goes over 'the very brink of constitutional power' and falls into the ugly abyss of racism." In a series of footnotes to his opinion, he now cited a number of "independent studies made by experts" to refute the racial and sociological "facts" that the Court had first presented in the Hirabayashi case to support the judgment of the military. The reasons advanced to justify the exclusion policy—the same reasons previously offered as the basis for the curfew order—were, Murphy correctly observed, "largely an accumulation of much of the misrepresentation, half-truths and insinuations

[28] Cf. *Hirabayashi* v. *U.S.*, 320 U.S. 81, pp. 109–114, and drafts of Murphy's proposed dissent in Box 132, Murphy Papers.

[29] *Korematsu* v. *U.S.*, 323 U.S. 214 (1944), 218. Jackson correctly noted in his dissent, "The Court is now saying that in *Hirabayashi* we did decide the very things we there said we were not deciding." *Ibid.*, p. 247.

[30] Murphy to Gene [Eugene Gressman], undated, Box 133, Murphy Papers.

that for years have been directed against Japanese-Americans by people with racial and economic prejudices," among whom was General DeWitt.[31] In *Korematsu*, Murphy was able to make partial amends for his troubled concurrence in *Hirabayashi* and to follow the line of reasoning and to reach the same conclusions as were embodied in his unpublished *Hirabayashi* dissent.

[31] *Korematsu* v. *U.S.*, 323 U.S. 214, pp. 233–242.

25

THE "FORGOTTEN YEARS" OF THE NEGRO REVOLUTION

Richard M. Dalfiume

In 1954 in Brown et al. *v.* Board of Education of Topeka et al. *the U. S. Supreme Court ruled that segregated schools were unconstitutional and, a year later, ordered such schools to desegregate "with all deliberate speed." The 1954 decision, written by Chief Justice Warren, for a unanimous Court, directly reversed the ruling promulgated in* Plessy *v.* Ferguson *(1896), which had established the legal principle of "separate but equal," based on the proposition that if equality of accommodations existed Negroes had no recourse under the equal protection of the laws clause of the Fourteenth Amendment. The decisions of the Warren Court and the controversy and violence that soon surrounded them served as a clarion call for young blacks all over the nation to join the struggle for equality in unprecedented numbers, thereby launching the civil rights movement of the 1950's and 1960's. As Richard Dalfiume points out in the article reprinted below, however, the separate but equal system of race relations had been under sharp attack for the preceding fifteen years.*

Richard M. Dalfiume's areas of specialization are recent American politics and black history. He has compiled a book of readings, American Politics Since 1945 *(Chicago, 1969), and is the author of* Desegregation of the U. S. Armed Forces: Fighting on Two Fronts, 1939–1953 *(Columbia, 1969). He is a member of the history department at the State University of New York at Binghamton.*

A recent president of the American Sociological Society addressed himself to a puzzling question about what we know as the Civil Rights Revolution: "Why did social scientists—and sociologists in particular—not foresee the explosion of collective action of Negro Americans toward full integration into American society?" He

Source: *Journal of American History*, Vol. 55, No. 1 (June 1968), pp. 90–106. Reprinted by permission of the Organization of American Historians.

pointed out that "it is the vigor and urgency of the Negro demand that is new, not its direction or supporting ideas."[1] Without arguing the point further, the lack of knowledge can be attributed to two groups—the ahistorical social scientists, and the historians who, until recently, have neglected modern Negro history.

The search for a "watershed" in recent Negro history ends at the years that comprised World War II, 1939–1945. James Baldwin has written of this period: "The treatment accorded the Negro during the Second World War marks, for me, a turning point in the Negro's relation to America. To put it briefly, and somewhat too simply, a certain hope died, a certain respect for white Americans faded."[2] Writing during World War II, Gunnar Myrdal predicted that the war would act as a "stimulant" to Negro protest, and he felt that "There is bound to be a redefinition of the Negro's status in America as a result of this War."[3] The Negro sociologist E. Franklin Frazier states that World War II marked the point where "The Negro was no longer willing to accept discrimination in employment and in housing without protest."[4] Charles E. Silberman writes that the war was a "turning point" in American race relations, in which "the seeds of the protest movements of the 1950s and 1960s were sown."[5] While a few writers have indicated the importance of these years in the recent Negro protest movement, the majority have failed to do so. Overlooking what went before, most recent books on the subject claim that a Negro "revolution" or "revolt" occurred in 1954, 1955, 1960, or 1963.[6] Because of the neglect of the war period, these years of transition in American race relations comprise the "forgotten years" of the Negro revolution.

To understand how the American Negro reacted to World War II, it is necessary to have some idea of the discrimination he faced. The defense build-up begun by the United States in 1940 was welcomed by Negroes who were disproportionately represented among the unemployed. Employment discrimination in the revived industries, however, was rampant. When Negroes sought jobs at aircraft factories where employers begged for workers, they were informed that "the Negro will be considered only as janitors and in other similar capacities. . . ."[7] Government-financed training programs to overcome the shortages of skilled workers discriminated against Negro trainees. When government agencies issued orders against such discrimination, they were ignored.[8]

1 Everett C. Hughes, "Race Relations and the Sociological Imagination," *American Sociological Review*, XXVIII (Dec. 1963), 879.

2 Quoted in J. Milton Yinger, *A Minority Group in American Society* (New York, 1965), 52. Many Negroes agreed with James Baldwin in recalling the bitterness they experienced. William Brink and Louis Harris, *The Negro Revolution in America* (New York, 1964), 50.

3 Gunnar Myrdal, *An American Dilemma: The Negro Problem and Modern Democracy* (New York, 1944), 756, 997.

4 E. Franklin Frazier, *The Negro in the United States* (rev. ed., New York, 1957), 682.

5 Charles E. Silberman, *Crisis in Black and White* (New York, 1964), 60, 65.

6 See, for example, Lewis M. Killian and Charles Grigg, *Racial Crisis in America* (Englewood Cliffs, 1964); Louis E. Lomax, *The Negro Revolt* (New York, 1962); Leonard Broom and Norval D. Glenn, *Transformation of the Negro American* (New York, 1965); Brink and Harris, *Negro Revolution in America.*

7 Quoted in Louis Coleridge Kesselman, *The Social Politics of FEPC: A Study in Reform Pressure Movements* (Chapel Hill, 1948), 7.

8 Charles H. Thompson, "The American Negro and the National Defense," *Journal of Negro Education*, IX (Oct. 1940), 547–52; Frazier, *Negro in the United*

Increasing defense preparations also meant an expansion of the armed forces. Here, as in industry, however, Negroes faced restrictions. Black Americans were assigned a minimal role and rigidly segregated. In the navy, Negroes could enlist only in the all-Negro messman's branch. The marine and the air corps excluded Negroes entirely. In the army, black Americans were prevented from enlisting, except for a few vacancies in the four regular army Negro units that had been created shortly after the Civil War; and the strength of these had been reduced drastically in the 1920s and 1930s.[9]

Although the most important bread-and-butter issue for Negroes in this period was employment discrimination, their position in the armed forces was an important symbol. If one could not participate fully in the defense of his country, he could not lay claim to the rights of a full-fledged citizen. The NAACP organ, the *Crisis*, expressed this idea in its demand for unrestricted participation in the armed forces: "this is no fight merely to wear a uniform. This is a struggle for status, a struggle to take democracy off of parchment and give it life."[10] Herbert Garfinkel, a student of Negro protest during this period, points out that "in many respects, the discriminatory practices against Negroes which characterized the military programs . . . cut deeper into Negro feelings than did employment discrimination."[11]

Added to the rebuffs from industry and the armed services were a hundred others. Negroes, anxious to contribute to the Red Cross blood program, were turned away. Despite the fact that white and Negro blood is the same biologically, it was deemed inadvisable "to collect and mix caucasian and Negro blood indiscriminantly."[12] When Negro citizens called upon the governor of Tennessee to appoint some black members to the state's draft boards, he told them: "This is a white man's country. . . . The Negro had nothing to do with the settling of America."[13] At a time when the United States claimed to be the last bulwark of democracy in a war-torn world, the legislature of Mississippi passed a law requiring different textbooks for Negro schools: all references to voting, elections, and democracy were to be excluded from the black student's books.[14]

The Negro morale at the beginning of World War II is also partly explained by his experience in World War I. Black America had gone into the war with high morale, generated by the belief that the democratic slogans literally meant what they said. Most Negroes succumbed to the "close ranks" strategy announced by the crusading NAACP editor, W. E. B. Du Bois, who advocated subduing racial grievances in order to give full support to winning the war. But the image of a new democratic order was smashed by the race riots, lynchings, and continued rigid

---

States, 599–606; Robert C. Weaver, "Racial Employment Trends in National Defense," *Phylon*, II (4th Quarter 1941), 337–58.

[9] See Richard M. Dalfiume, "Desegregation of the United States Armed Forces, 1939–1953" (doctoral dissertation, University of Missouri, 1966), 30–57; Ulysses Lee, *United States Army in World War II: Special Studies: The Employment of Negro Troops* (Washington, 1966), 32–87.

[10] "For Manhood in National Defense," *Crisis*, 47 (Dec. 1940), 375.

[11] Herbert Garfinkel, *When Negroes March: The March on Washington Movement in the Organizational Politics for FEPC* (Glencoe, Ill., 1959), 20.

[12] General James C. Magee, Surgeon General, to Assistant Secretary of War John J. McCloy, Sept. 3, 1941, ASW 291.2, Record Group 335 (National Archives); Pittsburgh *Courier*, Jan. 3, 1942.

[13] Pittsburgh *Courier*, Nov. 2, 1940.

[14] "Text Books in Mississippi," *Opportunity*, XVIII (April 1940), 99.

discrimination. The result was a mass trauma and a series of movements among Negroes in the 1920s which were characterized by a desire to withdraw from a white society which wanted little to do with them. When the war crisis of the 1940s came along, the bitter memories of World War I were recalled with the result that there was a built-in cynicism among Negroes toward the democratic slogans of the new war.[15]

Nevertheless, Negroes were part of the general population being stimulated to come to the defense of democracy in the world. When they responded and attempted to do their share, they were turned away. The result was a widespread feeling of frustration and a general decline of the Negro's morale toward the war effort, as compared with the rest of American society. But paradoxically, the Negro's general morale was both low and high.

While the morale of the Negro, as an American, was low in regard to the war effort, the Negro, as a member of a minority group, had high morale in his heightened race consciousness and determination to fight for a better position in American society. The same slogans which caused the Negro to react cynically also served to emphasize the disparity between the creed and the practice of democracy as far as Negro in America was concerned. Because of his position in society, the Negro reacted to the war both as an American and as a Negro. Discrimination against him had given rise to "a sickly, negative attitude toward national goals, but at the same time a vibrantly positive attitude toward racial aims and aspirations."[16]

When war broke out in Europe in 1939, many black Americans tended to adopt an isolationist attitude. Those taking this position viewed the war as a "white man's war." George Schuyler, the iconoclastic columnist, was a typical spokesman for this view: "So far as the colored peoples of the earth are concerned," Schuyler wrote, "it is a toss-up between the 'democracies' and the dictatorships. . . . [W]hat is there to choose between the rule of the British in Africa and the rule of the Germans in Austria?"[17] Another Negro columnist claimed that it was a blessing to have war so that whites could "mow one another down" rather than "have them quietly murder hundreds of thousands of Africans, East Indians and Chinese. . . ."[18] This kind of isolationism took the form of anti-colonialism, particularly against the British. There was some sympathy for France, however, because of its more liberal treatment of black citizens.[19]

[15] Kenneth B. Clark, "Morale of the Negro on the Home Front: World Wars I and II," *Journal of Negro Education,* XII (Summer 1943), 417–28; Walter White, " 'It's Our Country, Too': The Negro Demands the Right to Be Allowed to Fight for It," *Saturday Evening Post,* 213 (Dec. 14, 1940), 27, 61, 63, 66, 68; Metz T. P. Lochard, "Negroes and Defense," *Nation,* 152 (Jan. 4, 1941), 14–16.

[16] Cornelius L. Golightly, "Negro Higher Education and Democratic Negro Morale," *Journal of Negro Education,* XI (July 1942), 324. See also Horace R. Cayton, "Negro Morale," *Opportunity,* XIX (Dec. 1941), 371–75; Louis Wirth, "Morale and Minority Groups," *American Journal of Sociology,* XLVII (Nov. 1941), 415–33; Kenneth B. Clark, "Morale Among Negroes," Goodwin Watson, ed., *Civilian Morale* (Boston, 1942), 228–48; Arnold M. Rose, *The Negro's Morale: Group Identification and Protest* (Minneapolis, 1949), 5–7, 54–55, 122–24, 141–44.

[17] Pittsburgh *Courier,* Sept. 9, 1939.

[18] P. L. Prattis in *ibid.,* Sept. 2, 1939. Similar sentiments were expressed by Chicago *Defender* editorials, May 25, June 15, 1940.

[19] Pittsburgh *Courier,* Sept. 9, 16, 1939.

Another spur to isolationist sentiment was the obvious hypocrisy of calling for the defense of democracy abroad while it was not a reality at home. The NAACP bitterly expressed this point:

> THE CRISIS *is sorry for brutality, blood, and death among the people of Europe, just as we were sorry for China and Ethiopia. But the hysterical cries of the preachers of democracy for Europe leave us cold. We want democracy in Alabama and Arkansas, in Mississippi and Michigan, in the District of Columbia*—in the Senate of the United States.[20]

The editor of the Pittsburgh *Courier* proclaimed that Negroes had their "own war" at home "against oppression and exploitation from without and against disorganization and lack of confidence within"; and the Chicago *Defender* thought that "peace at home" should be the main concern of black Americans.[21]

Many Negroes agreed with columnist Schuyler that "Our war is not against Hitler in Europe, but against the Hitlers in America."[22] The isolationist view of the war in Europe and the antagonism toward Great Britain led to an attitude that was rather neutral toward the Nazis and the Japanese, or, in some extreme cases, pro-Axis. Appealing to this latent feeling, isolationist periodicals tried to gain Negro support in their struggle against American entrance into the war.[23] By 1940 there were also Negro cults such as the Ethiopian Pacific Movement, the World Wide Friends of Africa, the Brotherhood of Liberty for the Black People of America, and many others, which preached unity among the world's darker people, including Japanese. Many of these groups exploited the latent anti-Semitism common among Negroes in the urban ghettos by claiming that the racial policies of Germany were correct.[24]

Reports reached the public that some black Americans were expressing a vicarious pleasure over successes by the "yellow" Japanese and by Germany. In a quarrel with her employer in North Carolina, a Negro woman retorted: "I hope Hitler does come, because if he does he will get you first!" A Negro truck driver in Philadelphia was held on charges of treason after he was accused of telling a Negro soldier that he should not be in uniform and that "This is a white man's government and war and it's no damned good." After Pearl Harbor, a Negro sharecropper told his landlord: "By the way, Captain, I hear the Japs done declared war on you white folks." Another Negro declared that he was going to get his eyes slanted so that the next time a white man shoved him around he could fight back.[25]

[20] "Lynching and Liberty," *Crisis*, 47 (July 1940), 209.

[21] Pittsburgh *Courier*, Sept. 9, 1939; Chicago *Defender*, May 25, 1940.

[22] Pittsburgh *Courier*, Dec. 21, 1940.

[23] Lee, *The Employment of Negro Troops*, 65–67; Horace Mann Bond, "Should the Negro Care Who Wins the War?" *Annals*, CCXXIII (Sept. 1942), 81–84; Adam Clayton Powell, Jr., "Is This a 'White Man's War'?" *Common Sense*, XI (April 1942), 111–13.

[24] Roi Ottley, "A White Folk's War?" *Common Ground*, II (Spring 1942), 28–31, and *'New World A-Coming'* (Boston, 1943), 322–42; Lunnabelle Wedlock, *The Reaction of Negro Publications and Organizations to German Anti-Semitism* (Washington, 1942), 116–93; Alfred M. Lee, "Subversive Individuals of Minority Status," *Annals*, CCXXIII (Sept. 1942), 167–68.

[25] St. Clair Drake and Horace R. Cayton, *Black Metropolis* (New York, 1945), 744–45; Ottley, *'New World A-Coming'*, 306–10; Horace R. Cayton, "Fighting for White Folks?" *Nation*, 155 (Sept. 26, 1942), 267–70.

It is impossible to determine the extent of this kind of pro-Axis sentiment among Negroes, but it was widespread enough for the Negro press to make rather frequent mention of it.[26] In 1942 and 1943 the federal government did arrest the members of several pro-Japanese Negro cults in Chicago, New York, Newark, New Jersey, and East St. Louis, Illinois. Although the numbers involved were small, the evidence indicated that Japanese agents had been at work among these groups and had capitalized on Negro grievances.[27]

By the time of the Pearl Harbor attack, certain fundamental changes were taking place among American Negroes. Nowhere is this more evident than in a comparison of Negroes' reactions to World Wars I and II. The dominant opinion among them toward World War I was expressed by Du Bois. In World War II, most Negroes looked upon the earlier stand as a great mistake. The dominant attitude during World War II was that the Negro must fight for democracy on two fronts—at home as well as abroad. This opinion had first appeared in reaction to the discriminatory treatment of Negro soldiers;[28] but with the attack on Pearl Harbor, this idea, stated in many different ways, became the slogan of black America.[29]

American Negroes took advantage of the war to tie their racial demands to the ideology for which the war was being fought. Before Pearl Harbor, the Negro press frequently pointed out the similarity of American treatment of Negroes and Nazi Germany's treatment of minorities. In 1940, the Chicago *Defender* featured a mock invasion of the United States by Germany in which the Nazis were victorious because a fifth column of southern senators and other racists aided them.[30] Later the *Crisis* printed an editorial which compared the white supremacy doctrine in America to the Nazi plan for Negroes, a comparison which indicated a marked similarity.[31] Even the periodical of the conservative Urban League made such comparisons.[32]

26 "The Negro and Nazism," *Opportunity*, XVIII (July 1940), 194–95; Horace R. Cayton in Pittsburgh *Courier*, Dec. 20, 1941; J. A. Rodgers in *ibid.*, Dec. 27, 1941; Chandler Owen in Norfolk *Journal and Guide*, Dec. 13, 1941; report in Baltimore *Afro-American*, Nov. 21, 1942.

27 *New York Times*, Sept. 15, 22, 1942, Jan. 14, 28, 1943.

28 "Conference Resolutions," *Crisis*, 47 (Sept. 1940), 296; "Where the Negro Stands," *Opportunity*, XIX (April 1941), 98; Lester M. Jones, "The Editorial Policy of Negro Newspapers of 1917–18 as Compared with That of 1941–42," *Journal of Negro History*, XXIX (Jan. 1944), 24–31.

29 Baltimore *Afro-American*, Dec. 20, 1941, Feb. 7, 1942; Norfolk *Journal and Guide*, March 21, 1942; "Now Is the Time Not to Be Silent," *Crisis*, 49 (Jan. 1942), 7; "The Fate of Democracy," *Opportunity*, XX (Jan. 1942), 2. Two Negro newspapers adopted this theme for their war slogans. The Pittsburgh *Courier*, Feb. 14, 1942, initiated a "Double V" campaign—"victory over our enemies at home and victory over our enemies on the battlefields abroad." When a Negro was brutally lynched in Sikeston, Missouri, a few weeks after Pearl Harbor, the Chicago *Defender*, March 14, 1942, adopted as its war slogan: "Remember Pearl Harbor and Sikeston too." See also Ralph N. Davis, "The Negro Newspapers and the War," *Sociology and Social Research*, XXVII (May–June 1943), 373–80.

30 Chicago *Defender*, Sept. 25, 1940.

31 "Nazi Plan for Negroes Copies Southern U. S. A." *Crisis*, 48 (March 1941), 71.

32 "American Nazism," *Opportunity*, XIX (Feb. 1941), 35. See also editorials in Pittsburgh *Courier*, March 15, April 19, 26, 1941, May 30, 1942; Chicago *Defender*, Sept. 7, 1940; Norfolk *Journal and Guide*, April 19, 1941; Baltimore *Afro-American*, Feb. 17, 1940, Sept. 6, 1941.

Many Negroes adopted a paradoxical stand on the meaning of the war. At the same time that it was labeled a "white man's war," Negroes often stated that they were bound to benefit from it. For example, Schuyler could argue that the war was not for democracy, but "Peace means . . . a continuation of the status quo . . . which must be ended if the Negro is to get free." And accordingly, the longer the war the better: "Perhaps in the shuffle we who have been on the bottom of the deck for so long will find ourselves at the top."[33]

Cynicism and hope existed side by side in the Negro mind. Cynicism was often the attitude expressed after some outrageous example of discrimination. After Pearl Harbor, however, a mixture of hope and certainty—great changes favorable to the Negro would result from the war and things would never be the same again—became the dominant attitude. Hope was evident in the growing realization that the war provided the Negro with an excellent opportunity to prick the conscience of white America. "What an opportunity the crisis has been . . . for one to persuade, embarrass, compel and shame our government and our nation . . . into a more enlightened attitude toward a tenth of its people!" the Pittsburgh *Courier* proclaimed.[34] Certainty that a better life would result from the war was based on the belief that revolutionary forces had been released throughout the world. It was no longer a "white man's world," and the "myth of white invincibility" had been shattered for good.[35]

There was a growing protest against the racial status quo by black Americans; this was evidenced by the reevaluation of segregation in all sections of the country. In the North there was self-criticism of past acceptance of certain forms of segregation.[36] Southern Negroes became bolder in openly questioning the sacredness of segregation. In October 1942, a group of southern Negro leaders met in Durham, North Carolina, and issued a statement on race relations. In addition to endorsing the idea that the Negro should fight for democracy at home as well as abroad, these leaders called for complete equality for the Negro in American life. While recognizing the "strength and age" of the South's racial customs, the Durham meeting was "fundamentally opposed to the principle and practice of compulsory segregation in our American society." In addition, there were reports of deep discontent among southern Negro college students and evidence that political activity among the blacks of the South, particularly on the local level, was increasing.[37]

[33] Pittsburgh *Courier*, Oct. 5, 1940; George S. Schuyler, "A Long War Will Aid the Negro," *Crisis*, 50 (Nov. 1943), 328–29, 344. See also J. A. Rodgers in Pittsburgh *Courier*, June 28, 1941; Horace R. Cayton in *ibid*., March 22, 1941; Baltimore *Afro-American*, Sept. 12, 16, 1939; Guion Griffis Johnson, "The Impact of War Upon the Negro," *Journal of Negro Education*, X (July 1941), 596–611.

[34] Pittsburgh *Courier*, Jan. 10, Aug. 8, 1942. Charles S. Johnson, "The Negro and the Present Crisis," *Journal of Negro Education*, X (July 1941), 585–95. Opinion surveys indicated that most Negro soldiers expressed support for this kind of opportunism. Samuel A. Stouffer and others, *The American Soldier* (2 vols., Princeton, 1949), I, 516–17.

[35] Baltimore *Afro-American*, June 12, Oct. 31, 1942; Walter White in Pittsburgh *Courier*, May 23, 1942. The impact of world affairs on the American Negro is detailed in Harold R. Isaacs, *The New World of Negro Americans* (New York, 1963).

[36] See editorials in Pittsburgh *Courier*, Dec. 28, 1940; Feb. 1, June 28, 1941; May 30, 1942; Baltimore *Afro-American*, May 23, 1942.

[37] Charles S. Johnson, *To Stem This Tide* (Boston, 1943), 131–39; Malcolm S. MacLean, president of Hampton Institute, to Marvin H. McIntyre, Nov. 20, 1942,

The American Negro, stimulated by the democratic ideology of the war, was reexamining his position in American society. "It cannot be doubted that the spirit of American Negroes in all classes is different today from what it was a generation ago," Myrdal observed.[38] Part of this new spirit was an increased militancy, a readiness to protest loud and strong against grievances. The crisis gave Negroes more reason and opportunity to protest. Representative of all of the trends of black thought and action—the cynicism, the hope, the heightened race consciousness, the militancy—was the March on Washington Movement (MOWM).

The general idea of exerting mass pressure upon the government to end defense discrimination did not originate with A. Philip Randolph's call for a march on Washington, D.C., in early 1941.[39] Agitation for mass pressure had grown since the failure of a group of Negro leaders to gain any major concessions from President Franklin D. Roosevelt in September 1940.[40] Various organizations, such as the NAACP, the Committee for Participation of Negroes in the National Defense, and the Allied Committees on National Defense, held mass protest meetings around the country in late 1940 and early 1941.[41] The weeks passed and these efforts did not seem to have any appreciable impact on the government; Walter White, Randolph, and other Negro leaders could not even secure an appointment to see the President. "Bitterness grew at an alarming pace throughout the country," White recalled.[42]

It remained, however, for Randolph to consolidate this protest. In January 1941, he wrote an article for the Negro press which pointed out the failure of committees and individuals to achieve action against defense discrimination. "Only power can effect the enforcement and adoption of a given policy," Randolph noted; and "Power is the active principle of only the organized masses, the masses united for a definite purpose." To focus the weight of the black masses, he suggested that 10,000 Negroes march on Washington, D.C., with the slogan: "We loyal Negro-American citizens demand the right to work and fight for our country."[43]

This march appeal led to the formation of one of the most significant—though today almost forgotten—Negro protest movements. The MOWM pioneered what has become the common denominator of today's Negro revolt—"the spontaneous involvement of large masses of Negroes in a political protest."[44] Furthermore, as August Meier and Elliott Rudwick have recently pointed out, the MOWM clearly foreshadowed "the goals, tactics, and strategy of the mid-twentieth-century civil

OF 93, Roosevelt Papers (Franklin D. Roosevelt Library, Hyde Park); George B. Tindall, "The Significance of Howard W. Odum to Southern History: A Preliminary Estimate," *Journal of Southern History*, XXIV (Aug. 1958), 302. Anthropologist Hortense Powdermaker, *After Freedom: A Cultural Study of the Deep South* (New York, 1939), 331–33, 353, supports the observations of a tendency to rebel among the younger Negroes of the South. See also Ralph J. Bunche, "The Negro in the Political Life of the United States," *Journal of Negro Education*, X (July 1941), 567–84; Myrdal, *American Dilemma*, 499; Henry Lee Moon, *Balance of Power: The Negro Vote* (Garden City, 1948), 178–79.

38 Myrdal, *American Dilemma*, 744.

39 Garfinkel, *When Negroes March*, fails to emphasize this point.

40 Walter White, *A Man Called White* (New York, 1948), 186–87; "White House Blesses Jim Crow," *Crisis*, 47 (Nov. 1940), 350–51, 357; Dalfiume, "Desegregation of the United States Armed Forces, 1939–1953," 46–51.

41 Pittsburgh *Courier*, Dec. 7, 14, 21, 1940; Jan. 4, 25, Feb. 8, 1941.

42 White, *A Man Called White*, 189–90.

43 Pittsburgh *Courier*, Jan. 25, 1941.

44 Garfinkel, *When Negroes March*, 8.

rights movement." Whites were excluded purposely to make it an all-Negro movement; its main weapon was direct action on the part of the black masses. Furthermore, the MOWM took as its major concern the economic problems of urban slum-dwellers.[45]

Randolph's tactic of mass pressure through a demonstration of black power struck a response among the Negro masses. The number to march to Washington on July 1, 1941, was increased to 50,000, and only Roosevelt's agreement to issue an executive order establishing a President's Committee on Fair Employment Practices led to a cancellation of the march. Negroes then, and scholars later, generally interpreted this as a great victory. But the magnitude of the victory is diminished when one examines the original MOWM demands: an executive order forbidding government contracts to be awarded to a firm which practiced discrimination in hiring, an executive order abolishing discrimination in government defense training courses, an executive order requiring the United States Employment Service to supply workers without regard to race, an executive order abolishing segregation in the armed forces, an executive order abolishing discrimination and segregation on account of race in all departments of the federal government, and a request from the President to Congress to pass a law forbidding benefits of the National Labor Relations Act to unions denying Negroes membership. Regardless of the extent of the success of the MOWM, however, it represented something different in black protest. Unlike the older Negro movements, the MOWM had captured the imagination of the masses.[46]

Although overlooked by most recent writers on civil rights, a mass militancy became characteristic of the American Negro in World War II. This was symbolized by the MOWM and was the reason for its wide appeal. Furthermore, older Negro organizations found themselves pushed into militant stands. For example, the NAACP underwent a tremendous growth in its membership and became representative of the Negro masses for the first time in its history. From 355 branches and a membership of 50,556 in 1940, the NAACP grew to 1,073 branches with a membership of slightly less than 450,000 in 1946.[47] The editors of the Pitts-

[45] August Meier and Elliott M. Rudwick, *From Plantation to Ghetto: An Interpretative History of American Negroes* (New York, 1966), 222.

[46] "Proposals of the Negro March-On-Washington Committee to President Roosevelt for Urgent Consideration," June 21, 1941, OF 391, Roosevelt Papers. The standard versions of a Negro "victory" are Garfinkel, *When Negroes March;* Kesselman, *The Social Politics of FEPC;* and Louis Ruchames, *Race, Jobs, & Politics: The Story of FEPC* (New York, 1953). For a different interpretation, see Dalfiume, "Desegregation of the United States Armed Forces, 1939–1953," 172–77. The Negro press generally recognized that the MOWM represented something new. The Pittsburgh *Courier,* July 5, 1941, claimed: "We begin to feel at last that the day when we shall gain full rights . . . of American citizenship is now not far distant." The Chicago *Defender,* June 28, July 12, 1941, felt that the white man will be convinced that "the American black man has decided henceforth and forever to abandon the timid role of Uncle-Tomism in his struggle. . . ." The tactics of the MOWM had "demonstrated to the doubting Thomases among us that only mass action can pry open the iron doors that have been erected against America's black minority."

[47] Frazier, *The Negro in the United States,* 537; Charles Radford Lawrence, "Negro Organizations in Crisis: Depression, New Deal, World War II" (doctoral dissertation, Columbia University, 1953), 103; Myrdal, *American Dilemma,* 851–52. Such close observers of American race relations as Will Alexander, Edwin Em-

burgh *Courier* recognized that a new spirit was present in black America. In the past, Negroes

> *made the mistake of relying entirely upon the gratitude and sense of fair play of the American people. Now we are disillusioned. We have neither faith in promises, nor a high opinion of the integrity of the American people, where race is involved. Experience has taught us that we must rely primarily upon our own efforts. . . . That is why we protest, agitate, and demand that all forms of color prejudice be blotted out. . . .*[48]

By the time of the Japanese attack on Pearl Harbor, many in America, both inside and outside of the government, were worried over the state of Negro morale. There was fear that the Negro would be disloyal.[49] The depth of white ignorance about the causes for the Negro's cynicism and low morale is obvious from the fact that the black press was blamed for the widespread discontent. The double victory attitude constantly displayed in Negro newspapers throughout the war, and supported by most black Americans, was considered as verging on disloyalty by most whites. White America, ignorant of the American Negroes' reaction to World War I, thought that black citizens should subdue their grievances for the duration.

During World War II, there was pressure upon the White House and the justice department from within the federal government to indict some Negro editors for sedition and interference with the war effort. President Roosevelt refused to sanction this, however. There was also an attempt to deny newsprint to the more militant Negro newspapers, but the President put an end to this when the matter was brought to his attention.[50] The restriction of Negro newspapers from military installations became so widespread that the war department had to call a halt to

---

bree, and Charles S. Johnson recognized the changing character of Negro protest. They believed that "the characteristic movements among Negroes are now for the first time becoming proletarian, as contrasted to upper class or intellectual influence that was typical of previous movements. The present proletarian direction grows out of the increasing general feelings of protest against discrimination, especially in the armed forces and in our war activities generally. The present movements are led in part by such established leaders as A. Philip Randolph, Walter White, etc. There is likelihood (and danger) that the movement may be seized upon by some much more picturesque figure who may be less responsible and less interested in actual improvement of conditions. One of the most likely of the potential leaders is A. Clayton Powell, Jr." Memorandum of Conferences of Alexander, Johnson, and Embree on the Rosenwald Fund's Program in Race Relations, June 27, 1942, Race Relations folder, Rosenwald Fund Papers (Fisk University).

48 Pittsburgh *Courier*, Sept. 12, 1942. See also Roscoe E. Lewis, "The Role of Pressure Groups in Maintaining Morale Among Negroes," *Journal of Negro Education*, XII (Summer 1943), 464–73; Earl Brown, "American Negroes and the War," *Harper's Magazine*, 184 (April 1942), 545–52; Roi Ottley, "Negro Morale," *New Republic*, 105 (Nov. 10, 1941), 613–15; Thomas Sancton, "Something's Happened to the Negro," *New Republic*, 108 (Feb. 8, 1943), 175–79; Stanley High, "How the Negro Fights for Freedom," *Reader's Digest*, 41 (July 1942), 113–18; H. C. Brearley, "The Negro's New Belligerency," *Phylon*, V (4th Quarter 1944), 339–45.

49 Memorandum to Assistant Secretary of War McCloy from G-2, June 27, 1942, ASW 291.2, Record Group 335.

50 White, *A Man Called White*, 207–08; R. Keith Kane to Ulric Bell, May 14, 1942, OFF 992.11, Record Group 208; Memorandum to Robert A. Lovett from McCloy, March 6, 1942, ASW 291.2, Record Group 335.

this practice in 1943.[51] These critics failed to realize that, although serving to unify black opinion, the Negro press simply reflected the Negro mind.

One of the most widely publicized attacks on the Negro press was made by the southern white liberal, Virginius Dabney, editor of the Richmond *Times Dispatch*. He charged that "extremist" Negro newspapers and Negro leaders were "demanding an overnight revolution in race relations," and as a consequence they were "stirring up interracial hate." Dabney concluded his indictment by warning that "it is a foregone conclusion that if an attempt is made forcibly to abolish segregation throughout the South, violence and bloodshed will result."[52] The Negro press reacted vigorously to such charges. Admitting that there were "all-or-nothing" Negro leaders, the Norfolk *Journal and Guide* claimed they were created by the "nothing-at-all" attitude of whites.[53] The Chicago *Defender* and Baltimore *Afro-American* took the position that they were only pointing out the shortcomings of American democracy, and this was certainly not disloyal.[54] The NAACP and the Urban League claimed that it was patriotic for Negroes to protest against undemocratic practices, and those who sought to stifle this protest were the unpatriotic ones.[55]

The Negro masses simply did not support a strategy of moderating their grievances for the duration of the war. After attending an Office of Facts and Figures conference for Negro leaders in March 1942, Roy Wilkins of the NAACP wrote:

> *. . . it is a plain fact that no Negro leader with a constituency can face his*

[51] Baltimore *Afro-American*, Sept. 30, 1941; Pittsburgh *Courier*, March 8, 1941, Nov. 13, 1943. Assistant Secretary of War McCloy, who was also head of the war department's Advisory Committee on Negro Troop Policies, held a critical view of the Negro press that was common in the army. McCloy to Herbert Elliston, editor of the Washington *Post*, Aug. 5, 1943, ASW 292.2, Record Group 335.

[52] Virginius Dabney, "Nearer and Nearer the Precipice," *Atlantic Monthly*, 171 (Jan. 1943), 94–100; Virginius Dabney, "Press and Morale," *Saturday Review of Literature*, XXV (July 4, 1942), 5–6, 24–25.

[53] Norfolk *Journal and Guide*, Aug. 15, 1942. See also *Journal and Guide* editorials of Oct. 17, April 25, 1942; and March 6, 1943, for a defense of Negro militancy.

[54] Chicago *Defender*, Dec. 20, 1941; Baltimore *Afro-American*, Jan. 9, 1943.

[55] Pittsburgh *Courier*, May 8, June 19, 1943. A few conservative Negroes joined whites in criticizing the growing militancy. James E. Shepard, Negro president of North Carolina College for Negroes, asked the administration to do something to undercut the growing support of the militants among young Negroes: "Those who seek to stir them up about rights and not duties are their enemies." Shepard to Secretary of the Navy Frank Knox, Sept. 28, 1940, OF 93, Roosevelt Papers. Frederick D. Patterson, president of Tuskegee Institute, made it clear in his newspaper column and in talks with administration officials that he believed in all-out support for the war effort by Negroes regardless of segregation and discrimination. "Stimson Diary," Jan. 29, 1943 (Yale University Library), and columns by Patterson in the Pittsburgh *Courier*, Jan. 16, July 3, 1943. Such conservatives were bitterly attacked in the Negro press. The black leader who urged his people to relax their determination to win full participation in American life was a "misleader and a false prophet," the Norfolk *Journal and Guide*, May 2, 1942, proclaimed. Such people "endangered" the interests of Negroes by "compromising with the forces that promote and uphold segregation and discrimination," wrote the editor of the Chicago *Defender*, April 5, 1941. The *Crisis* charged that those Negroes who succumbed to segregation as "realism" provided a rationale for those whites who sought to perpetuate segregation. "Government Blesses Separatism," *Crisis*, 50 (April 1943), 105.

members today and ask full support for the war in the light of the atmosphere the government has created. Some Negro educators who are responsible only to their boards or trustees might do so, but the heads of no organized groups would dare do so.[56]

By 1942, the federal government began investigating Negro morale in order to find out what could be done to improve it. This project was undertaken by the Office of Facts and Figures and its successor, the Office of War Information.[57] Surveys by these agencies indicated that the great amount of national publicity given the defense program only served to increase the Negro's awareness that he was not participating fully in that program. Black Americans found it increasingly difficult to reconcile their treatment with the announced war aims. Urban Negroes were the most resentful over defense discrimination, particularly against the treatment accorded black members of the armed forces. Never before had Negroes been so united behind a cause: the war had served to focus their attention on their unequal status in American society. Black Americans were almost unanimous in wanting a show of good intention from the federal government that changes would be made in the racial status quo.[58]

The government's inclination to take steps to improve Negro morale, and the Negro's desire for change, were frustrated by the general attitude of white Americans. In 1942, after two years of militant agitation by Negroes, six out of ten white Americans felt that black Americans were satisfied with things the way they were and that Negroes were receiving all of the opportunities they deserved. More than half of all whites interviewed in the Northeast and West believed that there should be separate schools, separate restaurants, and separate neighborhoods for the races. A majority of whites in all parts of the country believed that the Negro would not be treated any better after the war than in 1942 and that the Negro's lesser role in society was due to his own shortcomings rather than anything the whites had done.[59] The white opposition to racial change may have provided the rationale for governmental inactivity. Furthermore, the white obstinance must have added to the bitterness of black Americans.

[56] Memorandum to White from Roy Wilkins, March 24, 1942, Stephen J. Spingarn Papers (Harry S Truman Library, Independence).

[57] Memorandum to Archibald MacLeish from Kane, Feb. 14, 1942; Bell to Embree, Feb. 23, 1942, OFF 002.11, Record Group 208. Some government agencies displayed timidity when it came to a subject as controversial as the race question. Jonathan Daniels, Assistant Director in Charge of Civilian Mobilization, Office of Civilian Defense, urged the creation of a Division of American Unity within the OCD, but his superiors decided Negro morale was "too hot a potato." Memoranda to James Landis, April 1, 7, 1942; Daniels to Howard W. Odum, Aug. 24, 1942, Jonathan Daniels Papers (University of North Carolina).

[58] "Reports from the Special Services Division Submitted April 23, 1942: Negro Organizations and the War Effort"; Cornelius Golightly, "Negro Morale in Boston," Special Services Division Report No. 7, May 19, 1942; Special Services Division Report No. 5, May 15, 1942: "Negro Conference at Lincoln University"; Special Services Division Memorandum, "Report on Recent Factors Increasing Negro-White Tension," Nov. 2, 1942. All are in OFF and OWI files in Record Group 44.

[59] "Intelligence Report: White Attitudes Toward Negroes," OWI, Bureau of Intelligence, Aug. 5, 1942; same title dated July 28, 1942, Record Group 44. Hazel Gaudet Erskine, "The Polls: Race Relations," *Public Opinion Quarterly*, XXVI (Spring 1962), 137–48.

Although few people recognized it, the war was working a revolution in American race relations. Sociologist Robert E. Park felt that the racial structure of society was "cracking," and the equilibrium reached after the Civil War seemed "to be under attack at a time and under conditions when it is particularly difficult to defend it."[60] Sociologist Howard W. Odum wrote from the South that there was "an unmeasurable and unbridgeable distance between the white South and the reasonable expectation of the Negro."[61] White southerners opposed to change in the racial mores sensed changes occurring among "their" Negroes. "Outsiders" from the North, Mrs. Franklin Roosevelt, and the Roosevelt Administration were all accused of attempting to undermine segregation under the pretense of wartime necessity.[62]

Racial tensions were common in all sections of the country during the war.[63] There were riots in 1943. Tensions were high because Negro Americans were challenging the status quo. When fourteen prominent Negroes, conservatives and liberals, southerners and northerners, were asked in 1944 what they thought the black American wanted, their responses were almost unanimous. Twelve of the fourteen said they thought that Negroes wanted full political equality, economic equality, equality of opportunity, and full social equality with the abolition of legal segregation.[64] The war had stimulated the race consciousness and the desire for change among Negroes.

Most American Negroes and their leaders wanted the government to institute a revolutionary change in its race policy. Whereas the policy had been acquiescence in segregation since the end of Reconstruction, the government was now asked to set the example for the rest of the nation by supporting integration. This was the demand voiced by the great majority of the Negro leaders called together in March 1942 by the Office of Facts and Figures.[65] *Crisis* magazine summarized the feelings of many black Americans: Negroes have "waited thus far in vain for some sharp and dramatic notice that this war is not to maintain the status quo here."[66]

The White House, and it was not alone, failed to respond to the revolutionary changes occurring among the nation's largest minority. When the Fraternal Council of Negro Churches called upon President Roosevelt to end discrimination in the defense industries and armed forces, the position taken was that "it would be very bad to give encouragement beyond the point where actual results can be accomplished."[67] Roosevelt did bestir himself over particularly outrageous inci-

[60] Robert E. Park, "Racial Ideologies," William Fielding Ogburn, ed., *American Society In Wartime* (Chicago, 1943), 174.

[61] Howard W. Odum, *Race and Rumors of Race: Challenge to American Crisis* (Chapel Hill, 1943), 7; for a similar view, see Johnson, *To Stem This Tide*, 67–68, 73, 89–107, 113, 117.

[62] John Temple Graves, "The Southern Negro and the War Crisis," *Virginia Quarterly Review*, 18 (Autumn 1942), 500–17; Clark Foreman, "Race Tension in the South," *New Republic*, 107 (Sept. 21, 1942), 340–42.

[63] Alfred McClung Lee and Norman Daymond Humphrey, *Race Riot* (New York, 1943); Carey McWilliams, "Race Tensions: Second Phase," *Common Ground*, IV (Autumn 1943), 7–12.

[64] Rayford W. Logan, ed., *What the Negro Wants* (Chapel Hill, 1944).

[65] Memorandum to White from Wilkins, March 23, 1942, Spingarn Papers; Pittsburgh *Courier*, March 28, 1942; Norfolk *Journal and Guide*, March 28, 1942.

[66] "U. S. A. Needs Sharp Break With the Past," *Crisis*, 49 (May 1942), 151.

[67] "A Statement to the President of the United States Concerning the Present World Crisis by Negro Church Leaders Called by the Executive Committee of the

dents. When Roland Hayes, a noted Negro singer, was beaten and jailed in a Georgia town, the President dashed off a note to his attorney general: "Will you have someone go down and check up . . . and see if any law was violated. I suggest you send a northerner."[68]

Roosevelt was not enthusiastic about major steps in the race relations field proposed by interested individuals within and without the government.[69] In February 1942 Edwin R. Embree of the Julius Rosenwald Fund, acutely aware of the growing crisis in American race relations, urged Roosevelt to create a commission of experts on race relations to advise him on what steps the government should take to improve matters. FDR's answer to this proposal indicates that he felt race relations was one of the reform areas that had to be sacrificed for the present in order to prosecute the war. He thought such a commission was "premature" and that "we must start winning the war . . . before we do much general planning for the future." The President believed that "there is a danger of such long-range planning becoming projects of wide influence in escape from the realities of war. I am not convinced that we can be realists about the war and planners for the future at this critical time."[70]

After the race riots of 1943, numerous proposals for a national committee on race relations were put forward; but FDR refused to change his position. Instead, the President simply appointed Jonathan Daniels to gather information from all government departments on current race tensions and what they were doing to combat them.[71] This suggestion for what would eventually become a President's

---

Fraternal Council of Negro Churches of America," Feb. 17, 1942; McIntyre to MacLean, Chairman of the President's Committee on Fair Employment Practice, Feb. 19, 1942, OF 93, Roosevelt Papers.

68 Memorandum to the Attorney General from the President, Aug. 26, 1942, OF 93, *ibid.*

69 Franklin Roosevelt's conservative and "leave well enough alone" attitude toward Negro rights is discussed in Arthur M. Schlesinger, Jr., *The Age of Roosevelt: The Politics of Upheaval* (Boston, 1960), 431; Frank Freidel, *F. D. R. and the South* (Baton Rouge, 1965), 73, 81, 97; Mary McLeod Bethune, "My Secret Talks with F. D. R.," *Ebony*, IV (April 1949), 42–51. Perhaps Roosevelt's conservative attitude is responsible for his privately expressed dislike of the NAACP. In 1943 Arthur B. Spingarn, president of the NAACP, asked him to write a letter praising the twenty-five years of service by White to that organization. On one version of the proposed letter there is an attached note which reads: "Miss Tully brought this in. Says the President doesn't think too much of this organization—not to be to[o] fulsome—tone it down a bit." Roosevelt to Spingarn, Oct. 1, 1943, PPF 1226, Roosevelt Papers.

70 Roosevelt to Embree, March 16, 1942, in answer to Embree to Roosevelt, Feb. 3, 1942, OF 93, Roosevelt Papers. In his covering letter to the President's secretary, Embree emphasized that his proposed commission should address itself to the problem of race around the world as well as at home: "A serious weakness both in America and among the united nations is the low morale of the 'colored peoples' to whom this war is being pictured as simply another struggle of the white man for domination of the world. This condition is becoming acute among the Negro group at home and among important allies abroad, especially the Chinese and the residents of Malaya, the East Indies, and the Philippines." Embree to McIntyre, Feb. 3, 1942, Commission on Race and Color folder, Rosenwald Fund Papers.

71 In June 1943, Embree and John Collier, Commissioner of Indian Affairs, developed an idea for a committee established by the President "to assume special responsibility in implementing the Bill of Rights of the Constitution, particularly in defending racial minorities at a time of crisis." Memorandum to Johnson and

Committee on Civil Rights would have to wait until a President recognized that a revolution in race relations was occurring and that action by the government could no longer be put off. In the interim, many would share the shallow reasoning of Secretary of War Stimson that the cause of racial tension was "the deliberate effort . . . on the part of certain radical leaders of the colored race to use the war for obtaining . . . race equality and interracial marriages. . . ."[72]

The hypocrisy and paradox involved in fighting a world war for the four freedoms and against aggression by an enemy preaching a master race ideology, while at the same time upholding racial segregation and white supremacy, were too obvious. The war crisis provided American Negroes with a unique opportunity to point out, for all to see, the difference between the American creed and practice. The democratic ideology and rhetoric with which the war was fought stimulated a sense of hope and certainty in black Americans that the old race structure was destroyed forever. In part, this confidence was also the result of the mass militancy and race consciousness that developed in these years. When the expected white acquiescence in a new racial order did not occur, the ground was prepared for the civil rights revolution of the 1950s and 1960s; the seeds were indeed sown in the World War II years.

Alexander from Embree, June 16, 1943, Race Relations folder, Rosenwald Fund Papers. See also John Collier and Saul K. Padover, "An Institute for Ethnic Democracy," *Common Ground*, IV (Autumn 1943), 3–7, for a more elaborate proposal.

Embree probably passed along his idea to Odum of the University of North Carolina so that he could discuss it with a fellow North Carolinian in the White House, Daniels, administrative assistant to the President. Odum and Daniels had a conference in August 1943 from which emerged a recommendation for a "President's Committee on Race and Minority Groups." Odum to Daniels, Aug. 23, 1943; Memorandum to Daniels from Odum, Aug. 30, 1943, Howard W. Odum Papers (University of North Carolina).

Although Daniels apparently gave Odum the impression that he was interested in a national committee, this was not the case. "It has been suggested that a committee of prominent men be named to study this situation," he wrote the President. "I am sure the naming of such a committee would not now halt the procession of angry outbreaks which are occurring. I doubt that any report could be made which would be so effective as a statement now from you would be. I am very much afraid, indeed, that any committee report would only serve as a new ground for controversy." Memorandum to the President from Daniels, Aug. 2, 1943, Daniels Papers. Roosevelt apparently agreed with Daniels, and Odum was informed that "My boss does not think well of the idea that we discussed." Daniels to Odum, Sept. 1, 1943, Odum Papers.

Daniels' appointment as White House coordinator of information on race relations was actually suggested by him to the President in June 1943. Memorandum to the President from Daniels, June 29, 1943, Daniels Papers. By July 1943, Roosevelt had approved of the new role for his administrative assistant, and Daniels was hard at work gathering information. Daniels to Secretary of War Stimson, July 28, 1943, ASW 291.2, Record Group 335.

[72] "Stimson Diary," June 24, 1943.

26

LEND-LEASE TO RUSSIA AND THE ORIGINS OF THE COLD WAR, 1944–1945

George C. Herring, Jr.

In March 1941 Congress enacted the Lend-Lease Act to help prospective allies and others in need of aid. Under its terms the United States eventually transferred to anti-Axis nations over fifty billion dollars in war materials and services. To avoid the pitfalls of foreign loans, which left a bitter diplomatic legacy after World War I, and at the same time recognizing the exhausted credit of the Allies, Franklin Roosevelt proposed that the nation lend or lease to any nation whose defense the president deemed vital for the defense of the United States war materials the beleagured nation needed to resist aggression. Under its provisions airplanes, tanks, artillery, and other supplies were shipped to Great Britain, Soviet Russia, and other nations fighting the Axis powers. In this essay George Herring reviews these activities as they pertained to Russia and examines some of the problems that arose, considering them with regard to tensions that developed between the two nations in the postwar period.

George Herring teaches diplomatic history at the University of Kentucky. His scholarly work is concerned with the origins of the Cold War. He has completed a manuscript on lend-lease and this article forms the basis of a chapter of this study. Currently he is helping to prepare for publication a portion of the wartime diary of Edward Stettinius, who was in charge of lend-lease operations until he became undersecretary of state in September of 1943.

On May 11, 1945, three days after the cessation of hostilities against Germany, President Harry S. Truman ordered a drastic cutback in lend-lease aid to the Soviet Union. The following day, civilian and military officials, zealously executing the

Source: *Journal of American History*, Vol. 56, No. 1 (June 1969), pp. 93–114. Reprinted by permission of the Organization of American Historians.

directive, halted loadings in port and even recalled several ships at sea bound for Russia. Truman's order naturally evoked loud protests from the Soviets. The Grand Alliance was disintegrating. Joseph Stalin interpreted the reduction of lend-lease as an American attempt to extort political concessions through economic pressure.

The full story behind this important policy decision has not been told.[1] In his *Memoirs*, Truman denied any intention of coercing the Russians. With the war in Europe ended, he argued, large-scale lend-lease shipments to the Soviet Union were no longer legally justifiable. The cutback applied to all nations, not just Russia; he had not intended the May 12 reduction to be so severe. When he had learned that his order had been interpreted too rigidly, Truman recalled, he had quickly corrected the mistake; and shipments to Russia had been resumed on as large a scale as possible.[2]

Those revisionist historians who have placed major responsibility for the Cold War on the United States have challenged Truman's explanation of the May 11 order and have cited the lend-lease cutbacks as one of the first of a series of provocative acts by his administration to coerce the Russians.[3] The fullest exposition of the revisionist thesis has been offered by Gar Alperovitz. He pinpoints the lend-lease cutback as the central element in Truman's "strategy of an immediate showdown" with the Soviets. Shortly after Truman took office, Alperovitz contends, Truman abandoned Franklin D. Roosevelt's policy of friendship and conciliation toward the Russians and embarked upon a "powerful foreign policy initiative aimed at reducing or eliminating Soviet influence from Europe." The drastic reduction of lend-lease after V-E Day was designed to achieve this objective. Alperovitz cites numerous conversations among Truman's advisers as evidence to prove that their major concern in cutting back lend-lease was the Soviet Union. The legal limitations on the use of lend-lease after V-E Day, he argues, were not rigid and were used by the administration only as a pretext for an act whose essential purpose was to coerce the Russians. A more flexible line on later Soviet requests for aid was taken only because the showdown strategy failed to produce a Soviet surrender and because the atomic bomb seemed to provide an instrument of coercion more powerful than economic pressure.[4]

The availability of new documentary evidence permits a detailed examination of the decision of May 11, 1945, to cut back aid to Russia. This evidence indicates that neither Truman's apology nor the revisionists' critique provides an adequate explanation for the decision. A full study of this important and controversial decision which places it in the context of American lend-lease policy for Russia and other Allied nations, considers it against the domestic political background in the

[1] The best accounts are in Herbert Feis, *Between War and Peace: The Potsdam Conference* (Princeton, 1960), 27–28, 329–30; and Martin F. Herz, *Beginnings of the Cold War* (Bloomington, 1966), 153–74.

[2] Harry S. Truman, *Memoirs by Harry S. Truman* (2 vols., Garden City, 1955–1956), I, 227–29.

[3] William Appleman Williams, *The Tragedy of American Diplomacy* (Cleveland, 1959), 241–43; D. F. Fleming, *The Cold War and Its Origins, 1917–1960* (2 vols., New York, 1961), I, 269–70; Lloyd C. Gardner, *Economic Aspects of New Deal Diplomacy* (Madison, 1964), 315–17.

[4] Gar Alperovitz, *Atomic Diplomacy: Hiroshima and Potsdam, The Use of the Atomic Bomb and the American Confrontation with Soviet Power* (New York, 1965), 19–40.

United States during the summer of 1945, and studies it in the light of the emerging conflict in Soviet-American relations, makes it possible to correct several misconceptions regarding the decision itself and to evaluate more accurately the significance of the lend-lease question in the origins of the Cold War.

To place the May 11 decision in perspective, it is necessary to consider the unique manner in which aid to Russia had been administered since its inception in 1941. After the Nazi invasion of Russia, Roosevelt attached special military importance to assisting the Soviets. He considered it essential to provide maximum support to operations on the Russian front; and until a second front could be opened, lend-lease was the only means of support available. During the course of the war, he seems also to have believed that American generosity in assisting the Russians would help break down the ingrained Soviet suspicion of the West, that it would convince the Russian leaders of American good will, and that it would provide a firm foundation for the Soviet-American cooperation upon which he came to base his hopes for a lasting peace.[5]

For these reasons, Roosevelt assigned highest priority to aid to Russia and took a close personal interest in the implementation of the Russian lend-lease program. Throughout the war he repeatedly impressed upon his aides the urgency of maintaining a steady and an increasing flow of supplies to the Soviets. When supply shortages or administrative red tape threatened to delay shipments, he exerted his personal influence to break the bottleneck. He relentlessly drove his subordinates to find sufficient shipping to transport supplies to Russia, and he even established a special committee, responsible directly to him and headed by his confidant Harry Hopkins, to oversee Soviet aid.[6]

Under the President's direct supervision, lend-lease to Russia was given a unique status. Lend-lease officials required other recipients of aid to file elaborate evidence which justified their need for and indicated their ability to use each item requested. Quarterly programs were established on the basis of this evidence, but these programs did not represent binding commitments. They were always subject to modification on the basis of changes in the availability of equipment or transport and changes in the strategic situation. As the military position of the Allies improved after mid-1944 and American troops took on a greater burden of the fighting, lend-lease to most nations was sharply reduced.[7]

None of these limitations applied to Russian lend-lease. Soviet requests were accepted at face value; no supporting evidence was required. These requests, compiled into annual programs called protocols, were represented as binding commitments and limited only by the availability of supplies and shipping. Difficulties in transporting supplies to Russia imposed severe limitations on the lend-lease program until 1943, but as the shipping crisis eased, protocol commitments steadily increased and were often exceeded.[8]

Roosevelt vigorously resisted any efforts to modify this unconditional aid policy.

[5] Franklin D. Roosevelt's attitudes can be seen in John M. Blum, *From the Morgenthau Diaries* (3 vols., Boston, 1959–1967), III, 80–87; Raymond H. Dawson, *The Decision to Aid Russia, 1941: Foreign Policy and Domestic Politics* (Chapel Hill, 1959); and George C. Herring, Jr., "Experiment in Foreign Aid: Lend-Lease, 1941–1945" (doctoral dissertation, University of Virginia, 1965), 232–78.

[6] Herring, "Experiment in Foreign Aid," 232–78.

[7] *Ibid.*, 148, 151–53, 441–43.

[8] *Ibid.*, 233–34; Department of State, *Report on War Aid Furnished by the United States to the U. S. S. R.* (Washington, 1945).

He rejected the proposals of air force officers to limit aircraft shipments to the Russians and quashed the army's efforts to get a *quid pro quo* in return for lend-lease aid. He politely ignored the warnings of his ambassador to Russia, Admiral William H. Standley, that the Soviets were taking advantage of his generosity. At the first meeting of the President's Soviet Protocol Committee, Hopkins stated that the unconditional aid policy had been established with some misgivings, but after extensive deliberation. It would be maintained, he continued, and should not be brought up for reconsideration.[9]

In 1944, however, as the Soviets took the offensive in Europe and political disputes began to divide the Allies, a number of Roosevelt's advisers questioned with increasing vigor the unconditional aid policy. The Russian military position was no longer desperate, and the Soviets seemed to be exploiting American generosity. They had ordered much equipment which they could not use and which reportedly had been wasted.[10] They had requested vast quantities of industrial equipment which could not be made operational before the end of the war and which was obviously intended for postwar reconstruction.[11] They were giving or selling to other countries American supplies or items similar to those received under lend-lease in order to boost their own political influence in Eastern Europe and the Middle East.[12]

The continued secretiveness of the Soviets suggested to some Americans that Roosevelt's policy had not succeeded in breaking the wall of suspicion which separated Russia from the West. More ominously, the pattern of Soviet policy toward Eastern Europe in 1944 seemed to indicate not only that the unconditional aid policy had failed to secure Russian-American friendship but also that it may have encouraged a more aggressive attitude on the part of the Soviets and deprived the United States of a bargaining lever to influence the shape of the postwar world. The President's advisers in Moscow, Ambassador W. Averell Harriman and Major General John H. Deane, chief of the United States Military Mission, warned their superiors in late 1944 that American generosity had been interpreted by the Soviets as a sign of weakness.[13] Deane cautioned General George C. Marshall that gratitude could not be banked in the Soviet Union and that the administration's policy of cooperation with Russia could not work unless it was based on mutual respect.[14]

[9] Richard K. Lukas, "Air Force Aspects of American Aid to the Soviet Union: The Crucial Years, 1941–1942" (doctoral dissertation, Florida State University, 1963), 376–77; William H. Standley and Arthur Ageton, *Admiral Ambassador to Russia* (New York, 1947), 239, 308, 351–60; Minutes of the first meeting of the President's Soviet Protocol Committee, Nov. 25, 1942, Edward R. Stettinius, Jr., Papers (University of Virginia, Charlottesville).

[10] John R. Deane, *The Strange Alliance: The Story of Our Efforts at Wartime Co-operation with Russia* (New York, 1947), 96–97.

[11] Minutes of the Executive Staff Committee, Office of Lend-Lease Administration, July 13, 1943; Edward R. Stettinius, Jr., memorandum to Dean Acheson, Dec. 27, 1943; Stettinius memorandum to Cordell Hull, Feb. 22, 1944, Stettinius Papers.

[12] W. Averell Harriman to Cordell Hull, Sept. 7, 1944, Department of State, *Foreign Relations of the United States: Diplomatic Papers, 1944* (7 vols., Washington, 1966–1967), IV, 1131.

[13] Harriman to Cordell Hull, March 13, 1944; Harriman to Harry L. Hopkins, Sept. 10, 1944, *ibid.*, 951, 988–90.

[14] John R. Deane to George C. Marshall, Dec. 2, 1944, Department of State, *Foreign Relations of the United States: Diplomatic Papers, The Conferences of Malta and Yalta* (Washington, 1955), 447–49.

Both Deane and Harriman as well as officials in Washington urged the President to modify the unconditional aid policy, to correct abuses that had developed, and to make clear to the Russians what the United States expected in return for its assistance. Harriman advised against drastic changes and proposed the adoption of a "firm but friendly *quid pro quo* approach." Deane, Harriman, and Secretary of the Navy Frank Knox suggested that the Russians should be required to justify their requests and to give limited concessions (in the form of improved communications and the exchange of weather and intelligence information) in return for lend-lease aid.[15] Moreover, Harriman urged that serious consideration be given to the use of lend-lease aid as a bargaining lever to protect American interests in Eastern Europe.[16]

Roosevelt adamantly opposed Harriman's proposal to use lend-lease aid as an instrument of pressure. The President explained to a group of congressional leaders on January 11, 1945, that the Russians had preponderant power in that region and that the United States was in no position to force the issue. In any event, he continued, a reduction or termination of aid to Russia would hurt the Allied war effort as much as it hurt the Soviets.[17] Further, as Cordell Hull recalled in his memoirs, he and the President feared that a termination of aid would threaten the prospect of a satisfactory postwar relationship with the Russians; even if Stalin did give in to American threats, there was no reason to expect that he would uphold his promises after the war ended and he no longer needed American aid.[18]

Despite rising protest within the administration, the President refused to approve any basic changes in Soviet lend-lease policy. Official remonstrances were submitted against Soviet re-transfers of lend-lease materials to other countries,[19] and an effort was made to prevent shipment of industrial equipment which could not be made operational before the war ended,[20] but these represented only minor changes. While the British lend-lease program was being reduced steadily, the United States exceeded protocol commitments to Russia; and Roosevelt continued to give Soviet lend-lease top priority.[21]

Roosevelt, who earnestly desired the Soviet Union to enter the war against Japan and to participate in a postwar collective security organization, apparently feared that any changes in lend-lease policy might jeopardize these objectives. In a very real sense, the President was a captive of his own decisions. Having once adopted a unique policy of economic assistance, he probably felt he could not

15 Harriman to Cordell Hull, March 2, 1944; Stettinius to Harriman, Feb. 25, 1944; Cordell Hull to Harriman, March 16, 1944, *Foreign Relations . . . , 1944*, IV, 1057–58, 1055–56, 1062–63; Franklin D. Roosevelt to Frank Knox, Feb. 19, 1944, quoted in cross-index sheet, OF 4117, Franklin D. Roosevelt Papers (Franklin D. Roosevelt Library, Hyde Park).

16 Harriman to Cordell Hull, March 13, 1944, *Foreign Relations . . . , 1944*, IV, 951.

17 Acheson memorandum to Stettinius, Jan. 11, 1945, Stettinius Papers.

18 Cordell Hull, *The Memoirs of Cordell Hull* (2 vols., New York, 1948), II, 1272–73.

19 Aide-Mémoire, Department of State to the Soviet Embassy, July 6, 1944, *Foreign Relations . . . , 1944*, IV, 1098–99.

20 Stettinius to Hopkins, June 30, 1943, Stettinius Papers.

21 President to Secretary of State, Jan. 5, 1945, Department of State, *Foreign Relations of the United States: Diplomatic Papers, 1945* (5 vols., Washington, 1967), V, 944.

modify it without risking a break in the tenuous relationship he had built with the Soviets over a three-year period.[22]

In an effort to cement this relationship, the President endorsed an ingenious plan for a lend-lease credit to bridge the gap between the end of lend-lease and the beginning of a comprehensive program of postwar aid for Russia. Based on section 3(c) of the Lend-Lease Act of 1943, this so-called 3(c) agreement allowed a steady flow of industrial equipment to Russia even if the equipment did not contribute directly to the war effort or could not be made operational before the end of the war. The agreement permitted the Russians to submit orders for large quantities of industrial equipment; orders shipped before the war ended would be provided on lend-lease; orders after that date, on credit.[23]

The 3(c) offer, later extended to other nations, was originated specifically for the Soviet Union and is a clear indication of the importance Roosevelt attached to economic aid as an instrument of Soviet-American amity. The termination of the 3(c) negotiations with the Soviets on March 24, 1945, is the only evidence that the course of Soviet policy after Yalta may have caused him to reconsider his economic policies. This evidence, however, is not at all conclusive. After months of haggling over terms, the Russians showed no inclination to accept the American offer and were seemingly confident that, if they persisted, they could get a better deal. By late March, American aid officials feared that the initiation of a 3(c) agreement so near the end of the war would be construed by Congress as a use of lend-lease for postwar purposes. Hence, Acting Secretary of State Joseph C. Grew and Foreign Economic Administrator Leo T. Crowley advised Roosevelt that the 3(c) offer should be withdrawn; the President concurred.[24]

Withdrawal of the 3(c) agreement cannot be taken as positive evidence that Roosevelt had decided to alter his policy toward the Soviets. Nor is there any evidence of how he intended to proceed after V-E Day, although it was clear to those administering lend-lease that legal limitations would require substantial adjustments in all programs when hostilities in Europe ceased. To keep within the law, the Joint Chiefs of Staff and the Foreign Economic Administration had developed detailed plans which provided for a sharp reduction in lend-lease shipments to all countries after V-E Day and limited subsequent shipments for use only in the war against Japan.[25] To avoid misunderstandings, Harriman had sought to include in the Fourth Soviet Supply Protocol (covering the period from June 1944 to June 1945) some provision for adjustment in the event of a German collapse.[26] But

[22] Hopkins' memorandum to General H. H. Arnold, Oct. 17, 1944, H. H. Arnold Papers (Manuscript Division, Library of Congress), rejects Arnold's suggestion for changes in the unconditional aid policy because such changes would be "untimely" in view of negotiations then taking place on Russian entry into the war against Japan.

[23] *Foreign Relations . . . , 1944*, IV, 1058–1158; Records of the Foreign Economic Administration, Administrator's File, Box 767 (National Archives).

[24] Joseph C. Grew and Leo T. Crowley memorandum for President, March 23, 1945, *Foreign Relations . . . , 1945*, V, 991.

[25] General C. M. Wesson memorandum for Crowley, Sept. 11, 1944, Records of the Foreign Economic Administration, Administrator's File, Box 819; memorandum, "Lend-Lease Policy with the Defeat of Germany," Sept. 5, 1944, Records of the Army Service Forces, Director of Materiel File, General Correspondence (National Archives).

[26] Minutes of the seventh meeting of the President's Soviet Protocol Committee, May 10, 1944, Records of the International Division, Army Service Forces, Central Decimal File, 334 PSPC, Vol. I, Military Records Section (National Archives).

Roosevelt had declined to approve these plans and in September 1944 had ordered all further planning stopped.[27] He offered no more guidance on the question.

Within several weeks after Truman assumed the presidency, it was clear that modifications in the Soviet aid program could not be postponed. The men to whom Truman turned for advice—those most intimately acquainted with the intricate operation of the lend-lease mechanism and those most knowledgeable about Soviet-American relations—agreed, although for different reasons, that the unconditional aid policy could no longer be justified. Crowley and the military officials responsible for handling the lend-lease program emphasized that the end of war in Europe would make it impossible to support continued shipments to Russia on the prevailing scale. Harriman, who had played a key role in shaping American-Soviet lend-lease policy from the accession of Truman to V-J Day, stressed diplomatic considerations.

In his dispatches from Moscow in early April and in discussions in Washington following Roosevelt's death, Harriman dramatized the breakdown in Soviet-American relations since Yalta. The Soviets' blatant violation of the Yalta agreements and the ruthless manner in which they extended their control over Eastern Europe left no doubt in Harriman's mind that they placed friendship with the United States secondary to the pursuit of their own interests. The extent of Soviet ambitions was uncertain, but, Harriman warned, the devastation of Europe posed a real danger that the Russians might dominate the continent. Harriman attributed the breakdown in cooperation at least in part to American policy. He was certain that the Soviets had interpreted as a sign of weakness the continued generous and considerate attitude that the United States had taken toward them despite their "disregard of our requests for cooperation in matters of interest to us."[28]

Harriman emphasized that cooperation with the Soviets could be achieved only if the United States dealt with the Russians on a "realistic basis" and adopted a position of firmness in defense of its own interests. Soviet-American cooperation could be secured only if the United States made it plain to the Russians that they could not expect cooperation on terms "laid down by them."[29] In addition, he recommended a concerted American effort to improve relations with the other Allied nations, to make them less dependent upon the Soviets, and to demonstrate to the Soviets that they could not play the Western nations off against each other. A close understanding among the other Allied nations, he argued, might force the Soviets to abandon their unilateral policies and to cooperate with the West.[30]

Specifically, Harriman urged that the United States begin immediately to adopt a position of firmness toward the Soviets, to select several cases where their actions were intolerable, and to make them realize that they could not continue their "present attitude except at great cost to themselves."[31] He suggested taking strong stands at first on minor issues in order to avoid giving the impression of a "major change in policy."[32] He also favored a gradual reorientation of American foreign economic policy toward "taking care of our western Allies and other areas under our

27 Memorandum, President to Department and Agency heads, Sept. 9, 1944, Stettinius Papers.

28 Harriman to Secretary of State, April 6, 1945, *Foreign Relations . . . , 1945*, V, 822.

29 *Ibid.*

30 *Ibid.*, 823–24.

31 *Ibid.*

32 Minutes, Secretary of State's Staff Committee, April 20, 1945, *ibid.*, 842.

responsibility first, allocating to Russia what may be left." He was hopeful that such a reorientation would help restore stability in Western Europe as a bulwark against Soviet expansion, that it would cement American relations with the Allies, and that it would discourage the Soviets from persisting in their unilateral policies. Russia's essential military requirements should be met, but the unconditional aid policy and the protocol system should be ended.[33]

Harriman urged continued efforts toward friendship with the Soviets, but always on a "quid pro quo basis." Truman agreed. "The only way to establish sound relations between Russia and ourselves," he remarked on April 20, was "on a give and take basis." Both men were confident that a tougher policy would not cause a break with the Soviets because the Russians urgently needed American aid for postwar reconstruction.[34]

The Truman administration carefully considered the possible military repercussions of a firmer posture toward Russia. The end of war in Europe was imminent, and it was agreed at a meeting on April 23 that no harm would be done the war effort if the Russians slowed down or ceased operations in Europe.[35] The war with Japan posed a more difficult problem. By late April, army planners had scaled down considerably earlier estimates of Japan's capacity to resist; this rendered Russian entry into the war less vital. Moreover, Harriman and Deane had repeatedly affirmed that the Soviets would enter the war to promote their own interests in Asia regardless of what the United States did. Marshall and Secretary of War Henry Stimson remained unconvinced and insisted at the April 23 meeting that the United States still needed Russian assistance to win the war and should not jeopardize that objective by a hard line on other issues. The consensus of Truman's advisers, however, seems to have been that Soviet entry into the war, while still desirable, was not essential and that, in any case, a tougher line on political issues would probably not affect Russian actions.[36]

The decision to modify the unconditional aid policy reflected the Truman administration's belief that Soviet-American cooperation could be established only if the United States adopted a stronger posture in its relations with the Russians. But, it should be emphasized, the policy would have been modified even had Roosevelt lived or had Russian-American relations been amicable. The exigencies of domestic politics and the legal limitations on the use of lend-lease aid left no alternative. Congress insisted that lend-lease must be used exclusively for military purposes and could not be used directly or indirectly for postwar relief, rehabilitation, or reconstruction. Truman and his advisers were keenly aware that any deviation from that position might provoke a rebellion in Congress and endanger acceptance of the proposed United Nations.

The lend-lease program had enjoyed broad popular support in the first years of the war, but opposition mounted in 1944 and 1945. The increasing expense of underwriting a global war, the widespread fear that the nation's resources were being exhausted, and the growing concern for America's economic well-being in the postwar era all contributed to that opposition. Businessmen resented continued

33 Harriman to Secretary of State, April 4, 1945, *ibid.*, 817–20.

34 Truman, *Memoirs*, I, 71.

35 William D. Leahy Diary, April 23, 1945, William D. Leahy Papers (Manuscript Division, Library of Congress).

36 *Ibid.*; Memorandum by Charles Bohlen of meeting at the White House, April 23, 1945, *Foreign Relations . . . , 1945*, V, 252–55.

government regulation of the economy and foreign trade, and rumors of waste and misuse of American supplies by recipient nations found a receptive audience as the American people began to feel the pinch of wartime shortages. Anti-New Deal congressmen played on these fears by denouncing lend-lease as the most colossal dole of all time and by predicting that it was only the "opening handout" of a "world-wide W.P.A."[37]

Americans grudgingly accepted the necessity of continuing lend-lease to win the war. But there was general agreement that it must cease with the termination of hostilities.[38] This viewpoint was clearly reflected in Congress. The Lend-Lease Act was extended in 1944 and 1945, but the debates grew louder and the majorities smaller.[39] With each extension, Congress reiterated that lend-lease was an instrument of war only and must be used for no other purposes. It must not extend "1 minute or $1 into the post-war period," Senator Arthur Vandenberg warned in 1940.[40]

The administration repeatedly assured the American people that lend-lease would be continued only so long as and to the extent that it contributed to the defeat of the Axis.[41] But recurrent rumors to the contrary fed popular suspicions. Fears were first raised in the summer of 1944 by reports that the British had requested a postwar extension of lend-lease. Then came rumors of a deal between Roosevelt and Winston Churchill at Quebec which involved six billion dollars of lend-lease for Britain after the defeat of Germany. Reports of a Russian request for postwar aid and leaks on the 3(c) negotiations with Russia and France heightened suspicions, and the publication of a final 3(c) agreement with France in February 1945 brought the issue to a head.[42]

When the administration presented the Lend-Lease Act for renewal in February 1945, it made a concerted effort to allay these fears. Crowley, defending the bill before House and Senate committees, repeatedly stated that lend-lease would be used only to prosecute the war and that any programs for postwar foreign aid would be sent to Congress for separate consideration.[43] He carefully explained that the administration had made no commitments for postwar assistance and emphasized that the Phase II agreement with Britain, and the French 3(c) agreement involved only war supplies and included adequate safeguards to protect American interests.[44]

[37] Herring, "Experiment in Foreign Aid," 401–14.

[38] See, for example, the comprehensive collection of editorial opinion on this question in OF 4193, Roosevelt Papers.

[39] Opposition to lend-lease grew so intense in 1944 that the London *Economist* warned of another resurgence of isolationism and ultra-nationalism in the United States at the end of the war. London *Economist*, 144 (April 1, 1944), 428.

[40] *Cong. Record*, 78 Cong., 2 Sess., 4097 (May 8, 1944).

[41] *Seventeenth Report to Congress on Lend-Lease Operations* (Washington, 1944), 7–8.

[42] National Association of Manufacturers, *NAM News*, XI (Aug. 5, 1944), 3; *New York Times*, Aug. 6, Nov. 1, 1944, Jan. 7, 26, March 1, 1945.

[43] House, *Hearings Before the Committee on Foreign Affairs, House of Representatives, on H.R. 2013, A Bill to Extend for One Year the Provisions of an Act to Promote the Defense of the United States, March 11, 1941*, 79th Cong., 1 Sess., 49, 53, 139, 141, 162; Senate, *Hearings Before the Committee on Foreign Relations, United States Senate, on H. R. 2013, An Act to Extend for One Year the Provisions of an Act to Promote the Defense of the United States, Approved March 11, 1941*, 79 Cong., 1 Sess., 7, 18, 19, 29, 30.

[44] House, *Hearings Before the Committee on Foreign Affairs, House of Representatives . . . 1941*, 139–42.

Democrats in the House and Senate accepted Crowley's assurances without challenge, but Republicans, both isolationists and internationalists, remained skeptical and demanded absolute guarantees that the authority granted the President under lend-lease would not be abused. House Republicans forced the administration to accept an amendment to the act which explicitly stated that lend-lease could not be used for postwar purposes. An exception was made that allowed execution of the 3(c) agreements.[45]

H. R. 2013 encountered still more difficulties in the Senate. Senator Robert A. Taft of Ohio argued that the exception in the House amendment nullified the effect of the amendment and permitted the President to send "indefinite amounts" of supplies abroad for postwar reconstruction under the guise of lend-lease. Taft proposed an amendment to eliminate the exception from the House amendment, thus requiring all lend-lease shipments to stop the instant the war ended. The Taft amendment gained vocal support in the Senate not only from isolationist Republicans William Langer, Kenneth Wherry, and Hugh Butler but also from Vandenberg and Joseph Ball, leaders of the internationalist wing of the party. The vote on the amendment followed partisan lines, and it was defeated by the narrowest of margins—a tie vote. Vice-President Truman voted and broke the tie.[46]

The debates on the extension of lend-lease in 1945 and the vote on the Taft amendment had a significant impact on the future formulation of lend-lease policy. The determination of Republicans to prevent any abuse of the lend-lease authority forced the administration to make unequivocal commitments. The implications of the debate extended far beyond the immediate issue of lend-lease to the entire internationalist program of Presidents Roosevelt and Truman. The vote on the Taft amendment especially was interpreted as foreshadowing a possible resurgence of isolationism in the Senate and underscored the need for caution lest the experience of 1919 and 1920 be repeated.[47]

This lesson was not lost on those who participated in the proceedings. Crowley had made emphatic pledges to Congress, and he repeatedly demonstrated his determination to honor them.[48] The army officers who were responsible for getting lend-lease appropriations from Congress recognized that adjustments had to be made in the program after V-E Day so that they could defend themselves before Congress.[49] Most important, Truman, who had cast the tie-breaking vote against the Taft amendment and signed the bill into law on April 17, was deeply impressed by the debate.[50] Facing the difficult task of steering Roosevelt's peace program through the Senate, Truman was acutely aware of the need to respect congressional sensitivities on lend-lease.

[45] *Cong. Record,* 79 Cong., 1 Sess., 2120–52 (March 13, 1945). Arthur Krock commented in the *New York Times,* March 14, 1945, that, without the amendment, extension of lend-lease might have been defeated or at least delayed indefinitely.

[46] *Cong. Record,* 79 Cong., 1 Sess., 3232–54 (April 10, 1945).

[47] Truman, *Memoirs,* I, 46.

[48] Crowley to Harry S. Truman, July 6, 1945, Records of the Foreign Economic Administration, Administrator's File, Box 794; Notes on Executive Policy Meetings, Foreign Economic Administration, March 1, 22, May 29, 1945, *ibid.,* Box 3174.

[49] General G. A. Lincoln to Marshall, May 11, 1945, Records of the Operations Division, War Department General Staff, ABC 400.3295 Russia (April 19, 1942), Sec. 3, World War Records Sections (National Archives, Alexandria, Virginia).

[50] Truman, *Memoirs,* I, 46, 97–98.

As V-E Day approached, there was no question but that the Russian lend-lease program had to be reduced. Shipments to the European theater would have to be cut off as quickly as possible and future commitments limited to those for Russian military operations in the Far East. Soviet requests for aid would have to be handled on the same basis as requests from other nations; requisitions would be accompanied by full information which justified need and would be approved on the basis of availability of supplies, the urgency of competing requests, and contribution to the war effort. This revised procedure would end the privileged status enjoyed by the Russians since 1941 and would entail a sharp reduction in lend-lease shipments. It would also indicate to the Soviets that the open-ended generosity of the Roosevelt era had ended and that henceforth Russian-American relations would be on a reciprocal basis.

It does not follow, however, that the administration intended to use economic aid as an instrument to coerce the Soviets into surrendering on the Eastern European question. Revisionists have argued that the special attention given Russian lend-lease by the administration in April and May of 1945 is clear indication that the revisions were designed primarily to pressure the Russians. It was in fact the unique status given Soviet aid by the Roosevelt administration that necessitated special handling as V-E Day approached.

It is quite true that some state department officials discussed the possibility of using lend-lease as an instrument of coercion.[51] Harriman himself had suggested that same possibility in 1944.[52] Those responsible for initiating the policy change were more cautious, however, because they feared that a rupture on the lend-lease issue might jeopardize the delicate negotiations then taking place at San Francisco on the Polish question and the organizational structure of the United Nations. At San Francisco on May 9, the day that Soviet Foreign Minister Vyacheslav Molotov left for Moscow with the Polish issue and the dispute over voting in the Security Council deadlocked, Harriman and Secretary of State Edward R. Stettinius, Jr., discussed the possible impact of the lend-lease reduction on other issues. They agreed that the United States should impress upon the Soviets the gravity for Russian American relations of the Polish issue, but no acts of pressure should be "suggested or considered" until after the San Francisco Conference. The necessary adjustments in the lend-lease program would be executed as tactfully as possible and "without any hint of relationship with the Polish or other political problems with the Soviet Union."[53] Stettinius advised the state department the same day that the United States should take a firm approach toward the Soviets on lend-lease and other issues, but should avoid "any implication of a threat or any indication of political bargaining."[54]

On May 10, 1945, Harriman conferred with Truman on the proposed changes in lend-lease policy.[55] The same day, Harriman met with representatives of all

[51] A war department representative at the May 10 meeting on lend-lease advised Marshall that there was an "implication in the State Department's discussion of the problem that lend-lease might be used as a political weapon in connection with difficulties in Central Europe." Lincoln to Marshall, May 11, 1945, Records of the Operations Division, ABC 400.3295 Russia (April 19, 1942), Sec. 3.

[52] See Note 16.

[53] Notes on conversation, Stettinius and Harriman, May 9, 1945, Stettinius Papers.

[54] Stettinius to Grew, May 9, 1945, *Foreign Relations . . . , 1945*, V, 998.

[55] Verbatim transcript of telephone conversation, Stettinius and Truman, May 10,

departments and agencies involved in the Soviet aid program to discuss the preparation of a memorandum for the President's signature which would precisely define the new policy. Regarding current commitments under the Fourth Protocol, it was agreed that the United States would supply only those items required for Soviet operations in the Far East and equipment needed to complete industrial plants already partially delivered. Other current and future programs would be evaluated in the context of competing demands and in terms of overall military situation, and all subsequent Soviet requests would have to be supported by information which justified need.[56]

On May 11, representatives of the state department and the Foreign Economic Administration drafted a memorandum for the President based on these principles. After securing Harriman's approval, Acting Secretary of State Grew and Crowley presented the memorandum to Truman. Both wanted to be sure that the President fully understood the implications of the order and that he would endorse it. Crowley predicted a sharp response from the Russians and "did not want them to be running all over town looking for help."[57] Grew and Crowley had little difficulty getting the President's approval. Apparently believing that the memorandum merely restated the ideas Harriman and Stettinius had discussed with him the day before, Truman, by his own recollection, signed it without even reading it.[58] At the same time, he approved a note to the Soviet embassy which advised simply that the end of the European war necessitated a readjustment of the lend-lease program and indicated the basic principles of that readjustment.[59]

Early in the morning of May 12, the Subcommittee on Shipping of the President's Soviet Protocol Committee met to implement Truman's order. A heated debate ensued. The May 11 memorandum stated that supplies on order for the Soviet which were not required for Far Eastern operations or to complete industrial plants would be "cut off immediately as far as physically practicable."[60] The Foreign Economic Administration representative on the subcommittee insisted on interpreting that phrase literally. Even ships at sea containing supplies for uses other than Far Eastern operations should be brought back, or the committee would have to explain why to Congress. The approach should be "when in doubt, hold," instead of "when in doubt, give."

Army officials disagreed and observed that this rigid approach would require calling back ships, unloading them and sorting supplies, then reloading only those supplies intended for the Far East. It was customary, they argued, that, once a shipment started, it continued to its destination, and deviation from this rule would cause chaos in the ports. But the Foreign Economic Administration stuck to

1945, Stettinius Papers. Truman told Stettinius that he "agreed entirely" with Harriman's proposal to reduce lend-lease to Russia.

56 International Division, Army Service Forces, "Lend-Lease as of September 30, 1945," II, 1043 (2 vols., unpublished manuscript in the Office of the Chief of Military History, Washington); memorandum prepared by Lincoln to be sent to Secretaries of War and Navy, May 11, 1945, Records of the Operations Division, ABC 400.3295 Russia (April 19, 1942), Sec. 3.

57 Grew, memorandum of conversation with Crowley, May 11, 1945, Joseph C. Grew Papers (Houghton Library, Harvard University).

58 Truman, *Memoirs*, I, 228.

59 Acting Secretary of State to Chargé of the Soviet Union, May 12, 1945, *Foreign Relations . . . , 1945*, V, 1000–01.

60 Memorandum by Acting Secretary of State and Foreign Economic Administrator to President, May 11, 1945, *ibid.*, 999–1000.

its position and received the backing of General John York, acting chairman of the Soviet Protocol Committee, who contended that Congress felt that the drastic action should be taken. The army acquiesced, and the subcommittee immediately issued orders to stop loading supplies for the Soviet Union and to recall ships at sea en route to Russia.[61]

The Foreign Economic Administration's zealous execution of the order caused consternation at San Francisco, in the state department, and in the Russian embassy. Stettinius later referred to the May 12 decision as an "untimely and incredible step."[62] When Harriman and Assistant Secretary of State Will Clayton learned what had happened, they were shocked. Harriman said that he had intended to cut off production of new supplies for the Soviets, but not shipments of supplies already programmed and ready for loading.[63] He immediately secured Truman's permission to countermand the order. The new orders allowed ships at sea to turn around once more, sent ships that were loaded on their way, and continued loadings of ships at berth.[64] The Soviets protested bitterly to the state department. Clayton attempted to explain that the action had been a mistake and that it had been corrected, but again he warned that the law required review and readjustment of all lend-lease programs on V-E Day.[65]

The May 12 decision had resulted in a serious diplomatic blunder. The cutoff did exactly what Harriman had sought to avoid: it gave the Soviets the impression that the United States was trying to force political concessions through economic pressure. Any adjustment after months of preferential treatment was bound to evoke loud protests from the Russians. But the rude, sudden, and drastic stoppage of shipments needlessly antagonized the Soviets at a critical period and gave them a splendid opportunity—which they exploited to the fullest—to accuse the United States of acting in bad faith.

In his Memoirs, Truman blamed the blunder on his own inexperience and on Grew and Crowley, whom he accused of taking policy-making into their own hands and of being motivated primarily by their dislike for the Russians.[66] Truman's charges are misleading at best. His *Memoirs* give the impression that the May 11 decision was made hastily and without much prior discussion. The evidence shows, however, that the decision was considered at length within the administration and

[61] Minutes of the twenty-ninth meeting of the President's Soviet Protocol Subcommittee on Shipping, May 12, 1945, Records of the Military Records Section, Edgerton Folder, Army Service Forces, Director of Materiel File, General Correspondence; General John Hull, transcript of telephone conversation with General John York, May 12, 1945, Records of the Operations Division, ABC 400.3295 Russia (April 19, 1942), Sec. 3.

[62] Edward R. Stettinius, Jr., *Roosevelt and the Russians: The Yalta Conference* (New York, 1949), 318.

[63] Lincoln memorandum for the record, May 14, 1945, Records of the Operations Division, ABC 400.3295 Russia (April 19, 1942), Sec. 3. A war department official who attended the May 10 meeting insisted that Harriman had said nothing about "cutting off" lend-lease for Russia. Lincoln to John Hull, May 13, 1945, *ibid.*

[64] Transcript of telephone conversation, John Hull to York, May 12, 1945, *ibid.*

[65] Lincoln memorandum for the record, May 14, 1945, *ibid.*

[66] Truman, *Memoirs*, I, 227-29. Truman later told Jonathan Daniels that "Crowley was as anti-Russian as Henry Wallace was pro-Russian." Jonathan Daniels, *The Man of Independence* (Philadelphia, 1950), 271.

that he was fully informed regarding these discussions. There is no evidence that Grew and Crowley attempted to undermine the policy agreed upon by Truman and Harriman. The record suggests rather that the blunder resulted primarily from the lack of a clear understanding among the President's advisers on exactly what measures were to be taken and from the rigid interpretation given the President's order by the Foreign Economic Administration and the Soviet Protocol Committee.

The hard line on Soviet lend-lease taken by Crowley and the Foreign Economic Administration seems to have stemmed more from a rigid legalism than from Russophobia. During the congressional hearings on the extension of lend-lease, Crowley had made unequivocal commitments that lend-lease was to be used only to prosecute the war. Imbued with an extremely narrow concept of executive authority and not concerned with the diplomatic impact of his actions, he waged an unrelenting battle to honor these commitments.[67] His crusade to limit post V-E Day lend-lease to the minimum, it should be emphasized, was not restricted to Russia, but applied to Britain and France as well.[68]

Finally, in assessment of responsibility for the May 12 blunder, Roosevelt must assume a large share of the burden. His unwillingness to face squarely the problem of lend-lease after V-E Day, his reluctance to present candidly to the American people and Congress the tremendous postwar economic needs of the Allied nations, and his refusal to prepare the Soviets adequately for the adjustments he knew would be necessary left his successor in a difficult position. Roosevelt's postponement of planning on these important issues had the effect of misleading the American people and antagonizing the Allies.

In considering lend-lease to Russia after V-E Day, it should be stressed that the United States fulfilled most of its commitments to support Russian Far Eastern operations and that it gave Soviet requests at least equal consideration with those of other nations. The question of future shipments was discussed in a series of meetings from May 12 to May 15. It was decided that no additional ships would be loaded in Atlantic or Gulf ports until cargo had been screened and items intended for Europe separated from those intended for the Far East. Crowley attempted to apply the same screening procedure in West Coast ports, but Harriman insisted on a more flexible approach which would allow ships scheduled for departure from West Coast ports during May and June to sail as planned on the premise that the route was *prima facie* evidence that the material was to be used in the Far East. Harriman won his point, although about 15 percent of these shipments was not included in specific commitments for the Far East.[69]

[67] In justifying his action, Crowley later wrote: "My long experience in government taught me that the Congress made the laws . . . any action on my part relating to the treatment of our Allies with regard to the reduction and discontinuance of Lend-Lease was that required by me in accordance with the laws of the United States." Crowley to Editor of *Life*, 39 (Nov. 14, 1955), 30.

[68] Notes on Executive Policy Meeting, May 29, 1945; Crowley to Truman, July 6, 1945, Records of the Foreign Economic Administration; Leahy Diary, June 29, 1945, Leahy Papers. At a cabinet meeting on July 6, 1945, Crowley conceded that the French desperately needed coal; but, he argued, it was important for them to show more initiative in helping themselves rather than doing nothing and placing the blame on the United States. Robert P. Patterson, notes on cabinet meeting, July 6, 1945, Robert P. Patterson Papers (Manuscript Division, Library of Congress).

[69] Minutes of the tenth meeting of the President's Soviet Protocol Committee, May 15, 1945, Records of the International Division, Army Service Forces, Cen-

The cutback in aid to Russia which resulted from the new policy was not immediately reflected in shipping. Shipments for the Far East had played a major part in the programs scheduled for May and June, and tonnage remained high during this period—May was the peak month for shipments to Russia during the war. But the statistics of procurement and production tell a different story. In the week of May 19 to May 26 alone, 435 requisitions with an estimated dollar value of $35,000,000 were cancelled by the Foreign Economic Administration. In January 1945, by contrast, 478 requisitions had been forwarded for procurement, and only seventy-five had been cancelled.[70]

It is not correct to conclude from these figures, however, that the Soviets were treated less favorably than the other Allies between V-E Day and V-J Day. In the second quarter of 1945, on the contrary, the dollar value of aid to Russia surpassed for the first time that of aid to the United Kingdom. In the third quarter, dollar values were about equal.[71] In late May, Churchill strongly protested to Truman against the sharp cutback in American aid to Britain, and in the same month the administration halted all lend-lease shipments to France when General Charles De Gaulle refused to evacuate a strip of Italian territory held by French troops.[72]

Further modifications were introduced in Russian aid policy as a result of the Hopkins-Stalin conversations in late May. The discussions ranged over a variety of issues, and Stalin made a special point of complaining about the "unfortunate and even brutal" manner in which lend-lease had been reduced. Hopkins carefully explained that the drastic action of May 12 did not represent a policy decision, but had been a "technical misunderstanding" by one government agency. He repeated that the law required a readjustment of the lend-lease program after V-E Day and reaffirmed the American commitment to assist Soviet Far Eastern operations.[73]

Stalin seems to have accepted Hopkins' explanation, and on the suggestion of Harriman, it was agreed that the ambassador should discuss the lend-lease question with Soviet Foreign Minister Molotov and Commissar of Foreign Trade Anastas Mikoyan. On May 28, the Soviets presented a detailed list of their supply requirements for the second half of 1945. Included in the list were requests for 1,000,000 tons of supplies originally promised in the Fourth Protocol, but not delivered before V-E Day, and requests for 570,000 tons of new items.[74]

Harriman and Deane viewed the requests sympathetically and urged their superiors to provide "timely and effective" support to Soviet Far Eastern operations, even at the risk of providing some items which could not be fully justified.[75]

---

tral Decimal File, 334 PSPC, Vol. II; Army Service Forces, "Lend-Lease," II, 1043–49.

[70] "Weekly News Letter No. 183, May 26, 1945"; "Weekly News Letter No. 185, June 9, 1945," USSR Branch, Records of the Foreign Economic Administration, Administrator's File, Box 818.

[71] *Twenty-First Report to Congress on Lend-Lease Operations* (Washington, 1946), 41.

[72] Truman, *Memoirs*, I, 241.

[73] Robert E. Sherwood, *Roosevelt and Hopkins: An Intimate History* (New York, 1948), 894–96.

[74] Army Services Forces, "Lend-Lease," II, 1043–49; Deane to War Department, May 28, 1945, *Foreign Relations . . . , 1945*, V, 1007–08.

[75] Deane to Protocol Committee, June 8, 1945, *Foreign Relations . . . , 1945*,

Deane selected a list of items which he was certain were "vitally important" to the Soviets and recommended their prompt shipment, even though the Soviets had not provided adequate justification of need.[76] Harriman urged the state department to consider seriously Russian requests for industrial equipment promised under the Fourth Protocol but not shipped at V-E Day, since Annex III (a section of the Protocol intended specifically to support Far Eastern operations) had not been intended to fill all Soviet needs for the war against Japan, but was a supplement to other requests. The ambassador also proposed that the state department reopen the 3(c) negotiations with the Russians, provided they entered the war against Japan, so that industrial equipment in the May 28 lists approved but unshipped at V-J Day could be delivered later on credit.[77]

The climate of opinion in Washington in May and June 1945, however, was uncongenial to any new requests for foreign aid. British supply officials reported to London that a "wave of economy" had swept over Washington after V-E Day.[78] Supply shortages were making it difficult to fill many requests for lend-lease.[79] Republicans in the House and Senate were charging the administration with a "breach of faith" by continuing shipments to Europe and to nations which had not yet declared war on Japan.[80] Crowley, vigorously supported by the President's chief of staff, Admiral William Leahy, was waging a veritable crusade to uphold to the letter his pledges to Congress by limiting shipments to those for specific use in the war against Japan.[81] The Joint Chiefs of Staff, who had greatly extended their control over lend-lease since Truman took office, were most concerned with accumulating supplies for American operations against Japan and were increasingly unsympathetic to Allied requests for assistance.[82] Beset with a multitude of domestic and foreign problems, and with his advisers divided, Truman delayed for weeks before establishing a firm policy for post V-E Day lend-lease. His decision closely followed the Crowley-Leahy approach.[83]

It is not surprising that the May 28 requests encountered extended delays. Harriman became so concerned that on June 21 he dispatched a personal message to Hopkins which urged him to secure "immediate action" on the Soviet re-

V, 1012–14. See also Harriman to Protocol Committee, June 11, 1945, *ibid.*, 1016–18.

[76] Harriman to Protocol Committee, June 11, 1945, *ibid.*, 1016.

[77] Harriman to Secretary of State, June 15, 1945, *ibid.*, 1025–26.

[78] H. Duncan Hall, *North American Supply* (London, 1955), 455–56.

[79] Civilian Production Administration, *Industrial Mobilization for War*. Vol. I: *Program and Administration* (Washington, 1947), 858, 873–87.

[80] *Cong. Record*, 79 Cong., 1 Sess., 4698–4700 (May 17, 1945); Washington *Post*, May 18, 1945. On May 31, the five Republicans who had sponsored the House amendment to the Lend-Lease Act expressed to Truman their concern that the lend-lease authority was being abused and warned that any attempt to aid the Allies through loopholes in the Lend-Lease Act would have "disastrous consequences." Reps. Robert B. Chiperfield, John M. Vorys, Karl E. Mundt, Bartel J. Jonkman, and Lawrence H. Smith to Truman, May 31, 1945, copy in Records of the Foreign Economic Administration.

[81] Leahy Diary, June 29, 1945, Leahy Papers; Hall, *North American Supply*, 455–56.

[82] William D. Leahy, *I Was There: The Personal Story of the Chief of Staff to Presidents Roosevelt and Truman Based on His Notes and Diaries Made at the Time* (New York, 1950), 410.

[83] Department of State, *Foreign Relations of the United States: Diplomatic Papers, The Conference of Berlin, 1945* (Washington, 1960), 818.

quests.[84] Finally, on June 27, the Joint Chiefs of Staff ruled that the United States would provide the Russians with items on the May 28 list which were approved by the Military Mission in Moscow and which could be procured and loaded on ship before August 31, 1945. Several weeks later, the date was extended to September 30, after which a new statement of policy was to be issued.[85]

The sudden advent of V-J Day rendered any new statement of policy unnecessary. As the first signs of Japanese capitulation reached Washington, the administration began planning the liquidation of the lend-lease program. On August 17, the President ordered the war and navy departments to end shipments of munitions to all lend-lease nations immediately; and three days later, he ordered all lend-lease operations terminated at once unless the recipient government agreed to purchase supplies for cash.[86]

The sudden termination of the lend-lease program after V-J Day required little adjustment in the Soviet aid program, since operations had been scheduled only through September 30.[87] Neither Annex III nor the approved items on the May 28 list had been completed when Truman ordered lend-lease stopped, but the American performance in Soviet supply from May to August was still creditable and compares favorably with performance on the British Phase II program during the same period. American shipments to Russia totalled more than 1,500,000 tons—over one fourth the volume shipped between July 1, 1944, and May 12, 1945, the peak period in Soviet supply. The United States shipped most of Annex III and the undelivered Fourth Protocol items requested on May 28. Only on the new requests of May 28 did shipments fall far short. Of the 570,000 tons requested, the war department approved for procurement only 185,000 tons, and about half of this was made available for shipment before V-J Day.[88] The Soviets agreed to pay cash for some of the remaining supplies and on October 15, 1945, concluded with the United States a "pipeline agreement" which allowed them to purchase on credit the bulk of supplies undelivered at V-J Day.[89]

The question of lend-lease forms an important chapter in the history of Soviet-American relations during the critical period from April to August 1945. After V-E Day, the Truman administration introduced a drastic change in Russian lend-lease policy which terminated Roosevelt's unconditional aid policy and placed the Soviet aid program on an equal basis with other programs. It cannot be implied from this, however, that the change resulted simply from Truman's accession to the presidency or entirely from the rising tension in Russian-American relations. On the contrary, the exigencies of domestic politics and Congress' determination that lend-lease should be used only to prosecute the war

84 Harriman to Hopkins, June 21, 1945, *Foreign Relations . . . , 1945*, V, 1026.

85 Acting Secretary of State to Chargé of the Soviet Union, June 27, 1945, *ibid.*, 1028–29.

86 Leahy Diary, Aug. 17, 1945, Leahy Papers; Truman, *Memoirs*, I, 476.

87 "Weekly News Letter No. 194, August 11, 1945," USSR Branch, Records of the Foreign Economic Administration, Administrator's File, Box 818.

88 Feis, *Between War and Peace*, 330; "Status of the Soviet Aid Program as of July 31, 1945," Records of the Foreign Economic Administration, Administrator's File, Box 818; Secretary of War to President, Aug. 11, 1945, Records of the Operations Division, 400.3295 Russia (April 19, 1942), Sec. 3; Army Service Forces, "Lend-Lease," II, 1043–49.

89 James F. Byrnes, telegram No. 1935 to American Embassy, Moscow, Aug. 31, 1945; Crowley to William Clayton, Oct. 15, 1945, Records of the Foreign Economic Administration, Administrator's File, Box 819.

would have necessitated a major change in the Russian aid program once the war in Europe ended. Roosevelt might have made the adjustment more smoothly, and he would probably have sent a personal explanation to Stalin, but the change would have been made.

Truman's decision to reduce lend-lease after V-E Day did not discriminate against the Soviets. It did not mark an abandonment of American attempts to cooperate with Russia, nor was it intended to coerce the Soviets. The lend-lease cutback was general; it applied to all nations. The reason the Russian aid program required separate handling before V-E Day was the unique status it had been given at the beginning of the war. The V-E Day decision hit the Soviets harder because aid to Russia had not, like aid to Britain, been gradually reduced after the summer of 1944. The termination of the unconditional aid policy did not mean that Truman had ended Roosevelt's policy of attempting to cooperate with the Russians. Harriman and Truman believed, on the contrary, that the unconditional aid policy had jeopardized that objective. Only if the United States demonstrated a determination to defend its own interests could a sound basis for postwar cooperation be constructed.

There is no evidence whatever that the May 11 decision was designed to drive the Russians from Eastern Europe. From time to time some of Truman's advisers had suggested such a course. But after V-E Day, Harriman had underscored the need for caution in handling lend-lease to avoid any break during the San Francisco Conference. The use of economic pressure was left open after the conference ended, but in the case of lend-lease aid it was not reconsidered. No attempt was made during the period from V-E Day to V-J Day to extort concessions, large or small, in return for American material.

Neither Harriman nor Truman intended the V-E Day slashes to be so drastic. This resulted from a misinterpretation of the May 11 directive by the Foreign Economic Administration and the Soviet Protocol Committee. The mistake was quickly corrected, however, and after V-E Day the United States did provide substantial aid for Soviet Far Eastern operations.

There can be no doubt that the May 12 reduction hurt the Russians economically. As Stalin admitted to Hopkins in May, however, the Soviets were aware that the end of war in Europe would force a substantial reduction in American assistance. The impact of the cutback could have been lessened by Soviet acceptance of the proposed 3(c) agreement, but the Russians lost this opportunity by trying to drive a hard bargain. In any event, the point of Stalin's protest to Hopkins was not the reduction of lend-lease, but the abrupt manner in which the reduction had been effected. Stalin had ample ground for complaint, but his talks with Hopkins, and Harriman's subsequent discussions with Molotov and Mikoyan, seem to have repaired at least some of the damage. On June 11, 1945, Stalin wired Truman a personal expression of gratitude for American aid, a move he had earlier told Hopkins would be impossible in view of the rude termination of lend-lease.[90]

The lend-lease question was an irritant in Soviet-American relations during

[90] Joseph V. Stalin to Truman, June 11, 1945, Ministry of Foreign Affairs, U. S. S. R., *Correspondence Between the Chairman of the Council of Ministers of the U. S. S. R. and the Presidents of the U. S. A. and the Prime Ministers of Great Britain During the Great Patriotic War of 1941–1945* (2 vols., Moscow, 1957), II, 244.

1945, but not a decisive issue in the origins of the Cold War. The conflict that developed over lend-lease aid was essentially a reflection of the deeper controversy over political issues. There is no evidence to suggest that a continuation of Roosevelt's lend-lease policy, had that been possible, would have made any substantial difference in the course of Soviet-American relations. It would certainly not have resolved the fundamental conflict over Eastern Europe. From the American point of view, however, the post V-E Day reduction was unavoidable. From the Russian point of view, the manner in which the reduction was handled was provocative. But it would be some years later, after Cold War divisions had hardened, before Soviet propagandists would turn on lend-lease as a "weapon of aggressive American imperialism."[91]

[91] A. Alexeyev, "Lend-Lease—Weapon of Aggressive American Imperialism," *Current Digest of the Soviet Press,* III (Sept. 8, 1951), 10.

27

AMERICAN PRISONERS OF WAR IN KOREA: A SECOND LOOK AT THE "SOMETHING NEW IN HISTORY" THEME

H. H. Wubben

The Korean War, lasting from 1950 to 1953, was the most controversial conflict in which American forces were engaged during the twentieth century prior to the Vietnam War. It was the nation's first modern effort to engage in a limited war, called a "Police Action" by President Truman, and it was the first war Americans fought under the aegis of a supranational organization. The United States put 1,600,000 servicemen into the war zones. It suffered losses of about 24,000 killed, 9,000 missing, 2,675 captured, and some 100,000 wounded. The war cost about $20 billion. After the first few months, in contrast to the national patriotism evident throughout World War II, the American public became apathetic, if not openly hostile toward the war. At the conclusion of the conflict 114,500 Chinese and 34,000 North Korean prisoners sought political asylum in South Korea, while 21 Americans elected to stay with their captors. Professor Wubben, in this article, devotes his attention to the controversial questions that arose during the conflict about the behavior of American prisoners of war in Korea, as a reflection upon American society.

H. H. Wubben teaches modern American history at Oregon State University and has published several articles.

Source: *American Quarterly*, Vol. 22, No. 1 (1970), pp. 3–19.

Americans have long been intrigued by speculations about their national character. In particular they have been receptive to assessments which credit them with immunity against certain human frailties, an immunity not possessed by most other peoples. Out of the Korean War came a controversy which impinged annoyingly upon such assessments and which provided grist for the mill of those who now preferred to believe that in recent decades the character had deteriorated.

Throughout the conflict reports coming out of North Korea indicated that the communists were subjecting American prisoners of war to a re-education process popularly described as "brainwashing." Prisoner returnees during Operation Little Switch in May and Operation Big Switch in August and September 1953 corroborated some of these reports. But it also became clear that such re-education was largely ineffective. Nevertheless, 21 prisoners chose not to return home. A few who did return admitted that they were "progressives," that is, men partially converted by the Chinese re-education program. Some who did not confess to such leanings faced accusations from other prisoners that they had taken the "progressive" line.

In addition it became apparent that a number of men had engaged in collaborative or criminal behavior detrimental to the welfare of their fellows. Consequently, the armed services made special efforts to find out what had happened. Psychiatrists and psychologists interviewed the newly-freed prisoners during the repatriation process and on the journey home. Intelligence officers also interviewed them, compiling dossiers on each man. Information acquired by these specialists eventually provided the data upon which subsequent formal studies of the prisoners and their behavior in captivity were based.

In 1955 came the official government view of the POW behavior issue, the report of the Secretary of Defense's Advisory Committee on Prisoners of War. But the committee's judgment was hardly definitive. On the one hand, the group declared, "the record [of the prisoners] seems fine indeed . . . they cannot be found wanting." On the other it concluded, "The Korean story must never be permitted to happen again."[1] Then in 1956 the Army issued a training pamphlet on the subejct of POW behavior. It was even more ambiguous. Readers learned that the Chinese "lenient policy" designed to lessen resistance "resulted in little or no active resistance to the enemy's indoctrination." Later, however, they read that the "large majority . . . resisted the enemy in the highest tradition of the service and of our country."[2]

Findings of the major formal studies, financed by or undertaken by the armed services in most cases, are much more satisfying to the scholar who desires more consistency in both raw material and analysis. These include research projects done for the Department of the Army, the Surgeon General's Office, the Air Force and the Walter Reed Army Institute of Research.[3] Also engaged in

[1] U.S. Department of Defense, *POW: the Fight Continues After the Battle, the Report of the Secretary of Defense's Advisory Committee on Prisoners of War* (Washington, D.C., 1955), pp. vi, 32.

[2] U.S. Department of the Army, *Communist Interrogation, Indoctrination and Exploitation of Prisoners of War*, Army Pamphlet No. 30-191 (Washington, D.C., 1956), pp. 21, 24.

[3] Examples of these respectively are the following. Julius Segal, *Factors Related to the Collaboration and Resistance Behavior of U.S. Army POWs in Korea* (Washington, D.C., Human Resources Research Office, George Washington University, 1956, HumRRO Tech. Rep. 33); Edgar H. Schein, W. E. Cooley and

examination of POW experiences was the Society for the Investigation of Human Ecology. The studies never achieved wide circulation although the research scientists who engaged in them reported their substance in professional journals.[4] Eventually one scholarly book-length treatment appeared. Albert Biderman's *March to Calumny*. Biderman, a sociologist who was active in several of these projects, demolished in a convincing manner those interpretations which accused the prisoners of being singularly deficient in the attributes expected of American servicemen unfortunate enough to become prisoners of war.[5]

The work of such specialists, however, has had little impact compared with that of those whose reports convey a largely, if not exclusively, negative version of the prisoners' actions during captivity. That version, in general, declares that American prisoners of war in Chinese and North Korean hands were morally weak and uncommitted to traditional American ideals. Consequently, some, though not a majority, were infected to a degree with the virus of communism. Furthermore, they were undisciplined. They were unwilling to aid each other in their travail. And they succumbed too easily under limited duress or no duress at all to the pressures of their captors to engage in collaborative behavior, including informing on each other. Their death rate, 38 percent, was the highest in history, and most deaths resulted from "give-up-itis" and lack of concern for one another among the prisoners themselves, not from communist mistreatment. Also, no prisoners successfully escaped from communist prison camps, a "first" in U.S. military experience. Other nationality groups, particularly the Turks, successfully resisted communist blandishments, and only the Marines among the Americans consistently adhered to patterns of honorable conduct. Finally, the POWs in Korea were the first Americans in captivity to so act, a "fact" which calls for a reassessment of mid-century American values and the culture which spawned them.[6]

Margaret T. Singer, *A Psychological Follow-Up of Former Prisoners of War of the Chinese Communists, Parts I and II* (Cambridge, Massachusetts Institute of Technology, 1961, 1962); Albert D. Biderman, *Communist Techniques of Coercive Interrogation* (Lackland Air Force Base, Texas, Air Force Personnel and Training Research Center, 1956, AFPTRC Development Report TN-56-132); Lee B. Grant, "Operation Big Switch: Medical Intelligence Processing" (Washington, D.C., Walter Reed Army Medical Center, mimeographed document, n.d.). Also Edgar H. Schein, *Some Observations on the Chinese Indoctrination Program for Prisoners of War* (Washington, D.C., Army Medical Service Graduate School, Walter Reed Army Medical Center, 1955, AMSGS-37-55).

[4] Major publications in scholarly journals include these: Albert Biderman, "Communist Attempts to Elicit False Confessions from Air Force Prisoners of War," *Bulletin of the New York Academy of Medicine*, XXXIII (1957), 616–25. Edgar H. Schein, "The Chinese Indoctrination Program for Prisoners of War: a Study of Attempted Brainwashing," *Psychiatry*, XIX (May 1956), 149–72. Schein, Winfred F. Hill, Harold L. Williams and Ardie Lubin, "Distinguishing Characteristics of Collaborators and Resisters Among American Prisoners of War," *Journal of Abnormal Social Psychology*, LV (1957), 197–201. See also special issue, "Brainwashing," *Journal of Social Issues*, XIII, No. 3 (1957); and Group for the Advancement of Psychiatry, *Methods of Forceful Indoctrination: Observations and Interviews* (New York, GAP Publications Office, 1957, GAP Symposium No. 4).

[5] Albert D. Biderman, *March to Calumny: The Story of American POW's in the Korean War* (New York, 1963). Anyone who has investigated this subject owes Biderman a considerable debt, as the writer of this article readily acknowledges. William L. White's *The Captives of Korea: An Unofficial White Paper* (New York, 1957), is a good journalistic treatment of the subject.

[6] Presumed to be most guilty of poor performance were Army and Air Force

Among those who accepted this as history, in part or in whole, were President Dwight Eisenhower, FBI Director J. Edgar Hoover and Senator Strom Thurmond of South Carolina. Political scientist Anthony Bouscaren saw the "record" as evidence that American education had flunked a significant test.[7] Another critic of education, Augustin Rudd, viewed the prisoner performance as evidence that the chickens of progressive education had come home to roost.[8] The editors of *Scouting* magazine in 1965 cited it in urging continued efforts to implant the ideals of the Boy Scout Code among youth in that organization.[9] And as late as 1968, California educator and political figure Max Rafferty employed it in some of his campaign literature during his senatorial race.[10]

These individuals, however, have not been so influential as two others in promoting this "history." They are late Eugene Kinkead, a free-lance writer, and Lt. Col. William E. Mayer, one of the psychiatrists who participated in the interviewing of the repatriates. Kinkead's major contribution was a book entitled *In Every War But One* which sold around fifteen thousand copies.[11] Lt. Col. Mayer's contributions, mainly public addresses, have won even wider circulation than Kinkead's, thanks to the tape recorder and the mimeograph.[12] Both men have modified from time to time their indictment of the prisoners, if not of recent trends in American society. Mayer, for instance, toward the end of one of his speeches said, "Finally, the great majority of men didn't become communists, didn't suffer any kind of moral breakdown, no matter what the communists did to them."[13] But by then the negative point had been so strongly stressed that few listeners were aware of his significant caveat.

---

prisoners, although it is allowed that the latter, beginning in 1952, were subjected to special attention by the Chinese who wanted germ warfare confessions. Because Air Force POWs underwent treatment which was unique in many aspects in the American captivity experience, and because it is the conduct of ground force troops which has been most called into question, this article deals primarily with the latter group of POWs.

[7] Anthony T. Bouscaren, "Korea, Test of American Education," *Catholic World*, CLXXXIII (Apr. 1956), 24–27.

[8] Augustin G. Rudd, *Bending the Twig: The Revolution in Education and its Effect on Our Children* (New York, 1957), p. 222.

[9] Rex Lucas, "Personally Speaking," *Scouting*, LIII (Jan. 1965), 3.

[10] See also Max Rafferty, "What's Happened to Patriotism?" *Reader's Digest*, LXXIX (Oct. 1961), 108.

[11] Eugene Kinkead, *In Every War But One* (New York, 1959). See also Kinkead, "A Reporter at Large: the Study of Something New in History," *The New Yorker* (Oct. 26, 1957), pp. 102–53. Biderman's *March to Calumny* is a devastating examination of the Kinkead book, but it sold only six thousand copies and is little known except to those who have made a serious effort to probe beneath the surface of the subject.

[12] William E. Mayer, tape of speech before San Francisco Commonwealth Club, n.d. See, also, interview with Mayer, "Why Did Many GI Captives Cave In?" *U.S. News and World Report*, XL (Feb. 24, 1956), 56–72; and Mayer, "The Moral Imperative: the Survival of Freedom," *Vital Speeches*, XIX (Feb. 15, 1963), 266–70. One of Mayer's leading critics has been Colorado University anthropologist John Greenway. See his article, "The Colonel's Korean 'Turncoats,'" *Nation* (Nov. 10, 1962), 302–5. Ironically, Greenway is editor of *The Journal of Folklore*. See also, Louis J. West, "Psychiatry, 'Brainwashing,' and the American Character," *American Journal of Psychiatry*, CXX (Mar. 1964), 842–50.

[13] Transcript of speech, "The New Weapon of Brainwashing," given at Tamalpais High School (California), n.d.

That they were not aware resulted from a number of circumstances. Many conservative Americans were disgruntled at the absence of a decisive American victory in the war. They blamed communist subversion at home for the result. This subversion in turn they blamed on "socialistic" influences originating in the 1930s which, they charged, had weakened the capacity and will of home, church and school to develop good character among the nation's youth. Thus, the prisoners served as evidence to verify their beliefs. Many liberals accepted the prisoners as examples of societal sickness also, although they rejected the communist subversion theme. They claimed that American materialism lay at the root of the problem. Both groups professed to view the prisoners with pity rather than scorn, as men who through no fault of their own were simply unfortunate products of a society on the verge of decay. Both were impressed by Mayer's credentials and the literate, entertaining manner in which he employed tendentious illustrations to document a general picture of moral and morale breakdown resulting from defective pre-captivity nurture. Given these general dispositions on the part of many Mayer listeners, it is no wonder that they let his muted but significantly qualifier slip by. They weren't interested in it. Finally many Americans, including academicians who would ordinarily have demanded more intellectual rigor in their own disciplines, simply took Mayer's and Kinkead's revelations at face value because they seemed to meet the test of reasonableness.

Historians have long known a great deal about the behavior of Americans in prisoner camps prior to the Korean War, particularly about prison behavior in World War II camps. As Peter Karsten wrote in the spring of 1965 issue of *Military Affairs*, the motivation and conduct of American servicemen, in or out of prison camps, have been a source of concern from the American Revolution to the present.[14] George Washington had numerous unkind words for defectors, mutineers and those of his forces who lacked "public spirit." The activities of the reluctant warriors of the War of 1812, the defectors and the short-term volunteers who departed the service when their time was up—if not sooner—wherever they were during the Mexican and Civil Wars, are a matter of record. "Give-up-itis," called "around the bends," was not unknown at Andersonville and Belle Isle. Draft dodgers and deserters numbered over 170,000 in World War I. By the early 1940s, "around the bends" had several new names, the most common being "Bamboo disease" and "fence complex."

Even in a "popular" war, World War II, the Army worried about the lack of dedication among its troops. Indoctrination programs were overhauled and beefed up with negligible success. A Social Science Research Council team which analyzed data collected by the Army during the war, concluded that the average soldier "gave little concern to the conflicting values underlying the military struggle . . . . [and] Although he showed a strong but tacit patriotism, this usually did not lead him in his thinking to subordinate his personal interests to the furtherance of ideal aims and values."[15]

As to moral and morale breakdown under severe conditions, two military physicians reported that in Japanese POW camps "moral integrity could be pretty well judged by inverse ratio to one's state of nutrition." And, they added, "Al-

14 Peter Karsten, "The American Democratic Citizen Soldier: Triumph or Disaster?" *Military Affairs*, XXX (Spring 1965), 34–40.

15 Samuel A. Stouffer et al., *The American Soldier: Combat and Its Aftermath* (New York [1965], 1949), p. 149.

though some of these prisoners sublimated their cravings by giving aid to their fellows, there was, in general, a lowering of moral standards. Food was often obtained by devious means at the expense of other prisoners." Though a buddy system did function to some extent, particularly among small cliques who shared both companionship and food, there were few group activities, and most men tended to be taciturn and seclusive. Being unable to defy their captors and survive, they expressed considerable verbal resentment toward each other. In particular they disparaged their own officers and their behavior.[16] Another physician, who was a prisoner himself in the Philippines and Japan, wrote that most POWs, whether sick or well, suffered periods of apathy or depression which, if not countered forcefully, would lead to death. "Giving up" occurred earliest and easiest among younger men as in Korea. In a sentence strikingly reminiscent of the Kinkead-Mayer critique, except that he omitted the "something new in history" theme, the physician wrote, "Failures in adjustment were most apparent in the 18-to-23-year-old group who had little or no previous experience and much overprotection. These men demonstrated marked inability to fight physical diseases and the initial shock of depression of captivity."[17]

Dr. Harold Wolff, a consultant to the Advisory Committee, reported that in World War II German prison camps where the pressures were much less severe than in Japanese and Korean camps, about 10 percent of the Americans "offered remarkably little resistance, if not outright collaboration." Wolff also noted that the escape record of Americans in World War II was not exceptional. Less than a dozen prisoners of the Japanese out of twenty-five to thirty thousand men escaped from permanent camps, all in the Philippines. Less than one hundred out of ninety-four thousand Americans captured by the Nazis successfully escaped from camps, of which less than half returned to Allied control.[18]

Autobiographical accounts of former World War II prisoners also tell much which shows that the Korean POW behavior was not unique. Edward Dobran, an airman held by the Germans, reported that a G.I. mess hall crew at his camp took care of itself well but skimped on the rest of the men's rations. Nor could those who apportioned food in the squads be trusted to do their job honestly more than a few days at a time. Dobran concluded, "In a place such as this, every man is strictly for himself. This sort of living and hardships showed what a human being is really made of. If you didn't look out for yourself here, nobody else did."[19]

Physician Alfred Weinstein's book-length recital of prison-camp life in the Philippines and Japan tells about a Marine officer's extensive collaboration with the Japanese and about the stealing of medicine by the same officer and some enlisted men medics at Cabanatuan. Some POW mechanics and truck drivers, put to work by the Japanese, lived high, using their positions to smuggle from Manila desperately needed food and medicine which they then sold for outrageous prices to the rest of the prisoners who were in dire need of both. Nor was Weinstein

[16] Stewart Wolf and Herbert S. Ripley, "Reactions Among Allied Prisoners of War Subjected to Three Years of Imprisonment and Torture by the Japanese," *American Journal of Psychiatry*, CIV (July 1947), 184–86.

[17] J. E. Nardini, "Survival Factors in American Prisoners of War of the Japanese," *American Journal of Psychiatry*, CIX (Oct. 1952), 244–46.

[18] Harold G. Wolff, "Every Man His Breaking Point—(?) the Conduct of Prisoners of War," *Military Medicine*, CXXV (Feb. 1960), 89–90.

[19] Edward Dobran, *P.O.W.: The Story of an American Prisoner of War During World War II* (New York, 1953), pp. 67–72.

complimentary about behavior in an officers' ward at a prisoner hospital at Cabanatuan. These officer-patients demanded so many special privileges, food and medicine because of their rank that the senior American officer had to break up the group by distributing the men throughout the other wards.[20] Also not complimentary about the self-seeking of a few officers incarcerated in Japan is Hugh Myers in a recently published memoir. Myers has described how four veteran Navy chiefs from the garrison at Guam assumed control over prison life at one stage in his POW experience when it became apparent that the officers were too concerned about their privileges, too inexperienced, or both, to do the job fairly or well.[21]

Nevertheless, in all the accounts discussed above which were written by men who had been POWs there is no tendency to denigrate American civilization because of the failings of a greater or lesser number of men in prison camps. Nor is it assumed by them that men under conditions of stress will uniformly conduct themselves in exemplary fashion. Weinstein, for instance, wrote, "Hard living, disease, and starvation made heroes out of few men. More frequently does it make animals out of men who, in the normal course of living would go through life with a clean slate."[22]

Two aspects of the Korean POW story, then, should be of particular interest to the historian. First, there is the fact that a poorly understood historical experience is interpreted in such a way that it makes a thoroughly inaccurate comparison between Americans past and Americans present. Second, there is the acceptance by the general public of this "nonhistory" as history, largely without the aid of historians. Critical to the development of these two aspects is the misuse of the data derived from the prisoners' experiences. This data, largely collected at the time of their repatriation, was not originally intended to provide raw material for behavioral or historical studies per se. It was, rather, gathered with the intention of providing information for possible court martial action against men accused of collaboration or criminal activity while in captivity, to identify men who merited commendation and decoration, and to identify repatriates who needed psychiatric care.[23]

Consequently, the generally accepted percentage classification of POWs by behavior, 5 percent resistor, 15 percent participator (or collaborator), and 80 percent middlemen, needs to be viewed more as suggestive than as absolutely definitive.[24] Biderman, for instance, reports that placement of a POW in the collaborator category required only that he be "accused of committing isolated but serious acts of collaboration" which could be corroborated. Placement in this category remained firm, moreover, even if the prisoner were otherwise regarded

[20] Alfred Weinstein, *Barbed-Wire Surgeon* (New York, 1948), pp. 111, 113, 120, 161.

[21] Hugh M. Myers, *Prisoner of War: World War II* (Portland, Ore., 1965), pp. 35, 54, 73–74.

[22] Weinstein, *Barbed-Wire Surgeon*, p. 229.

[23] Edgar Schein, "Epilogue: Something New in History?" in special issue, "Brainwashing," *Journal of Social Issues*, pp. 56–57. Biderman, *March to Calumny*, p. 40.

[24] Julius Segal, "Correlates of Collaboration and Resistance Behavior Among U.S. Army POW's in Korea," in "Brainwashing," *Journal of Social Issues*, pp. 32, 34. Segal, author of the Human Resources Research Office study (HumRRO report), notes these limitations in the data but tends to regard them as less important than Schein, "Epilogue," pp. 56–59, and Biderman, *March to Calumny*, pp. 205–14.

as having been a hard-case resistor throughout his captivity, as some of them were.[25]

With regard to the evidence that the POWs were peculiarly weak in moral fibre, uncommitted to American ideals and ignorant of the institutions and history of their country, a change in perspective is revealing. If one accepts the idea that it takes moral fibre to resist, actively *and* passively, ideological conversion attempts by a captor who is very concerned about "correct thoughts" and who has overwhelming power which he uses as it suits his purpose, then one must grant that most prisoners had it to some meaningful degree. The Chinese regarded passive resistance to indoctrination, including "going through the motions," as "insincere" and "stupid," if not actually reactionary behavior, as many of the scholars of POW behavior have noted. They made strenuous efforts to overcome such "insincerity" and "stupidity." But in May of 1952 they abandoned compulsory indoctrination, keeping classes only for the relatively small number of progressives. Their extensive efforts had resulted in disappointing returns among their stubborn captives.

Many prisoners did supply evidence that there was often a lack of discipline in their ranks. Autobiographies, both American and British, speak of a dog-eat-dog system prevailing during several of the "death marches" and in the temporary holding camps during the harsh winter of 1950–51. They also tell of prisoners in need being refused assistance by other prisoners. In these respects, however, they differ little from World War II POW memoirs which described the same kind of reaction to stress during those periods in which captivity conditions were the worst. Conversely, those who give testimony to such animalistic behavior also testify to behavior of a different order. Morris Wills, one of the original 21 who refused repatriation, only to return over a decade later, has written: "You really can't worry about the other fellow; you are at the line of existence yourself. If you go under that, you die. You would help each other if you could. Most would try; I wouldn't say all."[26]

"Reactionary" Lloyd Pate wrote in a similar, if more positive, vein. "After the first shock of our capture wore off, the G.I.'s with me on those Korean mountain roads began to act like soldiers this country could be proud of." He told of prisoners helping each other to keep up the pace when dropping out meant death; and he credited two such good Samaritans with saving his life.[27] Captive British journalist Philip Deane in one poignant passage revealed the context within which many prisoners faced life or death under brutal march conditions. In it he inadvertently answers many who charge that the prisoners "shamefully" aban-

[25] The post-repatriation plight of Cpl. Joseph Hammond, one of the most obstinate POWs, from the Chinese point of view, is instructive. See William Peters, "A Man's Fight for His Reputation," *Redbook* (Apr. 1958), 46–47, 89–94. Letter to author, Oct. 28, 1966, from Kathleen Lucey, legislative assistant to Rep. Thomas L. Ashley (Ohio), with enclosure: Ashley statement before House Judiciary Committee urging passage of a private bill in behalf of Hammond. Hammond's resistance record is touched on also in a British POW account, Francis S. Jones, *No Rice for Rebels* (London, 1956), pp. 200–1. Biderman, *March to Calumny*, pp. 63–66.

[26] Morris R. Wills, as told to J. Robert Moskin, *Turncoat: An American's 12 Years in Communist China* (Englewood Cliffs, N.J., 1968), p. 38.

[27] Lloyd W. Pate, as told to B. J. Cutler, *Reactionary!* (New York, 1956), pp. 34, 44, 51.

doned their weaker fellows en route. A young American lieutenant, faced with a bitter choice, allowed five men to drop out, in effect "abandoning" them, contrary to the orders of the North Korean march commander. He could not, he told the North Korean, order them carried because "That meant condemning the carriers to death from exhaustion." For this decision, the lieutenant's captors executed him on the spot.[28]

The same kinds of sources, supplemented again by the studies of research scientists and journalists, reveal that the physical duress to which prisoners allegedly succumbed so easily, presumably leading to widespread collaboration, ranged all the way from calculated manipulation of necessities of life to murder. One former prisoner labeled a reactionary by his captors told the author of many instances of physical brutality practiced by the Chinese. Among those brutalized were Chinese-appointed squad leaders who couldn't or wouldn't promote group compliance with the indoctrination program. Some, he maintained, were murdered. Others were subjected to severe beatings and then denied medical treatment for the injuries inflicted; death sometimes resulted. Some bad treatment, he declared, resulted from caprice, citing a case of one man in his squad, a "middleman" who underwent several nighttime beatings over a period of one month for no apparent reason.[29] Nevertheless, those who disparage prisoner behavior tend to take at face value the Chinese contention that they did not commit atrocities or torture their captives. An official U.S. Army report issued in June 1953, however, declared that after Chinese entrance into the war they were "fully as active as the North Koreans" in commission of war crimes.[30]

So far as the POW death rate, 38 percent, is concerned, this figure is speculative. It does not include atrocity deaths, which numbered over a thousand. Nor does it include well over two thousand missing in action. The Chinese kept no dependable records, and throughout much of the first year of the war the prisoners were in no position to do so themselves.[31] Whatever the true death rate, critics of the prisoners and of the alleged "softness" of American society see it as "too high." By implication they blame most of the deaths on prisoner negligence, or worse, on loss of will to live. Five prisoner physicians, however, reported otherwise shortly after the war. They wrote:

[28] Philip Deane, *I Was A Captive in Korea* (New York, 1953), p. 113. To cite all publications, autobiographical, scholarly or pertinent government documents which describe both positive and negative aspects of prisoner behavior would be impossible. A listing of useful titles, however, is in Albert Biderman, Barbara Heller and Paula Epstein, *A Selected Bibliography on Captivity Behavior* (Washington, D.C., Bureau of Social Science Research, 1961).

[29] The interviews were conducted by the author in 1966 on the campus of Oregon State University, Corvallis. The best catalog of the types of physical coercion employed against the prisoners is in William Peters, "More on Our POW's," *Reporter*, XX (Mar. 5, 1959), 39. See also, U.S. Congress, Senate, Committee on Government Operations. Permanent Subcommittee on Investigations. *Hearings Before the Subcommittee on Korean War Atrocities*, 83rd. Cong., 1st sess. (Washington, D.C., 1954), pp. 12–13. I have learned of no Americans who suffered the bamboo-splinters torture traditionally associated with Oriental captors. But one British naval officer was so tortured. See Dennis Lankford, *I Defy* (London, 1954), pp. 109–10.

[30] U.S. Department of the Army, War Crimes Division, Judge Advocate Section, Korean Communications Zone, *Extract of Interim Historical Report* (June 1953), p. 35. See also pp. 43–45, 49.

[31] Biderman, *March to Calumny*, pp. 93–101. This section deals with attempts to arrive at precise figures of American casualties.

The erroneous impression has been created that prisoners of war who were in good physical health gave up and died; this is not true. Every prisoner of war in Korea who died had suffered from malnutrition, exposure to cold, and continued harassment by the Communists. Contributing causes to the majority of deaths were prolonged cases of respiratory infection and diarrhea. Under such conditions, it is amazing not that there was a high death rate, but that there was a reasonably good rate of survival.[32]

Another example of misuse of data to demonstrate weakness on the part of the POWs and their nurture is the "no escape" theme. While it is true that no American successfully escaped from permanent prison camps in the Yalu River region, several hundred did escape before permanent camps were established, some after several months of captivity. From these camps, furthermore, at least 46 verifiable escape attempts involving nearly 4 percent of the POWs have been authenticated.[33] Nevertheless, both Mayer and Kinkead have insisted that failure to escape from permanent camps is significant. Mayer, in one speech, praised American prisoners in the Philippines for attempting and completing escapes despite the Japanese practice of putting prisoners in blood-brother groups of ten. If one escaped the rest were to be shot. But, according to Weinstein, the POWs took the Japanese at their word and established MP patrols to halt just such escape attempts.[34]

The assumption of Turkish superiority in POW camps also rests on a misreading of evidence. Turkish prisoners were, in the first place, a select group of volunteers. Furthermore, half of them were captured after the worst period of captivity was over, the winter of 1950–51. Well over 80 percent of the American POWs were not so fortunate. Turkish prisoners, unlike the Americans, were not split up. Officers and enlisted men remained together most of the time, an aid to maintenance of discipline. Nor were the Turks the objects of intense re-education

[32] Clarence L. Anderson et al., "Medical Experiences in Communist POW Camps in Korea: Experiences and Observations of Five American Medical Officers Who Were Prisoners of War," *Journal of the American Medical Association*, CLVI (Sept. 11, 1954), 121. Dr. Anderson, however, appears to be of two minds on the prevalence and causes of "give-up-itis." He later told Kinkead that it was one of the "worst problems" in one of the camps, Camp 5. He also leaned toward the interpretation that the POWs were a newer and weaker breed of Americans characterologically. See his analysis in Kinkead, *In Every War But One*, pp. 145, 148–49.

[33] Biderman, *March to Calumny*, pp. 52, 89. Chap. VI, pp. 84–90, "The Record of Escapes," discusses this subject in detail.

[34] Mayer, "The New Weapon of Brainwashing," transcript. Weinstein, *Barbed-Wire Surgeon*, p. 117. See also, Donald L. Baker, *Life-on-Rice* (New York, 1963), p. 26. It became apparent in the spring of 1968 that North Vietnam had taken advantage of public acceptance of contentions that "new breed" Americans lacked will and courage. On April 21 of that year an ABC television network late-news program showed a North Vietnamese film picturing security measures taken to prevent escape of some Americans confined in Hanoi. A coolly sarcastic English-speaking narrator pointed out the weak wooden doors, flimsy clasp locks and low walls surrounding the prison compound. The film then switched to a scene showing a captured airman being physically manhandled by angry civilians. The narrator's words and meaning were plain. Really courageous prisoners would make escape attempts. That they would be recaptured and treated roughly by an indignant Vietnamese civilian populace should be expected. Nevertheless, the prisoners should try, if they had any manhood left.

efforts as the Americans were. Yet, one Turk served on a peace committee. One refused to accept repatriation until he had a late change of heart. And some communist propaganda materials show Turkish involvement in communist-sponsored POW programs. In 1962, Brigadier General S. L. A. Marshall (ret.), military historian and author of *The River and the Gauntlet* and *Pork Chop Hill,* bluntly told a Senate subcommittee that the Turks were overrated. Said Marshall, "The story about the Turks being perfect prisoners is a continuation of the fable that they were perfect soldiers in the line which was not true at all."[35]

The assumption of Marine superiority to soldiers in prisoner-camp behavior also rests upon misreading of evidence. Marines may have retained more esprit de corps as prisoners, but they, like the Turks, were more of an elite unit. However, at Kanggye in 1951, some Marines made speeches, signed peace petitions (often with illegible signatures and wrong or misspelled names), and wrote articles for a "peace camp" paper called *The New Life.* Told by the Chinese that rewards for being a "good student" could include early release, some made up stories of hungry childhood and living on relief. Others said they joined the Corps in order to get decent food and clothing. Two described the criteria for a satisfactory article: "All you had to do was string stuff together in fairly coherent sentences such words as 'warmongers' . . . 'Wall Street big shots' . . . 'capitalistic bloodsuckers' and you had it made." Eighteen Marines and one soldier who convinced the Chinese of their "sincerity" eventually were selected for early repatriation. Taken close to the front, they crossed up their captors by escaping ahead of schedule.[36]

The experience of the eighteen Marines is discussed in a University of Maryland history master's thesis on Marine POWs in Korea by Lt. Col. Angus MacDonald. MacDonald notes with disapproval that the Marines gave far more information to their captors than name, rank and serial number. But he correctly views these as gambits designed to secure release from captivity.[37] The Army, however, seems to have taken a less pragmatic, and, consequently, more humorless view of similar efforts by its enlisted men.[38] MacDonald, on the other hand, does not deal adequately with the joint investigations of all services which, when concluded, revealed that only 11 percent of the Army repatriates compared with 26 percent of the Marine repatriates warranted further investigation on possible misconduct charges. Instead he quotes with approval an address by Lt. Col. Mayer which praised Marine performance, and by implication, criticized that

[35] U.S. Congress, Senate, Committee on Armed Services, *Military Cold War Education and Speech Review Policies, Hearings Before the Special Preparedness Subcommittee,* 87th Cong., 2nd. sess., 1962, III, 1242–43. Biderman, *March to Calumny,* pp. 159–62, gives the best concise summary of the Turkish performance, although nearly all other scholars writing on the subject of POW behavior have dealt with it too. For an interesting, highly technical study of the behavior of some groups of German POWs in Russian captivity during World War II, see Wilfred Olaf Reiners, *Conditional, Unconditional, and Longitudinal Collaboration: An Inquiry into the Dimensions of Prisoner-of-War Collaboration Behavior* (Ann Arbor, Mich.: University Microfilms, 1967).

[36] Harold H. Martin, "They Tried to Make Our Marines Love Stalin," *Saturday Evening Post* (Aug. 25, 1951), pp. 108–9.

[37] James Angus MacDonald, Jr., "The Problems of U.S. Marine Corps Prisoners of War in Korea" (M.A. thesis, University of Maryland, 1961). See pp. 60–84 of Chap. IV, "The Lenient Policy," and, particularly, pp. 68, 70, 84.

[38] See note 25 above.

of Army POWs.[39] Eventually both services made the further investigations suggested, the Army possibly applying a broader set of standards to define misconduct, since it initially cleared only 58 percent of the 11 percent thought to warrant further investigation. The Marines cleared 94 percent. Finally, only fourteen cases came up for trial, all Army cases, out of which eleven convictions resulted.[40]

In view of the commonly accepted belief that the Marines performed better than soldiers as POWs, it is interesting to note the comment by retired Air Corps Major General Delmar T. Spivey in a John A. Lejeune Forum on prisoner behavior. In this Marine-sponsored forum, Spivey, who while imprisoned in Germany during World War II was senior officer in the Central Compound of Stalag III, made the unrebutted statement that:

> *Even with all these things* ["*survival courses, physical conditioning programs, instruction in our American heritage, information about the enemy, courses and exercises designed to instill pride and self-respect and belief in one's service and country, and the assurance that our country will stand by an individual, both in combat and as a prisoner*"] . . . *we cannot assume that every fighting man will be completely prepared for his responsibilities as a prisoner. History is not on our side, and neither is human nature when we consider the past conduct of prisoners of war.*[41]

The conclusions of professional and semi-professional scholars and writers about American POW behavior are mixed. Stanley Elkins in his search for suggestive experience to support his description of the effects of a closed system on slave psychological development turned to the POWs. Unfortunately he exaggerated some of the findings of his source, Edgar Schein, one scholar involved in the POW studies. Elkins wrote of "profound changes in behavior and values" being "effected without physical torture or extreme deprivation" and of "large numbers" of American informers and men who cooperated in the indoctrination program.[42] But Schein said only that mandatory discussion and mutual criticism sessions which followed communist indoctrination lectures probably created "considerable doubt concerning ideological position in some of the men." They were, as a whole, he declared, "not very effective." Nor did he give any estimates of the numbers of informers or cooperators relative to the total POW population.[43]

[39] U.S. Department of Defense, *POW: The Fight Continues After the Battle*, p. 81. MacDonald, "Marine Corps Prisoners of War in Korea," pp. 236–37.

[40] U.S. Department of Defense, *POW: The Fight Continues After the Battle*, p. 82. "Misconduct in the Prison Camps: A Survey of the Law and an Analysis of the Korean Cases," *Columbia Law Review*, LVI (May 1956), 745–46, esp. note 256. Biderman, *March to Calumny*, p. 36.

[41] Robert B. Asprey, ed., "The Soldier and the Prisoner," The John A. Lejeune Forum, *Marine Corps Gazette*, IXL (May 1965), 40. Lt. Col. MacDonald and Col. James W. Keene, also of the Marines, were the other two participants in the Forum.

[42] *Slavery: A Problem in American Institutional and Intellectual Life* (New York [1963], 1959), note 99, p. 128.

[43] Edgar Schein, "Some Observations on Chinese Methods of Handling Prisoners of War," *Public Opinion Quarterly*, XX (Spring 1956), 326. Schein does note that the Chinese were successful in controlling large numbers of prisoners and creating social disorganization which enabled them to undermine supports to belief, preparatory to attempts at indoctrination. Schein also postulates that the indoctrination

Betty Friedan has seen the average Korean prisoner as an "apathetic, dependent, infantile, purposeless being . . . a new American man . . . reminiscent of the familiar 'feminine' personality."[44] Edgar Friedenberg described the POW as a new model of being, but an international one, not just American. He wrote, "this sort of young man is a character in existentialist novels and post-World War II Italian films."[45] Miss Friedan, however, discovered parallels closer to home. She found them in the youth of the 1950s, in their "new passivity," bored and passionless, demonstrated variously in: the annual springtime collegiate riots at Fort Lauderdale; a teen-age call girl service in a Long Island suburb; adolescent grave defilings in Bergen County, New Jersey; drug-taking parties in Westchester County, New York, and Connecticut; and the "helpless, apathetic state" of the female student body at Sarah Lawrence College.[46]

It is doubtful whether the typical Korean POW would recognize himself in all this. His schooling averaged somewhat less than nine years. His social class was hardly comfortable middle. And his withdrawal from activity was certainly in part a shrewd way of fending off the ubiquitous Chinese indoctrinators.

Among historians, Walter Hermes, author of the second volume of a projected five-volume official history of the war, took note of the Kinkead book. But he accepted Biderman's view, calling it a "convincing rebuttal" of Kinkead's thesis.[47] Robert Leckie, however, relied heavily on Kinkead and called the POW record "sorry . . . the worst in American history." Apathy, he declared, was responsible for the failure of any men to escape. But in the same paragraph he asserted that the Caucasian appearance of the Americans was the "more likely reason for this failure."[48] T. R. Fehrenbach, too, has generally taken a dim view of the prisoners' behavior. "Chemistry and culture," the Doolittle Board's democratization reforms and American education, among other culprits, were at fault, he wrote. His analysis of sources, like Leckie's, was less than rigorous.[49]

Harry Middleton, while acknowledging that the percentage of collaborators was

attempts might have been more successful had the Chinese instructors known their captive students and their material better and had the student-instructor ratio been lower. The lower ratio he deems important based on evidence from mainland China where indoctrination seems to have worked best when "students" self-police each other in their quest for ideological purity. It is, of course, debatable whether American G.I. prisoners would engage in an ideological struggle in the same fashion as Chinese "enemies of the state."

[44] *The Feminine Mystique* (New York, 1963), p. 386.

[45] *The Vanishing Adolescent* (New York [1963], 1959), p. 214.

[46] Friedan, pp. 284–85. Who were the sources for social psychologist Friedan and educational psychologist Friedenberg? Miss Friedan cited Kinkead. She cited Mayer. She cited Dr. Spock, who was presumably impressed by a Mayer speech. She cited Friedenberg, who, predictably, cited Kinkead. It's not only historians who quote each other.

[47] Walter G. Hermes, *Truce Tent and Fighting Front* (Washington, D.C., 1966), pp. 496–97.

[48] *Conflict: The History of the Korean War, 1950–1953* (New York, 1962), pp. 389–90.

[49] *This Kind of War: A Study in Unpreparedness* (New York, 1963), pp. 434–37, 461–68, 540–48. For an example of ambiguity in Fehrenbach cf. pp. 434 and 463. In the former he declared that the "Old Army," like that on Bataan, "exhausted and sick" in prison camp "would have spat upon its captors, despising them to the end." In the latter, however, he wrote "Americans and Britons in Japanese prisons retreated into dream worlds, and some informed on their buddies."

small, also looked askance at the prisoners' record. His book, though published later (1965) than Fehrenbach's narrative, displayed less acquaintance with or close reading of the available literature on the subject.[50] An English scholar, David Rees, in *Korea: The Limited War*, after devoting a lengthy chapter to the subject, leaned to the point of view that POW behavior was not unusual considering the fallible nature of man and considering the unique nature of the prisoners' experiences.[51] S. L. A. Marshall, a consultant to the Advisory Committee, is a defender of the prisoners.[52] And Russell Weigley in his *History of the United States Army* also concluded that the Korean POWs were not a discredit to the nation.[53]

In 1962, 21 scholars familiar with the POW behavior materials signed a paper entitled "Statement: To Set Straight the Korean POW Episode." This paper, drawn up by two of the signers, Edgar Schein and Raymond Bauer, who had worked extensively on the subject, directly refuted the popular version of the POW story expounded by Kinkead and Mayer. The "Statement" included these challenging assertions:

> *The behavior of the Korean prisoners did not compare unfavorably with that of their countrymen or with the behavior of people of other nations who have faced similar trials in the past.*
>
> *Instances of moral weakness, collaboration with the enemy, and failure to take care of fellow soldiers in Korea did not occur more frequently than in other wars where comparable conditions of physical and psychological hardship were present. Indeed, such instances appear to have been less prevalent than historical experience would lead us to expect.*
>
> *It is our opinion that any serious analysis of American society, its strengths and weaknesses, should rest on historically correct data. It is unfortunate that the Korean POW episode has been distorted to make the case for one view of American society. We hope that this Statement will be the first step toward setting the historical facts of this episode straight.*[54]

Historically correct data, however, were insufficient for many Americans in the 1950s and 1960s. They seemed to feel that any communist success at eliciting collaborative behavior or inducing ideological doubt among any American soldiers, no matter how small the number, signified a general American failure. Such failure to them was not to be taken lightly. It might reflect, after all, the existence of a more dangerous cancer in the American character than even they had suspected.

What is really "new in history," then, about the whole Korean POW episode?

First, never before Korea were American POWs confronted by a captor who worked hard to change their ideological persuasion. This point is worth a brief examination. Had American POWs of the Germans, for instance, been subjected to ideological thought reform efforts designed to inculcate virulent racist attitudes or to inculcate the idea that Germany was fighting the West's battle against

[50] *The Compact History of the Korean War* (New York, 1965), pp. 211–14.

[51] *Korea: The Limited War* (London, 1964), p. 346.

[52] Marshall signed the "statement" cited below in the text.

[53] (New York, 1967), pp. 520–21.

[54] This formal statement is found in Albert Biderman, "The Dangers of Negative Patriotism," *Harvard Business Review*, XL (Nov. 1962), 93–99.

communism, had these efforts taken place over the length of time and under circumstances comparable to those endured by the Korean POWs, there might be a rough basis for comparison. But those American POWs weren't so subjected. Dobran did report some anti-Semitism among his POW group upon which the Germans might have capitalized.[55] But one can speculate a little in the other direction that the American reaction to this divisive ploy might have been similar to that in one group of Negro POWs in Korea among whom the Chinese tried to foment ideological change by hammering upon the existence of racial discrimination in the United States. Wrote Lloyd Pate, "A few colored guys got up and said it was our business what we did in the United States and for the Chinks to mind their own damn business."[56]

Second, never before had the American public been so gullible as to believe that such a chimera as the enemy's self-proclaimed "lenient policy" was, in fact, lenient. During the first year of the war in particular the Chinese and North Koreans, often in systematic fashion, fostered brutalizing captivity conditions which were in significant part responsible for prisoner behavior which did not measure up to "ideal" standards.

And, finally, for the first time the public seemed to assume that such selfish undisciplined behavior as existed among the POWs was something new in American military experience and that it was a direct consequence of a characterological deterioration in the nation itself.

Whether or not such a deterioration has been taking place in American society, from the advent of the New Deal and the impact of progressive education as the critics strongly imply, is not under contention here. What is being contended, rather, is that if one really believes this and wants evidence to prove it, one will have to find examples other than among those Americans who died and those who survived in the prison camps of North Korea, 1950–53.

[55] Dobran, p. 62. See also former Alabama governor George Wallace's remark to a German-born American in Pittsburgh. "I'm sorry it was necessary for us to fight against those anti-communist nations [Germany and Japan]. I thought back then, Hell, we should have been in those trenches with the Germans, with yawl, fightin' them Bolsheviks." Marshall Frady, "George Wallace: The Angry Man's Candidate," *Saturday Evening Post* (June 29, 1968), pp. 47–48.

[56] Pate, p. 67.

28

THE "COMMUNIST-DOMINATED" UNIONS IN THE UNITED STATES SINCE 1950[1]

F. S. O'Brien

Organized labor in the period following World War II entered a new and challenging period. Faced with rising prices, it sought increased wages and in several instances engaged in strikes to keep up with the rising cost of living. Success in these initial ventures engendered the feeling that unions, thanks to favorable legislation, had grown too powerful. This feeling plus the existence of a few corrupt labor officials and the control of some unions by Communists led to mounting hostility and a call for congressional action to curb unions. Restrictive legislation was enacted in 1947, and at the same time organized labor sought to rid itself of crooks and Communists within its own ranks. In 1955 the AF of L and CIO merged, electing George Meany as president with Walter Reuther as vice-president heading the industrial union department. Despite this merger, organized workers, numbering some 18,000,000, faced many difficult problems. While the numbers of service and clerical employees increased, the proportion of manual workers in the labor force steadily declined. The advent of automation insured the fact that this proportion would drop even more precipitously. Decline in certain industries and the regional shift of others, together with the existence of large numbers of unorganized, underprivileged, and chiefly agricultural workers posed both problems and challenges to organized labor in the postwar period. One of the most critical issues the unions faced is the subject of this essay.

F. S. O'Brien is assistant professor of history at Williams College. Since the publication of this article he has served with the Brazil Development Assistance Program at the University of California.

---

[1] This subject was originally suggested to me by Professor George Hilton. I also wish to thank my colleague, John R. Eriksson, for helpful suggestions and criticisms.

Source: *Labor History*, Vol. 9, No. 2 (Spring 1968), pp. 184–209. Reprinted by permission of the author and publisher.

I

In the period between November 1949 and August 1950 the C.I.O. expelled eleven of its member unions. The leaders of these unions were accused of being members of the Communist Party in the United States or, at a minimum, Communist sympathizers, and of conducting the affairs of their unions in accordance with the dictates of the Communist Party rather than the policies of the C.I.O.

C.I.O. action had, of course, a significant impact on the subsequent history of each of these unions. Their experiences, however, have not been at all similar. Several have disappeared entirely, a few have merged or otherwise affiliated with other unions, and four of the original eleven are still in existence. This paper examines the record of each of these unions since 1950, and attempts to draw certain conclusions from their recent history.

II

It is first necessary to describe certain of the events which led up to these expulsions. This exposition will be brief, since the story of Communist penetration of the C.I.O. has already been thoroughly documented elsewhere.[2]

Throughout the 1920s and early 1930s the Communists attempted to form a separate (from the A.F.L.) Communist labor federation and also to "bore from within." Neither approach met with much success, though the Federation was itself experiencing considerable difficulties in retaining its membership.

When John L. Lewis led the Committee for Industrial Organization out of the A.F.L., the Communists were at first reluctant to join him. Having only recently re-entered the A.F.L. following their own unsuccessful fling at dual unionism, they feared that the C.I.O. would meet a similar fate. By early 1937, however, it had become evident that the C.I.O. would survive, and the Party decided that its best interest lay in joining the new federation. Accordingly, in May 1937, the Communist-led unions in the A.F.L. were ordered to affiliate.[3] In addition to these unions, hundreds of individual Party members also joined the C.I.O., and many were elected to offices in its newly formed unions. Communists also attained positions of influence in the national office of the C.I.O. as well as in the city and state industrial union councils. At the height of their power, the Communists were said to "dominate" or to have major influence in about 40 percent of all C.I.O. unions.[4]

The Communists strengthened their position within the C.I.O. during World War II,[5] but as relations between the United States and Russia deteriorated fol-

[2] See, in particular, David J. Saposs, *Communism in American Unions* (New York, McGraw-Hill, 1959); Max M. Kampelman, *The Communist Party vs. the CIO* (New York, Frederick A. Praeger, 1957); and Irving Howe and Lewis Coser, *The American Communist Party* (Boston, Beacon Press, 1957). See also Philip Taft, "Attempts to Radicalize the Labor Movement," *Industrial and Labor Relations Review*, I (July 1948), 580–592.

[3] Kampelman, *op. cit.*, 15.

[4] *Ibid.*, 18.

[5] During World War II the Communists attracted many new supporters; and Party membership reached an all-time high of around 80,000 in 1944. (Howe and Coser, *op. cit.*, 419.) While membership within the union movement grew also, the Communists lost some favor among organized labor because they advocated outlawing strikes for the duration, incentive pay plans and extensions of piece rates,

lowing the war and attitudes toward Soviet Communism hardened, a breach opened between the non-Communist and pro-Communist leaders within the C.I.O. Communist support of the Progressive Party in the 1948 presidential election was one of the most important causes of the split.[6] Another was the controversy over the World Federation of Trade Unions (W.F.T.U.).[7] Furthermore, the Communists were using the CIO News and other C.I.O. publications as vehicles for attacks on American foreign and domestic policies. Bitter objections were raised to this use of the C.I.O.'s name and to the implication that these views were held by a majority of C.I.O. members.

The final break did not come until 1950, though a number of individual C.I.O. unions—most notably the United Automobile Workers (U.A.W.) under Walter Reuther, the National Maritime Union (N.M.U.) under Joseph Curran,[8] and the Transport Workers Union (T.W.U.) under Michael Quill,[9]—were ridding themselves of Communist influences in the early post-war years. The remaining "Communist-dominated" unions encountered increasing difficulties in retaining their memberships in the face of raids by other C.I.O. and A.F.L. unions—and many entire locals were breaking away to join other unions. In addition, several of these unions were undergoing financial difficulties and falling behind in payments of per-capita dues to the C.I.O.

The United Farm Equipment and Metal Workers (F.E.) and the United Electrical, Radio and Machine Workers (U.E.) were under the heaviest attack. The F.E. had been involved in jurisdictional disputes with the U.A.W. for a number of years and had been ordered by the C.I.O. Executive Board to merge with the U.A.W. in 1945—an order that was rejected by F.E. leaders. In November 1948, the F.E. was again ordered to affiliate with the U.A.W. and a committee of C.I.O. vice-presidents was formed to "assist" in the merger. When the F.E. leaders refused to participate in the meetings of this committee, the C.I.O. Executive Board recommended that the F.E.'s charter be revoked at the next convention. Action against the U.E. had also become inevitable. This union had been making increasingly vehement attacks on C.I.O. officials, and at its September 1949 convention issued an ultimatum: the C.I.O. must punish those

---

speed-up on assembly lines and, finally, mobilization of labor. *Ibid.*, 413. See also Joel Seidman, "Labor Policy of the Communist Party during World War II," *Industrial and Labor Relations Review*, IV (October 1950), 55–69.

[6] At the January 1948 meeting of the C.I.O. Executive Board the Communists unsuccessfully sought to pass a resolution supporting Henry Wallace's candidacy. They then instructed their Communist-controlled C.I.O. unions to endorse Wallace anyway, and in the campaign these unions contributed money and personnel to the Progressive cause. Many C.I.O. leaders feared that a split in the labor vote would allow the Republicans to win the election and therefore the C.I.O., while not endorsing Truman officially, attacked Wallace repeatedly during the campaign.

[7] The C.I.O. had joined the W.F.T.U. when it was formed in 1945 but withdrew in January 1949, charging that the organization had been Communist-controlled from its inception. Subsequently the C.I.O., along with labor organizations from other western countries, participated in the founding of the International Confederation of Free Trade Unions; this action was bitterly opposed by the Communist faction in the C.I.O. For a detailed discussion of these events see Adolf Sturmthal, "The Crisis of the W.F.T.U.," *Industrial and Labor Relations Review*, I (July 1948), 624–638.

[8] See Philip Taft, "The Unlicensed Seafaring Unions," *Industrial and Labor Relations Review*, Vol. III (January 1950), 211.

[9] See Kampelman, *op. cit.*, 148–155.

unions that raided the U.E. or face the loss of U.E. per capita dues payments. Then, before the C.I.O. convention in November 1949, the U.E. and F.E. merged and announced their independence from the C.I.O. But the convention nevertheless carried out the formality of expulsion proceedings against both unions.

Philip Murray spoke out forcefully from the platform against Communism at this convention.[10] More importantly, the delegates amended the C.I.O. constitution to include the statement that, "no individual shall be eligible to serve either as an officer or as a member of the executive board who is a member of the Communist Party . . . or who consistently pursues policies and activities directed toward the achievement of the program or purposes of the Communist Party."[11] Finally, the C.I.O. Executive Board was given the power to expel any national or international union whose policies were "consistently directed toward the achievement of the program or purposes of the Communist Party."

In accordance with the above amendment, charges were brought against ten additional unions (though subsequently dropped in one case).[12] Hearings for the remaining nine unions were conducted by committees of the C.I.O. vice-presidents from December 1949 to August 1950. These hearings consisted primarily of testimony from union leaders who had formerly been members of the Communist Party or who were strongly anti-Communist, the reading into the record of public statements of union leaders suspected of Communist leanings, and examination of union newspapers and other publications for alleged pro-Communist statements. In most cases it was sufficient for the C.I.O.'s purpose to show that the union had publicly supported the official Communist Party line through two or more significant changes.

In each case the committee voted for expulsion. These expulsions were immediately carried out by the C.I.O. Executive Board, and approved by unanimous vote of the C.I.O. annual convention in November 1950. The expelled unions were granted the right of appeal at this convention, but none chose to do so.[13]

[10] Murray said, "There is room within the C.I.O. movement to differ about many subjects . . . but there is no room within the C.I.O. for Communism . . . the leaders of a small group of unions in the C.I.O. . . . whose membership is less than 10 percent of our total, have come to look upon their affiliation with the C.I.O. as a matter for their personal exploitation. They reject our basic policies; they flout the wishes of the majority; they obstruct our economic and legislative programs. No self-respecting organization can long tolerate this dangerous division . . . this voluntary association of labor unions can determine its own membership . . . the C.I.O. has the power to confer affiliation upon labor unions which wish to join our organization; it obviously has the power of disaffiliation over those organizations whose leaders' policies, statements and actions demonstrate their contempt and their hostility toward our general policies." C.I.O., *Proceedings of the 11th Constitutional Convention,* November 1949, 54 and 327.

[11] *Ibid.*, 240.

[12] These ten included all those discussed below. Also originally charged was the United Furniture Workers Union. However, there had been widespread opposition to the Communists in this union since 1946 and at the June 1950 Furniture workers convention, President Morris Pizer split with the pro-Communist majority on the executive board and was able to bring about the defeat of all left-wing candidates for office. See Kampelman, *op. cit.*, 161–2. Charges against the U.F.W. were dismissed by the C.I.O. on June 15, 1950.

[13] The National Union of Marine Cooks and Stewards did send a written appeal which was reviewed and denied.

The convention membership committee reported that the immediate loss in membership from the eleven expulsions (including F.E. and U.E.) was 675,000.[14] Philip Murray referred to a loss of 850,000 to 900,000[15] members, while other estimates varied from 500,000 to 1,000,000. These inconsistent figures are due to several factors (in addition to misinformation or deliberate misstatement). First, different estimates were based on reported membership in different years between 1946 and 1950 and, as stated above, most of the expelled unions were experiencing a membership decline during this period. Second, figures based on per-capita dues payments made to the C.I.O. could differ from those furnished to the Bureau of Labor Statistics. Finally, some estimates were based on the number of workers represented, which could vary substantially from actual membership in the absence of a union shop. Because of these discrepancies, and the absence of membership figures for some of the unions in various years, no attempt has been made to present statistics on membership of all the expelled unions for the same date. Table I reports membership for each of the unions at one or more times between 1946 and 1950, and for various years since 1950 for the unions which have continued in existence.

III

Since 1950 Communists both within and outside the labor movement have been under attack from the federal government, from the states, and from many other quarters. This story is well known and will not be retold here. But some of the legislation which has affected Communists in the labor movement might profitably be described.

The Taft-Hartley Act of 1947, Section 9h in particular, was among the most important statutes. It required an affidavit of every local and national union officer certifying that "he is not a member of the Communist Party or affiliated with such party, and that he does not believe in, and is not a member of or supports any organization that believes in or teaches the overthrow of the United States government by force or any illegal or unconstitutional methods." While many union leaders at first refused, on principle, to sign these affidavits, almost all, including the leaders of the expelled unions, had submitted them by the early 1950s. The National Labor Relations Board, with which the affidavits were filed, took the position that it could not rule on their validity but could only pass them on to the Justice Department for possible indictments for perjury. Because legal proof of Party membership was not easy to obtain, convictions for filing false affidavits were extremely difficult to secure; and there had only been twenty by the end of 1956.[16]

Among other legislation of this kind affecting unions, the Communist Control Act of 1954 (the Butler Act) amended the 1950 McCarran Act to provide that any *union* that had aided Communist-front groups within the prior three years, or whose leaders had been consistently identified with Communist groups in the prior two years, could be brought before the Subversive Activities Control Board (S.A.C.B.) and, if found to be "Communist-infiltrated," would lose all rights of

[14] C.I.O., *Proceedings of the 12th Constitutional Convention, November 1950*, 94.

[15] *Ibid.*, 21.

[16] *Fortune*, February, 1957, 101.

TABLE I

MEMBERSHIP OF "COMMUNIST-DOMINATED" UNIONS AT VARIOUS DATES, 1947–1962

Date		*A.C.A.*	*F.T.A.A.W*	*I.L.W.U.*	*I.U.F.A.W.*	*F. & L.W.*	*M.M.*	*N.U.M.C.S.*	*U.E.*	*F.E.*	*U.O.P.W.A.*	*U.P.W.*
Various Dates												
1946–1948	(1)		46,700						500,000	65,000	45,000	
1948	(2)			75,000	25,000		108,625	7,000			70,000	86,000
1948	(3)	10,000							400,000			
January-June												
1949 Average ...	(4)			65,000	25,000	100,000	91,400	6,000				
1951 Average	(5)			65,000				7,000				
1954 Average	(6)	7,000		65,000			100,000					
1955–1956												
Average	(7)	7,500		70,000			100,000		100,000			
1957–1958												
Average	(8)	8,000		56,000			100,000		160,000			
1959–1960												
Average	(9)	8,000		60,000			100,000		160,000			
1961–1962												
Average	(10)	7,500		60,000			75,000		163,000			

Sources:

(1) Kampelman, *The Communist Party vs. the C.I.O.*, 157, 158, 167, 173.
(2) Bureau of Labor Statistics, Bulletin #937, *Director of Labor Unions in the United States, June 1948.*
(3) *Fortune*, March, 1956.
(4) Bureau of Labor Statistics Bulletin #980, *Directory of Labor Unions in the United States, 1950.*
(5) Bureau of Labor Statistics Bulletin #1127, *Directory of Labor Unions in the United States, 1953.*
(6) Bureau of Labor Statistics Bulletin #1185, *Directory of National and International Labor Unions in the U. S., 1955.*
(7) Bureau of Labor Statistics Bulletin #1222, *Directory of National and International Labor Unions in the U. S., 1957.*
(8) Bureau of Labor Statistics Bulletin #1267, *Directory of National and International Labor Unions in the U. S., 1959.*
(9) Bureau of Labor Statistics Bulletin #1320, *Directory of National and International Labor Unions in the U. S., 1961.*
(10) Bureau of Labor Statistics Bulletin #1395, *Directory of National and International Labor Unions in the U. S., 1963.*

representation before the N.L.R.B. Following this, 20 percent of the union's membership could petition to the N.L.R.B. for an election to determine a new bargaining agent. Before this act, so long as the union's leaders had filed non-Communist affidavits under the Taft-Hartley Act, the union could not be denied the facilities of the N.L.R.B. The Butler Act thus made it possible for the government to move directly against the union itself instead of its leaders.[17]

Most recently, Section 504 of the Labor-Management Reporting and Disclosure Act of 1959 (the Landrum-Griffin Act) provided for a fine of $10,000 and/or imprisonment for one year for any union officer or member who failed to report Communist Party membership. This clause was intended to supersede the requirement for non-Communist affidavits under the Taft-Hartley Act.

Moreover, some firms during this period were firing employees who pleaded the Fifth Amendment regarding Party membership, a practice upheld by the N.L.R.B. and the courts.[18] As for the unions themselves, a 1954 Bureau of Labor Statistics survey of 100 union constitutions (these unions included 90 percent of total union membership at that time) showed that fifty-nine unions (with over 60 percent of total union membership) barred Communists from office and forty barred Communists from membership.[19]

IV

Against this background of government, business, and union hostility it is not surprising that the expelled unions experienced difficulties and that several quickly passed from the scene.[20] What is perhaps more surprising is that four have continued to survive, and that of these two have remained relatively strong and impervious to outside attacks. Because the fortunes of these unions have been so varied since 1950, they are described individually below.

1. Unions That Have Ceased to Function or Have Merged with Other Unions

United Public Workers The United Public Workers (U.P.W.) was formed in 1946 by a merger of the State, County and Municipal Workers (S.C.M.W.) and the United Federal Workers, both of which had been organized by the C.I.O. in the late 1930s. The president of the U.P.W. and former head of the S.C.M.W., Abraham Flaxer, was identified as a member of the Communist Party.[21] The union itself had a membership of about 80,000 before its expulsion from the C.I.O. but its post-1950 decline was exceedingly rapid. The C.I.O. chartered

[17] A.F.L. and C.I.O. unions were assumed by the act to be free from Communist influence and thus exempt from scrutiny.

[18] See Bruno Stein, "Loyalty and Security Cases in Arbitration," *Industrial and Labor Relations Review*, XVI (October 1963), 96–113.

[19] *Monthly Labor Review*, Vol. 77 (October 1954), 1097.

[20] Immediately following expulsion the newly independent unions considered the idea of founding a third labor federation, but no concrete result was achieved and the individual unions were left to follow separate courses of action. The party did not discourage attempts to affiliate with either C.I.O. or A.F.L. unions when this later became possible. Saposs, *op. cit.*, 209.

[21] Kampelman, *op. cit.*, 59 fn.

the Government and Civic Employees Organizing Committee on March 1, 1950, and this new union recaptured most of the U.P.W.'s membership—with only an estimated 2,500 die-hards remaining in the old organization by 1952.[22] The U.P.W. disbanded in February 1953; four remaining locals were chartered by the Teamsters Union, and the New York Teachers Union remained unaffiliated.[23]

United Office and Professional Workers of America and Food, Tobacco, Agricultural and Allied Workers The United Office and Professional Workers (U.O.P.W.A.) had originally been the Office Workers Union, a member of the Communist Trade Union Unity League in the early 1930s. It joined the A.F.L. when the T.U.U.L. was disbanded in 1935 and then joined the C.I.O. two years later. Its president, Lewis Merrill, broke with the Communists in December 1946, and attempted to purge them from the union. He was unsuccessful, however, and was himself purged, being succeeded by James H. Durkin under whose leadership the union remained "one of the most consistently pro-Communist unions in the C.I.O."[24] Membership of the U.O.P.W.A. declined from about 45,000 in 1946–47 to only 12,000 in 1949.[25]

The Food, Tobacco, Agricultural and Allied Workers Union (F.T.A.A.W.) also reported a membership decline in this period—from 46,700 in 1947, to 24,000 in 1948,[26] and to 22,600 in 1949.[27] Donald Henderson, president of the union, had been affiliated with the Communist Party since 1932.[28] In 1949 he was appointed the union's "National Administrative Director" in an attempt to avoid signing a non-Communist affidavit. But the N.L.R.B. challenged this move, and Henderson was forced to admit his Communist affiliation and to resign from the Party.

In 1950, following their expulsion from the C.I.O., the F.T.A.A.W. and the U.O.P.W.A. merged with the Distributive Workers Union (D.W.U.) to form the Distributive, Processing and Office Workers Union (D.P.O.W.U.).[29] The new D.P.O.W.U. president was Arthur Osman, Henderson was administrative director, and Durkin was secretary-treasurer. The union was estimated to have about 55,000 members at the time of formation, two-thirds of which came from the D.W.U.[30] In other words, the total membership of the F.T.A.A.W. and the U.O.P.W.A. combined had probably fallen by this time to under 20,000.

The C.I.O. had chartered the Insurance and Allied Workers Organizing

[22] *Fortune,* June 1952, 74. The Government and Civic Employees Organizing Committee merged with the A.F.L.-American Federation of State County and Municipal Employees in July 1956.

[23] Bureau of Labor Statistics, Bulletin No. 1185, *Directory of National and International Labor Unions in the United States, 1955,* 3.

[24] Kampelman, *op. cit.,* 96.

[25] *Ibid.,* 167.

[26] C.I.O., *Proceedings of the 10th Constitutional Convention, November 1948,* 164.

[27] Kampelman, *op. cit.,* 173.

[28] *Ibid.,* 174.

[29] The D.W.U. was formed in 1948 out of New York City Local No. 65 of the Retail, Wholesale and Department Store Union, which had withdrawn from the parent organization. This independent union, under Arthur Osman, was "one of the most completely Communist-controlled trade unions in the entire United States." *Ibid.,* 33.

[30] *Fortune,* November 1950, 52.

Committee in May 1950 to absorb the major part of the jurisdiction of the U.O.P.W.A.[31] and had turned over jurisdiction of the F.T.A.A.W. to the Retail, Wholesale and Department Store Union, the Brewery Workers Union, and the Packinghouse Workers Union—all of which were successful in making inroads in the memberships of the two expelled unions. Then, in 1954, the D.P.O.W.U. broke with the Communists and in May of that year Arthur Osman brought the membership back into the Retail, Wholesale and Department Store Union.[32]

International Union of Fur and Leather Workers The Fur Workers Union (F. & L.W.) was organized in 1912, joined the A.F.L. in 1913, and then withdrew from the A.F.L. in 1929 to join the Communist Trade Union Unity League. The A.F.L. established the Furriers' Joint Council as a competing union, but this organization was unable to win away many members of the Fur Workers and it ceased to function in 1932. With the T.U.U.L.'s dissolution the F. & L.W. returned to the A.F.L., but then left to join the C.I.O. in 1937. It merged with the C.I.O. Leather Workers two years later, and at the end of World War II was one of the strongest and largest Communist-led unions in the C.I.O., having approximately 100,000 members.[33]

The Fur and Leather Workers Union faced little outside union competition either before or after expulsion.[34] No new union was chartered by the C.I.O. to take over this jurisdiction, and the F. & L.W. lost only about 25 percent of its membership in the ensuing four years. Nevertheless, the F. & L.W. began to seek a merger with an A.F.L. or C.I.O. union in 1953 and, two years later, one was finally arranged with the A.F.L. Amalgamated Meat Cutters and Butcher Workmen of America. This proposal was strongly attacked by both the A.F.L. and C.I.O.,[35] but the Meat Cutters Union subjected the F. & L.W. to a thorough

[31] The Insurance and Allied Workers Organizing Committee was chartered in June 1953, as the Insurance Workers of America. The I.W.A. reported a membership of 12,000 in 1954 and 13,000 in 1955–56. In May 1959, the I.W.A. merged with the A.F.L. Insurance Agents International Union (11,000 members, 1955–56) to form the International Union of Insurance Workers (1961–62 membership 21,000). See Bureau of Labor Statistics, *Directory of National and International Unions in the United States*, Bulletin No. 1185, 3, 32; Bulletin No. 1222, 35; Bulletin No. 1267, 3; Bulletin No. 1395, 21.

[32] Bureau of Labor Statistics, Bulletin No. 1185, *op. cit.*, 3.

[33] For a detailed history of this union see Robert D. Leiter, "Fur Workers Union," *Industrial and Labor Relations Review*, III (January 1950), 163–186.

[34] Because of this lack of competition the union leaders did not sign Taft-Hartley affidavits until August 1950. Ben Gold, President of the union since 1925, announced his resignation from the Party to sign the affidavit. Gold was one of the few openly avowed Communists in the labor movement; he joined the Party in 1922, was for many years a member of the national committee of the Party, and twice ran for the New York State Assembly on the Communist ticket. He was tried and convicted of perjury in 1954 on the basis of his affidavit, but the Supreme Court ordered a new trial. A second trial was not held because the government dismissed the charges on the ground that certain material evidence was no longer available. *The New York Times*, May 10, 1957, 13. Gold resigned as president of the Fur and Leather Workers in October 1954, and returned to work in a fur shop. *Monthly Labor Review*, Vol. 77 (December 1954), 1367.

[35] At first the A.F.L. executive council voted unanimously to disapprove the merger. See *A.F.L. News Reporter*, December 17, 1954. The C.I.O. executive board criticized the Meat Cutters for the "unscrupulous opportunism with which

"de-Communization": the F. & L.W. was dissolved, its executive board disbanded, twenty-nine top union officials were removed from office, and former president Ben Gold and secretary-treasurer Irving Potash were barred from holding any future office in the Meat Cutters Union. The Meat Cutters had already adopted a constitutional clause which barred subversives from membership, and the merger agreement also provided that further evidence of Communist activity in the union's Fur Division over the next five years would be grounds for expulsion of the membership without trial. Furthermore, any Fur Division local found to be promoting Communist causes could be expelled and its treasury confiscated. With the enactment of these provisions the A.F.L. switched its position from condemnation to acquiescence,[36] but some observers still expressed doubt that all Communist influence had been eliminated from the Fur Division.[37]

International Union of Fishermen and Allied Workers The International Union of Fishermen and Allied Workers (I.U.F.A.W.) was formed in 1902 from a number of previously independent local unions on the West Coast. The I.U.F.A.W. joined the C.I.O. in 1938 and achieved a high degree of integration of local unions of fishermen from Alaska to Southern California by the end of World War II. Membership reached a peak of around 25,000 in 1947–48.

The I.U.F.A.W. came under the influence of Harry Bridges and the International Longshoremen's and Warehousemen's Union (I.L.W.U.) early in its history. A merger with the I.L.W.U. was proposed in 1949 and approved by a referendum vote of the I.U.F.A.W. membership. The I.L.W.U. also adopted a resolution supporting the merger and it was made effective on July 1, 1949. However, most of the fishermen have since been lost to the I.L.W.U.; in 1956 it was estimated that only 2,000 remained[38] and the I.L.W.U. now admits that it represents only a negligible number of fishermen.

The reasons for this decrease have had less to do with communism or inter-union raiding than with the declining fortunes of the West Coast fishing industry, which has suffered from competing foreign imports, from the restrictive actions of some Central and South American governments in protecting fishing grounds extending several hundred miles off their coasts, and from depletion of some sources of supply. A series of anti-trust decisions have also severely hampered collective bargaining in the industry.[39]

---

it is pushing a merger with the Communist-dominated Fur and Leather Workers." *C.I.O. News*, February 7, 1955.

[36] *A.F.L. News Reporter*, October 28, 1955. One 3,800 member local of the Fur and Leather Workers rejoined the C.I.O. at this time and was made the nucleus of a Leather Workers Organizing Committee (leadership of which was given to R. J. Thomas, former U.A.W. president who was defeated by Walter Reuther in 1946), now the Leather Workers International Union of America, but the bulk of the membership of the former Fur and Leather Workers Union has remained with the Meat Cutters.

[37] Saposs, *op. cit.*, 259.

[38] *Fortune*, March 1956, 206.

[39] See Roger L. Randall, "Labor Agreements in the West Coast Fishing Industry: Restraint of Trade or Basis of Industrial Stability?" *Industrial and Labor Relations Review*, III (July 1950), 514–541, and James A. Crutchfield, "Collective Bargaining in the Pacific Coast Fisheries: the Economic Issues," *Industrial and Labor Relations Review*, VIII (July 1955), 541–556.

National Union of Marine Cooks and Stewards The National Union of Marine Cooks and Stewards (N.U.M.C.S.), which represented cooks and stewards on West Coast ships, was founded as the Marine Cooks and Stewards of the Pacific in 1901 and joined the C.I.O. in the late 1930s. After expulsion in 1950, the C.I.O. turned over this jurisdiction to the National Maritime Union. At the same time the A.F.L. Seafarers International chartered a Marine Cooks and Stewards Division (S.I.U.-M.C.S.) for the specific purpose of capturing this membership.

Neither of these rival unions was successful in gaining an N.L.R.B. election against the N.U.M.C.S. when its contract expired in 1951, and the N.M.U. left the fight shortly thereafter. It had suffered from a lack of organization and had failed to generate any appeal among N.U.M.C.S. members, primarily because of the intense rivalry that has always existed between East and West Coast maritime unions.[40]

The S.I.U.-M.C.S. remained in the contest and finally gained an N.L.R.B. election in 1954. By this time the N.U.M.C.S. faced serious problems; the union treasury was depleted after four years of uninterrupted jurisdictional fighting, and president Hugh Bryson was under indictment for perjury in connection with his Taft-Hartley affidavit.[41] Fearing the N.U.M.C.S.'s imminent end, the I.L.W.U. entered the scene and attempted to organize the membership into its own hastily-created stewards branch. When the N.L.R.B. denied the I.L.W.U. a place on the ballot, both I.L.W.U. and N.U.M.C.S. leaders advised the workers to vote for "no union" rather than either N.U.M.C.S. or S.I.U.-M.C.S., and two thirds of the 2,000 cooks and stewards did so, thereby voting their union out of existence.[42] Another election was held in early 1955, this time between the I.L.W.U. and the S.I.U.; the S.I.U. petitioned the N.L.R.B. to hold the election among all unlicensed West Coast seamen—seamen and firemen as well as cooks and stewards—and the N.L.R.B. agreed to this request. Since the S.I.U. already represented unlicensed seamen and firemen on the West Coast, it was easy for them to defeat the I.L.W.U. by a margin of almost four to one.[43] It is probable that, had the stewards been allowed to vote separately, they would have chosen to join the I.L.W.U.[44]

United Farm Equipment and Metal Workers The United Farm Equipment and Metal Workers Union (F.E.) was established in 1938 by the C.I.O. Although the F.E. attained a membership of over 60,000 after World War II, the U.A.W. clearly dominated the farm machinery industry, representing over 90,000 of the 130,000 farm equipment workers employed in 1949. During the prolonged jurisdictional dispute between these unions from 1945 to 1949, the U.A.W. was able to capture over 20,000 F.E. members[45] and, after the U.E.-F.E. merger and their expulsion from the C.I.O. in 1949, the U.A.W. continued its

[40] The National Maritime Union is primarily an East Coast organization.
[41] Bryson was convicted in May 1955.
[42] For a complete discussion of these events, see Jane C. Record, "The Rise and Fall of a Maritime Union," *Industrial and Labor Relations Review*, X (October 1956), 81–92.
[43] *Ibid.*, 90.
[44] *Ibid.*, 91.
[45] *Fortune*, March 1956, 206.

successful raids on the F.E. membership. Some twenty-seven locals with about 30,000 members left U.E.-F.E. for the U.A.W. between 1949 and the end of 1955.[46] The final collapse of the F.E. came in March 1955 when the International Harvester local, largest remaining in the U.E.-F.E., disaffiliated and joined the U.A.W.[47] Clearly, therefore, the U.A.W. had assimilated almost the entire former F.E. membership.

2. Unions Still in Existence

American Communications Association The American Communications Association (A.C.A.) was formed in 1937 from the American Radio Telegraphists Association, which had been organized in 1931. The union's first president was Mervyn Rathbone who resigned in 1940 and later became secretary-treasurer of the California State C.I.O. organization, which was alleged to be under Communist leadership at that time.[48] He was succeeded in the A.C.A. by Joseph P. Selly, who had been leader of a Trade Union Unity League union of engineers and technicians. (Selly is still president of the A.C.A.[49])

One of the smaller unions in the C.I.O., with a membership of about 10,000 following World War II, the A.C.A. was able to survive because of the chaotic multi-union situation in the communications industry. The C.I.O. anticipated that, following expulsion, the membership of the A.C.A. would be recaptured by the Communications Workers of America and by the American Radio Association, an organization of anti-Communist dissidents that had left the A.C.A. in 1948. The A.C.A. was also threatened by the A.F.L. Commercial Telegraphers Union, which represents similar workers in the communications industry. But despite—or perhaps because of—this competition, the A.C.A. has managed to retain between 7,000 and 8,000 members. The bulk of its membership, some 4,000 workers, is employed at the New York Metropolitan Western Union Offices. The union also represents employees of Western Union International and RCA Communications Corporation. It was unsuccessfully challenged in 1962, by the Commercial Telegraphers Union in an N.L.R.B. election covering the New York Western Union local.

International Union of Mine, Mill and Smelter Workers The International Union of Mine, Mill and Smelter Workers (Mine-Mill) is the primary union of non-ferrous miners in the Western United States and Canada. It is the direct descendant of the colorful Western Federation of Miners, which had an intermittent association with the A.F.L. and the I.W.W. before joining the C.I.O. in 1937.

46 *Ibid.*, 206.

47 *The New York Times*, March 20, 1955, 50.

48 Kampelman, *op. cit.*, 196.

49 Selly and other officers of the A.C.A. were charged with membership in the Communist Party before the Senate Internal Security Committee and the House Un-American Activities Committee. A former vice-president of the union identified Selly as a member of the party in the 1930s. *The New York Times*, July 18, 1957, 2. Nevertheless, in October 1959, Selly reported to the Secretary of Labor that no officer or staff member of the A.C.A. was serving in the union in violation of Section 504 of the Landrum-Griffin Act. *ACA News*, October 1959, 1.

The union president in the late 1930s and early 1940s, Reid Robertson, had a long record of Communist-front activities. He was re-elected president in 1946 in a contested referendum election, despite the fact that he was reportedly unpopular with the members. However, because of this unpopularity and other controversies surrounding him, the union's executive board withdrew its support and Robertson resigned shortly after the election. He was succeeded by vice-president Maurice Travis, who had been expelled from the United Steelworkers Union for Communist activities.[50] Owing to opposition, Travis resigned at the 1947 convention. He was replaced by John Clark, but retained the post of secretary-treasurer, which enabled him to wield the real power in the union. Mine-Mill officers submitted Taft-Hartley affidavits in 1949. Travis, admitting Party membership, resigned "with the utmost reluctance and with a great sense of indignation" in order to sign the affidavit. Subsequently charged with perjury on his affidavit, he was charged with conspiracy to defraud the government by knowingly filing false affidavits.[51] So were thirteen other Mine-Mill officers, including James Durkin, formerly a Mine-Mill organizer, present secretary-treasurer Irving Dichter, and Albert Skinner, who became union president in 1963. (In further legal action, Mine-Mill was the first union to be charged with being "Communist-infiltrated" under the 1954 Communist Control Act.[52])

Membership in Mine-Mill dropped between 1945 and 1950, but it is difficult to know to what extent. Kampelman reports that in 1946–47 some forty to fifty

[50] See Kampelman, *op. cit.*, 177.

[51] Travis was convicted of perjury and sentenced to eight years in prison and fined $8,000. This conviction was reversed in the Tenth Circuit Court of Appeals in 1957 and a new trial ordered. On retrial in 1959 he was again convicted, but the Supreme Court voided his conviction in January 1961, on the grounds that, because the affidavit was originally filed in Washington, D. C., the trial should have been held there instead of in Denver, Colorado. He could not then be retried because of the three-year statute of limitations. *The New York Times*, January 17, 1961, 34. Travis had long before been retired on a pension by the union. Of the fourteen union leaders who were indicted for conspiracy in November, 1956, three pleaded *nolo contendere*, two cases were dismissed for lack of evidence, and nine—including Travis, Durkin, Dichter, and Skinner—were convicted in December 1959, sentenced to up to three years in prison and fined up to $2,000 each. (See *Mine-Mill Union*, April 1960, 1.) These convictions were reversed in Tenth Circuit Court of Appeals in March 1962. The court ruled that testimony of a key witness (concerning statements made by another person about the Communist Party's policy of having unions that were dominated by the party file false affidavits) was heresay. Charges against Durkin and one other officer of the union were dismissed while new trials were ordered for the remaining seven (*The New York Times*, March 6, 1962, 27). On retrial, one was found not guilty, but the other six, including Travis, Dichter and Skinner were found guilty and were sentenced to three years in prison and fined $2,000 each. These convictions have been appealed (*The New York Times*, September 21, 1963, 22).

[52] Charges were brought before the Subversive Activities Control Board by the Attorney General on July 28, 1955, but no action was taken in the case until 1957 and the government did not conclude its case until June 1960. In May 1962, the S.A.C.B. found Mine-Mill to be Communist-infiltrated, stating that, "It is quite clear that many important functionaries of respondent [the union] are and have been members of the Communist Party, and that other important functionaries are persons who are and have been amenable to the Communist Party." (*The New York Times*, May 5, 1962, 12.) These charges would, if upheld, make the union ineligible to represent employees before the N.L.R.B. The union has filed a petition with the S.A.C.B. requesting that the findings be set aside.

locals with 30,000 to 35,000 members, "a fourth of the total," broke away over the Communist issue.[53] Average dues-paying employed membership reported to the C.I.O. (for payment of per capita tax) dropped from slightly over 100,000 in the 1946–47 fiscal year to 44,000 in October 1949.[54] But it is impossible to estimate how much of this decline represented actual loss of membership and how much was deliberate under-reporting.

The C.I.O. entertained the hope that the membership would be taken over primarily by the U.A.W. and also by the United Steelworkers Union (U.S.W.), which had been conducting raids on Mine-Mill with some success in the South and in Minnesota's iron mines, but to little advantage in the non-ferrous mining areas of the Far-West. These two unions did, indeed, report, at the end of 1950, that they had "absorbed practically all of Mine-Mill"; but this statement was entirely untrue.[55]

During the early 1950s the Mine-Mill membership was courted by many unions—the U.A.W., U.S.W., United Mine Workers District 50, the Machinists, and others—but without success. This rivalry among unions, as in the case of the A.C.A., undoubtedly helped Mine-Mill to hold on. Throughout the '50s the union continued to report a membership of 100,000, but the 75,000 reported in 1963 is probably a more realistic figure for the entire period since 1950. Employment in copper, lead, and zinc production suffered in the mid and late '50s as over-production and foreign competition led to shutdowns, short work-weeks, layoffs, and prolonged strikes. Today the membership of Mine-Mill consists of some 30,000 copper miners employed primarily by the Anaconda, Kennecott, Revere and Phelps-Dodge companies in this country, about 30,000 miners in Canada,[56] and smaller numbers of lead and zinc miners.

Despite its relative success in retaining its membership, Mine-Mill has felt isolated and exposed as an independent union and has sought to return to the A.F.L.-C.I.O. In 1955 merger talks were held with the Steelworkers, Machinists, and Laborers unions, but in each case Mine-Mill was refused.[57] Mine-Mill has also sought a merger with the A.F.L. Metal Trades Department, the Molders, and the Operating Engineers without result.[58] In 1956 Mine-Mill signed a five-year mutual assistance pact with the Western Conference of Teamsters which was renewed in 1961, but this has not led to any formal affiliation.

[53] Kampelman, *op. cit.*, 183.

[54] *Ibid.*, 186.

[55] *Monthly Labor Review*, Volume 74 (January 1951), 11. In January 1954, the leaders of the Butte and Anaconda, Montana, locals, largest in Mine-Mill with a combined membership of over 7,000 at the time, took their locals out of Mine-Mill and into the U.S.W. However, this action was approved at a meeting of only 10 percent of the membership and in the subsequent N.L.R.B. election the members voted 2 to 1 to remain in Mine-Mill. See *Fortune*, February 1954, 82.

[56] Mine-Mill was also expelled by the Canadian Congress of Labor on grounds of Communist-domination. For a time during the 1950s the union made gains in Canada, but in recent years the Steelworkers have captured some of this membership. The most notable Steelworkers victory was won in 1962 at the International Nickel Corporation plant at Sudbury, Ontario, in an election involving over 14,000 employees. In this case the U.S.W. was able to win a close election only because of support from the Teamsters Union. See *Business Week*, July 17, 1962, 74–76.

[57] *Fortune*, March 1956, 206.

[58] Saposs, *op. cit.*, 255.

International Longshoremen's and Warehousemen's Union The I.L.W.U. was created in 1933 when the various West Coast longshoremen's locals were chartered by the International Longshoremen's Association (I.L.A.), which had been up to that time—as it remains today—primarily an East Coast organization. Harry Bridges, who had come to this country from Australia in 1920, rose to prominence in the West Coast maritime strike of 1934 and was elected West Coast president of I.L.A. in 1936. In June 1937, he led the West Coast organization out of the I.L.A. and into the C.I.O.

Of all the expelled unions the I.L.W.U. was probably the least affected by competition from other unions. No new organization was chartered by the C.I.O. to cover its jurisdiction and the I.L.A. "was thoroughly discredited, and its lackadaisical leadership was dis-interested in undertaking such a gigantic task."[59] There were some signs of a membership revolt against the union officers immediately following the expulsion, but they came to nothing; and Bridges and other I.L.W.U. leaders have retained their position despite extended prosecutions for alleged Communist affiliations.[60]

The I.L.W.U. today reports a membership of 60,000, only slightly below that of the pre-1950 period. While the present figure may be slightly overstated, it is nonetheless true that the I.L.W.U. has not suffered any loss of membership to A.F.L.-C.I.O. unions. Any decline has been due to the fact that the union has not been able to expand its membership into warehousing, while the number of jobs in longshoring and in the Hawaiian sugar and pineapple industries has declined

[59] *Ibid.*, 208.

[60] The Federal Government initiated an attempt to have Bridges deported as a Communist in 1939. In 1941 a Federal Immigration Commissioner ruled him a Communist and ordered him deported, but on appeal the Supreme Court cancelled this order in June 1945. On September 17, 1945, Bridges became a naturalized citizen of the United States and in 1949 he was indicted for perjury for swearing, when naturalized, that he had never been a member of the Communist Party. J. R. Robertson, I.L.G.W.U., first vice-president, and Henry Schmidt, I.L.G.W.U. international representative, were simultaneously charged with conspiracy as Bridges' character witnesses (*The New York Times*, April 2, 1950, IV., 1.). All three were convicted in April 1950; Bridges was sentenced to five years in prison; Schmidt and Robertson to two years each. In June 1953, the Supreme Court overturned this conviction on the ground that the three-year statute of limitations had expired before the indictments were delivered. (*The New York Times*, June 16, 1953, 1.). In December 1953, the government reopened civil proceedings to have Bridges deported on the ground that the naturalization decree had been obtained fraudulently, but in July 1955 the court found for Bridges, stating that "an exacting standard [of evidence]" was not met by the kind of witnesses which the government produced. (*The New York Times*, July 30, 1955, 1.) The Justice Department decided not to appeal this decision, admitting that "This closes out the Bridges case so far as the government is concerned." (*The New York Times*, October 1, 1955, 22.) Other officers of the union have also been prosecuted for alleged Communist Party membership. The head of the New Orleans local was convicted, in September 1956, of filing a false Taft-Hartley affidavit. Jack Hall, the union's regional director for Hawaii, was convicted of violation of the Smith Act in 1953, but the decision was reversed in 1958. Archie Brown, a member of the executive board of Local 10, was convicted, in April 1962, of having been a member of the Communist Party within the past five years while holding union office in violation of Section 504 of the Landrum-Griffin Act. (His was the first case tried under this section.) In an important decision the Ninth Circuit Court of Appeals overturned the conviction, holding the law unconstitutional as an invalid restraint on freedom of association. (*The New York Times*, November 19, 1964, 39.)

because of mechanization.[61] Present membership is divided roughly equally among three sectors: one-third in longshoring, one-third in warehousing, and one-third in the sugar and pineapple industries of Hawaii.[62] The I.L.W.U. maintains contracts with the Pacific Maritime Association, the major Hawaiian sugar and pineapple companies, and also represents Alaskan longshoremen, fishermen, and cold-storage and cannery workers. The union also has small locals of warehousemen in various inland cities.

While the I.L.W.U. has been able to retain its membership and bargaining strength as an independent union, it has made several attempts to re-enter the A.F.L.-C.I.O.[63] It had conducted merger negotiations with the Teamsters Union on various occasions during the '50s,[64] and Bridges at one time attempted "to insinuate his union into a merger with the International Longshoremen's Association."[65]

United Electrical, Radio and Machine Workers (UE) Organized by the C.I.O. in 1936, the U.E. drew upon company unions already established in the electrical equipment industry. The leaders of these company unions were not particularly well-entrenched and this provided an opportunity for Communist infiltration of the new organization. However, while James Matles, director of organization, and Julius Emspak, secretary-treasurer, came into the union from the Trade Union Unity League, the first president of the U.E. was James B. Carey, who has been long known as an outspoken anti-Communist. Alarmed at the increasing Communist influence within the union, Carey attempted to push a resolution through the union's 1941 convention that would allow locals to exclude Communists from office. But the resolution was defeated, and Carey was ousted from his own office.

[61] The I.L.W.U. has gained considerable favorable publicity for the agreement which it reached in October 1960, with the Pacific Maritime Association (the organization of West Coast ocean shippers) on mechanization of the waterfront. In exchange for giving up its restrictive work rules covering the introduction of new machinery, the number of men in longshoring gangs, the amount of cargo carried per crane load, the needless breaking down and restacking of pallets, etc., the union won the right to share in the savings from mechanization. The companies have paid to the union $5 million per year for five and one-half years beginning January 1, 1961. (A $1½ million pilot project was in effect in 1959–60.) The fund is used to provide a guaranteed thirty-five hour week for longshoremen and to pay early retirement benefits beginning at age sixty-five to those desiring them. For further details see *The New York Times*, May 27, 1963, 1; Max D. Kossoris, "Working Rules in West Coast Longshoring," *Monthly Labor Review* (January 1961), Vol. 84, 1–10; William Glazier, "Automation and the Longshoremen, A West Coast Solution," *The Atlantic*, Vol. 206 (December 1960), 57–61; and Charles C. Killingsworth, "The Modernization of West Coast Longshore Work Rules," *Industrial and Labor Relations Review*, XV (April 1962), 295–306.

[62] The I.L.W.U. now has an estimated 23,000 members in Hawaii, of whom some 21,000 are employed in the pineapple and sugar industries. While it had an estimated 30,000 members in Hawaii at the end of World War II, it is still by far the largest union in the state and is a potent economic and political force there. *Business Week*, September 7, 1963, 86.

[63] I.L.W.U. and A.F.L.-C.I.O. unions in Hawaii have been cooperating under a pact reached in 1962. *Business Week, op. cit.*, 92.

[64] *Fortune*, September 1958, 216.

[65] Saposs, *op. cit.*, 256. See also *Monthly Labor Review*, Vol. 82 (May 1959), 556.

He was succeeded by Albert Fitzgerald, who is still president of the U.E. Carey remained in the union as a local officer for a time, but soon was made C.I.O. secretary-treasurer and ceased to play an active role.[66]

At its peak following World War II, the U.E. had a membership of over 500,000, making it by far the largest of the expelled unions, but this membership fell away rapidly in the late 1940s. Hoping to recapture the U.E.'s entire rank and file, the C.I.O. chartered the International Union of Electrical Workers (I.U.E.) in November 1949. (The presidency of the I.U.E. was given to James Carey.) The I.U.E. reported a membership of 265,000 by 1952[67] and 425,000 in 1957.[68] In recent years, however, the I.U.E.'s membership has declined from the 400,000 level to under 300,000,[69] while the reported figures for the U.E. have actually indicated a gain in membership—from 100,000 in 1955–56 to 160,000 in the period 1957–1962.[70] While the initial decline of the U.E. was undoubtedly a crippling blow to the Communist Party's hopes of achieving and retaining real power in the American labor movement, and while the U.E. has been forced out of many of the General Electric and Westinghouse Electric plants where the bulk of its membership was once located,[71] it seems to have held on to about twenty to twenty-five percent of its original membership and perhaps to have slightly increased its membership in recent years; this despite sustained attacks from the I.U.E., the International Brotherhood of Electrical Workers, the Machinists, the U.A.W. and the U.S.W.

U.E. leadership has been under repeated government attack for alleged Communist activities. In December 1955, it became the second union to be charged

[66] Other anti-Communist members of the union formed the "U.E. Members for Democratic Action" in 1947 but their slate of officers was defeated by a margin of eight to one at the convention of that year. They were weakened in their fight by the fact that many entire locals were pulling out of U.E. to join the U.A.W. or the International Brotherhood of Electrical Workers (I.B.E.W.) of the A.F.L. See Kampelman, *op. cit.*, 132.

[67] *I.U.E. Workers Convention Report, 1952*, 339.

[68] *I.U.E. Workers Convention Report, 1957*, 219.

[69] Bureau of Labor Statistics Bulletin No. 1395, *op. cit.*, 18.

[70] The jump in U.E.-reported membership from 100,000 in 1955–56 to 160,000 for 1957–58 and subsequent years may have reflected a shift in reporting from actual membership to number of workers represented in collective bargaining agreement. (I.U.E. leaders estimated that U.E. membership was only about 75,000 in 1956 and less than 60,000 in 1957. See *I.U.E. Workers Convention Report, 1956*, 361, and *I.U.E. Workers Convention Report, 1957*, 219.) While the reported U.E. figure remained at about 160,000 between 1957–58 and 1961–62, U.E. leaders claimed a gain in contract representation of 55,000 between 1958 and 1964. See "Against the Mainstream: .Interview with James Matles of the U.E.," *Studies on the Left*, V, No. 1 (Winter 1965), 54. In September 1964, the U.E. claimed to *represent* 164,000 workers but admitted that dues-paying membership was about 100,000. (See *The New York Times*, September 15, 1964, 25.) These figures are admittedly conflicting (and perhaps confusing) but they do indicate that U.E. has at least held its own or slightly increased its membership in the past eight years.

[71] U.E. represented an estimated 100,000 GE employees before 1950. Following N.L.R.B. elections in 1950, I.U.E. had taken over 53,000 of these while U.E. still represented some 36,000. See *Communist Domination of Unions and National Security*, Hearings before a Sub-Committee of the Committee on Labor and Public Welfare, U. S. Senate, 82nd Congress, 2nd Session, 1952, 436. In 1960 U.E. was reported to represent about 57,000 GE and Westinghouse employees. (See *The New York Times*, September 13, 1960, 37).

with being "Communist-infiltrated." S.A.C.B. hearings were held in 1957 and 1958, but the charges were dropped in 1959 because certain key witnesses were unavailable and because a number of those whose membership had prompted the action had left the union.[72] Several U.E. officers have been tried and convicted of Communist affiliations, but most of these convictions have been set aside by higher courts.[73]

Although the U.E. has continued to launch bitter attacks at the C.I.O., the A.F.L., and especially the I.U.E., it has still sought to merge with other A.F.L.-C.I.O. unions. It approached the United Mine Workers, the Machinists, the Teamsters, and the I.U.E. in 1955, and also attempted to affiliate with the A.F.L., but was rebuffed in each instance.[74] In 1956 the U.E. offered to join the I.U.E. as an autonomous unit, but Carey stated that he would accept only the incorporation of U.E. members into existing I.U.E. locals and the negotiations collapsed.[75] (The U.E. is still seeking unity with the other major unions in the electrical and machine industry.[76])

V

Since this paper has dealt with events since 1950 and their impact, no conclusions are advanced concerning the initial entry of Communists and Communist-sympathizers into the C.I.O.[77] But a few conclusions may be drawn about the expulsions and their immediate aftermath.

First, it did seem inevitable that Communist and non-Communist elements within the C.I.O. should fall out after the war. Aside from the fact that many C.I.O. leaders were themselves ideologically opposed to Communism, most of them were able to perceive that organizations accused of being either pro-Communist or Communist-infiltrated would face serious and increasing difficulties in post-war America. The final break came not because the C.I.O. could tolerate no internal dissent from its official position on such largely peripheral issues as

[72] *The New York Times*, March 25, 1959, 8, and *Ibid.*, April 1, 1959, 29.

[73] Albert Fitzgerald, U.E. president, has not been accused of membership in the Communist Party. James Matles and Julius Emspak, director of organization and secretary-treasurer of U.E. respectively, were cited for contempt by a New York Federal Grand Jury in 1951 for failing to answer questions concerning alleged membership in the Communist Party, but the charges were later dismissed. Emspak was indicted and convicted of contempt of Congress for failing to answer questions of the House Un-American Activities Committee but the conviction was set aside by the Supreme Court in 1955. (Emspak died in April 1962, and was succeeded as secretary-treasurer by Matles). Matles was charged with falsely swearing that he was not a Communist when he was naturalized in 1934, and proceedings were undertaken in 1952 to deport him to his native Rumania. His citizenship was revoked in 1957, but his denaturalization was reversed by the Supreme Court in 1958. See *The New York Times*, March 27, 1957, 18, and *Ibid.*, April 8, 1958, 1. In a long-drawn-out case, John T. Gojack, a U.E. vice-president, was convicted in 1955 of contempt of Congress for failing to answer questions of a House Un-American Activities Sub-Committee. His conviction was overturned by the Supreme Court in May 1962, but he was re-convicted in October 1963, and his case is again under appeal.

[74] *Fortune*, June 1955, 61.

[75] *AFL-CIO News*, May 12, 1965.

[76] See "Against the Mainstream: . . ." *op. cit.*, 54.

[77] See Kampelman, *op. cit.*, Ch. 2. and Saposs, *op. cit.*, Chs. 13 and 14.

the Marshall Plan, the Atlantic Pact, the Greek Civil War, the Berlin Airlift, etc., but because the Communists and pro-Communists within the C.I.O. were making statements on such matters which could be (and were) interpreted by the public to represent the official C.I.O. position. Given the attitudes which prevailed in this country between 1948 and 1954, it would have been extremely difficult for an organization such as the C.I.O. to refuse to take action against known and suspected Communists within its ranks.[78] C.I.O. leaders did at first try reconciliation and compromise, but "that moment arrived when the domestic and international situation no longer brooked reconciliation."[79] Personal rivalries were also involved, to be sure, but primarily between pro-Communist and anti-Communist leadership factions within individual unions, rather than between Communist union leaders and the non-Communists on the C.I.O. Executive Board.

Secondly, the C.I.O. was forced to take some action against the Communists within its own house because Section 9h of the Taft-Hartley Act had largely failed to accomplish its purpose—to drive the Communist leaders out of the union movement. The affidavit was couched in the present tense; a union leader had only to swear that he "*is* not a member of the Communist Party." It was a simple matter for an individual to formally resign from the Party one day and to execute the affidavit the next day, and thus to remain technically within the law, a course followed by a number of Party members. (Some Communists resigned from the Party in order to remain in the union movement, but very few did the reverse.)

Third, once action was contemplated, the C.I.O. did not seem to seriously consider any alternative. The expulsions were carried out with such dispatch that the memberships could not possibly have been galvanized to the point of throwing off their leaders or leaving their unions for others: the threat of expulsion, so shortly before the fact, had no time to sink in. Why did the C.I.O. resort to actually expelling these unions, whose memberships were almost entirely non-Communist, in order to eliminate a few hundred or a few thousand Communist leaders? No entirely satisfactory answer can be offered. On the one hand, the C.I.O. constitution precluded direct interference in the internal affairs of member unions. Pressures of various sorts could have been applied, but an actual purge from above of national and local union officers would have been virtually impossible. Equally important, the C.I.O. did hope to recover later at least the majority of expelled union members.

This brings us to the final question concerning these expulsions: Could the C.I.O. have held a reasonable expectation of recapturing the entire expelled membership? The answer, based on the C.I.O.'s own actions, is clearly no. In only three cases—the U.E., the U.O.P.W.A. and the U.P.W.—did the C.I.O.

[78] While outside forces, such as public opinion, were vitally important, Kampelman undoubtedly overstates the situation when he says, "Not only was the integrity and survival of the trade union heritage at stake but more important was the national self-interest of the United States. For the C.I.O. to have remained aloof from the battle between Communism and democracy would have stopped it from playing any significant role on the American scene." Kampleman, *op. cit.*, 249. The C.I.O. also overstated in claiming that, "To put it bluntly—and factually—the C.I.O. in a year has broken the back of the Communist Party in the United States." *CIO News*, November 20, 1950, 4.

[79] Saposs, *op. cit.*, 225.

charter new unions, and in each of these cases the initial developments were, as stated above, favorable to the C.I.O.'s interests, although not always as anticipated. In five other instances, the jurisdictions were turned over to already-existing C.I.O. unions, but in only one did the assigned union successfully recover the membership for the C.I.O.—that of U.A.W. in its F.E. raids. Various C.I.O. unions made inroads on the former jurisdiction of the F.T.A.A.W. (and the remaining members returned to the C.I.O. through the D.P.O.W.U.), but other C.I.O. unions met with little success against the A.C.A., Mine-Mill, or the N.U.M.C.S. Finally, in the cases of the I.L.W.U. (and the Fishermens Union which merged with it) and the Fur and Leather Workers, no C.I.O. union was ever given explicit jurisdiction—some 150,000 or more C.I.O. members were seemingly written off completely.

With respect to events following the expulsions, an important question to ask is: Why did some of the expelled unions disappear quickly, while others remained in existence? The issue of Communism, it could be argued, played only an indirect role in these events. The rank-and-file of these (and of other) unions had not been noticeably stirred by the charge of Communist-infiltration; they have, in fact, played a largely passive role in the fight against Communists within their unions.[80] For one thing, they had heard the epithet "red" or "radical" frequently used to castigate their leaders. Like the proverbial cry of "wolf," these epithets had been used too frequently to have retained any real meaning. Moreover, union members seemed able to "compartmentalize their loyalties"[81]—to support their leaders on collective bargaining issues while ignoring their political recommendations. As Leiter has expressed it:

> *"Like the rank and file workers in other industries, members of the Fur Union are concerned with immediate improvements and pay little heed to the ultimate goals and objectives of the union leadership. The fact that Communists dominate the union has not frightened members. . . . Nor are they deeply interested in the part that the union plays in the larger labor movement, as long as wages go up, hours go down, and working conditions improve."*[82]

In other words, members are concerned first and foremost with obtaining that leadership which best serves their economic interests. And, while the Communists in the labor movement may have been Communists first and labor leaders second, they worked as hard as most other labor leaders to advance the economic interests of their members.[83] Union members generally support those leaders that have

[80] ". . . even when the charges are scandalous and the leader and his organization are alleged to be involved in unethical or perhaps unpatriotic practices, it may be difficult to stir the rank and file to action, so long as its special interests are not seriously affected." Saposs, *op. cit.*, 219.

[81] Kampelman, *op. cit.*, 253.

[82] Robert D. Leiter, "The Fur Workers Union," *op. cit.*, 186.

[83] In collective bargaining negotiations there was little to distinguish the approach of the Communist from that of the non-Communist labor leader—certainly the Communists were not obviously attempting to overthrow capitalism. In a slightly different connection, dealing with strikes, Philip Taft has stated, ". . . once in control of a union, Communist officers and their fellow travellers are not necessarily more militant in pursuing their aims, nor do Communist-officered unions engage in more strikes than do those officered by non- or anti-Communists."

"produced" in the past and that show promise of "producing" in the future. In general, those unions which succeeded in capturing members from an expelled union were the ones which promised a future performance on economic issues exceeding that which the rank-and-file could reasonably expect from its present union—because of size, effectiveness of leadership, relationship with management, freedom from legal harassment, etc.

While the membership of the expelled unions may have been apathetic over the Communist issues, their leadership was frequently weakened by it, and thus were made more vulnerable to raiding. For their officers were indicted and tried and, in some cases, fined and jailed for their Communist or alleged Communist affiliation; and all of these legal actions limited, to some degree, their effectiveness as active union leaders. In addition, union funds were exhausted in the legal defense of these officers and, finally, the unions were weakened when managements chose whether on ideological grounds or not, to cooperate with rival unions.[84]

We can further examine the surviving unions individually to analyze the factors which seem to have contributed to their survival.[85] First, the I.L.W.U., which has had a highly dynamic and effective leadership and, significantly, no rival union to challenge this leadership. Harry Bridges is today widely regarded as one of the most effective, perhaps even one of the most respected, labor leaders in the country. Further, the I.L.W.U. membership, at least in longshoring, constitutes, in Kerr and Siegel's term, "an isolated mass—a race apart."[86] Its members, that is, live in their own "community" with its own codes and social standards. The group is largely homogeneous because there is little occupational stratification; and it is immune to public opinion, being isolated from the public at large. Thus detached, the longshoring worker (on both the West and the East Coast) has been indifferent to the charges hurled at his union and its officials.

The leadership of Mine-Mill is generally acknowledged to have been less effec-

---

Philip Taft, "Ideologies and Industrial Conflict," in Arthur Kornhauser, Robert Dubin and Arthur M. Ross, editors, *Industrial Conflict* (New York, McGraw-Hill, 1954), 263.

[84] The entire subject of management relationships with the expelled unions is discussed in Saposs, *op. cit.*, Ch. 22. He deals primarily with the U.E.-I.U.E.-G.E. situation which was, to say the least, confused—both unions accused GE of favoring the other. GE probably leaned toward I.U.E. but not entirely on ideological grounds; this I.U.E.-U.E. rivalry has undoubtedly strengthened GE's hand in collective bargaining. In most instances management has quite naturally pursued its own economic interests. "Employers . . . were influenced primarily in their attitude toward Communists by immediate, practical considerations of plant harmony, advantageous labor relations, and effect on business prospects, rather than by the principle or ethics of having dealings with Communists." *Ibid.*, 227. In some cases employers were accused of favoring the Communist union on the ground that it was the weaker and thus easier to deal with. "Mine, Mill has been to a degree preferred by managements which reason that a weak Mine, Mill, even if dominated by the left wing, is to be desired over a more powerful unionism tied to the steel industry . . . the truth is that many managements throughout the industry, when speaking frankly, have said they prefer to bargain with Mine, Mill because it is relatively weak." Vernon H. Jensen, *Nonferrous Metals Industry Unionism*, 1932–1954 (Ithaca, N. Y., Cornell University Press, 1954), 305.

[85] The A.C.A. is not included in this discussion.

[86] Clark Kerr and Abraham Siegel, "The Interindustry Propensity to Strike—An International Comparison," in Kornhauser, Dubin and Ross, *op. cit.*, 191.

tive than the I.L.W.U.'s, but its members afford an even better example of an "isolated mass." In many western mining communities, the union hall is the center of social activity for the member and his family. In voting to change his union affiliation the worker would be undertaking to change an entire set of social and cultural relationships. Furthermore, Mine-Mill carried a long tradition of being the only union in its industry. The non-ferrous miners finally considered themselves to be distinct from coal miners or steelworkers and took pride in the militant history of their union. Their leaders had been radicals of one stripe or another from the days of "Big Bill" Haywood to the present, and called "reds" so often that the rank-and-file is unmoved by such charges. (A useful closing observation is that several unions have attempted raids on Mine-Mill, but the miners have still been at times able to cooperate with them in collective bargaining.)[87]

While the I.L.W.U. and Mine-Mill cases contain certain obvious features, the continued survival of the U.E. is perhaps more paradoxical and, therefore possibly more interesting. Obviously the U.E. has not been a complete success over the past fifteen years, but neither has it been a complete failure, and in recent years it seems to have made something of a comeback while the I.U.E. has been floundering.[88] It would be useful to discover just how the U.E. has been able to hold on to a hard-core membership and extend its appeal to some new members, despite the concerted efforts of the I.U.E., and U.A.W., and the I.B.E.W.[89]

No general answer to this question is attempted here, but a few comments are offered. The U.E. is a democratic union, as unions go, and its leaders seem dedicated and hard-working.[90] It employs only a relatively small number of organizers, relying primarily on the rank-and-file to spread organization in their immediate vicinity. It appeals to new members entirely in terms of local economic issues rather than ideologies.[91] For a further explanation of U.E. tenacity, historians will have to look elsewhere; perhaps sociologists and psychologists can help.

[87] Mine-Mill has repeatedly engaged in joint bargaining with the Metal Trades Unions, the railroad unions and even the U.S.W.

[88] As stated above, I.U.E. lost over 100,000 members between 1955–56 and 1961–62. I.U.E. has suffered a series of reverses in collective bargaining, particularly its capitulation to GE following a three-week strike in 1960. In the past three years the union has been torn by dissension among its leaders, culminating in the recent defeat of President Carey for re-election.

[89] The U.E. claims to have organized more than 125 new plants between 1958 and the end of 1964. (See "Against the Mainstream . . ." *op. cit.*, 54.) The reported number of U.E. locals increased from 115 in 1955–56 to 140 in 1961–62. (See Bureau of Labor Statistics Bulletin No. 1222, *op. cit.*, 33 and Bureau of Labor Statistics Bulletin No. 1395, *op. cit.*, 18,) The U.E. might face much more serious competition if Walter Reuther's recently proposed merger of the U.A.W. and I.U.E. were to take place. See *The New York Times*, February 10, 1965, 1.

[90] The U.E. constitution provides that no officer or employee of the union can earn more than the highest paid workman in the industry.

[91] "We find out what issues are bothering them, and contrast our program with that of other unions. We try to be specific. We use our contracts we've won in other places. We don't argue history, we try to show them how we work on specific issues." "Against the Mainstream . . ." *op. cit.*, 54.

29

THE FREEMAN ADMINISTRATION AND THE POOR

Don F. Hadwiger

American agriculture in the postwar period exhibited in acute form trends that were evident in the depressing decades prior to the conflict. By the 1970's no more than 10 percent of the American people lived on farms. Although more land was put into agricultural production, the number of farms continually declined. The average size of farms grew steadily larger, as small-scale operations became increasingly obsolete. Technological developments had made it impossible for unmechanized units to compete. In the postwar period rural electrification, just getting underway on a large scale in the New Deal period, brought power to more than 95 percent of the nation's farms, and widespread use of chemicals for plant nutrition, pesticides, and feed additives greatly added to production costs. Meanwhile, federal controls, emanating from the New Deal, eliminated many of the risks, especially for the large-scale farmers. Price and income support, in addition to soil conservation programs, stabilized for the established big operators one of man's most speculative occupations. The capital required to operate a farm, however, led some farm leaders to express fear for the future of farming operations on what once was traditionally called the family-sized farm. The dilemma of the surplus, eased somewhat through federal programs, continued to be a vexing problem for some farmers. American agriculture in the war and immediate postwar period, had enjoyed the most prosperous period in its history, but by the 1960's segments of rural America were experiencing economic conditions comparable to those of the Great Depression. Moreover, as this article makes clear, the abundance of American agriculture was not helping to combat poverty.

Initiated during the Kennedy administration, and loudly proclaimed as part of Lyndon Johnson's Great Society, was the War on Poverty. Included in it was a youth program designed to provide young people with job training, an urban and rural community action program, and a program attacking rural poverty. Although the poverty war achieved

Source: *Agricultural History,* Vol. 45, No. 1 (1971), pp. 21–32. Reprinted by permission of the author and the Agricultural History Society.

notable successes, it failed to assist many people in their efforts to improve their conditions within the framework of the American system.

Don F. Hadwiger is a professor of political science at Iowa State University. He is interested in "Civil Rights in the U.S. Department of Agriculture" and has presented papers and prepared articles on this theme with particular emphasis on the 1960's. He is the author of a recent book, Federal Wheat Commodity Programs *(Ames, 1970). In 1965 he was a research scholar in the U.S. Department of Agriculture.*

In May and June of 1968 a weeks-long demonstration took place outside the United States Department of Agriculture. It was one manifestation of the Poor People's campaign, and it came on the heels of Washington's major slum riot. Most of the demonstrators were black, and poor.

This was a most awkward confrontation for the liberal leadership of the USDA. The managers of the Poor People's campaign were not there to plead the cause of civil rights, but rather to bring to Secretary of Agriculture Orville Freeman's attention the victims of departmental policies. In 1967 the President's Commission on Rural Poverty had said "This nation has been largely oblivious to these 14 million impoverished people left behind in rural America . . . Instead of combating low incomes of rural people [agricultural programs] have helped to create wealthy landowners while bypassing the rural poor."[1] "Major programs have been discriminating against the poor farmers since the 1930's," wrote Charles Hardin for the National Advisory Commission on Food and Fiber, and he added, "Who will estimate the cost to the ideals that are supposed to make this country great?"[2]

The USDA's major benefits went mainly to those with "viable" commercial farms ($10,000 or more in sales), which included only about one percent of all Negro farmers.[3] Farm workers, as contrasted with farm owners and farm operators, received virtually no benefits from the Department of Agriculture, which meant that most Mexican-Americans were left out. In addition to class and occupational discrimination, according to careful observers, there existed explicit, pervasive, and unremitting race discrimination, both in employment and in services provided.

Leaders of the Poor People's campaign had a gut-awareness of this record, as indicated in their demands for an end to big farmer subsidies, for loans to small farmer cooperatives, for improvements in farm laborers' bargaining position, and for implementation of the recommendations of the U.S. Civil Rights Commission. But the protracted demonstrations at the USDA were intended to center attention on the hunger issue. Presumably Reverend Ralph Abernathy and other

[1] *The People Left Behind,* Report by the President's National Advisory Commission on Rural Poverty (Washington, D.C.: G.P.O., Sept. 1967), p. ix.

[2] Charles M. Hardin, *Food and Fiber in the Nation's Politics,* vol. 3 of the Technical Papers for the National Advisory Commission on Food and Fiber (Washington, D.C.: G.P.O., August 1967), p. 19.

[3] Of 868,908 farmers with sales of $10,000 or more, 7,036 were nonwhite operators living in the South, according to U.S. Department of Commerce, Bureau of Census, *1964 U.S. Census of Agriculture,* vol. 2, chap. 6, table 25; and chap. 8, table 26.

leaders felt the hunger problem was most urgent and most salient. They believed Freeman had the power to provide immediate substantial relief and that, since he was a liberal, he could be persuaded to do so. They were wrong.

Control over the programs at issue lay not mainly with Freeman but with senior members of three committees of the Congress. The agriculture committees of both houses, and the Agriculture Subcommittee of the House Appropriations Committee had been headed for many years by southerners representative of the white aristocracy, and of the commercial farmer class that had emerged in all great agricultural regions in the past three decades.

The rural achievers who captured the economic benefits of new technology were also competent to bend government to their ends. Government provided them bargaining power vis-à-vis other segments of the economy, and gave them a control over their workers which was quite extraordinary for the times. Inadvertently farm programs hastened the demise of the noncommercial farmer competitors. Yet the direct and indirect subsidies to the rural minority of commercial farmers were justified to the nation as based on the needs of all rural people. "It ain't the first time somebody has been used," said a USDA official, but American history probably reveals no more flagrant example. A measure of how well the system had socialized its functionaries was Freeman's statement scolding the Poor People's leaders for criticizing acreage subsidy programs: "When the farmer loses," he explained, "it is the poor, small farmer who suffers most."[4]

Substantial efforts to help the "forgotten man" were simply not tolerated, although the USDA has never been without a casual sprinkling of token projects. The civil rights revolution exposed the severe class discrimination which both Negroes and poor whites had experienced, and emphasized the Jim Crow practices under which Negroes alone had suffered.

The Department of Agriculture had indeed grown up white, like most American institutions. On the race issue it was rural southern white, because federal policy for each of the great agricultural regions had been written largely by its own representatives, and few black people farmed outside the South. Black colleges and black extension workers existed mainly to permit an easy exclusion of blacks from the regular system.

In Freeman's time the phalanx of southerners dominating each congressional agriculture committee wished to use the resources and jurisdiction of their federal agency to resist the civil rights revolution, and also to resist most aspects of the anti-poverty programs. Even the domestic food-assistance programs were to be used only to dispose of farm surpluses, to maintain a compliant and low-cost work force, and to bargain for urban votes on farm bills. This intent is revealed in a statement by Jamie Whitten, Chairman of the House Appropriations Subcommittee, speaking during the Benson era:

> *I am now of the opinion that the only way that we can get the Department to move fast enough to protect the farm prices and the income of the farmer is once again to transfer Section 32 funds[5] to the school lunch program so that they will have to use them.*[6]

[4] Letter from Freeman to Reverend Ralph Abernathy, 23 May 1968, copy in USDA history files.

[5] Section 32 funds are derived from tariff receipts and are for the purpose of increasing the use of U.S. farm products.

[6] U.S. Congress, House, Committee on Appropriations, *Department of Agri-*

Ten years later House Agriculture Committee member Paul Jones, from Missouri's cotton boot heel, voiced his and his chairman's warning against making concessions to the Poor People's campaign:

> *The thing is, as Mr. Poage said this morning, there are people like that big buck down at the city who said that he went to the so-called resurrection city to get away from that shovel. Well, I am getting tired of that, myself.*[7]

Orville Freeman as Secretary of Agriculture might at some point have challenged these men on these issues. But President Kennedy's first instructions to him were "Placate them," because Kennedy needed southern congressional votes on matters of higher priority than agricultural reform. At a crucial moment years later, Freeman got similar orders from President Johnson.[8]

Freeman moved right at the beginning to gain the complete confidence of Allen Ellender, a segregationist, conservative Democat from Louisiana, chairman of the Senate Agriculture and Forestry Committee; moderate Democrat Harold Cooley, chairman of the House Agriculture Committee; and Cooley's vice-chairman, W. R. Poage of Texas, an outspoken segregationist. Freeman also gained and maintained a good relationship with Mississippi Congressman Jamie Whitten, chairman of the Appropriations Subcommittee, who was an opponent of race-mixing, with a streak of paternalism. With support from these men Freeman achieved a major objective of the agricultural establishment—control of the surplus which had accumulated during the Benson era.

One partial solution of the surplus problem was to send large amounts of commodities overseas as food aid. Overseas shipments in 1965 and 1966 prevented severe famine in India, with incalculable benefits. Freeman weathered severe criticism from producers because he insisted on a safe margin of world wheat supplies.

Besides preventing famines Freeman sought developmental uses for surpluses sent abroad. In foreign food aid Freeman had found his mission. "Victory in [the War Against Hunger]," he said, "will save more lives than have been lost in all the wars of history."[9] But at home there were new moral and legal commitments that certainly posed a dilemma for a liberal Secretary of Agriculture whose President wished the USDA not to antagonize segregationists and conservatives. The federal government had discovered the "other Americans." Title VI of the Civil Rights Act of 1964 required integration in agency employment and services. In 1967 and 1968 domestic hunger became a major issue.

At least four initiatives seemed in order, given the resources of the Department, and the needs of the nation: to describe the conditions of poverty in rural America, and experiment with remedies; to seek a more equitable distribution of existing program benefits; to institute racial integration in USDA agencies and services;

---

culture Appropriations for 1959, Hearings, before a subcommittee of the Committee on Appropriations, 85th Cong., 2 sess., 1958, p. 1413.

[7] U.S. Congress, House, Committee on Agriculture, *Amend the Food Stamp Act of 1964, Hearings,* 90th Cong., 2 sess., 1968, p. 11.

[8] Nick Kotz, *Let Them Eat Promises* (Englewood Cliffs, N.J.: Prentice-Hall, 1969), pp. 147–92.

[9] U.S. Congress, House, Committee on Agriculture, *World War on Hunger, Hearings,* 89th Cong., 2 sess., 1966, p. 188.

and to develop adequate family food assistance and school lunch programs. What Freeman actually did in each of these areas will be discussed, beginning with the research and experimentation initiative.

To gain information about the problems of rural America, and to find solutions, was a mandate of the Hatch Act, from whose subsidies a magnificent research establishment was developed in the land-grant colleges and then in the USDA. The Act provided for research on "the problems of agriculture in its broadest aspects and such investigations which have for their purpose the development and improvement of the rural home and rural life, and the maximum contribution of agriculture to the welfare of the consumer, as may be deemed advisable, having due regard to the varying conditions and needs of the respective states."[10] For more than half a century since then, agricultural research has been "pragmatic," in the sense that it has operated without social perspectives, and in response to bureaucratic and political pressures. The research product was appraised by a committee of insiders in 1965. They found much research on agricultural production, and little on rural society.[11]

Public agricultural research can be credited in large part with the abundant product of commercial agriculture, but the effects of technological change had a dark side which public research was not encouraged to observe. Efforts to provide an honest comprehensive picture of rural life during and after modernization, and to devise programs of social action—these have been nipped in the bud. A short history of these efforts is needed in order to appreciate Freeman's dilemma.

During the New Deal, a number of experimental programs to recognize and help the rural poor were developed under the Farm Security Administration. The FSA was dismembered at the earliest opportunity by white southerners in Congress and in the Farm Bureau, with plenty of assistance from midwestern conservatives.[12] Such was also the fate of land-use planning committees which were supposed to become a means by which rural communities could plan their own futures.

No less a threat to the South's peculiar institutions was the USDA's Bureau of Agricultural Economics (BAE), a group of ambitious social scientists, headed by Howard Tolley, whose mission in 1945 was to prepare for changes in postwar agriculture. The BAE produced a so-called "conversion program for the Cotton South," which would have de-emphasized cotton, diversified southern agriculture, and provided job training for industry so that those moving out of southern agriculture could find work nearby.[13] This plan was labeled a "socialistic" scheme at that time and provoked the wrath of Representative Whitten and the other cotton congressmen.[14] Midwestern Republicans joined them in demanding that the BAE be disciplined. Secretary Clinton Anderson reorganized the BAE in accord with

[10] Quoted in *Report of a Study Sponsored Jointly by Association of State Universities and Land Grant Colleges and U.S. Department of Agriculture, A National Program of Research for Agriculture* (October 1966), pp. 32–33.

[11] Ibid., pp. 55–57.

[12] See Grant McConnell, *The Decline of Agrarian Democracy* (Berkeley: University of California Press, 1953), and Sidney Baldwin, *Poverty and Politics* (Chapel Hill: University of North Carolina Press, 1968).

[13] Richard S. Kirkendall, *Social Scientists and Farm Politics in the Age of Roosevelt* (Columbia, Missouri: University of Missouri Press, 1966), pp. 227–28.

[14] Ibid.

the advice of Representative Whitten, and the principals in that agency fled to distinguished careers in the universities and elsewhere, or hunched down in the USDA bureaucracy. Congressman Whitten's advice was to be applied thenceforth, as he reminded Freeman in 1961:

> *I would say for the record that in past years we had some problems with the old Bureau of Agricultural Economics. At one time some of their social studies and other things were, to say the least, not very popular up at this level. It looked to us as if those things were getting over into the policy field, that perhaps some undue influence was exercised on action programs by the theorists and economic groups.*
>
> *It reached the point where it was extremely difficult for the Bureau of Agricultural Economics to get proper financing through the Congress. I don't mean that that will be the experience in the future, and I don't say it in any way to upset your plans at all. But it is always good for all of us to read history. May I suggest that reading a little history might keep our new bureau in the proper field of activity, if the feelings of Congress are like they were some years ago.*[15]

Whitten and associates have continued their role as research chiefs, overseeing a federal-supported establishment that includes most of the available expertise on rural America.

Whitten has ignored requests for more adequate human nutrition research. Vast areas of the rural landscape are either off-limits or are covered on tiptoe, and research items have been phrased so as to avoid committee biases. Questions which were politically unresearchable have been passed over. A USDA scholar recently wrote a fine book on the freedoms enjoyed by participants in the farm economy.[16] Farm workers were not mentioned. Was "freedom" relevant to them? Certainly; and the author was at a loss to explain the omission, only observing that earlier writings also excluded farm workers.

Directors and researchers in the land grant college experiment stations also moved into harmony with congressmen and local potentates, whose desires were often interpreted as the authentic voice of "society." Natural scientists who tended to dominate the experiment stations avoided social research that might embarrass the various interests that supported the colleges. Criticism of the system was clearly aberrant behavior, best engaged in by pseudonym, as in the book *Poor Damn Janeth*.[17]

The USDA and the experiment stations have proved that much first-rate research can be done in an atmosphere of censorship, but when large sectors of reality and a whole race of people—even a whole class of people—are given almost no research priority and cannot be studied objectively, then the results of such research cannot be the basis of a good society.

For the record, there were a few studies and surveys of social conditions in rural

[15] U.S. Congress, House, Committee on Appropriations, *Department of Agriculture Appropriations for 1962, Hearings,* before a subcommittee of the Committee on Appropriations, 87th Cong., 1 sess., 1961, p. 70.

[16] Harold F. Breimyer, *Individual Freedom and the Economic Organization of Agriculture* (Urbana: University of Illinois Press, 1965).

[17] Ira Dietrich, pseud., *Poor Damn Janeth* (Madison, Wisconsin: Bascom House, 1967).

America, begun under Freeman, adequate in terms of their objectives.[18] These studies produced economic data crying for complementary sociological data. They provided opportunities for analysis and needs for verification. They also showed the need for analysis of the effects of federal policies, but the USDA's Economic Research Service was generally not permitted to undertake such subjects.

When we move on from research to the question of distributing benefits more equitably, we find that the Department of Agriculture had major responsibility for certain aspects of the rural poverty scene, including rural housing and rural community development. Freeman did push for an agency to stimulate community development but finally backed down in deference to conservatives such as Whitten, who registered disapproval and denied appropriation requests. The USDA housing agency, Farmers Home Administration, was a remnant of the Farm Security Administration. Its housing record in the period 1960–1968 is suggested in the findings in a USDA social research publication, as follows:

> *Rural housing had improved considerably since 1960, but the condition of housing occupied by the rural poor may not have improved very much. . . . Over 95% of the homes built were constructed by families with incomes over $6,000 a year. Also, most of the repairs were of a minor nature and made to standard homes.*[19]

In 1960 there were 4.8 million families in rural substandard housing,[20] but the number of annual housing starts and rehabilitations financed was only 1 percent of that need, even in the peak year of 1968.[21] By 1969 Farmers Home had been given workable programs providing subsidized loans under legislation developed by the congressional banking and currency committees. Loan activities had tripled since 1960, by any measure, but annual requests for increased staff had been rejected or pared down by the House Appropriations Subcommittee. As a result, overworked local staffs complained that they could not adequately process existing applications, and they were reluctant to encourage others to apply.

The Department of Agriculture was also charged with providing adequate food, for urbanites as well as farmers, for poor as well as better-off Americans. The story of food for the poor can be told only briefly here.[22]

Initially, President Kennedy's administration seemed intent on alleviating hunger at home. Kennedy, as a Senator in 1959, had presented testimony that included evidence of widespread domestic malnutrition. He was criticized then by President Eisenhower for his campaign statement that some Americans go to

18 For example, USDA, Economic Research Service, *Rural Poverty in Three Southern Regions: Mississippi Delta, Ozarks, Southeast Coastal Plain,* Agricultural Economic Report 176 (Washington, D.C.: GPO, 1970), *Characteristics of Human Resources in Rural Southeast Coastal Plain . . . with Emphasis on the Poor,* Agricultural Economic Report 155 (1970), and *Human Resources in the Rural Mississippi Delta . . . with Emphasis on the Poor,* Agricultural Economic Report 170 (1970).

19 USDA, Economic Research Service, *Status of Rural Housing in the United States* (Washington, D.C.: GPO, 1968), p. iii.

20 Ibid., p. 5.

21 According to USDA-FHA, the agency financed approximately 50,000 housing starts or rehabilitations in 1968.

22 For a fuller amount of domestic food programs under Freeman, see Kotz, *Let Them Eat Promises.*

bed hungry. In his first official act Kennedy enriched the domestic commodity distribution package for needy families, but from that point on progress was slow or negative from the viewpoint of food recipients. Distributed food remained an unwieldly grab-bag of inadequate nutritional value. Freeman worked strenuously for a food stamp program, which was tried out and then enacted in 1964. Participation was low—far less than under the commodity program—because of the terms. Those eligible determined that they could not afford stamps, and the bonus received was so small in many cases as to be barely worth the inconvenience and embarrassment. From 1964 to 1967 the administration doggedly implanted food stamps in the counties where commodities had been before, and in a few others, at first ignoring those areas where local governments did not wish to participate. It was clear from Freeman's statements, from the USDA's sales pitch, and from practice, that food stamps were a program to suit agricultural producers, welfare agencies, grocers, and local power structures. The administration preferred to believe that the program served most of those in need, and preferred not to test that belief very thoroughly.[23] When people started inquiring in 1967 and 1968 they found little relationship between the USDA's programs and the nutritional needs of low-income America. It was a major scandal, and a group of hunger-fighters, supported by labor groups and the liberal Field Foundation, made the most of it.

Freeman might have joined them, calling for a better understanding of food programs and food needs, and publicly demanding the resources needed for a good program. Instead he became defensive. He reacted first to the Clark subcommittee of the Senate Labor and Public Welfare Committee, whose members included Senator Robert Kennedy. This subcommittee had been informed that there was hunger in Mississippi, and had observed it first-hand. Testifying before this group Freeman engaged in a "shouting match" with Senator Jacob Javits of New York, charging that there was hunger in New York as well as in Mississippi, and then was unable to prove it when pressed to do so by Javits and the press.[24] Freeman immediately became the darling of the Mississippi congressmen because he had noted with satisfaction that every Mississippi county had a food program.

Meanwhile a Citizen's Board of Inquiry had been formed by the hunger-fighters. This Board issued its report, *Hunger USA*, late in the spring of 1968. It was a journalistic rather than a scientific report, but nonetheless persuasive. It revealed widespread hunger and cited by chapter and verse a number of inadequacies of the food programs. Another report, *Our Daily Bread*, sponsored by several women's organizations, concluded that the school lunch program failed to reach low-income families. Freeman agreed with the southerners that *Hunger USA* misrepresented conditions of hunger and malnutrition in the United States.[25] Nevertheless, in the midst of the disclosures, the USDA acted to require all poor counties to have a food program and to establish guidelines to make sure that free school lunches were provided as required by law.

Freeman was unable to absorb two new waves of criticism that broke on him in late May of 1968. Columbia Broadcasting System presented an hour-long docu-

[23] Ibid., chap. 4.

[24] *New York Times*, 14 July 1967, p. 12.

[25] U.S. Congress, House, Committee on Agriculture, *Amend the Food Stamp Act of 1964, Hearings*, 90th Cong., 2 sess., 1968, p. 92.

mentary, a shocker called *Hunger USA*, which indicted the food programs. Hours later Reverend Ralph Abernathy and his Poor People were knocking on the door of the Department of Agriculture, making demands for immediate action.

Freeman published an outraged letter to Frank Stanton of CBS, charging that their television presentation was a "travesty on objective reporting" and demanding equal time. Stanton responded that Freeman's main complaint was that the USDA had been given too much blame and too little credit. Stanton said, "The issue of hunger in America transcends the superficial issue of assessing blame for its continued existence." When Freeman fired back another request for equal time, Stanton's response was to air *Hunger USA* again and to make the film available on Capitol Hill so that all lawmakers might have a chance to view it.

The Poor People's leaders had decided to emphasize food program changes, downgrading other demands. They were deeply concerned about hunger and better prepared to talk about it, and the issue was by this time highly visible. They must have hoped that Freeman had the power and the will to make immediate concessions on this issue. The Poor People suggested several changes: run dual programs so those who could not afford stamps could pick up commodities; provide free stamps for the poor; improve the commodity food package; and require all poor counties to have at least one program. The last suggestion was well on the way to fulfillment. On other points discussed below, Freeman's responses were expedient.

The Poor People charged that $200 million in funds were available to make these changes, in the "Section 32" fund deriving from tariff receipts. Freeman said that this money was not his to spend, presumably because of understandings with the President and Congress. He said dual programs and free stamps were illegal, as indicated by legislative intent expressed during the development of the law, but Freeman's statements had been a major factor in determining the content of that legislative history. Freeman did not want to be as generous to poor people when the provisions were enacted as the Poor People's leaders now wanted him to be. So he kept telling them he could not act because he did not have the authority or the money, and yet he maintained—before, after, and even during the Poor People's campaign—that he did not want any more authority or resources, with one exception: he wanted more money for the food stamp program. While the siege was going on, Freeman raised his requested food stamp increase from $20 million to $100 million, and told the House Agriculture Committee that an efficient program would cost about $1.5 billion, compared with $360 million being spent for both programs at that time.

According to Nick Kotz, Freeman tried repeatedly during this time to get President Johnson's support for increased food-stamp funding, but was hardly able to get messages through to him, much less convince him. Johnson, in turn, was being pressured by Whitten and others. When Vice President Hubert Humphrey asked the President to promise larger amounts for food stamps, Johnson replied, according to Kotz, "I've given my word to Congress [on cutting spending]. If you can get Congress to do something, fine, but we've made a commitment. We've talked to Ellender, Poage, and Whitten. I'm not going to be the one to break that agreement. That's what they're waiting for up there. If I break the agreement, we'll never get anything else through Congress."[26]

[26] Kotz, *Let Them Eat Promises*, pp. 147–92.

The strategy of relying upon the liberal conscience and public opinion against entrenched power had not worked, at least over the short run.

On the issue of race discrimination, the Poor People's demands were based mainly on a 1965 study by the U.S. Civil Rights Commission. Surveying employment practices in major USDA agencies the Commission had found that virtually all employees in responsible positions at all levels were white. With respect to distribution of program benefits by race, the Commission noted that the combination of government programs and inputs of technology had left Negroes progressively worse off. It concluded, "there is unmistakable evidence that racial discrimination has served to accelerate the displacement and impoverishment of the Negro farmer."[27] The Commission found evidence of discrimination in the distribution of acreage allotments under farm commodity programs. It noted that services offered by Farmers Home Administration and the Cooperative Extension Services were on a Jim Crow basis, with minority services being inferior in quality and scale and even completely different in substance from those received by white farmers.[28] Many other instances of discrimination were cited.

Freeman used this report as a measure of the actions needed to fulfill his responsibilities under the Civil Rights Act of 1964. He established a departmental committee and a citizen's committee to supervise implementation of the Commission recommendations. By 1968 many things had been done—particularly to abolish segregated meetings and other forms of overt segregation—but the underlying inequality in services and employment remained. Freeman's citizens' committee concluded that he had been the unhappy victim of much stalling and deceitfulness: "Secretary Freeman is and has been completely sincere in his desire to achieve full equality and opportunity in departmental programs and employment. We feel we share with him the frustrations stemming from the failure of the department to meet the ideal of that full equality."

The Civil Rights Commission, also in a 1968 review, was not willing to concede that Freeman had tried hard. Its executive director concluded, "Possibly one of the most enduring impressions of the Commission throughout its various opportunities to observe the Department of Agriculture over the last four years is that officials charged with administering agricultural programs do not feel and have not been told that equal opportunity is a matter of highest priority in their work."[29] Freeman took strong exception to that statement.

The monitoring instruments of the USDA tended to hide discrimination rather than to disclose it—for example, the compliance certification signed by a local officer, and the use of local or agency officers to supervise compliance by their own agencies. The picture of compliance presented from these procedures was very different from the facts revealed by statistical data on minority participation and reports of investigations by the USDA's office of the Inspector General. The Civil Rights Commission said, "Civil Rights audits conducted so far by the

[27] U.S. Commission on Civil Rights, *Equal Opportunity in Farm Programs: An Appraisal of Services Rendered by Agencies of the United States Department of Agriculture* (Washington, D.C.: GPO, 1965), p. 99.

[28] Ibid., pp. 38–67.

[29] Letter from Howard A. Glickstein to Secretary Freeman, dated 17 January 1969, which appeared in U.S. Congress, Senate, Select Committee on Nutrition and Human Needs, *Nutrition and Human Needs, Hearings*, 91st Cong., 1 sess., 1969, pt. 8, p. 2684.

OIG (Office of Inspector General) have demonstrated extensive noncompliance and overall program weakness in several agencies. These findings are in sharp contrast to the picture of compliance presented in other reporting activities of the Department."[30] But the USDA's Office of Inspector General had no power to take action on what it found, and in practice little or no action was taken.

Therefore the Commission urged the development of a strong enforcing agency under the Secretary. Freeman had appointed an assistant for civil rights who was without specific authority and specific funding. In the absence of a vigorous office that could spot noncompliance and could improve the compliance criteria, the procedures became formalities, and the criteria became bureaucratic rationalizations. Congressional committees which had been keen to catch the Department playing the fool in its grain-storage operations had far more reason to investigate its civil rights record. This record can be illustrated by findings with respect to two major agencies—the Cooperative Extension Service and the Agricultural Stabilization and Conservation Service.

The Extension Service began as a federal–local–Farm Bureau partnership designed to bring information from the land-grant colleges to dirt farmers that would help them improve their farms, environment, and society. However, Extension became the nearly exclusive property of the farmers that it had first served, and then became almost a superfluity for these commercial farmers who no longer needed an intermediary to the sources of technical knowledge. Tightly controlled farmer committees or county governments ran the county extension offices, often enforcing their prejudices against new ideas or activities suggested by the state extension office. But state extension offices received a magnificent federal subsidy, especially in southern states, based upon the size of rural populations.

Following the 1965 Civil Rights Report, Freeman took steps to integrate the southern services. Three years later the Civil Rights Commission did a study of the Alabama Extension Service, whose integration plans had been submitted to the USDA. By that time black and white extension workers shared local facilities, and some white 4-H clubs had one or more black members. Negroes did not share positions of authority, and of 112 employees in the State Extension office, only 8 were Negroes. Negroes did not receive equal salaries for equal work, even though they often had higher academic degrees and more experience. Job classifications for Negroes were different and less impressive. To illustrate: two Negro women workers were known as district home agents, with salaries of $10,800, while their four white counterparts were known as associate extension district chairman, with salaries of $12,000. The Negro women served twice as many counties as the whites. The Commission noted that no chief county extension agent was Negro[31] (none was Negro anywhere in the U.S.).

Services to farmers, while formally integrated, were virtually segregated in practice, the Commission found. Potential workload of the average Negro male extension agent (workload calculated as the number of Negro farm operators and farm

[30] U.S. Commission on Civil Rights, Staff Paper, *The Mechanism for Implementing and Enforcing Title VI of the Civil Rights Act of 1964: U.S. Department of Agriculture* (July 1968), p. 35, which appeared in U.S. Congress, Senate, Select Committee on Nutrition and Human Needs, *Nutrition and Human Needs, Hearings*, 91st Cong., 1 sess., 1969, pt. 8, p. 2704.

[31] *Hearing before the U.S. Commission on Civil Rights, held in Montgomery, Alabama, April 27–May 2, 1968* (Washington, D.C.: GPO, 1969), pp. 748–49.

boys) was about six times that of the white agent, and the same was true for women agents. In this way, Alabama Extension divided its 1967 federal subsidy between the races, a subsidy amounting to $2.6 million dollars, or 41.4 percent of the total state Extension budget.[32]

Integration in the Agricultural Stabilization and Conservation Service, the agency which distributes farm program subsidies, perhaps got even more approving winks from southerners. Some Negro farmers were elected to the ASC community committees, whose only practical function is as an electoral body to select the three-member county ASC committees. This indirect election system produced only three Negro county committeemen in the whole of the United States in 1968. But even that record was better than the system for appointing state and local managers. The appointed state ASC chairmen, who hire the staffs, were white in all cases, as were the majority on all the three-man state committees. A few states had one Negro state committee member who had been selected by state politicians. In 1968 the local ASC office managers, who are the people really in charge at the county level, were white in all U.S. counties having a significant number (10 percent or more) of Negro farm operators, and the farmer fieldmen who are the crucial link in the organization network and who tend to organize local elections, were also all white. Therefore the big farm agency was still lily-white when Freeman left it, except for some Negroes in meaningless positions, and a few selected Negroes in positions proximate to power.

The Poor People's campaign of 1968 provided occasion to consider the record of USDA service to blacks and to all of the rural poor. The bedraggled serenaders who marched around the USDA in 1968 represented the rural poor who were being counted as beneficiaries of programs they may never have heard of, which were being run by and mostly for that class of farmers with above-average incomes. The demonstrators were Negro Americans who for generations had, with poor whites, done the work on southern farms, and they also represented Mexican-Americans who had done the stoop labor everywhere, and poor whites who made up the majority of those now disinherited from their work role in agriculture.

It was not as if no one knew that these people had been excluded from both the economic system and the political system. The BAE's 1945 Conversion Plan for the Cotton South had recognized this, had proposed to do something about it, and had been firmly put to rest. Other earlier USDA initiatives had met the same fate. Exclusion of these people had turned out to be a fact that had to be lived with, at least for a while. But by the 1960s blacks as well as many others had decided they would no longer tolerate an environment of overriding race discrimination and inequality. The USDA liberals did not join in that decision. The USDA administration, when the national spotlight fell upon it, did not come forward to enlighten the American people about poverty, racism, and hunger in rural America. It did not wholeheartedly join the black Americans and other liberal groups but kept them at arms length and in retrospect was an instrument in frustrating their efforts to achieve substantial remedies within the system.

[32] Ibid., p. 757.

30

THE "MEGAMACHINE" BEHIND THE MERCURY SPACECRAFT

Loyd S. Swenson, Jr.

"America is today in the midst of a transition," wrote Zbigniew Brzezinski in 1968. "U. S. society is leaving the phase of spontaneity and is entering a more self-conscious stage; ceasing to be an industrial society, it is becoming the first technocratic one." A society marked by the technical organization of modes of ordinary life was becoming evident in the efforts in the decade of the 1960's to conquer space.

In 1958, within a year of the dramatic launching of Sputnik by the Soviet Union, Congress created a National Aeronautics and Space Administration (NASA). In 1959 a Soviet space vehicle hit the moon and another photographed its dark side. Two years later, Soviet Major Yuri Gagarin was hurled into orbit, circled the earth in a space capsule, and returned safely. Within a month of this Soviet spectacular space triumph, President John F. Kennedy, appearing before Congress, said: "I believe that this nation should commit itself to achieving the goal before this decade is out, of landing a man on the moon and returning him safely to earth. No single space project in this period will be more impressive to mankind or more important for the long-range exploration of space; and none will be so difficult or expensive to accomplish." In July of 1969, eight years later, this vision was fulfilled with the successful landing of Apollo 11 on the moon. Almost all American ventures into space, from the first suborbital flight of Alan B. Shepard, Jr., in 1961 to his moon-landing in 1970, have been characterized by near perfection in a multitude of bureaucratic and scientific operations. An aspect of the technocratic society that Brzezinski envisioned is examined in this article, which concentrates on an early phase of the American space program.

Loyd S. Swenson, Jr., teaches the modern history of science and technology at the University of Houston. Previously he served as a historian with the NASA Manned Spacecraft Center. He is the coauthor of a history of Project Mercury published by the Government Printing Office in 1966.

Source: American Quarterly, Vol. 21, No. 2 (1969), pp. 210–227.

Space technology and social criticism have become joint and acute concerns in the seventh decade of the 20th century. The exploration of space and the exploitation of Earth both have excited imaginations and emotions and have led to some serious rethinking on the meaning of life, liberty and learning. Although the interrelationships between space and society can only be dimly perceived as yet, their interactions may become less obscure if we conceive the adventure into space in terms of the advent of two new kinds of giant engines: the physical propulsion systems produced by rocket technology and the human social system derived from industrial culture.

In his recent book *The Myth of the Machine,* Lewis Mumford argues that the "megamachine" of human social organization, and not tool-making, has been the most powerful determinant in cultural evolution. He defines the "megamachine" as an archetypal engine composed of human parts which can be deployed either in mechanically organized creative work or in destructive military wastefulness. Mumford's latest thesis holds that such "megamachines" through "megatechnics" have achieved all the monumental wonders of the world and have molded the main events in human history. Mumford sees the building of the Egyptian pyramids as "precise static equivalents" of our launching of space rockets, "both devices for securing, at an extravagant cost, a passage to Heaven for the favored few."[1] This judgment fails logically but succeeds metaphorically in evoking an image of a "megamachine" of interested people behind manned spaceflight attempts to date.

A decade after the launching of Earth's first artificial moon and seven years after man's first orbital circumnavigation, both of these premier Soviet achievements remain mysterious in detail to the western world. Current events in space continue to make more history than has been written. Space technology as well as the space sciences and especially manned spaceflights have developed so rapidly and grown so complex that few have been able to see beyond the personalities of the first space pilots. American achievements in the first decade of the space age have been impressive also, but information about U.S. space accomplishments is so plentiful that the noise often seems to occlude information. To understand ourselves and where we may be headed, we need to study in depth, comparatively if possible and extensively if not, the social, economic and technological history of the beginnings of space exploration.[2]

[1] *The Myth of the Machine: Technics and Human Development* (New York, 1967), pp. 12, 34, 221. See also Peter Ritner, *The Society of Space* (New York, 1961); Kenneth E. Boulding, *The Meaning of the 20th Century: The Great Transition* (New York, 1964); John K. Galbraith, *The New Industrial State* (Boston, 1967); Harold D. Lasswell, "The Social Consequences of the Space Age," in *Fifth National Conference on the Peaceful Uses of Space,* NASA SP-82 (Washington, 1966), pp. 194–99; Barbara Ward, *Spaceship Earth* (New York, 1966).

[2] One may best begin an overview of the U. S. national space program by consulting Eugene M. Emme, *Aeronautics and Astronautics: An American Chronology of Science and Technology in the Exploration of Space, 1915–1960* (Washington, 1961), followed by the yearly series of chronologies prepared by the NASA Historical Staff: *Aeronautical and Astronautical Events of 1961* (Washington, 1962); *Astronautical and Aeronautical Events of 1962* (Washington, 1963); *Astronautics and Aeronautics: Chronology on Science, Technology and Policy, 1963, 1964, 1965* (Washington, 1964–66). For the Soviet program, see Ari Shternfeld, *Soviet Space Science* (2nd rev. ed.; New York, 1959); Alfred J.

Gagarin, Shepard, Grissom, Titov and Glenn were individual names that conjured visions, among organization men in industrial societies during 1961 and 1962, of heroics unparalleled. These first cosmonauts and astronauts, as everyone knew, did not actively propel themselves into space. Rather, they passively were boosted by a different kind of "megamachine"—ballistic missiles called rockets—and by intricate governmental, industrial and technological organizations—in short, by "megamachines" of their nation-states.[3]

Without detracting from the active and often saving roles of the first space pilots to their missions, most people recognize that these early spacemen were military emissaries, sent forth on peaceful missions to test the limits of human capabilities. These pilots volunteered to act as scouts, but they were commandeered also. The states of various technological arts on Earth as well as the agencies of their political states determined virtually every action of the first astronauts. Mission control centers, flight systems, engineering, and operations divisions, space task forces, military and civilian space agencies, aerospace industrial workers, political representatives, executive statesmen and public opinion—all to varying degrees called the shots into space. Although Soviet experience and practice in these respects are not yet fully open to view, they may be presumed to be socially similar to those of the U.S. National Aeronautics and Space Administration (NASA). Understanding the spaceflights of our era may be achieved in various ways; one neglected approach is the study of the "megamachine" or of the social structure of the earthbound men of space. This is where most of the action was, and is, and here social organization and human organisms conspired to begin man's functional conquest of space.[4]

Project Mercury, the first American manned spaceflight series, was many things to many people. Most obviously, it was a gamble in the international power struggle between the United States and the Soviet Union. But it was more of a response than a challenge in inaugurating the manned space race, because the arms race had long since been extended into space by ballistic missiles.

The purpose of the present study is to assay a few of the ways government-industry relations affected technology in the development of the Mercury space-

---

Zaehringer, *Soviet Space Technology* (New York, 1961), and *A Casebook on Soviet Astronautics*, ed. F. J. Krieger (2 vols.; Santa Monica, Calif., 1956–57).

[3] For an excellent study of the organizational complexities of the U. S. space program, see Robert L. Rosholt, *An Administrative History of NASA, 1958–1963*, NASA SP-4101 (Washington, 1966). For a bibliography on both American and Soviet literature, see "History of Aeronautics and Astronautics: A Preliminary Bibliography," NASA HHR-24, comp. Katherine M. Dickson (Washington, 1967).

[4] A good biographical series of portraits is to be found in Shirley Thomas, *Men of Space* (7 vols.; Philadelphia, 1960–65). Guides to the literature and concerns of science and public policy may be approached through *Science and Society*, ed. Norman Kaplan (Chicago, 1965); *Science and Society in the United States*, eds. David D. Van Tassel and Michael G. Hall (Homewood, Ill., 1966); *The Politics of American Science: 1939 to the Present*, eds. James L. Penick Jr., C. W. Pursell Jr. et al. (Chicago, 1965), and J. Stefan Dupré and Sanford A. Lakoff, *Science and the Nation: Policy and Politics* (Englewood Cliffs, N. J., 1962). Cf. Alexander G. Korol, *Soviet Research and Development: Its Organization, Personnel, and Funds* (Cambridge, 1965). For more specifically technological literature, see *Modern Technology and Civilization: An Introduction to Human Problems in the Machine Age*, ed. Charles R. Walker (New York, 1962) and *The New Technology and Human Values*, ed. John G. Burke (Belmont, Calif., 1966).

craft. This subject is intrinsically complicated, but it appears small, like the Mercury capsule itself, compared to the scale of problems that arise in analyses of larger projects, such as the development of the Atlas intercontinental ballistic missile (ICBM) or of the nuclear submarine or of the successor programs to Mercury—Projects Gemini and Apollo. By excluding any serious consideration here of the converse problem of how technical demands molded and limited government-industry relations, this paper will restrict itself to a partial synthesis.[5]

Members of the "megamachine" behind Mercury saw themselves as teammates. Accordingly, two guiding questions here are: What was the Mercury team? and, How did that team function? The latter question is especially contingent upon perspective given by recent events, including the sterling completion of Project Gemini and the tragic deaths of the first Apollo flight crew in training. Both questions were prefigured by a former title of this study, "Governmental Design and Industrial Development of the Mercury Spacecraft," but neither these questions nor the answers here given should be considered definitive.

It is no mere coincidence that the titles of the two most famous stories of personal exploits in the history of American aviation are "*We*" and *We Seven*. Both books were published immediately after sensational flights that dramatized the courage of individual pilots and symbolized technological leaps that established the years of 1927 and of 1961 as milestones in the history of human mobility. The "aeronautical *We*" bequeathed by Charles A. Lindbergh's autobiographical account of his trans-Atlantic flight in 1927 appropriately was expanded to the astronautical *We Seven* "by the astronauts themselves" in 1962. Ghost-written by *Life* magazine editors, the astronauts' first book, like Lindbergh's first literary effort, was titled to call attention to the team that made the flights possible and to the symbiosis of man and machine. Many members of the American aerospace community today remember vividly Lindbergh's most famous flight, even though they may have forgotten the teamwork and social inventions that made the flight possible. Despite his renunciation in later life of the symbiosis of man and machine, Lindbergh's solo voyage in the *Spirit of St. Louis* still commands respect from the engineers and pilots who are moving from aeronautics into astronautics.[6]

But such has been American social reorganization since 1927, with urban-industrial, military-industrial and governmental-industrial complexes ever accelerating, that few common categories of analysis, like big business, big government

[5] A more detailed study of the interrelationships between social organizations and technical necessities in Mercury may be found in "Part Two—Development" of Loyd S. Swenson Jr., James M. Grimwood and Charles C. Alexander, *This New Ocean: A History of Project Mercury* (Washington: NASA SP-4201, 1966).

[6] Charles A. Lindbergh, *"WE": The Famous Flier's Own Story of His Life and His Transatlantic Flight . . .* (New York, 1927), and *We Seven, by the Astronauts Themselves*, ed. John Dille (New York, 1962). Cf. Lindbergh, *The Spirit of St. Louis* (New York, 1955); *Of Flight and Life* (New York, 1948) and most recently his article, "The Wisdom of Wildness," *Life*, LXIII (Dec. 22, 1967), 8–10. See also my paper "Lindbergh's *Spirit of St. Louis* and Shepard's *Freedom 7*: Parallels and Poles in Aircraft and Spacecraft Technology and Testing, 1927–1961," Society for the History of Technology, San Francisco, Dec. 29, 1965. See also John W. Ward's percipient essay, "The Meaning of Lindbergh's Flight," *American Quarterly*, X (Spring 1958), 3–16.

or big labor, big science or big military, help one to understand technology and social change since World War II. Policy problems arising from the phenomena of burgeoning corporate technology, wherein delicate distinctions between governmental, academic, military and industrial groups become increasingly blurred, are growing into much bigger political issues. Since NASA symbolizes most obviously today the intricacy of government-managed technology, its manned spaceflight program (often but erroneously thought to be the whole of its concern) is the target of many critics.[7] Among the individual men who worked to put the first Americans into space, however, Mercury seemed to have generated stronger professional pride than institutional loyalties. Its novel and urgent goal of putting a man in orbit gave every participant, no matter how specialized, a sense of creative responsibility.[8]

Project Mercury evolved from an aeronautical experiment into a truly national program. It necessitated cooperation between NASA, the military services, scientific institutions and private industry in a multitude of ways. Designing, engineering and managing the teamwork for the bell-shaped Mercury spacecraft itself was largely a four-year, one agency-one company affair, but designing and manufacturing about forty thousand components for some seventeen major subsystems of the spacecraft had to be more widely contracted. Integrating components and individualizing subsystems for each mission, testing and proving the dependability of the launch rockets and other pyrotechnics, insuring the compatibility of spacecraft and launcher, and proving the whole spacecraft-booster and spacecraft-recovery system to be operational before risking a manned flight—all this and much more was involved, and so the NASA managers called for and received the expertise of the nation as needed.

When the seven original astronauts reported to NASA and donned civilian clothes in mid-1959, they had to be trained, equipped and conditioned, literally, to act passively and to react reflexively. NASA, the Navy, the State Department and the communications industry had to establish a global network of tracking stations to monitor and perchance to command the orbiting ballistic capsule. Leaders of the manned space program had to appear repeatedly before Congressional committees and the American public to enlist financial, political and moral

[7] For critiques of NASA that err by overgeneralization, see Edwin Diamond, *The Rise and Fall of the Space Age* and Amitai Etzioni, *The Moon-Doggle: Domestic and International Implications of the Space Race* (both Garden City, N.Y., 1964), and H. L. Nieburg, *In the Name of Science* (Chicago, 1966), pp. 3–60. On the other hand, far too personal and yet insightful is Oriana Fallaci, *If the Sun Dies* (New York, 1966). For classic guidance on the problem of social vs. personal invention, see Abbot Payson Usher, *A History of Mechanical Inventions* (rev. ed.; Boston, 1954), pp. 1–83. For an influential analysis of American cultural and social sectors, see Max Lerner, *America as a Civilization: Life and Thought in the United States Today* (New York, 1957), esp. pp. 207–64.

[8] On specialization vs. creativity, see Robert L. Barre, "Some Social Implications of Organizing for a Space Effort," Conference on Space Science and Space Law, Norman, Okla., June 20, 1963. On pride vs. prestige, see Vernon Van Dyke, *Pride and Power: The Rationale of the Space Program* (Urbana, Ill., 1964). For an interesting general theory on creativity as motivational energy, see Norman W. Storer, *The Social System of Science* (New York, 1966) and for an insightful critique, see John Ziman, *Public Knowledge: An Essay Concerning the Social Dimension of Science* (Cambridge, 1968).

support for Project Mercury. All of this activity took place under the scrutiny of a public increasingly impatient with schedule slippages and hardware failures, both of which were plentiful.

Project Mercury was often compared with the Manhattan Project and with the Atlas ICBM development. These three major technological programs have been paramount examples of the type of consortium among government, industry and university that has provided for the common defense and promoted the general welfare of the nation since 1940. The principle of compartmentalization that was used to protect the military-industrial secrets of the Manhattan Project and the principle of concurrency that served the Defense Department and Air Force to insure technological supremacy by parallel developmental efforts cannot be said to have characterized Mercury. If they applied at all, these principles, extreme examples of the division of labor and of deliberately fostered simultaneity of invention, were only incidental and peripheral to the Space Task Group that managed Mercury.[9]

The only truly adequate structural-functional comparison for Project Mercury is Project Vostok. Lacking the information to compare Mercury with Vostok, many American observers have turned to historical analogies and homologies. The insights to be gleaned from comparisons of manned space exploration with previous experiences ought not to be disparaged, even though they are limited.[10] People ask themselves for parallels from history to aid and comfort their adaptation to a future that is already present. As man accelerates into a virtually unknown universe, various commentators have suggested a wide range of somewhat appropriate analogies to guide expectations, temper fears and bolster hopes.

And what is the best analogy to the birth of manned spaceflight? Is it with life rising up out of the sea, or with primates becoming bipedal? Is it with Egyptian pyramid-builders, or Gothic cathedral construction? Is it with Leif Ericson, Christopher Columbus or Ferdinand Magellan, or generally with the great age of discovery and exploration in the 16th and 17th centuries? Is it with the Montgolfier or Wright brothers or Lindbergh? Is it with railroad overexpansion into the American West, or with the American completion of the Panama Canal, or the construction of Boulder (Hoover) Dam, or the Tennessee Valley Authority (TVA)?[11]

[9] On "compartmentalization," see Richard G. Hewlett and Oscar E. Anderson Jr., *The New World, 1939/1946,* Vol. I of *A History of the United States Atomic Energy Commission* (University Park, Pa., 1962), pp. 227–38. On "concurrency," see Ernest G. Schwiebert, *A History of the U.S. Air Force Ballistic Missiles* (New York, 1965).

[10] See the interesting suggestions presented in *The Railroad and the Space Program: An Exploration in Historical Analogy,* ed. Bruce Mazlish (Cambridge, 1965). For a literate defense of the prestige factor and propagandistic value of NASA's activities, see Harold L. Goodwin, *The Images of Space* (New York, 1965). See parallel accounts by William R. Shelton, *American Space Exploration: The First Decade* (Boston, 1967) and *Soviet Space Exploration: The First Decade* (New York, 1968).

[11] So far as historical homologies go (and that is not far), I personally prefer to compare Mercury with the Panama Canal and Boulder Dam, each of which cost about the same in money, time and engineering effort. Typical of the space impact literature that so often seeks analogies are the essays in *Space: Its Impact on Man and Society,* ed. Lillian Levy (New York, 1965). See also my paper "The Fertile Crescent: The South's Role in the National Space Program," *Southwestern Historical Quarterly,* LXXI (Jan. 1968), 377–92.

Because most of these complex events are vivid only to a few memories, the burden of comparative criticism commonly falls on the Manhattan and Atlas Projects. Not only are both within living recollection but also a few men participated in all three. Furthermore, government-industry-university relations are commonly thought to be unique in recent American experience, and the social sciences applied to science itself and to technology are not yet widely enough respected to provide useful correlations. Whether or not the history of technology and of science can balance both social trends and psychological leadership remains to be proved. Neither social inventions nor personal innovations alone can provide satisfying explanations for the dawning aerospace revolution.[12]

Imagining a God's-eye view of the problem posed by man's attempt to escape from Earth and see the Universe, we may profit by looking down an exponential ladder from Mankind as a whole to the primary pair of individual minds that made Mercury move. There are, we are told, almost half again more than two billion people on Earth pressing for living space, and about two hundred million people reside in the United States, some twenty million of whom were the kind of young adult males who might have qualified (conceivably) as astronauts. There were approximately two million people who may be said to have participated in the Mercury Program at one time or another, and something like two hundred thousand workers in the American aerospace industry directly contributed goods or services for Mercury. Roughly twenty thousand people were involved in the Mercury operations team, including the recovery forces, but only about two thousand people might be called critical decision-makers at some point in the Mercury Program. Roughly two hundred managers in government and industry maintained the continuity of the program and worried over reliability, cost and scheduling requirements, whereas the initial manned ballistic satellite design came from a small team of about twenty scientists and engineers. Finally, two men, Maxime A. Faget and John F. Yardley, representing the Space Task Group and McDonnell Aircraft Corporation respectively, are most respected within the aerospace community as being the chief designer and the chief developer of the Project Mercury spacecraft.

Significantly, perhaps, the Soviet space program likewise has been symbolized operationally by two individuals, a "Chief Theoretician" and a "Chief Designer," who may be the honored academicians Valentin Petrovich Glushko and Sergei Pavlovich Korolyov.[13] In contrast to the Mercury capsule (so obviously an out-

[12] For convenient guides to literature on the social and psychological dimensions of innovation, see *The Sociology of Science*, eds. Bernard Barber and Walter Hirsch (Glencoe, Ill., 1962) and *Scientific·Creativity: Its Recognition and Development*, eds. Calvin W. Taylor and Frank Barron (New York, 1963). For still other dimensions, see *The Coming of the Space Age*, ed. Arthur C. Clarke (New York, 1967).

[13] See Theodore Shabad, "Talk in Moscow Names 2 as Top Space Planners," *New York Times*, Nov. 11, 1963. Whatever these titles mean (they may refer primarily to rocketry or to administration), Glushko was a pioneer liquid-fuel rocket designer and Korolyov was an early mechanical and structural engineer in rocketry. For a glimpse of the Soviet "megamachine" for space exploration that contradicts Shabad, see S. Yu Protsyuk, "The Development of Aircraft and Rocket Design in the Ukraine," NASA Technical Translation TT F-10, 749 (Feb. 1967) from *Ukrainian Engineering News*, XVII (1966), 79–93; on the other hand, see also M. K. Tikhonravov *et al.*, "Ten Years of Space Research in the USSR," NASA Technical Translation TT F-11,500 (Feb. 1968).

growth of aircraft technology), however, the Soviet's first spacecraft was a massive shell that seems to have derived more from the bathyspheres of deep-diving oceanographic techniques. This difference clearly reflected the Soviet advantage in having rocket booster power. But the design must also have been a conscious choice. The range of alternative configuration designs available to Mercury planners was far more limited by the technical necessities imposed by the Atlas rocket.

During the decade of transformation of guided missiles into intercontinental ballistic rockets, the United States government was, of course, operating a monopolistic market as customer, paymaster and regulator for the production of ever-larger and more sophisticated rocket boosters, payloads and weapons systems.[14] Research and development activities by the Department of Defense, however, were notoriously inefficient and poorly organized. The old military services continued to use the arsenal and national laboratory institutions that had served the Army and Navy well since the Civil War, but the Air Force preferred to rely almost exclusively on the aerospace industry itself and on derivative not-for-profit management corporations for the research and development work of creating new weapons systems. This difference in approach meant that the Army and Navy supported directly more applied research and development, whereas the Air Force bought more of its research from the academic and industrial sectors and directly supported in-house work aimed at development and operations. American foreign policy was tied to the concepts of massive retaliation and deterrence utilizing a Strategic Air Command equipped with nuclear weapons. Ballistic missilery and second-strike capabilities grew out of the paradox of possessing too much power to be useful. President Eisenhower knew how closely welded became the military and industry during his administration, and his famous farewell address warned of the threats posed by a "military-industrial complex" and by a "scientific-technological elite" to free institutions.[15]

After the challenge flung into orbit around the Earth by Sputniks I and II in 1957, the United States responded in part with passage of the National Aeronautics and Space Act of 1958. Deliberately choosing to create a new civilian space agency based on the nucleus of expertise accumulated since 1920 by the National Advisory Committee for Aeronautics (NACA), instead of using military proposals and industrial management for space exploration, the Congress and President elected to create a new mission-oriented agency, unlike either the Atomic Energy Commission or the military services. NASA was given a mandate to conceive the designs and to contract with industry for the development of the vehicles and equipment necessary to explore space. Air Force research and development precedents would be followed in many cases, of course, but neither the Air Force nor the Department of Defense could now set space policy.

[14] This is the thesis of an article by Robin Higham, "Government, Companies, and National Defense: British Aeronautical Experience, 1918–1945, as the Basis for a 'Broad Hypothesis,'" *Business History Review*, XXXIX (Autumn 1965), 323–47.

[15] Morton J. Peck and F. M. Scherer, *The Weapons Acquisition Process: An Economic Analysis* (Cambridge, 1962); see also I. B. Holley Jr., *Buying Aircraft: Materiel Procurement for the Army Air Forces* (Washington, 1964). Eisenhower quoted and studied, *American Military Thought*, ed. Walter Mills (Indianapolis, 1966), pp. 495–514.

Although each of the military services and several aerospace companies had invested much study in the man-in-space problem, civilian aeronautical engineers from NACA were authorized to do the job. In October 1958, NACA became NASA and some thirty-five of these men became the Space Task Group, established informally to achieve manned orbital circumnavigation as soon, as cheaply and as safely as possible. Already for six months they had been experimenting and testing various components so that they had a plan, a purpose and a nascent program in operation, not just on paper. Under the leadership of Robert R. Gilruth at Langley Field, Virginia, and of Hugh L. Dryden and Abe Silverstein in Washington, the Space Task Group quickly implemented the specific ideas of the young man known to his colleagues as Max Faget.

The manned rocket idea, as well as the manned ballistic satellite idea, had been perennial fantasies long before the Russian K. E. Tsiolkovskiy, the German Hermann Oberth and the American Robert H. Goddard had suggested some real possibilities for space travel. But in 1957 and early 1958, the idea of a manned nosecone, launched by an ICBM into orbit and capable of reliable recovery, was not widely envisioned. The X-15 rocket research glider or some sort of dynamic soaring vehicle was a far more popular conception, especially among Air Force advocates. But Max Faget and his civilian colleagues successfully sold their ideas for a manned satellite boosted by the "bare Atlas" ICBM and based on the ballistic reentry principle. Theirs was the design for the drag configuration, for a contoured couch, an attitude control, retrorocket and escape systems, and for parachute descent. Their specifications in these areas were essentially carried through to completion in the operational Mercury spacecraft. In only two respects did their original expectations fall significantly short of later developments. One of these problems, the development of an ablative or meltable heatshield instead of a heat sink thermal buffer, was resolved within a year of the start of the program. The other problem, the development of a worldwide tracking and communications network, evolved under the separate responsibility of another NASA organization.[16]

Prior to the assignment and authorization of Project Mercury there were, of course, many differences of approach, attitudes and concerns between government and industry, between various government centers, between the Air Force and NACA, between Washington and field centers, and between lobbyists of many sorts, institutional as well as individual. A careful study of this confused situation in 1956 and 1957 seems to show that interservice rivalry was no more rampant than intercenter competition. NACA's Virginia center at Langley Laboratory was strong on structures and pilotless aircraft research, NACA's Ames Laboratory in California was strongest in aerodynamical theory, and the NACA center at Cleveland, Ohio, namely, the Lewis Laboratory, was chiefly concerned with propulsion. The Air Force, likewise, had various groups competing for precedence. Within Langley itself a six-month intracenter competition between three schools of aeronautical engineers was finally resolved in favor of the Faget approach.

Faget was in 1958 the 37-year-old head of the Performance Aerodynamics Branch of the Pilotless Aircraft Research Division of the NACA Langley Labora-

[16] See *This New Ocean*, pp. 55–132. The Goddard Space Flight Center at Greenbelt, Md., gradually took on the tracking and communication responsibilities: see Alfred Rosenthal, *The Early Years: Goddard Space Flight Center Historical Origins and Activities through December 1962* (Washington, 1964).

tory in Hampton, Virginia. He was the son of an honored physician in the U.S. Public Health Service, a graduate in mechanical engineering from Louisiana State University in 1943, and a veteran of the Navy's submarine service before he had joined the Langley staff in 1946. Having made a number of important innovations both in technological hardware and in the software of analytical techniques, Faget had proven an invaluable lieutenant to Robert R. Gilruth and his group of applied scientists (or pure engineers) observing and telemetering data from vehicles in free flight. Faget's seminal paper of April 1958 was co-authored by B. J. Garland and J. J. Buglia, but Faget's primacy and delivery of it led directly to the American wingless nonlifting manned satellite.[17]

Meanwhile, advanced design groups within industry likewise had their differences of opinion until the designs were frozen in the fall of 1958. Although aviation companies showed twice as much interest in the manned ballistic satellite bidding as they had in the X-15 project competition, there were only eleven and one-half industrial proposals for the Mercury prime contract. Government evaluators of the bids were so anxious to avoid charges of favoritism that they lost several months of lead time between the design and development phases.

Project Mercury was never a crash program, in the sense that the compartmentalized Manhattan Project for the development of the atomic bomb or the ICBM program stressing concurrency had been. The assignment of a "DX" (the highest) industrial priority rating in the late spring of 1959 did, however, put the man-in-space project on a par with the development of a super-rocket engine and thereby bestowed invaluable industrial prestige to the Space Task Group and to McDonnell Aircraft Corporation. The Mercury contract award had been a surprise to much of the industry when announced in January 1959, but everything still hinged on the qualification flight tests of the General Dynamics Corporation's fragile yet potent Atlas rocket, primarily as an operational ICBM and secondarily as a manned launch vehicle. In such operational programs, big government and big industry had long since learned to work together intimately in the name of national defense.[18]

Aircraft corporations that had become missile and electronic companies during the 1950s had learned to expect low production runs and high overhead costs as a result of research and development contracts. But paradoxically, quality control for guided missiles was not as important as for manned aircraft, since in case of actually having to use them, quantity could make up for lack of quality. On the other hand, some aerospace companies, like McDonnell Corporation which was

[17] *This New Ocean*, pp. 86–90; cf. p. 489. The basic Mercury conceptual paper by Faget, Garland and Buglia is "Preliminary Studies of Manned Satellites—Wingless Configurations: Non-lifting" in "*NACA Conference on High-Speed Aerodynamics:* Ames Aeronautical Laboratory, Moffett Field, Calif., Mar. 18, 19, 20, 1958: A Compilation of the Papers Presented." In addition to Faget, NASA later honored eight other men as Mercury inventors: Andre J. Meyer Jr., William Bland, Alan B. Kehlet, Willard S. Blanchard, Robert G. Chilton, Jerome B. Hammack, Caldwell C. Johnson and Jack C. Heberlig. See Bob Gordon, "Inventions Undergo Long Process before Patents Finally Awarded," [MSC] *Space News Roundup*, IV, No. 2 (Nov. 11, 1966).

[18] *This New Ocean*, pp. 133–59, 178–208. For a typical overview of the government-industry agglomeration in R&D for space, see William Gilman, *Science U.S.A.* (New York, 1965).

still supplying manned jet aircraft for the Navy in quantity, suddenly discovered vast new qualitative requirements for the small production runs of spacecraft that had to be "gold-plated" for manned occupancy. This meant new kinds of engineering tradeoffs among the points of the triangle of industrial aerospace managers' concerns: reliability, cost and schedules. It also meant that NASA research and development contracts would be more prestigious than profitable at first. Whether that would change in the future depended upon the success of the Project and on continuing political support for the space program.[19]

The founder of McDonnell Aircraft Corporation said in his annual report for 1959 that "there is no need to stampede away from the aircraft business."[20] Indeed it was a small select crew of design engineers turning into development engineers and of developmental engineers turning into production engineers who worked on the first twelve spacecraft. As the contract evolved and some three thousand suppliers came in to assist with subcontracts for supply of parts for the capsule, contract administration was handled by Logan T. MacMillan and later by Walter F. Burke. Another man took the informal lead in the industrial response to the governmental design.

John F. Yardley was the person who became the closest counterpart in the McDonnell manufactory to Max Faget in the NACA-NASA organization. Just as Faget may be considered the chief designer of the Mercury capsule, so Yardley may be called its chief developer. Neither the civil servant Faget nor the McDonnell engineer Yardley was the nominal leader of the vast platoon within which each worked, but both sparked the technical talents of their fellow workers and maintained continuous engineering leadership from design through the final development of the Mercury hardware. By telephone, teletype and face-to-face, Faget and Yardley consulted each other about thousands of detailed design and development decisions involved in producing the first set of Mercury spacecraft during 1959 and 1960.

John Yardley held a master's degree in applied mechanics, had worked for McDonnell since 1946 as a stress analyst, strength engineer and project leader, and had participated with the company's Advanced Design Group from the beginning of their interest in a manned ballistic satellite. Yardley was exceptionally talented in his energetic capacity for work and for synthesizing technical knowledge. Yardley and Faget made hundreds of bilateral agreements on their own responsibility, but larger decisions regarding the development of systems or interaction between subsystems were reserved for the seventeen different working groups in the Task Group and the ten or so at McDonnell.[21]

As time passed into 1961, Yardley stayed with Mercury while Faget moved

[19] See *Aerospace Facts and Figures, 1962,* ed. Ben S. Lee (Washington, 1962) [Yearbook for Aerospace Industries Association of America, Inc.], pp. 1–28. An interesting analytical study of these matters is Herman O. Stekler, *The Structure and Performance of the Aerospace Industry* (Berkeley, 1965). See also, J. Stefan Dupré and W. Eric Gustafson, "Contracting for Defense: Private Firms and the Public Interest," *Political Science Quarterly*, LXXVII (June 1962), 161–77.

[20] Cited in *This New Ocean*, p. 191, fn 50. See also Stekler, pp. 42–78, 154–96. Cf. Edwin H. Rutkowski, *The Politics of Military Aviation Procurement, 1926–1934: A Study in the Political Assertion of Consensual Values* (Columbus, Ohio, 1966).

[21] *Ibid.*, p. 190. John F. Yardley, interview with L.S.S., Aug.-Sept. 1964, St. Louis, Mo.

toward the design of Apollo. Meanwhile, James Chamberlin, a senior Canadian aeronautical engineer, joined the Task Group, inaugurated an elaborate capsule coordination system and gradually replaced Faget in relations with Yardley. From this new collaboration came a set of designs for a "Mercury Mark II," better known today as the Gemini spacecraft.

Manufacturing difficulties abounded in building the Mercury spacecraft, not least of which were the habitability changes demanded by the astronauts, the lack of microminiaturization and the "pancake" approach to the architecture of subsystems. The cost consciousness of the Space Task Group and the reliability question at NASA headquarters were probably more irksome than the controversial patent policies of NASA and the late entry of the Wernher von Braun team with their Redstone launch vehicle into the NASA family. The timing of flight events in the Mercury Program must be explained largely by facing this problem: Why was the first Mercury-Redstone flight allowed to slip past the first Mercury-Atlas flight? This is a difficult question to answer satisfactorily now, but two proximate reasons have been given. Fabrication difficulties with the capsule together with differences in "reliability" interpretations among the Mercury teammates were the two primary reasons why Gagarin rather than Shepard was the first man in space.[22]

At first, "psychological confidence" in the readiness of the Mercury spacecraft to fly was supposed to be built up in three stages: developmental tests, qualification tests and flight tests. Both government and industry inspectors were to certify testing at all three levels, but midway through qualification tests in 1960, a new level of proof was established for most of the hardware. Called "reliability testing," this level of proof came to require life-tests on many components and was supposed to raise the so-called "confidence coefficients" for readiness decisions. Project Orbit, an elaborate reliability ground-test program, was introduced at McDonnell to simulate each mission in environmental chambers with a facsimile spacecraft.[23]

Concurrently differences in professional background cost much time and effort. Polarization over reliability questions came less between government and industry than between mathematicians and engineers, windtunnel vs. flight-test experts, old Air Force vs. new NASA procedures, headquarters vs. field center attitudes, physicians vs. physicists, systems engineers vs. components specialists, and logical vs. empirical personalities. Philosophical issues in probability theory, symbolized by the relative frequency school and the degree of confidence school, were problematic throughout 1960 and 1961. The immense enlargement of McDonnell's preflight operations checkout group at Cape Canaveral was another indication that failure would not be tolerated but that success could not be guaranteed. Still, it was always the rocket boosters, and not the manned capsule, that were considered most dangerous.

One example of a technical debate involving reliability that was to prove por-

[22] My paper "Project Mercury: A Case History in Contemporary Technology," given at the joint meeting of the American Association for the Advancement of Science and the Society for the History of Technology, Washington, D.C., Dec. 27, 1966, detailed the second answer to this question as found in *This New Ocean*, pp. 322–30.

[23] *Ibid.*, pp. 112, 178, 256, 265, 269–71, 491.

tentous long after Project Mercury was consigned to history was that surrounding the decision in 1959 to use low-pressure pure oxygen in the cabin atmosphere. The important issue of whether to provide a "shirtsleeve" cabin air environment or to follow the experience of military aviation with pressure suits and pure oxygen supplies was decided in favor of the latter position for several compelling reasons. Faget and Yardley, together with most of their colleagues who studied the alternatives, found the disadvantages of a mixed gas environment too great a risk. They chose, therefore, to use the more "reliable" pure oxygen system at 5 p.s.i. ambient pressure. This Environmental Control System worked quite well throughout Mercury, and with few essential modifications, throughout Project Gemini. But its very success was partly responsible for the accidental sacrifice of three astronauts in 1967 before Apollo ever left its launching pad.[24]

When astronauts Shepard, Grissom and Glenn finally took their rides into space, they proved themselves as test pilots, and they proved the effectiveness of the governmental design and industrial development of the Mercury spacecraft. They did not, however, validate or justify any single economic or managerial philosophy. Compromises had been too frequent for that. The relations generally between government and industry had been mutually satisfying, steadily improving and closely personal on all levels throughout the Project. Only by specifying levels of analyses and specific contentions could one find systemic faults. Except for the fact that it failed to beat the Russians, Mercury was a magnificent operational success.[25]

Within four years between 1959 and 1963, the 35 members of the original Space Task Group that had designed Project Mercury evolved into the Manned Spacecraft Center consisting of more than thirty-five hundred people. Meanwhile, this growing group had relocated from Virginia to Texas, redesigned Mercury as Gemini and moved far toward Apollo spacecraft designs as mission planning for a moon landing was authorized. McDonnell Aircraft Corporation, providing most of the development and production engineers and facilities, built 24 Mercury spacecraft through the work of less than a thousand picked men out of its twenty-four thousand personnel. Spare parts and ground support equipment eventually required as much McDonnell effort at the Florida Cape as in St. Louis, and the prime contractor eventually received almost $143 million for Mercury, but by that time McDonnell engineers were developing the "Mercury Mark II."

The Mercury team-at-large waxed with the Mercury mission and waned slightly with the wait for Gemini flights. "The Mercury team" was often characterized by the press as consisting of over two million people and (considering the space race competition) as representing the whole American population. Although such claims would be congenial to Mumford's concept of the "megamachine," they are too broad to be technologically meaningful, and yet it is too narrow to credit merely such segments as the Atlas team, the Mercury spacecraft team and the network team for the success of the program. Compared to the programs that

[24] *Ibid.*, pp. 225–26, explains the reasons for the choice of a pure oxygen Environmental Control System.

[25] Historiographical problems presented by Mercury as a success story were analyzed in my paper, "Americans in Orbit: A Partial Report of the Historiography of Project Mercury," History of Science Society, annual meeting, Philadelphia, Dec. 29, 1963.

followed Mercury, the first team was small, compact and intimate, spurred by an awesome adventure, cooperative as well as competitive, and animated by virtually equal concerns for safety, cost and schedules.

While political pressures forced most NASA contracts after Mercury from the Cost-Plus-Fixed-Fee into the Cost-Plus-Incentive-Fee mold, the research and development nature of all the manned spaceflight endeavors means that they have all been more experimental than profitable. Exploring technology was as much Mercury's purpose as exploring space. Hence, criteria for its assessment should be multidimensional. Bruce Mazlish recently suggested six such dimensions for the complex social invention represented by NASA's evolving "space program" as a whole. Using his schema, I should say that the manned spaceflight program seems to be far more important technologically than economically, more significant socially than managerially, and perhaps most influential psychologically. The political effects, if discernible at all, cannot be matched by the basic change manned spaceflight has wrought on the psyches of our children. Indeed, it may well be argued by future historians that the most important single impact of Sputnik was on American public education policies. NASA and the national space program have contributed to the American cultural taste for speed, power, pride and freedom, but vicarious spaceflight by millions of television viewers was inaugurated, like the Project itself, more as a response than as a challenge to the successive Soviet coups in space.[26]

Although technical constraints such as limited booster power affected the development of Mercury more than social constraints, a number of conclusions have been offered regarding the way government-industry relations affected technology and vice versa. Most significant perhaps were the size of the team, the cost and the time required: peak figures were 2,020,528 for manpower, $400,658,000 for grand total costs, and 55 months for the Project's lifetime. The celebrated squabble in the headlines at the end of the program was judged a "rather small tempest in a rather large teapot." McDonnell and NASA engineers worked so well together that their corporate identities were subsumed to the Mercury team. They learned together what had to be done to balance a man on a missile, send him up and around and bring him down safely. The award of the Gemini spacecraft contract on a sole-source basis to McDonnell is evidence enough for that.[27]

Conversely, the lessons learned from the new technology ranged from upgrading all test and control standards to the use of Program Evaluation and Review Technique (PERT), the incentive-type contract, and other management tools. Space technology required many applications of systems, engineering, operations analyses, automatic checkout equipment and environmental vacuum chambers

[26] These six categories of analysis are borrowed from Mazlish, *The Railroad and the Space Program*, pp. 1–52, and ranked here in order of estimated strength of impact. For some comparative data see Proceedings, *Conference on Space-Age Planning*, NASA SP-40 (Washington, 1963), pp. 147–71 *et passim*. For a more conventional multidimensional analysis, see Hugo A. Meier, "American Technology and the Nineteenth Century World," *American Quarterly*, X (Summer 1958), 116–30. For a comparative critique of the Mumford and Mazlish theses discussed here, see Theodore A. Wertime, "Culture and Continuity: A Commentary on Mazlish and Mumford," *Technology and Culture*, IX (Apr. 1968), 203–12.

[27] *This New Ocean*, Epilogue, pp. 505–11. See also *Mercury Project Summary Including Results of the Fourth Manned Orbital Flight*, NASA SP-45 (Washington, 1963), pp. 1–31, 365–68.

that were not envisioned in the 1950s. Indeed, the history of Project Gemini, now under way, will probably provide the best evidence of the lessons learned from the shortcomings of Mercury. The Gemini spacecraft, at least, was designed by both McDonnell and NASA-MSC engineers in close accord with the criticisms of James Chamberlin. Development and operations by the government-industry team were continuous and virtually indistinguishable. The complete record of the Gemini-Titan flights speaks well for the effectiveness of this arrangement.[28]

Project Apollo is so vastly much larger, more complicated and sophisticated in all respects that neither Mercury nor Gemini offers more than an elementary understanding of its design and development. The various generations of the enormous Saturn booster which Apollo is using are the first U.S. rockets to be man-rated, made for human occupancy from initial design onward. And whereas the Apollo command module became suspect after Astronauts Grissom, White and Chaffee lost their lives, the 24 technical subcommittees of the accident investigating board indicated in microcosm the size and scope of the ground-based "megamachine" necessary to shoot the moon.[29] Apollo 8's circumlunar mission during Christmas 1968 surely must rank as one of the "good Earth's" most significant emanations.

Some critics of the great "moondoggle," like Mumford, compare the space Olympics to pyramid-building or even to less respectable activities. Their voices are often in the best tradition of western social criticism, and yet their songs are often no more than the fashionable despair of those who class themselves in the better half of only two cultures. National commitments to space exploration do present profound questions of priorities among social values, problems of allocation of resources scarce even to affluent societies, and dilemmas enough to vex the best of moral and political philosophers as well as those philosophers of efficiency who are called space scientists and engineers.

Both cynical critics of and zealous apologists for space exploration agree, however, that a "megamachine" of interested people has grown up behind the space program. Manpower devoted to rocket power has blazed a highway into the sky, and that action itself is stupendous enough to blind us to the actors. Whether one sees the "megamachine" behind Mercury and Apollo as triumphant, menacing or merely ambiguous depends largely on how one views the question: "Must the miracle of the person succumb to the order of the ant hill?"[30]

[28] At work on a Gemini history at the Manned Spacecraft Center and the University of Houston are James M. Grimwood and Barton C. Hacker.

[29] It is perhaps noteworthy that McDonnell Aircraft Corporation has no part of the Apollo spacecraft contract, neither of the Command nor of the Lunar Excursion Module. On the Apollo accident of Jan. 27, 1967, see the seven-part report by U.S. Senate Committee on Aeronautical and Space Sciences, 90th Cong., 1st Sess., Hearings and Recommendations of Apollo 204 Review Board, Mar.-May 1967.

[30] The question is Lynn White, Jr.'s, in his essay " 'Civilizing' the Engineer by 'Civilizing' the Humanist" in *Engineering: Its Role and Function in Human Society*, eds. William H. Davenport and Daniel Rosenthal (New York, 1967), p. 143. See also Jacques Ellul, *The Technological Society*, trans. John Wilkinson (New York, 1964); Edward B. Roberts, *The Dynamics of Research and Development* (New York, 1966); *Science and Culture: A Study of Cohesive and Disjunctive Forces*, ed. Gerald Holton (Boston, 1965); *Science as a Cultural Force*, ed. Harry Woolf (Baltimore, 1964).

Certainly the national space program, including manned exploration of the moon but also much more, excites the imagination and curiosity of almost all of mankind. Probably two of the largest "megamachines" in history, those of the Soviet Union and of the United States, are now at work on the effort to explore the moon and near space. In the last analysis, it is surely an article of faith to believe that the technological, managerial, social and imaginative returns from the space investment will far surpass the political, social and economic costs of the present. The success of the Mercury spacecraft fathered that of Gemini and fostered the hope of Apollo. The makers of Mercury functioned as a team, and that team for the most part is still functioning.

31
OL' LYNDON—AND JFK

William Appleman Williams

In a 1971 interview that touched upon a broad range of problems, Herman Kahn, the distinguished defense analyst, commented on "the low morale of Western democracies," claiming "we have forgotten how to stand up for our rights; we have lost the sense for recognizing central policy issues." In America, there was also "a permanent crisis of leadership." Men of ability were simply not available in high places to grapple with both persistent problems and new issues.

The following essay-review by Professor Williams of Lyndon Johnson's own account of his presidency is concerned with this crisis of leadership. By his concise, provocative, often caustic but nevertheless sympathetic evaluation of President Johnson's administration, Professor Williams refutes in part Mr. Kahn's comment by showing how even a man of great ability, occupying the most powerful office in the country, can be trapped by past policies, misled by his advisers, and dazzled by his own ambitions into pursuing a course of action that is self-destructive and seriously damaging to the nation. Though less contained than Kennedy's Camelotian chivalry, Johnson's heroics are the more tragic.

William Appleman Williams, a professor of history at Oregon State University, is undoubtedly the dean of the present-day critics of American foreign policy. In a series of provocative books and articles he has raised penetrating and challenging questions about the conduct of foreign policy throughout American history. Among his more important books are The Tragedy of American Diplomacy *(Cleveland, 1959);* The Roots of the Modern American Empire *(New York, 1969);* American-Russian Relations, 1781–1947 *(New York, 1952); and* The Shaping of American Foreign Policy: Readings and Documents in American Foreign Relations *(Chicago, 1956).*

Source: William Appleman Williams, *Some Presidents: From Wilson to Nixon* (New York: The New York Review, 1972), pp. 83–107. Reprinted with permission from *The New York Review of Books*.

The issue here is how we read a document. For how we read determines what we learn.

So far, at any rate, we have not been learning much from this slyly honest witness. Mostly we have heard a frustrated (and therefore angry) complaint that Ol' Lyndon did not go naked down to the river and confess his sins in chants of unconditional surrender. But then I remember Abbie Hoffman's belated admission that Revolution for the Hell of It is a contradiction in terms, and it struck me that Lyndon went to the river before Abbie. I have a feeling that the comparison may tell us as much about the weakness of the left during its most striking opportunity since it blew the Great Depression as all the books that will ever be written on the subject.

We face, on another front, the precious vanguard of sophisticated nags who fill the page with put-downs of the man. They scan the document to cull footnotes for a priori conclusions of such profundity as that LBJ was not JFK. My, how the computers must be overheating under the load of all those Brownie Points coming in from the Ivy League. The one relevant aspect of John Kenneth Galbraith's egoistic digression is his honesty about the supercilious arrogance of such elitist evasions.[1] If the Liberal Establishment were prepared to lead us plebs into the Golden Age, it would have neither the time nor the need to belabor Lyndon and his merely human torments. Having won the battle at the crossroads with their shiny new crossbows, the prodigies would be fingering the Grail.

Alas.

Rather, thank God. (Remember the Bay of Pigs, the Green Berets, the Missile Madness, and the noble call to Define Ourselves in Terms of the State?)

Next there will be many readers of the witness who will try to use it as the cornerstone for their own ambitious architecture. You know: the dreary academic-bureaucratic strategy of constructing one's own career upon a critique of another's labor. If you have that much leisure, and are hung up on reading, you can relax about what to do for the next decade.

So we are left with the most difficult alternative (there *is* a double meaning there, but it will have to wait for another essay). The only way forward is to make the effort to read with skepticism, compassion, and a readiness to recognize a truth we did not expect to find. That is, try to be a historian. Or, if you (like me) prefer the idiom of Thucydides, try to be a citizen. Meaning read Lyndon to understand better what we have wrought, and how we misbent the iron, in order to undo what we came to feel (when manipulated through appeals to our good intentions and our egos) was our finest hour.

Extremely difficult and terribly painful.

But Lyndon has given us some leverage, and it is crucial to use it carefully: "I make no pretense of having written a complete and definitive history of my Presidency. I have tried, rather, to review that period from a President's point of view—reflecting a President's personal and political philosophy. . . . I have not written these chapters to say, 'This is how it was,' but to say, 'This is how I saw it from my vantage point.' "[2]

[1] J. K. Galbraith, "Seeing Things Through for JFK," *Saturday Review* (November 6, 1971).

[2] Lyndon Baines Johnson, *The Vantage Point: Perspectives of the Presidency, 1963–1969* (Holt, Rinehart & Winston, 1971), p. ix.

That is an honest and basically accurate description of his book *The Vantage Point*. It is not in any sense a complete account of his Presidency, even from his point of view, and some of the gaps (as in the treatment of civil rights, black-white relations, and crime) are so panoramic as to remind one of Johnson's own ranch. But therein lies the essential usefulness of the volume: it is conclusive evidence of how the Vietnam War had fuzzed his mind. At the end of his tenure he saw everything as skewed by the pain of that traumatic wound to his conception of America. Just so: his distorted vision should help us see clearly how our imperial foreign policy has twisted our best perceptions and subverted our good intentions, and thereby carried us to the edge of disaster.

In a very real sense, that is, Johnson is telling us, however unconsciously or indirectly, about how our failure to sustain and extend the social movement created by Eugene Debs left us with nothing but the traditional solution to our problems: open the door to another frontier while defending those already settled. For that is the only possible way to sustain market place. liberalism. Johnson happened to be the man who was President when that truth worked itself out in front of our eyes—and with our lives.[3]

But Johnson tells us even more. He gives us a crucial insight into what it means to be a white Southerner who accepts and tries to adapt to the victory of the North. For he saw first and always as a *Southern* white who grew up wandering hither and yon across that no-man's land that divides the lowers from the maybe middles. He knew want and work, and learned what the constancy of both did to his parents and his neighbors. That prism-prison distorts some truths, but it clarifies others that the rest of us seldom glimpse—let alone see and feel and therefore know.

One of those is an excruciating awareness of the rest of the country's pervasive anger and contempt toward the South (that backward slough). Acknowledge and live with that truth as a Northern white and you begin to understand Johnson.[4] The visceral essay on the white Southerner as a second-class citizen has yet to be written. C. Vann Woodward is just too damn polite. And Norman Mailer has not considered it important enough. But if you wonder about their hawkish bellicosity, for example, remember that they alone among us have been defeated and occupied, and then kept down economically, politically, and emotionally for yet another century.

Then put that Southern consciousness of being first among the damned into a male with a great and earthy zest for life who has suffered a heart attack; and then make that man President because the young and handsome symbol of Northern power and smug self-satisfaction has been murdered while visiting a backward and unruly Southern fief. I think you have to take that man seriously when he says he was of a mind not to tempt the gods in 1964. Of course he was torn. Hell, yes, he wanted victory in his—and his beloved South's—own right, but I have a strong sense that he would have gone home if Lady Bird had said the bags were packed. Her lines about becoming the handy dart board for all the

[3] I considered these points to be obvious, or at any rate clearly implied by the rest of my remarks, when I first wrote this essay. I have made them explicit because some readers seemed to think I was apologizing for Johnson when instead I was—and am—trying to indicate in a humane way how we can all learn from his terror and failure.

[4] Johnson, *The Vantage Point*, pp. 18, 89, 95, 155.

tension and anger, and about the drinking, are masterpieces: the South is *finally here* and the sex is going, Love; so if you do not challenge Fate, the booze will get you. In that league, Ms. Camelot is a spectator who does not even know the name of the game. It sure as hell is not touch football.

I am glad he stayed. That does not mean I like what happened. I am glad he stayed because what he did at home (especially in trying openly to help the blacks and the poor), and what he did in Vietnam after the attack on the Marines at Danang, finally brought us to the visceral confrontation with ourselves that offers us a chance to break out of our traditional outlook. Given all that has gone before, I do not think that option could open up in any other way. And the Kennedys (and maybe even another white Northern Establishment man) might well have finessed the mess into another classic American victory.

Dear God.

It is easy to discount Johnson's concern and determination to help the poor and the old and the other put-downs. You have heard it many times: "Oh, that just comes naturally to a populist." But many poor boys—probably most—forget those other people once they scratch and claw their way into the front row at the feed trough. The primary issue here, though it takes a bit of care to confront it directly, is how the programs reveal the limits of white Northern liberalism. We must begin, though, with Johnson's knowledge of how to move the system. That was the product of his white Southern experience: if they will not let you run it from the top, then learn how to control it from the side. Others from the South could have maneuvered the legislative victories just about as effectively if they had cared. And, so far as *whites* are concerned, some of them do care.

So the populist answer is not enough. For Johnson included the blacks and other nobodies. Not just up *to* the crunch, but *through* the crunch. The way he tells us how he began to transcend the color line is beautiful. His black driver asked him (after he had become a member of the Congress) to stop taking the dog along on the numerous trips back and forth to Texas. It was hard enough, he explained, just barrelin' through in three days. But a black man was utterly beaten down because of all those extra hours spent looking for a place to piss—let alone to eat and sleep—and it was just too damn much, even if you are a good man, Mr. Lyndon, for a black man with a dog. And his soul confrontation with his fellow white Southerners during an address to the Congress remains a great moment.[5]

> *"What happened in Selma is part of a far greater movement which reaches into every section and state of America. It is the effort of American Negroes to secure for themselves the full blessings of American life."*
>
> *I paused for breath. In that fleeting moment my thoughts turned to the picket line in Birmingham, the sit-ins in North Carolina, the marches in Selma. . . .*
>
> *I raised my arms.*
>
> *"Their cause must be our cause too. Because it is not just Negroes, but really it is all of us who must overcome the crippling legacy of bigotry and injustice. And . . . we . . . shall . . . overcome."*

And here, in this memoir, he does what few other whites of any section have

[5] Ibid., pp. 154–155; then see pp. 29, 39, 73, 157.

done. He admits publicly that he was wrong about black power. No radical chic here: just poor white Southerner gittin' on down the line.[6]

> *When asked about black power in 1966, I responded: "I am not interested in black power or white power. What I am concerned with is democratic power, with a small d." As I look back now, that answer seems totally insufficient. It is easy for a white man to say he is "not interested in black power or white power." Black power had a different meaning to the black man, who recently had had to seek the white world's approval and for whom success had come largely on white people's terms. To such a man, black power meant a great deal—in areas that mattered the most—dignity, pride, and self-awareness.*

What we come down to, then, are the concepts that guided Ol' Lyndon. And those were the product of orthodox Northern white liberalism. The program was simply the ideas of the New and Fair Deals pushed to their limits. And, underlying all, the American Zen Buddhism of *growth*. The nonviolent, nondisruptive way to solve all problems. "The economic pie was big enough for everyone—and growing much faster than our population."[7] But it did not work for Franklin Delano Roosevelt or Harry S Truman, and it did not work for Lyndon Baines Johnson.

This fallacy is tucked away in the classical capitalist assumption (and prayer) that growth will mask the inequitable and irrational use and distribution of resources, as well as meet the demands of increasing population and the cry from everyone for more goodies. Another difficulty was that not even Ol' Lyndon could forever override the Southerners and Northerners who demanded duly sanitized and processed representatives when the past seemed about to push us into the present in such matters as community initiative and control of community affairs.[8] But the gut truth of it is that the Great Society was what Franklin Roosevelt should have proposed in 1936. It was too little and too late in 1963.

None of that can be dumped on Lyndon. Unless, of course, you simply prefer your rulers to spend their childhood in upstate New York or Cape Cod rather than in Texas. Only a thimbleful of radicals and utopians were offering anything significantly more imaginative and fundamental. If the Great Society was Camelot's program, then the New Frontier was nothing more than the liberal intellectuals whoopin' it up back at The Old Stamping Ground.[9] If it was mostly Johnson, as I think it was, then he deserves credit for striving to do all that was possible within the orthodoxy he had been taught.

In any event, it was Johnson rather than Kennedy who moved the system. The Kennedy machine was like a freeway cruiser: beautiful on the way to the White House or the moon, but of little help in getting coal to Grandma in the snow. A full appreciation of Lyndon's contraption, which would make either

[6] Ibid., first see pp. 155–162 and 164–165; then p. 167.
[7] Ibid., p. 30.
[8] Ibid., p. 83.
[9] Here the mind-bending essay is W. I. Susman, "The Persistence of American Reform," in *American Reform: The Ambiguous Legacy*, edited by D. Walden (Yellow Springs, Ohio: The Ampersand Press, 1967), pp. 94–108.

kind of trip, depends upon an understanding of two of the assumptions behind the Constitution.

One holds that the Constitution enables a majority (even a strong plurality) of the people to do almost anything they want to do if and when they function as citizens. The other promises that when the people do not act as citizens nothing terribly bad can happen because of the carefully designed structural baffles (and the size of the empire) that prevent any man or group from appropriating total power, and because the government will in any event be managed in trust by the best available men who sit in the Senate and the White House. The first proposition is largely true. The second is demonstrably false. And therein lies the trouble.

Johnson does not discuss the problem in those formal terms in *The Vantage Point* (though I have little doubt that he could). But he does let us see what happens when the people stay home glued to the tube. It is very simple. The men charged with the responsibilities in the Senate and the White House have to distort and manipulate (and thereby weaken) the basically representative system to cope with immediate needs and to try to fulfill the public's expression of its wishes when it last performed as an assembly of citizens.

All very understandable. And all very dangerous. First, it means that the honest custodians have to bargain in a closed environment (the Congress) with other minds closed to almost everything except the bullheaded self-interest of those who define citizenship as die-hard protection of their self-defined welfare. Second, the powers of the Presidency are fudged and fudged again in order to do what the sometime citizenry said it wanted during its last venture into self-government. It all comes down to creeping benevolent despotism—with serious limits on the opportunity to be benevolent.

Very bad news. Even if (as with Johnson) your hero is Franklin Roosevelt.[10] Perhaps particularly if Roosevelt is your patron saint. For that means you as acolyte have to develop on your own the inner strength to engage the people in serious dialogue when they finally arouse themselves as citizens. Franklin is a poor guide for that trip. A dialogue is not a Fireside Chat. He never said anything as gutsy about the blacks as Lyndon did—or did anything as meaningful to help them. And Roosevelt set the pattern for easing the nation into war through disingenuous maneuvers.[11]

So we come to Vietnam (and the Dominican Republic).

Remember whom we have at the bar. A Southern poor white who molded himself in the image of an upstate New York aristocrat and *that* kind of *noblesse oblige*, and then came to power because a Massachusetts *nouveau riche* (and *that* kind of pseudo *noblesse oblige*) had been killed in the heart of his own Texas. Foreign policy offers such a man the *one and only* basis for taking the oath with any confidence that he is truly an American in his own right. Foreign policy is the magic key. For there he *is* in tune. He is a child of his age.

Lyndon's critics are wrong. He was not unprepared for foreign policy, he was instead miseducated with masterful efficiency by the white Northern elite that had dominated the conduct of foreign affairs since 1865.

> *Like most men and women of my generation, I felt strongly that World War II might have been avoided if the United States in the 1930s had not*

[10] Johnson, *The Vantage Point,* pp. 70, 81, 104, 324, 327, 345.

[11] Or was it Wilson?

given such an uncertain signal of its likely response to aggression in Europe and Asia.

Then consider the projection of that outlook in his May 23, 1961, report to Kennedy on his mission to Asia.

> *1. The battle against Communism must be joined in Southeast Asia with strength and determination to achieve success there—or the United States, inevitably, must surrender the Pacific and take up our defenses on our own shores. . . . 3. There is no alternative to United States leadership in Southeast Asia. . . . 8. . . . The basic decision in Southeast Asia is here. We must decide whether to help these countries to the best of our ability or throw in the towel in the area and pull back our defenses to San Francisco and a "Fortress America" concept.*[12]

Along the way, the teaching continued. After Roosevelt, the instructor was Truman. The haberdasher as town tutor: bringing the insights of Wilson and the two Roosevelts to Main Street.

> *It must be the policy of the United States to support free peoples who are resisting attempted subjugation by armed minorities or by outside pressure. . . . We must assist free peoples to work out their own destinies in their own way. . . . Collapse of free institutions and loss of independence would be disastrous not only for them but for the world.*[13]
>
> *Our foreign relations, political and economic, are indivisible. . . . We are the giant of the economic world. . . . The choice is ours. . . . So our devotion to freedom of enterprise, in the United States, has deeper roots than a desire to protest the profits of ownership. It is part and parcel of what we call American.*[14]

The various elements in that outlook, first brought together by Wilson, were tightly integrated by the white Northern elite in National Security Council Document 68 (prepared during the winter of 1949–1950). The gospel as amended and interpreted by Dean G. Acheson, associated bishops, and consulting Protestant Jesuits. If the true American faith is to be maintained and advanced, "the nation must be determined, at whatever cost or sacrifice, to preserve at home and abroad those conditions of life in which those objectives can survive and prosper." The United States will be the sun, "with other free nations in variable orbits around it." This "means the virtual abandonment by the United States of trying to distinguish between national and global security. . . . Security must henceforth become the dominant element in the national budget, and other elements must be accommodated to it."[15] Underlying it all, of course, were the assumptions that Washington was the Holy See of the new empire and that America possessed the necessary power.

[12] Johnson, *The Vantage Point*, p. 46, 147–148; *The Pentagon Papers* (Bantam, 1971), pp. 128–129.
[13] Truman, March 12, 1947 (The Truman Doctrine).
[14] Truman, March 6, 1947 (address at Baylor University).
[15] C. Phillips, *The Truman Presidency: The History of a Triumphant Succession* (Macmillan, 1966), pp. 306–308.

Here again, as with the explanation of Johnson as populist, we need to move carefully to undo the facile, unfair, and misleading charges that Vietnam was Johnson's war. First, it is impossible to separate domestic from foreign affairs. Second, NSC-68 is the classic expression of the American projection of that truth into absurdity: for America to be well, the entire world must take the patented American remedy and then follow the American diet. Third, the absurdity cannot be laid in the lap of Lyndon Baines Johnson. Even Townsend Hoopes acknowledges that Johnson was educated in that idiom and that Kennedy bequeathed him advisers who thought "about the external world in the simplistic terms of appeasement versus military resolve."[16] Hoopes is so excited, relieved, and impressed by his own awakening from the nightmare that he not only blames Johnson for the wrong things but totally ignores those brave souls who had been warning about the impending disaster through the long and lonely night. Finally, the major point is to learn from Johnson's sad experience in carrying the absurdity to its insane conclusion.

Truman took us a good way down that path by going to war in Korea without so much as a courtesy call on the Congress. The Congress seemed to have forgotten that he was supposed to come by, but that does not absolve HST. For a time, nothing happened. Then, slowly and cautiously, almost as though they were learning to walk after a year in traction, some Americans began to act as citizens. The ensuing protest against the Korean War was not dramatic, but it was significant and ultimately influential. The crucial weakness of that opposition was that it focused narrowly on the war rather than on the war as the expression of the underlying outlook of liberal capitalism.

Truman met no resistance as he simultaneously implemented the *Weltanschauung* in Indochina, even though the antiwar sentiment clearly affected the election of 1952.[17] Thus the possibility of a serious reconsideration of the traditional approach that would lead on to different action depended wholly upon the wild chance that the President, or a significant number of other established leaders, would be jarred enough by the war, or by the antiwar feeling, to question orthodox assumptions and policies.

Wonder of wonders, a boy from Kansas who stayed human through West Point did gingerly approach that heresy. Dwight David Eisenhower occasionally talked bluntly in private about the possibility of direct intervention in Indochina (and allowed John Foster Dulles to preach about it far too much), but the key fact is that he acted very cautiously.[18] He made no irreversible commitment, and did not trap himself by exposing advisers to enemy fire. And there is something more: for, in spite of his failure to confront Joseph McCarthy quickly or decisively enough, he did not appease the wild man from Wisconsin by embarking on overseas adventures.

There was an important bit of Hoover in Eisenhower: the kind of perception, for example, that enabled Hoover to tell Truman in 1945 to relax and concentrate on improving life in the United States and the Western Hemisphere. And also the sense of proportion and confidence that allowed Ike to say simply that

[16] T. Hoopes, *The Limits of Intervention* (McKay, 1969), pp. 6–7, 15–16. But also see C. L. Cooper, *The Lost Crusade: America in Vietnam* (Dodd, Mead, 1970), p. 13.
[17] Cooper, *The Lost Crusade*, p. 63.
[18] Ibid., pp. 134–137.

the United States should not overreact to criticism, or to annoying but secondary policy actions by other nations. For that matter, Hoover's strong attack of December 20, 1950, against the Truman approach was an important factor in opening the sometimes pointed discussion of global interventionism that set the background for the election of 1952; and once elected Eisenhower revealed himself in action to be far closer to Hoover than to Dulles.

John Fitzgerald Kennedy was of a different breed. He charged on to honor orthodoxy and to revive the activism of Truman. In foreign affairs, at any rate, he displayed little understanding of either the virtue or the sanity of going slow. Even of doing nothing. He agreed (in 1956) with Dulles that it would be wrong to hold elections throughout Vietnam. He described the make-believe government below the seventeenth parallel as the

> *. . . cornerstone of the Free World in Southeast Asia, the Keystone to the arch, the finger in the dike. . . . Moreover, the independence of Free Vietnam is crucial to the free world in fields other than the military. Her economy is essential to the economy of all of Southeast Asia; and her political liberty is an inspiration to those seeking to obtain or maintain their liberty in all parts of Asia—and indeed the world. The fundamental tenets of this nation's foreign policy, in short, depend in considerable measure upon a strong and free Vietnamese nation.*[19]

Four years later, campaigning against Richard Milhous Nixon, he attacked the Eisenhower failure to oust Fidel Castro as symptomatic of the Republican inability to deal toughly with Russia. Castro was "a source of maximum danger." "Those [like Nixon] who say they will stand up to Khrushchev have not demonstrated the ability to stand up to Mr. Castro." As for the main show, Kennedy argued that it was urgent to initiate a major increase in military spending because of the nature of the enemy and his great advantage in missiles: "There is very little time. The enemy is lean and hungry and the United States is the only strong sentinel at the gate."[20]

Once elected, Kennedy quickly surrounded himself with zealous "watchmen on the walls of freedom" and launched a major effort to strengthen and refine the orthodox counterrevolutionary policy by applying the relevant manipulatory insights and techniques of the social sciences, and by adopting centralized and computerized management.[21] It may help in understanding Robert S. McNamara to approach him as the white Northern equivalent of Lyndon B. Johnson. That is, the white Northern middle-class boy who became corporation manager and then took on the challenge of controlling the military by asserting American control of the world without relying on the Joint Chiefs of Staff.

19 Ibid., pp. 150, 168.

20 Here I extend the original version of this essay to offer more information and to clarify rather cryptic discussions of several important points. The publishing schedule for this collection made it impossible to do that in an essay on R. J. Walton's *Cold War and Revolution: The Foreign Policy of John F. Kennedy* (Viking Press, 1972). Walton offers a coherent interpretation of Kennedy, though his major points have been presented by others in less integrated fashion. His sense of the meaning of Kennedy's famous speech at American University, however, is particularly keen.

21 Cooper, *The Lost Crusade*, p. 207; A. Austin, *The President's War* (Lippincott, 1971), pp. 30–31.

Jackie had hardly filled the second closet of her wardrobe before JFK was striding down the road that led to war in Vietnam. The first move involved Laos. Kennedy promptly defined that lovely lazy land as being essential to American security, and then began to act on that view with such a slow-witted analysis and heavy-handed interference that open military intervention was a real possibility for a period of months.

Next came the opening phase of the military build-up which, in spite of official admission that the missile gap did not exist, finally topped-out at about $6 billion. The first requests were made when Kennedy and his advisers interpreted Russia's exploratory bid to unfreeze the Berlin stalemate as posing a dire threat to the United States. More young men were requisitioned to serve the state in military tasks, more reserve units were activated, various regular units were placed on high alert, and a request for $207 million momentarily took the issue of civil defense out of mothballs. Happily, the Russians did not overreact in the same fashion.

Then came the Bay of Pigs. In view of all the debate about whether or not Kennedy would have walked on and on into the Vietnam quagmire (as Johnson did), it is fair to explore the question of Eisenhower and the exile force that he allowed Nixon and the Dulles Brothers to organize. My view is this: in the crunch Eisenhower would not have authorized an invasion. First, because of his aversion to armed intervention per se. Second, because his military expertise would have informed him that Castro did not pose a threat to the security of the United States. Third, because as an unusually sensitive and responsible commanding officer, he would not have sent 1,500 men on such an operation without American support. And fourth, the necessity of American involvement would have reinforced his deep reluctance to order more Americans to die.

Nixon is different. Scarily so. I am sure that in 1961 he would have gone in with everything required. Which would have been a hell-of-a-lot more than he would have assumed was necessary, and which might therefore have produced the first Vietnam. So give Kennedy his due: he did not do *that*.

But what Kennedy did do was considerably more than enough to warrant grave criticism; and his action surely trapped Johnson and the rest of us for what seems an eternity of shame and agony. The heart of the trouble was that Kennedy could not step back and put the relationship between Castro, the United States, and himself in perspective. There are several ways to explain it: if you are hooked on psycho-history, then it is the *machismo* rivalry (including Kennedy's uncertainty and insecurity about what to do inside the United States) that will strike you; if you stress ideology, then it is the faith in Christian corporate capitalism as the true and necessary way (Kennedy as Wilson); if you prefer class analysis it is the inability of any President, whatever his best intentions and hopes, to say no to the orthodoxies of corporate capitalism unless he has been elected by a social movement with strength and imagination; and if you emphasize politics, then it is a combination of knowing that Nixon probably *did* beat you in Illinois and Texas, and the necessity of honoring your rhetoric to establish your credibility in order to be re-elected.

Whichever of those options you choose, the central point here is that the Cuban Missile Crisis was a direct result of the Bay of Pigs. Kennedy did not learn from that error and failure. He did not let go. He lacked the imagination and courage to re-examine the white Northern liberal catechism and go to the people with a confession that would revive them as citizens. Instead, he took the by-pass.

The cop-out in the guise of tough-mindedness: No More Cubas. As if a sane man would undertake always to win.

That made him a hostage of the right, and trapped him into settling for less than his *own* aspirations. One undertakes to stay in power to do good for the people by drastically narrowing one's definition of the good. Thus Cuba remained under "our most careful surveillance." He gave serious consideration to any proposal that seemed likely to blot out the defeat. There was open talk of another invasion, and he persistently discussed the assassination of Castro.

Irony of ironies.

Terror of terrors.

Everyone who cared knew about those discussions. After all, you only had to read one of five: *The Nation, The New York Times, The Congressional Record, I. F. Stone's Weekly,* or the *Washington Post.* And if you had even the loosest kind of connection, you were privy to reputed (and undoubtedly distorted) quotations. Khrushchev and Castro had very good connections, and they were understandably and increasingly scared.

So they asked for assurances that there would be no reworked replay. Kennedy gave them nothing, not even the back of his mind. So then the missiles were moved in to italicize two points: revolutions in small countries are no longer the exclusive business of the United States, and we Russians think it is time you Americans also lived inside the parabola of nuclear missiles so that you will learn by doing (so to speak) that you are not unique.

The missiles, as Theodore C. Sorenson has so eloquently explained (McNamara and others were typically more prosaic in making the same point), "did not substantially alter the strategic balance *in fact.*" At this point, given what we know, I think Khrushchev initially made one of two mistakes: either he overestimated Kennedy and assumed that the President would open private talks about Cuba and other matters; or he counted on the shock of the missiles to accomplish the same objective.

Either way, Khrushchev was wrong. But he adjusted quickly and effectively, realizing that Kennedy was not a man who was capable of making the first gesture. So he did. We are all indebted to Khrushchev for recognizing his man, and for being himself a human being able to accept what seemed to be a public defeat in order to attain important objectives.

The confrontation with Khrushchev may have been the most important, if limited, learning experience in the life of John Fitzgerald Kennedy. For he grasped the vital point that America was no longer a nation with the power to impose its will upon a small nation if another superpower takes the poor and the weak under its nuclear umbrella. Ike knew that, but he was not a teacher; and Kennedy's concept of courage was not sophisticated enough to include Hoover.

So it was Khrushchev who tutored Kennedy for the famous speech at American University. It was lovely. More beautiful than he realized, however, for while he publicly unzipped the Truman Doctrine as it affected direct confrontations between nuclear powers, he had not learned the other lesson from Cuba: a social movement can unzip a nuclear empire.

So on he went into Vietnam. "We are not going to withdraw" from Vietnam: "for us to withdraw . . . would mean a collapse not only of South Vietnam but Southeast Asia." Dominoes with a shot of Irish whisky. That crusading zeal manifested itself, sooner than later, in a steady expansion of American troops who were exposed to combat and who had been imbued with the true faith "to revolutionize the economy and political structure of the provinces . . . during their one-year tour of duty."[22] Read revolutionize to mean Americanize, and read advisers-in-the-field-exposed-to-enemy-fire to mean votes in the pocket of Barry M. Goldwater and Associates.[23] Kennedy had defined himself into the trap of having to win abroad to win at home.

That put Johnson in the position of a man wandering down an arroyo with a cloudburst moving in behind the hills. Given all the elements that had been unleashed, the wonder is that he went so slow.[24] It says a good bit about the man. True, I would not have gone at all, and of course neither would you, but that is not the issue. To stop at that point is to engage in the worst kind of self-indulgence.

So we are not yet done.

At a crucial juncture, Johnson did do less than was in him. I do not mean that I think he was capable of drawing on hidden and inner resources to transcend the outlook he had been taught and which he had internalized as his own. The point is that he did not honor, after the first direct attacks on American units, his own commitment to the existing system. That is the only solid ground for criticism. Meaning that it is so easy to fault a man for not breaking free of his own views that it is pointless. But it is something quite different when a man does not honor his own code.

There *were* excruciating circumstances. The assassination, and the coming to power as a proxy. And all those "advisers" in Vietnam, with ever more of them being killed. Johnson had not selected a single major adviser in America, and had not sent a single adviser to Vietnam. Even so, in spite of the liberal orthodoxy and the clamor from the right, those problems might have been fuzzed enough to fold the tent.

That became extremely difficult after the assassination and the nomination of Goldwater. Still, Johnson gave it a try. I do not think that the Tonkin Gulf Boo-Boo was the point of no return. Being an Academy man, I say simply that the Navy looks bad. We did fire first, and there is no such thing as a warning shot between two men of war.[25]

In the beginning, moreover, Johnson was not a Truman. Not even a Roosevelt. And certainly not a Kennedy saying yes to the Bay of Pigs in the secrecy of his clique. Johnson *did* go to the Congress. At that point, looking back, I think that all of us who defined the problem as centering on Johnson made the mistake of personalizing the political process. If we believe in self-government, that is to say, then we should insist upon the power of the representative bodies, and control them by our involvement as citizens, rather than lusting after a hero to whom we can hand over even more authority. And that means building a social movement to elect a man or woman of our persuasion instead of simply humiliating a man

22 Cooper, *The Lost Crusade*, pp. 211, 207.

23 Austin, *The President's War*, pp. 30, 43, 104. On the same trap in the Dominican Revolution, consult J. Slater, *Intervention and Negotiation* (Harper & Row, 1907), pp. 16–17, 32, 199. Then see *The Vantage Point*, pp. 19, 42, 197–198, 201–202, 280.

24 Here read *The Lost Crusade*.

25 *The President's War*: it has to be read through.

who is the natural product of a system that we assume to be incapable of defining and dealing with the real problems.

If we are serious about radical reform (let alone revolution), then we need to become a bit more sophisticated about the North Vietnamese and the VC. They have every right to decide their own strategy and tactics. And we can wish them success within the framework of an honest (if disturbed) commitment to the principle of self-determination. But we also need to learn, for our own purposes, how the leaders of the Establishment respond to such a frontal challenge.

The February, 1965, decision by the North Vietnamese or the VC (or both) to mount persistent frontal attacks on American units is understandable. I might very well have supported the same policy if I had endured those previous twenty years as a Vietnamese. But there are many ways to win, and the key to choosing among them is a knowledge of one's opponent. And I think they could have won the quiet way—sooner and with vastly less cost to their own country.

But if you push Ol' Lyndon you are in trouble with an aroused poor Southern white who has accommodated to defeat by becoming a Northerner.

And it blinded him, fogged his mind, and the only message he got was the one already inside: we have the power to finish the job.

So at that juncture he was neither candid nor shrewd. He did not go back to the Congress, and he did not withdraw the American combat units.

He had blanked out what he had written to Kennedy in May, 1961. "At some point we may be faced with the further decision of whether we commit major United States forces to the area or cut our losses and withdraw. . . . We must remain master in this decision."[26]

Only much later, after the white Northern liberal orthodoxy had run its course into horror, did Johnson's mind begin to clear. The public, first aroused by the students, began slowly to come awake and act as citizens with a will to "remain master in this decision." Then Têt. Lyndon goes on for pages about how the situation was stabilized, but most of it should be read as an unconscious record of the way he came to terms with the truth that it was all over.

So he went to the river.

He argues cogently that his push for the blacks and the poor had more than a bit to do with the last trip to Texas. Forcing the nation to confront the truth that the nobodies were somebodies did strengthen the right. It is a paradox appropriate to our ongoing moment of truth. The left moved us onto the road out of the war but the right retained the initiative at home.

To Robert Kennedy, Johnson was brave and honest.[27]

"I'm not that pure, but I am scared."

I see no point in belaboring Ol' Lyndon anymore.

The responsibility and the opportunities are now ours.

[26] *Pentagon Papers,* p. 130.
[27] Johnson, *The Vantage Point,* p. 541.